Karl C. Garrison, Ph.D., George Peabody College for Teachers, is Professor of Education at the University of Georgia. He previously taught at North Carolina State College, Teachers College of Connecticut, Georgia State College for Women, and was Dean of Instruction at Maryland State Teachers College, Frostburg. Professor Garrison is author of several textbooks in the field of educational psychology.

Dewey G. Force, Jr., Ph.D., University of Michigan, is Associate Professor of Educational Psychology at the University of Minnesota. He previously taught at the Rackham School of Special Education, Michigan State Normal College, Ypsilanti, and the University of Georgia. Since 1948, Professor Force has devoted himself to the field of special education.

THE PSYCHOLOGY
OF
EXCEPTIONAL
CHILDREN

KARL C. GARRISON
UNIVERSITY OF GEORGIA

DEWEY G. FORCE, JR.
UNIVERSITY OF MINNESOTA

Fourth Edition

THE RONALD PRESS COMPANY • NEW YORK

Library of Congress Catalog Card Number: 65–21809

PREFACE

The purpose of this book is to bring together in systematic form much of the pertinent knowledge of exceptional children that bears on their education. It has been designed as a textbook for both students enrolled in departments of education and departments of psychology and as a source of reference for teachers in service. Emphasis is placed on the contribution that the classroom teacher can make to the education and welfare of the exceptional child.

Increased attention is given to educational provisions for exceptional children; and the roles of the home, community, school, and other forces and conditions that affect the lives of exceptional children are emphasized. Attempts have been made throughout to view the exceptional child as an individual with needs and problems not significantly different in nature from the so-called average child.

Developmental theory has been stressed throughout. Behavior and development are regarded as processes of continuing interaction between an organism and its environment—a process in which the individual constantly strives to maintain an adjustive balance. The implications of this viewpoint are that a child must be viewed as a unified whole rather than a multiplicity of parts, and that his growth and development can be understood and guided best when his complete history is known.

The authors wish to acknowledge the cooperation extended by authors and publishers in granting permission to reprint excerpts from published works cited in the text. Both students and teachers who used the previous edition have offered helpful suggestions. We express our indebtedness to them and especially to Professor Malcolm B. McCoy, Program for Exceptional Children, of the University of Georgia, for helpful suggestions offered in connection with Chapters 7, 8, and 9.

KARL C. GARRISON
DEWEY G. FORCE, JR.

May, 1965

CONTENTS

Part IV

Physical Disability

Part V

Neurological and Other Physiological Impairment

Part VI

Emotional and Social Adjustment

THE PSYCHOLOGY

OF

EXCEPTIONAL

CHILDREN

I

CHILDREN:
HUMAN RESOURCES

Most of the scientific data on exceptional children is of a relatively recent date, stemming largely from the wide range of studies dealing with various phases of child growth and development. Also, progress in medical science has led to a better understanding of many of the ills and problems that affect children. The psychologist and educator are interested in how children differ, what factors influence individual differences, and how to develop a program best suited to the total growth of each individual child. The statistician raises questions about the degree of differences, the distribution of abilities, and relationships. He is interested in methods of measuring differences and in the reliability and validity of such measures.

In Chapter 1 the exceptional child is defined and a number of different categories of exceptional children are presented. Methods for identifying exceptional children are described along with methods most widely used by investigators in studying children, especially those classified as exceptional. The philosophy and scope of services of special education are presented in Chapter 2. Administrative matters, parental considerations, multiple disabilities, and scope of services are discussed in this chapter.

GENERAL INTRODUCTION–
CHILD STUDY

The raw material for the American democracy of tomorrow is the millions of children and youth of today. The wealth, power, and spiritual force of this nation lie in the infinitely varied potentialities of these boys and girls. The development of human resources represents the major task of schools. Children cannot be neglected without disastrous consequences. If the human resources present in growing boys and girls are to have the fullest and most complete utilization, all children must be guided in their maturation and development. In each decade of the present century the hopes of the nation's founders and early leaders for educated citizens have been increasingly realized. The necessity for an educated citizenry has become almost universally accepted.

School enrollment has more than kept pace with the growth of population during the twentieth century. Increased enrollment has brought forth increased diversity in the school population. Where children handicapped in the learning of verbal materials formerly dropped out of school at an early age, they now remain in school until the compulsory retaining age or beyond. In the past many children who were emotionally and socially maladjusted often dropped out of school at an early age. The physically handicapped were frequently discouraged from going to school; or, if they entered school, they often dropped out before graduation.

Following World War II, increased interest developed in handicapped persons, particularly in the mentally retarded child. Among the forces responsible for recent advancements are the efforts of organized parent groups to bring the problems of handicapped children to public attention and to secure for these children more adequate educational, vocational, and recreational opportunities. As a result of working together, parents of handicapped children have developed a better understanding of the problems of their children and have influenced educational administrators in the development of more adequate programs.

The children to be considered in this book are those who deviate sufficiently from the average that they need special attention and consideration if they are to be able to develop their potentials. These are referred to as exceptional children. They are not basically different in their characteristics from other children. They have the same psychological needs of all children, but their disabilities and differences emphasize certain needs or create special needs of which schools and society must be aware in planning appropriate educational experiences.

INDIVIDUAL DIFFERENCES IN CHILDREN

A wide range of individual differences will be found among any group of children in any characteristic or ability. Such differences among pupils have been recognized by teachers from the beginning of a formal education program and even before. Early viewpoints concerning the nature and causes of these differences were indefinite and confused, and many misconceptions arose concerning them (Peterson, 1935). Some of these erroneous impressions have persisted for years and continue to influence practices and thinking regarding the training of children.

How Children Differ. Individual differences can be observed among children of the same age in height, weight, motor skills, mental ability, or social development. Children of the same family vary considerably in different abilities and in growth characteristics. This is illustrated in the growth curves of the heights of five sisters presented in Fig. 1–1 (Ford, 1958). Pertinent information on individual differences will be presented in subsequent chapters dealing with intellectual

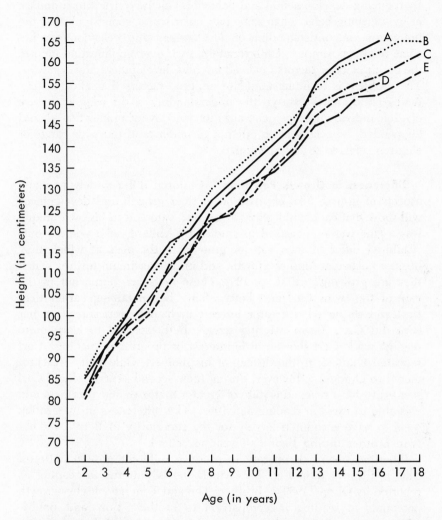

Fig. 1–1. Individual growth curves for height of five sisters. (After Ford, 1958.)

growth and characteristics, perceptual development, conceptualization, motor coordination and development, visual abilities, auditory abilities, emotional characteristics, socialization, and other abilities and characteristics.

There are those who would ascribe all aspects of behavior to a single force or condition, or to a combination of forces and conditions.

By reducing developmental and behavioral characteristics to formulas, or by ascribing behavior to some particular cause, some think that the prediction and understanding of development and behavior may become relatively simple. Unfortunately, such oversimplification ignores the multiplicity of factors involved in child development and behavior. The problem is to understand the multiple factors that affect a particular child and to gain greater understanding of the complex nature of each individual. Overgeneralization and oversimplification should be avoided, especially in an attempt to understand the wide range of children referred to as exceptional.

Differences in Growth Potentials. Children differ widely in many aspects of growth. An observation of their growth and development will show that each child grows at his own rate and in his own unique way. This was emphasized in studies by Millard, who pointed out: "Children differ in their rate of growth, in the ages at which they begin a particular kind of growth, and in the maximum toward which they are growing" (1951, p. 12). These facts are borne out in the case of the twins Carl and Betty. Betty began talking earlier than Carl and displayed a greater interest in having stories read to her than did Carl. Upon entering school, Betty seemed to learn quite readily, while Carl showed little interest or progress in reading. Carl repeated Grade 1, to the dismay of his mother, while Betty was promoted to Grade 2. However, during their second year in school Carl seemed to have reached a state of greater maturity and readiness and was able to excel in reading activities. The differences in maturation seem to have accounted largely for the superiority of Betty over her twin brother during their first year at school.

Inherited potentials operate to produce different growth patterns. This is illustrated in Fig. 1–2, which shows patterns in reading as reported by Olson (1959). Brothers Tim and Tom have higher growth potentials in reading in comparison to brothers Billy and Bobby. Olson points out that this higher level for learning of Tim and Tom is further borne out from measurements that show them to be superior in other kinds of growth. Differences in experiences do not account for such wide variations as those shown in Fig. 1–2. All four boys had favorable home and school environments. Tim and Billy, the older brothers of Tom and Bobby, were in the same grades together and in the same room in school. The boys were children of parents of preferred status with superior home and cultural conditions. Such differences can best be accounted for on the basis of inherent potentialities for development. It appears that heredity sets limits to one's

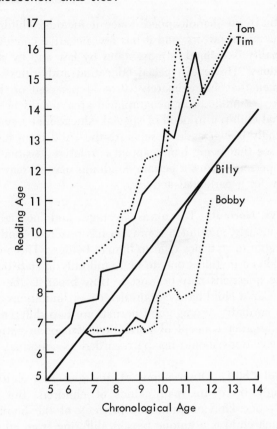

Fig. 1–2. Individual differences in reading patterns. (Olson, 1959.)

development in any direction. The challenge to the teacher is to see that each child is given the opportunity to develop in harmony with his potentialities for growth. This requires that special consideration be given to the exceptional child if he is to develop to his maximum capacity.

THE EXCEPTIONAL CHILD

Any estimate of the number of exceptional children will depend upon the kinds of deviations included under the term "exceptional," the degree of deviation that makes a child exceptional, and the kinds of special educational provisions thought necessary. The dictionary definition of the term "exceptional" refers to anything that is extraordinary, unusual, or outstanding in some way. It is a more inclusive term than the term "handicapped" since it includes children at both extremes on certain factors, and it has few negative connotations.

Exceptionality is defined in most states by law and by state education regulations. However, special education authorities are in general agreement that approximately 10 to 15 per cent of the children in almost any community or geographical area should be considered as exceptional children in need of special educational service. Efforts are increasingly being made to separate the child from his condition in order to see that being handicapped is relative to situations rather than to the person. Thus, a certain condition may or may not handicap a person for a particular activity.

Average vs. Normal. The terms "average" and "normal" are often used synonymously, and much confusion has resulted. Both terms are more applicable to statistics than to human beings. The notion of the average child is a mythical one, to be found only in statistical calculations. These questions may be raised: How broad is the concept of normality? Can a child have certain defects or limitations and still be regarded as normal? Average and normal are two different concepts. We need a broader concept of normality. Except in extreme cases, individual deviations should not be regarded as abnormal.

The Special Child. Observations of any group of children reveal that seemingly there are many kinds of children. But essentially there is only one kind of child—the progeny of the human species. However, each child is a unique person, differing from all other children. The label "normal" has been given to some children; the label "abnormal" has been given to others. However, all normal children may be regarded as abnormal in some ways, while all abnormal children may be regarded as normal in some attributes. Concerning this, Doll (1963) states:

Hence the limitations to growth, development, and learning may better be considered as merely deviant than as incurably pathological. In this context, the special child is a child with personal attributes, commonly referred to as handicaps, which constitute or impose restrictions to learning or doing not usually shared by others. Some of these are skeletal, some neuromuscular, sensory, emotional, intellectual, cultural, aptitudinal, behavioral, linguistic, and so on. But some special children are gifted, being superior or talented in these same attributes. [P. 275.]

Needs of the Special Child. It has become rather general to state that the needs of the exceptional child are the same as those for normal children. In many ways this is true, especially in those things essential to the life and development of children in a particular culture. However, his designation as *special* implies in itself that he is deviant in some respects. This deviation is bound to bring forth some differential needs, or differences in potency of certain needs. Thus, in the desire for acceptance of the special child at home, at school, and in the community, the fact must not be overlooked that he has certain attributes that set him apart from others. These unusual needs call for special consideration on the part of those persons concerned with his guidance and education. The importance of acceptance of the special child has been set forth by Doll (1963) as follows:

This is indeed a need of every child, but the usual child finds it forthcoming without demand. The very fanfare with which we press for this acceptance of the special child emphasizes his deviation, since so often his other needs are accentuated by his overall rejection as a person. [P. 278.]

Children with handicaps, like other children, live in a world that extends beyond their immediate family. They must learn how to protect themselves from the physical hazards that exist in their environment. They must also learn to be social beings. This means that they must assimilate the culture in which they are born and must learn to conform to a reasonable degree to the social forces they encounter. Social acceptance achieved through the formation of good habit patterns is a measure of a child's success in his social development. It is also a basis for self-confidence on the part of the individual and social adjustments in social situations. Concerning the importance of identifying with other children, Carr (1959) states:

. . . important as it is, the time comes when the acceptance of parents does not substitute for association and friendship with other children. The child needs to have a sense of belonging as an equal; if he cannot achieve this, his feelings may be a more serious handicap than the physical one. Often it is not necessary or even desirable that his associates and friends be children with like handicaps. Sometimes it is. . . . Special classes in schools make it possible for children to have many of their associations in a normal setting. [P. 252.]

Likewise, the importance of the need for achievement should be recognized by the teacher. As a general principle, virtually all children can achieve if materials and methods are used suitable to their abilities and motives. Crandall *et al.* (1960) have set forth a conceptual framework for the study of children, based on the abilities and needs of children. They state:

It is evident that all children, as they emerge from the initial helplessness of infancy, gradually develop motivations and skills to achieve an ever-increasing variety of goals. During early childhood, as a child's capacities mature and new learning situations are faced, the need for achievement emerges from genetically prior need systems. [P. 788.]

SCIENTIFIC METHODS OF CHILD STUDY

Various aspects of child development and behavior have received increased attention in recent decades. Methods developed for the study of normal children have been refined and adapted to the study of groups of children who deviate from the normal. Also, new techniques have been developed and used for studying groups of exceptional children. Many research studies dealing with the use of various methods and instruments for studying exceptional children have been conducted. These serve to furnish the educator, psychologist, and psychiatrist with valuable tools for helping to understand exceptional children better.

The complexity of the human organism that is the child and the myriad factors that influence his growth and development have prevented any one method of child study from becoming accepted as the major or most important one. Present studies seem to be moving further away from the generalized observations of the past, and more emphasis is being placed on systematic recording of specific patterns of behavior. The development of statistical methods for analyzing and interpreting data has resulted in more precise and specific evaluations. A brief description is presented in the following pages of the methods for studying children that are most commonly used today. In some cases applications are made to exceptional children.

The Genetic or Longitudinal Method. The genetic or longitudinal method of studying children is concerned with the development of a particular characteristic or attribute throughout a given period of time. The method seeks to ascertain the day-to-day, week-to-week, or month-to-month relationship of specific attributes to the individual's pattern and rate of growth. This method is especially useful for studying handicapped children. Therapy and educational planning should be concerned not only with a diagnosis of the child's present condition, but with the developmental history of the difficulty or difficulties encountered by the child.

Gesell and Halverson's (1942) work with infants and young children, in which motion-picture photography was used, is an excellent example of refinements made in the use of observations in longitudinal studies. Their work furnished useful materials dealing with the development of posture and locomotion. Tapes and recordings have furnished good materials about children's voices, while motion pictures have been used to show lip and jaw movements in the production of speech.

Recognition that the child grows in a "whole setting" must be taken into consideration in studying children. Observations of the child in the home setting, the school setting, and the playground setting are frequently made by psychiatrists, psychologists, and others in their attempt to gain a better understanding of the dynamics of child behavior. Through long-time observations certain behavior patterns may be seen to occur again and again and may become a basis for prediction of future behavior.

One difficulty with the genetic or longitudinal study lies in the need for long-term continuous observation, evaluation, and study which it requires. Clinicians, child psychologists, and others working with exceptional children recognize the value of behavioral and developmental data collected over a period of time in arriving at a better understanding of the individual child. Thus, they frequently have to depend upon data from interviews with parents, school records, or medical histories. Frequently such data, especially those obtained from interviews with parents, are not only inaccurate but actually misleading. Although the longitudinal method has furnished perhaps the most valid data available about the development of children, it frequently has limited use for those attempting to understand the exact nature of a child's problem.

The Normative-Survey Method. If the genetic method may be thought of as representing a longitudinal approach, the normative-survey method represents a cross-sectional approach to studying children. Essentially, the normative-survey method attempts to study one or more characteristics in a group that is thought to be a representative sample of the total population. If a researcher desired to know how the height and weight of ten-year-old girls differ from the height and weight of ten-year-old boys, he might determine these differences by obtaining a representative sample of ten-year-olds and then weighing and measuring each of the selected children. Through the use of standard statistical techniques he could determine the averages and variances of each of the two groups. Similarities and differences thus could be found. Another scholar might seek to compare the mathematics achievements of fifth-grade boys and girls. A third research worker might seek to discover whether the typical six-year-old child is able to perform certain hand-eye coordinated tasks that are related to the mastery of handwriting skills.

Through the use of cross-sectional studies averages or norms have been obtained. A criticism frequently made of the normative-survey method is that the sample that is studied rarely satisfies all of the criteria of being truly representative of the total population from which it is drawn. Generalizations are subject to much probability of error. Furthermore, extensive growth studies conducted during the past several decades show that each child's development is unique, and that it must be determined in relation to his own rate of growth, rather than according to standards based upon group averages. In studying the growth patterns of exceptional children, where there are often great differences in growth, it is especially difficult to assess the meaning of cross-sectional data for an individual child.

The Case Study.   The case study or clinical method of child study has developed largely as a result of efforts on the part of specialists to understand and to assist children who have special problems. It is widely used by child psychologists, child psychiatrists, remedial specialists, speech correctionists, counselors, and social workers. The procedure may be viewed as being somewhat analogous to the genetic method in reverse; that is, it starts from the present and delves into the past developmental history of the particular child being studied. Essentially, the case study seeks to study intensely a wide range of factors that may have contributed to, or may have had some bearing upon, the development of the child. Usually it is hoped that such intensive study will reveal something about the etiology of the child's difficulty, as well as furnish clues for proper handling. Although complete case studies ideally require a team approach that involves a number of specialists, school teachers are finding it increasingly helpful to gather more accurate and pertinent information about their pupils. The typical case study generally includes the following information:

1. *Family history.* Usually information is obtained regarding the physical and mental health of the various members of the family. The health history is often important in helping to determine whether the child's present condition might be due to genetic factors such as heredity. Instances of mental retardation, tendency toward heart disease, and cases of mental illness should be noted.

2. *Prenatal and birth history.* Since human development begins with conception, it is important to learn something about the environmental conditions that might have affected the child prior to birth. Infections, injuries, toxemias, poor nutrition, or other complications during pregnancy may affect the prenatal development of the child. Similarly, unusual birth conditions, such as prolonged labor, prematurity, and difficult delivery, may have resulted in brain damage or otherwise affected the child's development.

3. *Developmental history.* An understanding of the child's past developmental pattern often is helpful in understanding present problems and conditions. A knowledge of the child's motor, language, and physical development usually is valuable. Illnesses and injuries, food habits, toilet training—all provide valuable clues.

4. *Personal and social history.* A knowledge of the child's social adjustments helps the clinician or teacher to understand better his present needs and behavior. Habits of eating, sleeping, and playing should be noted. Skills he has mastered should be recorded. A knowledge of the child's abilities, interests, likes and dislikes, and play activities helps to present a useful background for understanding the immediate problems.

5. *Educational history.* The progress the child has made in his schoolwork and the difficulties he has encountered while progressing through kindergarten and each grade provide information of great use in diagnosing his problems. General achievement, results of standardized tests, grades attained, attendance record, and special abilities or disabilities are important factors to consider.

Usually it is necessary to obtain additional data to supplement the case history. Physical, neurological, psychological, and psychiatric examinations sometimes are needed to furnish additional information about the child, his needs, and his conditions.

Although the case study is invaluable in studying individual children, it has certain limitations. First, it is time consuming and is limited to the investigation of an individual child. It is difficult to generalize on the basis of a single case history or even to generalize on the basis of several case histories. Clinicians, however, constantly identify significant factors that support prevalent theories or that lead them to subsequent theorizing. Second, a complete case study requires the services of specialists. Teachers cannot hope to function as specialists with competencies in all the different areas that deal with child behavior and development. However, as special services designed to aid the teacher in his work with children who have special difficulties continue to become more prevalent in school systems, it is likely that the case study will play an increasingly important role in child study.

Experimental Methods. These methods have been employed in many investigations dealing with the behavior and development of children. Two general types of experimental methods are used in studying children: the single group and the parallel group. The single-group method studies a single individual or one group of individuals, while the parallel-group method makes use of two or more groups in studying a specific problem. Essentially, the experimental methods seek to test a specific hypothesis by carefully controlling all variables except the one being studied.

Watson and Rayner (1920) used the single-group method in demonstrating the conditionability of emotional responses during infancy. In this study a single infant was used as the subject. Gordon (1959) employed a single-group method in studying children's concept of the self. In the investigation by Gordon teams were assigned to judge individual children. Children in the elementary school were observed without the observers being seen by the children. Lippitt (1940) used one-way vision screens for observing the effects of democratic and autocratic social atmospheres on the behavior of children. The parallel-group method of experimentation was employed in this study. A distinguishing feature of the experimental method is the active role of the experimenter as he attempts to control variables in the environmental situation in which the subjects are exposed. The lack of adequate controls of different forces operating is perhaps the greatest criticism that can be made of the use of the parallel-group method. This will be pointed out in later chapters in connection with treating problems of exceptional children in which the experimental method is employed.

The experimental method often has little immediate or practical use for the clinician, school psychologist, or teacher. However, data gathered in a clinic under controlled conditions may ultimately furnish the clinician or specialist with clues to the nature of certain problems encountered and methods of dealing with such problems. The clinician is both a scientist and a practitioner. His effectiveness need not suffer from his scientific efforts. Such efforts, when directed toward a better understanding of a child's problems, should make his work more effective.

Psychoanalytic Methods. An important influence upon modern child psychology has come out of the work of Sigmund Freud, the father of psychoanalysis, and others inspired by his work. The psychoanalytic interview was originally developed as a method for studying adults suffering from conflicts and other emotional disturbances. It was Anna Freud (1928) in particular who emphasized the principle that neurotic symptoms appearing in adults are the result of childhood experiences.

Psychoanalysis is essentially a method of reconstructing the individual's past through examining in detail the behavior and experiences of an individual. The psychologist notes irregularities, evasions, and deceptions in the behavior of the individual. Play activities of children furnish valuable data for analysis and interpretation. Through such data the investigator hopes to find the conscious and unconscious forces in behavior. Data obtained by the methods used in psychoanalysis are extremely hard to evaluate, although such data may be very important in arriving at a better understanding of the dynamic forces in the child's life. The method should be supplemented with data from other sources since it is dependent upon interpretations of observed behaviors and verbalizations. In order to overcome the difficulties inherent in the verbalized nature of psychoanalysis, a variety of projective techniques and other somewhat unstructured devices have been developed to study the personalities of children. The techniques that stem largely from psychoanalytic methods have been generally accepted as research instruments and are useful in studying psychological problems of children and adults.

IDENTIFYING EXCEPTIONAL CHILDREN

Much progress has been made in the past two or three decades in the development of instruments and procedures for better understanding the abilities, characteristics, and needs of children with special abilities, limitations, and problems. If exceptional children are to receive the optimum benefits from special treatment and training, it seems important that they be identified at an early age.

Systematic Observations. It was pointed out earlier that observations over a relatively long period of time have been found useful in studying exceptional children and adolescents. Observations during infancy will reveal the presence or absence of sensory and motor difficulties. Infantile autism, regarded by some clinicians as the earliest form of schizophrenia, may be detected during early infancy by the clinician through systematic observations. Mongolism, and other conditions that are congenital in nature, may also be detected at an early stage by the clinician. Through systematic observations of a child who is having difficulties with certain aspects of the school program, the teacher or clinician may be able to detect ways in which the child is significantly different from other children of his age or maturity level. Although the child may not appear physically different from other children, certain meaningful differences may appear when systematic observations of his behavior are made in the classroom or on the playground. Reading, spelling, language, and arithmetic are frequently sources of confusion and difficulty for the mentally retarded child. The child handicapped by visual difficulty, a hearing defect, or lowered vitality is also likely to encounter difficulties in his learning activities; but systematic observation will reveal that the difficulties encountered by these children are usually quite different from those encountered by the mentally retarded child.

The school-age child crippled by poliomyelitis but with average mental ability will be able to understand directions, comprehend meanings, and participate in many group activities. The young mentally retarded child not only will fail to learn to read and spell at the normal age, but also will not understand directions given in classroom situations, and will fail to comprehend certain complex activities encountered on the playground and elsewhere. In general he finds it simpler to play with younger children and may withdraw from active participation with members of his age group. He will catch on to the rules of the game only after repeated trials, and then may make many incorrect responses in situations where generalizations of the rules are required. He may display good memory for concrete items in a given situation, and this is often mistaken for general intelligence.

Minor physical defects must be identified, or the child's behavior may be misunderstood. Children with defective hearing are often accused of being slow learners or inattentive, and children with lowered vitality are occasionally referred to as lazy or inattentive. Laziness, inattentiveness, and lack of interest should be regarded as symptomatic of difficulties. Careful observation of such children will reveal the level of their intelligence, or specific language problems, and will result in a better understanding of the specific nature of the difficulty. Dupont has dramatically indicated the need for concern about emotional symptoms, too, with this pointed suggestion: "We propose nothing less that someday at least, all school age children be given emotional examinations just as they now receive physical examinations as a routine part of their school enrollment" (1957, p. 10).

School Records. Cumulative school records furnish a useful source of data in identifying potential learning problems as well as academic and creative abilities. Accurate, complete, and objective developmental records for individual exceptional children furnish a valuable source of research materials for the school psychologist, and, more important, they furnish an invaluable source of information for the teacher and counselor. Such records should include achievement test results, evidence of classroom performance, psychological test data, health history, family history, anecdotal records that reveal unusual characteristics, and other data useful to the teacher, counselor, school psychologist, and others concerned with the education, guidance, and therapy for the individual children.

In addition to the more standardized and formal records maintained by the school, many teachers find it helpful to supplement such records with additional records—formal and informal in nature. Such records contain additional data about the student's activities and achievements in the given subject or grade; his work habits; attitudes toward self, classmates, and school; and social adjustments. Samples of pupils' work, anecdotal materials, and observations by the individual teachers furnish valuable information about individual pupils that cannot be gathered by more formal procedures. Such information is invaluable in understanding a child's difficulties along with the complex and interrelated factors that operate in the individual child at any given time.

Educational and Psychological Tests. Educational and psychological testing are not new. As a result of the vast amount of research in progress in the area of testing, new devices are continually appearing. Many of the newer tests may be used with handicapped children, sometimes with some slight adaptations. Because of the specific nature of most standardized tests, they have been found useful for measuring certain aspects of an individual's educational achievement or mental development. An objective test score on the content of a health course, however, cannot safely be used as a criterion for determining the health attitudes and practices of a group of junior high school pupils. Achievement tests not only furnish us an evaluation of an individual's general educational development in certain directions, but also provide information about some phases of this development.

Achievement tests have been developed to measure the amount of information, knowledge, understanding, or skill that a pupil has acquired in certain areas. Tests have been developed for all traditional subjects such as reading, language, arithmetic, spelling, and science. Within more recent years there has been an expansion of tests to cover the various subjects of the secondary school curriculum. There has also been an enlargement of the scope of achievement tests to include applications of knowledge, appreciation, and problem-solving abilities.

Some standardized tests of schoolroom learning are actually batteries of subtests that cover the major academic fields of learning. The *California Achievement Tests,* the *Cooperative General Culture Tests,* the *Iowa Educational Development Tests,* the *Metropolitan Achievement Tests,* and the *Stanford Achievement Tests* are examples of test batteries. Ordinarily, subtests in these batteries can be purchased separately, administered individually, and interpreted as separate tests. Figure 1–3 shows a diagnostic achievement profile of a seventh-grade pupil on the *Metropolitan Achievement Tests,* Elementary Battery. Such a profile furnishes the teacher with important information about the strong and weak points of individual pupils.

Since intelligence as an "inborn capacity" is largely an abstraction, any attempt to measure it must be based upon a functional definition or set of assumptions. Newland refers to *manifest intelligence* as book-learning aptitude and *basic intelligence* as the true potential of the child. Intelligence tests administered under desirable conditions furnish a rough basis for estimating a child's manifest, or functional, intelligence. *They do not give an IQ that can be filed away as the final answer to the child's mental capacity.* Concerning this distinction, Newland (1952) states:

> In most if not all cases, *the basic capacity of a child is an inference.* It is in making this inference that the psychological sheep are separated from the test-giving goats. Good clinical training and experience with many kinds of children are needed to provide the basis for such clinical inferences. No test is ever wrong. No test result is ever wrong. What usually is wrong is the inference drawn from the results on a given test in a given situation. [P. 53.]

The *Wechsler Intelligence Scale for Children* is a valuable addition to the limited number of individual tests available for measuring intelligence of children. Considerable research has already been done on its predictive efficiency. Data available reveal significant differences in IQ results between it and the Stanford-Binet, in spite of the high correlations found between them. Pastovic and Guthrie (1951)

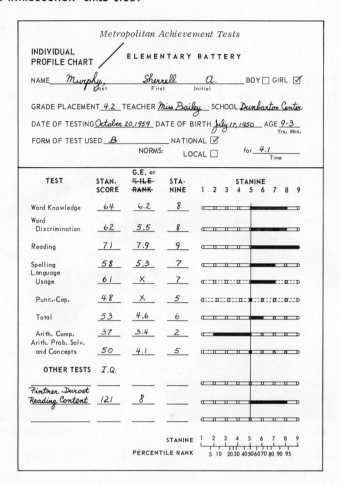

Fig. 1–3. Individual Profile Chart of a fourth-grade pupil on the *Metropolitan Achievement Tests.* (Copyright 1960 by Harcourt, Brace and World, Inc., New York, and used by permission.)

conclude that "the WISC IQ should not be interpreted as equivalent to Binet IQ at age levels below ten years since the WISC score is consistently lower than that of the Binet" (p. 385). The limits of the IQ values given for the Wechsler full scale are from 46 to 154, which means that the scale cannot be used successfully with individuals who rank above or below these limits.

About the time the first revisions of the Binet tests were being made, some psychologists developed performance tests as substitutes for verbal scales of the Binet type. The various correlational studies

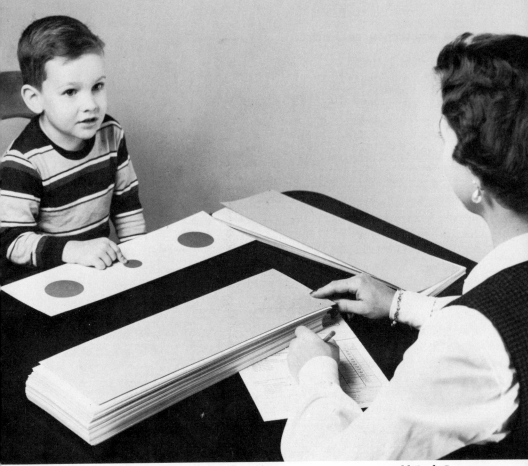

Individual testing is essential in determining the mental ability of children and adolescents.

made between results on these tests and those obtained from revised Binet tests have shown that it is sounder practice to regard these performance tests as supplements rather than substitutes for the Binet tests. In cases involving diagnosis of mental deficiency, it is often advisable to supplement the Stanford-Binet or a similar test with performance tests in order to check on the possible influence of language, educational, and cultural factors on the individual's intelligence test score. Some evidence has been found that indicates that mentally retarded children obtain somewhat higher ratings on performance scales than on the Stanford-Binet or other tests in which language might play an important part. Some of the most widely used performance scales are:

The Arthur Point Scale of Performance Tests
Carl Hollow Square Scale
Cornell-Coxe Performance Ability Scale
Ferguson Form Boards

Group tests are easily administered and save considerable time, since they can be given to many children at the same time. They are frequently used as screening devices. A study by Slutsky *et al.* (1952) dealt with the use of a group intelligence test as a screening device in the selection of mentally retarded children for placement in special classes. The Stanford-Binet IQ's of 868 third-grade children who had obtained low scores (IQ's 76 and below) on the *Otis Quick-Scoring Alpha Mental Test* were studied and analyzed. The mean IQ obtained by the group on the Otis test was 68.90, while the mean IQ obtained on the Stanford-Binet test was 77.37. A consideration of the individual results for the group showed that 342 children (almost 40 per cent) obtained Stanford-Binet IQ's of 75 or below. According to the results presented in Table 1–1, if an Otis IQ of 60 were used as a cutoff point, 81 per cent of the children tested would have had a Stanford-Binet IQ of 75 or below. These results indicate that the

TABLE 1–1

Relationship Between Otis Quick-scoring Alpha and Stanford-Binet
Intelligence Quotients

Otis IQ	N	Cumulative Per Cent of Stanford-Binet IQ's	
		75 or Below	Above 75
75–76	143	39	61
73–74	150	44	56
71–72	129	49	51
69–70	103	51	49
67–68	91	56	44
65–66	56	62	38
63–64	56	67	33
61–62	56	74	26
59–60	31	81	19
57–58	28	85	15
55–56	13	88	12
53–54	3	92	8
51–52	4	96	4
50 and below	5	100	0

SOURCE: After Slutzky *et al.* (1952).

group test may well serve as a device for screening pupils for individual testing. The results do not, however, indicate how many children with Stanford-Binet IQ's below 75 would be missed by such a screening device. This factor should be recognized in considering results obtained from any screening device, and perhaps suggests the necessity for different kinds of screening devices or for interpreting the results of group testing with extreme caution.

For exceptional children there is a strong need for the development of tests in which the validity is directly related to the group on which it is to be used (Gallagher and Moss, 1963). This has led to the development of specialized instruments for certain groups of exceptional children. Tests of special aptitude are useful in identifying individuals with special abilities. However, in considering their use with different groups of exceptional children, such tests are of little use without modification. Because of the difficulty of the reading material and the standardized directions, available clerical aptitude tests are seldom suitable for mentally retarded individuals. On the other hand, existing mechanical aptitude tests are useful for mentally retarded individuals since most of them will be trained for unskilled and semiskilled jobs.

Aptitude tests may be divided roughly into two types: paper-and-pencil and manipulative. The *MacQuarrie Test for Mechanical Ability*, a paper-and-pencil test, requires no reading; however, the standardized directions for some parts are too difficult for severely retarded persons.

Measuring Personality. Three widely used methods for measuring personality and personality adjustments are (1) personality inventories, (2) rating scales, and (3) projective techniques. Some of these are referred to in connection with the personality and personalities difficulties of exceptional children. Personality inventories are self-rating questionnaires that deal not only with overt behavior such as that found in emotional display, but also with the person's own feelings about himself as noted in introspection. The subject is given a list of questions relating to different aspects of behavior. They are stated in such a way that they can be answered by "Yes," "No," or "Uncertain." Illustrative items used in personality inventories are as follows:

Are your feelings easily hurt?	Yes	No	Uncertain
Do you worry over possible misfortunes?	Yes	No	Uncertain
Are you easily moved to tears?	Yes	No	Uncertain

It should be pointed out that personality inventories are not sufficiently reliable and valid to be used as a final measure of a child's personality characteristics. Some tests have a "lie score" which indicates whether the testee has been untruthful in answering the questions, but this does not provide a correction factor. Tests of this sort may be useful in diagnosis but are of questionable value in general personality measurement (Ellis, 1953).

One of the best-known personality inventories is the *Minnesota Multiphasic Personality Inventory,* which is used to classify people into clinical types. It contains over 500 questions directed at nine dimensions of personality. These are (1) hypochondria (undue concern about bodily complaints), (2) depression, (3) hysteria, (4) psychopathic deviation (disregard of social motives), (5) paranoia (suspiciousness), (6) masculinity-femininity, (7) hypomania (excessive activity), (8) psychasthenia, and (9) schizophrenia. A high score on any trait indicates symptoms that should be further investigated.

Rating techniques are of two general types. The first of these may be referred to as the rank-order type, since the individual is ranked for some trait or characteristic with reference to others being rated. In such a case the individuals would be ranked as *first, second, third,* etc. The second type has often been referred to as a graphic rating scale. The individual is rated graphically—along a line—for some trait, with numbers or verbal descriptions being placed at points where he seems to belong. For example, the child may be rated for thoughtfulness as *often thoughtful, usually thoughtful, sometimes thoughtful, seldom thoughtful,* or *never thoughtful.* Such ratings are commonly given children by their parents, teachers, and others. However, one should be cautious in generalizing from one situation to another about the existence of a particular trait. Goodenough (1949) refers to an unpublished study carried out at the Institute of Child Welfare of the University of Minnesota that bears out the need for this caution. Only a moderate relationship was found between the indexes of talking obtained for nursery school children in different situations. An outstanding example cited was a nursery school child who scarcely uttered a word during her three years of attendance at the nursery school but who had a very high index of talkativeness at home. Thus, even during the nursery school stage, individuals play different roles in different social-field environments.

Projective techniques avoid direct questions and subjective ratings in an effort to arrive at the nature of personality. Rather, these procedures confront the subject with a stimulus for the purpose of so ordering his perceptions or responses that they will reflect the dynamics and structure of his personality. The best known and most widely studied of these techniques is the *Rorschach Ink-Blot Test*. This consists of a series of cards, on each of which is an irregularly shaped ink blot. The subject is asked "What might this be?" or "What does this look like to you?" The subject then gives his interpretation. The examiner notes the responses given, the number of different ones, and their quality and completeness. Needless to say, the value of such a test will depend largely upon the skill and ability of the examiner who interprets the responses. This test has a distinct advantage over many other projective techniques in that the stimulus itself provides very little of the interpretation. The subject's responses are determined by personal experiences and by the direction of his emotional and mental reactions. This has been borne out by the wide range of responses obtained from subjects having different levels of maturity or cultural background.

The interpretation of Rorschach ink blots is not standardized and there are no norms. The greatest usefulness of the test is in revealing markedly deviant personalities. Enthusiastic Rorschach exponents recognize that the test is in need of further experimental research, particularly in regard to method of scoring, normative studies, and longitudinal studies.

Another projective technique that has been widely used is the *Thematic Apperception Test*, commonly referred to as TAT. This test consists of a series of pictures, usually including people, about which the subject being tested is instructed to tell a story. The pictures are shown one at a time, with no time limit. This test is employed primarily in clinical studies of the maladjusted and abnormal.

A variety of projective devices appeared after the Rorschach and TAT tests had found considerable favor among students of clinical and abnormal psychology. Many of these are still in the experimental stage.

There is evidence, both theoretical and practical, that all these tests based upon free associations and responses provide some bases for interpreting the personal and social needs of the individual. One of the major criticisms of projective techniques centers about their lack of objectivity—they rely upon subjective evaluation of the individual's responses. This criticism has merit. Caution should be observed, however, in attempting to arrive at a quantitative score for all aspects of personality. Because of its intangible and interdependent nature, personality is difficult and perhaps impossible to describe in purely quantitative terms.

The Complete-Survey Procedure. A complete survey by a team of specially trained consultants will identify more problems than are located through teacher referrals. This does not mean that referrals should not be made and used in finding physically handicapped children. The classroom teacher is usually able to recognize outstanding problems, but many borderline cases are not detected. These children must be reached and treated if they are to make the most of their potentialities.

The complete-survey procedure was used in testing 15,000 children in six counties of Tennessee for hearing and speech defects (Foote and Stecher, 1953). A portable pure-tone audiometer was used under a variety of circumstances. In one-room schools the testing was done in the classroom, with all children present. The testing procedure was first explained to all the children and then each child was screened in turn. In the larger schools a quiet room was chosen for the testing, such as the library, gymnasium, or auditorium. When the school had no electricity available for the operation of the audiometer, the testing was done in some church or farmhouse.

The complete-survey procedure has also been used in determining the visual problems of schoolchildren, in connection with programs of visual conservation and treatment. Likewise, X rays have been widely used in recent years in locating children who may be suffering from tuberculosis or from allied conditions. Dental surveys, nutritional surveys, and surveys by mental hygienists are increasingly being used to locate children needing special consideration and treatment. However, the complete-survey procedure that has been most widely used involves the use of mental tests. A large percentage of schools give intelligence tests periodically in order to determine the level of intelligence of the entire school population. The results of these tests, supplemented by those given to individual cases in the community needing special care and treatment, furnish a complete survey of the intelligence levels of the school-age population.

In addition to mental, aptitude, and personality tests which are widely used, there are many motor and sensory tests available. A complete survey will include in addition to psychological and educational tests the following:

1. Individual audiometric sweep testing of all pupils, with special provisions for retesting those showing a 9 or 10 decibel loss or greater in the speech range.
2. Visual-acuity testing of all pupils, with further tests or referral of those showing evidences of visual difficulties.
3. Location of pupils with physical disabilities, and special examinations or referral of those with suspected disabilities.
4. Speech survey conducted by trained personnel with individual tests on spontaneous and directed speech. Pupils who appear to have speech problems should be examined more carefully.
5. Medical tests to determine disabilities and health conditions that interfere with normal activities.

SUMMARY

The major purpose of child psychologists is to describe, interrelate, and predict the behavior and development of children as accurately as methods for gathering data will permit. In order to do these tasks more successfully, various methods have been devised for gathering data about individual children. The longitudinal method was early devised for gathering data that made it possible to determine the nature of individual growth curves and thus to predict more accurately the physical growth and development of individuals from birth to maturity.

Tests have been developed to measure different abilities, aptitudes, and personal characteristics. Most of these tests were designed for individuals who are growing and developing in a normal or average environmental condition. Results from such tests reveal that rarely are the tests completely suitable for exceptional children. Thus, efforts have been made to modify existing tests and to develop new tests especially designed for particular groups of individuals.

Rating scales and personality inventories are widely used in measuring personality characteristics and development. Projective techniques have been devised and widely used in an attempt to measure characteristic responses of individuals that are not measured by existing psychological tests and personality inventories. Although considerable research has been done in the development of such techniques and in the interpretation of results obtained, much remains to be done before projective techniques reach the level of objectivity needed for accurate evaluation and prediction.

Since the individual must be viewed as an interrelated whole, the case-study method of studying the individual child appears to offer great promise. This method may make use of any or all of the other methods suggested for gathering data on individual children, and may also use the resources of various agencies. The completeness of the case study will be determined by a number of factors, including (1) the purpose of the study, (2) the training of the person making the study, (3) the resources available for making the study, and (4) the cooperation of others in conducting the study.

The application of various methods to the study of handicapped children requires, in addition to an understanding of methods of studying children, a knowledge of exceptional children. Such a knowledge will enable the investigator to adapt methods to the characteristics of the children being studied. There is a further need on the part of those studying exceptional children to determine the qualitative as well as the quantitative nature of individual differences. As a result of clinical studies of exceptional children, increased attention is being given to the qualitative aspects. This may be observed in connection with qualitative studies of the vocabulary development of the child. The increased use of projective techniques and anecdotal records is a further indication of the recognition of the importance of qualitative aspects of behavior. Much interest is manifested today in qualitative differences in family relations and in social-class status.

CHAPTER REFERENCES

CARR, LELA B. (1959). Problems confronting parents of children with handicaps. *Except. Child.,* 25:251–55.

CRANDALL, V. J., KATKOVSKY, W., and PRESTON, ANNE (1960). A conceptual formulation for some research on children's achievement development. *Child Developm.,* 31:787–97.

DOLL, E. A. (1963). Adultation of the special child. *Except. Child.,* 29:275–80.

DUPONT, H. J. (1957). Emotional maladjustment and special education. *Except. Child.,* 24:10–15.

ELLIS, A. (1953). Recent research with personality inventories. *J. consult. Psychol.,* 17: 45–49.

FOOTE, R. M., and STECHER, SYLVIA (1953). Toward better speech and hearing. *Child* (June–July), pp. 154–57.

FORD, E. H. R. (1958). Growth in height of ten siblings. *Hum. Biol.,* 30:108–19.

FREUD, ANNA (1928). Introduction to the technique of child analysis. *Nerv. ment. Disord. Monogr.,* No. 48.

GALLAGHER, J. J., and MOSS, J. W. (1963). New concepts of intelligence and their effects on exceptional children. *Except. Child.,* 30:1–5.

GESELL, A., and HALVERSON, H. M. (1942). The daily maturation of infant behavior. A cinema study of postures, movements and laterality. *J. genet. Psychol.*, 61:3–32.

GOODENOUGH, FLORENCE L. (1949). The appraisal of child personality. *Psychol. Rev.*, 56:123–31.

GORDON, I. J. (1959). Inferring children's concepts of self: interobserver reliability. Paper presented at the Southeast. Psychol. Assn., St. Augustine, Florida, April 24, 1959.

LIPPITT, R. (1940). An experimental study of the effect of democratic and authoritarian group atmosphere. *Univer. Iowa Stud. Child Welf.*, Vol. 16, No. 1.

MILLARD, C. V. (1951). *Child growth and development in the elementary school.* Boston: D. C. Heath.

NEWLAND, T. E. (1952). Are exceptional children tested or assessed? *Except. Child.*, 19:51–55.

OLSON, W. C. (1959). *Child development.* (2nd ed.) Boston: D. C. Heath.

PASTOVIC, J. J., and GUTHRIE, G. M. (1951). Some evidence on the validity of WISC. *J. consult. Psychol.*, 15:385–86.

PETERSON, J. (1935). *Early conceptions and tests of intelligence.* Yonkers, N.Y.: World Book Co.

SLUTSKY, J. E., JUSTMAN, J., and WRIGHTSTONE, J. W. (1952). The use of a group intelligence test as a screening device for the selection of mentally retarded children for placement in special classes. *Amer. J. ment. Def.*, 57:106–8.

WATSON, J. B., and RAYNER, R. (1920). Conditioned emotional reactions. *J. exp. Psychol.*, 3:1–14.

SELECTED READINGS

ANDERSON, J. B. (1954). Methods of child study. In L. CARMICHAEL (ed.), *Manual of child psychology.* (2d ed.) New York: Wiley.

BERNARD, H. W. (1962). *Human development in western culture.* Boston: Allyn & Bacon. Chap. 1.

GARRISON, K. C., and KINGSTON, A. J. (1964). *Child psychology.* New York: Scribner's. Chap. 1.

JENKINS, J. J., and PATERSON, D. G. (1962). *Studies in individual differences.* London: Methuen.

MUSSEN, P. H. (ed.) (1960). *Handbook of research in child development.* New York: Wiley.

NEWLAND, T. E. (1963). Psychological assessment of exceptional children and youth. In W. A. CRUICKSHANK (ed.), *Psychology of exceptional children and youth.* (2d ed.) Englewood Cliffs, N.J.: Prentice-Hall.

OLSON, W. C. (1959). *Child development.* (2d ed.) Boston: D. C. Heath. Chap. 1.

PEARSON, G. H. J. (1949). *Emotional disorders of children.* New York: Norton. Chap. 1.

STONE, J. L., and CHURCH, J. (1957). *Childhood and adolescence.* New York: Random House. Chap. 14.

THOMPSON, G. E. (1962). *Child psychology.* (Rev. ed.) Boston: Houghton Mifflin. Chaps. 1 and 2.

THORPE, L. P., and CRUZE, W. W. (1962). *Developmental psychology.* (2d ed.) New York: Ronald. Chap. 1.

VENESS, THELMA (1962). *Studies in individual differences.* London: Methuen.

An annotated, select list of recent references to exceptional children is presented on pages 539–40.

2

SPECIAL EDUCATION

In recent years the field of special education has greatly accelerated in development as parents, educators, and the general public have become convinced that exceptional children have potentialities and needs that cannot be met through general education but that require special efforts on the part of teachers and other professional personnel. The growth of special services has been phenomenal, and yet much remains to be done in various parts of the country and for children with particular conditions that may handicap them educationally, socially, or vocationally.

PHILOSOPHY

A philosophy has gradually evolved that expresses the hopes and purposes of special education and the convictions of those who call themselves special educators. While society frequently needs to be convinced about how "normal" the handicapped person may be, nonetheless, the person with a disability may have special needs that he and others must recognize and seek to meet. Graham (1961), an acknowledged spokesman for special education, has said:

The realization that a child's handicap represents only a minority part of him reflects one of the noteworthy trends in the education of the handicapped which has occurred in the last half century. Now we understand also that the education of the handicapped child must be a continuing process because, like the normal child, he learns and acquires skills by his efforts day after day, year after year. [P. 48.]

Scope of Special Education.   In an attempt to determine the scope of special education, Hodgson (1964) submitted a questionnaire containing a list of physical, intellectual, and learning characteristics to a group of educators consisting of school administrators, specialists in special education, and members of the state department of education. The respondents were requested to indicate approval or rejection of each item as a function of special education. A tabulation and analysis of the results of this study indicated that special education should include the following classifications and educational provisions (p. 197):

Gifted	Orthopedically handicapped
Mentally retarded	Chronic medical problems
Mentally deficient	Hospital teaching
Emotionally disturbed and/or so-	Home teaching
cially disturbed	Deaf
Blind	Hard of hearing
Partially seeing	Speech reading
Cerebral palsied	Speech correction

Differences were noted in the responses of school administrators, specialists in special education, and members of the state department of education. The professors of school administration were least inclined to include the gifted and mentally deficient (IQ range of 0 to 50) as classifications in special education. State department of education members and the specialists, however, were in general agreement that these categories should be the responsibility of a public school department of special education.

Special education seeks to meet the unusual needs that any child may have without labeling the person as different from all other human beings. Thus, to say that the exceptional child is basically like other children is quite true. He has the same physiological and psychological needs as have all other human beings (Carr, 1959). However, to meet these human needs, when a child has a disability, may require a very special effort on his part and/or by those concerned with his welfare.

Understanding the Exceptional Child.   In order to understand the exceptional child, it is useful figuratively to separate the child from his condition or disability. Efforts to understand persons who are blind may be more profitable than attempts to understand "the blind" as a group because of the great individual variations among persons with this particular label. Special educators have become increasingly more concerned with how a specific disability interferes with functioning for each exceptional child than they are with placing each child in some appropriate, diagnostic category such as "the retarded."

Because of the visibility of his condition, the child with cerebral palsy may be seen as more handicapped than he actually is, or needs to be. On the other hand, the child with a hearing loss appears to be quite normal but, in fact, may be quite handicapped for oral communication. This latter point also means that being handicapped is to be seen as more relevant to *situations* than to *persons*. The blind child may be handicapped for reading in the usual style and must learn braille, but he may not be handicapped at all in moving about his familiar home in the dark of night. The mentally retarded child is most handicapped in the usual school setting, where a premium is placed on intellect and problem-solving ability; but many retarded children can learn skills, when taught in modified fashion, that allow for independence and vocational success as adults. To say "Hire the handicapped; it's good business" may thus not be literally correct because it places the emphasis on disability. If it is good business to hire handicapped persons, it is certainly not because of their disabilities but because they have abilities or have developed skills that may be used vocationally, and they are placed in employment situations where their disability becomes largely irrelevant.

The range of problems to be found among exceptional children means that instruction generally must be provided in smaller groups or on an individual basis. While a child may have a chief disability, frequently he will have multiple disabilities that complicate instruction. In the survey conducted by Wishik (1956) in Georgia, multiple disability was found to be present in a majority of the sample studied.

Educational Placement. Two assumptions underlie the educational placement of exceptional children. (1) A careful and complete evaluation, conducted by competent personnel, is essential to the accurate determination of the special needs that a child may have. This means more than a cursory screening or "one-shot" examination by minimally qualified personnel. (2) Once his special needs are identified, the kind of placement that seems best for this particular exceptional child should be provided. There must be alternatives that go beyond the regular classroom with no special service or residential placement that often is largely custodial. Careful identification and suitable placement have been called *selective placement* in that the kind of placement is chosen that best serves a particular child and his unique needs. If the best kind of placement does not exist in a given community, then steps must be taken to develop such a facility or service.

While many exceptional children may not become "normal" or cured of their disability or condition, their special needs will, hopefully, change or be reduced through special education. Thus, no placement should be seen as permanent but should be open to periodic review when new evidence may be considered. Any placement is being increasingly seen as a flexible matter for all exceptional children. Further, placement in the community in a relatively normal kind of educational setting is generally seen as the goal or ideal placement. Graham (1956) has emphasized this latter point in his remark:

Special education does not relieve the regular school teacher of responsibility for the exceptional child. It offers special services to supplement the regular school program.

State regulations on special-class size have come to reflect official concern for the numbers of exceptional children who might profitably be educated together. Fifteen is a frequent limit to the size of a class for educable, mentally retarded children. Presumably, such a limit increases the possibility of homogeneity; but new special-class teachers quickly become aware of the heterogeneity possible in a group of this number unless multiple criteria are used for selecting the "right" 15 children for his class.

PROGRESS

In 1952 Mackie outlined five continuing problems in special education. These were (1) extension of programs to wider age groups, (2) closer home-school relations, (3) more teachers, (4) more adequate financial appropriations, and (5) closer teamwork among related agencies.

Since 1952 there has been marked progress in each of these areas. Programs have been extended to include preschool children as well as youth of high school and postschool age. The parents of exceptional children have increasingly been seen as partners of special

teachers in the planning and implementation of programs appropriate
to their children's special needs. Progress in training teachers of exceptional children is reflected in the growing numbers of children
being served. Improved patterns of state reimbursement and the
availability of federal funds have stimulated research, the expansion
of direct services, and college and university programs. Public and
private agencies are continuously seeking ways to cooperate and to
redefine services that will further benefit exceptional children.

Table 2–1 shows the special education enrollments in local public
school systems reported nationally for February, 1958.

TABLE 2–1

Special Education Enrollments in Local Public School Systems, February, 1958

Area of Exceptionality	Number of Pupils
Blind	2,844
Partially seeing	8,598
Deaf	6,424
Hard of hearing	13,113
Speech impaired	486,944
Crippled	29,311
Special health problems	23,077
Socially and emotionally maladjusted	28,260
Mentally retarded (upper range)	201,406
Mentally retarded (middle range)	16,779
Gifted	52,269
Other	13,041
Total	882,066

SOURCE: Mackie and Robbins (1961).

Mackie (1962) pointed out that the number served in 1958 was
about one-fourth of those estimated to need special education. This
is contrasted with 15 per cent (Mackie, 1952) in need of special
services who were reported as receiving such services in 1952. This
figure is further contrasted with the figure of 10 per cent (Martens,
1944) obtaining needed services as reported in 1944.

This expansion is one measure of the public's concern for educational provisions for *all* children who may be served by the schools.
It is also a measure of the progress toward the goal of special programs
for all exceptional children who need such programs. The nearly
900,000 children enrolled in 1958 were served through a variety of
special education programs with the full-time, self-contained special

class being just one of the ways by which special education was provided. While about 750 public school systems had special education programs in 1935, the figure was doubled by 1948, and was up to 3,700 programs in 1958.

In commenting about continuing roadblocks to progress in the field, Mackie (1962) again pointed out the critical shortage of professionally qualified special educators that still exists when she remarked, "It is estimated that 200,000 are needed and only about 50,000 are available" (p. 10).

An examination of the special education program in one state in the 1952–1962 decade illustrates the dimensions of growth that are reflected in other states. Home instruction was first offered in Minnesota in 1952 with 1,292 children served by 342 teachers. In the 1961–1962 school year 2,775 children were tutored at home by 1,407 teachers. The number of Minnesota children and professional personnel serving them in this and other special education programs in the 1952–1953 and 1961–1962 school years may be seen in Table 2–2.

TABLE 2–2

Minnesota's Exceptional Children and Personnel Serving Them in
1952–1953 and 1961–1962

Category	Children		Personnel	
	1952–1953	1961–1962	1952–1953	1961–1962
Speech problems	5,060	14,290	48	184
Mentally retarded	2,499	6,266	153	531
Crippled	485	427	31	126
Hearing impaired	206	337	21	63
Visually impaired	278	252	26	64
Emotionally disturbed and neurologically impaired	–	625	–	63
Hospital-homebound	1,292	2,775	342	1,407*
Other essential personnel			–	140
Totals	9,820	24,972	621	2,578

* 1,369 of these are part-time personnel teaching home instruction.

SOURCE: After Reynolds (1954) and Stenswick (1961–1962).

Programs for mentally retarded children, children with speech problems, and services to homebound and hospitalized children showed the greatest numerical growth. Programs in several other areas of special education showed little change in the numbers of children but striking increases in the number and qualifications of personnel serving them. Public school programs for Minnesota's emotionally disturbed and neurologically impaired children were initiated in 1958 and indicate the nature and extent of progress in special education.

Progress in special education in Minnesota was made possible by a number of interrelated developments illustrative of conditions generally necessary for improvement of programs for exceptional children.

1. Increased legislative interest was stimulated by parent groups, professional educators, and representatives of health agencies and residential institutions, and resulted in a Legislative Interim Commission to study the problem in the 1955–1957 biennium. Of several sweeping recommendations to the 1957 Legislature, all were adopted.

2. Major changes in the state's education laws made the responsibility for special education clear. The provision of suitable special education programs was made mandatory for all educable handicapped children rather than permissive, as had previously been the case.

3. Changes were made in state regulations to make financial incentives and reimbursement much more attractive to school districts that were establishing programs.

4. A major development in the Minnesota Department of Education was the establishment of a Special Education Section with several qualified consulting personnel. Prior to 1957 there had been a part-time Supervisor of Special Education for the state. By 1962 there was a Director, an Assistant Director, and four full-time consultant positions.

5. Qualified personnel were added to the faculties at the University of Minnesota and at three of the five state colleges to train teachers and other specialists for positions in the field; no year-round programs for training special teachers existed in the state before 1957. By 1964 the University of Minnesota had eleven full-time faculty in special education and was training personnel in all fields of special education and at all levels of training from the baccalaureate through the doctorate.

Yearly increments in the numbers of exceptional children served in Minnesota public schools in the ten-year period are seen in Table 2–3. A notable acceleration and differentiation of programs can be seen after 1957, with greatest numerical growth in the 1957–1960 period.

Continuing growth may be observed in the figures of Table 2–4 which indicate the numbers of exceptional children served by full- and part-time special personnel for 1962–1963 and for the 1963–1964 school year.

TABLE 2–3

Exceptional Children Served in Minnesota Public Schools, 1952–1962

Category	1952–1953	1953–1954	1954–1955	1955–1956	1956–1957	1957–1958	1958–1959	1959–1960	1960–1961	1961–1962
Speech correction	5,060	5,914	6,949	7,255	7,422	7,924	9,942	11,551	12,425	14,290
Educable retarded	–	–	–	–	–	–	–	–	5,229	5,839
Trainable retarded	–	–	–	–	–	–	–	–	368	427
(together)	2,499	2,834	2,872	3,179	3,504	3,806	4,582	5,085		
Crippled	485	474	441	428	405	397	442	442	428	427
Hearing impaired	206	193	209	190	215	253	254	238	299	337
Visually impaired	278	254	267	275	256	259	257	228	235	252
Emotionally disturbed	–	–	–	–	–	–	652	486	365	568
Neurologically impaired	–	–	–	–	–	–	+SLD	+SLD	98	57
Home-hospital	1,292	1,323	1,278	1,299	1,233	1,732	1,856	2,481	2,716	2,775
Total	9,820	10,992	12,016	12,626	13,035	14,371	17,985	20,511	22,163	24,972

SOURCE: Adapted from Annual Reports of Recommendations for Reimbursement Aid of State Funds—Special Education, 1952–1962.

TABLE 2–4

Exceptional Children Served by Full- and Part-Time Special
Personnel, 1962–1964

	1962–1963			1963–1964		
	Pupils	Personnel		Pupils	Personnel	
Category		Full-Time	Part-Time		Full-Time	Part-Time
Speech correction	15,712	128	98	16,392	144	120
Educable mentally retarded	6,341	477	53	6,803	495	85
Trainable mentally retarded	435	51	13	483	55	16
Crippled	468	103	57	490	111	55
Hearing impaired	355	44	48	412	49	59
Visually impaired	224	22	43	239	20	47
SLD (Special learning disabilities)	942	30	71	1,366	39	141
Home-hospital	3,021	39	1,648	3,316	75	1,916
Other essential personnel	–	123	50	–	136	50
Total	27,498	1,017	2,081	29,501	1,124	2,489

SOURCE: Adapted from Annual Reports of *Recommendations for Reimbursement Aid of State Funds—Special Education*, 1962–1963 and 1963–1964.

Growth in the numbers of special personnel serving exceptional children in Minnesota may be seen in Table 2–5. Underscores indicate the years in which new teacher training programs were organized or efforts accelerated in existing programs. Occupational therapists and physical therapists and other part-time professional personnel were included in the numbers of specialists serving crippled children in 1961–1962. The apparent fluctuations in the numbers of "other essential personnel" is due to counting procedures and categorization of services. There were over four times as many specialists serving exceptional children through special education in Minnesota in 1961–1962 as there were ten years earlier.

Special legislative funds were given to the University of Minnesota and to three of the state colleges, Mankato, Moorhead, and St. Cloud, in 1957 to establish programs in special education as well as $40,000 of scholarship moneys given to the University in the 1957–1959 period. These funds were largely used for summer scholarships and had a marked effect on the numerical development of special education programs for retarded children within the state.

Table 2–6 indicates another basis for noting the growth of special education in Minnesota. The 1956–1957 school year was just prior to the many changes in the state program outlined here.

Similar illustrations of dramatic growth may be seen in other sec-

TABLE 2–5

Professional Personnel Serving Exceptional Children in Minnesota Public Schools, 1952–1962

Category	1952–1953	1953–1954	1954–1955	1955–1956	1956–1957	1957–1958	1958–1959	1959–1960	1960–1961	1961–1962
Speech correction	48	52	64	69	78	77	105	116	155	174
Educable retarded	–	–	–	197	192	–	–	–	403	473
Trainable retarded (together)	153	166	181	17	20	242	306	373	42	58
Crippled	31	31	33	34	26	25	29	39	44	126
Hearing impaired	21	20	24	23	24	26	29	30	43	63
Visually impaired	26	26	25	26	25	25	27	30	33	64
Emotionally disturbed	–	–	–	–	–	–	14	11	14	43
Neurologically impaired								+SLD	8	20
Home-hospital	342	398	413	422	398	514	791	1,091	1,310	1,407
Other essential personnel	–	–	–	–	–	165	213	272	–	140
Total	621	693	740	771	763	909	1,514	1,962	2,052	2,578

SOURCE: Adapted from Annual Reports of *Recommendations for Reimbursement Aid of State Funds—Special Education, 1952–1962.*

41

TABLE 2–6

Statistics Comparing Special Education Programs in Minnesota for
the School Years 1956–1957 and 1961–1962

	1956–1957	1961–1962	Per Cent Increase
Number of counties providing at least one special class (not including home-hospital instruction)	32 (87)	82 (87)	156
Number of districts providing at least one special class (not including home-hospital instruction)	57 (480+)	243 (480+)*	326
Total number of pupils served	13,055	24,971	91
Total personnel employed in reimbursable positions	763	2,578	238
Total cost	$2,465,422.20	$6,396,695.99	159
Total state aid	$1,547,798.98	$3,439,989.93	122

SOURCE: Special Education Section, Minnesota Department of Education, March 8, 1963, Memo to Representative Bassett, Attachment No. 4, p. 1.

* Many providing for children from other districts in cooperative, interdistrict programs.

tions of the United States. Based on a 1958 survey of exceptional children in local school programs, Mackie and Robbins (1960) state: ". . . figures represent a rate of growth three times that of local public elementary and secondary school enrollments during the same period" (p. 14).

The crucial shortage of trained persons to staff special education programs for exceptional children has been closely related to the equally critical shortage of college and university personnel qualified to conduct programs of teacher preparation. Mackie *et al.* (1963) reported 225 institutions with minimal sequences in some area of special education in 1961–1962 compared to 122 institutions eight years earlier in 1953–1954. Courses have often developed by expediency or been outlined on paper and first taught by some experienced special-class teacher in the field through a summer workshop or short course. Gradually, full-time college personnel with doctoral level training have been obtained to coordinate the course offerings and to provide year-round opportunities for teacher training.

About the federally sponsored 85–926 Graduate Fellowship Program in Mental Retardation, which was started in 1959 to run for a ten-year period in an effort to train leadership personnel, Mackie (1962) has said:

Although it is too soon for the full influence of the program to be felt, some results are already apparent; it is contributing to the recruitment of personnel to work in the field of mental retardation; many of the Fellows have already completed their preparation and are working full-time; and graduate programs in colleges and universities have been strengthened by the full-time employment of staff in this field. [P. 11.]

The training of teachers of hearing impaired children was quickly accelerated by Public Law 87–276, although recruitment of students to newer programs poses some problems. During the 1962–1963 school year, 43 colleges and universities had 154 stipend holders at the undergraduate level and 292 at the graduate level (Hoag, 1963).

The enactment of Public Law 88–164 just prior to President Kennedy's assassination promised further and even more dramatic acceleration of services and college and university training programs in all areas of special education and from the undergraduate through the doctoral and postdoctoral levels. Almost $50,000,000 was provided for training and demonstration projects and $6,000,000 for research in special education during the 1963–1966 period. A Division on Exceptional Children was established within the U.S. Office of Education with branches concerned with (1) children with physical and sensory handicaps, (2) children who are mentally retarded and emotionally disturbed, and (3) research and demonstration—all under the distinguished direction of Dr. Sam Kirk.

Progress of another sort is seen in Krugman's (1962) listing of the added services provided for exceptional children in New York State in recent years:

Classes for trainable mentally retarded children
Extension of education for educable mentally retarded to age twenty-one
Special provision for culturally deprived children
Special provision for non-English speaking children
Provision for the education of emotionally disturbed children
Many additions for physically handicapped children's education
Reimbursement for out-of-state education when in-state facilities are not available
New provisions for transportation of exceptional children
Many new types of reimbursement for exceptional children
Work camp and other camp-type or residential facilities for socially and emotionally disturbed adolescents
Many additions to vocational rehabilitation provisions [P. 246.]

In 1954 the Southern Regional Education Board appointed a Commission on the Training of Teachers of Handicapped Children which studied the results of a survey by Dunn *et al.* (1955) and then draw up a series of recommendations for regional cooperation. Later the Western Interstate Commission for Higher Education conducted a similar survey and made a series of recommendations that have further enhanced regional planning and the development of high-quality teacher preparation programs in special education.

With the expansion of direct services to exceptional children, the numbers served, and the increased numbers of specially trained personnel, there has also come the necessity for the broadening and improvement of consultant and supervisory efforts at both the local and state levels. Blessing (1960) has described the function and role of the modern state department of education as being both consultive and administrative. As new programs are established, the understanding, compliance, and reporting in line with established administrative regulations and standards is important; but as programs develop, matters of curriculum or program, objectives, and teaching methodology take precedence and require qualified consultant help at both the local and state levels.

While progress in special education has been made along many lines in recent years, much remains to be accomplished, and other facets of advancement in the field might well have been considered in this section. However, only two further comments are made. The stimulation to progress provided by individual parents and by local and state associations and the National Association for Retarded Children is particularly noteworthy as was President Kennedy's strong personal interest before his untimely death.

PROGRAMS

Historically, educational provisions for exceptional children have moved from the residential setting, often far removed from the community, to community placement in special classes in regular schools or to placement in regular classes with a variety of ancillary special services. The notion of free and compulsory education for all who are educable took hold in the early 1900's. A companion notion is that of equality of opportunity, which is reflected in the Supreme Court's 1954 decision relative to segregation of Negroes in school. Equality of educational opportunity has often been denied those exceptional children who could not profit from the typical classroom program. The changing social-democratic philosophy accompanied by the improved economy of our country has affected the role, function, and scope of education. Today it is generally recognized that special provisions must be made for those children who are exceptional, although the *form* of the provisions may be hotly debated. Since special provisions cost more than those for normal children, the states and the federal government have sought ways to make such services feasible. There is fairly general agreement that over 12 per cent of our school-age population is unable to profit sufficiently from the usual educational program and must have special provisions of some sort.

The pattern of enrollment in special education programs, as determined by Mackie and Robbins (1961), is presented in Fig. 2–1. The variety of provisions from field to field within special education is readily apparent. There is considerable variation to be found in programs in different states and different school systems, also. As yet there is little research evidence or professional consensus as to what constitutes an optimum program in any of the fields. There often is professional disagreement in what constitutes an exceptional child and when he needs special provisions.

Reynolds (1962) has sought to provide a single frame of reference for the variety of special educational programs that have become possible. His schematic presentation is seen in Fig. 2–2. It may be seen that this presents the broad range of types of special education programs in organized fashion and that the residential school and the special class are just two of a number of alternatives that should become available in considering suitable placement for every exceptional child. The magnitude of the continuing task before special education may be inferred from the statement, "The strategy proposed here requires variety and range in programs for all handicapping areas, continuing assessment procedures to assure changes in placement at appropriate times, and coordinated planning and placement services covering all areas" (Reynolds, 1962, p. 368).

Mackie's (1962) added comment that another major roadblock to adequate educational opportunity is the lack of scientifically tested knowledge on how best to provide instruction for exceptional children underscores the importance of accelerated research efforts in this field. Connor (1963) cites the following concept preliminary to administrative and instructional provisions for exceptional children:

Special education in all of its areas of exceptionality is an aspect of the instructional function of regular education. Its relationship with the wel-

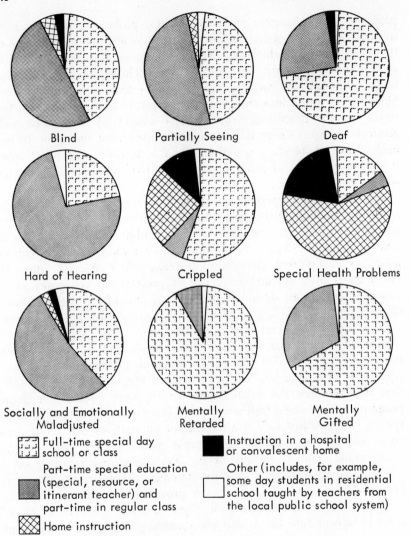

Fig. 2–1. Class placement of handicapped schoolchildren. (Mackie and Robbins, 1961.)

fare, guidance, clinical or medical professions, and governmental services are necessary, but subordinate to the main purpose of teaching handicapped and gifted children and helping them to develop into first class citizens. [P. 432.]

Materials are presented in subsequent chapters bearing on educational provisions for the different categories of exceptional children.

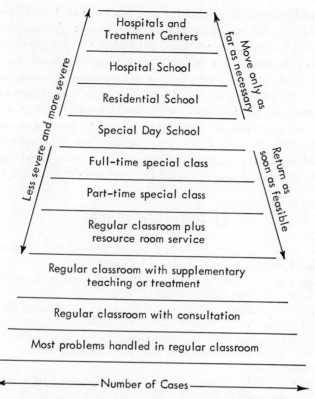

Fig. 2–2. Organizational framework of special education programs. (Reynolds, 1962.)

Quantitative growth in the field of special education is quite apparent; increased concern for the quality of programs for exceptional children is essential if the field of special education is to show continued progress.

SUMMARY

The unusual characteristics of exceptional children provide the basis for the development of an area of education called special education. Over the years a philosophy of special education has evolved that insists that exceptional children are very similar to other children in many needs and quite different from other children in some of the special needs produced by a variety of conditions and disabilities. Thus, special education has developed. Progress in special education was accelerated after World War I and again after World War II; but recent years have seen almost phenomenal growth as reflected in broader programs, expanded teacher preparation opportunities, programs for training leadership personnel, more effective state and national leadership, increased funds for programs, new facilities, and research in the field. All of these developments have been stimulated by increased professional interest, organized parent efforts, and attention by national leaders. At present a variety of programs may be seen across the country; but geographic, population, and monetary factors still make for uneven development of suitable educational opportunities for each exceptional child.

CHAPTER REFERENCES

BLESSING, K. R. (1960). Providing special educational services for exceptional youth. *Except. Child.*, 26:395–400, 408.

CARR, LELA B. (1959). Problems confronting parents of children with handicaps. *Except. Child.*, 25:251–55.

CONNOR, L. E. (1963). Preliminaries to a theory of administration for special education. *Except. Child.*, 29:431–36.

DUNN, L. M., GEER, W. C., and GODWIN, W. L. (1955). *Teachers for the South's handicapped children*. Atlanta: Southern Regional Education Board.

GRAHAM, R. (1956). Sixteen steps in the philosophy of special education for exceptional children. Mimeographed.

GRAHAM, R. (1961). Handicapped and normal children are more alike than different. *NEA J.*, 50:48–50.

HOAG, R. L. (1963). Training for teachers of the dead. *Sch. Life*, 45:18–20, 30.

HODGSON, F. M. (1964). Special education—facts and attitudes. *Except. Child.*, 30:196–201.

KRUGMAN, M. (1962). An administrator speaks on current trends in special education in New York City. *Except. Child.*, 28:245–48.

MACKIE, ROMAINE P. (1952). *Some problems in the education of handicapped children*. U.S. Office of Education Leaflet No. 112. Federal Security Agency. Washington, D.C.: U.S. Government Printing Office.

MACKIE, ROMAINE P. (1962). Education of exceptional children; program, progress, problems. *Sch. Life*, 44:10–12.

MACKIE, ROMAINE P., NEUBER, MARGARET A., and HUNTER, PATRICIA P. (1963). College and university programs for the preparation of teachers of exceptional children. *Sch. Life*, 45:29–35.

MACKIE, ROMAINE P., and ROBBINS, PATRICIA P. (1960). Exceptional children in local public schools. *Sch. Life*, 43:14.

MACKIE, ROMAINE P., and ROBBINS, PATRICIA P. (1961). *Exceptional children and youth: chart book of special education enrollments in public day school of the United States.* Washington: U.S. Government Printing Office.

MARTENS, ELISE H. (1944). *Needs of Exceptional Children.* U.S. Office of Education Leaflet No. 74. Washington: U.S. Government Printing Office.

REYNOLDS, M. C. (1954). Education for the handicapped. *Minn. Educ. Assn. J.,* pp. 24–25, 36.

REYNOLDS, M. C. (1962). A framework for considering some issues in special education. *Except. Child.,* 28:367–70.

STENSWICK, E. (1961–1962). Recommended reimbursement aid of state funds, special education, September 12, 1962. Dittoed.

WISHIK, S. M. (1956). Handicapped children in Georgia: a study of prevalence, disability, needs, and resources. *Amer. J. publ. Hlth,* 46:195–203.

SELECTED READINGS

DUNN, L. M. (ed.) (1963). *Exceptional children in the schools.* New York: Holt, Rinehart & Winston, 1963. Chap. 1.

HUNT, J. T. (1963). The education of exceptional children. *Rev. educ. Res.* (February).

KIRK, S. A. (1962). *Educating exceptional children.* Boston: Houghton Mifflin. Chap. 1.

II

INTELLECTUAL
DEVIATIONS

The exceptional children considered in this section include those who are mentally retarded and generally inferior to average children in their intellectual development and those who are gifted in intellectual development or who have special talents and are generally superior when compared to average children.

In Chapter 3 various aspects of mental retardation are considered: definitions, numbers, degrees of defect, etiology, adjustment problems, learning problems, and psychological needs. In Chapter 4 educational provisions and guidance of the mentally retarded are presented with special consideration given to vocational training and adult adjustment. In Chapter 5 giftedness, creativity, high achievement, and special talents are discussed with emphasis on identification, numbers, characteristics, and adjustment problems. Chapter 6 considers educational provisions and guidance for children who are creative or otherwise gifted.

3

MENTALLY RETARDED
CHILDREN

DEFINITION AND CLASSIFICATION

Definition of Terms. The term "mental retardation" is used here to include all degrees of intellectual deficit. Although other terms have been used in attempts at clarification of the concept of retarded mental development, interchangeability of terms has frequently led to increased confusion. Terminology becomes further confused when these several labels are assigned to quantitative and qualitative differences *within* the broad area of mental retardation.

Among terms that have been used are "mentally inferior," "slow learner," "mentally atypical," "backward," "subnormal," "mentally handicapped," or "feebleminded." Sometimes these terms have been used in a highly specialized manner and sometimes in a broad, general way.

The task of actually defining the condition of mental retardation has not been simple, either. Most earlier definitions of the condition have been descriptive of the results rather than of the basic condition itself. The following extract from Hegge (1952) suggests some of the difficulties of definition.

Much as in the case of normal people the mentally retarded are what they are, and will become what they will become, as a result of the inter- action of organism and psyche with the social and physical environment— in each instance the interaction of a unique individual with an experience which is unique for him. Perhaps the most satisfactory point of view is to regard the mentally retarded group as consisting largely of essentially normal people whose output of mental ability places them at the lower end of a distribution of normal traits. We do, indeed, expect them to grow up and function with and as normal people, provided they receive specialized and skilled assistance.

In the total picture of mental retardation we can at present discern no details which are universally unique for the mentally retarded mind; as a result, the total picture itself cannot be sharply distinguished from that of the borderline or dull normal. Whether a dividing line is made in terms of test scores or in terms of underlying mental processes, the exact point of division must be arbitrary. One source of difficulty is that the test scores do not show the underlying modes of intellectual functioning. The other difficulty arises from the fact that the mental processes and associated be- havior and achievements are not different in kind but in degree—when the highest among the mentally retarded and the lowest among the dull normal are compared. [P. 22.]

Sarason (1955) attempted to relate the definition of serious mental retardation to an impairment of the central nervous system. He states:

The term mental deficiency refers to individuals who are socially inade- quate as a result of an intellectual defect which is a reflection of an im- pairment of the central nervous system which is essentially incurable. The condition has existed from birth or from shortly thereafter. The mentally defective individual will always be in need of supervision and assistance. Although many benefit from special training programs—they can improve the quality of their performance—it is not expected that they will be able to fend for themselves socially and vocationally. [P. 442.]

The definition published in 1952 by the Committee on Nomenclature and Statistics of the American Psychiatric Association (1952) had an important influence in recent considerations of mental retardation. Concerning mental retardation with no specific brain involvement, the Committee stated:

Here will be classified those cases presenting primarily a defect of in- telligence existing since birth, without demonstrated organic brain disease or known as familial or "idiopathic" mental deficiencies. The degree of intelligence defect will be specified as *mild, moderate,* or *severe,* and the current I.Q. rating with the name of the test used will be added to the diagnosis. In general, *mild* refers to functional (vocational) impairment, as would be expected with I.Q.'s approximately 70 to 85; *moderate* is used for functional impairment requiring special training and guidance, such as would be expected of I.Q.'s of about 50–70; *severe* refers to the functional impairment requiring custodial or complete protective care, as would be expected with I.Q.'s below 50. The degree of defect is estimated from other factors than merely psychological test scores, namely, consideration of cultural, physical and emotional determinants, as well as school, vocational and social effectiveness. [Pp. 23–24.]

The development of the parent movement and increased special educational provisions for mentally retarded children combined to produce the need for terms and definitions that have more practical meaning for both parents and educators. Thus, the terms "educable," "trainable," and "totally dependent" have come into rather wide usage. While these terms have also brought some confusion, their careful definition has provided a greatly enlightened basis for the expansion of realistic educational services to children who are mentally retarded.

The following characterizations are taken from a report on study projects for trainable mentally handicapped children, issued by Vernon L. Nickell, Superintendent of Public Instruction, state of Illinois (1954). This report used the term "mentally handicapped" to indicate the broad group of children who are mentally retarded.

The Educable Mentally Handicapped: Educable mentally handicapped children are those who, because of slow mental development, are unable to profit sufficiently from the program of the regular elementary school. They can, however, learn many things in a special class. Their retardation is such that they are able to learn some of the academic skills such as reading, writing, and arithmetic. This is why they are called "educable."

They are capable of acquiring second, third, or fourth grade achievement by the age of sixteen. They can learn to work and in most instances can become self-supporting at the adult level. In general they have the following characteristics: (1) They are able to learn second to fourth-grade subject matter by the age of sixteen. (2) They do not begin to learn to read or to understand formal arithmetic until some time between nine and twelve years of age. (3) They develop mentally from one-half to three-fourths as fast as an average child. (4) Their progress in school is likewise about one-half to three-fourths the rate of the average child. After they begin to read, for example, they progress about half as fast as a normal child. If they begin to learn to read at the age of ten, they probably can gain three or four grades in the next six years. (5) Although their vocabularies will be limited, their speech and language will be adequate in most ordinary situations. (6) In most instances they can learn to get along with people. (7) They can learn to do unskilled or semi-skilled work and can usually support themselves at the adult level.

The Trainable Mentally Handicapped Child: In contrast to the educable mentally handicapped, the trainable mentally handicapped children are more retarded and cannot learn academic skills. We may define trainable mentally handicapped children as those who are developing at such a slow rate that they are unable to profit from the program of instruction for the educable mentally handicapped, but who have potentialities for learning (1) self care, (2) social adjustment in the family and neighborhood, and (3) economic usefulness in the home, in a residential school, or in a sheltered environment.

The characteristics of such children may be listed as follows: (1) they are capable of eventually learning self care in dressing, undressing, eating, toileting, keeping clean, and in other necessary skills which will make them independent of their parents in the regular routines of living; (2) they are capable of learning to get along in the family and in the immediate neighborhood by learning to share, respect property rights, and in general to cooperate with their families or with the neighbors; (3) they are capable of learning to assist in chores around the house or in doing a routine task for some remuneration in a sheltered environment and under supervision; (4) their mental development is approximately one-quarter to one-half that of an average child; (5) they are generally not capable of learning academic skills such as reading and arithmetic beyond the rote learning of some words or simple numbers; (6) their speech and language abilities are distinctly limited; (7) they can eventually learn to protect themselves from common dangers; and (8) they will require some care, supervision, and economic support throughout their lives.

The Totally Dependent Mentally Handicapped Child: Totally dependent children are those who, because of very severe mental retardation, are unable to be trained in total self care, socialization, or economic usefulness, and who need continuing help in taking care of their personal needs. Such children require almost complete care and complete supervision throughout their lives, since they are unable to survive without help. In general, these children (1) require assistance in dressing, undressing, toileting, and eating throughout their lives; (2) require protection from dangers; (3) are incapable of learning to participate socially with others; (4) develop at less than one-quarter the rate of the average child; and (5) have inadequate speech and language—either absent or limited to a few elementary words or phrases. [P. 3.]

The term "marginally independent" has been used to refer to the adult prognosis for the educable retarded child who has had appropriate educational opportunities; the term "semidependent" has been used to predict the adult status for the trainable retarded child who has had special education.

In recent years the National Association for Retarded Children and the American Association on Mental Deficiency have joined to suggest more suitable terms than "educable" and "trainable" since these terms mainly have reference to school-age children and mental retardation is a lifetime concern to the family and a variety of social agencies. Thus, the terms "mildly retarded," "moderately retarded," and "severely retarded" are finding greater usage with special educators being chiefly concerned with the "mildly retarded" and "moderately retarded."

The general definition given by Heber (1959) and accepted by the American Association on Mental Deficiency reads: "Mental retardation refers to subaverage general intellectual functioning which originates during the developmental period and is associated with impairment in one or more of the following: (1) maturation, (2) learning, and (3) social adjustment" (p. 3).

In amplification of meaning of the various words used in the definition, Heber further comments:

Because of the different roles of maturation, learning, and social adjustment for the pre-school, school, and post-school aged groups, the definition specifies that it is necessary for the sub-average intellectual functioning to be reflected by impairment in only one of these three aspects of adaptive behavior in order to confirm a diagnosis of mental retardation. In actual practice, however, it will be found that a great percentage of individuals diagnosed as mentally retarded will be impaired, or have a history of impairment, in all three areas of adaptation. [P. 4.]

The rate of intellectual development is thought to be slower than normally expected, hence the label "mentally retarded." This retardation is manifested in social and intellectual behavior in a manner that marks the retardate as less able to manage than society ordinarily expects.

In another answer to the question "What is a retarded child?" Begab (1963) has stated:

His defect originates during the developmental years of his life and is associated with an impairment of his adaptation to the norms and expectations of society. In this impairment, the retarded child may range from total incapacity to a level of self-sufficiency that makes him relatively indistinguishable from others. . . .

The two dimensions by which retardation is defined—intelligence and behavior—are relative qualities and subject to change in many cases. Who functions as retarded is determined in large measure by the standards and tolerance of the community and by the importance it attaches to intellectual prowess. [P. 29.]

While children categorized as *slow learners* (75–90 IQ approximately) develop somewhat slower than normal children, they are not usually considered mentally retarded or within the province of special education. Further, emotional disturbance or social maladjustment may produce educational retardation, but mental retardation and mental illness are not synonymous. Where cultural depriva-

tion operates to produce educational retardation, these children will
often appear to be mentally retarded; but appropriate environmental
stimulation may alter this picture considerably.

Mental Retardation from a Quantitative Viewpoint. Two main
criteria have been used for determining mental retardation. The first
makes use of tested intellectual ability or test scores. The classification of mental retardation based on Binet age levels tentatively
adopted in 1910 by the American Association for the Study of the
Feeble-minded has been widely followed in the United States. According to Binet, the IQ's of idiots range from 0 to approximately 25,
those of imbeciles range from 25 to approximately 45 or 50, and those
of the moron group range from 50 to approximately 75. Children
with IQ's between 75 and 90 are generally regarded as borderline
cases. Roughly comparable quantitative labels of significance to
educators would be:

1. Totally dependent mentally handicapped—IQ 0–35
2. Trainable mentally handicapped—IQ 35–55
3. Educable mentally handicapped—IQ 55–75
4. Slow learners—IQ 75–90

The second criterion concerns the social competence of the individual. Individuals continuously unable to adjust to what is regarded
as a minimum level of independence have been classified as severely
retarded. Social age is used as one basis for classification and training. The importance of social competence is implied in this statement from Doll (1942):

More specifically, the clinical evaluation of particular attributes of individuality, such as intelligence, achievement, attitudes, aptitudes, personality, health, and the like, is designed to evaluate variables related to
social competence or threats to its successful expression. [P. 49.]

Limitations of Low IQ As a Criterion. Although a low measured
IQ is often the most frequently used single basis for determining
mental retardation, it should be used with extreme caution. One
should not identify a child as mentally retarded simply because he
scored below an IQ of 75 on either a group or individual intelligence
test. There are several reasons for exercising caution.

1. Results from different intelligence tests are not wholly in agreement. What should be concluded about a child's intelligence when

results on a performance test, such as the *Arthur Point Scale,* yield an IQ of 92, while those obtained from the *Stanford-Binet Tests* give an IQ of 65?

A random sample of 50 children was selected from the eight- and nine-year-olds in the third and fourth grades and given the *Stanford-Binet Intelligence Tests (Form L)* and the *Wechsler Intelligence Scale for Children* (Arnold and Wagner, 1955). Stanford-Binet administration preceded the Wechsler administration for one-half of the subjects, while the Wechsler administration was given first to the other half of the sample. The findings from this study, presented in Table 3–1, are in agreement with results from previous studies, which indicated that there is a substantial agreement between the two scales

TABLE 3–1

Correlations Between Wechsler Intelligence Scale for Children and Stanford-Binet Scale

	Correlation of WISC		
Item Correlated	Verbal	Performance	Total
Mental age with scaled score	.77	.69	.81
IQ	.85	.75	.88
IQ corrected	.88	.74	.90

Source: Arnold and Wagner (1955).

when the Wechsler full scale IQ's and verbal scale IQ's are correlated with Stanford-Binet IQ's. On the other hand, correlations between the Wechsler Performance Scale IQ's and the Stanford-Binet IQ's are only moderate, ranging from .35 to .80 as reported in the summary of studies presented by Freeman (1955). Furthermore, in studies of the mentally retarded the Wechsler Scale has yielded somewhat higher IQ's, while at the upper level of mental ability the Stanford-Binet scale yielded higher IQ's.

2. Although it is assumed that the rate of intellectual development, as expressed by an IQ, is relatively constant, various studies show that the IQ's of children and adults are not *completely* constant. Early studies of the intelligence scores of children reared in a very restricted environment showed a progressive reduction in IQ with increased age. Closely related to this is a study by Speer (1940) of the mental development of children of mentally retarded mothers. He noted that the longer the child remained in a given environment, the more his IQ assumed the level characteristic of the environment.

Fig. 3–1. The *Arthur Point Scale of Performance Tests,* Revised Form II. The scale provides a means of measuring the intellectual abilities of deaf children, those suffering reading disabilities or other language difficulties, the culturally deprived, and the non-English-speaking. It is primarily non-language in nature. (Courtesy The Psychological Corporation.)

The longer children of mothers identified as mentally retarded remained with their mothers, the lower the tested IQ's of the children became. Table 3–2 shows this relationship.

The Charles (1953) study of 151 individuals previously diagnosed as mentally retarded furnishes information on inferences sometimes drawn from intelligence test scores. These individuals were carefully studied some 15 years after a diagnosis of mental retardation. Public school records of retest data available for 73 of the 151 children showed that many of these children were actually "dull" or environmentally handicapped rather than truly mentally retarded. They were most handicapped on verbal tests and in the ability to do academic work at school.

TABLE 3–2

Effects of Feeble-minded Mothers on Intelligence of Children
After Birth

Age of Child	N	Median IQ
0–2	12	100.5
3–5	19	83.7
6–8	12	74.6
9–11	9	71.5
12–15	16	53.1

SOURCE: After Speer (1940).

The results of this and similar studies emphasize the importance of careful clinical judgment in interpreting intelligence test scores. The following case of L. V., reported by Charles, illustrates a subject with a low verbal IQ and a normal performance IQ reared in an environment where schooling, reading, and language abilities in general were very inferior:

L. V. Female, age 42; 1916 Binet: 68 IQ. Wechsler-Bellevue: verbal scale 68 IQ, performance scale 105 IQ, full scale 85 IQ.

L. V. is a neat and rather attractive widow with five children. Three daughters aged eight to 15 are in school, an older daughter is married, and a son is overseas with the Army. The subject's early background was unfavorable even for this group of subjects. Her mother was married at least three times and according to the 1935 data card was "probably related to more feeble-minded individuals than any other person in Lincoln except the R's—and she is related to them indirectly."

The subject spent the years of 1918 to 1921 in the State Home for Dependent Children. She completed the fifth grade in the Lincoln schools. She was married in 1925, divorced in 1926, and remarried in 1927. In the same year she was accused of cohabiting with an older man, and her husband was accused of cohabiting with a widow. She has no other public record of delinquency. Since her husband's death four years ago, she has been employed as a baker. She has supported her family alone since her husband's death except for a very little relief in 1950. The home is a one-story frame house finished with imitation brick siding and a new basement which was constructed in 1950. She reports that she owns it "except for a few payments." The furniture is old but the interior of the house is fairly neat and clean. A friendly relationship seemed apparent between mother and children. During the test she made the comment quoted earlier, relevant to her lack of ability with words but facility with her hands. In view of her test scores and achievements, it seems a good summary of her ability. [Pp. 56–57.]

3. The IQ obtained from most tests is determined from a composite score obtained from performance on a variety of tasks. Jastak (1949)

made use of 12 separate scales, representing as many purported mental abilities, for securing psychometric patterns. By testing such a number of different abilities, he discovered wide intra-individual psychometric patterns. The scores of three adolescent patients examined at the Delaware State Mental Hygiene Clinic are presented in Table 3–3. These patients have identical IQ's—62. The traditional

TABLE 3-3

The Results of Three Clinic Cases on the Psychometric Patterns

Name of Test	Standard Scores		
	Case A	Case B	Case C
1. Vocabulary	97	55	66
2. Oral Reading	50	50	66
3. Information	88	49	60
4. Analogies	78	56	59
5. Comprehension	71	63	62
6. Picture Anomalies	50	103	52
7. Picture Reasoning	57	74	64
8. Form Boards	45	99	58
9. Drawings	53	64	65
10. Symbol Substitutions	42	47	63
11. Mental Arithmetic	49	52	67
12. Digit Span	65	33	61
Range of Scores	42–97	33–103	52–67
Average IQ	62	62	62

Source: Jastak (1949).

method of diagnosis would classify each of these as mentally retarded at the educable level. However, a careful study of the three cases shows that individual A has a vocabulary equivalent to that of the average adult, while his information is not far below that of the average. On the picture anomalies and form boards, individual B scored within the average range. The ratings for individual C are all below 70. The question then is: "What is the potential mental ability or intelligence of each of these three cases?"

Inadequacy of Social Competence As Criterion. The social criterion was early used in an attempt to furnish a legal definition of mental retardation. A weakness in the use of this criterion is the subjective method of arriving at a definition of the point where an individual is designated mentally retarded. For example, just how is one to judge a social inability or failure? How much social failure is compatible with being normal, and how much means mental retardation? How should the individual be judged who succeeds in learning from books but fails to acquire habits conducive to good social adjustment?

The nature, severity, and duration of failure are determined by the individual's inherent characteristics, his past experiences, the complexity of his environment, and his present circumstances. It was pointed out earlier that when an apparently mentally retarded child is shifted from an unfavorable to a favorable environment, pronounced changes in IQ may be obtained. There may also be significant changes in attitudes and behavior. The child may further change from being one who consistently fails or does not try to one who consistently succeeds and displays considerable initiative and energy. An individual may, because of his past experiences, fit admirably into one environment and fail miserably in another. Is he normal in the one situation and mentally retarded in the other? One should not confuse mental retardation with maladjustment, which will be given special consideration in Part VI.

In addition to classification by quantitative deficits, there are other schemes for classifying mental retardation.

Neuropsychiatric Classification. A number of psychiatrists regard the psychometric approach as too limited for an adequate diagnosis and have suggested a medical or physiological appraisal as an essential aspect. In the determination of potential for training or educability, the individual intelligence test is most useful with the mildly or moderately mentally retarded individual; it is of very limited value for the extremely retarded. Furthermore, the IQ alone throws no light on the etiology of mental retardation.

Using the results of 250 postmortem examinations of individuals classified as idiots or imbeciles, Benda et al. (1951) concluded:

Thus an analysis of severe mental defects demonstrates that all cases correspond to different neuropsychiatric conditions that are all characterized by pathology of the central nervous system. There is no condition that cannot be expressed in terms of developmental or metabolic brain pathology. [P. 722.]

According to this concept, the normal variations of human intelligence are grouped around a mean IQ of 100 and fall between 70 and 130. A small percentage between 55 and 70 are classed as an intellectually inadequate group. However, the neuropsychiatric classification is actually concerned with causes. It is concerned with the severer forms of mental retardation—those with IQ ratings below a range of 45 to 55. Four groups of neuropsychiatric disorders may be identified:

Prenatal developmental disorders, 40 per cent
Traumatic "birth injuries," 25 per cent
Metabolic disorders, neoplastic malformations, so-called degenerative diseases, and psychoses, 20 per cent
Infectious diseases, 15 per cent [Benda *et al.*, p. 724.]

Classification by Clinical Types. Among the clinical types of mental retardation that have been differentiated are mongolism (Down's syndrome), cretinism, microcephalus, and hydrocephalus. The number and quality of the physical signs vary from case to case, and the amount of intellectual retardation also varies. However, the combination of rather characteristic signs leads to an inference of mental retardation in most cases. Since the amount of mental retardation is not often proportional to the number of signs, it is important to have careful psychological evaluation rather than to put much stock in the way a particular child may look. Mongolism and cretinism will be discussed later in this chapter.

Clinical Syndromes Mistaken for Mental Retardation. Early childhood schizophrenia is sometimes mistaken for mental retardation. In such cases the behavior of the child during the early years appears normal, followed by a gradual and progressive change. Some characteristics of the child's behavior have been described by Angus (1948). The parents become concerned about the child's schoolwork as well as his lack of interest in school. The apparently indifferent child may be accused of being lazy. Lack of interest in school may be accompanied by a changed attitude toward himself as well as toward the members of his family. His lack of interest in his own personal appearance and his apparent dependence upon the parents but with a lack of emotional attachment present a confusing picture. Since the abnormal development of the schizoid is progressive in nature, his condition may go unnoticed or be mistaken for mental retardation during childhood. (For further discussion of childhood schizophrenia see Chapter 17.)

Endogenous-exogenous Classification. Cases of mental retardation attributable to acute or chronic brain syndromes, as described by the Committee on Nomenclature of the American Association on Mental Deficiency (1952), are sometimes referred to as exogenous, while those cases where no such condition appears are labeled endogenous.

According to Strauss (1939), who first presented this distinction, endogenous cases involve:

Any mental defective in whose immediate family (grandparents, parents, or siblings) there occur one or more cases of mental defect and in whose case history there is no evidence of brain disease or injury. [P. 63.]

Exogenous cases involve:

Any mental defective in whose immediate family there is no history of mental deficiency and whose case history indicates a prenatal, natal, or postnatal disease or injury which appears to have damaged the brain. There should be a strong probability that this brain defect is the cause of his mental retardation. [P. 63.]

The endogenous-exogenous distinction may have some importance for medical treatment or determining prognosis. An injury may produce greater intellectual deficit. However, the endogenous-exogenous distinction has been found to have little relevance for educational planning. The term "brain injured" has often been substituted for "exogenous" with rather confusing results. Does the term refer to cause or effect? Certain behavioral and psychological symptoms of importance to the educator and psychologist have been found to result from brain damage, but not always. And in some cases the symptoms may be present with no manifest brain pathology. On the other hand, a child may have a demonstrable brain injury with none or few of the symptoms that concern educators. Neurological impairment, including the so-called Strauss Syndrome, will be considered further in Chapter 13.

Trends in Classification. Later studies have led to important changes in earlier concepts of classification. A statistical analysis of the neuropathic finding in 543 autopsied cases by Malamud (1954) bears on this problem. He concluded that "an etiological classification of the mental deficiencies is not warranted in the present state of our knowledge" (p. 447). The difficulties in classification appear in part as a result of similarities between the different groups and in part as a result of the inadequacy of medical histories of the cases.

For many years mental retardation was looked upon as a single condition—existing from birth or from an early age—that caused the individual to function at a lower intellectual level. The advent of psychological tests, particularly the *Stanford-Binet Tests*, led to labeling those with an IQ below 70 as mentally retarded. Mental retardation is now known to be not a single type of subnormality but a great variety of conditions classified under the same general heading. A variety of behavior patterns and mental characteristics may be observed. Individuals with mental retardation of non-organic origin are generally capable of learning and developing to a greater degree than those whose retardation results from organic pathological conditions (Cassel, 1949).

Prevalence of Mental Retardation. The 3 per cent estimate of the National Association for Retarded Children is commonly cited as a basis for determining the incidence of mental retardation in any particular community setting. A further breakdown of this 3 per cent estimate suggests that 25 per 1,000 are educable retarded, 4 per 1,000 are trainable retarded, and 1 per 1,000 are totally dependent. Numbers of educable retardates will vary with socioeconomic circumstances and with particular IQ limits that may be imposed.

Data showing the number of mentally retarded children enrolled in public schools and in homes and residential schools vary considerably from state to state. The extent to which programs are provided for mentally retarded children is largely dependent upon the attitudes, state regulations, and financial abilities of the different states. Legal definitions of mental retardation also have an important bearing on this matter. Bateman and Kirk (1963) summarized several prevalence studies and pointed out:

. . . that the number of children enrolled in community classes depends on: (a) the adequacy and ability of institutions to accommodate severely retarded children; (b) the lower limits of eligibility; (c) the existence of adequate programs for the educable mentally retarded; and (d) the problem of transportation. [P. 8.]

It has been conservatively estimated that for every mentally retarded person placed in a state institution, there are approximately ten remaining in the community. Roselle (1955) has estimated that there are between 19 and 26 mentally retarded for every 1,000 children of school age. These estimates for the educable retarded, trainable retarded, and severely retarded are presented in Table 3–4. These parallel approximately the estimates published by the National Association for Retarded Children.

To determine the incidence of trainable mentally retarded children in the school-age population, pilot studies (Wirtz and Guenther, 1957) were conducted in five selected communities in Illinois and three in Michigan. The intelligence quotient range of 25 to 49 inclusive was

TABLE 3–4

Estimated Mental Retardation in School-Age Population,
Ages Five to Seventeen

Level	Number per 100,000
Mildly retarded (educable)	1,500–2,000
Moderately retarded (trainable)	300–450
Severely retarded	100–150

SOURCE: After Roselle (1955).

used as a basis for determining the "trainable mentally handicapped." These children were described as those possessing the potentialities for learning (1) self-care, (2) social adjustment at home and in the neighborhood, and (3) economic usefulness at home, in a sheltered environment, or under close supervision.

In each of the communities surveyed the results were thought to represent minimal figures, since it was possible that some children were missed in the surveys. The community groups were very similar when one Michigan community with a private institution was eliminated from the total survey. On the basis of the results of this study, it appears that for 1,000 school-age children, there are 1 to 2 trainable mentally handicapped children in the community and 1 in an institution. The grand totals showed 2.98 trainable mentally handicapped children per 1,000 school-age population. Rather similar deductions were reached from Illinois data, which estimated 1.49 trainable retarded per 1,000 school-age children living in the local communities and .85 per 1,000 in institutions, yielding a total estimate of 2.34 trainable retarded children per 1,000 school-age population in Illinois (Bateman and Kirk, 1963).

Sex Differences in Prevalence of Mental Retardation. Statistics have consistently shown that more males than females are placed in special, public school classes or are admitted to institutions for the mentally retarded. The obvious conclusion then might be that mental retardation is more prevalent among males than among females. This conclusion might be sound if there were not selective factors in operation. One hypothesis that has been advanced is that social factors operate to bring more male cases to the attention of the schools and other agencies, and therefore the incidence of male retardation in institutions and special classes is higher than for females.

Data presented by Malzberg (1953) of the enrollment in institutions for the mentally retarded in New York State (see Table 3–5) indicate a preponderance of males at all age levels. Among the first admissions during a three-year period, the ratio was 129.6 males to

TABLE 3–5

Ratio of Males to Females Among First Admissions to New York State Schools for Mental Defectives

Age Group	General Population Ratio		First-Admission Ratio	
	M	F	M	F
Under five years of age	104.3	100	142.4	100
Five to nine years	103.9	100	168.9	100
Ten to fourteen years	104.4	100	148.2	100
Over fifteen years	92.9	100	80.6	100

SOURCE: After Malzberg (1953).

100 females, while the total institution population ratio was 95.4 males to 100 females. A study of data on the age of first admission shows that the greatest sex differences appear among the young age groups, where cultural and social forces would normally operate least as selective factors in bringing one or the other sex to the attention of the authorities.

IDENTIFICATION OF MENTALLY RETARDED CHILDREN

In an attempt to discover the diagnostic value of the *Stanford-Binet Tests* for mentally retarded children, many investigators have compared the performance of mentally retarded and normal children of the same mental age. One study (Thompson and Magaret, 1947) compared the performance of 441 mentally retarded with 1,326 normal children on Form L of the 1937 *Stanford Revision of the Binet Test*. Table 3–6 shows the test items on which the mental retardates did significantly better than the normals, and those items on which the normal children registered superiority.

Early Diagnosis. There are differences of opinion about the value of intelligence tests in determining a child's intelligence during the first two years. However, in mentally retarded children, there is generally a history of lateness in reaching various stages of development during infancy and early childhood, except in cases where the mental retardation results from trauma, encephalitis, or other postnatal con-

TABLE 3–6

Items on Stanford-Binet Scale (Form L) That Differentiate Defectives
from Normals with a P of .01 or Less

Location	Name of Item	Mental Ages
Items on Which Defectives Surpass Normals		
III, 1	Stringing beads	3
III, 5	Drawing a circle	3
V, 2	Folding a triangle	4–5 **
V, 4	Drawing a square	4–6
VI, 1	Vocabulary	5–6
VI, 2	Bead chain	4–7
VII, 1	Picture absurdities I	5–7
VIII, 2 *	Wet Fall	6–7
VIII, 5	Comprehension IV	6–9
X, 2	Picture absurdities II	7–10
XI, 1	Memory for designs	8–10
XIII, 4	Problems of fact	8–10
Items on Which Normals Surpass Defectives		
II ½, A	Identification by name	3
III, 6	Three digits forward	3–4
III ½, 5	Identification by use	3–4
IV, A	Sentence memory I	4–5
IV ½, 2	Four digits forward	4–6
VI, 5	Picture comparison	5–8
VII, 3	Drawing a diamond	6–9
VII, 5	Opposite analogies I	6–10
VII, 6	Five digits forward	6–10
VIII, 2 *	Wet Fall	8–10
VIII, 4	Similarities and differences	7–10
VIII, 6	Sentence memory III	6–10
IX, 4	Rhymes	8–10
IX, 6	Four digits reversed	7–10
X, 4	Reasons I	8–10
X, 6	Six digits forward	8–10
XII, 2	Verbal absurdities II	9–10
XII, 6	Minkus completion	9–10
XIV, 5	Directions I	9–10

* This one item is easier for mental defectives of mental ages six and seven than for six- and seven-year-old normals. It is easier for normal eight-, nine-, and ten-year-olds than for mental defectives of mental ages eight, nine, and ten. It is the only item examined that shows significant differences in opposite directions at different mental age levels.

** To be read 4 to 5 years.

SOURCE: After Thompson and Magaret (1947).

ditions. Since many normal children may be slower in certain activities, such as sitting, walking, or talking, a developmental examination must cover all fields of development. Some special features of mental retardation that may be apparent early have been described by Illingworth (1955):

The first sign of abnormality noted is likely to be the child's lateness in watching his mother's face when she talks to him (an average 4-weeks-old baby watches his mother's face intently as she speaks to him, often opening and closing his mouth and bobbing his head up and down). He will be late in smiling, and in head control, as shown by pulling him to the sitting position, placing him in the prone, or holding him off the couch with the hand under his abdomen. The average 6-weeks-old baby when he is held in the latter position should be able for a few seconds to hold his head up so that its plane is in that of the long axis of the trunk. As he grows older his defective head control becomes progressively more obvious. It is the most important early objective sign of abnormality.

Other features of note in the retarded baby, other than the obvious signs of general retardation, include the lateness in following with the eyes and of taking notice, which so often leads to an erroneous diagnosis of blindness; lateness in turning the head to sound (3 months in an average baby), which often leads to an incorrect diagnosis of deafness; lateness in stopping to drool and to mouth objects (both usually achieved at about 12 months in an average baby, with occasional exceptions in the succeeding weeks); the persistence of the reciprocal kick long after the age of 9 months when it is normally lost; and, more important than any of these, the general disinterestedness of the baby, the lack of prolonged concentration, and the slowness with which acts are performed. [P. 3.]

Speech and language retardation has been widely used as a partial basis for diagnosing mental retardation during early childhood. Brown (1955) suggested that lack of development in the early use of words in the young child may serve as a clue to possible mental retardation. A child who is slow in learning to talk or has a speech disorder is likely to be regarded as low in intelligence or retarded. This tendency is especially in evidence when the child is retarded in speech but shows normal progress in other directions. Concerning this, McCarthy (1960) states:

It is safe to say that mentally defective children are always delayed in the onset of speech, and their articulation and sentence structure are usually of poor quality. All children who speak late are not, however, mentally retarded, for there are many reasons for delay in talking, and even some very bright children have not talked until three or three-and-a-half years of age. However, intellectually gifted children are usually early and efficient speakers and early speech is a very good index of mental precocity. [P. 11.]

The importance of obtaining a total psychological profile of the child has been emphasized by Sarason and Sarason (1945):

1. A psychological examination should include several measures of intelligence of the individual type of test. The tests should be chosen so that an adequate picture of verbal conceptual, visual-motor, and memory functioning can be obtained. The status of academic achievement should also be ascertained.

2. The personality organization should be carefully evaluated by means of projective techniques such as the Rorschach or Thematic Apperception Tests. The relation in each case between intelligence and personality should be sought. . . .

3. Each test should be analyzed to see to what extent there is an internal consistency in the results and to determine, if possible, to which clinical picture the test pattern shows most resemblance. . . .

4. Test results should be interpreted in the light of the outstanding features of the past or present environment which might have affected functioning and are reflected in the examination. . . .

5. All the foregoing information should be brought together so that one gets a total picture in which all features of the examination are related. [P. 323.]

However, the dangers of generalizing from a single test score or of assuming consistency in test results are pointed out by Illingworth (1961) who states:

In my opinion the correlation between test scores in infancy and in later years will never be high, except in the case of subnormal infants. The reasons for this opinion are many. The diagnosis of mental subnormality in infancy is much easier than the diagnosis of mental superiority. The history-taking, examination, and especially the interpretation of the findings, demand interest in the subject, experience, and the willingness to learn from experience. There are special difficulties in handicapped children, especially those with athetosis. Delayed maturation, in individual fields or in development as a whole, is relatively common, so that fairly considerable backwardness in the early weeks may be followed by average or superior progress later. Degenerative diseases, including hypsarrhythmia, cannot be anticipated, nor can the occurrence of other conditions which damage the intellectual functions, such as meningitis, encephalitis, head injury, lead poisoning, or hypoglycaemia. The child's intellectual progress may be retarded by environmental deficiencies, such as emotional deprivation, so that although one's assessment of his developmental potential may have been accurate, he subsequently functions at a sub-optimal level. Conversely, an exceptionally good environment may lead to an unexpected improvement in a child's performance. Children may appear to be severely retarded after an attack of encephalitis, and yet make a remarkable recovery later. Repeated examinations are not always possible, so that the rate of development cannot be assessed. [P. 214.]

CHARACTERISTICS OF MENTALLY RETARDED CHILDREN

Learning Characteristics. What are the learning characteristics of the child who is significantly below average in intellectual ability? The fact that intelligence is defined in terms closely related to learning ability answers the question in a general way. The concept of mental age in terms of learning ability suggests that the learning ability of a twelve-year-old child with a mental age of ten might be roughly the same as that of the average ten-year-old. The ability of mentally retarded children to understand certain arithmetic processes was compared with that of normal children of the same mental age in a study by Cruickshank (1948). Two groups of 15 boys each were used for this study. The mentally retarded boys made up the experimental group, while the control group consisted of boys of average mental ability. Comparison of the two groups show that they were equated for mental age and arithmetic age.

	Mean C.A.	Mean M.A.	Mean Arithmetic Age
Experimental group	14.29	10.06	9.73
Control group	9.09	9.96	9.84

The arithmetic test consisted of two parts. Part I was based on 20 simple verbal problems, and the subjects were asked merely to designate how the problem should be worked. An example will illustrate this.

> You know the price of an apple. You know the price of an orange. How do you find the cost of both?

Part II consisted of the 20 problems used in Part I, but the boys were instructed to give the answer.

The performances of the control group and the experimental group were analyzed for each fundamental operation. In all four operations the control group was definitely superior to the experimental group. The results presented by Cruickshank provide a good basis for generalization. He states:

> There is observable from the results of Parts I and II a significant difference between the ability of the two groups to name processes in the abstract presentation and to work the problem when presented in a more concrete fashion, although the difference in favor of the control group is much smaller in this latter comparison. There is a pronounced difference

in the ability of the experimental group to solve problems when presented in the concrete rather than abstract form. Both the experimental and control groups show similar abilities to solve concrete rather than abstract problems in a study reported earlier dealing with the ability of mentally retarded children to isolate extraneous materials in arithmetic problems. [P. 288.]

The mentally retarded child is inferior to the normal child in learning complex and abstract materials. This inferiority may be first apparent when he enters school, but it becomes more observable as he progresses to more complex kinds of learning. The mentally retarded child is generally unable to compete successfully with others of his age in the traditional school subjects. His deficiency is most marked in activities requiring reading and listening comprehension, following complex directions, gaining insight into problem situations, and generalizing from rules and principles encountered in his schoolwork.

It has been observed that mentally retarded children frequently have difficulty in expressing time relations. Engle and Hamlett (1952) studied the ability of mentally deficient children to handle clock and calendar situations by presenting them a set of 18 questions related to such situations. A correlation of .57 was found between total scores for the 177 mentally retarded patients and mental age. The scores for a group of mentally retarded adults with a mean mental age of seven years and seven months were found to be about equal to those of normal children midway between eight and nine years of age. These findings point to the need for careful teaching of time concepts by concrete methods.

Comparative studies of the learning ability of mentally retarded and average children of the same mental age show the mentally retarded child to be equal to the average child of his mental age level on tests involving concrete materials. When simple tasks of a performance type are used, there is a low correlation between intelligence and performance by a group of children of the same mental age. Using the factor analysis approach, Swineford (1948) compared the performance of normal and retarded children. Retarded subjects were found to be most markedly inferior in the general factor, with a smaller degree of inferiority in the verbal factor and with no inferiority in the spatial factor.

Language Skills. A study reported by Catalano and McCarthy (1954) explored the feasibility of using certain measures of infant speech in the prediction of later intellectual status. Correlations were obtained between recordings of prelinguistic utterances of children

ranging in age from six to eighteen months with IQ's obtained from
the administration of the Stanford-Binet 31.3 months after the time of
recordings of speech. All of the correlations between the various
indices of infant speech and later IQ were positive, with measures of
consonant development yielding the highest correlation.

One should not generalize too readily about the child's mental development from his early speech development, although studies do
show a high percentage of speech defects among institutionalized
mentally retarded children and one sees a greater incidence of poor
speech among retarded children than among normal children.

In a study of the articulation profile of mentally retarded schoolchildren, Russell (1952) used 209 pupils from 18 classes in Kern
County, California. A test developed for use in this study was composed of objects that served as stimuli for eliciting the desired response. In some cases it was not practical to use objects; so pictures
were used. In all, 80 objects and 20 pictures made up the test items.

Comparisons were made between the articulatory patterns of the
209 mentally retarded subjects and a control group of children from
the general school population who were matched in chronological age.
The percentages of three types of errors for the two groups are presented in Table 3–7. While the articulation of consonants by the

TABLE 3–7

Comparison of Mentally Retarded and Normal Children in Percentage
of Errors in Articulation of Consonants

Type of Error	Mentally Retarded Group	Matched Group
Substitutions	51.4	35.9
Omissions	15.2	4.4
Indistinct sounds	33.4	59.7

SOURCE: After Russell (1952).

mentally retarded group shows a greater incidence of errors in the
substitution category, the control group showed a greater error preference for indistinct or otherwise carelessly articulated sounds. Since
there is a tendency in American speech to slight the consonant in the
final position, it was often difficult to determine in many cases whether
errors in such consonants as "d," "b," and "t" should be classified as
indistinct sounds or omissions. This may account for some differences
found in the results of studies bearing on this problem. A comparison

of the articulatory patterns for the two groups of children revealed a great similarity of the consonant sound errors common to the two groups. The mentally retarded group seemed to make more infantile articulatory sounds and a larger number of defective articulatory sounds than did the normal children.

The speech of 74 children enrolled in the St. Coletta School for Exceptional Children was studied by Schlanger (1953). Available information on 68 of the children indicated that the mean age for the onset of comprehensible speech was slightly over three years. The general speech testing of the children showed this distribution of speech defects: voice defects, 62 per cent; articulatory defects, 57 per cent; stuttering, 20 per cent. Sound substitutions accounted for more than 10 per cent of the total number of sounds tested. The defective consonant sounds found most frequently in these children were the same as, and in approximately the same order as, those reported in an earlier study by Poole (1934) for younger children.

Even children who are slightly retarded may have greater speech difficulty than normal children. Moskowitz (1948) suggested that the slow learner (the child with an IQ between 75 and 90) will be inferior to the average child in speech and writing skills. He tends to have few ideas, make incomplete sentences, and phrase his statements poorly. Not only is he inferior to the average child in his language activities, but he also usually displays a lack of interest in activities that require language skills other than the simplest ones that he has developed through everyday experiences in connection with concrete situations.

Physical and Motor Development. Walking and talking are developmental processes that, under favorable conditions, indicate roughly the rapidity with which the child is progressing toward maturity. Likewise, dentition has been found useful in appraising the child's developmental status. The data from a study by Flory (1936), presented in Table 3–8, furnish evidence of the relation between physical development and the mentality of the child. The evidence appears to be sufficient to warrant the conclusion that retardation in walking and talking is directly related to the amount of mental retardation present.

In a critical review of studies of motor function and physical fitness in mental retardates, Stein (1963) mentions four studies of a variety of motor skill tasks in which "All . . . of these descriptive studies found rather consistently that the mentally retarded performed at lower levels than their normal peer comparison groups" (p. 233).

TABLE 3–8

Average Age (in Months) at Which Mentally Retarded Boys Walked, Talked, and Erupted First Teeth

Levels	Walking			Talking			Teething		
	N	Mean	S.D.	N	Mean	S.D.	N	Mean	S.D.
Idiot	145	30.20	16.7	46	27.15	21.3	46	8.22	3.0
Imbecile	184	24.32	12.7	118	39.42	20.4	61	10.91	6.6
Moron	141	19.97	10.3	64	27.06	14.0	53	10.18	6.6
All classes	470	24.83	13.8	228	36.84	19.7	160	9.75	5.6

SOURCE: After Flory (1936).

Upon examining the results of several studies, Stein (1963) further concluded:

In general the evidence supported the hypothesis of a significant positive relationship between mental age and motor proficiency. [P. 237.]

. . . .

It appears that the complexity of the movements and the associated intellectual action necessary to carry out the movements could be greater factors in limiting the motor performance of the retardate than the lack of motor ability *per se.* [P. 234.]

. . . .

Today many retardates would also have to be classified as physically underdeveloped. [P. 232.]

A study reported by Cantor and Stacey (1951) dealt with manipulative dexterity of mental retardates. The subjects of this study consisted of 175 male retardates ranging in age from fourteen to eighteen years. Their IQ's obtained from the revised Stanford-Binet test, ranged from 42 to 82, with a mean of 64.8. Manipulative dexterity was measured by the *Purdue-Pegboard,* administered individually by the three-trial method.

A comparison of the performances of groups at three IQ levels (those with IQ's of 42–59, or 60–69, and of 70–82) is presented in Table 3–9. The 70–82 IQ group appears to be better than the 42–59 IQ group in every case, while the 60–69 IQ group is generally better than the 42–59 IQ group.

The performance of the 175 mental retardates also failed to compare favorably with that of two groups of normal males (865 industrial men and 456 male veterans).

Differences in Etiological Groups. Various studies have attempted to reveal qualitative and quantitative differences in functioning of re-

TABLE 3–9

Comparison of Means and Standard Deviation in Manipulative
Dexterity Test of Three IQ Groups for Each Operation

Measure	IQ 70–82 (N = 52)	IQ 60–69 (N = 80)	IQ 42–59 (N = 43)
Right hand, one trial			
Mean	14.77	14.59	13.63
S. D.	1.55	2.18	2.26
Right hand, three trials (total)			
Mean	46.17	45.50	42.60
S. D.	4.10	5.98	6.55
Left hand, one trial			
Mean	14.25	14.27	13.35
S. D.	1.83	2.19	2.32
Left hand, three trials (total)			
Mean	43.92	43.90	40.47
S. D.	4.60	5.68	6.05
Both hands, one trial			
Mean	11.92	11.42	10.65
S. D.	1.61	1.87	2.07
R + L + B, one trial (total)			
Mean	126.62	124.50	115.72
S. D.	11.67	15.33	16.85
Assembly, three trials (total)			
Mean	97.38	92.69	85.13
S. D.	12.74	16.94	19.95

SOURCE: After Cantor and Stacey (1951).

tarded children from different etiological groups. A study reported by Cassel and Riggs (1953) was concerned with this problem. Three groups were designated as organic, familial, and unexplained. The unexplained consisted of those whose family history and early years were such that neither familial nor organic factors were thought to be present. The *Vineland Social Maturity Scale* was used to gather information about the daily behavior and social competence of the subjects. No significant differences were found between groups for the items on the scale including Dressing, Socialization, Occupation, and Communication. The organic group was especially low on activities dependent upon visual-motor coordination and a practical, goal-directed approach to living. The unexplained cases were unique in that they were very poor where effort, dependability, responsibility, and contribution to community welfare are involved. Their personality structures have been described as *dependent* and *egocentric*. Closely related to this are the results of a study by Rain (1952) in which it was noted that non-familial, exogenous children develop social competence at a slower rate than familial, endogenous children.

MONGOLISM

Mongolism, or Down's Syndrome, is a so-called clinical type of mental retardation in which there is a rather typical combination of physical signs and moderate to severe intellectual deficit. The condition was first described by Langdon Down in 1866. Apparently conflicting evidence over the years has led to a variety of theories regarding its etiology. Benda (1946) concluded that mongolism was the result of insufficient functioning of the pituitary gland. Advanced maternal age has often been noted as having some relationship to the occurrence of mongolism.

The invention of the electron microscope opened up some new possibilities for exploration. In 1956, chromosomal research by Tjio and Levan determined conclusively that man has 46 chromosomes rather than 48 in the cells of his body. In 1959 it was determined that there is an extra chromosome in cases of mongolism; and, as Gottesman (1963) points out: "It has since been established rather conclusively that mongolism is associated with an extra chromosome at pair 21 for a karyotype with 47 chromosomes" (p. 283). Even more recently it has been found that, while the twenty-first pair of chromosomes is somehow involved, there are variations in the involvement, which leads to the present belief that mongolism may be either inherited through the mother or may be the result of a genetic accident (mutation) at conception.

Prevalence. About 10 per cent of all institutionalized mental retardates are classified as mongoloid. Beidleman's (1945) report based on observations in the Lying-in Hospital of Boston over a period of 14 years revealed an average of 3.4 mongoloids per 1,000 births. This is a higher percentage than reported in most other studies. Gottesman (1963) cites an incidence of about 1 in 700 births and confirms the figure of 10 per cent of institutional populations with this diagnosis.

While the life expectancy is shorter than normal and has been estimated in the past as 10 to 20 years, better medical care and "wonder drugs" have made it difficult to say with any certainty just how long the average mongoloid now lives. It has been pointed out that the life span of the mongoloid has greatly increased and that many now live well beyond the age of twenty.

Intellectual Development. Numerous studies have dealt with the intellectual development of mongoloids. The question has been raised:

What is the intellectual level of the majority of mongoloids at or near maturity?

The mental age distribution of 62 patients of sixteen years of age and more, based on results of the Stanford-Binet Test, is given in Table 3–10. Almost half (47 per cent) of the patients had a mental

TABLE 3–10

Mental Age Distribution of Mongoloid Patients of Sixteen Years
of Age and More

Mental Age	No.	Per Cent
0 to 2 years, 11 months	29	47
3 years to 3 years, 11 months	18	29
4 years to 4 years, 11 months	7	11
5 years to 5 years, 11 months	6	9
6 years to 6 years, 11 months	1	2
7 years to 7 years, 11 months	1	2
Total	62	100

SOURCE: Durling (1952).

level below three years and were therefore psychologically classified as idiots.

There are significant peculiarities in the mental growth curves of mongoloids. First are the great irregularities noted in the curves, with considerable variations in pattern for different individuals. Many mongoloids have a very slow rate of mental development. However, it seems safe to say that a mongoloid child with low-measured mentality at the age of two to five years is most likely to have a relatively low rating at later dates. The mental growth curves of the 62 cases studied by Durling (1952) were divided into three classes:

1. Those reaching the peak of mental development at a chronological age of less than sixteen years
2. Those reaching the peak around an age of eighteen years
3. Those reaching the peak of development after an age of twenty years

Speech development of the mongoloid lags behind walking, and pronunciation and articulation are usually poor. In many cases the speech of the mongoloid is so indistinct that only those closely associated with him are able to understand it. The speech is likely to remain close to the two- or three-year level, although the vocabulary is affected by the nature of the environment. Treatment has been found to have some value, particularly in producing a more pleasant voice. In a large percentage of cases mongolism is accompanied by secondary defects, including thyroid deficiency. Thyroid treatment has been found useful for these cases insofar as the disturbances are a result of thyroid deficiency, but is of no value in the treatment of the mongolism itself.

Physical Growth Pattern. The mongoloid infant is deficient in skeletal growth, and this prenatal deficiency is extended into the child's postnatal life. However, measurements show that the mongoloid child at birth is within the normal range for height, although a large number of cases are below average. Retardation in growth becomes more conspicuous during the first two or three years, when complete arrest may be observed for several months. In the following ten years the growth rate may be nearly normal. However, the slow rate of the early years gives these children a delayed start that causes them to be smaller than normal children. Furthermore, growth in height ceases at an early age, so that retardation becomes more apparent after ages twelve or thirteen. Benda (1946) reports that only eight boys in his study reached a height of over 150 centimeters (about 5 feet), and these represented borderline cases. No mongoloid girls exceeded 150 centimeters in height. Thus, mongoloids in their late teens resemble in height children who are between nine and fourteen years of age.

The weight of mongoloids at birth and during the first year is below that of normal babies. During the next three or four years their weight tends to approximate that of normal children, while after five years most mongoloids are overweight, especially when compared with other children of their height.

Gonadal deficiency is conspicuous among mongoloids. At the age when manifestations of gonadal development are most observable in normal children, there is a lack of sexual development among mongoloids. As a group they are deprived of adrenal-gonadal activity, which normally plays an important role from the beginning of pubescence until forty years or later. These unfinished children appear to skip the active years of the teens, twenties, thirties, and forties. They become old at an age when others are in their active years. The skin becomes wrinkled and dry, the blood vessels show fatty degeneration, and all bodily functions become sluggish in nature.

A normative survey of the developmental patterns of 79 mongoloids in two state institutions and a home group consisting of 24 cases was conducted by McNeill (1954). He found that the development of stature was greater than the development of muscular strength, while the development of muscular strength was greater than social, mental, vocabulary, or motor development. Social development was more advanced than mental development; the majority of the mongoloids in his sample were classified as idiots (IQ below 25). This level of intelligence is significantly lower than that found in other studies that included non-institutionalized cases.

In summarizing the findings of various studies on the characteristics of children with mongolism, Bateman and Kirk (1963) point out:

Probably due to selection factors, the mongoloid children living at home were superior to those in institutions on both mental and physical traits. As a group the mongols were below average in height and eye-hand coordination. Mental growth showed a drop below other areas, and social maturity was a little higher than mental development. Language functions were among the lowest of the mongoloid's abilities. [P. 23.]

CRETINISM

The cretin, who is dwarflike in physical development, is disabled as a result of atrophy or inactivity of the thyroid gland. Since the thyroid gland is important in regulating nutrition, physical growth—including the development of the brain—is affected. The surface of the brain is frequently characterized by simple convolutions. This brain damage is accompanied by delayed puberty and by special learning and personality characteristics.

Cretinism is a condition characterized by a deficiency in iodine secretion from the thyroid gland. Therefore, it is also known as hypothyroidism. It accounts for a little less than 1 per cent of institutionalized mental retardates. In some respects the cretin resembles the mongoloid, so that the conditions are sometimes confused. Differential factors are presented in Table 3–11.

While goitrous sporadic cretinism is thought to be genetically determined, the discordance of non-goitrous cretinism in monozygotic twins reported by Pickering and Konlischer (1956) suggests that this type is not genetically determined. Rather, it appears to be directly related to influences of environmental factors on the development of the thyroid cells in the fetus. Three patterns of thyroid pathology have been observed: (1) thyroid aplasia, which is a congenital condition; (2) athyroidism, resulting from a later loss of thyroid function; and (3) thyroid dysfunction, resulting from a degenerated goiter.

The cretin has thyroid aplasia. The clinical picture is quite uni-

TABLE 3–11

Differential Factors in Mongolism and Cretinism

Factor	Mongolism	Cretinism
Recognizable	At birth	After two to three months
Body growth	Retarded	Retarded
Head	Brachycephalic	Normal size
Eyes	Upward, outward slant	Puffy
Osseus orbits	Smaller than normal	Normal
Epicanthus	Present at inner angle	Not present
Nose	Small; bridge under-developed	Normal
Tongue	Scrotal, may protrude	Thick, large, protrudes
Hands	Short; incurved fifth finger	Short, square
Feet	First and second toes widely spaced	Short, square
Skin	Occasionally dry	Very dry, pale, coarse
Hair	Variable	Very dry, and coarse
Tone	Poor, marked joint laxity	Unchanged
Constipation	Uncommon	Marked
Congenital anomalies	Frequent, heart and eyes	Umbilical hernia
Ossification	Slight or no delay	Marked delay
B.M.R.	Normal	Decreased
Serum iodine	Normal	Decreased
Cholesterol	Normal	Decreased

SOURCE: Yannet (1954).

form, making every case a member of a common group, that of "sporadic cretinism." The adult is a dwarf, his standing height usually being less than 40 or 42 inches. The shortness of standing height may be accentuated by the curved spine and the laxity of the hip joints. The movements of the cretin are slow and awkward, with a waddling or shuffling gait. The head is relatively large, the extremities are short and broad, and the hands and feet are stumpy and deformed. The trunk is short, but compared with the extremities is relatively long.

The abdomen is round and protruding. In females the breasts are usually small and infantile throughout life, although some females develop huge breasts. Puberty is late in appearing, and many cretins are sterile. The skin is cool, dry, and loose or puffy, suggesting heart or kidney disease. The nails are thick, brittle, and short. Cretins are heavy eaters and consequently obese, but they usually suffer from general muscular weakness and clumsiness.

While congenital thyroid aplasia represents a well-defined clinical entity, the loss of thyroid function may occur at any time of development. The older the child, the less will be the mental retardation and the thyrogenic deficiency. A traumatic or infectious factor at birth or shortly afterward may produce a picture of cretinism that cannot readily be distinguished from the thyroid aplastic case.

The mental development of the cretin will be dependent upon the amount of thyroid activity that remains, or upon the early administration of thyroxin. However, the results of treatment cannot be judged by the mental development of the child alone, since heredity sets the limits here in the same manner that limits are set for normal children. Treatment is more likely to affect the physical symptoms than to improve mentality.

Degeneration of the thyroid may occur at any time. When the thyroid is destroyed by infectious diseases after birth, it is replaced by fibrous tissue. Endemic cretinism is due to a degeneration of a hypertrophic thyroid, if present, or to an absence of it and should not be confused with thyroid hyperplasia or goiter.

Thyroid Deficiency and Intellectual Retardation. The child born with thyroid deficiency is incompletely developed. He is more susceptible to injury even during the birth period than is the child with normal thyroid function. Thyroid treatment may be beneficial to the individual in altering conditions resulting from thyroid deficiency, but will not be worthwhile in the treatment of a condition resulting from birth injury such as brain damage. The untreated cretin may not learn to speak, although he may utter some indistinct sounds in a low-pitched voice.

The term "cretinism" has been closely associated with dwarfism and mental retardation prevalent in certain mountainous geographical areas. However, these individuals vary in degrees of physical and mental retardation. In many cases retarded individuals in certain geographical areas are classified as cretins, whereas the mentally retarded in other areas are referred to as feeble-minded. Thus, a large number of feeble-minded in areas of iodine deficiency are classified as cretins but should be classified otherwise. The incidence of endemic cretinism is not higher than 2 per cent of all degrees of mental retardation.

SOCIAL-EMOTIONAL ADJUSTMENT

Children who are mentally retarded are likely to develop social-emotional adjustment problems as they strive to win acceptance and to satisfy the psychological needs that they have in common with all children. Their intellectual deficit handicaps them in interpreting all kinds of experiences that are important to normal social-emotional growth. Webster (1963) has noted important differences between the emotional development of young mentally retarded children and normal children. He states:

Practically all retarded children we have observed show poor development in their capacity to make emotionally significant distinctions between the familiar and the nonfamiliar, between friends and strangers, between persons and places or between persons and inanimate objects.

The retarded child's emotional development is impaired by a difficulty in finding new solutions for old conflicts and frustrations. We have noted an impairment in the capacity for spontaneous displacement of drives to new interests. There is a tendency toward repetition and inflexibility in solving emotional problems just as in other functions. [Pp. 39–40.]

From a series of studies of motivation and personality Cromwell (1961) points out the developmental aspects of personality in mentally retarded children and notes: "Personality and behavior patterns develop in many mentally retarded children which tend to lower their social and intellectual efficiency a measure below what we would already expect on the basis of constitutional impairments" (p. 47). Cromwell presents a useful theoretical framework for viewing personality development in mentally retarded children that involves learning and social-learning theory. He indicates that the same basic laws of learning apply to all children, but that failure experiences in retardates have a different effect than in normal children. The following remark of Cromwell's seems appropriately directed to the teacher who wonders why such a child does not try harder if he fails on a particular task. Cromwell states: "It has been further discussed as to how experiences of failure may be more prevalent among retarded children and may lead to passive-avoidant behavior, lack of responsiveness to failure, and decreased effort in the face of failure" (p. 51). There is hope, however, when Cromwell further suggests: "The growth of a higher level motivational system of success-striving and the ability to see success-failure meanings develop gradually with age and conceptual ability of the children. Different rates of growth are expected in retarded and normal individuals" (p. 51).

The close relationship between emotional maladjustments and reading failure has led to confusion. Children who are presumed to be dull because of educational retardation may actually be suffering from serious frustration and emotional maladjustment. Emotional problems thus keep them from showing their true mental ability.

The Western Ohio Studies furnish useful information about the effect of mental and educational retardation upon the personality development of children (Mangus, 1950). A survey was made of all third- and sixth-grade children in one county. The results showed a preponderance of adjustment problems among boys and girls seriously retarded in their schoolwork. The evidence indicated that a series of failures led directly to maladjustment. Mentally retarded pupils may become further retarded as the years of schooling pass. The repetition of one or two grades in the elementary school may not enable these children to succeed in later years when they are in high school, and it tends to throw them with an age group younger than their own. This may cause a strong sense of failure to develop in them. Results of studies of pupils who have not been promoted because of failure to learn show an excessive number of problem cases. The futility of grade repetition as a remedy for educational retardation was studied a number of years ago by Grace Arthur (1936). She found that pupils repeating the first grade did no better than first-grade beginners of the same mental age. It has been suggested by Arthur and others that reading might well be deferred by many children until they have reached sufficient mental maturity for learning to read successfully. The school has an important influence in the friendship formation of children and adolescents. Thus, the role of the mentally retarded child in the social structure of his class should be indicative of his general social adjustment under the existing educational program. The question of segregation versus non-segregation of mentally retarded children has caused considerable controversy for years. Recent studies have dealt with different aspects of this problem. However, results have been somewhat conflicting. One argument against segregation is that it is undemocratic and places a mark of inferiority on the individuals of the segregated group. Those in favor of segregation point out that segregation follows democratic principles in that equal educational opportunities are provided; for equal educational opportunity does not mean that the same type of education is provided for all children, but rather that each child should be furnished educational opportunities and experiences commensurate with his abilities.

Segregation is also not simply a matter of placing the child in a separate room. A child cannot be more truly segregated from others than to be placed in a room where he meets with continuous failures while other children are experiencing a series of successes. Thus, the mentally handicapped child may be rather completely segregated by being placed in a regular classroom where little consideration is given to his needs and abilities. Johnson (1950) designed a study to investigate the social position of mentally retarded children who were in the regular grades. Using a sociometric instrument and some other measures, he compared mentally retarded with typical children in grades 1 to 5. He found the mean social quotient of the mentally handicapped to be significantly lower than that of the typical group. The mentally retarded were also found to be less accepted in their classes and more rejected than were the typical children. Johnson analyzed the results of his study as follows:

(1) The mentally handicapped children were usually rejected because of their behavior in the classroom, on the playground, and away from the school. The majority of the reasons given for their rejection were due to various kinds of compensatory behavior, such as bullying, fighting, misbehaving, showing off, swearing, lying, cheating, etc. These behaviorisms may well have been the result of the mentally handicapped child's inability to compete in school and in intellectual situations.

(2) The mentally handicapped children were not usually rejected because of poor academic achievement or because they were over age. . . . [Pp. 60–89.]

A study conducted by Martin (1953) also dealt with this problem. Records from children in Grades 5 through 8 in 15 parochial schools were studied to locate children with intelligence quotients ranging from 50 to 75. Schools were selected for study from three broadly defined socioeconomic levels—underprivileged, middle, and upper classes. The extent of acceptance, isolation, and rejection was obtained from a sociometric instrument administered to each class.

A comparison of the acceptance and rejection scores of the 145 children making up the mentally retarded group with a similar number of pupils of average and above-average mental ability, matched for school, grade level, and sex, is presented in Table 3–12. No significant sex differences in acceptance were noted. Statistically significant differences in acceptance scores were obtained between the mentally retarded and control groups. These differences appeared in connection with schoolwork and play activities. In each case the differences were in favor of the control group, indicating a less favorable acceptance for the mentally retarded. A further comparison was made between the acceptance of groups from different socioeconomic levels. The results showed that at each socioeconomic level, the differences in acceptability between the mentally retarded and control groups were in favor of the control group.

Mentally retarded pupils were not only isolated by their peers, but were actively rejected by them. This rejection seemed to result from

TABLE 3–12

Acceptance Scores Made by Boys and Girls in Mentally Retarded and Control Groups

Group		No.	Mean Acceptance Score		
			Work	Play	Total
Boys:	Retarded	84	−1.1	−.9	−1.1
	Control	84	.4	.5	.5
Girls:	Retarded	61	−1.2	−.9	−1.1
	Control	61	.7	.6	.7
Total:	Retarded	145	−1.2	−.9	−1.1
	Control	145	.7	.6	.7

SOURCE: After Martin (1953).

behavior patterns involving aggressiveness, a finding in harmony with results reported by Johnson concerning children of the lower elementary grades. Such patterns may be compensatory in nature, since mentally retarded pupils in competition with average and above average are more likely to meet with failure. Martin also noted that the mean attitude-toward-school scores decreased as the level of intelligence decreased. Pupils with IQ's below 80 expressed significantly less favorable attitudes toward school than did pupils whose IQ's were above 80, while those with IQ's above 110 expressed more favorable attitudes than did those with IQ's below 110. Intelligence quotient, teacher rating, and social acceptance were the factors most closely associated with attitude toward school.

The question may be raised: Is the mentally retarded child isolated and rejected in schools that emphasize social adjustment, often referred to as progressive schools? Johnson and Kirk (1950) present data from such a school. These data revealed that mentally retarded children were no more accepted in these classes than in traditional classes.

Various studies have shown that differences in adjustment among the mentally retarded are closely related to differences in the nature of family relations. Abel (1940) concluded from a study of the vocational adjustment of mentally retarded girls:

The successful girls had a home in which they were not rejected psychologically. Often the fathers treated them severely, particularly in restricting their recreational opportunities. But almost every girl had a sympathetic mother. These mothers were often harassed by hard work both in their homes and in a factory, but nevertheless they genuinely loved their daughters and shared their lives with them. . . .

Among the 17 girls who were failures, 14 came from severely unfavorable homes, homes in which they were rejected by the mother, driven and dominated too much by one or both parents, and from a situation where too much responsibility was thrown on their shoulders without any accompanying affection and guidance. Two of these girls became sex offenders, one ran away. One girl was institutionalized by her mother to get her out of the way. Another girl came from a home of much higher intelligence than her own, a home in which her intellectual limitations were not accepted. It is interesting that we had two girls in the successful group who had parents and siblings of considerably higher intelligence than themselves, but in these homes the mother in the one case, and the stepmother in the other, were understanding and showed genuine affection for the girls. [P. 71.]

In a series of studies on the effect of the severely retarded child on his family, Farber (1960) found that the sex of the child and his placement had a definite effect on the marital integration of the parents. Marital integration was lower when the retarded child was a boy and was at home. As the retarded boy grew older, his disruptive influence on marital integration increased. Marital integration scores of parents were *higher* with (1) a mentally retarded girl at home, (2) a mentally retarded girl in an institution, or (3) a mentally retarded boy in an institution than for a mentally retarded boy at home.

In a further study of sibling relationships, Farber and Jenné (1963) found that the sex of the retardate, his placement, and the sex of the normal sibling were factors in adjusting to this situation within the family. Bateman and Kirk (1963) summarized Farber's earlier findings as follows:

1. As the retarded child grew older, his status in the sibling group changed so that he was regarded as the youngest child. . . .
2. Normal brothers and sisters who interacted with their retarded sibling differed in their life goals from other siblings.
3. The adjustment of normal siblings was unaffected by the sex of the retarded child or social status of the family, but was influenced adversely by a high degree of dependence on the part of the retarded child. Sisters tended to be better adjusted when the retarded child was institutionalized than when the retarded child was at home while the opposite was true of brothers as they seemed less well adjusted when the retarded child was institutionalized. [Pp. 47–48.]

A retarded boy placed more stress on the family than did a retarded girl; institutionalization of the retarded child reduced pressures on parents and sisters of the retarded child; religion and social status were significant factors in determining the family's ability to manage the child at home. [P. 49.]

Far from being a simple choice, the decision to place a child in a residential facility was found to be very complicated. This may be implied from the statement, "The decision of the parents to institutionalize a severely retarded child was shown to be related to demographic-ecological, social organizational, and social psychological variables" (Bateman and Kirk, 1963, p. 49).

Blodgett (1964) reports essentially similar findings from her study of 90 normal adolescent siblings of retarded children. She indicates:

One noticeable conclusion is that retarded brothers cause more conflicts than retarded sisters, and that boys are more resentful and critical of retarded brothers than they are of retarded sisters. Girls are more critical of retarded brothers than sisters, but not nearly as harsh as boys. Both boys and girls are less critical of retarded sisters. [P. 2.]

As a result of her experiences in parent counseling and her research findings, Blodgett (1964) makes these suggestions to parents on how best to help normal siblings of retarded children:

1. Recognize the importance of your own attitudes in determining those of your other children.
2. With younger normal children, be aware of their confusion, uncertainty, ambivalence of feeling. Help them feel that this is acceptable to you; recognize that their criticalness of you may be partly uncertainty about how important they are to you, and loved by you.
3. Be aware of the heightened conflict between same-sex siblings when they are boys and opposite-sex siblings when the retarded one is a boy and the normal one is a girl. Be aware of the greater difficulty boys have in talking about the problem, and the greater protectiveness both boys and girls have toward retarded girls.
4. Be especially watchful about the amount of responsibility given to normal girls with regard to the retarded member.
5. Take the teeners into your confidence with regard to future planning; this is an area of considerable concern to them.
6. Permit and encourage teeners to express their feelings, doubts, conflicts, etc., rather than hiding them.
7. Be watchful how you divide your attention among your children.
8. Be watchful of how family group activities may be hampered by the retarded child, and strive to find a balance.
9. In view of the tremendous frequency of ambivalent attitudes, be watchful whether the normal teens are having trouble forming consistent philosophies and values in other areas, too.
10. Try to resolve your inter-parent differences and work out consistent policies. [P. 3.]

SUMMARY

Several generalizations develop from the discussion in this chapter. There is no clear line of demarcation between the mentally retarded and the normal child. There are no clear lines of demarcation between the different levels of mental retardation. Mental retardation is not a unique condition, but appears under varying circumstances and conditions.

While the terms "educable" and "trainable" have usefulness in considering school-age retardates, the terms "mildly retarded," "moderately retarded," and "severely retarded" are coming into greater usage among parents and professional personnel concerned with the lifetime needs of each retardate. Apparently, some 200 or more specific etiological factors operate to produce mental retardation with a large number of cases still to be found in the category of "cause unknown." Etiological factors may be grouped as follows:

1. Those resulting from hereditary factors, often referred to as familial (endogenous)
2. Those resulting from brain injury, infection, glandular deficiencies, toxic conditions, and other accidents and diseases (exogenous)
3. Those resulting from impoverished or non-stimulating environmental conditions
4. Those resulting from varied combinations of these three conditions

Where mental retardation is present from birth, there is usually a history of lateness in reaching various landmarks in development during infancy and early childhood. A larger percentage of boys than girls are listed as mentally retarded. There are both qualitative and quantitative differences in the functioning of retarded children from different etiological groups. A high percentage of speech defects is to be found among retarded children.

The limitations of the IQ as a rigorous criterion of mental retardation have been known for some time, but the effects of cultural deprivation and failure experiences on test scores, behavior, and school achievement are just beginning to be scrutinized carefully.

The National Association for Retarded Children's estimate of 3 per cent is frequently mentioned in any consideration of the prevalence of mental retardation, with the great majority of the mildly retarded to be found in communities in which about one-fourth to one-half are served by organized special education programs.

The differences between the learning ability of children classed as mentally retarded and the learning ability of average children are most pronounced in those activities that involve reasoning and problem-solving in which symbols are used. It has been pointed out that mentally retarded children are generally slower in starting to walk and talk. They do not show a superiority in mechanical or motor performance (they are usually slightly inferior in such activities); but they can compete more successfully in these tasks than in the more abstract and symbolic performances, and in some cases they may show pronounced abilities.

Two of the most common clinical types of retardation, mongolism and cretinism, were considered briefly. The social-emotional adjustment problems of mental retardates were considered in some detail within the contexts of school and family settings. The behavior of a retardate in the school setting might be predicted from the amount of educational frustration and social isolation he encounters as he tries to learn what is required of him. It has been further noted that the sex of the retardate and normal siblings, as well as placement of the retardate in the family or residential setting, are factors to be considered in noting the adjustments of all family members among whom one is retarded.

CHAPTER REFERENCES

ABEL, T. M. (1940). A study of a group of subnormal girls successfully adjusted in industry and the community. *Amer. J. ment. Def.,* 45:66–72.

ANGUS, L. R. (1948). Schizophrenia and schizoid conditions of students in a special school. *Amer. J. ment. Def.,* 53:227–38.

ARNOLD, F. C., and WAGNER, WINIFRED K. (1955). A comparison of Wechsler children's scale and Stanford-Binet scores for eight- and nine-year-olds. *J. exp. Educ.,* 34:91–94.

ARTHUR, GRACE (1936). A study of the achievement of sixty grade I repeaters as compared with that of non-repeaters of the same mental age. *J. exp. Educ.,* 5:203–5.

BATEMAN, BARBARA D., and KIRK, S. A. (1963). *Ten years of research at the Institute for Research on Exceptional Children, University of Illinois, 1952–1962.* Mimeographed.

BEGAB, M. J. (1963). What is a retarded child? *Together,* Vol. 7, No. 11, 29.

BEIDLEMAN, B. (1945). Mongolism. *Amer. J. ment. Def.,* 50:35–53.

BENDA, C. E. (1946). *Mongolism and cretinism*. New York: Grune & Stratton.

BENDA, C. E., MALCOLM, J. F., and CHIPMAN, CATHERINE E. (1951). The inadequacy of present-day concepts of mental deficiency and mental illness in child psychiatry. *Amer. J. Psychiat.*, 107:721–29.

BLODGETT, HARRIET (1964). Dr. Blodgett presents study. *Parentalk*, March, Vol. 12, pp. 2–3.

BROWN, S. F. (1955). A note on speech retardation in mental deficiency. *Pediatrics*, 16: 272–73.

CANTOR, G. N., and STACEY, C. L. (1951). Manipulative dexterity in mental defectives. *Amer. J. ment. Def.*, 56:401–10.

CASSEL, MARGARET E. (1949). Note on pseudo-feeblemindedness. *Train. Sch. Bull.*, 46:119–26.

CASSEL, MARGARET E., and RIGGS, MARGARET M. (1953). Comparison of three etiological groups of mentally retarded children on the Vineland Social Maturity Scale. *Amer. J. ment. Def.*, 58:162–69.

CATALANO, F. L., and McCARTHY, DOROTHEA (1954). Infant speech as a possible predictor of later intelligence. *J. Psychol.*, 38:203–9.

CHARLES, D. C. (1953). Ability and accomplishment of persons earlier judged mentally deficient. *Genet. Psychol. Monogr.*, 47:9–71.

COMMITTEE ON NOMENCLATURE AND STATISTICS OF THE AMERICAN PSYCHIATRIC ASSOCIATION (1952). *Diagnostic and statistical manual* [for] *mental disorders*. Washington, D.C.: The Association.

CROMWELL, R. L. (1961). Selected aspects of personality development in mentally retarded children. *Except. Child.*, 28:44–51.

CRUICKSHANK, W. M. (1948). Arithmetic ability of mentally retarded children. II. Understanding arithmetic processes. *J. educ. Res.*, 42:279–88.

DOLL, E. A. (1942). Social age as a basis for classification and training. *Amer. J. ment. Def.*, 47:49.

DURLING, D. (1952). Mental growth curves in untreated institutionalized mongoloid patients. *Amer. J. ment. Def.*, 56:578–88.

ENGLE, T. L., and HAMLETT, IONA C. (1952). Comparison of mental defectives and normal children in ability to handle clock and calendar situations. *Amer. J. ment. Def.*, 58:655–63.

FARBER, B. (1960). *Family organization and crisis: maintenance of integration in families with a severely retarded child*. Monographs of the Society for Research in Child Development, Vol. 25, No. 1.

FARBER, B., and JENNÉ, W. C. (1963). Interaction with retarded siblings and life goals of children. *Marriage & Fam. Liv.*, 25:91–98.

FLORY, C. D. (1936). *The physical growth of mentally deficient boys*. Monographs of the Society for Research in Child Development, Vol. 1, No. 6.

FREEMAN, F. S. (1955). *Theory and practice of psychological testing*. (Rev. ed.) New York: Holt, Rinehart & Winston.

GOTTESMAN, I. I. (1963). Genetic aspects of intelligent behavior. In N. ELLIS (ed.), *Handbook of Mental Deficiency*. New York: McGraw-Hill.

HEBER, R. (1959). *A manual on terminology and classification in mental retardation*. Monograph Supplement to *Amer. J. ment. Def.*, Vol. 64.

HEGGE, T. G. (1952). Psychological aspects of mental retardation. In S. G. DiMICHAEL (ed.), *Vocational rehabilitation of the mentally retarded*. Washington, D.C.: U.S. Government Printing Office.

ILLINGWORTH, R. S. (1955). Mental retardation in the infant and preschool child. *Brit. med. J.*, No. 4930, p. 3.

ILLINGWORTH, R. S. (1961). The predictive value of developmental tests in the first year, with special reference to the diagnosis of mental subnormality. *J. Child Psychol. Psychiat.*, 2:210–15.

JASTAK, J. (1949). A rigorous criterion of feeblemindedness. *J. abnorm. soc. Psychol.*, 44:367–78.

JOHNSON, G. O. (1950). A study of the social position of mentally handicapped children in the regular grades. *Amer. J. ment. Def.*, 55:60–89.

JOHNSON, G. O., and KIRK, S. A. (1950). Are mentally handicapped children segregated in the regular grades? *Except. Child.*, 17:65–68, 87.

McCARTHY, DOROTHEA (1960). Language development. *Monogr. Soc. Res. Child Developm.*, 25:5–6.

McNEILL, W. D. D. (1954). Developmental patterns of mongoloid children: a study of certain aspects of their development. Unpublished doctor's dissertation, Univer. of Illinois.

MALAMUD, N. (1954). Recent trends in classification of neuropathological findings in mental deficiency. *Amer. J. ment. Def.*, 58:438–47.

MALZBERG, B. (1953). Sex differences in the prevalence of mental deficiency. *Amer. J. ment. Def.*, 58:301–5.

MANGUS, A. R. (1950). Effect of mental and educational retardation on personality development of children. *Amer. J. ment. Def.*, 55:208–12.

MARTIN, SR. M. ALOYSE (1953). Social acceptance and attitude toward school of mentally retarded pupils in regular classes. Unpublished doctor's dissertation, Univer. of Southern California.

MOSKOWITZ, M. (1948). Teaching the slow learner. *Sch. Rev.*, 16:477.

NICKELL, V. L. (1954). *Report on study for trainable mentally handicapped children*. Springfield, Ill.: Superintendent of Public Instruction.

PICKERING, D. E., and KONLISCHER, NINA. (1956). Discordance of cretinism in monozygotic twins. *Amer. J. Dis. Child.*, 92:63–65.

POOLE, I. (1934). Genetic development of articulation of consonant sounds in speech. *Element. Eng. Rev.*, 11:159–61.

RAIN, MARGARET E. (1952). Development of social maturity in familial and non-familial mentally deficient children. *Train. Sch. Bull.*, 48:177–85.

ROSELLE, E. N. (1955). New horizons for the mentally retarded when a school looks at the problem as a whole. *Amer. J. ment. Def.*, 59:359–73.

RUSSELL, H. K. (1952). Articulation profile of 209 mentally retarded school children. Unpublished master's thesis, San Francisco State Coll.

SARASON, ESTHER K., and SARASON, S. B. (1945). A problem in diagnosing feeblemindedness. *J. abnorm. soc. Psychol.*, 40:323–29.

SARASON, S. B. (1955). Mentally retarded and mentally defective children: major psycho-social problems. In W. CRUICKSHANK (ed.), *Psychology of exceptional children and youth.* New York: Prentice-Hall.

SCHLANGER, B. B. (1953). Speech measurements of institutionalized mentally handicapped children. *Amer. J. ment. Def.*, 18:114–22.

SPEER, G. S. (1940). The mental development of children of feebleminded and normal mothers. *Thirty-ninth yearbook of the National Society for the Study of Education,* Part II, 309–14.

STEIN, J. U. (1963). Motor function and physical fitness of the mentally retarded: a critical review. *Rehabilit. Lit.*, 24:230–41, 263.

STRAUSS, A. A. (1939). Typology in mental deficiency: its clinical, psychological and educational implications. *Proc. Amer. Assn. ment. Def.*, 44:85–90.

SWINEFORD, F. (1948). *A study in factor analysis.* Supplementary Educational Monographs, No. 67. Chicago: Univer. of Chicago Press.

THOMPSON, CLARE W., and MAGARET, ANN (1947). Differential test responses of normals and mental defectives. *J. abnorm. soc. Psychol.*, 42:285–93.

TJIO, J. H., and LEVAN, A. (1956). The chromosome number of man. *Hereditas,* 42:1–6.

WEBSTER, T. C. (1963). Problems of emotional development in young retarded children. *Amer. J. Psychiat.*, 120:37–43.

WIRTZ, M. A., and GUENTHER, R. (1957). The incidence of trainable mentally handicapped children. *Except. Child.*, 23:171–72, 175.

YANNET, H. (1954). Mental deficiency. In W. E. NELSON (ed.), *Textbook of Pediatrics.* (6th ed.) Philadelphia: W. B. Saunders.

SELECTED READINGS

CAIN, L. F., and LEVINE, S. (1963). *Effects of community and institutional school programs on trainable mentally retarded children.* CEC Research Monograph, Series B, No. B-1.

ELLIS, N. (ed.) (1963). *Handbook of mental deficiency: psychological theory and research.* New York: McGraw-Hill.

GARDNER, W. I., and NISONGER, H. W. (1962). *A manual on program development in mental retardation.* A monograph supplement to the *Amer. J. ment. Def.*, Vol. 66.

HUNT, J. McV. (1961). *Intelligence and experience.* New York: Ronald.

MAUTNER, H. (1959). *Mental retardation; its care, treatment and physiological base.* London: Pergamon.

PRESIDENT'S PANEL ON MENTAL RETARDATION (L. MAYO, Chairman) (1962). *A proposed program for national action to combat mental retardation.* Washington: U.S. Government Printing Office.

U.S. DEPARTMENT OF HEALTH, EDUCATION, AND WELFARE (1962). *Mental retardation, activities of the U.S. department of health, education, and welfare.* Washington, D.C.: U.S. Government Printing Office.

WRIGHT, S. W., and TARJAN, G. (1963). Progress in pediatrics: mental retardation. *Amer. J. Dis. Child.,* 105:511–26.

For additional special materials on the mentally retarded, the reader is referred to the American Association on Mental Deficiency, Inc., and the National Association for Retarded Children.

4

EDUCATING THE
MENTALLY RETARDED

Special educational provisions for mentally retarded children have followed an interesting course over the years. Historically, where such children were excluded from regular education programs, residential placement often existed as the only alternative given to parents. Around the turn of the century special classes for the mentally retarded first began to develop in public schools, usually in larger communities. The approach to placement has often been essentially negative, with emphasis on what a particular child could not do. This has superimposed social retardation on the other problems that the mentally retarded child has had. Recent years have seen a trend away from residential placement to community placement and services with the range of services broadened and improved at an accelerated rate. Fraenkel (1961) asserts that:

It is clear to see that the old stereotypes, the old beliefs, and the old concepts about the capabilities of the mentally retarded child, adolescent, and adult no longer have substance. In fact, our prior focus on the retardate's inability, his incapacity, or his disability has, in many instances, prevented many of the mentally retarded from achieving their full potential. [P. 99.]

The 1960 White House Conference on Children and Youth noted the following range of community services that have become available in recent years.

Diagnostic and treatment centers
Public health services
Preschool nurseries
Day-care (activity) centers
Special education
Avocational and prevocational services
Sheltered workshops and other opportunities
Vocational guidance, counseling, habilitation, and rehabilitation
  services
Foster homes, residential treatment centers
Recreational opportunities, in existing programs where feasible, or
  in special programs as needed; camps
Parent counseling and homemaker services
Opportunities for religious participation

Gardner and Nisonger (1962) prepared a manual on program development in mental retardation subtitled *Guidelines in Planning, Development, and Coordination of Programs for the Mentally Retarded at State and Local Levels,* in which some 25 crucial issues in program development were considered in detail. In their Foreword the authors point out:

The guidelines presented are based on the assumption that sound program development depends in large measure upon clarity of program objectives, careful assessment of the needs and potentials of retarded individuals to be served, effective methods of treatment, training and care based upon scientific knowledge, adequately trained personnel, sound program planning and the development of effective methods of evaluation and research. [P. iii.]

Within recent years special educational provisions for school-age, educable mentally retarded children in local communities have either been permitted or required by state regulation. New York City had its first organized classes for trainable mentally retarded children in 1928 (Lynch and Scharf, 1957). While the arguments still exist about public school responsibility for the education of trainable retardates, many states and communities have organized special educational provisions for them through their schools. The National Association for Retarded Children has had a notable influence in the development of all special educational provisions for retarded children. The NARC

Official Policy on Education (Baldini, 1963) clearly enunciates their position on educational provisions:

1. The provision of educational opportunities for retarded children of school age is the responsibility of public school systems.
2. It is the responsibility of State Departments of Education or Public Instruction to establish standards, provide leadership and professional guidance and grant financial aid to public school systems in developing day school programs for the retarded throughout the state.
3. Teachers of the retarded should be highly qualified individuals who are especially trained to work with the retarded. Toward this end the NARC will lend every effort to seek improved and expanded teacher training facilities throughout the nation and to encourage an increasing number of qualified students to enter this field.
4. Educational programs for the retarded should be such that they fit the needs and abilities of each individual child and help him to develop to his fullest potential.
5. School classes conducted by state and local units of NARC should be on a temporary demonstration basis. In those cases where it is necessary for a unit to provide educational opportunities for the retarded, units should pursue a simultaneous major effort to have such facilities taken over by public school systems.
6. Each NARC unit has the duty to cooperate with the school boards in its area in implementing the programs necessary to provide the retarded with meaningful educational opportunities.
7. NARC will provide professional consultation in order to facilitate the realization of NARC policies in regard to education of the retarded. [P. 4.]

EDUCATIONAL NEEDS

The educational development of the mentally retarded child follows the same general pattern as that of the average child; however, he needs more time to learn new materials at different stages of his development. He needs more first-hand experiences with things about him before beginning his reading; and he should not be expected to grasp new ideas and recognize differences in words as quickly as the average and superior child, or to see relationships as readily.

Basic Needs. The basic needs of the mentally retarded child are not different from those of other children. Likewise, the essential educational needs of the mentally retarded child are not wholly different; although the emphasis should be on a more practical program rather than the traditional academic curriculum. Garrison (1952) reported that an educational program directed toward the development of social skills and attitudes contributed to adjustive behavior of mentally retarded children. He noted that within the range of mental development of the class studied, the IQ per se was not a differentiating factor in predicting which social skills and attitudes could be developed. These seem to be "soaked up" from the social milieu in which the child grows, participates, and develops. It is at this point in particular that the child who grows up in an unwholesome and impoverished environment may develop unfavorable attitudes.

Whether the goal is education for living or education for making a living, exceptional children will profit most from a program that takes into consideration the individuality of each child and is directed toward the development of well-adjusted personalities. In the case of vocational training "more attention is given to the simpler skills considered a part of prevocational training than to the more complicated skills involved in vocational training" (Geer, 1952).

The learning characteristics and problems of children vary with their maturation, motivation and intellectual development. Mental age furnishes a basis for determining at about what level a child is capable of functioning in learning activities at a particular time. The mentally retarded child is inferior in his ability to learn many things when he enters school at the age of six. He is definitely not ready to learn to read. The teacher finds it impossible to teach pupils with mental ages of four and five years the same skills and content that children with mental ages of six years and more are able to learn. As retarded children grow older, the rate of mental growth ordinarily continues to lag behind that of the average child. This condition creates a challenging problem that the teacher may not be able to solve in a regular class through ordinary group instructional procedures and the curriculum materials available for the particular grade that he teaches.

In structuring the curriculum for mentally handicapped children, Martens (1950) attempted to integrate the subjects of the elementary school into broad areas of experience. This unit plan of teaching seems to be especially appropriate either for the special class or for the regular class in which the mentally retarded child may be found. It furnishes common experiences around which children of different abilities can contribute according to their interests and developmental level. It also furnishes concrete experiences that may give richer meaning to other learning in the classroom. The curriculum for the educable mentally retarded should be plotted on a broad horizontal level rather than along the steeper vertical ascendancy that typifies the curriculum for the normal child. This implies that the mentally retarded child will not be able to handle concepts as broad or complex, or to reach such heights in abstract thinking, problem-solving, and creative activities, as would ordinarily be the case for the average or above-average child.

Special Needs. In the ordinary classroom the mentally retarded child may differ greatly from the normal child in his motivation for learning. Any difference is likely to be the result of acquired reactions and attitudes that have evolved as a result of his retardation rather than innate differences in needs. The mentally retarded child is continuously exposed to intellectual competition in which he is inevitably the loser. Being the loser over a period of time can have a devastating influence upon his adjustment and personality characteristics.

When the mentally retarded child faces the task of learning to read, write, and do number work of a level of difficulty for which he is not ready, he is likely to display avoidance reactions rather than the eagerness characteristic of his more competent associates. Thus, negative attitudes appear among mentally retarded children in varying degrees, depending upon the nature and degree of their mental retardation and upon how the children have been understood and dealt with in the past. One of the outstanding problems faced by those dealing with mentally retarded children is to help them overcome these motivational blocks. The mentally retarded child is faced with a need for bolstering his ego and for developing a feeling of personal worth. He is likely to feel frustrated and needs to succeed in *some* tasks regarded by himself and others as worthwhile.

Other needs that are prominent among mentally retarded children are those common to all children, such as the needs for emotional security, to love and be loved, to be worthy in a group, to be worthy in their own estimate, to be accepted by their peers, to know their assets and limitations, to develop emotional control, and to be effective in their social relations.

EDUCATIONAL PROVISIONS

Special Classes. Increasing numbers of schools are attempting to provide, by means of special classes, for the needs of children whose educational progress is erratic, puzzling, and retarded. In some states, school systems are required by law to set up special classes for educable

Special Education Department, Charlotte-Mecklenburg County Schools

Educable mentally retarded pupils can acquire usable skills in a school where special provisions are made for their education.

mentally retarded children. Special class provisions for trainable retarded children have come largely through parent pressure. An increasing number of these children are being trained in the public
schools, while the training of others is provided through private
auspices. The purposes for establishing classes for trainable mentally
retarded children are summarized by the U.S. Office of Education
(1952) in the following extract.

1. While a very small percentage of the more severely retarded group,
even under optimum training conditions, may be able to achieve a limited
degree of self-direction (and a few may be able to participate in sheltered
workshop activities when these are available), a larger number will achieve
a moderate degree of personal and social development and become economically useful in their own homes. For these children the class will
provide training experiences that will enable them to develop to the fullest
extent possible the limited abilities which they possess.

2. Lack of responsiveness because of severe conflicts, social immaturity,
physical involvements, or speech retardation may result in inadequate
measurements of intellectual ability and influence the examiner to reserve
his judgment relative to the potentials of a number of mentally retarded
children. These children may respond more adequately to repeated testing
procedures after effective socializing experiences have been provided. A
few may eventually become candidates for the regular special class groups
for educable children. For such children the training class may afford
opportunities for observation and further study. . . .

3. Another purpose of the class for the severely mentally retarded will
necessarily involve its screening functions, for not all of the children assigned on the basis of initial tests and preliminary observations will prove
capable of training and personal adjustment in a public-school situation.
Only observation over an extended period during which stimulating experiences are provided will allow the teacher and psychologist to render an
adequate evaluation of certain pupils' potentials for training. Undoubtedly,
a substantial number of the children referred for training-class placement
will require eventual institutional care. A corollary of this purpose is that
the training class must provide opportunities for the counseling of parents
in regard to institutional placements in those instances in which pupils do
not indicate the necessary capacity for growth and development. . . .
it is important to recognize that the purposes of the training class go beyond
what it can offer the pupil and extend to the needs of parents for understanding and guidance. [P. 10.]

The following conclusions were drawn from the Goldstein (1956)
study of the lower limits of eligibility for classes of trainable mentally
retarded children:

1. When the Kuhlmann IQ is below 25, the probability that the child
will be retained in the class is low enough to warrant ineligibility.
2. When the Kuhlmann IQ is between 25 and 35, other criteria should

be considered before the child is declared ineligible. These criteria are mental age below two years, social age below three years, and social quotient under 35.

3. When the Kuhlmann IQ is above 35, the probability that the child will be retained in the class is very high. At this level, an exhaustive psychometric evaluation of the child for establishing eligibility does not appear to be necessary. The data contributing most in determining eligibility are those denoting soical behavior, motor ability, and sensory acuity and perception. [P. 227.]

The goals to which programs for trainable retarded children must be directed include:

1. *Adequate habits of personal behavior.*—The pupil should be able to control his behavior according to acceptable standards. Habits of cleanliness, health, and eating should not be offensive when he is observed by others. He should be able to remove and put on his clothing.

2. *Efficient communicative skills.*—The pupil must be responsive to ordinary conversation and able to communicate his needs and interests to others.

3. *Useful coordinations.*—The development of coordinations will include a normal walking gait, the maintenance of a healthful posture, and the ability to perform common tasks with his hands.

4. *Acceptable habits of work.*—The pupil must learn to enjoy useful and satisfying occupations. Being helpful to others and willing to perform common tasks will be essential if he is to achieve any degree of independence and economic usefulness. In addition, he must develop ability to see a very simple project through to completion. Pride in the achievement of simple tasks is as essential to the adequate adjustment of the severely retarded child as is the satisfaction growing out of greater achievement enjoyed by more capable children.

5. *Adjustment to social situations.*—The severely retarded child cannot perform as an isolate if he is to achieve any degree of competence for social living. He must learn to respect the rights and property of others, become able to tolerate the behavior of other pupils, and be willing to participate in simple group activities. Whether his participation is to be limited to the family group and the immediate neighborhood or to a larger world in which he will be employed in a useful occupation, his adjustment will be inadequate unless he can learn to enjoy social participation.

6. *Willingness to follow directions.*—The severely retarded child will be constantly under the supervision of others who are capable of guiding his activities. Unlike his more normal peers who can accept responsibilities for independent action, he will be subject to much direction. Responsiveness to direction necessarily must be one of his most valuable attributes. Therefore, the program must put particular emphasis upon this type of training. [U.S. Office of Education, 1952, p. 12.]

Since work with mentally retarded pupils must be individualized to a very marked degree, the size of the class should not be large. For trainable retarded children it should be kept below 10. Classes for educable retarded children may have approximately 15 members at the elementary age levels and 15 to 18 at the secondary age level. The classroom should be large, with extra space for the different types of material to be used in the activities that are important in any instructional program designed for special needs and abilities of the pupils. There must be sufficient room for the pupils to move about freely and to be able to carry on their activities individually and collectively.

Advantages as well as disadvantages of special classes have been discussed here. In considering the possibility of placement, the welfare of both the individual and the group must be taken into account. The organization is of far less importance than the spirit of understanding, cooperation, and desire to develop that permeates the group.

Melcher and Blessing (1957) have described efforts to bring special education to retarded children in the rural areas of Wisconsin through the development of regional centers where there are special classes under county direction, but with cooperative arrangements for transportation and other services.

Modifications of Special-Class Plan for Small Community. In the smaller school, where only one special class may be possible, there are circumstances in which it may be better to allow the young mentally retarded child to remain in the regular primary grades rather than to assign him to the special class. The decision will depend upon factors such as (1) the resourcefulness of the teachers, (2) space available, (3) equipment for special activities, (4) age-range in the special class, and (5) a cooperative school personnel.

Strong arguments for special-class placement have been found in the results of sociometric studies of mental retardates in regular classes. For some time it has been known that definite selection factors are at work in determining which retarded children are placed in special classes. The preponderance of boys and the greater number of special classes in poorer sections point rather clearly to social-emotional maladjustment and cultural-environmental disadvantage as complicating factors in school adjustment.

Johnson (1950) and Miller (1956) observed that mentally retarded pupils were unsuccessful in their peer relationships. In their studies they were rejected and isolated, although they were enrolled in regular classes with average children. Johnson (1961) attributes the adjustment difficulties of mentally retarded pupils to unsuccessful compensatory reactions related to failure and frustration. Their peers did not, according to Johnson, reject them because they lacked ability to perform schoolwork, but because of their behavior, which included objectionable traits such as fighting, cheating, and lying. Martin (1953) found similar conditions in the parochial school setting. As shown in Table 4–1, the normal (control) group received significantly higher acceptance scores on her sociometric instrument.

TABLE 4–1

Acceptance Scores Made by Boys and Girls in Mentally
Retarded and Control Groups

Group		Mean Acceptance Score			
		Number	Work	Play	Total
Boys:	Retarded	84	−1.1	−.9	−1.1
	Control	84	.4	.5	.5
Girls:	Retarded	61	−1.2	−.9	−1.1
	Control	61	.7	.6	.7
Total:	Retarded	145	−1.2	−.9	−1.1
	Control	145	.7	.6	.7

SOURCE: After Martin (1953).

Deno (1963) analyzed enrollments in special classes for educable mentally retarded children in Minneapolis, Minnesota, over a 30-year period to see what changes had occurred in the ability characteristics of pupils assigned to such classes.

Among several conclusions were the following:

1. There has been a steady increase of enrollment of pupils in our public school classes for the educable retarded.
2. There seems to be a clear tendency toward inclusion of more cases at the extremes of the educable range.
3. The median IQ has dropped significantly at the elementary level over the last ten years.
4. There is beginning to be a flattening of the distribution of IQ's in educable classes. The concentration of cases between 75 and 80 is less pronounced.

While the removal of a mentally retarded child from a regular class may contribute somewhat to the homogeneity of the regular class, the erroneous assumption is often made that in the special class the retardate will be with others "like himself" and that the special teacher somehow has a homogeneous group. While the special teacher has fewer children in his class, the range and variety of characteristics and problems still make for an extremely heterogeneous class, as any special teacher will verify. The task of teaching is thus complicated on several dimensions. Classes for trainable retardates are usually self-contained and may have a great variation in age within a single group. Classes for educable retardates usually have a smaller age range, because of the numbers of possible clients, and are self-contained for younger children with increasing opportunities and degrees of integration as these children grow older.

From her analysis of special class enrollments Deno (1963) also notes a distinction *within* the educable group that bears further investigation:

The data suggest that our special classes are becoming progressively less homogeneous as a teaching unit. The real significance of the trends which are evident is in the fact that the pupil with an IQ above 80 is fundamentally different in important characteristics and needs from the one with an IQ below 65. The latter is likely to be obviously defective in functioning and have more conspicuously deviant appearance and behavior. The pupils above 80 IQ are probably emotionally disturbed, brain-damaged, victims of social deprivation or remediable instructional failures rather than retarded in the classical sense. The fact that this makes for a different teaching situation is regrettable but of less importance than the fact that these two groups need a different kind of program and curricula. [P. 8.]

Deno (1963) then recommends:

. . . that we work toward a specially designed, possibly more centralized program for pupils below 65 IQ and emphasize remedial work and an adapted curriculum for those of higher IQ. The latter group may well be continued on our present plan of integration in regular classes for some of their work. The lower ability group may do better on a more segregated plan. [P. 8.]

Jordan (1960) studied the sociometric status of educable retarded children within special classes and found that IQ and social status were positively related. Her over-all status findings confirmed Johnson's results for regular classes; the children lowest in IQ occupy low social positions.

Importance of Integration. The concept of increased integration of the handicapped into regular class activities has been emphasized by Cruickshank (1955). There are many examples of such programs today. Among these may be mentioned the Harvey Lowrey School, Dearborn, Michigan, and the Ann Kellogg School, Battle Creek, Michigan. Such integration may mean placement of the individual handicapped child within a class of normal children. For mentally retarded children increased integration means inclusion of members of special classes in selected activities of regular classes. This requires first of all an understanding of the program by teachers, pupils, parents, and the community. Any integration can best be brought about when a conscious effort is made to interpret such a program to all possible participants. In-service workshops, group meetings, field trips, visiting speakers, visual aids, school and community projects, and other means embracing group dynamics are useful for developing an understanding and more accepting attitude.

The policy often followed to secure increased integration is to segregate children only in those areas where they are seriously handicapped (Rodman, 1952). For the mentally retarded these areas will include the skill subjects of reading, arithmetic, spelling, and writing. Physical education may be taken in the classes with the regular children. However, integration for less-academic subjects may present some organizational difficulties for the regular class teacher, and the special teacher should be willing to take certain children with problems from the regular class on an exchange basis. Stein (1963) sounds a note of caution about integration with normal children for physical activities when he states:

Indiscriminate placement of the mentally handicapped in physical education classes has disregarded such factors as the inability of retarded children to play naturally or spontaneously as do normal children and ignored the findings of research dealing with physical and motor abilities, physical fitness, and motor proficiency of normals and retardates alike. [P. 232.]

Mentally retarded children should also participate on the student council, safety patrol, and other school-related activities. It was pointed out in Chapter 3 that educable mentally retarded children as a group are not significantly inferior in simple motor skills. They are frequently able to participate successfully in different aspects of the school program where verbal skills and problem-solving of a complex or abstract nature are not important.

Educational Provisions for Mentally Retarded Adolescents. It appears that the elementary teacher is generally more sensitive to the needs and problems of mentally retarded children and preadolescents than is the high school teacher. There are several factors that may account for this difference. In the first place, it appears likely that elementary teachers are more pupil-minded than are secondary teachers. In the second place, the elementary teacher usually comes into closer contact with the pupils because of the nature of the class-room plan of organization. Thus, the more subject-minded secondary teacher often overlooks the special needs and problems of the mentally retarded adolescent.

It has been pointed out that the emotional needs of the mentally retarded individual are not especially different from those of normal children. With growth into adolescence peer relations and peer ap-proval become increasingly important. The educable or trainable re-tarded adolescent should be placed in situations where he will be able to satisfy his needs for achievement as well as for belongingness and peer approval. Some recommendations for a high school program for the educable mentally retarded might include:

1. Accept the child at his own level and plan for specialized instruction in terms of his own ability to achieve.
2. Assimilate him in the regular high school student body in all activities in which he can profitably participate.
3. Recognize and provide for his needs for belongingness, security, and a feeling of personal worth.
4. Emphasize practical learning, as contrasted with theoretical knowledge.
5. Relate experiences to the home, community, health and sanita-tion, leisure-time activities, and associations with other people, and to a definite job objective when possible.
6. Promote largely upon the basis of physical and social maturity, even when there is a serious intellectual deficiency.
7. Provide for some sort of graduation as a means of recognizing even limited achievement.

Dinger (1961) studied the postschool adjustment of former stu-dents of special classes in Altoona, Pennsylvania. A random sample of 614 names was selected from 1,500 names on file. Of those selected, 421 were located and 333 (79.3 per cent) of these provided data for analysis. In an effort to determine which positive adjustments were being made by former pupils of classes for the educable retarded, Dinger interviewed 100 of the 144 subjects who met his criteria of being employed and living in Altoona. He also analyzed the jobs of these 100 subjects and talked with their employers. Dinger found that a diploma was an aid to job-getting. Most were employed in unskilled or semiskilled jobs. For most subjects their present job had been their only employment. Most got jobs through friends and relatives. Half had annual incomes higher than beginning teachers with four years of college training. The average wage was $3,327.

Special Education Department, Charlotte-Mecklenburg County Schools

The educational program for junior high educable mentally retarded must include experiences of a concrete nature that are meaningful to the pupils.

Dinger found little correlation between wages and IQ (.21) or between wages and chronological age (.29) for these successful graduates of a special education program. The Dinger study points out several implications for high school programs and has several specific recommendations for planning school programs at the secondary level.

In summarizing the results of other follow-up studies, Fraenkel (1961) points out:

. . . [figures] seem to indicate that most mentally retarded persons rehabilitated into employment will work in service occupations, unskilled jobs, and semiskilled work. About a fourth of all retarded ready for competitive employment will secure employment in clerical, sales, and kindred jobs, skilled jobs, and agricultural work and as family workers or homemakers. [P. 102.]

The Mentally Retarded in Residential Schools. The first American institution for the mentally retarded was established in Barre, Massachusetts, in July, 1848. Others followed, under either state or private control, until today 49 states have public residential institutions. The false notion that when a child is placed in a state institution his intellectual condition is hopeless is still all too prevalent. This idea may result from the fact that (1) in the early days, these institutions were referred to as "places for training idiotic children"; and (2) the more extreme cases (especially those from unfortunate home and environmental conditions) are the ones that often are placed in such institutions. Undoubtedly, many of the children placed in institutions for the mentally retarded are incapable of being trained for adequate social and economic adjustments, and a large percentage of the others will need constant guidance and supervision throughout life. But it is equally true that there are many in our public schools who are incapable, for one reason or another, of ever becoming completely independent of financial support and social guidance. It was pointed out in Chapter 3 that a fairly accurate classification of the degrees of mental retardation can be made and a total evaluation should serve as a basis for the placement of a child in a residential school for the mentally retarded and for his program of training once he is placed in such an institution. There is increasing emphasis on the different roles of residential institutions. Will children need *custodial care* or *semicustodial care?* Which children need a *training* program? Concerning the program in residential schools for the educable retarded, Martens (1939) early noted:

The plan of school activities in residential schools can best be compared with the program of special classes for mentally retarded children in day schools. There is the same need for making the material of instruction simple and concrete, familiar to the pupil's experience and within his comprehension. There is the same emphasis upon the development of his sensory and motor abilities, the same need for consideration of "the whole child," and all his idiosyncrasies, defects, interests, and emotions. In fact, the residential school has a distinct advantage over the day school in that it has the *whole child* the *whole day* and the *whole year*. [P. 238.]

A primary objective in the education of pupils in residential schools should be good health. Physical defects and various conditions contributing to poor physical and mental health should be given first consideration. Educational efforts toward the development of sensory and motor abilities and good sensorimotor coordination should receive a great deal of attention, for it has been shown that mentally retarded boys and girls are able to do these types of work better than more verbal and abstract types. The heights to which physical skills can be developed among the mentally retarded has been demonstrated by some of the work done in physical education. Although there may not be much transfer in manual abilities, such skills do provide a partial basis for further growth, for socialization, and for the development of desirable mental and emotional attitudes. Although academic skills should not be neglected, these are valuable only insofar as the pupil can grasp and apply them to the experiences of daily living.

In the past there has been reluctance among parents to place a child in an institution, even though individual situations would indicate such placement to be desirable. This problem has received significant attention through the development of organized parent groups and their concerted efforts at dealing with the situation in a more realistic way than in the past. Some parents still have tremendous difficulty in attempting to solve such problems on other than a sentimental or strongly emotional basis, but many parents are increasingly experiencing the release from tension that comes from sharing their problems through affiliation with those facing similar problems. The activities of local groups affiliated with the National Association for Retarded Children are contributing greatly to improved attitudes toward mental retardation, residential placement, and special education programs.

One sobering note concerning special education programs for trainable retardates in the residential setting comes from the results of the Cain-Levine study (1961) of trainable retardates in residential and community settings. They comment:

The school within the institution apparently cannot counteract the pervasive lack of stimulation by providing a few hours of training each day.

Further, it is questionable whether the school within the institution can carry out a consistent and systematic program for trainable mentally retarded children, as institutions are presently constituted. [P. 48.]

Cain and Levine studied school and non-school differences for groups of 182 trainable subjects. Composition of the sample may be seen in Table 4–2.

TABLE 4–2

Composition of Community and Institutional Control and Experimental
Groups by Sex and Diagnostic Classification

		Sex		Diagnostic Classification [*]		
Group	N	Male	Female	Mongo-loid	Organic	Undiffer-entiated
Community						
Control	46	24	22	17	12	14
Experimental	63	31	32	31	18	14
Institution						
Control	33	23	10	19	9	12
Experimental	40	30	10	8	9	16

[*] The child's classification was provided by the family physician or clinic. This information was not available for some subjects.
SOURCE: Cain and Levine (1961).

Within settings the groups were comparable, but between settings the groups were not comparable, although all children met the criteria set for this particular study. Notable findings were that the trainable child in the community became more socially competent than the child in the residential setting, that trainable children not in community programs also grew in social competence.

Three quotations from the Cain-Levine study (1961) will serve to highlight their conclusions:

There was a significant increase in the social competency development for the community children attending public school classes and for community children not attending such classes. However, social competency scores did not differ between these two groups of children. [P. 44.]

.   .   .   .

. . . that public and institutional programs, as they are now conducted, do not foster the social competency development of trainable retarded children beyond that of children not attending such programs. [P. 47.]

.   .   .   .

The data of this study support the point of view that the institution is not as desirable a setting as is an adequate home environment for the development of trainable mentally retarded children. [P. 49.]

They made a number of recommendations including (1) improved teacher training programs, (2) detailed curriculum planning for each child, and (3) research on the learning abilities of trainable mentally retarded children.

GUIDANCE AND VOCATIONAL ADJUSTMENT

Guiding the Mentally Retarded. There is a growing tendency to organize all educational programs to suit the needs and conditions confronting individual children rather than compelling pupils to conform to some rigid system designed and controlled by standards. Educational provisions for the mentally retarded child should aim:

1. To help him understand his abilities and limitations and to guide him in the development of his abilities
2. To teach him to live happily with himself and others
3. To develop in him the attitudes, ideals, and habits of emotional control necessary for adequate social adjustment
4. To help him cultivate an interest in a wide variety of things that he will encounter in his daily living—friends, nature, sports, music, and the like
5. To develop in him the desire to be of service to his classmates and others

The guidance techniques used in special education should be similar to those employed in the regular school program, with some adjustments made to meet the special needs of the mentally retarded child. Guidance should start as early as possible and be continuous, since guidance looks toward the development of each child in accordance with his potentials for growth and learning. Teachers and counselors should realize that the difficulties of childhood and adolescence may be intensified in the mentally retarded.

Concerning the guidance of the mentally retarded in high school, Daly and Cain (1953) have stated:

The educational guidance of mentally retarded students should help them to understand themselves and their limitations, to accept the special class program which is designed to make possible and profitable their stay in secondary school, to select each term two or three subjects from a restricted list of electives that are within their range of ability and adapted to their needs, and to adjust satisfactorily in these two or three classes in the regular high-school program. [P. 151.]

Special education at all levels should endeavor to bring about favorable personal and social adjustments, and to build a favorable attitude toward the world of people and work. Too often the mentally retarded adolescent develops a feeling that the world of work will be closed to him, and such a fear becomes the basis of maladjustment.

Vocational Adjustments. In academic areas educable mentally retarded children cannot achieve the degree of skill and knowledge and understanding of which the average child is capable. Therefore, the emphasis should be placed upon the development of a pleasing personality and upon adequacy in the occupational and social areas. These individuals are capable, in most cases, of acquiring the social and vocational skills that will enable them to take their places as cooperative and contributing members of our society.

Studies of New York workers show that 60 to 80 per cent of them lost their jobs for non-manual reasons rather than for poor vocational skills. For this reason, Michael-Smith (1951) listed the following personality traits to be developed in retarded children along with their vocational training:

1. Competent to perform routine work
2. Able to look after own health
3. Loyal to employers
4. Willing to assume new duties
5. Systematic in carrying out own work
6. Ability to control temper—maintain an even disposition
7. Cautious and careful to avoid danger
8. Optimistic
9. Obedient
10. Flexible
11. Personally attractive
12. Strong physically
13. Normal physically
14. Capable of remembering what he has been told
15. Dexterous [Pp. 108–9.]

In a study by Charles (1953), 151 individuals who had been identified as mentally retarded about 15 years earlier were carefully studied. At the time of the study, nine subjects were institutionalized, about 80 per cent of the total subjects studied were unmarried, and about four-fifths of the married subjects had children. The types of homes ranged from filthy shacks to costly new homes with beautifully landscaped grounds. The majority were reasonably clean and not considered detrimental to community health. Most of the group were regularly employed. Of the gainfully employed, half had been at the same job or type of work from 3 to 20 years. Labor was the most common job for the males, and most females were listed as house-keepers.

During World War II, Hegge (1944) studied a group of boys with an average age of seventeen years and an average Stanford-Binet IQ of 71 and found that 88 per cent of them were employed and were financially independent of family and relief. Their wages were generally good, and some of the boys were employed in skilled occupations. He concluded from this study that higher-grade mentally retarded individuals could become adjusted on a job if given a chance to adapt in their own way at a time when competition with more intelligent and effective personalities is reduced. Inability to impress an employer at first sight or to adapt to a job so readily as to be acceptable when there is keen competition for jobs does not necessarily imply lack of capacity to handle some responsibilities after a longer period of experience under guidance.

Factors Contributing to Vocational Success. A number of studies have dealt with the characteristics needed by the mentally retarded for successful occupational adjustment. These studies have shown consistently that the characteristics needed are the same as those needed by anyone. Coakley (1945) found, from a study of occupational adjustment of the mentally retarded, that these factors are the major obstacles to vocational success: lack of punctuality, absenteeism, poor quality of work, and inability to get along with other workers. These results have been verified in later studies. There is a relatively high correlation between intelligence and gross occupational areas. Thus, care must be taken to guide the mentally handicapped into vocational areas that do not require a high degree of intelligence.

Evidence that the non-academic student need not become a liability to society is furnished from a follow-up study (McIntosh, 1949) of Jarvis School for Boys, Toronto. Because intelligence tests were given to students before admission to this school, IQ's at the time of admission were available. A survey of 1,000 cases was conducted over a ten-year period. The IQ range of the group is shown in Table 4–3. The largest group fell in the 71–75 IQ range, and 65.2 per cent were between 66 and 80. Of the 611 boys over nineteen years of age in 1945, 44.2 per cent were in the armed services. Eight of these were killed in action.

The weekly income distribution of the graduates is shown in Table

TABLE 4–3

Distribution of Intelligence Quotients of 1,000 Boys at Time of
Admission to Jarvis School, Toronto

IQ	Number	Percentage
40–50	4	0.4
51–55	15	1.5
56–60	51	5.1
61–65	68	6.8
66–70	166	16.6
71–75	275	27.5
76–80	211	21.1
81–85	96	9.6
86–90	35	3.5
91–95	22	2.2
96–100	10	1.0
101 or more	8	0.8
IQ not available	39	3.9

SOURCE: After McIntosh (1949).

4–4. These data should be interpreted in light of the fact that 54.7
per cent of these wage earners were twenty-one years of age or under.
Nevertheless, 20 per cent of the graduates were earning the same as
or more than the average weekly earnings for industrial workers of
Toronto at that time.

TABLE 4–4

Distribution of Weekly Wage Earnings of 1,000 Boys After
Graduating from Jarvis School, Toronto

Amount Earned	Number	Percentage
Less than $15.00	29	2.9
16–20	136	13.6
21–25	187	18.7
26–30	193	19.3
31–35	179	17.9
36–40	96	9.6
41–45	47	4.7
46–50	34	3.4
51 or more	22	2.2
Miscellaneous	77	7.7

SOURCE: After McIntosh (1949).

How well do the lowest IQ groups do when they leave school?
The results show that graduates having the highest IQ's are more

likely to earn the most money; however, 75.8 per cent of those with IQ's of less than 60 were self-supporting, and 27 per cent had been on the job three years or more. In an interview study Porter and Milazzo (1958) compared for social competence and economic efficiency mentally retarded adults who had attended a special class with those who had attended regular class. There was a favorable advantage for the special-class "graduates" both in frequency of employment and in conformity to social standards.

Job Adjustment Problems. The mentally retarded youth, on his first job in particular, tends to fall into the role of the "dumbbell" or the "rube." He may be the butt of jokes and teasing that can bring him much discomfort. Supervised work experience supplemented by careful vocational orientation and counseling at school would do much to alleviate these problems. In a study of 80 closed cases of mentally retarded workers, Peckham (1952) noted ten different kinds of prominent job adjustment problems. Listed in order of frequency of occurrence, these were:

1. Lack of acceptance by fellow employees (teasing, etc.).
2. Lack of social and vocational sophistication.
3. Salary dissatisfaction.
4. Inability to budget properly.
5. Lack of initiative and job responsibility.
6. Job quitting for capricious reasons without preparation for the future.
7. Parental unrealism about client capacities.
8. Client unrealism about personal capacities.
9. Illiteracy.
10. Family over-protection.

DeProspo (1954) reported some of the jobs in which mentally retarded adolescents and youths in New York City were then engaged. These may be seen in Table 4–5. While the occupational trend is toward workers with higher levels of skills and knowledge, all kinds and levels of skills and jobs are needed to operate our complex industrial society. The increase in service workers and helpers attest to the fact that a wide range of non-manufacturing jobs are closely inter-related to our industrial urban society. An important task for teachers and others concerned with the education and guidance of the mentally handicapped is to recognize the potentials of these pupils in relation to the wide range of jobs available.

TABLE 4–5

Jobs of Mentally Retarded Adolescents and Youths in New York City, 1954

Job		IQ	Salary	Time on Job
Publishing houses				
Helping in the bindery	Girl	60	$30 wk.	3 mos.
Cutter in book bindery	Girl	70	25	11 mos.
Packing books	Girl	72	26	1 yr. 10 mos.
Inserter envelopes	Girl	75	32	1 yr.
Puts cover on books	Girl	60	30	1 yr. 5 mos.
Lifting books for packing	Boy	58	32	1 yr.
Food handling				
Bus girl–large dept. store rest.		64	35	7 mos.
Dishwasher and bus boy		72	35	6 mos.
Cafeteria worker	Boy	72	30	2 yrs.
Waitress		75	27	7 mos.
Hospital area				
Nurses aide	Girl	65	31	2 yrs. 5 mos.
Tray attendant	Girl	65	30	1 mo.
Messenger	Girl	73	36	1 yr. 2 mos.
Kitchen helper	Boy	52	30	3 mos.
Bus boy		64	30	1 yr.
Garment trades				
Folding pillow cases	Girl	62	30	6 mos.
Floor girl		66	37	1 yr.
Delivery	Boy	52	30	6 mos.
Foot treadle operator	Girl	67	85¢ hr.	1 mo.
Miscellaneous				
Assembler of ven. blinds	Girl	73	32	6 mos.
Packing of costume jewelry	Girl	72	33	1 yr.
Sprayer of flowers	Boy	72	32	5 mos.
Packing china	Boy	70	35	5 mos.
Stock girl		65	34	7 mos.
Costume jewelry (prong)	Girl	67	30	3 mos.
Porter	Boy	71	38	1 yr. 9 mos.
Pin boy		56	Part time	
File clerk dry cleaners	Girl	68	36	1 yr.
Helper furniture factory	Boy	58	80¢ hr.	7 mos.
Mechanics helper	Boy	58	40	6 mos.
Helper–storm windows	Boy	66	46	2 mos.
Packing cigarettes	Boy	66	36	1 yr.
Truck driver helper	Boy	ND	45	1 yr.
Elevator operator	Boy	67	46	3 mos.
Laundry worker	Boy	68	31	7 mos.

SOURCE: After DeProspo (1954).

SUMMARY

While residential placement was the earliest special service provided for the mentally retarded, a wide range of community services, including special classes for both educable and trainable retarded children, has become available since the turn of the century. The development of community services has been accelerated since World War II through the efforts of various professional groups, the federal and state governments, and the activities of the National Association for Retarded Children. Mental retardation is seen as producing a wide variety of special educational needs in which academic skills are less emphasized than are the development of social competence and vocational skills.

Special classes for mentally retarded children are seen as usually more heterogeneous than might be desired with positive results occurring only when there are good teachers and good programs designed specifically for the particular group of students enrolled. Some integration with normal children is felt to be desirable for a variety of reasons that so far have not yielded to scientific investigation.

Educational programs in residential institutions and educational programs for trainable retarded children are being modified and improved in the light of research findings. Educational programs at the secondary school level are developing slowly as time passes since the establishment of special classes in the elementary school setting. The content of secondary school programs is being modified in the light of results obtained from follow-up studies of mentally retarded adults.

A summary of the results of various studies of vocational opportunities and adjustments of mentally retarded individuals indicate the following:

1. The majority of the mentally retarded are capable of learning and performing a wide range of skills.
2. The majority of the mentally retarded can, through proper guidance, become self-supporting and become useful citizens.
3. The great bulk of the mentally retarded work at service jobs and in other areas requiring a low level of skill.
4. The IQ bears little relation to success on the job when a realistic approach is made to the type of work the mentally retarded are capable of performing.
5. Personal-social skills are more important for life adjustment and vocational success than mechanical ability.

CHAPTER REFERENCES

BALDINI, J. J. (1963). Quality of education emphasized. *Child. Limited,* Vol. 12, No. 4, 4.

CAIN, L. F., and LEVINE, S. (1961). *A study of the effects of community and institutional school classes for trainable mentally retarded children.* San Francisco: San Francisco State College.

CHARLES, D. C. (1953). Ability and accomplishment of persons earlier judged mentally deficient. *Genet. Psychol. Monogr.*, 47:9–71.

COAKLEY, FRANCES (1945). Study of feebleminded wards employed in war industry. *Amer. J. ment. Def.*, 50:301–6.

CRUICKSHANK, W. M. (1955). New horizons in education of the handicapped child. *Amer. J. publ. Hlth*, 45:306–11.

DALY, FLORA M., and CAIN, L. F. (1953). Mentally retarded students in California secondary schools. *Bull. Calif. State Dep. Educ.*, Vol. 22, No. 7.

DENO, EVELYN. (1963). Changes in composition of Minneapolis special classes for the educable retarded over a thirty year span. Dittoed. February 14, 1963.

DEPROSPO, C. J. (1954). Opportunities for the exceptional child. *The Adolescent Exceptional Child.* Proceedings of the 1954 Spring Conference of the Child Research Clinic of the Woods Schools, pp. 25–26.

DINGER, J. C. (1961). Post-school adjustment of former educable retarded pupils. *Except. Child.*, 27:353–60.

FRAENKEL, W. A. (1961). Planning the vocational future of the mentally retarded. *Rehabilit. Lit.*, 22:98–104.

GARDNER, W. I., and NISONGER, H. W. (1962). *A manual on program development in mental retardation.* A monograph supplement to the *Amer. J. ment. Def.*, Vol. 66.

GARRISON, I. K. (1952). The development of social skills and attitudes. *Amer. J. ment. Def.*, 56:338–43.

GEER, W. C. (1952). Education of mentally retarded children. *Amer. J. ment. Def.*, 56:560–69.

GOLDSTEIN, H. (1956). Lower limits of eligibility for classes for trainable children. *Except. Child.*, 22:226–27.

HEGGE, T. G. (1944). Occupational status of higher-grade mental defectives in the present emergency. *Amer. J. ment. Def.*, 14:207–13.

JOHNSON, G. O. (1950). A study of the social position of mentally handicapped children in the regular grades. *Amer. J. ment. Def.*, 55:60–89.

JOHNSON, G. O. (1961). *A comparative study of the personal and social adjustment of mentally handicapped children placed in special classes with mentally handicapped children who remain in regular classes.* Syracuse, N.Y.: Syracuse University Research Institute, Office of Research in Special Education and Rehabilitation.

JORDAN, JUNE B. (1960). Intelligence as a factor in social position—a study in special classes for the mentally handicapped. Unpublished doctor's dissertation, Univer. of Illinois.

LYNCH, KATHERINE D., and SCHARF, L. (1957). More help for the less able—historical review of education for the retarded. *NEA J.*, 46:336–38.

MCINTOSH, W. J. (1949). Follow-up study of 1,000 non-academic boys. *J. except. Child.*, 15:166–70.

MARTENS, ELISE H. (1939). Residential schools for mentally retarded. *Sch. Life*, 24:238.

MARTENS, ELISE H. (ed.) (1950). *Curriculum adjustments for mentally retarded children*. Washington, D.C.: U.S. Office of Education.

MARTIN, SR. M. ALOYSE (1953). Social acceptance and attitude toward school of mentally retarded pupils in regular classes. Unpublished doctor's dissertation, Univer. of Southern California.

MELCHER, J., and BLESSING, K. (1957). Special education for rural retarded youth. *Except. Child.*, 23:207–210, 214.

MICHAEL-SMITH, H. (1951). Personality training in vocational education for the retarded child. *J. except. Child.*, 17:108–10.

MILLER, R. V. (1956). Social status and sociometric differences among mentally superior, mentally typical, and mentally retarded children. *Except. Child.*, 23:114–19.

PECKHAM, R. A. (1952). Problems in job adjustment of the mentally retarded. *Amer. J. ment. Def.*, 56:448–53.

PORTER, R. B., and MILAZZO, T. C. (1958). A comparison of mentally retarded adults who attended special classes with those who attended regular school classes. *Except. Child.*, 24:410–12, 420.

RODMAN, J. T. (1952). *The organization of a special class for the mentally retarded at Bret Harte School*. A field study, San Francisco State College.

STEIN, J. U. (1963). Motor function and physical fitness of the mentally retarded: a critical review. *Rehabilit. Lit.*, 24:230–41, 263.

U.S. OFFICE OF EDUCATION (1952). *The forward look: The severely retarded child goes to school*. Washington, D.C.: U.S. Government Printing Office.

WHITE HOUSE CONFERENCE ON CHILDREN AND YOUTH (1960). *Recommendations: Composite Reports of Forum Findings, March 27–April 2, 1960*. Resolution No. 582. Washington, D.C.: U.S. Government Printing Office.

SELECTED READINGS

BAKER, H. J. (1959). *Introduction to exceptional children*. (3d ed.) New York: Macmillan. Chap. 15.

DUNN, L. M. (ed.) (1963). *Exceptional children in the schools*. New York: Holt, Rinehart & Winston. Chaps. 2 and 3.

GARTON, MALINDA D. (1964). *Teaching the educable mentally retarded —practical methods*. (2d ed.) Springfield, Ill.: Charles C Thomas.

INGRAM, CHRISTINE P. (1960). *Education of the slow learning child*. (3d ed.) New York: Ronald.

KIRK, S. A. (1962). *Educating exceptional children*. Boston: Houghton Mifflin. Chaps. 3, 4, and 5.

PERRY, NATALIE (1960). *Teaching the mentally retarded child*. New York: Columbia Univer. Press.

ROSENZWEIG, L. E., and LONG, JULIA (1960). *Understanding and teaching the dependent retarded child.* Darien, Conn.: Educational Publishing.

WILLIAMS, H. M. (1960). The retarded child goes to school. *U.S. Office of Education Pamphlet No. 123.* Washington, D.C.: U.S. Government Printing Office.

WILLIAMS, H. M. (1961). Education of the severely retarded child: classroom programs. *U.S. Off. Educ. Bull., No. 20.*

5

GIFTED CHILDREN

"Precocity is a morbid condition, and those manifesting it often lack vitality and resisting power." While this statement is typical of popular opinion years ago in regard to the physical characteristics of the gifted child, there were those persons who had early reached entirely different conclusions. In 1875, Francis Galton (1891) had declared:

> There is a prevalent belief that men of genius are unhealthy, puny beings—all brain and no muscle—weak-sighted, and generally of poor constitutions. . . . A collection of living magnates in various branches of intellectual achievement is always a feast to my eyes; being, as they are, such massive, vigorous, capable-looking animals. [P. 331.]

The cartoonist's conception of a mental prodigy as a wizened, bespectacled youngster with hollow chest is extravagantly wrong. Gifted children are usually stronger, larger, and healthier than those of average intellectual abilities. Abundant evidence from research studies indicates clearly that the gifted child compares favorably to his peers in almost all traits and characteristics that may be measured.

IDENTIFICATION

Definition and Classification. About 1920, Terman presented the notion that an extraordinarily high IQ was indicative of genius. In his early search for gifted children, Terman *et al.* (1925) set forth an IQ of 140 on the *Stanford Revision of the Binet Test* as the provisional lower limit for inclusion of children below the eleven-year age group. Some allowance was made for older children, since the brightest children of these groups were found to be graded too low on the Stanford-Binet scale. The standards thus set were as follows:

Below 11 years	I.Q. 140
11 to 11½ years	I.Q. 139
11½ to 12 years	I.Q. 138
12 to 12½ years	I.Q. 137
12½ to 13 years	I.Q. 136
13 to 13½ years	I.Q. 134
13½ to 14 years	I.Q. 132

Giftedness may also be characterized by special abilities of a high order that may not necessarily be associated with high general intellectual ability or an extremely high score on an intelligence test. In this connection, Witty (1940b) suggested that if creative work of a high order, rather than scholastic attainment, was to be the final measure of the gifted, it was questionable whether the intelligence test is a suitable instrument. Thus, creative ability and originality introduce a concept of the gifted that relates more to the dynamics of behavior than to scores obtained from taking an intelligence test. Witty stated:

It is evident, then, that an acceptable criterion for giftedness must be sought primarily outside the provinces covered by the intelligence test. For the content of the intelligence test is patently lacking in situations which disclose originality or creativity. [P. 505.]

Later, Witty (1958) defined giftedness in broad social terms when he stated that a child was gifted whose "performance in a potentially valuable line of human activity is consistently remarkable."

In his recent book, Durr (1964) emphasizes school achievement when he defines giftedness as applying ". . . to those students who have a very high level of academic aptitude, either demonstrated or potential" (p. 16).

The relationship of creative abilities and high intellectual ability has come into question and been studied extensively in recent years. Many of the characteristics that are used to describe the creative child may be found among the characteristics ordinarily listed for gifted children. However, studies of the relationships of creativity,

A favorable school environment fosters the development of creative expression.

high intellect, and achievement have produced some important delineations among these facets of intelligence.

Of creativity, Torrance (1963) has said:

. . . creativity may be defined in many ways. It is usually defined in terms of either a process or a product, but may also be defined in terms of a personality or an environmental condition. . . . [Torrance defines] creativity as the process of sensing problems or gaps in information, forming ideas or hypotheses, testing and modifying these hypotheses, and communicating the results. . . . Creativity is sometimes contrasted to conformity. . . . Such concepts as curiosity, imagination, discovery, innovation, and invention are also prominent in discussions of creativity. [P. 4.]

Finally, Lucito (1963) proposed a further definition of giftedness, based upon Guilford's conception of intellect, that emphasizes what Lucito terms productive-evaluative thinking:

The gifted are those students whose potential intellectual powers are at such a high ideational level in both productive and evaluative thinking that it can be reasonably assumed they could be the future problem solvers, innovators, and evaluators of the culture if adequate educational experiences are provided. [P. 184.]

In Lucito's view, *production* and *evaluation* depend upon *cognition* and *memory;* and he thus focuses attention directly on the potential problem-solvers and innovators. Since any IQ or percentage definition would seem to omit many such children from consideration, Torrance's (1963) suggestion about a minimum level of measured intellect for creativity bears mention. He states:

Recent studies have shown that if we identify as gifted those scoring in the upper 20 percent on an intelligence test, we would eliminate about 70 percent of those who will score in the upper 20 percent on a measure of creativity. . . . Many research workers are convinced that cut-off points at 135 IQ and above, as used in most programs for intellectually gifted children, are too high. Several estimates place the minimal level at 120. [P. 9.]

Discovery by Tests. Following the development of individual intelligence tests, children with an IQ of 130 or higher were classified as gifted. Early studies indicated that these children constituted about 1 per cent of the school population. It has been suggested by some students that the IQ is generally very useful for identifying those children who are high in abstract or verbal intelligence. Bowman (1950) felt that students in the 95th percentile or beyond on the *Primary Mental Abilities Test* and the *Iowa Educational Development Test* should be listed as superior. However, there is evidence that such tests have limited value for evaluating the intellectual abilities of children reared in an impoverished environment. Furthermore, since there is a negligible relationship between intelligence test scores and measures of ability in music, art, and other special areas, such tests alone cannot lead to the identification of children with unusual talent.

When administered by a trained person, individual intelligence tests are certainly more valid for measuring intelligence accurately than are group intelligence tests. Since any single examination will measure only a limited sample of an individual's mental behavior, however, a single test score should not be used as the only basis for determining a child's mental level when an important educational decision is to be made. Furthermore, test scores obtained when children are very young—preschool and primary grade children—are less reliable and valid than those obtained at a later date. In the appraisal of the child's mental ability, it is advisable to supplement test scores with other data on such items as age of talking, size of vocabulary, school marks, educational test scores, subjective ratings, and other pertinent data. In addition, these data must always be interpreted in the light of the child's chronological age and cultural background.

Many procedures have been developed for measuring various creative thinking abilities, but these are often unstandardized and have been used primarily in research rather than for the identification of children who might benefit from special educational procedures. Types of tasks used in the elementary school setting include:

Perceptions of inkblots
Picture construction from dots, circles, squares, parallel lines, incomplete figures, and shapes of colored paper
Verbalizations while painting
Symbolizations of words by lines
Designs for standardized materials
Ideas for product improvement
Consequences problems and asking and guessing
Guessing sounds or constructing images from sounds
[Torrance, 1963]

As Torrance (1963) indicates, "Performances are usually scored for such qualities as fluency, flexibility, originality, and elaboration" (p. 8).

Piers et al. (1960) used some of Guilford's experimental creativity tests with 114 seventh- and eighth-grade students of superior intelligence and achievement in an effort to determine usefulness of these tests with younger children, to determine sex and grade differences, and to determine amount of agreement between measures of creativity and teacher ratings.

The tests were found suitable for subjects of these ages; there were no marked sex differences in test performance; and there was very low correlation of teacher ratings and test scores.

Reports of Teachers and Others. Teachers come into close contact with children in classroom activities, where various kinds of learning take place. Thus, teachers should be in a good position to identify gifted children and those with special abilities. However, if the judgments of teachers were relied upon exclusively, many gifted children would go undetected. In a study by Terman et al. (1925), only 15.7 per cent of the children nominated by teachers, each selected as the most intelligent in his class, were found to be qualified

for inclusion in the gifted group. Additional training in child psychology and methods of evaluating behavior and development should
lead to improved accuracy of teacher judgments.

Reports of parents are of some value in estimating the intelligence
of their children, although the effects of parental bias usually run
very high in such reports. Terman and Oden (1947) found that
early indications of superior intelligence noted by parents were quick
understanding; extensive information; unusual and extensive vocabulary; excessive curiosity; and unusual interest in reading materials,
including atlases and encyclopedias. Among factors that may lead
parents and others astray in their judgments are—in addition to bias
—failure to keep in mind the total picture of the child's behavior and
lack of norms or standards upon which to pass judgment.

More recently, Pegnato and Birch (1959) compared seven methods
of locating gifted children in a metropolitan junior high school of
1,400 students. Of 781 children nominated by all screening methods,
only 94 had Stanford-Binet IQ's above 135. Only about half of the
gifted children appeared among teachers' nominations, and they
thus concluded that little reliance should be placed on teacher nominations in screening for giftedness.

Chambers (1959) conducted two simultaneous studies of four
groups (80 subjects) of upper elementary school children in an attempt to find an effective group method of screening intellectually
gifted children to obviate the need for a full-scale WISC for every
child referred. By using the group *SRA Primary Mental Abilities
Test,* elementary form, with a cutoff score of 117, plus the verbal subtests of the WISC, 60 per cent of the non-superior children could be
eliminated from further consideration.

Age-Grade Status.   In the Terman *et al.* (1925) study, one of the
errors frequently observed in teachers was a failure to take into consideration the chronological age of the child. This failing was allowed
for by Terman and his collaborators in their selection of children for
additional testing. Concerning the value of information on the age-
grade status of a child, Terman and Oden (1947) state: "If you are
allowed only one method of locating the highest IQ in a classroom,
your chance of getting the right child is better if you merely look in
the class register and take the youngest rather than trust the teacher's
judgment" (p. 6). It is unlikely that this method of identifying
gifted children would operate effectively under conditions where
most children are rigidly promoted one grade annually.

CHARACTERISTICS

Learning Characteristics. The learning characteristics of gifted children have frequently been studied and identified through contrast with normal or mentally retarded children. The performance of bright and retarded children varying in chronological age but similar in mental age was studied by Ramaseshan (1950). The bright children excelled in verbal meaning and reasoning, while the retarded subjects performed better on tasks involving space and word fluency.

Greenfield (1955) found significant differences in the problem-solving process of bright and dull eleven-year-old girls. Each group studied was composed of 25 girls, with IQ's ranging from 120 to 150 for the bright group and from 77 to 100 for the dull group. The problem-solving characteristics of the subjects were classified into four major areas for analysis and study:

I. Understanding the requirements of the problem, i.e., comprehension of directions and statement of the problem
II. Understanding the ideas contained in the problem
III. General approach to the solution of the problem
IV. Personal factors in the solution of problems

In the first three areas, the differences between the bright and dull children were found to be statistically significant, with the dull children failing to perform adequately in these respects. The dull children more often introduced personal factors into their problem-solving and were less able to bring relevant knowledge to bear on the problem. The bright children showed less care and system in their problem-solving in that they selected one of the choices and then attempted to justify it. Also, they more frequently changed their solution after a reconsideration of a problem.

A seven-year-old child with an IQ of 145 was observed in learning activities while at play. A great deal of originality was manifested in constructing a play cafeteria, with the trays, food line, and cash register present in an orderly manner. Even a sign—CAFETERIA—was placed nearby to indicate that this was a place for eating. Such mental characteristics as memory, orderly association, advanced school abilities, as shown in activities requiring spelling and arithmetic, as well as good insight into the total pattern situation were revealed. The gifted child fills in the missing parts. He is able to recognize, on the basis of the part-whole relations or a pattern relation, the nature of the completed pattern. This is an important distinction between the learning of gifted and of average children and has been referred to as "insight."

Gifted eleven-year-old children from the Hunter College Elementary School, a laboratory school for gifted children, showed a general superiority in abilities in art judgment, music memory, science, and mathematical abilities when measured by standardized tests (Wilson, 1953). They showed unusual understanding in science and excelled in school performance in general. Their superiority was least marked in musical accomplishment as measured by the Kwalwasser-Ruch Test. The results showed pronounced individual variability among the gifted children in the various abilities and in comparison with each other.

Physical Traits. The "typical" mentally superior child is usually slightly above the average for his age level in height, weight, and other measures of physical development. He is also usually somewhat stronger and healthier than average children. Terman and his colleagues (1925) found that gifted children were, as a group, equal or superior to average boys and girls in health and physical energy to almost the same degree as in other traits.

The chief interest of a study reported by Laycock and Caylor (1964) was to find out if gifted children would be larger in physical measurements than their less-gifted siblings. The sample used for the study consisted of 81 pairs of siblings from the Riverside (California) public schools. The five bodily measurements presented in Table 5–1 were made on each subject. The mean differences, although slightly favorable to the gifted, were not statistically significant. The results of

TABLE 5–1

Mean Differences Between Siblings in Anthropometric Measurements

| | Mean Standard Score [*] | | Mean Difference |
	Average Sibling	Gifted Sibling	Gifted-Average
Weight	47.15	47.88	.73
Height	48.19	48.78	.59
Biacromial	43.85	44.27	.42
Bi-iliac	47.41	48.87	1.46
Leg	47.60	49.33	1.73

[*] These are transformed scores.
SOURCE: Laycock and Caylor (1964).

this study support the viewpoint that the gifted child most likely comes from a privileged home where all children, including non-gifted siblings, grow bigger physically than more typical children.

The findings from the first Science Talent Search (Edgerton *et al.*, 1947) substantiate those of Terman, Hollingworth, and others relative to the superior physical status of gifted individuals. In the first search, 3,175 high school students, out of a total of 14,000 for whom entrance materials were requested, submitted complete entries. The male students among the 300 who were either winners or who received honorable mention were compared with other entrants and with army inductees. Comparisons for height and weight yielded the following results:

	Average Height (Inches)	Average Weight (Pounds)
Highest STS students	70.31	153.05
Other STS students	70.01	153.85
Army inductees	68.14	144.76

The insignificant weight difference in favor of the "other" group of STS students may be accounted for by the fact that they averaged approximately 2.5 months older than the highest STS group. In a three-year follow-up study of the two STS groups, the highest STS group was significantly superior in physical condition, except for the first year, in which this group had a significant excess of defective vision. Comparison of those from the two STS groups reporting no defects with results from the Selective Service inductees indicated that both STS groups were superior with respect to freedom from physical defects.

Concerning the characteristics of the gifted or academically talented, Stalnaker (1961), then President of the National Merit Scholarship Corporation, described them as:

. . . heavier and physically and mentally healthier than those of average intelligence. They have greater interest in people, showing less tendency to withdraw, and show greater confidence. They are less tense, less anxious and less given to depression. [P. 198.]

Reading Ability and Interests. The clearest difference between gifted children and average children is in reading and other scholastic pursuits. A study conducted by Barbe (1952) dealt with the reading interests and habits of 1,030 gifted high school students. Each of his subjects had obtained an IQ of 130 or higher on either the

Henmon-Nelson Tests of Mental Ability or the *California Tests of Mental Maturity.*

A study of the early reading of these students revealed that 47 per cent of the girls and 33 per cent of the boys had learned to read before entering school. This finding is in harmony with the Terman and Oden (1940) study in which almost half of the gifted children had learned to read before entering school. The majority of the 1,030 gifted students studied by Barbe were taught to read by their first-grade teacher. The mother was listed as having taught 18 per cent of the students to read, and the father 5 per cent. Three per cent said that they taught themselves to read. One boy reported that he learned to read sign posts and road maps for diversion while traveling by car. The group average for amount of time spent weekly in reading was six hours, with the boys averaging five hours and the girls averaging seven. However, 75 per cent did very little reading during the week, which should be a matter of concern when it is realized that these are the intellectually gifted among the high school population. Over 80 per cent of the students stated that they enjoy reading. The wide range of choices of reading interests is shown in Table 5-2. Mystery and biography were listed among the top three choices by both boys and girls. Seven of the highest interests listed by the two groups appeared in both lists. Animal stories, teen-age books, and stories dealing with social problems were in the girls' list but not in the boys'. Western stories and comics were in the boys' list but not in the girls'.

Ten per cent of the boys and 14 per cent of the girls in Barbe's study reported that they never used the school library. Only 17 per cent of the students said that they used it once a week or more. Thirty-eight per cent of the boys and 12 per cent of the girls reported that they never used the public library, and only 13 per cent of the students said that they used it at least once a week.

School Achievement. One cannot accurately predict achievement from a study of aptitude or intelligence. One of the most interesting of the early studies bearing on this is reported by Pyle and Snadden (1929). It indicated the overlap found between the brightest and dullest students in a Detroit senior high school on three of a series of nine ideational tests. Overlapping was also indicated by the graphs of the results of three or four motor-learning tests. These experiments used only 31 bright students and 12 dull ones, but similar results have been found more recently by investigators performing comparable experiments with larger groups of children.

TABLE 5–2

Reading of Gifted Children

Boys	Girls
Type of Reading Most Enjoyed	
Mystery	Historical fiction
Biography	Modern novels
History	Biography
Historical fiction	Mystery
Comics	Teen-age books
Science	Sports
Modern novels	Animals
Sports	Science
Humor	History
Western	Social problems
Magazines Read	
Life	Life
Saturday Evening Post	Seventeen
Reader's Digest	Saturday Evening Post
Time	Reader's Digest
Collier's	Ladies' Home Journal
Look	Time
Coronet	Senior Prom
Newsweek	Collier's
Holiday	Cosmopolitan
Quick	Newsweek

SOURCE: After Barbe (1952).

A study of the records of a group of gifted children was reported by Lamson (1935). Their early school records were analyzed in relation to their final high school achievements. The gifted children were approximately two years younger than a control group of children, both upon entering high school and upon graduating. In both the State Regents' examination and the school record, the gifted children were significantly superior. An extensive follow-up study of a large group of gifted children was conducted under the direction of Terman and is reported in the third volume of his *Genetic Studies of Genius*. Seven years after the original study of 1,000 children, data were gathered on 587 of them.

At the time of the follow-up study, 74 per cent of the boys and 84 per cent of the girls were accelerated in school. Of the 352 subjects who were then attending high school, failures in schoolwork were negligible in number, and almost one-half the marks earned were "A." On the *Iowa High School Content Examination,* only 10 per cent of the unselected high school seniors rated as high as the *average* senior of the gifted group. Practically all the gifted children graduated from high school, and from 80 to 90 per cent of those graduating entered or planned to enter college. In college, members of the gifted group earned considerably more than their proportionate share of scholarships, fellowships, and other honors.

Leta Hollingworth's follow-up studies of children with extremely high IQ's lead to some interesting and worthwhile conclusions relative to what may be expected from those with various degrees of high intelligence (1942). She noted that those who test around 140 IQ (Stanford-Binet) in childhood are likely to be around the 75th percentile of college graduates; while those who test around 160 IQ may be expected to show some noteworthy accomplishments, such as winning honors in a first-class college. In the case of her investigations of children with IQ's of 180 or higher, she notes:

This is perhaps the most significant fact to be derived from data: that the children who test at and above 180 IQ constitute the "top" among college graduates. They are the students of whom one may confidently predict that they will win honors and prizes for intellectual work. [P. 249.]

Personality Traits. In the work of Terman and his collaborators (1925), sufficient experimental evidence was presented to indicate that intellectual precocity is not in any manner an indication by itself of an antisocial or negative or undesirable personality. While all the data were not wholly objective—a fact that was recognized by Terman and his co-workers—they were quite significant. Historically, there has been a rather common notion that most geniuses are "freaks" or are unstable in nature. These opinions have been arrived at inductively from a few observations of either one or several particular geniuses who were more or less atypical, and thus all people of genius are judged to be similar. The studies mentioned show very clearly that if one attempts to make even a careful subjective analysis or evaluation of the personality traits of gifted children, these children will usually obtain personality ratings above the average for other children of the same age.

A comparative study of the characteristics of bright and dull pupils was conducted by Lightfoot (1951). The bright group consisted of 48 pupils with IQ's from 120 to 200, with a median of 147; and the dull group consisted of 56 children with IQ's ranging from 68 to 104, with a median of 88. The groups were carefully rated on 40 personality characteristics. The mean ratings of the two groups on certain characteristics in which they were markedly different are presented in Fig. 5-1. The means were found to be farthest apart on

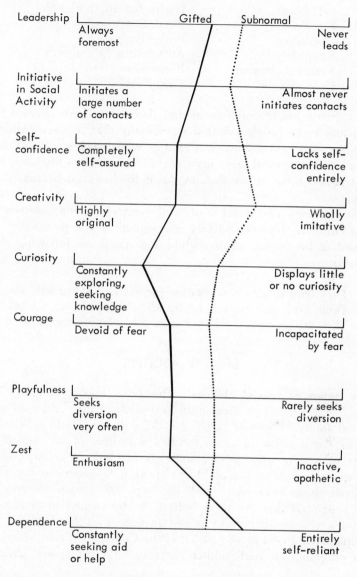

Fig. 5–1. Mean or median ratings assigned mentally gifted and mentally subnormal groups on personality ratings. (Lightfoot, 1951.)

creativity, self-confidence, and curiosity. The attributes for which the differences between the means were not statistically different were:

Selfishness	Desire for appropriation
Emotionality	Physical aggression
Obedience	Protectiveness
Kindliness	Antagonism to authority
Verbal aggression	Reticence
Defensiveness	Exclusiveness

As a group, bright children are less inclined to have nervous disorders and to be poorly adjusted emotionally than average children. When excessive nervousness does exist or when some emotional characteristics are observed, the causes should be sought in the home and school environment rather than in the individual's intellectual superiority.

In a summary of several studies of creativity among elementary school children, Torrance (1959) commented on the personality adjustment of the highly creative child and noted the following characteristics:

1. They tend to have a reputation for having wild or silly ideas.
2. Their work is characterized by ideas "off the beaten track."
3. They are characterized by humor and playfulness.

SPECIAL ABILITIES

The Nature of Special Abilities. The terms "special abilities," "aptitude," and "talent" are often used in describing the child with some unusual ability. Freeman (1955) has defined an aptitude as "a condition or combination of characteristics indicative of an individual's ability to acquire with training some specific knowledge, skill, or set of responses, such as the ability to speak a language, to become a musician, to do mechanical work, etc." (p. 306). Some investigators have suggested that the term "gifted" be broadened to include individuals with unusual ability in certain areas (Pritchard, 1952). For example, Havighurst et al. (1955), in the Community Youth Development program, screened children with the following special abilities:

1. High intelligence
2. Creative abilities in art, music, literature, writing, etc.
3. Special abilities in a socially useful area, such as mechanics, science, athletics, human relations, and civic and social organizations
4. Creative talent, or the ability to apply new and novel methods to the solution of problems

A portion of the resources present in the newborn child are selected by environmental conditions and favored in a progressive determination of the growing individual. There exists in every normal child a number of lines of specialization or patterns of abilities that may be selected for development, while other elements are sacrificed since they are not selected. But when early talent reveals itself, there is a strong likelihood that this will be reinforced by favorable recognition and opportunities for exercise if the environment is favorable. The absence of achievement in some area of life is not necessarily indicative of lack of talent in that area. Seashore (1942) said of this:

It has been shown that, by well-directed experiment, we can often discover and certify the presence of a high order of talent in individuals who are not themselves aware of its existence and whose associates have observed no evidence of it. [P. 170.]

Unevenness of Abilities. Ability in music, mechanics, drawing, arithmetic computation, and rote memory is not perfectly correlated with general intelligence. In the case of each of these abilities, it is possible to find subjects of inferior general intelligence who can perform better than the average person. However, when children are classified according to general intelligence, there is revealed positive correlation among their capacities. Thus, if a child is above average in one performance, he will probably fall on the high side of average in other performances undertaken; but, as Terman has shown, the correlation is by no means perfect. So a gifted child may be found who is especially efficient in some capacities, but he may fall below the average in certain other capacities.

It is known that superior and creative talent in music and representational drawings are related to intellectuality. Terman claims that the great musical composers and the great artists have been gifted in intellect and imagination. All the young musicians and artists of genuine accomplishment whom he studied have had, without exception, high intelligence quotients. There are, however, considerable variations in abilities within a single individual.

A study of psychological profiles indicates that one cannot predict with any great degree of accuracy the extent of one ability from the presence of another. These profiles show individual patterns of all types. Two individuals with the same total score on an intelligence test may differ considerably from each other in the composition of intelligence. One may have a high score on items of a verbal nature and a low score on the numerical and space items. *The California Tests of Mental Maturity* provides for a total numerical score and a total verbal score. Thus, such a test provides, in part, for the measurement of special abilities and becomes diagnostic in nature.

The task of identifying the talented child may be a very difficult one. The child with a strong interest in art, poetry, or science, but lacking in ability and interest in reading, spelling, and arithmetic, may be mistakenly identified by the teacher and others as retarded. The story of Thomas Edison's early school experiences is still pertinent today. After his first two months in school, Edison's mother was advised that he could not learn. She then took him from school and allowed him to learn for himself under her general direction and encouragement.

Art Ability and Intelligence. Symbolic and analytical drawings and caricatures require a high degree of skill as well as superior intelligence. Many children with high intelligence lack these special skills. There are, however, certain elementary skills of a sensory or motor nature related to drawing that do not require a high level of intelligence. Tiebout and Meier (1936) conducted a study in order to determine the relationship of intelligence to artistic ability, both in the degree to which it is present in the child population and as it was manifested in superior performance at the high school level and in actual achievement of artists. For the first phase of the study, 100 children from each of the first seven grades were used as subjects. For the second phase, two selected groups were used. The first of these consisted of 72 junior and senior high school students who had been rated as artistically superior. The second group was composed of 51 artists of recognized achievement. The study with the grade school children yielded the conclusion: "Artistic ability is a special ability in the sense of being only somewhat related to general intelligence, as measured by established tests" (p. 123). In the study of the individuals who were artistically superior, it was found that both the recognized artists and the high school group had superior intelligence, as indicated by their average IQ's. "It appears that the use of artistic potentialities in the achievement of marked success in art is *dependent to a certain extent on intellectual capacity*" (p. 123).

This relationship has been shown in connection with the development, analysis, and interpretation of intelligence tests. There are some phases of art ability that are dependent upon a clustering of certain specific abilities; however, the dependence of art ability on insight, creative thinking, and associational thought—all of which are closely identified with intelligence—has been demonstrated in a number of studies.

A study by Bottorf (1946) revealed that good general intelligence is important in attaining success in art and that those with the lowest IQ's have little chance of attaining much success but are not precluded from moderate success. Among college students, a positive relationship was obtained between art test scores and grades in other subjects. However, there was considerable inconsistency in their grades in other subjects. Bottorf (1946) concluded: "Those receiving the highest art scores as a group appeared to excel in a few subjects, be lower in a few, and vary in attainment in the others" (p. 423).

Aptitude in Creative Writing. It was suggested earlier that a close relationship exists between results on group intelligence tests and verbal ability tests. However, Thurstone and other students, through the factor-analysis technique, showed that verbal ability exists as a special trait or ability. From biographical data, there is evidence that unusual language abilities may appear at a relatively early age. The phenomenon is illustrated in the case of Minou Drouet, a poetic genius. Minou became a subject of much controversy when she was eight years of age. She lived in Brittany with her foster mother and wrote many poems prior to her eighth birthday. When a volume of these was published, many critics claimed that an eight-year-old child could not write such poems and accused her foster mother of writing them. How, they asked, could an eight-year-old write such a poem as:

> I love the water, which doesn't endure
> which never finishes a sentence
> which never has the same stomach
> the same voice.
>
> MINOU DROUET

As a test of her ability, Minou agreed to take a special test for membership in the Society of Authors, Composers, and Music Publishers. She was then placed in a room and given a topic on which to write. In 25 minutes she wrote a poem, "Paris Sky," which consists of 36 lines (*Life*, 1956). On the basis of this poem, she was awarded membership in the society.

Special Abilities As Drives. Special ability can supply the motive for a child's self-improvement in both personality growth and school adjustment. The teacher may show the pupil how a career he has chosen requires the development of certain qualities and abilities and how the work of the school day is linked to these traits. He may cite the achievements of those who have succeeded in the child's field of interest as indicative of their ability in certain subjects. The child who is interested in singing as a career can be shown the practical value of studying modern foreign languages, and the child who wants to draw can be shown the value of spelling. Once the pupil begins to see some value in schoolwork he becomes interested in other activities of the school day. Minor personality changes can be encouraged if the youngster is convinced that such changes may make success in the desired field a little easier.

The bright child is likely to lose interest in his schoolwork if some outlet is not provided for his extra ability. When a special talent is present, his aptitude may well be utilized for providing such an outlet. The development of aptitudes then becomes an important and potent drive in the development of a well-organized and more forceful personality.

ADJUSTMENT PROBLEMS

Many of the more recent generalizations about the adjustments of gifted children and adolescents were developed from the research with 1,000 gifted children by Burks et al. (1930). They recognized that mentally superior children were often faced with difficult problems of social adjustments. They stated:

It is in the case of the child with extraordinarily high IQ that the social problem is most acute. If the IQ is 180, the intellectual level at six is almost on a par with that of the average eleven-year-old, and at ten or eleven is not far from that of the average high school graduate. Physical development, on the other hand, is not likely to be accelerated more than 10 per cent, and social development probably not more than 20 or 30 per cent. The inevitable result is that the child of 180 IQ has one of the most difficult jobs of social adjustment that any human being is ever called upon to meet. [Pp. 264–65.]

Getzels and Jackson's (1958) studies have shown significant differences between adolescents exceptionally high in intelligence but not equally high in creativity and those exceptionally high in creativity but not equally high in intelligence. Their results show that teachers prefer those high in intelligence but not equally high in creativity. Significant differences also appear in the fantasy production of the two groups—the highly creative adolescents expressing more imaginative, humorous, and original ideas in their themes. High creative adolescents, as compared with high IQ adolescents, are more rebellious and less given to conformity. This leads to more conflicts with teachers at school.

It has been claimed that the pupil younger than his classmates is quite likely to suffer in social development, especially during the adolescent period when an age difference of even one year is very significant. This will vary considerably, however, according to the physical, mental, and general social qualities of the child. It is very difficult to set forth a formula for the treatment and promotion of the mentally alert child. Eurich (1939) has shown that the youngest student is not handicapped scholastically, even as he progresses into college. On the contrary, he continues to do superior academic work. The danger of lack of social development that may result from too rapid promotion has been suggested by some students of child development. However, where provisions are not made in the school curriculum for the care of such pupils through sectioning or a more enriched curriculum, there are real dangers in holding the child back. Such bad habits as indifference, laziness, or acts of mischief may develop.

One situation that is likely to impose social and emotional strain upon the intellectually superior child is his acceleration in school, which almost always breaks up his normal social relations with other children of his own age and inevitably puts him into a group of children too big to play with him and too mature in their interests for him to fit into their social grouping. It is only when a brilliant child is actually large and mature for his age that he may be accelerated at all without this liability. The degree to which extra promotions are desirable depends in part upon non-intellectual characteristics of each individual brilliant child.

The gifted child who is less mature in his interests than others of the group often develops an attitude of indifference toward the activities of the group as a whole, but he may be able to find comfort and needed friendship in activities with others of the group who likewise reveal a less-mature interest. In the latter instance, such children will not be seriously affected by the time lag in their maturity. Such friendships should be encouraged at this stage.

Inner World of the Gifted Adolescent. Various techniques have been used for studying the problems and inner feelings of gifted adolescents. Anecdotal records obtained from observations of the behavior and comments of adolescents in the classroom, on the playground, or at home furnish information about their inner feelings; and interviews conducted by trained counselors may furnish valuable information about their problems. Perhaps the projective technique in the hands of an individual trained in its use will give us the greatest insight into their inner world.

Compositions were used by Strang (1950) to explore the inner world of 300 high school pupils with IQ's over 120. Many problems related to growing up were described in these compositions. The four types of problems most frequently mentioned were: feelings of inferiority and inadequacy; unsatisfactory human relations; failure to realize intellectual potentialities; and difficulty in choosing, preparing for, and entering a vocation.

Feelings of Inferiority and Inadequacy. It seems strange that gifted children might suffer from feelings of inferiority. However, they sometimes feel inferior or inadequate in certain activities. The most frequent source of their feeling of inadequacy, especially among boys, stems from relative slowness in achieving success in physical skills, including sports. Although the gifted are not handicapped in acquiring physical skills, they do not experience the advantage in learning these skills that they experience in activities involving reasoning, abstract thinking, and verbal skills.

A common source of inferiority feeling is the anxiety of parents. Parental pressure is placed upon gifted children to make good grades at school, to win special honors, and otherwise do meritorious work. This composition of a fourteen-year-old girl, describing her feelings in response to parental pressures, illustrates the operation of such pressures in producing problems:

I am afraid that I will be afraid to face my mother when I come home this afternoon. For within the next hour I will hear from our school's Guidance Counselor whether I passed the test to my preferred high school.

I am afraid because my mother has taken the attitude that this test means life or death to my career. She will promptly inform my father at the dinner table whether I failed or passed.

And if I failed—what then? I had better keep silent for my father and mother would argue about dad not teaching me this; and mother not being more strict.

For the next few days I would have to keep silent, minding my own business while mother and father bicker all night long. It may sound funny to an outsider, but unfortunately it is the truth. If I speak out and defend myself, such defense would be useless, for fresh arguments and attacks would be pointed against me. [Strang, 1950, p. 99.]

Development of Interests. Outstanding characteristics of the interests of the mentally gifted are their wide range and their transitory

Creative expression may be observed at different age levels and through varied media. It is encouraged in an atmosphere that provides guidance without inhibiting self-expression.

Metairie Park County Day School

nature. According to genetic case studies of interests from childhood through adolescence, early fixation and permanence were more common among those of less intelligence. The interests of the mentally gifted boys and girls were more unstable. Witty (1940a) conducted a follow-up study of a group of 50 children with a median IQ of 153. He found a continued superiority of the group in their home and school adjustments, and a wide range of interests as well as strong interests in relation to their general life activities.

As mentally gifted children progress through the elementary school into the junior high school, there is an increasing tendency for them to prefer academic subjects. This choice may be accounted for by their continued greater success in studies that require abstract thinking, the use of symbols, and the use of ideas based upon symbols. There is the ever-present danger of the mentally gifted narrowing their interests too greatly if they are not encouraged to enter into pursuits other than those of the academic curriculum. Today, high schools are tending to develop a wider range of wholesome and useful interests among the mentally gifted since the staff is constantly relating the program to activities of the community and are training boys and girls for life through guidance in living.

SUMMARY

The problem of definition and terminology appears in any study of the gifted child. Terman and others used intelligence tests to identify gifted children. Studies show that persons selected by tests as gifted at a relatively early age tend to maintain their superiority when older. Children talented in the arts, mechanics, and motor skills, or who display unusual creative abilities, are now being studied but are often neglected in our educational programs. Favorable home conditions, good educational opportunities, good health, and a stimulating environment are factors that favor the development of a child's full potentialities.

Mentally superior children are above the average for their age level in various measures of physical development. They are also above average for their age level in such character and personality qualities as self-confidence, will and perseverance, desire to excel, conscientiousness, truthfulness, originality, desire to know, generosity and unselfishness, cheerfulness and optimism, and leadership.

In school tasks and school-related tasks, gifted children show their greatest superiority. A large percentage of gifted children learn to read before entering school, often with a minimum of guidance. The scholastic achievement of gifted children is significantly above that of average children of the same age level. Growth curves show this to be true at all grade levels. These students go on to win scholastic honors far out of proportion to what would be expected of them on the basis of their comparative numbers.

The testing movement, aided by developments of statistical techniques for studying test data, has revealed the presence of a number of special abilities not too closely related to intelligence and largely unrelated to each other. By means of tests designed to measure various aptitudes, individual profiles may be secured. The unevenness of abilities is observable from a study of a number of individual aptitude profiles. Considerable research has been conducted in recent years in attempts to ascertain the aptitudes needed for the performance of certain tasks or for attaining success in specific pursuits. The results of such studies are very important in educational and vocational guidance and are being used in connection with many selection programs.

As a group, gifted children are less inclined to have nervous disorders and to be poorly adjusted emotionally than are average children. They display a keen interest in play and engage in a wider range of play and creative activities than average children do. In the realm of social adjustments, the gifted child's problems may become most acute.

CHAPTER REFERENCES

BARBE, W. (1952). A study of the reading of gifted high-school students. *Educ. Administr. Supervis.*, 38:148–54.

BOTTORF, EDNA (1946). Study comparing art abilities and general intelligence of college students. *J. educ. Psychol.*, 37:398–426.

BOWMAN, LILLIE (1950). A program of self-evaluation at the tenth grade level. *Calif. J. educ. Res.*, 1:1–7.

BURKS, BARBARA S., JENSEN, DOROTHEA W., and TERMAN, L. M. (1930). *The promise of youth.* Vol. 3. *Genetic studies of genius.* Stanford, Calif.: Stanford Univer. Press.

CHAMBERS, J. A. (1959). Preliminary screening methods in the identification of intellectually superior children. *Except. Child.*, 26:145–50.

DROUET, MINOU (no date). *Arbre, mon ami.* Paris: René Julliard.

DURR, W. K. (1964). *The gifted student.* New York: Oxford Univer. Press.

EDGERTON, H. A, BRITT, S. H., and NORMAN, R. D. (1947). Physical differences between ranking and non-ranking contestants in the first annual Science Talent Search. *Amer. J. Anthrop.*, 5:435–52.

EURICH, A. C. (1939). Youth in the colleges. *Thirty-eighth yearbook of the National Society for the Study of Education,* Part II. Chicago: Univer. of Chicago Press. Pp. 73–86.

FREEMAN, F. S. (1955). *Theory and practice of psychological testing.* New York: Holt, Rinehart & Winston.

GALTON, F. (1891). *Hereditary genius.* (Rev. ed.) New York: Appleton-Century-Crofts.

GETZELS, J. W., and JACKSON, P. W. (1958). The highly creative and highly intelligent adolescent: an attempt at differentiation. Paper read at APA Convention, Washington, D.C., September, 1958.

GREENFIELD, LOIS B. (1955). Problem-solving processes of bright and dull eleven-year-old girls. Unpublished doctor's dissertation, Univer. of California.

HAVIGHURST, R. J., STIVERS, E., and DEHAAN, R. F. (1955). *A survey of the education of gifted children.* Supplementary Educational Monographs, No. 83. Chicago: Univer. of Chicago Press.

HOLLINGWORTH, LETA S. (1942). *Children above 180 IQ.* Yonkers, N.Y.: World Book Co.

LAMSON, E. E. (1935). High school achievement of fifty-six gifted children. *J. genet. Psychol.,* 47:233–38.

LAYCOCK, F., and CAYLOR, J. S. (1964). Physiques of gifted children and their less gifted siblings. *Child Developm.,* 35:63–74.

LIGHTFOOT, G. F. (1951). Personality characteristics of bright and dull children. *Contributions to education, No. 969.* New York: Teachers Coll., Columbia Univer., Bureau of Publications.

LUCITO, L. J. (1963). Gifted children. In L. DUNN (ed.), *Exceptional children in the schools.* New York: Holt, Rinehart & Winston.

PEGNATO, C. V., and BIRCH, J. W. (1959). Locating gifted children in junior high school. *Except. Child.,* 25:300–304.

PIERS, ELLEN, DANIELS, JACQUELINE M., and QUACKENBUSH, J. F. (1960). The identification of creativity in adolescents. *J. educ. Psychol.,* 51:346–51.

PRITCHARD, MIRIAM C. (1952). Total school planning for the gifted child. *Except. Child.,* 18:107–10, 128.

Proof of a prodigy. *Life,* Feb. 13, 1956, p. 53.

RAMASESHAN, R. S. (1950). A note on the validity of the mental age concept. *J. educ. Psychol.,* 41:56–58.

SEASHORE, C. E. (1942). Talent. *Sch. & Soc.,* 55:169–73.

STALNAKER, J. M. (1961). Ability more than IQ. *Sci. Newsltr,* 79:198.

STRANG, RUTH (1950). Inner world of gifted adolescents. *Except. Child.,* 16:97–101, 125.

TERMAN, L. M., and ODEN, MELITA H. (1940). Status of the California gifted group at the end of sixteen years. *Thirty-ninth yearbook of the National Society for the Study of Education,* Part I. Chicago: Univer. of Chicago Press. Pp. 67–89.

TERMAN, L. M., and ODEN, MELITA H. (1947). *The gifted child grows up.* Vol. 4. *Genetic studies of genius.* Stanford, Calif.: Stanford Univer. Press.

TERMAN, L. M. et al. (1925). *Mental and physical traits of a thousand gifted children.* Vol. 1. *Genetic studies of genius.* Stanford, Calif.: Stanford Univer. Press.

TIEBOUT, CAROLYN, and MEIER, N. C. (1936). Artistic ability and general intelligence. *Psychol. Monogr.,* 48:95–125.

TORRANCE, E. P. (1959). Current research on the nature of creative talent. *J. counsel. Psychol.,* 6:309–16.

TORRANCE, E. P. (1963). *Creativity.* Washington, D.C.: National Education Association.

WILSON, F. T. (1953). Some special ability test scores of gifted children. *J. genet. Psychol.,* 82:59–68.

WITTY, P. (1940a). A genetic study of fifty gifted children. *Intelligence: its nature and nurture. Thirty-ninth yearbook of the National Society for the Study of Education*, Part II. Chicago: Univer. of Chicago Press.

WITTY, P. (1940b). Contributions to the I.Q. controversy from the study of superior deviates. *Sch. & Soc.*, 51:503–8.

WITTY, P. (1958). Who are the gifted? *Education for the gifted. Fifty-seventh yearbook of the National Society for the Study of Education*, Part II. Chicago: Univer. of Chicago Press.

SELECTED READINGS

See Selected Readings for Chapter 6, pages 178-179.

6

EDUCATIONAL PROVISIONS AND GUIDANCE FOR THE GIFTED

In the previous chapter, the gifted child was described as one with superior ability in scholastic endeavors, with superior insight into complex problems, and with superior powers of concentration and sustained attention. He is likely to be more original in his approach to various problems and, if given a challenging situation, to show more initiative and intellectual curiosity. He tends to be self-critical and may need help in achieving self-understanding. His superior potentialities cannot develop in a vacuum, and neither can it be assured that he will develop in optimum fashion without special consideration and guidance. Gifted boys and girls need careful instruction and attention as superior individuals. If they are to have opportunities to develop in accordance with their potentialities, they must be identified early and given continuous stimulation and suitable educational experiences.

Wrenn (1949), through the National Manpower Commission studies, pointed out that relatively few gifted and capable young people from the lower socioeconomic groups had adequate educational opportunities. Particularly disturbing is the finding that a large percentage of these young people never finish high school. A follow-up investigation of the top 16 per cent of Minnesota high school graduates revealed that nine years after graduation only 45 per cent had received the bachelor's degree, and only 8 per cent had earned an advanced degree. This finding was in harmony with results obtained earlier from a follow-up study of the more select Stanford group of gifted children. Although the Stanford children tended to maintain their superior mental status and showed performance of high rank in adulthood, 10 per cent of them never entered college and only 60 per cent actually graduated. Several "flunked out" of college only to return later or to enter some educational pursuit in line with their interests, in which they then made good records.

Teachers have often been satisfied with a pupil's accomplishments as long as he is doing work that meets or excels some minimum standard. Thus, Jane is allowed to run errands for the teacher or to spend time loitering in the classroom or library. Lorge (1954) has suggested that the special education of the superior child should begin as soon as he is identified. He states: "It is a hope that the intellectual élite will be identified somewhere between his sixth and ninth birthday. For all those identified, a special curriculum, under the guidance of specially trained and intellectually superior teachers, is a requisite" (p. 6). Perhaps the greatest value of early identification is an awareness among teachers and parents of superior potentialities in certain pupils. Consciousness among teachers of such existing potentialities may lead them to a positive consideration of the needs of such pupils. With a minimum of guidance by trained and understanding teachers, many of these pupils can develop their potential abilities to a much greater degree. This is illustrated in Fig. 6–1, which shows that the amount of time spent in teacher-directed study is inversely related to the level of the IQ.

SPECIAL EDUCATIONAL PROVISIONS FOR THE GIFTED

Because of the wider range of subject offerings in high school compared with that in the elementary school, one might expect the high school to make better provisions for the gifted. It has been observed that the superior students usually pursue an academic curriculum consisting of a modern language, algebra, geometry, and other subjects largely designed to prepare them for college. However, special educational provisions need to be offered gifted children in the elementary school years. Various administrative methods that may be used in schools are: (1) acceleration, (2) grouping, (3) enrichment in the regular class, and (4) elective courses.

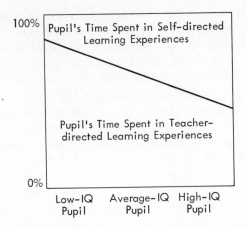

Fig. 6–1. Relationship between mental ability of students and need for teacher-directed learning experiences.

Acceleration. Historically, the first special educational provision for the mentally superior child was to permit him to skip one or more grades after he had mastered the work at one level. This procedure was designed (1) to save the child from possible frustration as a result of remaining with slower-learning pupils, (2) to save the teacher the task of making special provisions for his instruction, and (3) to perhaps save money for the school district. A major criticism of this procedure was early voiced by Leta Hollingworth (1931):

> If the child be accelerated in the regular class to the point where he can function with real interest intellectually, he will be out of harmony with the classroom situation in other important respects. A child of eight years graded with twelve-year-olds is out of his depth socially and physically, though able to do intellectual work as well as they can. [P. 443.]

Considerable controversy has arisen around the practice of acceleration. However, research bearing on such practice seems to point to the soundness of the conclusions stated by Terman and Oden (1947):

> No universal law can be laid down governing the amount of acceleration desirable. Some gifted children are less injured by accelerations of three or four years than others by one or two years. . . . It is our opinion that children of a 135 IQ or higher should be promoted sufficiently to permit college entrance by the age of seventeen at the latest, and that a majority in a group would be better off to enter college at sixteen. [Pp. 279–80.]

In a more recent report, Trusler (1949) recommended a moderate degree of acceleration. Strang (1955) has stated, "A certain amount of acceleration, individually determined, enables gifted children to contribute to society for a longer period of years" (p. 515).

Jack Birch (1954) presented data on 43 mentally advanced children who were accelerated one full year in school-age grade placement by being admitted to school from 1 to 105 days earlier than the general admission age of five years, seven months. The development of these children was studied by follow-up statements from their principals and teachers. The responses were then evaluated as positive, positive-questionable, negative-questionable, and negative. A tabulation of the evaluations revealed that the preponderance of ratings were on the combined positive and positive-questionable side for all children, and no child had a majority of ratings on the negative and negative-questionable side. A further study of the evaluation showed that where some negative and negative-questionable responses or ratings were made, these judgments tended to be given during the first year of school and that later evaluations of the same child swung toward the positive side. This study furnishes further support for the viewpoints of Witty, Pressey, Terman, Strang, and others who have stated that where careful consideration on an individual basis is made, acceleration may be useful as early as the first year in school.

Another form of acceleration is that of advanced or early entrance into college. The Ford Foundation has sponsored scholarships for gifted youth who have finished two years of the four-year high school program. Follow-up studies of these youth in college show that they succeed academically without any apparent injury to their personal and social adjustments. In 1932, the University of Buffalo originated an experiment designed to develop a program of acceleration for those students of superior ability who found college orientation courses repetitious after superior scholastic attainments in high school (Barbour, 1954). Certain departments constructed examinations, in many cases similar to those given at the end of a particular course, for evaluating the educational achievement of those superior students. As of February, 1954, nearly 2,000 entrants had taken one or more of these examinations. Under grants from the Carnegie Foundation and the Ford Foundation, the results of this program have been carefully evaluated. Ninety per cent of those who took three or more such examinations felt they had benefited and would repeat the performance or try out for more advanced credits if they were doing it again. A follow-up study of the graduates indicated that those who took these examinations tended to pursue postgraduate or professional studies.

The Jones-Ortner study (1954) indicated that age alone, as an index of general maturity, is not an adequate gauge of intellectual accomplishment, or of readiness for college. It seems likely that in the better high schools, special sections in English, history, or mathematics may be set up for superior students. In such instances, superior students could avoid the boredom often associated with these courses the first year at college and at the same time pursue courses that offered them a greater challenge.

Morgan (1959) conducted a study to determine predictors for successful acceleration. Subjects were 23 gifted children, mean Stanford-Binet IQ of 149, between six and thirteen years in Grades 2 through 8, of whom 12 were accelerated over a three-year period and 11 were not. Two years later, three predictors (academic achievement, physical development, and attitude of parents) were considered through a detailed questionnaire given to the parents. The accelerates equaled the non-accelerates in school achievement, surpassed them in academic distinction and social leadership, and tended to have better emotional adjustment. Morgan concluded that these three criteria were useful predictors of successful acceleration in the elementary school.

McCandless (1957) cites Hobson's study of 550 underaged admittees who were compared with 3,891 other children who graduated from the Brookline (Massachusetts) public schools between 1946 and 1955. The chief conclusion was that moderately early admission to school for bright children is advantageous.

In summarizing the research on early admission to school for mentally advanced children, Reynolds, Birch, and Tuseth (1962) conclude:

. . . that early admission to school of mentally advanced children who are within a year of the ordinary school-entrance age and who are generally mature is to their advantage. Although there are needs for further research, there are few issues in education on which the research evidence now available is so clear and so universally favorable to a particular solution. [P. 17.]

In an article in the *NEA Journal* (1960), the advantages and disadvantages that Passow stresses include the following:

ADVANTAGES

1. Acceleration provides the gifted with opportunities commensurate with their ability to progress and places them in the grade corresponding to level of maturity rather than to chronological age.
2. Students should be allowed to acquire educational attainments in the shortest time needed. Since research shows little correlation between achievement in a given area and the time devoted to its study, gifted children should be encouraged to proceed at their own rate.
3. Indications are that a person's outstanding creative accomplishments are products of an early adult life. This peak of creativity is used to great-

est advantage when students are enabled to complete their educational preparation and to enter productive careers earlier than would be possible in a rigid system of grade progress.

4. Emotional maladjustments may result from keeping children in classes which do not challenge them. Achieving below potential ability is probably more harmful than the temporary difficulties attendant upon being placed with somewhat older students.

5. Acceleration is a form of enrichment; the time saved in mastering fundamental learnings makes possible more work in a given field, or additional work in other areas of interest.

6. The saving of a year or more enables a student to complete advanced or graduate work without having to delay marriage and independent living.

7. If able students are allowed to save a year or more in their public schooling, the consequent lowering in school years and school costs, and increased man-years of productivity will result in lower costs and significant savings for students, parents, schools, and communities. [Pp. 22–23.]

DISADVANTAGES

1. Rich learning experiences do not necessarily come from a fixed pattern of subject matter. Although the time spent on particular activities can be decreased, studies in depth and breadth also contribute an essential ingredient to the learning process.

2. There are better ways of eliminating the boredom resulting from lack of challenge than reducing time spent in class.

3. Intellectual maturity may not go hand in hand with social and emotional maturity when younger students are placed with older ones. This may result in a denial of leadership opportunities to those whose physical or social maturity is less than that of older students.

4. Acceleration may deny bright students the time and opportunity to think, reflect, explore, and appreciate. The pressures for rapid progress may result in a curtailment of creativity.

5. Students with like mental age but different chronological age may perform qualitatively quite differently; the more difficult work provided for the gifted child through acceleration may not necessarily yield more appropriate experiences.

6. Equal acceleration in all areas does not take into account differences in rates of maturation. A student ready for rapid progress in one area may not be ready for it in another area.

7. Acceleration tends to separate the gifted from his age peers and to emphasize differences in ability. This separation may lead to undesirable social and behavior patterns.

8. Pure skipping may leave serious gaps in the student's learnings, which, in turn, may affect his later educational attainments. [P. 23.]

Homogeneous Grouping. Many psychologists have proposed, for schools large enough to organize them, the special class for gifted children or a form of homogeneous grouping in which the students are sectioned in accordance with their ability. In support for such a procedure, it is pointed out that greater opportunity for earned group leadership is available, that the materials and methods can be better adapted to the abilities of the pupils, and that increased psychological benefits can be derived from cooperating and competing with peers of more nearly equal ability.

The New York City high schools have experimented with three grouping devices for educating gifted children. These are: (1) the Honor Classes, (2) the Honor School, and (3) the Specialized School. Youngert (1938) suggested three problems or questions to be considered in the organization of a special class. First, what scholastic attainments will be realized that are not realized in the ordinary class? Second, what will be the resultant attitude of the students of the class, those excluded, and the teachers? Third, what will be the general teaching situation and the total school program?

In an evaluation of acceleration in the special-class setting, Justman (1954) studied 95 matched pairs of intellectually gifted students selected from 11 normal-progress and 11 special-progress classes in nine junior high schools located in comparable middle-class neighborhoods in New York City. He found that (1) separation generally brought superior educational achievement to that attained by equally gifted children who remained in normal-progress groups; (2) acceleration by a period of one year at the junior high school level was not accompanied by loss in those areas to which his appraisal was directed (mathematics, science, social studies, work-study skills, and language arts); and (3) separation of intellectually gifted children into homogeneous special-progress groups on the junior high school level had some value.

The establishment of special classes for gifted students is impractical in small high schools where there are too few pupils for such classes. Acceleration or grouping within regular classes may be the only practical solution. In high schools of 700 or more pupils, special classes may be possible, especially in such subjects as English, social science, and science. The slower pupils usually eliminate themselves in mathematics before they reach the junior or senior year. Cathell (1955) describes a program of Honors English designed for superior high school students. An important phase of the work of the class consisted of reading, both for class and out-of-class activity. Before the school term ends in the spring, each student is given a comprehensive reading list correlated with the year's literature study. Thus, many of the young people are able to do a great deal of guided reading during the summer months.

A more advanced and more comprehensive literary anthology is used by the Honors English group than is used by the other English classes. "Students plan their own outside reading program, based upon the list compiled by the teacher but with the addition of other books that the student may wish to include" (p. 335). With this special class, creative writing offers an incentive for many students, while TV programs have their appeal to others. One of the best outcomes was that "the class learned how to do reference work honestly, how to use facts without copying the author's words, when to cite and when to quote and the importance of recognizing contradictory references and authors' prejudices" (p. 335).

In Public School 233, Brooklyn, 30 pupils were selected as intellectually gifted and placed in a special section of Grade 7. These pupils were kept together for two years, during which time they were given an enriched program along with greater responsibilities. The school provided twenty-five dollars a year in extra supplies, gave the pupils opportunity for service in the school community, guided them as to curriculum suitable to their needs and interests, and kept them as an integral part of the school (Brown, 1949).

In the adjusted curriculum, the children learned everything prescribed for normal children. However, course work was not in the regular sequence. Some of the prescribed topics were studied from a more mature viewpoint. New materials, often different in content, were added. Instead of making elaborate notebooks for themselves, the children jointly undertook major service tasks for the school community. Their first major task was that of painting the flags of the United Nations for the school. This task provided opportunities for studying and reflecting on history, current events, applied mathematics, and color. Another project was that of writing a constitution for the general organization of their school. This activity was correlated with that of studying the United States Constitution, which was thus made more meaningful. In addition, these work projects provided opportunities for the pupils to experience and grow through cooperative planning and action in activities for the welfare of the school. This latter value is most important for the intellectually gifted, who should be trained so that they can take a more active part as leaders in a democratic community. Another major task undertaken by the children was the formation and maintenance of a nature room. This also served the school community. Brown (1949) has discussed this as follows:

They began this project late in their VII B term and continued it through their eighth year. Any child or class in the school may come to the nature room to look, to read, or to borrow material. The intellectually gifted class divided itself into eight committees: insects, plants, aquatic life, birds, animals (mammals), minerals, industry, and records. Each committee set up, cared for, and found out as much as it could about its particular area. The committees rotated as curators-of-the-day. In this way, even though the individual child became most familiar with his own area, he also had to have more than a passing acquaintance with the other areas because he had to act as guide for visiting classes. [P. 383.]

A study by Abramson (1959) investigated the relationship between ability grouping in high school and subsequent progress in college. Subjects were 318 students who had completed the college sophomore year in a liberal arts program or its equivalent and who had graduated from four high schools that met the requirements for special schools or classes (IQ of 115 or higher and general achievement above the 80th percentile). Among the findings were:

1. No significant differences in grade point averages earned by students who had been members of ability groups in high school and students not grouped by ability.
2. Grade point averages considered by levels of intelligence differed significantly without regard to the school attended.

Abramson (1959) thus concluded:

1. No superiority of preparation for college could be claimed for either the special high school or honors class as contrasted with the comprehensive high school with heterogeneous grouping of students.
2. Over-all achievement was associated with levels of intelligence rather than with the particular high school attended.
3. Since high school ability grouping showed no effect on academic achievement in college, further research should center on curricula and methods of teaching.
4. Preparation for college is only one educational aim, and school objectives should include more suitable systems of evaluation, including departure from current practices.

Intraclass Grouping. There are a number of possible advantages inherent in intraclass grouping. The alert teacher will recognize variations in interests and abilities and will automatically conduct a sort of grouping so as to render the schoolwork more effective. Group projects, individualized work, contract methods, and socialized recitations can be adapted to intraclass groupings. The work of all the children must, in the final analysis, be planned, graded, and checked by the teacher. Where there is intragrouping, this may be done more effectively than if no grouping were present. Intraclass grouping presents a problem for the teacher of the heterogeneous group, however, that is greater than would be the case for the more homogeneous group.

Intraclass grouping will furnish opportunities for leadership and for individual pupils to apply their knowledge, experiences, special abilities, and intelligence in a very desirable manner if the teacher knows her pupils and enlists their interest and help in planning units of experience. Martens (1946) has described a unit on Norway carried out by a fourth-grade class of 40 children. These children varied in IQ from 93 to 126, with most of them between 105 and 115. Most of these children came from homes with above-average cultural and economic advantages.

The unit on Norway grew out of the travel of some of the children. Their discussion periods led to talks of modes of transportation and communication. In gathering information about the geographical and historical background of transportation, they became interested in the unusual boats of the Vikings. The adventurous folk of the North have always held a lure for children, and the class voted to study the homeland of these people.

In order to make learning happier and more effective, the class was divided into three groups. One group was to study the geographical aspects of the country; one was to delve into the history of the country and the ancestry of the modern Norwegians; and the third group was for scientifically minded pupils who wished to take up some of the scientific wonders connected with the country. Each child was allowed to sign up for the work in which he was most interested. Seeking the novel, the children called themselves Historians, Scientists, and Geographers.

The Historians, Scientists, and Geographers worked as three separate groups for research and group discussions on many problems selected by the children. All information offered was talked over. When facts were doubted, it was necessary to turn back to books. A special section of the blackboard was set aside which was titled "Information, please." All questions were listed here until further information had been secured about them. There were helpful criticisms and suggestions from the entire group. Many levels of informational books were necessary because the groups varied in reading ability. Much mimeographed material was used in addition.

In order to insure a feeling of class integration, each group was asked to report its findings to the class as a whole. Such reports were made two or three times a week, at any time when the group had something vital to share. Each child kept an individual book, recording anything of interest that had been done in his group. When reports were made by other groups, the children tried to become proficient in note taking, as the reporting group always planned a short check-up of the facts that had been brought out.

Places where the Vikings sought adventures were found, and their routes were traced. The children became reasonably familiar with geographical terms, such as zones, circles, and climates. Maps and atlases became part of their research equipment. Charts of interesting items were made. These were kept in a very large book made of beaverboard and were used in all reports given by the individual groups.

Four clubs were organized on the basis of the interests and talents of the children. The Reading Club made a study of Norse mythology. They read, told, and dramatized many of the old sagas. The Poetry Club searched for poems about Norway and the Norwegians, and they wrote some of their own poetry.

The Music Club was led by three children who were most talented in music. Its members studied the lives and works of Norwegian musicians. They listened to and interpreted the story and the music of the "Peer Gynt Suite," and some of them played sections of the suite on the piano for a class recital.

The Art Club studied the beauties of the scenery of Norway and tried to interpret it through the medium of crayons and paint. A child exceedingly talented in art led this group. Quiet and shy by nature, she was able to overcome in part her tendency to shrink into herself by lending a helping hand for club meetings.

As the culmination of the unit on Norway, Longfellow's poem, "The Passing of Balder," was read and dramatized. The Poetry Club had studied this poem, and the Reading Club read the Norse myth telling of Balder the Beautiful. The class reworked the story into scenes, characters were selected, and the action was pantomimed. Words were then set to action and written down as a guide. Committees took over the responsibility for the final performance in relation to publicity, program, costumes, and properties. Everyone had a vital part in contributing to the success of the performance. But, most important of all for intercultural education, everyone learned to appreciate the vigorous people of the Northland, their accomplishments in the face of hardships, their music and their art, and their fine human qualities as friends to all mankind. [Pp. 47–48.]

Unless carefully planned and executed, intraclass grouping may promote habits of laziness and superficial thinking among gifted children. The gifted child needs materials that will challenge his abilities. There is evidence that forced retardation, such as is often practiced with mentally superior children, does not slow up school achievement as much as some educators claim. Though the child may become bored with much of the work of the school, and though he may be forced to remain out of school because of certain extenuating circumstances, and though the parents may actually permit him to be away from school a considerable amount of time and to engage in other experiences, nevertheless he continues to develop and his achievement tends to keep pace with his superior mental ability. Terman and

Oden (1947) found that there was very little relation to be found between achievement test scores and the number of years and months superior ten-year-olds had attended school.

Enrichment in Regular Class. All plans for special provisions for the education of gifted children are based on possible enrichment of the curriculum, although acceleration also emphasizes advancing through the different levels of learning at a more rapid pace than that of the average child. In the enriched program in the regular class, the gifted child will not be separated from the others but will be working at different aspects of common problems or projects. He may be doing square root while the others are struggling with long division, or he may be using watercolors while the others are drawing with crayons. The following are a few of the various ways of enriching the program for gifted children:

1. Provide special instruction in music, art, industrial arts, and other specialized fields.
2. Provide honors or advanced classes to supplement regular classroom instruction.
3. Organize and conduct special clubs or afternoon and evening classes.
4. Allow talented students to take extra courses as electives in fields of their abilities and interests.
5. Help talented students make use of community agencies, such as museums, libraries, and arts and crafts classes.

The enriched program for gifted children in the Colfax School of Pittsburgh, described by Wolfe (1948), attempts to provide for the complete development of each gifted child:

The junior workshop is for children in grades one to three, and the senior workshop for those in grades four through six. In order to keep their mental and social development in healthy balance, these gifted children are assigned to regular grade homerooms where they participate in brief morning exercises and homeroom activities. They leave their homerooms to spend the morning in the workshop where they receive their academic training and engage in enrichment activities.

In the afternoon they rejoin their own age groups for the special subjects of art, music, science, library, gymnasium, and swimming. Correlating their workshop activities with classes of their own age groups keeps these gifted children from forming an isolated clique.

The atmosphere of the workshops is informal. Children move about freely and consult one another when necessary. About half of the time spent in the workshop is devoted to mastering the requirements for the curriculum for their respective grades. They work in groups under the guidance of pupil leaders, discussing their assignments and checking their work. [P. 27.]

The inclusion of extracurricular activities in the program for the gifted child offers limitless possibilities and has been used by alert teachers. The organization and administration of such activities will do a great deal toward providing a more balanced program for gifted children. Teachers and others have presented some rather exhaustive plans for utilizing time and abilities in extracurricular pursuits. Some of the activities suggested are newspapers, forestry, mechanics, arts and crafts, and radio. One can readily see the possibilities of using various types of activities, depending upon local conditions and interests of the children. Trips to local industries, large stores, museums, and farms, as well as to other points of scientific and cultural value, may be taken to good advantage.

In a study whose purpose was to evaluate the effectiveness of a case-study approach for adjusting the environment of highly gifted children in the elementary school, Gallagher et al. (1960) found a wide range of adjustments. Subjects were 29 boys and 25 girls who had individual IQ scores above 150 for whom various placements, projects, and activities were devised over a three-year period. The procedures had the obvious effect of increasing teacher understanding of the needs and characteristics of each child, and parents were generally enthusiastic about the schools' efforts. It was concluded that adjustments for gifted children in the regular classroom might be unproductive unless (1) additional psychological staff is employed for diagnostic services, (2) there is a curriculum specialist to help supplement teachers' skills, (3) there is a program of grouping to help children who are in positions of relative intellectual isolation, (4) plans are developed to enlist more effective aid from parents, and (5) there is an attempt to provide a more enriched environment for the gifted child.

From a study of the acceptance and performance of 117 gifted children among a random sample of 771 classmates in three elementary schools, Williams (1958) concluded that the performance of gifted children is generally affected by considerations of group acceptance.

Baldauf (1959) attempted to answer the question, "Do mentally advanced students show significant educational gains from a curriculum enrichment program in the regular classroom?" in a study of 95 pupils (IQ's over 125 on the *California Mental Maturity Tests*) from Grades 4 through 7 in two elementary schools and one junior high school who were compared with a control group in two other elementary schools and one junior high school. The experimental group had special curriculum material taught by teachers with special training by a special curriculum resource consultant over a period of a year with test-retest data obtained on the pupils.

The chief conclusions were that the enrichment program had no adverse effect and allowed significant gain in some cases; and that the enrichment program may not have supplied sufficient challenge to these gifted students, many of whom saw it as either interesting or uninteresting busy work.

In his explorations of the development of creative thinking, Torrance (1960b) studied groups of children from the kindergarten level through graduate school students. Certain conclusions seem especially relevant to professional personnel in the elementary school. Torrance found that:

1. Highly creative individuals tend to alienate their peers and elders.
2. The highly creative child is more of a disturbing element in elementary classrooms than are his less creative peers.
3. The guidance worker needs to help the highly creative child cultivate those personality traits that are essential to his creativity, and help him to reduce the sanctions of his peers.
4. Measures of creativity and intelligence are both needed in the identification of giftedness.

SPECIAL EDUCATIONAL PROVISIONS FOR THE TALENTED

In Chapter 5, it was pointed out that the several abilities of a particular individual may be far from equal. While it is true that children with high intelligence test scores are in general superior in a number of areas, there are many children with special ability or talent in one skill and little more than average ability in most other skills. A successful program for gifted children must make some provision for these children. This has been accomplished in several schools, usually through (1) special groupings; (2) special provision for individual instruction within particular groups; or (3) extraclass activities, such as clubs. The purpose of all three provisions is the same —the discovery and development of a variety of talents. The Portland, Oregon, public school program includes a wide range of activities. Children with superior ability in graphic art, music, mechanical arts, dramatics, creative writing, rhythms, or social leadership are identified and given specialized instruction in special groups. The New York

City schools also offer programs designed to develop a wide range of talents. Several specialized high schools offer work in art, music, sciences, mathematics, and special vocational skills.

Development of Musical Abilities. Individual differences in musical ability, interests, and needs can well be taken care of in the high school program by offering two types of courses in music—"appreciation" courses and "amateur performance" courses. For pupils who display special ability in voice, violin, piano, or other musical instruments, both individual and group performance training courses may be provided. The group performance training is often provided through the orchestra, band, or glee club. The more complex work may be organized around individual needs and abilities. When, however, certain ambitious pupils coming into these group courses on trial prove naturally untalented or indifferent learners, these children should be removed and guided into activities where they can perform more successfully.

The public schools of Berkeley (Havighurst, *et al.*, 1955) offer, as part of the educational development program for gifted children, special activities in music. The Berkeley program has been described as follows:

The talented music student, whether he intends to pursue music as an avocation or as a vocation, has many opportunities available to him in the Berkeley schools. Provision is made at the elementary level for excellence in instrumental music by the organization of an All-City Orchestra which meets outside school and plays music of a more challenging type than would be possible at the local school level. In the choral field, glee clubs have been organized in practically all the schools. . . .

There is also an All-City Orchestra at the junior high school level, and each school has a boys' and girls' glee club. Talent shows are presented, and the school music teachers work with the classroom teachers to provide opportunities for members to perform before their classmates.

At the senior high school level, orchestra, band, and swing band afford opportunities for the student excelling in instrumental music. For the serious vocal student there is the A Capella Choir. Classes in harmony and composition are offered, and creative work is presented in an annual concert. A music club prepares concerts. Annual talent shows perform for radio and television audiences, service clubs, churches, and other community organizations. . . . [P. 38.]

Some "performance power" instruction can also well be made for those less talented in music—perhaps in the nature of chorus and popular group singing. These courses might be organized into special classes with a definite schedule. Musical enthusiasts who know very little about individual differences and special needs for other types of educational training would advise giving the majority of high school pupils amateur performance courses. On the basis of evidence now available, however, it appears that not more than 15 to 25 per cent of the usual high school population needs or can profit to any marked degree from the special performance courses in music.

The situation regarding music appreciation seems to be different. Practically all American adults today listen to a great amount of music, just as they read a mass of current news and literature. However, relatively few have been trained to seek out those types of musical material within their level or capacity for appreciation. Very few listeners have received training in the discrimination of the various types of music. It is at this point that academic musicians or the professional teachers and critics of music fail in their understanding of human nature and desires. There is a definite need for intensive education toward improved appreciation for those less gifted in the ability to perform.

Development of Art Abilities. Art ability may be detected by the alert teacher as early as the kindergarten stage of the child's educational development, and various tests have been developed for helping teachers and others evaluate art ability among elementary and high school pupils more readily and more accurately. Through individualized instruction, the artistically talented child in the elementary grades may be able to develop his art abilities in harmony with his interests, needs, and maturational level.

Special instruction in art is more widely available than is instruction in most other special areas. Such instruction may take the form of a special class or school, or art instruction offered by out-of-school agencies. The High School of Music and Art, New York City (Havighurst *et al.*, 1955) is one example of a specialized academic high school that provides a program for those who are talented in the fields of music and art. For each student, either music or art is the chief subject of interest in addition to regular academic studies. Students are admitted from all parts of the city during their eighth or ninth year at school. Entrance examinations are designed to test for potential ability, not for acquired techniques.

The course in art includes three or four years of studio practice with instruction in crafts and a year of art survey. The first year is exploratory, giving the student an opportunity for creative expression with a variety of media. The second year is devoted to a study of drawing, color, and composition in special media such as oil and watercolor. The third year provides opportunity for specialization. The student may choose architecture, painting, graphic arts, advertising arts, or sculpture. He may elect costume design, textiles, stage design, or ceramics. [P. 81.]

The Art Museum of Worcester, Massachusetts (Havighurst *et al.,* 1955) offers, as a part of a larger program, professional instruction in art for children and youth from four through eighteen years of age. The classes are free and open to all young people of the community and surrounding areas. The subjects taught are painting, drawing, block printing, and modeling with clay and other materials.

Children who are interested and have ability are encouraged to join the late-afternoon classes, which are less crowded than those on Saturday and offer more individual attention. A class in oil painting, for youths of fifteen to eighteen years, attracts those of more than ordinary ability. Such students are encouraged to enter the school of the Worcester Art Museum, where they can continue the study of art professionally. [P. 60.]

An extensive program is also offered during the summer months.

Development of Ability in Creative Writing. The program for gifted children in Portland, Oregon (Havighurst *et al.,* 1955), features a comprehensive plan for the identification and development of special abilities in music, art, leadership, and other creative activities, including writing and drama. This development is accomplished in the elementary schools by enrichment in the regular class program and through the formation of special classes. In the high schools participating in the program, enrichment in the regular classroom, special sections of regular classes, and elective seminars are employed to carry out the program. "As students leave the elementary schools, eighth-grade teachers and principals make recommendations to the high schools concerning students whom they feel to be intellectually gifted or to possess special talent. . . ." (P. 88.) Such community resources as the radio and television stations, the art museum, and the city library have been most helpful in making it possible for students to receive special help and training.

The writing of original prose and verse is an essential component of all areas of learning at Public School No. 241 of New York City (Havighurst *et al.,* 1955), which is one of the city's elementary schools that operates a special program for intellectually gifted children. "In addition to original booklets, the children write and direct their own plays, puppet shows, and operettas for class, school and community presentation. The children also produce a school magazine in which their creative writing is published. . . ." (P. 74.) The radio and speech classes, including such organizations as the Broadcasting Guilds, are means for stimulating students with special interests and abilities in drama and speaking. A three- or five-minute newscast may be given at the beginning of each period, with individual students writing, timing, and reading their own news reports. The better programs and more talented students may be selected to appear on radio or television. Again, educational programs are most effective when they are closely integrated into the total life pattern of the community or city. Community resources for the development of creative abilities are available in all communities. Teachers should be on the alert to discover and use the resources of the particular community in which he or she is teaching.

Development of Science Talent. Through special classes for students with special ability and interest in science, many high school students are given advanced and specialized training in different branches of science. In schools that emphasize science throughout the entire curriculum, special abilities in science are developed. Different science clubs participate in many activities, including science fairs of various kinds. Sometimes there are community resources available that help in stimulating special interest on the part of superior and talented boys and girls. There is a growing recognition of the importance of clubs, out-of-school agencies, and community resources as possible means for stimulating and developing science talent.

GUIDANCE AND COUNSELING FOR THE GIFTED

Follow-up Studies. What happens to child geniuses? A long-range study by Terman and Oden (1947) furnishes useful information on this question. A follow-up of gifted children in their sample revealed that approximately 84 per cent of the men and 93 per cent of the women earned high school grades required for admission to top-ranking colleges and universities (A or B grades). More than 80 per cent of both men and women participated in extracurricular activities when in high school. Honor society membership was held by 38 per cent of the men and 55 per cent of the women. They held offices and displayed leadership in student affairs to a larger degree than would be expected from their numbers in the student body. These achievements are still more impressive in light of the fact that the mean age of these gifted children at high school graduation was more than a year below the average for California high school seniors.

Educational and employment records were unfavorably influenced in many cases by the fact that these students finished high school during the 1930's—the depression years. However, 90 per cent of the men and 67 per cent of the women continued their education beyond high school and graduated from college. These figures are about eight times as large as that for the general population. (It should be pointed out, as a partial explanation for this, that the majority of these individuals came from homes and neighborhoods that were above average on a socioeconomic scale.) Of those graduating from college, 68 per cent of the men and 60 per cent of the women returned for graduate study. The average grades in college, while superior, were not always as high as might have been expected from the students' marked superiority in intelligence. A number of factors were found to account for this. An analysis of causes of unsatisfactory work was made for a number of cases. One case cited by Terman and Oden (1947) illustrates the most common cause:

M 1582 (Binet I.Q. 168) entered college at the age of fifteen years and ten months. He had stayed out of school one semester between high school and college, having graduated at midyear. Although he got along satisfactorily in his social relationships in high school and had no serious personality difficulties, he had been left out of things to some extent because of his youth and studiousness. He determined to overcome this in college, with the result that his scholastic interests diminished and most of his attention was given to having a good time. He was disqualified at the end of his freshman year, but after working for a year he returned to college, got his bachelor's degree at twenty, and entered graduate school. After completing his work for a medical degree he was appointed to an important position in a university medical school. He had already published a number of papers on his research studies. He served during the war, first as a medical officer in the field, later as the director of a medical research laboratory for the Army. [Pp. 159–60.]

A study by Witty and Theman (1943) of 82 mentally superior Negro youths identified in elementary school as having Stanford-Binet IQ's ranging from 120 to 200 substantiated an earlier finding of Terman and others. The average scores on high school achievement tests of those with an IQ of 140 or more were significantly higher than the average for the entire group. The educational attainment of these superior Negro youths, as measured by teachers' marks and rank in graduation class, was found to be similar to that reported for superior white boys and girls. The Negro youth exhibited even stronger interest in school than did gifted white pupils of the Terman study. Interest in school subjects varied, with English mentioned most often, followed by science and chemistry, French, and history.

Success in any school task is in large measure dependent upon mental maturity (which enables the pupil to respond intelligently to ideas and problems); a background sufficiently rich in experience; habits of concentration, attention, persistence, and self-reliance; and an ability to think and understand sufficiently developed to interpret and use ideas presented through written symbols. The many studies on this problem that have been made reveal correlations that range from .20 to above .75 between grades obtained and intelligence tests scores. The size of such correlations will depend upon a number of variables, among which may be motivation, nature of subject matter, study periods, teaching procedures, and criteria for grades. Too much attention to the achievement of superior children is neither wholesome for them nor in the best interests of the average and below-average group. This idea was brought forth early by Samuel R. Hall in his *Lectures on School-Keeping* (1829) when he stated:

If rewards are given at all, let them be "rewards of merit" and not rewards of intellectual capacity. The dull of apprehension are not to be punished for being so, neither do the more gifted merit praise for what they have received from the hand of God.

Need for Educational and Vocational Guidance. Surveys of school dropouts show that many able students never finish high school and that a large percentage never enter college. While many superior secondary school graduates fail to continue their education for financial reasons, it seems likely that an even larger number lack interest in or motivation for going to college. Interest in going to college is closely related to the parents' occupation and education and to the amount of discussion of college activities in the home and by school personnel. In a survey reported by Cole (1956), only about 25 per cent of the 9,689 able seniors reported having had "quite a lot" of discussion with teachers or counselors, while 18 per cent said they had none at all.

When able students who were planning to go to college were asked why they wanted to go, 40 per cent of the boys and 30 per cent of the girls stated that the most important reason was that the degree was needed for the work they intended to follow. Another 11 per cent gave as the most important reason the financial advantage that a college degree would give to them. Only 5 per cent of the boys and 9 per cent of the girls gave enjoyment of study as the most important reason.

The results of the study also revealed the vocational aspirations and interests of this cross-section of able high school seniors. The students were asked what they would like to be within 15 years if hard work would bring success in their chosen careers. The answers to this question are presented in Table 6–1. Only a small percentage of the boys were interested in "white collar" jobs and skilled labor, while 18 per cent of the girls expressed a desire for such jobs. The large percentage of boys interested in engineering and business possibly reflects financial interest.

Guiding the Superior Pupil. The emotional needs of the superior pupil are certainly similar to those of inferior and average children. However, methods of meeting these needs may not be the same. Teachers should know the learning characteristics of individual children and adjust their methods and materials in harmony with these characteristics. There are many gifted children whose educational aspirations are quite mediocre and far below their capabilities. Griswold (1954) has stated: "While over half of the nation's youth finishes high school, a fifth (of the whole) goes on to some form of higher education. Of the top quarter in intellectual ability . . . 20

TABLE 6–1

Idealized Vocational Aspirations of High School Students
(Top 30 Per Cent in Ability)

Vocations	Boys	Girls
Engineering	26%	0%
Professional, non-specified	8	5
Physical science	6	1
Biological science	1	0
Social science	1	1
Medical professional	8	3
Law and politics	4	1
Literature and arts	3	8
Religion and social welfare	2	4
Education	4	20
Technical workers	3	2
Medical technical workers	0	12
Business technical	2	0
Farm	4	1
Business	10	5
White collar	4	18
Skilled labor	4	0
Other labor (including housewife)	1	12
Miscellaneous	9	6

SOURCE: After Cole (1956).

per cent do not continue for financial reasons and 40 per cent for lack of motivation" (p. 147). The superior child should understand his capabilities and should be guided in setting goals in harmony with his abilities. Failure to do this leads to personal maladjustments and a gross waste of human resources.

Earlier it was suggested that gifted children should be encouraged to participate in activities outside the classroom. The capacities that the gifted child possesses can reach their highest expression when the individual is healthy in mind and body. The school should be aware and not unconsciously foster mental health difficulties among gifted children and adolescents by:

1. Thwarting their drive for obtaining satisfaction from school success
2. Reinforcing any feeling of social inferiority or inadequacy that may have been acquired because of social rejection
3. Encouraging them to concentrate on intellectual achievements as a compensation for social rejection
4. Fostering egotism and excessive desire for praise, showing them off
5. Promoting infantilism

Gowan (1960) has summarized the characteristics and role of the counselor who is to work successfully with gifted children and indicates that the senior high school period is critical in that lack of proper guidance may do a great disservice to the gifted child.

The creative and academic performances of a group of talented adolescents were studied by Holland (1961) who obtained a random sampling of National Merit Finalists (649 boys, 345 girls, and their parents) that was then polled and tested by mail. The relationship between three criteria of academic and creative performance and 72 personal, demographic, and parental variables were actually examined.

According to Holland (1961):

The results suggest that creative performance at the high school level occurs more frequently among students who are independent, intellectual, expressive, asocial, consciously original, and who have high aspirations for future achievement. Students who are persevering, sociable, responsible, and whose parents hold somewhat authoritarian attitudes and values are more frequently academic achievers. The negligible relationships found between academic aptitude and creative performance at a high aptitude level suggests that we need to use nonintellectual criteria in the selection of students for scholarships and fellowships. [P. 147.]

Counseling Program. No particular counseling program can be recommended to the exclusion of others. The nature of the program will be affected by a number of factors, including the size of the school, size of classes, specialized services available, and training of the teachers. Whatever the conditions and combination of resources available, counseling of the gifted should provide the following:

A. The granting of credit by examination to gifted pupils who can demonstrate prior mastery of the content of required courses. This is especially important during the last two years of high school. The time thus saved usually should be devoted to enrichment activities.

B. Enrichment opportunities for the gifted in the creative arts, industrial arts, and home arts, and the counseling of gifted pupils into those areas.

C. Enrichment opportunities in athletics, dramatics, debate, student government, and other co-curricular areas, and the counseling of gifted pupils into them.

D. Sufficient flexibility to permit the skipping of gifted pupils from one grade to the next, when after careful individual study it is determined that the skipping is needed.

E. Cautious experimentation in the introduction of college freshman work to selected 12th grade gifted pupils, thus permitting them to achieve advance standing when they enroll at college.

F. Long-distance planning with gifted students and their parents, so they will be qualified for college entrance and may proceed with the specialized professional training their abilities permit.

G. Special help to the gifted in qualifying for and obtaining college scholarships.

H. Careful avoidance of anything which will attach the label of "Genius" or which will otherwise stigmatize gifted pupils in the minds of their associates.

I. A referral service which will make possible psychiatric study and treatment for the most disturbed gifted pupils. [Barbour, 1954, pp. 478–79.]

The Role of the Teacher. No system of instruction or program designed for the gifted will be any better than the teachers entrusted with carrying out the program. It was suggested earlier that the gifted have been neglected to a marked degree. Teachers often recognize as superior only those who have won scholarship honors or are apparently well adjusted in their educational activities and social relations. At the same time, teachers subscribe to a philosophy of equality of educational opportunity and extol the notion that the "whole" child goes to school and that he should be given the opportunity to develop his potentialities. Some of the special needs of teachers of gifted children may be summarized as follows:

1. They must first be able to identify giftedness in the classroom and elsewhere, if they are to make provisions for the maximum development of children's potentialities.

2. They must have a thorough understanding of child development, so as to provide sound guidance and teaching in harmony with the needs and maturational level of each individual child.
3. They must have a thorough understanding of the principles of learning, especially as these principles apply to the learning of gifted children.
4. They must have superior skill in group dynamics and counseling techniques. The teacher must be able to motivate the gifted to superior performance without fostering egotism on the part of the learner.
5. They should have a wide cultural background, a well-adjusted personality, and a balanced program of living in their own lives.

CURRICULUM AND ACHIEVEMENT

Creative Children. Torrance (1959) pointed out that it is the school's job to help highly creative children to be less obnoxious without sacrificing their creativity. He indicates that creativity is important to healthy personality development, that it contributes to the acquisition of information, that it is essential in the application of knowledge, and that it is important to our society that creative talent be identified, developed, and utilized properly.

As the result of efforts to encourage 100 upper elementary school children to jot down creative ideas and to increase individual valuation of personal creative thinking ability, Torrance (1960a) points out that, since most children get their ideas in the classroom and write there, the educational setting should be suited to the identification, stimulation, and development of creative thinking and writing abilities.

In commenting on research findings on creative characteristics, Taylor (1961) indicates that many present academic programs are geared to memorization and non-creative activities and work habits and that the development of creativity in students should be strongly emphasized as a goal throughout the entire educational programs in many fields of science.

Motivation and Achievement. In a comparative study of achievers (A) and underachievers (U), Frankel (1960) selected and matched 50 pairs of white boys drawn from the senior class of a New York City high school where each pair consisted of an achiever and an underachiever matched on the three criteria of equivalent IQ, school entrance examination score, and chronological age to answer the general question, "Why do students of seemingly similar high intellectual ability perform so differently academically?"

Frankel found distinctly different interest patterns between groups. The U's were less happy at school, less conforming, and had poor attendance records; while the A's were more conforming, did not break rules, and participated in extracurricular events and activities. The A's had done significantly better than the U's in junior high school. In conclusion, Frankel (1960) stated, "It appears probable that the factors relating to scholastic underachievement of this group may have been operating before these students entered the junior high school" (p. 180).

At the junior high school level, Drews and Tehan (1957) found that mothers of high achievers were more authoritarian and restrictive in their treatment of their children than mothers of low achievers. A *Parental Attitude Scale* was given to mothers of 40 junior high school students (IQ's of 130+) and to mothers of 28 students (IQ's from 93 to 120), and the answers to 30 questions were analyzed in terms of a Dominating Scale, a Possessive Scale, and an Ignoring Scale. These findings are consistent with some findings reported earlier on parent attitudes and achievement.

Academically Superior Students and College Attendance. Increased college attendance is reflected in the greater percentage of academically superior high school students who go on to college. Estimates by Berdie (1954) indicated that about 50 per cent of the superior students were going on to college in the early 1950's. Little (1960) conducted a two-year study of academically talented seniors graduating from Wisconsin high schools. He found that approximately 80 per cent of the boys and 60 per cent of the girls in the top quarter of their class, by class rank and test scores, were either in college or planned to enroll. Ten per cent of the non-college boys and 30 per cent of the non-college girls stated that they would not attend college even if they had the money. Five per cent of the non-college students reported that they were not in college because they could not afford it. Non-college-going peers, indifference toward school, and low levels of parental education were factors that were found to outweigh living in a college community, the opportunity to attend college while living at home, the size and strength of the high school program, and even family income.

The results of the study by Little (1960) are supported by those of McDaniel and Forenback (1960), involving the top 15 per cent of Kentucky's 1959 high school seniors who participated in a statewide testing program. The findings indicated that 76 per cent of the students from the top 15 per cent of the class entered college. Simmons (1963) found from a study of academically superior high school students in Georgia that 88 per cent planned to attend college and that approximately the same percentage actually entered college in the fall following their graduation. This study supports the trend for an increasing percentage of academically superior students to attend college. The relationship of background factors related to college attendance indicated some significant differences between superior students who entered college and those who did not enter college. The following factors were significantly related to college attendance:

1. S.A.T. Scores.
2. Yearly income of the family.
3. Extent of student-parent discussion of college plans.
4. Occupational level of the father.
5. Educational level of the father.
6. Educational level of the mother.
7. Parental attitude concerning student's college attendance.
8. Number of siblings, particularly older siblings.
9. Size of high school attended.
10. Presence of a guidance counselor in the high school.
11. Extent of student-faculty discussion of college plans.
12. Type of institution preferred for post high school training.
13. Preference regarding the attending of a local junior college.
14. Preference for a job rather than college after high school.
15. Marital status was for girls highly significant.
16. Preference for armed forces rather than college was for boys highly significant.

In summary, the factors revealed as being significant in their relation to, and influence on, the student's college plans and actual college attendance were of several types. For both boys and girls, the family background appeared to be most important with such factors as the family financial condition, parental attitude, parental educational level, and number of siblings (particularly older siblings) being the most notable. Another important variable was the desire of the student for activities other than college, such as work, or in the case of girls, marriage, or for boys, the armed forces. With respect to high school background factors, the size of the school attended along with faculty interest in the student's college plans seemed to be closely related to both the student's planning for and subsequently going to college.

Stivers (1958) conducted a study in a midwestern high school in a city of 40,000 population. Research was centered on the top 25 per cent of the boys and girls in the tenth grade. The final group consisted of 86 students, 45 girls and 41 boys. Each student was questioned directly and indirectly about his plans for school and work. On the basis of the responses, students were classified as "motivated for college" and "not motivated for college." Stivers' study disclosed that the students who were well motivated for college at the tenth-grade level were not significantly higher in social class but did have a significantly greater need for achievement. Basically, the significant differences between the motivated and the non-motivated students were in the number and variety of persons who held up the goal of higher education. It was found that the higher motivated group had a higher composite score on tests of ability to succeed in school. The students who wanted to go to college had a higher score on the communality scale of the *California Psychological Inventory*. The students who were college bound had higher scores on the achievement-via-independence scale of this same test.

The results of a study by Morrow and Wilson (1961) support the hypothesis that bright high-achieving high school boys engage in more sharing activities, ideas, and confidence; are more approving and trusting, affectionate, and encouraging (not pressuring) with regard to achievement; are less restrictive and severe; and enjoy more acceptance of parental standards. Thus, family morale seems to foster academic achievement among bright high school boys by fostering positive attitudes toward teachers and school and interest in intellectual pursuits.

In a descriptive summary of the National Merit Scholarship Program, Stalnaker (1961) pointed out the Corporation's concern for talent loss and suggested that: "Apart from financial need, lack of motivation appears to be the primary cause of qualified students not going on to college (p. 522).

SUMMARY

Schools are increasingly making specific efforts to meet the educational needs of gifted children and adolescents. Such efforts are being manifested in a variety of ways, the most important of which are the following: (1) acceleration or rapid promotion or early admission, (2) enriched educational environment, (3) special grouping, (4) differentiated curricula, (5) enlarged extraclass program at school, and (6) specialized classes and schools. Regardless of the procedure employed, the psychological needs of gifted pupils are basically similar to those of other pupils. This fact should always be kept in mind by those concerned with the education and guidance of these children and adolescents.

Follow-up studies of the gifted show that some of them never develop into well-rounded personalities of worth and substance, although they may be numbered among leaders in the world of art, music, and science. If gifted boys and girls are to make the most of their capacities, they must be guided in the understanding of their potentialities and motivated to develop them for their own happiness as well as the welfare of society.

The notion that gifted pupils will be able to get along without guidance is unsound. Various studies referred to in this and the previous chapter show that many of them are faced with difficult adjustment problems. A large percentage of gifted students are not adequately motivated by the ordinary school program.

There is need for a broader conception of the gifted. Many students display unusual ability in some particular area. There is a need to identify these pupils at an early age and guide them toward a more complete realization of their true potentialities. The optimum development of the gifted will depend upon (1) early identification, (2) motivation and goals commensurate with their abilities, and (3) opportunities to participate in a wide variety of activities.

CHAPTER REFERENCES

ABRAMSON, D. S. (1959). The effectiveness of grouping for students of high ability. *Educ. Res. Bull.*, 38:169–83.

BALDAUF, R. J. (1959). A comparison of the extent of educational growth of mentally advanced pupils in the Cedar Rapids experiment. *J. educ. Res.*, 52:181–83.

BARBOUR, R. (1954). Counseling gifted high school pupils. *Calif. J. second. Educ.*, 29:476–82.

BERDIE, R. (1954). *After high school—what?* Minneapolis: Univer. of Minnesota Press.

BIRCH, J. W. (1954). Early school admission for mentally advanced children. *Except. Child.*, 21:84–87.

BROWN, M. V. (1949). Teaching an intellectually gifted group. *Element. Sch. J.*, 49:380–94.

CATHELL, DOROTHY (1955). Honors English: a break for bright students. *Clearing House*, 29:335.

Cole, C. C., Jr. (1956). *Encouraging scientific talent.* New York: College Entrance Examination Board.

Drews, Elizabeth M., and Tehan, J. E. (1957). Parental attitudes and academic achievement. *J. clin. Psychol.*, 13:328–32.

Frankel, E. (1960). A comparative study of achieving and underachieving high school boys of high intellectual ability. *J. educ. Res.*, 53: 173–80.

Gallagher, J. J., Greenman, M., Kearns, M., and King, A. (1960). Individual classroom adjustments for gifted children in elementary schools. *Except. Child.*, 26:409–22.

Gowan, J. C. (1960). Organization of guidance for gifted children. *Personnel & Guidance J.*, 39:275–79.

Griswold, E. W. (1954). *Essays on education.* New Haven: Yale Univer. Press.

Havighurst, R. J., Stivers, E., and DeHaan, R. F. (1955). *A survey of the education of gifted children.* Supplementary Educational Monographs, No. 83. Chicago: Univer. of Chicago Press.

Holland, J. (1961). Creative and academic performance among talented adolescents. *J. educ. Psychol.*, 52:136–47.

Hollingworth, Leta S. (1931). Personality development of special class children. *Univer. Pa. Bull., 18th annu. Schoolmen's Wk. Proc.*, Vol. 18, p. 443.

Jones, E. S., and Ortner, Gloria K. (1954). Advanced standing for superior students through examinations at the beginning of their college careers. *NEA J.* (Feb.), p. 107.

Justman, J. (1954). Academic achievement of intellectually gifted accelerants and non-accelerants in junior high school. *Sch. Rev.*, 62:142–50.

Little, J. K. (1960). Wisconsin study of academically talented high school graduates; their college plans and progress. In N. E. Brown (ed.), *Incentives and obstacles to higher education.* Washington, D.C.: Council on Education.

Lorge, I. (1954). Social gains in the special education of the gifted. *Sch. Soc.*, 79:4–7.

McCandless, B. R. (1957). Should a bright child start school before he is five? *Education*, 77:37–75.

McDaniel, E. D., and Forenback, Mary S. (1960). *Kentucky's top 15 per cent, a study of the college attendance patterns of superior high school students.* Special Research Report, Kentucky Cooperative Counseling and Testing Service. Lexington, Ky.: Univer. of Kentucky.

Martens, Elise H. (1946). *Curriculum adjustments for gifted children.* U.S. Office of Education Bulletin No. 1. Washington, D.C.: U.S. Government Printing Office.

Morgan, Antonia B. (1959). Critical factors in the academic acceleration of gifted children, a follow-up study. *Psychol. Rep.*, 5:649–53.

MORROW, W. R., and WILSON, R. C. (1961). Family relations of bright high-achieving and under-achieving high school boys. *Child Developm,.* 32:501–10.

Promotion—accelerating the academically talented. *NEA J.,* Vol. 49, No. 4 (1960), 22–23.

REYNOLDS, M. C., BIRCH, J. W., and TUSETH, ALICE A. (1962). Review of research on early admission. In M. C. Reynolds (ed.), *Early admission for mentally advanced children.* Washington, D.C.: Council for Exceptional Children. Pp. 7–17.

SIMMONS, N. G. (1963). College going plans and actual college attendance of academically superior high school seniors in Georgia. Unpublished doctor's dissertation, Univer. of Georgia.

STALNAKER, J. M. (1961). Recognizing and encouraging talent. *Amer. Psychologist,* 16:513–22.

STIVERS, E. (1958). Motivation for college in high school boys. *Sch. Rev.,* 66:341–50.

STRANG, RUTH (1955). Psychology of gifted children and youth. In W. M. CRUICKSHANK (ed.), *Psychology of exceptional children and youth.* Englewood Cliffs, N.J.: Prentice-Hall.

TAYLOR, C. W. (1961). Research findings on creative characteristics. *Stud. Art Educ.,* 3:9–17.

TERMAN, L. M., and ODEN, MELITA H. (1947). *The gifted child grows up.* Vol. 4. *Genetic studies of genius.* Stanford, Calif.: Stanford Univ. Press.

TORRANCE, E. P. (1959). Current research on the nature of creative talent. *J. counsel. Psychol.,* 6:309–16.

TORRANCE, E. P. (1960a). Creative thinking in the language arts. *Educ. Leadership,* 18:13–18.

TORRANCE, E. P. (1960b). Explorations in creative thinking. *Education,* 81:216–20.

TRUSLER, J. W. (1949). Pupil acceleration in elementary schools. *Grade Tchr.,* 67:96–98.

WILLIAMS, META F. (1958). Acceptance and performance among gifted elementary school children. *Educ. Res. Bull.,* 37:216–20.

WITTY, P., and THEMAN, VIOLA (1943). A follow-up study of educational attainment of gifted Negroes. *J. educ. Psychol.,* 34:35–47.

WOLFE, VERONICA (1948). Special workshops enrich school day for gifted children. *Sch. Mgmt.,* 17:27.

WRENN, G. C. (1949). Potential research talent in the sciences based on intelligence quotients of Ph.D.'s. *Educ. Rec.,* 30:5–22.

YOUNGERT, E. (1938). Is it desirable to organize special classes for gifted students? *Tchrs. Coll. Rec.,* 39:375–88.

SELECTED READINGS

ANDERSON, H. H. (ed.) (1959). *Creativity and its cultivation.* New York: Harper & Row.

BISH, C. E. (1961). The academically talented. *NEA J.,* 50:33–37.

BRANDWEIN, P. F. (1955). *The gifted student as future scientist.* New York: Harcourt, Brace & World.

BRYAN, J. N. (1962). Education of the gifted. *Sch. Life,* 44:12–15.

CARTER, H. D. (1960). Gifted children. In CHESTER HARRIS (ed.), *Encyclopedia of educational research.* New York: Macmillan. Pp. 583–93.

CROW, L. D., and CROW, ALICE (1963). *Educating the academically able —a book of readings.* New York: McKay.

DEHAAN, R. F., and HAVIGHURST, R. J. (1957). *Educating gifted children.* Chicago: Univer. of Chicago Press.

DURR, W. K. (1964). *The gifted student.* New York: Oxford Univer. Press.

DURR, W. K., and COLLIER, C. C. (1960). Recent research on the gifted. *Education,* 81:163–70.

FARBER, S. M., and WILSON, R. H. L. (eds.) (1963). *Conflict and creativity.* New York: McGraw-Hill.

FREEHILL, M. F. (1961). *Gifted children.* New York: Macmillan.

GALLAGHER, J. J. (1964). *Teaching the gifted child.* Boston: Allyn & Bacon.

GREER, EDITH (1963). The academically talented. *Sch. Life,* 45:9–12.

HAVIGHURST, R. J., STIVERS, E., and DEHAAN, R. F. (1955). *A survey of the education of gifted children.* Supplementary Monographs, No. 83. Chicago: Univer. of Chicago Press.

HENRY, N. B. (ed.) (1958). *Education for the gifted.* Chicago: Univer. of Chicago Press.

HOLLINGWORTH, LETA (1942). *Children above 180 IQ.* Yonkers, N.Y.: World Book Co.

JUSTMAN, J. (1960). Some unmet problems in the education of the gifted. *Except. Child.,* 26:436–41.

REYNOLDS, M. C. (ed.) (1962). *Early school admission for mentally advanced children.* Washington, D.C.: Council for Exceptional Children, National Education Association.

SCHIEFELE, M. (1953). *The gifted child in the regular classroom.* New York: Teachers Coll., Columbia Univer., Bureau of Publications.

STERN, HELEN G. (1962). Guidance for the underachiever in high school. *NEA J.,* 51:24–26.

SUMPTION, M. R. (1941). *Three hundred gifted children.* Yonkers, N.Y.: World Book Co.

TORRANCE, E. P. (1962). *Guiding creative talent.* Englewood Cliffs, N.J.: Prentice-Hall.

TORRANCE, E. P. (1963). *Creativity.* Washington: National Education Association.

WARD, V. S. (1961). *Educating the gifted—an axiomatic approach.* Columbus, Ohio: C. E. Merrill.

WITTY, P. (ed.) (1951). *The gifted child.* Boston: D. C. Heath.

III

ORAL AND
AURAL HANDICAPS

In Part III the special characteristics of children with speech and hearing problems are presented along with therapy in school situations. The vast amount of recent research on these problems has furnished valuable information useful to parents, teachers, clinicians, and others concerned with the education, guidance, and therapy of children with problems of speech or hearing.

Children with defective speech are described in Chapter 7. The speech difficulties described include articulatory defects, stuttering, and such speech problems as pitch, nasality, delayed speech, cleft palate, and impairment resulting from damage to the central nervous system. Attention is given to remedial measures used in the correction of speech difficulties.

Chapter 8 deals with the definitions, etiology, and methods of identifying children with defective hearing, along with special characteristics of children classified as hard of hearing or deaf. In Chapter 9 current educational provisions for hard-of-hearing and deaf children are presented along with materials dealing with occupational adjustment of these individuals.

7

DEFECTIVE SPEECH

Most children are born with the physiological mechanism essential for vocalization. Early vocalization, which appears to be reflex in nature, occurs as a part of an infant's undifferentiated mass activity. The early cries and sounds rapidly give way to a large repertoire of sounds and vocalizations. Selective vocal responses develop rapidly. Reports on the babbling sounds of infants indicate that they engage in spontaneous cooing between the second and fourth month. Concerning language development, McCarthy states (1960):

A variety of syllables are heard between the fourth and sixth months of life, and by the tenth month most babies begin to imitate the sounds and voices of others, . . . The earliest noncrying speech sounds are vowels with about four different vowels heard during the first two months, and thereafter, about one more vowel is added every two months for the first year of life. The rest of the vowels are added to the repertoire more slowly during the second year of life. . . . It is also of interest to note that the number of different consonants exceeds the number of different vowels at about one year, and this is approximately the age at which normal babies speak their first word. [Pp. 5–6.]

SPEECH—ITS NATURE AND DEVELOPMENT

Components of Speech. In order to understand the complexity of the act involved in thinking and talking, one must understand its beginning and final fixation and integration. The process of developing elementary speech habits is similar to, though more complex than, the process of learning to walk. Both are dependent in part upon the maturation of the muscles involved in the performance of the act. The most individualistic of all the components of speech is *resonance*. The anatomical structure of the speech mechanism of each individual is different from that of each other individual (Martmer, 1959). Thus, no two voices are alike in all respects. Emotional, physiological, and psychological differences among individuals contribute to differences in voice quality. Fairbanks (1959) states:

Its sources of variation lie in the generation of the vocal-fold tone and in the transmission of the tone through the vocal channel. [P. 170.]

One may note in the voice of a single speaker variations in harshness, breathiness, hoarseness, and nasality. The prominence of any of these deviations will vary significantly in relation to the physical and emotional states of the individual.

Development of Speech. The child is equipped, through biological heredity, to make all the muscular and nervous adjustments necessary to walking and talking. With growth and stimulation a greater variety of prelinguistic utterances occur. As he reacts to people and to objects in his environment, words related to these people and objects take on meaning. Thus, it might be said that a child's language development appears as a result of the interaction between him and his environment, of which language is a part. Karlin (1958) has further emphasized that:

From a phylogenetic point of view, speech is the newest of man's skills. For its normal development one must have a normal functioning brain, adequate hearing, normal peripheral anatomical structures used in speech, and also a stimulating environment. [P. 370.]

The idea that speech is a form of behavior that has to be learned indicates the importance of guidance and motivation of the child during the early years when speech habits are being formed. Milisen *et al.* (1954) has developed a theory of speech learning that emphasizes good listening and a desire to communicate on the part of the individual learner. When speech is made satisfying and rewarding to the child, he will get satisfaction from speaking and will engage in more speaking activities. The amount of speaking a child does is extremely important to those concerned with his training. Babies who show the most rapid development of speech sounds are the ones who coo and babble the most and who get attention from their parents through these vocal expressions. The teacher who wants to improve a child's speech will first try to motivate him to talk as much as possible and to secure satisfaction and enjoyment from talking. This, however, does not mean that no other guidance will be needed; there are some things that the child should be encouraged to do and some things that he should not do.

Speech Disorders. Speech is produced by the movements of the organs of articulation, that is, the jaws, lips, tongue, and soft palate. Any failure of these organs to make the correct movements may result in an articulatory defect. A child's speech is closely associated with his aspirations, his attitudes, and his feelings. Speech is part of his general behavior patterns. It can never be separated from the *self*. Anything that affects a child's well-being will also affect his speech. Thus, the child who is having difficulty with his speech may also be struggling with other problems.

Disorders of speech may result from organic defects or conditions such as cleft palate, cerebral palsy, nasal obstruction, muscle paralysis, and laryngeal difficulties. Speech and language disorders have been classified by Karlin (1958) as follows:

(1) Delayed speech—retardation in acquisition and use of words
(2) Articulatory disorders—the distortion, omission, and substitution of consonant sounds
(3) Voice disorders—the absence of voice or abnormal production of the qualities (intensity, pitch, or melody) of voice
(4) Cluttering—rapid speech, associated with slurring and distortion of sounds
(5) Stuttering—disorganization of the rhythmic flow of speech
(6) Aphasia—disorders of linguistic symbolization [P. 372.]

A broad twofold classification of speech problems might differentiate between (1) those that are fundamentally organic in origin, and that are known as physiological defects, and (2) those that are psychological in origin and known as functional or psychogenic disorders. Accurate classification of speech disorders into special types is not always possible. The etiology of a particular disorder may be organic in nature, as would be the case of a disorder that appeared as a result of injury to certain parts of the upper temporal lobe of the brain or the lower part of the frontal lobe (Broca's area). A case with which the senior author is familiar illustrates this. A college student slipped, fell, and injured his head. Although the fall was not fatal, it did damage his brain to the extent that he was unable to speak words although he could recall words and their meaning and could actually write them. This condition is known as motor aphasia. There was a slow but gradual improvement.

Often a speech difficulty that is strictly organic in origin becomes functional in nature as a result of the way the subject reacts to the difficulty. In cases where he reacts with intense fear, or perhaps even with a feeling of satisfaction, the condition may tend to persist or even become more severe. Functional disorders may, on the other hand, appear without any particular organic basis. The child who finds lisping a source of satisfaction may continue to lisp. This may eventually become habitual and such a part of the total personality that it might come to be wrongly regarded as organic as well as functional.

There will be no attempt here to organize speech disorders into a particular classification. Special consideration will be given to major defects found among school children. The following types will be presented: (1) articulatory defects, (2) stuttering, (3) special voice disorders (dysphonias; namely, nasality, huskiness, and harshness). Other types of disorders that should be mentioned are delayed speech, non-talking (aphonia), aphasia (loss or impairment of ability of expression or of comprehending language because of brain injury), and defects due to a cleft palate or cleft lip. Speech defects associated with hearing loss and cerebral palsy will not be considered since they are treated elsewhere.

Prevalence of Speech Difficulties. The number of children with speech defects is almost as large as the total of those with all other types of handicaps combined. However, the incidence of speech difficulties varies considerably from school to school, depending in a large measure upon the standards used for identifying speech-handicapped pupils. One of the most comprehensive surveys of speech problems was the New England survey conducted by nurses, teachers, doctors, and others (Pronovost, 1951). From this survey of 87,288 children speech problems were found among 7.8 per cent. According to a report of the American Speech and Hearing Association Committee on the Midcentury White House Conference on Children and Youth (1952), a minimum of 5 per cent of the school-age population (ages five to twenty-one) have serious defects of speech or a hearing condition with which a speech defect is associated.

According to the results of a survey conducted by a Committee on Legislation of the American Speech and Hearing Association, 5 per cent of school-age children had defective speech (1959). The Committee estimated that in the year 1960 at least 3,000,000 children in the United States would require remedial attention. The results of this report are summarized in Table 7–1. Johnson (1959) estimates that if all children who would benefit from both speech and hearing services were included, the per cent would be approximately doubled.

TABLE 7–1

Estimated Number and Per Cent of School-Age Children per 10,000 with Each Type of Speech or Hearing Problem

Type of Problem	Number of Children	Per Cent of Children
Articulation	300	3.0
Stuttering	100	1.0
Voice	10	.1
Cleft-palate speech	10	.1
Cerebral palsy speech	10	.1
Retarded speech development	20	.2
Speech problems due to hearing impairment	50	.5

SOURCE: American Speech and Hearing Association (1959).

It will be noted that articulation problems comprise the largest number with speech problems due to hearing impairment being second largest. It is likely that among children with less severe or moderate speech problems this per cent would more than double, while certain other speech problems would not increase so much as a result of more severe screening.

Over 75 per cent of the speech problems among secondary school students relate to consonant and vowel production. These articulation errors may be classified as being largely functional in nature. However, some speech problems may result from irregular teeth, malocclusions, or other organic factors.

The Non-verbal Child. If the teacher or clinician is not familiar with the many problems that arise that involve speech, he is likely to be very confused and present misleading diagnoses or conclusions. For in this group of "problem children" are to be found many different primary diagnoses: mental retardation, hearing defects of various types and origins, brain damage, emotional disturbances, restricted cultural opportunities, and problems of a genetic origin. The child who gives clinical evidence of retarded language development may be suffering from delayed onset of speech; however, the youngster who, "for a variety of reasons, has been unable to develop understanding of language and inner language has a more serious problem than a simple delay in speech" (McWilliams, 1959, p. 420).

The first problem faced by the speech pathologist is that of diagnosis. This should be done as early as it is possible to conduct the needed testing. It is likely that it may need to be done at different stages in the child's development. From the standpoint of the cooperation of parents as well as therapeutic work with the child, this should be done as early as the parent expresses a concern about the child's language development. In this way the pitfall of the teacher or other professional worker of acting as a comforter with the expression "He'll outgrow it" can be avoided. The period of examination should begin with as accurate a history of the child's development as can be obtained. This means that the parent should be encouraged to talk freely, and this serves as good therapy for a troubled parent as well as to provide useful information for the examiner. This should be followed by other examinations usually made in a speech clinic—audiological analysis, mental testing, visual testing, tests of motor coordination, studies of emotional reactions, and other pertinent information that may be obtained through careful interviews with parents and observations of the child.

ARTICULATORY DEFECTS AND DISORDERS

Some investigators of speech defects among children point out that most disorders are articulatory in symptom and functional in origin (Powers, 1957). Clinical evidence has increasingly stressed the emotional and personality factors that appear among children as symptoms of functional speech disorders referred to as "baby talk," "delayed speech," and "speech inhibition" (Russell, 1944).

Immature Speech. The substitution of one sound for another frequently occurs among preschool and first-grade children. Sally, a bright and alert youngster, substitutes w for l and r. Instead of "road" she says "woad," and instead of "lamb" she says "wamb." Tom says "tat" for "cat." The normal process of maturation, along with correct examples, will usually remedy these conditions. In this connection Davis (1938) has presented data relative to the ages at which most children are able to articulate certain sounds. S's and z's are listed at two age levels, since distortions in these sounds appear among many children at the eight-year level when they lose their front teeth.

3.5 years: *b, p, m, w, h*
4.5 years: *t, d, n, g, k, ng, y*
5.5 years: *f, v, s, z*
6.5 years: *zh, sh, l, th* as in *then*
8.0 years: *s, z, r, wh*

Roe and Milisen (1942) noted that substitutions tend to characterize the faulty speech of children from Grades 1 to 6. They noted that there was an improvement in the articulation of individual consonants up to the fourth grade indicating that growth and maturation eliminated many sound errors in the lower grades. They point out, however, that "sound discrimination and speech improvement are needed in all grades as a means of improving the speech of a majority of children" (p. 45).

Lisping appears especially among preschool children and in the lower grades. It includes the inability to pronounce certain letter sounds or combinations of letter sounds and a tendency to omit, transpose, or make slurring sounds. This constitutes the most characteristic feature of baby talk and is found to a greater or lesser degree among very young children. Those sounds requiring tongue-tip and fine, coordinated movements are, usually, the easiest sounds for children to produce. These include the *p, b, m,* and *o* sounds. Other sounds in order of chronological development and probably in order of difficulty of production, are *h, w, t, d, n, k, g, j, f, v, t, z, dz, l, s, z, hu,* and *r* (Mecham *et al.*, 1960, p. 159). When lisping persists beyond the age of five or six years, it might be considered abnormal. The frequency of this condition decreases rapidly in the upper grades of the school. The undue persistence of lisping may be attributed to (1) lack of practice in the proper use of the articulatory organs, due to bad models in the child's language environment; (2) damage to auditory pathways from end organs to higher centers; (3) incomplete development of the speech organs; (4) anatomical abnormalities of teeth, lips, tongue, jaws, soft or hard palate, nasal or pharyngeal cavities, etc.; (5) a general deficiency of the motor centers; or (6) poor listening habits.

Articulation Profile. A number of studies have indicated a low positive relationship between intelligence and speech defects. Craig surveyed the speech of 692 children enrolled in the first, second, third, and fourth grades of four Negro schools in Augusta, Georgia (1951). She found that at the fourth-grade level the intelligence of children with severe speech problems tended to fall below measured intellectual ability of the normal group. There is also considerable evidence that children with defective speech tend to be retarded in their schoolwork. Various studies bearing on the relation between reading ability and speech show that a substantial relationship exists between reading and speech defects.

The articulation profiles of 209 mentally retarded school children from ages seven years, three months, up to seventeen years, five months, in 18 classes in Kern County, California, were studied by Russell (1952). The IQ range of the group was from 40 to 79, with a mean IQ of 65.5. A comparison of the distribution of types of articulation errors between this group and a matched group of normal school-age children shows that, while the articulation of consonants by the mentally retarded group showed a greater incidence of error, the matched group of children manifested a greater number of errors typified by indistinct or otherwise carelessly articulated sounds. In the case of vowel errors Russell noted that there were approximately four times as many distorted sounds among the retarded than among the matched group. No significant sex differences in articulation errors were noted. The mean number of errors on the complete test for boys was 14.7, while that for the girls was 12.9.

The purpose of a study reported by FitzSimons (1958) was to determine if children with articulation problems differed from normal-speaking children in ways other than in the speech disorder syndrome. Data were gathered from two matched groups: a control group of 70 children with normal speech and an experimental group of children with diffuse, non-organic articulatory problems. Data were gathered relative to their family background, habit disorders, and educational factors. In addition, projective and non-projective test results were analyzed for both groups.

Significantly more members of the problem group had experienced abnormal birth conditions, bottle feeding, early weaning, early implementation and accomplishment of toilet training, early occurrence of childhood diseases, and delay in both locomotion and communication attempts. A comparison of the two groups on the presence of conduct and habit disorders is shown in Table 7–2. Destructiveness, eating and food problems, fears, jealousy, nervousness, refusal to obey, showing off, shyness, sleeplessness, temper tantrums, and thumb sucking were present to a significantly greater extent among the children with articulatory disorders than among children of the control group.

Unsatisfactory school grades in health habits, work habits, and

TABLE 7–2

Comparison of Articulation and Normal Samples on Presence
of Conduct and Habit Disorders

Conduct and Habit Disorders	Articulation Sample	Normal Sample	Chi Square
Destructiveness	18	2	14.93 *
Eating and food problems	39	2	47.22 *
Enuresis	9	3	3.28
Fears	21	10	5.01 *
Fingernail biting	7	11	1.10
Hurting pets	1	0	.11
Jealousy	6	3	5.08 *
Lying	6	1	3.77
Nervousness	53	22	27.60 *
Refusal to obey	27	7	15.54 *
Showing off	30	6	21.54 *
Shyness	31	13	10.74 *
Sleeplessness	6	1	3.77
Temper tantrums	35	8	24.47 *
Thumb sucking	34	15	11.33 *

* Significant at .05 level.
SOURCE: FitzSimons (1958).

language, as well as unsatisfactory scores in reading readiness status
and reading grade placement, were significantly more frequent among
the children with articulatory disorders. An analysis of the *Children's
Apperception Test* protocols showed that the children with articulatory disorders "exceeded to a significant degree the normal group
in aggression, fears and anxieties, and perception of parents as
authoritarian. The mean number of positive outcomes was significantly greater for the normal children" (p. 485).

Behavior Patterns and Articulatory Defects. The modern conception
of speech is that the entire self is involved in speech activities. Thus,
one would expect to find a relationship between certain behavior
patterns and special speech problems. A study reported by Solomon
(1961) was designed to test the possible relationship between functional articulatory speech defects in children and certain personality
and behavior patterns. Forty-nine boys and girls with functional
defects of articulation were matched in pairs with a control group of
normals. Mothers of both groups were asked to describe their children's behavior over the past two years in the following areas of child
development and personality: (1) eating behavior, (2) sleeping behavior, (3) toilet training, (4) fears and anxieties, (5) comfort pat-

tern, (6) tension, (7) aggression, (8) dependency, and (9) peer relations. Four of the nine selected behavior areas, in addition to the over-all adjustment rating, were found to show differences between the two groups that were significant at the .01 level or better. These were sleeping, fears and anxieties, peer relations, and tension. Solomon concludes: "The speech-defective group tended to be passive children who internalized their responses and were characterized by submissiveness, timidity, and a need for approval" (p. 378).

The results of this study indicate that functional speech problems of children are not isolated phenomena but part of a total adjustive pattern. This would suggest a broadening of the speech correction program so as to include the child's behavior and adjustments at home and elsewhere.

First-grade children with severe articulatory defects were used in a study by Jenkins and Lohr (1964) designed to determine the relation between articulatory disorders and motor ability. These children were matched for age, sex, and IQ with a control group of normal-speaking children. Both groups were given the *Oseretsky Tests of Motor Proficiency*.[1] The results for the two groups were analyzed and compared for mean motor ages. The comparisons shown in Fig. 7–1 show that the control group consistently excelled the experimental group in each task. However, the wide distribution of motor quotients in both groups indicates that motor ability should be assessed separately for each individual studied.

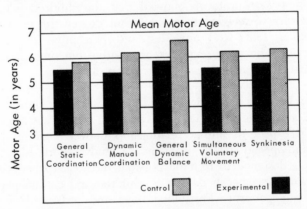

Fig. 7–1. Comparison of mean motor ages achieved by each group in each category.

[1] The *Oseretsky Tests of Motor Proficiency* are described more fully in Buros' *Mental Measurements Yearbook* (Highland Park, N.J.: Gryphon Press).

Dickson (1962) found that children who retain speech errors are inferior in motor tasks as measured by the *Oseretsky Tests of Motor Proficiency* to children who outgrow speech errors. There are also indications from his study that "mothers of children who retain speech errors tend toward emotional immaturity and instability more than mothers of children who outgrow speech errors" (p. 270).

Testing Articulation Proficiency. Barker and England (1962) developed a detailed scale for articulation measurement that includes separate categories for every consonant blend, as well as the vowel and consonant sounds. A simplified scale has also been constructed that requires less time for computation of the final score. A test form for the *Arizona Articulation Proficiency Score* is shown in Fig. 7–2. Numerical values are assigned according to their frequency of occurrence in American speech. These sounds have also been arranged in developmental order to furnish an indication of the subject's articulation age.

By use of speech charts, such as the *Arizona Articulation Proficiency Score* or the *Fletcher Chart* (1953, p. 87), differential diagnosis can be made of those speech difficulties arising from hearing loss as distinguished from those stemming from other causes.

Individual speech examinations were given by Mase (1946) to 581 boys in the fifth and sixth grades of the Trenton, New Jersey, public schools. Among this number 53 boys were found who had two or more sound substitutions and/or omissions exclusive of lisping. These boys were normal in hearing ability, physical development, emotional stability, and intelligence. They were carefully matched with control subjects, who showed no speech defects, on the basis of chronological age, mental age, social background, academic achievement, and socioeconomic status. Both groups were tested for the following factors: (1) auditory acuity, (2) memory span, (3) coordination of the muscles that control the articulators, (4) coordination of gross muscles, (5) tonal memory and rhythm, and (6) auditory articulatory discrimination.

No significant differences were found between the two groups on any of these six factors. This does not mean that these factors were not operative in causing the defect. It does mean, however, that none of the factors was present in an excessive amount, according to the tests used, among those with articulatory speech defects. A stated conclusion of this study was that a child with a functional articulatory speech defect does not necessarily lack skill in any of these six factors.

Consonants							Vowels				
Age	Phonetic Symbol	Error			Value		Age	Phonetic Symbol	Key Word	Error	Value
		I	M	F	Single	Total					
3	[n]				2.0	6.0	3	[i]	tree		2.5
	[m]				1.0	3.0		[ɪ]	pig		6.0
	[w]			▓	1.0	2.0		[ɛ]	bed		3.0
	[p]				0.5	1.5		[æ]	cat		3.0
	[h]			▓	1.0	2.0		[ɑ]	clock		2.0
4	[k]				1.0	3.0		[ʌ]	drum		1.5
	[f]				0.5	1.5		[ə]	zebra		7.0
	[b]				0.5	1.5		[u]	soup		2.5
	[g]				0.5	1.5		[ʊ]	book		1.0
5	[d]				1.0	3.0		[ou]	nose		2.0
	[j]			▓	1.0	2.0		[eɪ]	cake		2.0
6	[l]				1.5	4.5		[aɪ]	pie		3.0
	[l] blends				0.5	1.5		[au]	cow		0.5
	[ŋ]	▓			0.5	1.0		[ɝ]	bird		0.5
	[t]				2.0	6.0	6	[ɚ]	hammer		2.0
	[r]			▓	0.5	1.0		[ɛɚ]	hair		0.5
	[r] blends			▓	0.5	1.0		[aɚ]	car		0.5
	[dʒ]		▓	▓	0.5	0.5		[ɔɚ]	horse		3.5
	[tʃ]			▓	0.5	0.5		[ɪɚ]	ear		0.5
7	[ʃ]	▓		▓	0.5	0.5		[ɔ]	saw		1.5
	[z]				0.5	1.5					
	[θ]		▓	▓	0.5	0.5					
	[s]				1.0	3.0					
	[s] blends				0.5	1.5					
	[y]				0.5	1.5					
8	[ð]				1.0	3.0					
	[hw]		▓	▓	0.5	0.5					

Vowel Total _____

+Consonant Total   +_____

Grand Total   _____

100.0

Consonant Total_____   −_____

= AAPS

Indicate sound substitutions by noting the substituted sound, omissions by —, distortions by X. ▓ means not tested in that position.

Fig. 7–2. Arizona Articulation Proficiency Score.

Correction of Articulatory Defects. If the correction of any speech defect is to be effective, it must be based upon the nature and cause of such a condition. In those cases where the organic condition of the speech organs is faulty, any correctional program should first remedy that physical defect if possible. Most cleft palates can be corrected by surgery with little danger to the child. If this is done early in life, speech disorders from such a condition may usually be corrected. For young school children auditory discrimination activities related to reading may improve articulation. A study by Weaver *et al.* (1960), using the *Gates Reading Readiness Test* and articulation tests as measures of performance, confirmed a positive relationship between reading readiness and competency in speech, although a common underlying causal factor was not determined. For articulatory problems that persist beyond first grade the services of a trained speech therapist are likely to be needed for satisfactory correction.

The first essential in the correction of a defect of a functional nature is to secure the cooperation of the child. The child must develop an intense desire for better articulation. Since the careless speaker, as a rule, lacks a desire for clear enunciation, this motivation becomes one of the most important parts of the training. His friends often speak of this carelessness, and he uses it as a device for getting favorable responses. The student must be convinced that careful speech is a generally accepted index of culture and refinement; that, in every worthwhile field of business, advancement often depends upon it; and that it is usually a prerequisite for social acceptance among the majority of educated people. After a genuine desire for good speech has been established, it is comparatively easy to acquire correct habits through guidance and practice.

It has been emphasized that the child learns most of his speech through imitation. Thus, it is important for parents and teachers to practice good speech habits. The classroom teacher needs to see how his efforts may supplement those of the speech correctionist in the elimination of articulatory defects. Black and Eastman (1961) have described some of the many opportunities available in schools for the enrichment of a speech correction program in regular classrooms, through special services, the wise use of instructional materials, and within fine and applied arts. Hahn (1958) and Hinman (1960) have also indicated the scope of the teacher's responsibility in not only identifying potential speech problems in his pupils but in working carefully with his pupils in the elimination of errors and the improvement of speech.

Special Education Department, Charlotte-Mecklenburg County Schools

Children with speech problems need special help by teachers trained in this work.

STUTTERING

Speech is an unstable function. It frequently reflects the emotional and temperamental make-up of an individual. When the speech and language patterns of the child are in the formative stage, emotional and social pressures may be reflected in the type of non-fluent speech labelled as stuttering.

General Nature of Stuttering. Stuttering may be described as the repetitions, blockage, or interruption of speech sounds accompanied by physical tension. This condition is readily diagnosed. Williams *et al.* (1963) noted from a careful study of 24 college-age stutterers that the use of audio cues alone is sufficient for securing useful and reliable data on the frequency and severity of stuttering.

The young child stutterer, while prolonging a sound, may thrust his head forward and up, with the muscles of the neck strained, and display increased tension. When the child enters school, the condition may be aggravated by various pressures encountered at school. Stuttering usually is thought to have its onset between the ages of two and four, and frequently experiences in this period have a deep-seated effect upon the individual. Stuttering appears to perpetuate itself as a result of the fears and anxieties established relative to it. It differs from lisping in that it frequently increases at least up to the age of ten or eleven years. Stuttering has consistently been found to be more frequent among boys than among girls.

Data gathered on stuttering among African children attending schools in Orlando Township, Johannesburg, revealed a sex ratio of 3.28 boys to 1.00 girls (Aaron, 1962). This is fairly consistent with that reported for European stutterers. The ratio of male to female stutterers as reported by three investigators are as follows: 4.40 to 1.00 (Morgenstern, 1953), 3.09 to 1.00 (Louttit and Halls, 1963), 3.00 to 1.00 (Milisen and Johnson, 1936).

Primary and Secondary Stuttering. Bluemel (1932) advanced the notion that the development of stuttering went through two fairly well-defined stages—primary and secondary. At a later stage Johnson (1942) pointed out that it was difficult to distinguish primary stuttering from normal non-fluency. Other students found the concept of primary stuttering a confusing one. In 1957 Bluemel revised his definition of primary stuttering. In his revised definition he no longer separated stuttering into two distinct stages, but suggested that in the secondary stage the primary symptoms are not replaced, but additional symptoms appear.

Bloodstein (1961) has furnished a review of these developmental concepts with a good description of the roles of tension and frustration in the development of stuttering. He writes:

It may probably be said of almost any action which one has learned to perform that if it is approached with the conviction that it will demand all one's ability, or more, and that it is extremely important to succeed, two things are particularly likely to happen: (a) the action is likely to be begun with more muscular tension than is necessary and (b) there may be a tendency to perform the action in fragments, that is, to do part of it because the whole thing appears too difficult. It is just such reactions of tension and fragmentation which the symptoms of stuttering appear to represent. [Pp. 71–72.]

In a study reported by Shehan *et al.* (1962) 48 secondary stutterers, ranging in age from eleven to forty-four years, were given a
sheet of paper with the following instructions: "Draw whatever you
think most adequately represents your behavior immediately *before*
(or *during*, or *after*) a moment of stuttering" (p. 131). The graphic
presentations were then studied by 12 judges—6 speech clinicians and
6 classroom teachers. The drawings, ranked on four variables,
showed a relatively high degree of tension, shame-humiliation,
sadness-dejection, and guilt feelings.

Etiology of Stuttering. In an early study comparing stuttering and
non-stuttering children, Johnson (1942) obtained information on 46
stutterers between the ages of two and nine years and a control group
of non-stutterers. His data dealt mainly with the developmental history of the two groups of children. The results showed a relatively
similar developmental history although more stutterers were present
in the families of the stutterers than of non-stutterers. A comparison
of data on the family histories of 204 stutterers with similar histories
of 204 non-stutterers furnish evidence of a possible genetic basis for
stuttering (West *et al.*, 1939). From an analysis of more than 6,000
members of family lines it was found that there were almost 6 times
as many stutterers in the stutterers' families. The parents and grandparents from these families stuttered in 14 times as many cases as in
families of non-stutterers. That some children of a family where
one of the parents is inclined to stutter develop the tendency to
stutter, while others from the family do not, might indicate that imitation alone is not a sufficient explanation for the onset of stuttering.
Apparently there may be a hereditary constitutional condition present
in some individuals that causes them to develop the habit more readily
than the average person would.

It seems unlikely, however, that a child would develop the habit
of stuttering if his general environment were completely satisfactory.
An environmental factor or condition that interferes with the development of unified motor habits coordinated with one's personal and
social habits would be unfavorable for the development of good
speech habits. The effects of a complex home condition leading to
feelings of rejection are shown in the case of a ten-year-old boy
reported by Tarrasch (1951):

A boy of ten years was referred to the clinic by the county nurse because of stammering and was treated from May until October, 1948. The
family situation was good and the school and the boy's mother both co-
operated well in treatment. During therapy it was revealed that the child's

stammering was an expression of his hostility toward his sisters and his mother because it seemed to him that the sisters were preferred to him and that he was inferior to them. He was ridiculed both at home and at school and felt rejected. His sisters were held up to him as shining examples and his school work suffered because he felt he could not compete with them.

In the treatment room the boy was able to get rid of some of his hostility through such aggressive play as shooting at targets, hammering and banging. He also found that such constructive play as building, drawing and finger painting helped release his muscular tension and speaking became easier for him. The therapist listened carefully when he attempted to speak and waited patiently until he had finished. He was never interrupted. Gradually he was able to confide in her and to tell her of his struggles at home to gain his mother's and father's respect and affection, and of his difficulty in trying to cope with the ridicule and hostility of his two sisters. It was not long before he began to realize that he had found someone who understood him and wanted to help him. With the security thus gained he was able to express himself with less fear and inhibition. The situation was much helped by the treatment of the mother who gained insight into the boy's needs and understood that he must have from her encouragement and reassurance, that he should be supported when he wanted to speak up in the presence of his sisters, and that he must not be ridiculed by them. [Pp. 235–36.]

Therapy. Based upon their theory of early childhood experiences as the background for stuttering, Wyatt and Herzan (1962) developed and investigated three principles of therapy:

(1) Therapy with a stuttering child should be initiated as soon as possible after the appearance of compulsive repetition of sounds and syllables; (2) therapeutic techniques should be specific for children of different ages and in different stages of stuttering; (3) the mother of the stuttering child should be included in the therapeutic process. [Pp. 645–46.]

Wyatt (1958) contends that therapy with young children must include both mother and child if the best results are to be obtained. Both need to undergo a learning experience. In such a case therapy consists of providing mother and child with help and experiences that will help them improve their mutual communication and adaptation rather than of "speech exercises" or drills.

In such a program mothers become co-therapists. Therapists must at all time beware of being regarded as superior mothers. Some mothers take readily to the role of co-therapists while other mothers must be trained for such a role. This second group of mothers are sometimes difficult problems and may present an almost insurmountable difficulty to therapy for the stuttering child.

The results of the pilot study by Wyatt and Herzan (1962) were most encouraging. However, it should be emphasized that the techniques employed by the therapists should be adapted to the age of the child being treated. Therapy will be more economical and effective if undertaken as soon as possible after the appearance of compulsive repetitions in a child's speech. For preventive purposes teachers, therapists, and others should be aware of the impact of the child of his separation from his mother during the second or third year, when language is being acquired. They should also be aware of the seriousness of separation from the mother in the case of the dependent child when he first enters school. A psychodynamically oriented theory of remedial work with stuttering children and their mothers can be carried out in the kindergarten and elementary school, provided the therapist has adequate psychological training and experience in working with children of different ages and with adults, and provided he can enlist the cooperation of the school administration and teachers in permitting individual treatment.

SPECIAL VOICE DEFECTS

A good speaking voice should be loud enough to meet the needs of the ordinary speaking situation, should be of a pitch appropriate to the age and sex of the individual, have appropriate resonance (nasality), be clear, and have some variation in intensity and pitch.

Nasality results from the excess passage of air through the nasal cavities. The structure that effects the closure is the *uvula*, or soft palate, which is further aided in the direct partial closure by air pressure, which may effect a more complete closure. When, therefore, the lips are not firmly closed (or the tongue and palate as the case may be), this pressure will not exist and the closure of the nasal passage is consequently incomplete. Thus, air passes through the nasal passage and, during the period when sounds are made, produces nasality. If, on the other hand, the lips are firmly closed for the sound of *p* or *b*, there will be no nasality nor will the preceding or following vowel be nasalized. Practice in the precise, delicate, and effective movements of the muscles involved in pronunciation is the best procedure for correcting nasality.

Voices that are not clear in tone are sometimes referred to as harsh or husky. Harsh voice is generally considered in relation to excessive muscular strain and effort involved in voice production. This viewpoint is based upon clinical observations and reports of fatigue following excessive speaking by individuals with such a voice (Curtis, 1956, p. 177). Such conditions may also result from some organic defect in the vocal folds themselves or in the muscles that control them. The developmental causes of such deficiencies or irregularities may be hereditary.

DELAYED SPEECH

The normal range of time for speech development has been suggested as a result of a number of studies bearing on this problem. However, it is not possible to state a precise time at which "delay is significant." Morley *et al.* (1955) reported data on the main conditions accounting for delayed speech in 278 children referred to them supposedly for this condition. These causes are given in Table 7–3.

TABLE 7–3

Causes of Delayed Speech in 278 Children

Cause		Number
Deafness		110
Developmental aphasia		72
Transient	49	
Prolonged	23	
Mental deficiency		71
Cerebral palsy		22
Mental illness		3

SOURCE: After Morley *et al.* (1955).

In a continuing study of 1,000 children from all social classes in Newcastle (England) from which the data for Table 7–3 were obtained, there were 4 children at the age of six with delayed speech, and 3 of these were mentally defective. This observation supports materials presented in Chapter 3 relative to the close relation between speech development and mental deficiency. Even in the case of the selected data from a speech department, such as those presented in Table 7–3, the predominant position of mental retardation in the delayed development of speech may be noted.

Aphasia. Aphasia is defined by Morley *et al.* (1955) as "a breakdown in the comprehension of words giving rise to a disturbance of thought and a disorder of language" (p. 463). It is defined by Barger (1953) as a generic term "Indicating faulty functioning of one or more faculties in the cerebral areas concerned with specialized language culture" (p. 167). In children the process is primarily a failure to develop the central process of speech. The group of children classified by Morley et al. as aphasic did not develop any recognizable words until two years or later, or phrases until four years or later. Even when they did develop, their development was slow and there was an obvious poverty of language. Those referred to in Table 7–3 as transient developmental aphasia developed fairly quickly and successfully after the age of four. These children were normal in intelligence and hearing and showed no evidence of cerebral palsy. It is with the group of children classified as prolonged aphasia that careful diagnosis and treatment is especially important. It seems likely that many children in this group have a real cerebral disorder. With these children overanxiety on the part of parents or teachers may retard rather than assist the child in his speech development. If the use of expressive speech is delayed beyond the age of six years, the child's personal and educational development will be seriously impaired.

The condition appears with varying degrees of intensity and may account for more educational deviation than has ordinarily been recognized. It appears among boys eight times more frequently than among girls. Berry and Eisenson (1956) have pointed out that "the child with a hearing loss will respond more consistently to sounds, if they are loud enough to be heard, than will the aphasic child" (p. 422). Aphasia rather than mental retardation is to be suspected in relation to the following characteristics: (1) easily distracted, (2) greater persistence and perseveration, (3) emotional lability, and (4) lower frustration tolerance.

The case of A. H., reported by Morley et al. (1955), illustrates the nature of expressive aphasia:

A. H., aged 10, is the second child of intelligent professional parents. His birth was normal and general development satisfactory. Words began at 20 months, but phrases did not follow until after 4. At 6 he still avoided the use of verbs, and, though willing to tell a story with gusto, got it thoroughly muddled through omitting, transposing, and mispronouncing his words. He has normal hearing and comprehension, and at 8 years and 10 months his IQ was 120.

He is, however, a tense, restless boy, and recovery may have been delayed by his personality and the parents' desire for rapid improvement and academic success. . . . When he knows exactly what he wants to say his speech is sensible and clear; when he cannot get the word or cannot get the right one, distortions and substitutions occur and speech is jumbled and confused. In writing he expresses himself much more clearly. We consider this boy has an expressive aphasia, perhaps arising in part from a poor auditory memory for speech. [P. 466.]

Damage to the Central Nervous System. There are certain speech problems associated with bulbar poliomyelitis, cerebral palsy, and other impairments involving the central nervous system. (The relation of speech problems to cerebral palsy will be presented in Chapter 14.) Speech training for such children consists primarily of modified therapy applied to the muscles used in speaking. Bulbar polio may affect the muscles of breathing, although this speech difficulty has become far less frequent with better preventive measures against poliomyelitis.

MALFORMATIONS

Cleft Palate or Cleft Lip. Children with cleft palate or cleft lips make up a significant group of those who may have speech problems. The American Dental Association estimates that 1 child in every 700 has this condition. The upper lip may have a bilateral or unilateral cleft. The hard or soft palate may be involved in varying degrees. The amount and kind of speech disturbance is directly related to the extent and location of the malformation. When the soft palate alone is involved, the sounds that will be affected are those of *k*, *g*, and *ng*. If the upper gum ridge and upper lip are also involved, such sounds as *b*, *m*, *p*, *t*, *s*, and *z* will be affected.

Data presented by Tretsven (1963) show the incidence of cleft palate varies with different groups. The results, presented in Table 7–4, show that cleft palate is relatively high among Montana Indians.

TABLE 7–4

Incidence of Cleft Lip and Palate for Different Groups

Study Subjects	Incidence
Tretsven (1963) Montana Indians	1:276
(1956–1960) Montana non-Indians	1:583
Wisconsin (1952)	1:770
Los Angeles Hospital (1955)	1:1,030
U.S. Children's Bureau (1953)	1:1,000
California (1955)	1:851
Pennsylvania (1951)	1:750

SOURCE: After Tretsven (1963).

The results for the other groups are somewhat consistent with estimates of the American Dental Association.

Training in articulation will tend to improve generally the speech of the patient with a cleft palate. Berry (1949) suggests that a lingual anomaly is closely associated with palatal clefts. She observed that the rapidity of the tongue movement of cleft-palate children was below normal. In a test of the mobility of the tip of the tongue less than 2 per cent of the children could produce a tongue tap or trill. Although Dingman (1963) indicates that initial corrective surgery on a cleft lip is now being generally done at ten to fourteen days of age and first stage surgery on a cleft palate is being carried out at eighteen to twenty months of age, a careful dental program is needed for treatment of carious teeth and possible misalignment; and a speech evaluation and correction may still become necessary at a later date.

Other Malformations. For speech to be normal, the upper jaw must protrude slightly in front of the lower when the jaws are closed. In case the lower jaw does not come forward fairly close to the upper, or if the lower jaw protrudes in front of the upper, certain sounds will be defective. Sometimes the formation of the teeth will prevent the jaws from coming together as they normally should and defective speech sounds are the result. Such conditions may be treated by surgery or through bracing the teeth.

ACCEPTANCE

The hypothesis has been brought forth that the child with a speech problem is generally more frequently rejected by his peers than other children. There is also the question of acceptance by parents, especially the mother, during the early years. Several recent studies have provided useful materials dealing with problems of acceptance. These studies are notable in that acceptance will have an important bearing on the child's personal development.

Parental Acceptance or Rejection. Clinical observations, based upon individual and group psychotherapy, suggest that one of the strongest feelings of stutterers is that of rejection by their parents, especially the mother. McCarthy (1960) noted that parents of stutterers are tense and perfectionistic, perhaps as a disguise for rejection.

Kinstler (1961) attacked this problem through a maternal attitude scale, developed in an attempt to differentiate between the attitudes of mothers of stutterers and of non-stutterers. The scale was administered to a group of 30 mothers of male stutterers and a control group of 30 mothers of male non-stutterers. Statistically significant differences between the two groups of mothers were obtained. The following conclusions were derived from this study:

(a) Mothers of young male stutterers reject their children covertly far more but overtly far less than do the mothers of normal speakers. (b) Mothers of stutterers accept their children covertly less and overtly only slightly less than do mothers of normal speakers. [P. 155.]

The results of this study have important implications for those attempting speech therapy for children with speech problems. The problem of enlisting the cooperative efforts of the parents both overtly and covertly is most important, especially in light of the fact that speech difficulties (especially stuttering) are so closely related to the child's interpersonal relations at home.

Acceptance-Rejection by Peers. The child with a speech problem is generally presumed to be more frequently rejected by his peers than other children. A study reported by Woods and Carrow (1959) was designed to test this assumption through administering a sociometric test employing the criteria of play, work, and friendship to 1,524 elementary public school children in Grades 2 through 5. A comparison of the choice-rejection scores of the speech-defective and non-speech-defective children are presented in Table 7–5. The

TABLE 7–5

Mean Choice-Rejection Scores on Criteria 1 (play),
2 (work), and 3 (friendship)

Criterion	Group	Grade			
		2	3	4	5
1	Speech-defective	98.30	97.86	99.71	93.00
	Non-speech-defective	100.83	100.42	100.98	100.40
2	Speech-defective	100.48	98.90	101.86	93.67
	Non-speech-defective	100.17	100.36	101.21	100.69
3	Speech-defective	98.82	97.79	99.00	91.11
	Non-speech-defective	100.93	100.54	101.29	100.71

SOURCE: Woods and Carrow (1959).

results showed that the speech-defective children made lower mean scores than the non-speech-defective on all three criteria, except

Criterion 2 (work), in Grades 2 and 4. The results of this study support the hypothesis that the child with a speech defect tends to be less acceptable to his peers in the elementary school than the non-speech-defective child. The acceptance in the case of work in the classroom indicates that the child who makes high grades may be cultivated as a workmate, although he is given little or no consideration as a playmate at recess.

EVALUATING PROGRESS OF THE CHILD

Two methods have been described by Bangs (1961) for studying the progress of children with language or speech problems: (1) clinical judgments and (2) psychometric retest. The interval of time between re-evaluations will depend upon the nature of the language difficulty or problem and the needs of the child.

Clinical Evaluation Record. Report cards are usually thought of as a means of telling parents how well their children are doing in school. Such reporting also furnishes the teacher or clinician with needed information about the progress of the child and his assets and liabilities. Norms on the behavior of children at various age levels serve as a useful reference for teachers, clinicians, and speech pathologists.

Psychometric Retest. The clinical evaluation record plus the psychometric battery of tests used as a retest device will furnish data on each child's progress. The scarcity of different forms of standardized tests suitable for preschool children with language difficulties has made it necessary to use the same battery for retest purposes. The value of cumulative data for diagnostic and training purposes has been demonstrated by many speech teachers and speech pathologists.

Case history taking and medical reports are essential, especially in severe or complicated cases. However, there is a need for additional information as a basis for therapy and educational guidance. For example, the clinician or teacher needs information relative to social maturity, oral language usage, visual-motor perceptual skills, work habits, dependence-independence, and self concept. The *Case History Questionnaire* developed for use in the speech and hearing clinic of the University of Georgia, presented in Fig. 7–3, furnishes a relatively complete developmental history of the child. Such a history when correlated with the nature and history of the speech problem provides valuable information to the therapist. Case-study histories

CASE HISTORY QUESTIONNAIRE
Speech and Hearing Clinic, University of Georgia

I. ROUTINE IDENTIFICATION

NAME OF CASE_____ AGE_____ BIRTHDATE _____ SEX_____
NAME OR PERSON GIVING INFORMATION_____ DATE_____
ADDRESS OF CASE _____ PHONE _____
ADDRESS OF PERSON GIVING INFORMATION_____ PHONE _____

II. DESCRIPTION OF DEVIATION

1. Does he attempt to talk?_____
2. Is his speech understandable by parents?_____ By strangers?_____
3. Does he make some sounds the wrong way?_____ If so, what ones?_____
_____
4. Does he hesitate and/or repeat sounds or words a great deal?_____
5. Does he "get stuck" in attempting to say words? _____
6. Do you suspect a hearing loss?_____ Why? _____
7. Is the voice too weak?_____
8. Is the voice too high in pitch?_____ Too low? _____
9. Is the quality unpleasant?_____ If so, describe _____
10. Is the speech too fast?_____ Too slow?_____
11. Is there some physical cause for the above answers?_____
_____

III. DEVELOPMENTAL FACTORS

A. Birth History

1. What was mother's condition during pregnancy?_____
2. Was the delivery normal?_____ Prolonged?_____
   Instruments used?_____ Caesarian?_____
3. Was there evidence of injury at birth?_____ What?_____
4. Were there evidences of weakness or poor health at birth?_____
   What?_____

B. Growth

1. Was he ever a feeding problem?_____ When?_____
   How severe?_____
2. Has he increased in height normally?_____
   Has he gained weight normally?_____
3. Age of teething_____

C. Locomotion

1. Age of sitting up_____ Age of creeping_____ Age of walking_____
2. Does he seem to have normal coordination for his age?_____

D. Speech Development

1. Did he babble and coo during the first ten months?_____
2. At what age did he use single words meaningfully?_____
   Age for short sentences_____

Fig. 7–3. A case history questionnaire.

E. Social Development

1. Does he have opportunity to play with children?_____
   What ages?_____ How many?_____
2. Does he like to play with children or would he rather play alone?_____
3. At what age did he start feeding himself?_____ Dressing himself?_____
   Caring for self at the toilet?_____

IV. MEDICAL HISTORY

A. List diseases and their effects and severity:

Diseases	Ages	Severity and Effects

B. List severe injuries, ages, and effects:

Injuries	Ages	Severity and Effects

C. List operations and ages for each:

Operations	Ages

D. List kind and number of physical examinations child has had — please give doctor's name and address whenever possible:

E. A doctor's report would be appreciated — please have family physician report on the enclosed blank:

Fig. 7–3. A case history questionnaire (*continued*).

V. SCHOOL HISTORY (FOR CHILDREN)

A. Status

1. Age entered_____ 2. Present grade_____
3. Are there any subjects that are especially difficult for him?_____
4. Has he been a serious behavior problem any time at school?_____
5. With reference to #3, what subjects have been difficult?_____
_____

B. Attendance

1. Has attendance been regular?_____
2. How many schools has he attended?_____

C. Speech Correction

1. Has he received any special work on speech or hearing in the school?_____
2. How much or how long?_____
3. What was done?_____

VI. Home

A. Family

1. Father's name_____
2. Mother's name_____
3. Brothers' names and ages_____
_____
4. Sisters' names and ages_____
_____
5. Others in household_____
_____

B. Housing

1. Underline the type of dwelling you have:
   House   Apartment   Other
2. How many rooms does the dwelling have?_____
3. Is it shared with another family?_____
4. Do you own the home?_____

C. Neighborhood

1. Encircle all words that best describe your neighborhood – add any others that you wish:

   residential   business   crowded   rural

   poor   average   well-to-do

2. Encircle all words which best describe the play facilities for your child:

   nearby playground   large yard   small yard   no yard

   several children near own age   some children near own age

   no children near own age   playroom in house

   playmates of same sex   playmates of opposite sex

   many toys   some toys   few toys   no toys

Fig. 7–3. A case history questionnaire (*continued*).

furnish a sounder basis for guiding the child in his personal, social, and educational development.

SUMMARY

There are several types of speech defects and many causes of such difficulties. These have at times been classified as (1) those that are fundamentally organic in origin and (2) those that are of a psychological nature. The major defects found among schoolchildren are articulatory defects, stuttering, and voice defects. Several other types have been described in this chapter, including delayed speech and aphasia. The number of children with speech difficulties will vary considerably from school to school, depending in part upon the standards used for identifying speech-handicapped children.

Articulatory defects head the list in both the elementary school and the high school, with over 75 per cent of the speech problems among secondary school students relating to consonant and vowel production. Articulatory problems are largely functional in nature, although some are related to irregular teeth, malocclusions, or other organic factors. Prevention of most of these defects is easier than cure. Such prevention should begin during early childhood.

The solution of the problem of stuttering is an educational one, not one that is to be determined by drugs, operations, and the like. The stutterer's curriculum is of secondary importance, but the establishment of more adequate speech habits and healthier social attitudes is of major consequence. This problem is closely identified with that of mental hygiene. Despite his handicap, the stuttering child should be made to feel that he is an integral member of the school body. His talents and abilities should be utilized to make him a useful citizen, to create respect for him on the part of others, and to inspire self-confidence.

CHAPTER REFERENCES

AARON, MYRTLE L. (1962). The nature and incidence of stuttering among a Bantu group of school-going children. *J. Speech & Hearing Disord.,* 27:116–28.

AMERICAN SPEECH AND HEARING ASSOCIATION COMMITTEE ON LEGISLATION (1959). Need for speech pathologists. *ASHA,* 1:138–39, 161–67.

AMERICAN SPEECH AND HEARING ASSOCIATION COMMITTEE ON THE MID-CENTURY WHITE HOUSE CONFERENCE ON CHILDREN AND YOUTH (1952).

Speech disorders and speech correction. *J. Speech & Hearing Disord.*, 17:129–37.

BANGS, TINA E. (1961). Evaluating children with language delay. *J. Speech & Hearing Disord.*, 26:6–18.

BARGER, W. C. (1953). An experimental approach to aphasic and to non-reading children. *Amer. J. Orthopsychiat.*, 23:158–70.

BARKER, JANET, and ENGLAND, G. (1962). A numerical measure of articulation: further developments. *J. Speech & Hearing Disord.*, 27:23–27.

BERRY, MILDRED F. (1949). Lingual anomalies associated with palatal clefts. *J. Hearing & Speech Disord.*, 14:359–62.

BERRY, MILDRED F., and EISENSON, J. (1956). *Speech disorders.* New York: Appleton-Century-Crofts.

BLACK, MARTHA E., and EASTMAN, M. (1961). Utilizing public school resources in speech correction programs. *Except. Child.*, 28:205–11.

BLOODSTEIN, O. (1961). The development of stuttering: III. Theoretical and clinical implications. *J. Speech & Hearing Disord.*, 26:67–82.

BLUEMEL, C. S. (1932). Primary and secondary stuttering. *Quart. J. Speech,* 18:187–200.

BLUEMEL, C. S. (1957). *The riddle of stuttering.* Danville, Ill.: Interstate.

CRAIG, R. SUE (1951). The nature and frequency of speech defects among first, second, third, and fourth grade children in four negro schools of Augusta, Georgia. Unpublished doctor's dissertation, Northwestern Univer.

CURTIS, J. F. (1956). Disorders of voice. In W. JOHNSON (ed.), *Speech handicapped school children.* (Rev. ed.) New York: Harper & Row.

DAVIS, IRENE P. (1938). The speech aspects of reading readiness. *Newer practices in reading in the elementary school.* Seventeenth Yearbook, Department of Elementary School Principals. Washington, D.C.: National Education Association. Pp. 282–89.

DICKSON, S. (1962). Differences between children who spontaneously outgrow and children who retain functional articulation errors. *J. Speech & Hearing Res.*, 5:263–71.

DINGMAN, R. O. (1963). Modern concepts of the treatment of cleft lip and cleft palate. *Rehabilit. Lit.*, 24:144–46.

FAIRBANKS, G. (1960). *Voice and articulation drillbook,* 2nd ed. New York: Harper & Row.

FITZSIMONS, RUTH M. (1958). Developmental, psychosocial, and educational factors in children with articulation problems. *Child Developm.*, 29:481–89.

FLETCHER, H. (1953). *Speech and hearing in communication.* New York: Van Nostrand.

HAHN, ELISE (1958). Speech defects are every teacher's responsibility. *NEA J.*, 47:39–41.

HINMAN, MARY P. (1960). Speech education—the teacher and the specialist. *NEA J.,* 49:24–25.

JENKINS, EDNA, and LOHR, FRANCES E. (1964). Severe articulation disorders and motor ability. *J. Speech & Hearing Disord.,* 29:286–92.

JOHNSON, W. (1942). A study of the onset and development of stuttering. *J. Speech & Hearing Disord.,* 7:251–57.

JOHNSON, W. (1959). *Children with speech and hearing impairment.* U.S. Office of Education Bulletin, No. 5. Washington, D.C.: U.S. Government Printing Office.

KARLIN, I. (1958). Speech and language handicapped children. *J. Dis. Child.,* 95:370–76.

KINSTLER, D. B. (1961). Covert and overt maternal rejection in stuttering. *J. Speech & Hearing Disord.,* 26:145–55.

LOUTTIT, C., and HALLS, E. C. (1936). Survey of speech defects among public school children in Indiana. *J. Speech & Hearing Disord.,* 1:73–80.

MCCARTHY, DOROTHEA (1960). Language development. *Monogr. Soc. Res. Child Developm.,* 25:5–6.

MCWILLIAMS, BETTY J. (1959). The non-verbal child. *Except. Child.,* 25:420–23, 440.

MARTMER, E. E. (1959). *The child with a handicap.* Springfield, Ill.: Charles C Thomas. P. 133.

MASE, D. J. (1946). Etiology of articulatory speech defects. *Contributions to Education,* No. 921. New York: Teachers Coll., Columbia Univer., Bureau of Publications.

MECHAM, M. J., BERKO, M. J., and BERKO, F. G. (1960). *Speech therapy in cerebral palsy.* Springfield, Ill.: Charles C Thomas.

MILISEN, R., and JOHNSON, W. (1936). A comparative study of stutterers, former stutterers, and normal speakers whose handedness has been changed. *Arch. Speech,* 1:61–86.

MILISEN, R. L., *et al.* (1954). The disorders of articulation: a systematic clinical and experimental approach. *J. Speech & Hearing Disord.* Monograph Supplement No. 4.

MORGENSTERN, J. J. (1953). Psychological and social factors in children's stammering. Unpublished doctor's dissertation, Univer. of Edinburgh.

MORLEY, MURIEL, COURT, D., MILLER, H., and GARSIDE, R. F. (1955). Delayed speech and developmental aphasia. *Brit. med. J.* (Aug. 20), pp. 463–67.

POWERS, MARGARET H. (1957). Functional disorders of articulation—symptomatology and etiology. In L. E. TRAVIS (ed.), *Handbook of speech pathology.* New York: Appleton-Century-Crofts.

PRONOVOST, W. (1951). A survey of services for the speech and hearing handicapped in New England. *J. Speech & Hearing Disord.,* 16:148–56.

ROE, VIVIAN, and MILISEN, R. (1942). The effect of maturation upon defective articulation in elementary grades. *J. Speech & Hearing Disord.*, 7:37–50.

RUSSELL, H. K. (1952). *Articulation profile of 209 mentally retarded children.* Seminar in Special Education Report, San Francisco State College.

SHEEHAN, J. G., CORTESE, P. A., and HADLEY, R. G. (1962). Guilt, shame, and tension in graphic projections of stuttering. *J. Speech & Hearing Disord.*, 27:129–39.

SOLOMON, A. L. (1961). Personality and behavior patterns of children with functional defects of articulation. *Child Developm.*, 32:731–37.

TARRASCH, HERTHA (1951). Results of child guidance work in two county clinics. *J. Child Psychiat.*, 2:229–43.

TRETSVEN, VENUS E. (1963). Incidence of cleft lip and palate in Montana Indians. *J. Speech & Hearing Disord.*, 28:52–57.

WEAVER, C. H., FURBEE, CATHERINE, and EVERHART, R. W. (1960). Paternal occupational class and articulatory defects in children. *J. Speech & Hearing Disord.*, 25:171–75.

WEST, R., NELSON, S., and BERRY, MILDRED (1939). The heredity of stuttering. *Quart. J. Speech*, 25:23–30.

WILLIAMS, D. E., WARK, MICHELLE, and MINIFIE, F. D. (1963). Ratings of stuttering by audio, visual, and audiovisual cases. *J. Speech & Hearing Res.*, 6:91–100.

WOODS, SR. FRANCES J., and CARROW, SR. MARY A. (1959). The choice-rejection status of speech defective children. *Except. Child.*, 25:279–83.

WYATT, GERTRUDE L. (1958). A developmental crisis theory of stuttering. Vol. 1. *Language and Speech.* Teddington, Middlesex, England: Robert Draper, Ltd.

WYATT, GERTRUDE L., and HERZAN, HELEN M. (1962). Therapy with stuttering children and their mothers. *Am. J. Orthopsychiat.*, 32:645–59.

SELECTED READINGS

BARBARA, D. A. (1958). *Stuttering—a psychodynamic approach.* London: Hutchinson.

DELACATO, C. H. (1962). *The diagnosis and treatment of speech and reading problems.* Springfield, Ill.: Charles C Thomas.

JOHNSON, W. (1961). *Stuttering and what you can do about it.* Minneapolis: Univer. of Minnesota Press.

JOHNSON, W., DARLEY, F. L., and SPRIESTERBACH, D. C. (1963). *Diagnostic methods in speech pathology.* New York: Harper & Row.

MORLEY, MURIEL (1957). *The development and disorders of speech in childhood.* Edinburgh: E. & S. Livingstone.

MURPHY, A. T., and FITZSIMONS, RUTH M. (1960). *Stuttering and personality dynamics: play therapy, projective therapy, and counseling.* New York: Ronald.

TRAVIS, L. E. (ed.) (1957). *Handbook of speech pathology.* New York: Appleton-Century-Crofts.

8

DEFECTIVE HEARING

HEARING: ITS NATURE AND PROBLEMS

Those who hear spoken language and enjoy music and other sounds are fortunate. Until recently one who could not hear was often condemned to a lonely existence. There were few schools available to him. He was often referred to as a "dummy"—or as "deaf and dumb," with the emphasis implicitly on "dumb." It was not known that he could learn to talk, or that his speech impairment was largely due to inability to hear.

There is no accurate record of just how many children have significant hearing losses, but it is generally estimated that there are well over 500,000. Some estimates place the number as considerably over 1,000,000. Concerning the estimates, McCabe (1963) states: "Extensive screening programs among school children have demonstrated an incidence of 3 per cent to 6 per cent for mild to moderate hearing loss. The number of children requiring auditory education has been estimated at 0.2 per cent to 0.4 per cent" (p. 470). The great majority of hard-of-hearing children have sufficient hearing to enable them to learn to communicate in a natural manner, that is, by listening and speaking. Their hearing losses vary from mild or moderate to severe. Most of them are receiving their education in the regular classroom, frequently unaware of their difficulties.

Definition and Classification. Who are the hard of hearing? Or, more specifically, just where is the line to be drawn between the normal, the hard of hearing, and the deaf? It is highly important to both researchers and educators to have a workable definition of the deaf and hard of hearing. The Committee on Hearing of the National Research Council has prepared a general classification of hearing losses based upon a person's hearing level—his threshold or lowest point at which he begins to detect sound stated in decibels. The scale of degrees of hearing loss is shown in Table 8–1. While such

TABLE 8–1

Scale of Degrees of Hearing Loss

Class	Name	Loss for Speech, in Decibels *	Remarks
A	Normal	Not more than 15 in *worse* ear	Both ears within normal limits; no difficulty with faint speech
B	Near normal	More than 15 but not more than 30 in *either* ear	Has difficulty only with faint speech
C	Mild impairment	More than 30 but not more than 45 in *better* ear	Has difficulty with normal speech but not with loud speech
D	Serious impairment	More than 45 but not more than 60 in *better* ear	Has difficulty even with loud speech
E	Severe impairment	More than 60 but not more than 90 in *better* ear	Can hear only amplified speech
F	Profound impairment	More than 90 in *better* ear	Cannot understand even amplified speech
G	Total loss of hearing in *both* ears		Cannot hear any sound

* The classes are defined by "decibels loss of hearing for speech." Until suitable technical facilities for direct measurement by speech audiometry are available, the loss of hearing for speech shall be calculated from pure-tone air-conduction measurements by averaging the hearing losses at 500, 1,000, and 2,000 cycles per second, or at 512, 1,024, and 2,048 cycles per second if the available audiometers are so calibrated. A person should be classified one class lower than indicated by the average value if, with an average loss of 10 decibels or more, his hearing loss for any one of the three frequencies is greater by 25 decibels (or more) than the least of his three losses.

data give information that may be useful, especially for some physiological problems, they do not furnish useful data to clinical and educational psychologists concerning the effects that a sensory impairment has on a particular pupil's behavior and learning. A wide disparity in definitions of a non-quantitative nature have been offered, some of which are based upon the ability to speak and understand speech;

others are based upon categories of functional and non-functional hearing status. The set of definitions suggested by Wooden (1963) furnish a useful classification that includes several important and inclusive personal variables.

The *deaf* are those in whom the sense of hearing, either with or without a hearing aid, is insufficient for interpreting speech. The *prelanguage deaf* are those in whom deafness *preceded* a firm establishment of language and speech. The *postlanguage deaf* are those in whom deafness occurred *after* good language and speech had been acquired.

The *hard of hearing* are those in whom the loss of hearing is educationally significant, but whose residual hearing is sufficient for interpreting speech with—if not without—a hearing aid.

A *natural-language group* is one composed of the hard of hearing and those postlanguage deaf who have retained their normally acquired speech and language. [P. 344.]

How the Ear Works.   Sounds have their beginning as vibrations of air waves. The outer ear is the mechanism for collecting the vibrations and directing them to the inner ear, where nerve impulses are set up and transmitted to the brain. The ears are delicate organs, extremely sensitive and readily susceptible to disorders of one sort or another. Once a loss of hearing occurs in one or both ears, there is great danger of a permanent defect. Progress toward deafness may be slow, but it gradually approaches serious impairment. Of course, not all forms of deafness have this history. Some are congenital, that is, present at birth. The exact causes of some types of hearing loss cannot be determined.

The ear consists of three parts: the outer, the middle, and the inner. The outer ear includes the visible part and the corridor or passageway, called the external canal. Wax glands in the outer ear and canal protect the eardrum from excessive moisture or dryness. A screen of hairs at the entrance of the canal protects the ear mechanism against dust and other foreign substances. At the inner end of this canal is a membrane known as the tympanum or eardrum. Beyond this membrane, in the middle ear, are found three tiny bones, or ossicles. Sound waves that enter the outer ear strike the tympanic membrane and set it vibrating. This motion causes the ossicles of the middle ear to vibrate also, concentrating the motion at a small opening at the inner end of the middle ear. The fluid in the inner ear transmits the vibrations to nerve endings in the inner ear and then to the auditory nerves. Considering the nature of sound and the physiological details of the structure of the inner ear suggests that different parts of the organ are attuned to vibrations of various frequencies or pitches.

Sound waves of slow vibration are interpreted as tones of low pitch, and sound waves of more rapid vibration are heard as tones of higher pitch. Sensitivity is greatest in the middle-tone range, where the normal human ear can identify approximately 325 different degrees of intensity of a single tone.

Auditory perception results when impulses traverse the auditory nerves to the brain. It is generally recognized that the auditory acuity of the small child is incompletely developed. As the child grows older, the mechanisms involved in hearing begin to show signs of greater maturity, and the ability to hear improves. This is a function that is closely associated with the development of voice and speech. Hearing impairments usually appear early in the life of a child. These are sometimes classified as (1) nerve deafness or (2) conductive deafness. Nerve deafness is the loss of sensitivity in the nerve endings in the inner ear; those sensitive to the higher pitched tones are usually first to be lost. Conductive deafness may result from an obstruction in the middle or outer ear. This condition affects the individual in such a manner that the sounds seem to resemble those produced by voices in an adjoining room with the door closed.

Types of Deafness. Medical science classifies types of deafness according to the part of the physiology involved. *Conductive deafness* refers to hearing difficulties involving the outer and middle ear, whereas *perceptive deafness* involves malfunctioning in the inner ear. If the difficulty arises as a result of pathology in the brain, the condition is referred to as *central deafness.* A fourth form of deafness may appear from undue emotional strain and is classified as *psychic deafness,* or *hysterical deafness.* This condition, of psychogenic origin, is very difficult to diagnose and treat medically.

An etiological classification that has been used frequently, in connection with both impaired hearing and deafness, is *congenital deafness* and *acquired deafness.* This classification is based upon time of onset, in that congenital conditions are those that are presumed to have occurred before birth, and acquired conditions those that developed after birth. Such a classification furnishes little understanding of causal factors, however. Ventry and Chaiklin (1962) employ the term "functional hearing loss" to denote "audiometric discrepancies that do not have an apparent organic etiology" (p. 251). This may mean that the examiner was unable to account for the loss on an organic basis. This also allows for the possibility that subsequent examinations with new or more refined instruments will reveal an organic condition to account for the hearing loss. Thus, the term "functional," as suggested by Ventry and Chaiklin, is not the antonym of "organic" or the synonym of "psychogenic."

Some Conditions Confused with Deafness. Conditions that may cause certain symptoms of deafness include aphasia, mental deficiency, and faulty auditory perception. A careful differential diagnosis of these conditions early in life should include an evaluation of the child's total behavior symptomatology (Myklebust, 1951). Aphasic children often give no response to sound at the pain level of intensity. Monses (1959) defines aphasia as follows: "Aphasia is the inability to use and/or understand spoken language, and is the result of damage or defect in the central nervous system" (p. 395). She warns, however, that we should always be aware of the likelihood of multiple handicaps, and that aphasia may exist along with mental retardation, deafness, emotional disturbances, or some other handicapping condition. The final determination of whether or not aphasia is present along with another condition such as deafness lies in the child's response to different teaching procedures. The aphasic deaf child will fail to learn by methods currently used in teaching oral communication to the deaf.

In sensory aphasia the child does not understand spoken language and is thus not able to use speech for communication. It is in receptive or sensory aphasia that questions relative to hearing impairment are most likely to arise, and the problem of determining such a child's auditory acuity is most difficult.

The child with psychic disturbances may "shut out" sounds in the same fashion that he fails to respond to other stimuli. This usually occurs among children with deep-seated emotional disorders and is a form of withdrawal from the world of reality, which includes sounds. In general behavior these children are very different from deaf children, however. This condition may appear very early in life and is usually attributed to undesirable or inadequate experiences. Some of the characteristics associated with psychic deafness of a child are:

1. His history reveals behavior problems rather than a problem of hearing impairment.
2. He usually has good voice quality.
3. His parents have normal hearing in most cases.
4. The child gives evidence of hearing at times at home.
5. His laughter and gait are more like those of children with normal hearing than those of hard-of-hearing and deaf children.
6. He responds to sounds of low intensity often, while showing no response to sounds of high intensity.

The mentally defective child who is not talking at the age of thirty months may be thought to be partially deaf. An example is Lonnie, whose case was called to the attention of the senior author of this book.

Lonnie was brought to my attention at the age of 32 months. It was evident from his responses to intelligence test items that he was mentally deficient. An IQ of approximately 45 was obtained from administering the *Revised Stanford-Binet Scale.*

The mother was especially concerned about Lonnie's inability to talk and had had him examined for hearing and other physical conditions on two or more occasions. Lonnie's baby sister, approximately one year of age at this time, was already beginning to form a few words and appeared to get most of the attention of the mother. Lonnie was perhaps less responsive in his motor activities and social responses than one would normally expect for a child of this age with an IQ of 45. It seems likely that an unfavorable attitude on the part of the mother toward Lonnie's condition may have aggravated the case.

Identifying the Child Who Is Hard of Hearing. Studies by Curry (1954), Geyer and Yankauer (1956), and Kodman (1956) show that classroom teachers incorrectly identify the normal-hearing child as well as those with mild to severe hearing loss. In a later study by Kodman, Schneck, Stockdell, Thompson, and Spies (1958) a comparison was made of parents, teachers, and audiometers as detectors of school children who needed medical and/or educational attention for a mild to severe hearing loss. The results showed that audiometric examinations were far superior to either parents or teachers in the identification of such children.

Another study by Kodman *et al.* (1959) took into consideration socioeconomic status of the parents in judgments of parents, teachers, and audiometric tests for identifying children with hearing loss. Two samples of pupils were drawn from different occupational and income groups—the occupational groupings of the two samples are shown in Table 8–2. In Table 8–3 is shown the number of hearing loss pupils identified correctly by the three methods under study. The criterion for a hearing loss was two or more thresholds 15 decibels or greater in either or both ears, by pure-tone audiometry for the octave frequencies from 250–8,000 cycles. Parents from the two socioeconomic levels and the classroom teachers were significantly inferior to pure-tone audiometry in identifying elementary school children with mild to severe hearing losses. It would seem that while parents and teachers are not accurate in identifying such children, their ratings or recommendations relative to children with hearing losses should be sought—partially as a screening device.

TABLE 8–2

Classification of the Two Samples Based on Father's Occupation

Categories	Percentage Values	
	Garrison Sample	Caywood Sample
I. Professional	1.5	31.1
II. Clerical and Sales	1.8	22.4
III. Skilled Labor	18.7	21.9
IV. Service	2.7	4.8
V. Farming	17.8	2.2
VI. Semiskilled Labor	14.8	5.7
VII. Unskilled Labor	6.5	1.8
VIII. Unemployed	15.1	9.2
IX. Unclassified	21.1	0.8

SOURCE: Kodman *et al.* (1959).

TABLE 8–3

Number of Children Identified as Having Hearing Losses by the Three Methods Used

	Number	Per Cent
A. Garrison sample (N 427)		
Audiometer	45	10.5
Teachers	7	1.6
Parents	9	2.1
B. Caywood sample (N 289)		
Audiometer	24	8.3
Teachers	4	1.4
Parents	5	1.7

SOURCE: Kodman *et al.* (1959).

Since any effective educational program for hard-of-hearing children presupposes an identification of such children, teachers should be on the lookout for certain symptoms that characterize the hard-of-hearing child. The following check list of symptoms may be helpful in finding children who are in need of more careful examination:

1. Behavior
   a) Tilts head at an angle to get better sound
   b) Listless and inattentive
   c) Fails to respond when questioned
   d) Shows defects in speech, especially where phonetics are important
   e) Peculiar voice qualities, often high pitched

    f) Avoids people
    g) Tends to run his words together
    h) Has poor oral reading ability
    i) Has poor general scholarship in relation to IQ
    j) Usually talks louder than is necessary
    k) Watches face (especially mouth and lips) of speaker
2. Appearance
    a) Deformities of the outer ear
    b) Discharging ear
    c) Muscular tension when listening
    d) Mouth breathing
    e) Blank facial expression when spoken to
    f) Chronic catarrhal condition
3. Complaints by the child
    a) Buzzing or ringing noises in the head
    b) Earache
    c) Nausea or dizziness
    d) Inability to understand directions
    e) Headaches in the sinus area

Testing the Child's Hearing. It is not necessary to wait for the appearance of observable symptoms of hearing difficulty before referring a child to special services for tests. Scientific tests have been developed to measure hearing ability at different pitch levels. The most widely used tests are (1) noisemakers, (2) tuning forks, (3) speech audiometry, (4) pure-tone audiometry (objective), and (5) pure-tone audiometry (subjective). However, the most useful element in any testing situation is the tester with training, experience, and clinical ability. A particular test is a tool, and no tool is better than the person using it. The clinician usually employs a battery of tests in making a complete evaluation of the child's hearing.

Noisemakers of various types are the oldest method used for testing hearing. They are still widely used. A serious criticism of most noisemakers is that they are not calibrated (Clark, 1956). Their main value is to tell the tester whether or not the child can hear. Noisemakers should not be used to determine the child's degree of hearing ability. The tuning fork is frequently used for a quick approximation of hearing ability and to detect high-tone deafness as well as testing for bone conduction. This method is, however, subject to the problem that it begins to lose sound intensity immediately after the tuning fork is struck. This would provide a real obstacle to the child with a short attention span.

Speech audiometry can be very useful in determining hearing

levels. Speech audiometry is especially useful in determining the speech level of mentally retarded children since many of these children may be extremely difficult to test by subjective pure-tone audiometry, especially the younger children and the more severely mentally retarded. Sortini and Flake (1953) made use of toys in testing the hearing level of preschool children. In this the child is asked to pick up or identify certain toys. Sometimes a child responds by picking up the correct toy even though the examiner has been unable to get the child to say a word.

Pure-tone audiometry is divided into two major approaches: objective and subjective. The most widely used objective method is psychogalvanometry. A pure tone from a standard audiometer is sounded in the child's ear, followed by a mild electric shock. The child soon becomes conditioned so that when he hears a tone a change in skin resistance results. The change is automatically recorded on a moving sheet. The threshold of audition for the different frequencies can be ascertained and recorded in decibels once this conditioning is well established. Such a test may be used with children as young as nine to ten months and should be extremely useful with children from one to five years of age. According to Sortini (1960) this method has been found to be of value in

. . . excluding deafness as an etiological factor in an existing speech delay with mentally retarded children, and in aiding the diagnosis of aphasia. GSR testing has been used to exclude deafness as a significant factor in an existing speech delay with emotionally disturbed children—as well as assisting us in the diagnosis of malingerers and psychogenic deafness. [Pp. 537–38.]

Subjective pure-tone audiometry has been found to be useful for testing normal children in that rapport between the examiner and the child is easily obtained. A major difficulty frequently arises from not allowing sufficient time between the presentation of the stimulus and the response. This is especially true in the testing of cerebral-palsied children.

An individual pure-tone audiometric threshold test is recommended as a follow-up for those failing any screening test. The validity of audiometric test results tends to vary directly with the age of the child. Using the pure-tone audiometer with sweep checks at six frequencies, Hardy (1955) reported the percentage of correct referrals to an otological clinic at different age levels as follows:

Five- to seven-year-olds—79 per cent correct
Eight- to ten-year-olds—84 per cent correct

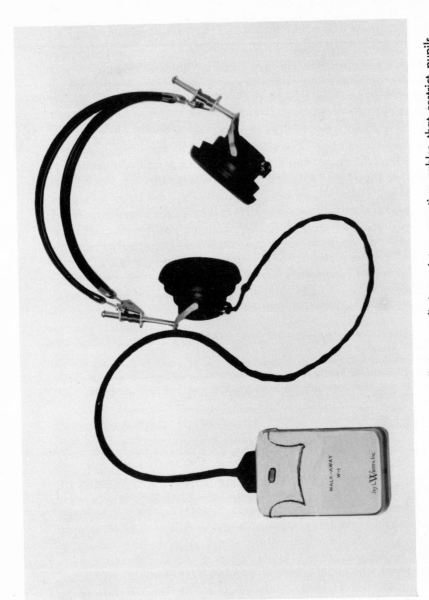

Fig. 8–1. The W-1 Warren Walk-Aways eliminate interconnecting cables that restrict pupils to their desk. (Courtesy Jay L. Warren, Inc.)

Eleven- and twelve-year-olds—89 per cent correct
Thirteen years and older—94 per cent correct

In the hands of experienced testers, pure-tone audiometers are very useful diagnostic instruments for children of school age. Roach (1954) lists two important reasons for using pure-tone audiometers:

1. To locate children with defective hearing in order to refer them to the medical profession for treatments, and
2. To furnish a basis for planning the educational placement and training for those children whose hearing acuity is not restored to normal or near normal conditions through medical services. [P. 330.]

Deaf and Sensory Aphasic Children. Clinicians are sometimes baffled when faced with the problem of differentiating between children who cannot hear sound and those who under some conditions seem to be able to hear but who are not able to utilize their auditory sensations. These children are referred to as those characterized by sensory aphasia. Such children frequently react to audiometric examination in a manner similar to that of deaf children (Goldstein *et al.*, 1958). This confusion in clinically differentiating a diagnosis of deafness and sensory aphasia led Olson (1961) to introduce a children's language test into the diagnostic procedure. The *Illinois Test of Language Ability* was administered to two groups of children— 25 deaf and 27 sensory aphasic children. The deaf children achieved an adjusted mean score on each of the nine subtests that was higher than the scores of the sensory aphasic group. On four of the nine subtests the differences in the scores in favor of the deaf group were statistically significant. These tests were (1) visual-motor association, (2) auditory receptive, (3) vocal expressive, and (4) auditory vocal grammatical. It seems, then, that a standardized language test, such as the *Illinois Test of Language Ability*, should be helpful in a differential diagnosis of deafness and sensory aphasia in children.

Causes of Deafness. The actual causes of deafness in many cases have not been known. However, scientific advances have furnished us with a better understanding of factors and conditions that contribute to deafness than was known several decades ago. In any discussion of the causes of deafness it is necessary to define terms. One of the most misused terms is the term "congenital." The word congenital refers to the time of acquisition in that any condition present at birth is congenital. This does not necessarily mean that the condition is inherited, although it may be inherited if it is congenital.

Furthermore, deafness that was not present at birth and is not congenital may be inherited deafness as a result of gene structure even if it appears at a later stage. This has been observed especially among older people in which it appears that deafness in old age runs in families.

The term "endogenous," which means produced from within, and resulting from internal causes, and the term "exogenous," which means originating from without, and due to external causes, are more accurate terms. Deafness resulting from maternal infection during pregnancy would be a case of congenital deafness, but it would be exogenous since it was produced from without the organism. A study bearing on the causes of deafness was reported by Brill (1961) involving 656 pupils enrolled in the California School for the Deaf from September, 1958, to December, 1960. The causes of deafness among these children are presented in Table 8–4. In a subsequent study

TABLE 8–4

Causes of Deafness in 656 Pupils at the California School for the Deaf, Riverside, September, 1958–December, 1960

Causes or Conditions	Number		Per Cent
Both parents deaf	52		
Hearing parents and deaf siblings	101		
Other deaf relatives	35		
Total of above (all congenital)		188	28.5
Congenital/no deaf relatives		261	39.9
Total possible endogenous		449	68.3
Rubella	46		
Probable Rh	15		
Total—Congenital/exogenous		61	
Adventitious		146	
Total possible exogenous		207	31.7

SOURCE: Brill (1961).

Sank and Kallman (1963) made a genetic analysis of 8,200 deaf residents over twelve years of age in New York State and found that approximately one-half of all cases were genetically determined. A comparison of the results of these studies with those obtained from earlier studies indicates that the proportion of endogenous deafness to exogenous deafness has been increasing, and that it has always been proportionately higher than reported. The decreased percentage of exogenous deafness can best be accounted for through medical advancements that have brought under control many of the infectious diseases of childhood that accounted for about 15 per cent of the entire population of totally deaf or severely hard-of-hearing children (Davis and Silverman, 1960; Brill, 1964).

Perceptive deafness was defined earlier as a form of deafness resulting from injury to the nerve endings found in the cochlea. It may also result from certain infectious diseases that produce high fevers. Sometimes a child is born with perceptive deafness because the mother had German measles during the early months of her pregnancy. Bordley (1958) concluded from a study of 1,152 children examined at the Hearing and Speech Center of Johns Hopkins Medical Institution that "the etiological factors of paramount interest, at the present time, should include: viral infections of the pre-natal and post-natal periods; oxygenization around the time of birth; blood incompatibility; prematurity; and the hazards of being born" (p. 172).

Any condition that impedes normal movement of the bones of the middle ear would produce conductive deafness. One of the most common causes of conductive deafness is otosclerosis, in which the last bone in the chain to the inner ear becomes immobilized and is unable to transmit the mechanical vibrations to the fluid in the inner ear. Other factors or conditions that may interfere with hearing are tumors, impacted wax in the outer ear, infections in the inner ear, and scarred or inelastic drum membranes resulting from abscesses in the middle ear.

Apart from hereditary deafness, defects of hearing have three main causes: (1) diseased conditions of the nose and throat, (2) infectious diseases, and (3) stoppage of the outer ear canal. The first of these is by far the most important and accounts for considerably more than half of all cases. The conditions of the nose and throat most frequently involved are adenoids, enlarged tonsils, and chronic catarrh. Most cases of acquired deafness in children are due, directly or indirectly, to diseased conditions of the nose and throat. Adenoid growths overlying the Eustachian tube openings not only cause impaired hearing but also cause repeated infection of the tubes and middle ear. Infected tonsils, paranasal sinusitis, and upper respiratory infections cause considerable middle ear ailments which in turn may lead to deafness. Neglected colds, chronic catarrhal conditions, and infectious diseases that affect the throat (measles, scarlet fever, and diphtheria) are also causes of hearing loss. There are some diseases—such as measles—that are frequently complicated by discharging ears. If the ear is allowed to drain over a period of time, there is a tendency for any hearing impairment to become permanent although the ear may stop discharging at a later date.

In the past the eardrum was often punctured to relieve the patient's suffering from a nose or throat infection. When this is done, there is danger of infection from the outside since there is nothing to block the entrance of disease germs to the middle ear. However, the development of various antibiotics to combat infections has to a large degree eliminated the necessity for puncturing the eardrum.

Summarizing, it may be said:

1. Deafness nearly always has its origin in childhood.
2. In the vast majority of cases it is due to diseased conditions of the nose or throat and is therefore usually preventable.
3. The source of the trouble may be either (1) some chronic disorder of the throat, such as adenoids, enlarged tonsils, catarrh, etc., or (2) an acute infectious disease that involves the throat, usually scarlet fever, measles, or diphtheria.
4. Wax accumulations and injuries to the eardrum are occasionally causes of deafness.

SOME CHARACTERISTICS OF CHILDREN WHO HAVE DEFECTIVE HEARING

Certain characteristics are often found in those who are deaf and hard of hearing. They are frequently inattentive, imperfect in speech, bewildered and baffled in expression, sensitive, and aloof. They may complain of earaches, have discharging ears, and tend to hold their heads in peculiar positions. Theirs is often a world of isolation from normal social relationships.

Socioeconomic Status. A study reported by Fiedler (1951) was concerned with the socioeconomic status of a group of children with hearing defects. The number of social agency contacts for 50 children with hearing difficulties and the number of contacts for a control group of children with no hearing difficulties were compared. The results revealed that the group with defective hearing had a significantly larger number of contacts with agencies giving financial aid and health services, and with other community agencies, than did the control group. Therefore, interpretations of the personality and the mental and educational development of hard-of-hearing children in comparison with other groups must take into account the total environmental setting.

Hardy (1954) also studied the relationship of socioeconomic factors and hearing defects, using as subjects 36,692 pupils in the kindergarten, first, fourth, sixth, and eighth grades of 98 public elementary schools of Chicago. The incidence of hearing impairment as determined by an otologist was estimated at 2 per cent of the school population. No sex differences were found. Socioeconomic background was estimated from housing conditions, monthly rent, median family income, and population character, according to the 1950 census. No attempt was made to secure a complete cross section of Chicago's pupil population. More than half of the children in the group studied were from the poor section of the city.

The findings do not bear out the hypothesis that impaired hearing is most frequently associated with low socioeconomic conditions. In fact, the trend appears to be in the opposite direction. The highest frequency of impairment was found among native-born white children and the lowest among children from overcrowded conditions found in the non-white areas.

Elser (1959) compared the social position of hearing-handicapped children in school with that of hearing children. The subjects consisted of 45 hearing-handicapped children and 1,213 children without hearing handicaps enrolled in the third through the seventh grades. A variety of tests designed to measure the social position of children in classrooms were administered. The results revealed that the hearing handicapped as a group was not as well accepted by their peers as other children. There was, however, a very wide range of acceptance of hearing-handicapped children, indicating that other factors also enter into acceptance-rejection scores.

Multiple Anomalies. Danish *et al.* (1963) reviewed the medical records of 499 students in the Pennsylvania School for the Deaf to determine the frequency of congenital anomalies. The records of the children studied were divided into three groups: (1) acquired deafness, (2) congenital, non-hereditary deafness, and (3) congenital deafness, apparently hereditary. There was a greater incidence of associated defects among those children who became deaf following some illness or accident than among those congenitally deaf. Differences were also noted in the types of defects when the congenitally acquired deaf were compared with the congenitally hereditary deaf.

Speech Development. The child with congenital deafness will remain without speech or language until these are developed through special teaching. Thus, there is likely to be a serious educational lag if he is not given special help during the preschool period. The language disability of the deaf child is perhaps a greater handicap than the physical fact of deafness. The spontaneous speech sounds of deaf-born, five-year-old children were studied at the Iowa School for the Deaf over a period of more than two years (Carr, 1953). Three transcriptions of 30 breath units each were made for each of the 48 subjects studied, making a total of 144 recordings. The results showed that these deaf-born children used many spontaneous speech sounds in their undirected vocalization. These speech sounds were natural in quality and were uttered in a manner free from the strain and self-consciousness often present in the taught speech of deaf-born children. The spontaneous development of vowel and consonant sounds in these children did not continue much beyond the level of hearing infants of twelve to thirteen months.

Children who become severely deaf from disease or some other condition after the acquisition of speech have more meaningful language concepts and greater verbal language ability than those of the same age born deaf. The time of the loss of hearing, the degree of hearing difficulty, and psychological factors connected with the disability have important bearings on the speech development of the child with impaired hearing.

Mental Ability. Modern efforts to determine the mental competence of children who are hard of hearing had their beginning with Pintner and Paterson, although Greenberg had made measurements of the mentality of the deaf at the Institute for the Improved Instruction of the Deaf as early as 1889 (Pintner and Paterson, 1916). Pintner and Paterson made use of the form board in their studies of deaf children and those who were hard of hearing. They early concluded from these studies that, on the average, deaf children were slightly inferior to normal children in performance ability. Considerable progress has been made in measuring the mental ability of the handicapped since that time; new techniques have been developed and less emphasis is placed on the IQ as the most important objective in psychological testing. Furthermore, increased attention is being given to the qualitative aspects of responses to items on the individual test. Studies by Frisina (1955) show that the intellectual functioning of the deaf child is not significantly different from that of the hearing child when the verbal aspects are controlled. This is shown on results from such tests as the Performance Scale of the *Wechsler Intelligence Scale for Children,* the *Arthur Point Scale of Performance Tests* (Forms 1 and 2), the *Chicago Non-Verbal,* the *Nebraska Test of Learning Aptitude,* the *Drever-Collins Performance Scale,* and somewhat similar tests. However, on tests of intellectual functioning of a more abstract nature the deaf child functions less efficiently than his hearing counterpart. Thus, Oleron (1950) concluded from his study of the intelligence of deaf children "that the deaf show an inferiority in the sphere of abstract thought" (p. 191). This he attributed to the close connection that exists between ordinary language usage and abstract thought.

Murphy (1957) has pointed out that deaf children fall within the range of normal intelligence test scores on the *Wechsler Intelligence Scale for Children.* Results secured on the *Wechsler-Bellevue Scale* with deaf pupils in a residential school are shown in Table 8–5. The results show that the average deaf child of this study scored at the average level on the performance section at all age levels, whereas all age groups were significantly below average on the verbal part of the scale. These data indicate that the achievement of the deaf children on the verbal test was about two-thirds that of hearing children. This ratio was maintained from the twelfth to the seventeenth year chronologically.

TABLE 8–5

Intelligence Quotients for Deaf Children on the *Wechsler-Bellevue Scale*

Age	N	Verbal		Performance	
		Mean	S. D.	Mean	S. D.
12	18	64.6	14.3	102.2	15.1
13	16	60.6	11.4	104.8	13.2
14	16	62.6	14.7	98.5	14.8
15	15	69.9	12.0	102.0	14.5
16	10	73.5	13.6	100.5	12.1
17	10	70.9	10.8	103.0	9.9
Total	85	66.5	13.7	101.8	14.5

SOURCE: After Murphy (1957).

A further analysis of the results revealed no differences by sex or by etiology. As a group they were inferior on the verbal scale. However, the age progression on the performance scale was sufficiently above the average for hearing children that by twenty years of age there was no inferiority on the total scale score. The trend for the deaf child to score above average on certain mental tests of a non-abstract nature is in harmony with the earlier results of Frisina (1955) and Oleron (1950).

Motor Ability. Motor proficiency and mechanical ability of deaf children have received considerable attention in connection with educational and vocational guidance. Early studies by Long (1932) and

Morsh (1936) indicated that, with the exception of balance, there is no significant difference in motor ability between deaf and hearing subjects.

The balance sense of children and adolescents with defective hearing was studied by Dixon (1950). A modification of the *Springfield Walking Beam Test* was used for measuring dynamic balance, while a modification of the *Bass Stick Test* was used for measuring static balance. A correlation of .78 was obtained between the scores made on the two tests, indicating that good dynamic balance is usually accompanied by good static balance. A negative correlation (−.42) was obtained between the degree of hearing loss in the better ear and ability to balance, indicating the greater the loss the poorer the balance. A further analysis of the relationship revealed that the congenitally deaf children were superior in balance to those becoming deaf through disease. It appears likely that diseases that have an adverse effect upon hearing may also have an adverse effect on balance, since the physiological structures involved in equilibrium and hearing are so close to each other in the inner ear.

Myklebust (1960) made use of the *Heath Railwalking Test* in studying the motor ability of deaf children. Results obtained from comparing deaf children with hearing children revealed a significant inferiority of the deaf children at all ages from seven through fifteen years. He concluded further that "the deaf are inferior in early life and, although they show progressive maturation, do not attain normal ability in locomotor coordination" (p. 190).

The *Heath Railwalking Test* furnishes a measure of only one aspect of motor development—locomotor coordination. Batteries of tests designed to measure motor development or motor proficiency have been slow to develop. The *Oseretsky Tests of Motor Proficiency* include six areas of motor function: general static, dynamic manual, general dynamic, speed, simultaneous movement, and synkinesia (Doll, 1946). The findings from a pilot study in which the Oseretsky Tests were administered to 30 boys and 20 girls at a public residential school are presented in Fig. 8–2 (Myklebust, 1960). The age range of these children was from eight through fourteen years. Both sexes and the total group scored a motor age of 9.50 years, while their mean chronological age was 11.1 years. The results in Fig. 8–2 show that the deaf children were lowest on general static and speed and were highest on synkinesia which involves involuntary movements in one part of the body while voluntary movements are being made by another part. This may be noted in the involuntary movement of one hand while the other hand is involved in a voluntary act. The general dynamic

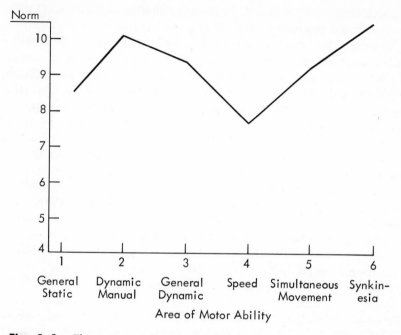

Fig. 8–2. The motor profile for deaf children on the *Oseretsky Tests of Motor Proficiency.* (Myklebust, *Psychology of deafness,* Grune & Stratton, Inc., 1960, by permission.)

task requires coordination of the general type found in the *Heath Railwalking Test* in which deaf children were found to be inferior in an earlier study.

Personality Adjustments. Personality inventories, widely used in studying personality characteristics of children, are of questionable validity when used with deaf children, since the responses are so completely dependent upon language. Levine (1963) noted from a vocabulary analysis of several inventories used with the deaf that the tests were "above the reading vocabulary comprehension of the deaf as a group and even further removed from their reading concept level" (p. 504). The projective technique seems to be better suited for studying the personality of deaf children. Rorschach personality patterns have been obtained from a variety of groups differing in age, background, education, and socioeconomic levels. Levine concludes: "Despite these differences, they are generally characterized by: (1) conceptual deficiencies; (2) emotional immaturity; (3) rigidity and egocentricity; (4) deficient social adaptability; and (5) constricted interests and motivations" (p. 505).

One must be careful in drawing conclusions relative to the effects of a hearing handicap in itself on the personality development of a child. Differences found between the personality of hearing-handicapped children and children with normal hearing will be affected by other personal characteristics of the individual child and by the nature of parental and educational guidance. The results of a study by Avery (1948), in which the *Vineland Social Maturity Scale* was used with acoustically handicapped children, refute earlier conclusions that indicated that the acoustically handicapped child is inferior in social maturity. Bowyer *et al.* (1963) concluded that perhaps mental age is the most important consideration for adjustment in children with the physical handicap involving hearing.

The age at which the hearing loss occurs will have an important bearing on the child's personal and social adjustments. This is clearly implied in the study by Frisina (1959) in his description of the role of ambition in the organization of behavior. He states:

Prejudices, biases, and other cultural subtleties are introduced and developed largely through the ability to hear. Verbal language, i.e., a system of verbal symbols, emerges spontaneously principally because of hearing. . . . It is significant that audition provides the primary means through which hearing children develop and use language during the first six years of life. It is not until the hearing child learns to read that a visual symbol system begins to influence further language development and its elaboration.

In the hearing child, audition and vision begin to interact during the early weeks of life. However, insofar as visual symbols are concerned, it is chiefly through hearing that verbal language emerges during the first years of life. . . . to understand the important contribution hearing makes to emotional and physical growth during the early years serves to emphasize the multidimensional problems likely to result from early deafness. [Pp. 94–95.]

SUMMARY

Estimates of the numbers of children with hearing difficulties vary considerably, depending in part upon the criteria used for classifying children with such difficulties. Audiometric tests are needed to identify correctly children with severe hearing loss, which is essential for an effective educational program for the hard of hearing. Language tests have been introduced to differentiate deafness and sensory aphasia.

The terms "endogenous" and "exogenous" have been used for classifying deafness arising from internal causes and external causes respectively. Studies show that about two-thirds of the causes of deafness may be classified as endogenous with the proportion of endogenous deafness to exogenous deafness on the increase. In either case deafness nearly always has its origin in childhood, with a large percentage of instances due to diseased conditions of the nose and throat, which are, therefore, preventable.

Hearing-handicapped children as a group are not as well accepted by peers as other children. The congenitally deaf child will remain without speech or language until these are developed through special training. The time of the loss of hearing, the degree of hearing difficulty, and the social and psychological factors connected with the disability have important bearings on the educational, psychological, and social development of the child.

The deaf child is seriously handicapped in intellectual functioning on tests involving abstractions. On motor tests deaf children score lowest on general static and speed tests and highest on tests of synkinesia. There is also evidence that acoustically handicapped children are socially more immature than other children.

CHAPTER REFERENCES

AVERY, CHARLOTTE (1948). Social competence of pre-school accoustically handicapped children. *Except. Child.*, 15:71–76, 88.

BORDLEY, J. E. (1958). The etiology of deafness in young children. In SIR A. EWING (ed.), *The modern educational treatment of deafness.* Washington, D.C.: The Volta Bureau.

BOWYER, L. R., MARSHALL, A., and WEDDELL, K. (1963). The relative personality adjustment of severely deaf and partially deaf children. *Brit. J. educ. Psychol.*, 33:85–87.

BRILL, R. G. (1961). Hereditary aspects of deafness. *Volta Rev.*, 63:168–75.

BRILL, R. G. (1964). Deafness and the genetic factor. *Amer. Ann. Deaf*, 108:359–73.

CARR, JOSEPHINE (1953). An investigation of the spontaneous speech of five-year-old deaf born children. *J. Speech & Hearing Disord.*, 18:22–29.

CLARK, J. T. (1956). Testing hearing of children with noisemakers—a myth. *Except. Child.*, 22:326–27, 341.

CURRY, E. T. (1954). Are teachers good judges of their pupils' hearing? *Except. Child.*, 21:15–17.

DANISH, J. M., TILLSON, J. K., and LEXITAN, M. (1963). Multiple anomalies in congenitally deaf children. *Eugen. Quart.*, 10:12–24.

DAVIS, H., and SILVERMAN, S. R. (eds.) (1960). *Hearing and deafness.* (Rev. ed.) New York: Holt, Rinehart & Winston.

DIXON, BARBARA C. (1950). A study of balance of audio-defective children and adults. Unpublished master's thesis, Boston Univer.

DOLL, E. A. (1946). *Oseretsky tests of motor proficiency.* Minneapolis: Educational Test Bureau. Pp. 1–47.

ELSER, R. P. (1959). The social position of hearing handicapped children in the regular grades. *Except. Child.,* 25:305–9.

FIEDLER, MIRIAM F. (1951). A study of the socio-economic status of a group of public school children with hearing defects. *Child Developm.,* 22:193–98.

FRISINA, D. R. (1955). A psychological study of the mentally retarded deaf child. Unpublished doctoral thesis, Northwestern Univer.

FRISINA, D. R. (1959). Some problems confronting children with deafness. *Except. Child.,* 26:94–98.

GEYER, MARGARET L., and YANKAUER, A. (1956). Teacher judgments of hearing loss in children. *J. Speech & Hearing Disord.,* 21:482–86.

GOLDSTEIN, R., LANDAU, W., and KLEFFNER, F. (1958). Neurologic assessment of some deaf and aphasic children. *Ann. Otol. Rhinol. Laryngol.,* 67:468–79.

HARDY, MARTHA C. (1954). Socio-economic background of children with impaired hearing. *Child Developm.,* 25:295–308.

HARDY, MARTHA C. (1955). Outcomes of a hearing and vision conservation program demonstration in a metropolitan school system. *J. Sch. Health,* 25:6–12.

KODMAN, F. (1956). Identification of hearing loss by the classroom teacher. *Laryngoscope,* 66:1346–347.

KODMAN, F., POWERS, T. R., PHILIP, P. P., and WHEELER, G. N. (1958). An investigation of hearing loss in mentally retarded children and adults. *Amer. J. ment. Def.,* 63:46–63.

KODMAN, F., SCHNECK, P. E., STOCKDELL, K. G., THOMPSON, W. V., and SPIES, C. (1958). Identification of hearing loss by parents, teachers and audiometers. *Eye, Ear, Nose, Throat Mon.,* 37:103–5.

KODMAN, F., SPIES, C., STOCKDELL, K., and SEDLACEK, G. (1959). Socio-economic status and observer identification of hearing loss in school children. *Except. Child.,* 26:176–79, 188.

LEVINE, EDNA S. (1963). Studies in psychological evaluation of the deaf. *Volta Rev.,* 65:496–512.

LONG, J. (1932). *Motor abilities of deaf children. Contributions to education,* No. 514. New York: Teachers Coll., Columbia Univer., Bureau of Publications.

McCABE, B. F. (1963). The etiology of deafness. *Volta Rev.,* 65:471–77.

MONSES, EDNA K. (1959). Aphasia and deafness in children. *Except. Child.,* 25:395–99, 409.

MORSH, J. (1936). Motor performance of the deaf. *Comp. Psychol. Monogr.,* No. 66.

MURPHY, K. P. (1957). Tests of abilities and attainments. In Sir A. EWING (ed.), *Educational guidance and the deaf child.* Washington, D.C.: The Volta Bureau.

MYKLEBUST, H. R. (1951). Differential diagnosis of deafness in young children. *Except. Child.,* 17:97–101, 117.

MYKLEBUST, H. R. (1960). *The psychology of deafness.* New York: Grune & Stratton.

OLERON, P. (1950). A study of the intelligence of the deaf. *Amer. Ann. Deaf,* 95:179–94.

OLSON, J. L. (1961). Deaf and sensory aphasic children. *Except. Child.,* 27:422–24.

PINTNER, R., and PATERSON, D. G. (1916). Form board ability of young deaf and hearing children. *Am. Ann. Deaf,* 61:148–89.

ROACH, R. E. (1954). Considerations in education of children with various degrees of hearing loss. *Except. Child.,* 20:330–35, 358.

SANK, DIANE, and KALLMAN, F. J. (1963). The role of heredity in early total deafness. *Volta Rev.,* 65:461–70.

SORTINI, A. J. (1960). Hearing evaluation of brain-damaged children. *Volta Rev.,* 62:536–40.

SORTINI, A. J., and FLAKE, C. G. (1953). Speech audiometry testing for pre-school children. *Laryngoscope,* 63:991–97.

VENTRY, I. M., and CHAIKLIN, J. B. (1962). Functional hearing loss: a problem in terminology, *ASHA Journal of the American Speech and Hearing Association,* 4:251–54.

WOODEN, H. Z. (1963). Deaf and hard of hearing children. In L. E. DUNN (ed.), *Exceptional children in the schools.* New York: Holt, Rinehart & Winston.

SELECTED READINGS

BARBARA, D. A. (ed.) (1960). *Psychological and psychiatric aspects of speech and hearing.* Springfield, Ill.: Charles C Thomas.

DAVIS, H., and SILVERMAN, S. R. (eds.) (1960). *Hearing and deafness.* (Rev. ed.) New York: Holt, Rinehart & Winston.

DiCARLO, L. M., and DOLPHIN, JANE (1962). Social adjustment and personality development of deaf children: a review of literature. In E. P. TRAPP and P. HIMELSTEIN (eds.), *Readings on the exceptional child.* New York: Appleton-Century-Crofts.

EWING, SIR A. (1957). *Educational guidance and the deaf child.* Washington, D.C.: The Volta Bureau.

JORDAN, T. E. (1962). *The exceptional child.* Columbus, Ohio: C. E. Merrill. Chap. 4.

KIRK, S. A. (1962). *Educating exceptional children.* Boston: Houghton Mifflin. Chap. 6.

LAVOS, G. (1955). Evaluating the intelligence of the deaf. In FRAMP-

TON and GALL (eds.), *Special education for the exceptional.* Vol. 3. Boston: Porter E. Sargent.

LEVINE, EDNA S. (1960). *The psychology of deafness.* New York: Columbia Univer. Press.

MEYERSON, L. (1963). A psychology of impaired hearing. In W. M. CRUICKSHANK (ed.), *Psychology of exceptional children and youth.* (2d ed.) Englewood Cliffs, N.J.: Prentice-Hall. Chap. 3.

MYKLEBUST, H. R. (1960). *The psychology of deafness.* New York: Grune & Stratton.

ROACH, R. E. (1960). The meaning of severe deafness in the life of the young child. In J. F. MAGARY and J. R. EICHORN (eds.), *The exceptional child.* New York: Holt, Rinehart & Winston.

RONNEI, ELEANOR C. (1955). The hard of hearing. In FRAMPTON and GALL (eds.), *Special education for the exceptional.* Vol. 3. Boston: Porter E. Sargent.

STRENG, ALICE (1960). The child who is hard of hearing. In J. F. MAGARY and J. R. EICHORN (eds.), *The exceptional child.* New York: Holt, Rinehart & Winston.

For further information about various problems of the deaf and hard of hearing, write the following organizations:

Alexander Graham Bell Association for the Deaf, Inc., Washington, D.C., which publishes *The Volta Review.*

American Hearing Society, Washington, D.C.

9

HEARING-HANDICAPPED CHILDREN

Children with varying types and degrees of hearing losses are enrolled in regular classes in schools. Where periodic hearing examinations are not given, many of these children's problems are never identified. Teachers who are ignorant of a child's hearing disability may label the child as dull or stupid. On the other hand, both parents and teachers are quite likely to overprotect or segregate the child with hearing difficulty, in spite of the fact that he needs an opportunity to develop socially and emotionally through group activities with his peers.

Many of these children may be in need of medical treatment, others need hearing aids, and those with severe loss need special instruction through special classes. Table 9-1 shows the enrollment in schools and special classes in 1955 and 1960. The largest group of deaf children shown in Table 9-1 are enrolled in public residential schools, while the largest group of hard-of-hearing children are in day classes in public schools.

NEED FOR UNDERSTANDING THE CHILD

Much emphasis has been given in recent years to the need of teachers to understand the pupils with whom he is directly concerned

TABLE 9–1

Enrollment in Schools and Classes for Deaf and Hard of
Hearing, 1955 and 1960

Kind of School	1955			1960		
	Number of Schools	Deaf	Hard of Hearing	Number of Schools	Deaf	Hard of Hearing
Public residential schools	72	12,436	1,665	72	13,911	1,778
Day schools	10	1,147	325	10	1,714	346
Day classes in public schools	200	2,866	1,408	254	4,282	2,671
Denominational and private residential schools and classes	50	1,540	273	64	1,676	473
Schools and classes for the multiple handicapped	11			15		
Total	343	17,989	3,671	415	21,583	5,268

SOURCES: *American Annals of the Deaf,* 101 (January, 1956): 222; *Ibid.,* 106
(January, 1961): 162.

in the teaching-learning situation. The teacher of the hearing-handicapped child should understand the child's background, his educational record, his psychological characteristics, his family history, his
medical history, and the nature and extent of hearing loss present.
It is also important for the teacher to understand something of the
nature of the child's self concept, his aspirations, and his needs.

Studying the Child. One of the first needs of the teacher of hard-
of-hearing or deaf children is to know the pupils he is to teach. He
should be acquainted with the audiological evaluation of each child.
He should review the health record of each child, and study carefully
the educational background of each individual. Following this, he
should follow through with his own evaluation of the present educational status of each child. He should be especially concerned with
each child's speechreading ability at the present time. Standardized
speechreading tests should be used, if they are available.[1]

Other questions suggested by Miller (1957) that should concern
the teacher are:

What is the child's speech development pattern at the present?
What is his speech discrimination ability?

[1] See, for example, Mary Rose Costello, Study of Speech-Reading as a Developing Language Process in Deaf and Hard of Hearing Children. Unpublished doctor's dissertation, Northwestern Univer.

What is his language ability or level?
What is expected of the child by the classroom teacher?

The education of the deaf in Great Britain follows a general accept-ance of a standard system of classification formulated in 1938 by the Committee of Inquiry into Problems Relating to Children with De-fective Hearing. The classification takes into account both the decibel loss and the child's ability with speech and language. The following is a brief summarized version of the classification presented by Finnett (1957):

Grade I—(a) Hearing loss up to 35 decibels; (b) Speech and language normal.
Grade IIA—(a) Hearing loss between 35–60 decibels; (b) Speech and language fair to good.
Grade IIB—(a) Hearing loss between 35–60 decibels; (b) Speech and language fair to poor.
Grade III—(a) Hearing loss greater than 60 decibels; (b) Little or no naturally acquired speech and language. [Pp. 205–6.]

An educational and psychological profile is especially helpful to the teacher in evaluating the child's strengths and weaknesses as well as his personality characteristics and adjustments. It has been noted that hard-of-hearing children obtain scores on personality inventories and rating scales markedly similar to those obtained by normally hearing children (Madden, 1931). However, Meyerson (1963) has pointed out that hearing loss or deafness frequently places the child in antagonistic overlapping role situations. These have an im-portant bearing on his personal and social adjustments. Kirk de-scribes three children with differing degrees of hearing loss (1962). The greatest difference noted was in social maturity. Many studies have shown that the deaf child is very seriously handicapped in his social relations and displays considerable social immaturity. Some of this stems from the overprotection received at the hands of the mother or other adult.

The Use of an Appraisal Profile. A special committee in Maryland has furnished a Child's Appraisal Profile, which has been useful as medical criteria for describing the child and for educational prognosis and planning. The definitions of categories of impairment are pre-sented by Hardy (1960):

DEFINITION OF CATEGORIES OF IMPAIRMENT

Physical Motor   Function of vital organs and details of cross and fine coordination in daily activities, such as walking, climb-ing stairs, eating, dressing, and toilet activities.

Social   Awareness of, and relations with, peers, family and
                    others.

Emotional   Stability in adjustment to various situations.

Sensory Motor   Details of function of peripheral nervous system.

Intellectual   Details of function of central nervous system relative
                    to language and speech facility, auditory perception,
                    understanding of verbal and printed symbols, memory,
                    and other aspects of intellectual behaviour which would
                    affect learning. [P. 18/7.]

Within these categories five levels of gradation are employed so that a total rating may be obtained. This should be most helpful to the educator who is able to interpret the findings on a particular child and combine these with his own observations and experiences with the child. Hardy states:

At stake here is the concept that "deafness" is not a simple entity involving prescribed capacities and behavioral bents, but a highly variable state, in that a wide variety of neurophysiologic and psychophysiologic patterns and potentials may be present. [P. 18/9.]

While it is generally true that hearing-handicapped children who have the most residual hearing are the ones who most likely will achieve the greatest ease in oral communication, studies and experiences by educators and clinicians have shown that the degree of hearing loss is not the only important factor that should be considered in predicting the deaf child's ability to learn. The ability to develop good auditory discrimination is important for the child's learning to lip-read and to talk. Closely related to this, Monses (1959) states:

Just as we know there are children with normal hearing who cannot use oral communication because of aphasia, we must assume that there may also be children with impaired hearing who also have aphasia. In the diagnostic process we must always be aware of the possibility of dual or multiple handicaps. [P. 397.]

Psychometric appraisals are helpful to the educator in planning an educational program for a group of children, Kodman et al. (1962) concluded from their study that the *Columbia Mental Maturity Scale* may be used as a screening device with deaf children functioning at a mental age of six or above. The Scale was judged to be only partially successful with six- to eight-year-old children. The obtained

IQ's ranged from 40 to 135 with a mean of approximately 88. Cerebral-palsied children, as well as other brain-damaged children, are frequently handicapped in hearing. This was noted by Dunsdon in a study of 27 children (1952, p. 84). Only 2 of the 27 could be said to have normal hearing. Two other children registered a loss of slightly less than 10 per cent, while 5 of the children registered a loss in excess of 20 per cent.

EDUCATIONAL PROVISIONS FOR THE HEARING HANDICAPPED

After the children needing help are identified, provisions must be made for their treatment and education. Such provisions should be based upon an accurate diagnosis of their needs and capabilities. Children found to have a hearing loss should be referred to an otologist, who determines the nature of the disability and, where possible, administers the needed medical treatment. For example, he may find that infected adenoids or tonsils are adversely affecting the child's health, including hearing. Also, he may find that there is a condition needing further medical diagnosis. In any case, the otologist is an important part of a team in the diagnosis and treatment of the hard-of-hearing child.

Educational Planning. The planning of an educational program for the hearing-handicapped child must first of all take into consideration the degree of the handicap. Certainly the educational program for the hard-of-hearing child will be different from that for the deaf. Brill (1957) has contended that hard-of-hearing children should be educated in schools with hearing children with a special supplementary program, while:

Deaf children should be educated with other deaf children in a school where there are enough other deaf children to have a well graded and complete program and a qualified staff. [P. 198.]

Early enrollment in the nursery school or kindergarten is very important for the hard-of-hearing child so that he can learn to work and play in group activities as other children do. The educational program should be based upon the special needs of each child. For some—those whose hearing is severely impaired—a carefully selected hearing aid may be beneficial. Auditory training should be given to enable the users of hearing aids to make the most of such instruments.

Special instruction in speechreading is important for the young school-child, and the child should be allowed to move about freely in the classroom without fear of disciplinary action or embarrassment.

Although it is usually necessary to separate a child for speechreading lessons and help in the use of hearing aids, it seems psychologically and educationally desirable for the child to associate as much as possible with children who hear normally. Children with defective hearing may need special help in some phases of their schoolwork, especially the language arts.

It is a common occurrence to find that children who are hard of hearing are listed among those with speech problems. However, children with mild hearing losses and those whose hearing difficulties developed after the age at which speech was well established are not likely to have speech defects. Many of the very hard-of-hearing children may be guided in developing intelligible speech if they are given special help during the preschool and early school years.

Roach (1954) has suggested the following program of instruction for children with varying degrees of hearing loss:

1. The improvement of language comprehension
2. The use of a hearing aid when needed
3. Auditory training to furnish maximum efficiency in the use of the hearing aid
4. Lip reading instruction in order that vision may help the child in the process of understanding oral communication
5. Speech therapy to help the child express himself more clearly.
6. Education of the parents and family concerning the child's problems so that the home climate may be conducive to educational and social maturity. [P. 358.]

In recent years the residential schools have become to a greater degree an integral part of the public school system, legally and professionally. As a result, various cooperative arrangements between residential and day centers have been developed by different states and school systems. Also, unusual arrangements may be found between the residential schools and the regular schools. For example, the Michigan School for the Deaf sponsors rehabilitation programs for the hard-of-hearing children of the state for whom no local facilities are available (Poulos, 1961). Children are enrolled whose hearing impairments are great enough to cause unsatisfactory work in regular school classes but not sufficient to cause them to be enrolled in a special-class program.

Integration of the Hearing Handicapped into Regular Classes. The results of integrating hearing-handicapped children show that many factors are involved in evaluating the program. Motto and Wawrzaszek (1963) analyzed the research evidence available on the integration of hearing-impaired children in an effort to (1) categorize scientifically supportable information and (2) clarify problems that require further research attention. Their findings are summarized as follows:

1. The hearing handicapped are not as accepted socially in integrated classrooms as non-handicapped children. There is a trend to support the generalization that hearing handicapped tend also to occupy a social position of neutrality rather than of rejection.

2. It has been assumed that one of the primary objectives of integration is the development of adequate communication competencies. By attending classes with non-handicapped children, the deaf will, it is hypothesized, imitate the model presented by normal children. This would result in a speech pattern with proper rhythm, inflection and quality which characteristically are deficient in the speech of the deaf. There is insufficient research evidence to support or reject this hypothesis.

3. It has been hypothesized that children with moderate hearing losses are more readily integrated into regular classrooms than are those with profound hearing losses. Although some supporting evidence has been presented, there is a critical lack of information regarding the relationship between severity of disability and response to integration experiences.

4. Several writers have stressed the importance of communication skills as a prerequisite for integration. Our analysis of the literature indicates no organized research to verify this belief; and at the present time, this generalization is accepted on the basis of teacher observation, conjecture, and perhaps wish-fulfillment.

5. Although the rationale has remained nebulous, it has been hypothesized that integration of the deaf into regular classrooms will result in significant increments of educational achievement. There is an absence of supporting evidence for this belief.

6. Several writers have implied that through integration the hearing handicapped child could achieve at the level of comparable non-handicapped children. It is as unrealistic to expect the deaf child to compete in social and academic performance with his non-handicapped peers as it would be to expect a physically handicapped individual to compete in a foot race with normal classmates. It is entirely possible that the deaf child can benefit significantly from integration experiences, yet never achieve the mean of non-handicapped performance.

7. The factor of pace of integration has been overlooked in previous studies. Abrupt integration appears to be contra-indicated, and a sequential, gradually increasing exposure to non-handicapped peers seems to be in order. [P. 129.]

Classroom Provisions. In order to minimize the likelihood of educational retardation among those pupils with impaired hearing who
are to be found in almost every classroom, certain unfavorable conditions should be avoided. The child should be assigned a front seat
on the side of the room near the windows. In order to make it possible for him to follow the teacher's speech as well as possible while
instruction is being given, the light should fall on the teacher so that
the child may have a full view of his face. In order that undue attention shall not be given to the child's handicap, the teacher should
insist upon clear enunciation from all the children in the room, thus
benefiting not only the handicapped child but other members of the
class as well, for certain speech habits are improved through such
practice. The child who is hard of hearing should be permitted to
turn around so that he can see the faces of the other children when
they speak.

He may even be encouraged to undertake a definite study of lipreading, for through steady practice and patience the skill is acquired.
It has been suggested that he practice the pronunciation of words with
a mirror at home in order to familiarize himself with the formation
of words as they are spoken. It is a common observation that, through
sheer force of necessity, people who are hard of hearing closely watch
the face of a speaker and sometimes develop skill at speechreading
without knowing how they do it. In this way they may become able
to carry on a conversation without discernible difficulty.

In a study of 17 children who were hard of hearing and who were
given instruction in speechreading for from one to three years, 47
per cent of the group showed an increase in IQ, 41 per cent showed
no change, and 11 per cent showed a decrease (Hofsommer, 1936).
Among 76 per cent of the group, definite improvements in classroom
achievement were noted. Among 16 children who were hard of hearing but who were not given instruction in lipreading because of lack
of parental cooperation, none showed an increase in IQ during the
same period, but 75 per cent showed a decrease. Only 18.7 per cent
made classroom improvement, and all individuals in this group presented definite personality problems.

Only those children who show the effects of deficient hearing in their
schoolwork will need to be given special instruction, and this will not
be needed when these pupils have acquired enough facility in speechreading so that they are able to profit from ordinary methods of teaching. In some cities a specially trained teacher goes from school to
school giving instruction in speechreading individually or to small
groups composed of not more than six pupils. The length of the in-

struction periods ranges from 30 to 45 minutes, and meetings are held from one to four times a week. This has brought good results. A child can thus continue with his regular classwork, and he and his room teacher are intelligently advised of his needs. Parents are satisfied since their child has not been marked as too different from other pupils in the school.

The Use of Hearing Aids. In 1940 the National Research Council sponsored a series of investigations of the educational and psychological value of individual hearing aids for children (1944). Studies reported results from hard-of-hearing children who were attending regular public school classes in greater New York and Jersey City. The original 104 subjects were divided into two experimental groups of 26 each and two control groups of 26 each. Experimental subjects wore hearing aids while the control subjects did not. Each of the 26 children in the first experimental group was paired with a child of the same sex, chronological age, mental age, and amount and kind of hearing loss in a control group (matched pairs). The second experimental group was matched as a group with the second control group (matched groups).

Subjects were tested at the beginning and at the end of the study with achievement and personality tests. Case studies were made and speech was also studied. Pupils wearing hearing aids differed considerably in the extent to which they used their aids. Results indicated no significant differences between experimental and control groups in scores on the achievement and personality tests. Analysis of interviews with subjects and their parents showed a trend toward improved school and social adjustment for the children who wore hearing aids.

The early experience of the Division of Special Education in Baltimore seems to provide a sound basis for dealing with the hard of hearing (Whildin). In 1940 a hearing aid class was begun with a trained full-time teacher in charge. This class was made up of pupils from nine to fourteen years of age having an IQ range from 53 to 130. The special teacher was responsible for teaching lipreading, speech correction, ear hygiene, the adjustment and care of the hearing aid, and other special matters directly related to the hard-of-hearing condition. Through a cooperative arrangement with the program for the regular grades, all classes except English were taught by regular classroom teachers. This experiment extended over a period of more than a year and a half, during which 38 children were assigned to the class, although at no one time were more than 20 enrolled. Of this group of 38 children, all but 4 were able to pass the regular work of their grade. Further investigations showed that many other children were in need of special educational help. The experiences of the Division indicated that when these children were fitted with hearing aids and given instruction in lipreading, they were better able to adjust in regular classes with normal children. Thus, in Baltimore the special hearing class as such was discontinued a little less than two years after the experiment had been begun. Children were placed in the regular classes where they would normally be, but were provided with hearing aids and given special instruction in lipreading and speech twice each week.

These results suggest the need for special teachers who will be able to help the child to develop correct speech, who can provide lipreading instruction, and who can assist in adjusting hearing aids to the needs of the pupil. These experiences further suggest the need for the regular classroom teachers to recognize the problem and thus be in better position to deal with it intelligently and with patience. The education of the child who is hard of hearing involves considerations not present in the instruction that is provided for the normal pupil. He needs the sympathetic understanding of a teacher who is familiar with his characteristics. This does not mean that the teacher, or even the parent, should permit sympathy to become pity, for that might encourage the development of self-pity in the child. But a considerate teacher who recognizes a child's difficulties, who is eager to guide him in his responses so that he will be able to adjust more completely and more satisfactorily to the world of which he is a part, may be able, through the use of helpful procedures and useful materials, to make for better and more wholesome adjustments in the growing child.

Shorewood, Wisconsin, is an example of a small community that developed a good program for children with impairing hearing. As of 1958–1959 three teachers and one speech therapist give instruction to the 30 hearing-handicapped children who are enrolled in the Shorewood Public Schools. Their hearing losses range from mild through moderate to profound. The program has been defined by Streng (1958) as follows:

Shorewood Health Department has for many years been responsible for the screening testing, in which all children are tested annually by the public health nurses assisted by health volunteers. Otological referral and follow-up are the responsibilities of the Health Department. Free hearing aid evaluative service is available to children at the University of Wisconsin at Milwaukee and many parents avail themselves of it. A psychological evaluation is a prerequisite for enrollment in the program for hearing handicapped children. When all available information is brought together, educational placement is made according to the child's needs by the groups involved in evaluating him.

Children with mild hearing losses remain in the regular classes and receive special help from the speech therapist. In contrast, children with profound losses generally begin their school lives at the age of three in the special classes. During the kindergarten years they go, one to a class-room, into the regular kindergartens for socialization purposes. Later they take art and physical education with children of their own ages. As they grow older and their ability to communicate improves they begin to go to regular classes for subjects in which they excel. It might be arithmetic for one child or social studies for another. At the high school level these children begin by taking courses in home economics and manual arts, as well as physical education with the regular classes, and each year one major academic subject is added to their programs. By the time they are ready to be graduated they are taking all their work in the regular high school. . . . Children with moderate losses who are unable to maintain the pace of the regular classroom are often transferred to the special classes until they have been able to catch up or until they have been able to make certain educational and personal adjustments which will enable them to return to the regular classrooms. [P. 76.]

Prevention of Hearing Difficulties. Any program of education and general health should include provisions for the conservation of hear-ing and the prevention of deafness. An important reason for exerting caution with any disease that may involve the hearing mechanism is the possibility of developing hearing difficulties or deafness. Children should be taught the dangers of colds and proper methods of caring for themselves when infected. Likewise, the importance of proper diet and rest as fortification against disease should be impressed upon them. It is no longer assumed that every child must necessarily have the so-called children's diseases. Rather, it is essential to safeguard children from exposure to all communicable diseases, such as scarlet fever, measles, meningitis, diphtheria, whooping cough, and even common colds, that may be contributing factors to deafness. More-over, too much cannot be said about protecting the ears during illness, for it is so easy through sheer carelessness to permit serious conse-quences to the ears to follow the disease itself. There are some special preventive measures that should become habitual with school-children. Parents and teachers should foster the development of such habits.

1. Teach the child how to blow his nose gently, with both nostrils open.
2. Teach the child how to protect his ears when swimming.

3. Never neglect earache or abscessed ears.
4. Teach children how to clear up a chronic cold.
5. See that all children practice good ear hygiene.

If early medical treatment is to be a means of conserving hearing, then any hearing loss must be detected in its incipient stages. The most important time to apply preventive measures is during the early period of the child's life; therefore, symptoms of hearing loss, if detected by the teacher or anyone else working with the child, should be called to the attention of the parents in order that prompt treatment may be given by a physician or an otologist.

When an infection of the middle ear continues over a long period of time, it is referred to as *otitis media*. Continued infection may result from a lack of proper drainage of the ear or from excessive granulation inside. When such a condition exists, a medical specialist is needed in order to insure proper care. Through adequate medical care of acute *otitis media* in the early stages, a large number of cases of handicapping degrees of deafness could be prevented. Otologists point out that serious conditions may develop when acute *otitis media* is neglected. This fact should be made known to teachers and parents, for no method of therapy has been developed whereby the results of neglect can be remedied.

EDUCATIONAL PROVISIONS FOR DEAF CHILDREN

While the majority of hard-of-hearing children may benefit from special educational provisions either in or close to regular classes, such placement is hardly possible for deaf children. They have no functional hearing, experience great difficulty in learning language concepts, and frequently cannot learn intelligible oral communication. For these and other reasons deaf children are almost universally taught in either special day classes organized for them in large school systems or in special classes in residential schools organized exclusively for the deaf.

Residual Hearing in the Educative Process. Although it has been shown that very few so-called deaf children are totally deaf to sound, this does not imply that all the remainder have sufficient residual hearing for education in regular classes. How far along the continuum it is necessary to go in order to treat the child as deaf is not always easy to determine. This was implied in Chapter 8. It is, however, important for the teacher to have a clear and complete knowledge of the extent and limitations of a child's hearing. A study by Strizver (1958) revealed that "profoundly deaf children are able to discriminate among tones of different frequencies provided the differences are sufficiently large" (p. 304). Pitch discrimination was more difficult for the profoundly deaf children at higher frequencies. Those children who could discriminate pitch differences around 500 cps were better in discriminating speech than those with poor or no speech discrimination.

Watson (1961) has pointed out that there are three factors to be considered: (1) the residual hearing of the child, (2) the nature of speech, and (3) the capabilities of hearing aid equipment. These factors are interacting, a situation schematically presented in Fig. 9–1.

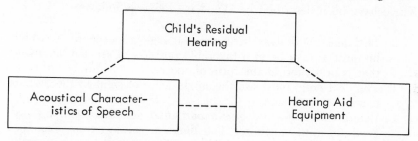

Fig. 9–1. A triangle of interacting factors that serve as the basis for the education of children with residual hearing.

This triangle furnishes the basis for studying the use of residual aids in the education of the child. Hearing aids are articles of scientific equipment that should be furnished on the basis of the child's needs and personal characteristics. The child's residual hearing may be obtained by means of a pure-tone audiometer. Too often the teacher is unaware of the information being obtained by the child and educational practice is based upon the acoustical characteristics of the child's speech without any consideration of the triangle of interacting factors.

Special Language Problems of the Deaf. Wooden (1964) points out, "The young child learns his first language through associating a symbolization of it with illustrating meanings or concepts" (p. 334). This presents a difficulty for the deaf child who is deprived of an important sensory avenue to language learning, forcing him to depend largely upon visual impressions. Some educators have suggested that the deaf child should be talked to from infancy so that speechreading will become his inner language. Certainly many of the difficulties involved in the education of deaf children would be solved if speechreading could be developed by this process. There is, however, a major problem concerned with this method. Speechreading is perhaps the weakest of the receptive media (Wooden, 1962, p. 157). Many adults who lose their hearing ability never learn to recognize on the lips language they have been using. Furthermore, Pauls (1960) has pointed out that only approximately one-third of the speech sounds are clearly visible in speechreading. There are also the homophonous words that look alike on the lips. Wooden concludes that "speech reading would not seem to hold promise as an initial language-teaching medium" (p. 157).

The teaching of language to the deaf involves factors and conditions other than those found in teaching language to hearing children. These have been described by Wooden (1962) as follows:

1. The deaf child lives in a non-language atmosphere in which he must always be in a favorable position to see any language that is presented in the form of speech.
2. The deaf child must use the single sense of sight in the dramatization of language.
3. Before the deaf child gets a particular connotation of a word fixed, he must encounter it in different settings from that normally used by hearing children. The normally hearing child receives a multitude of language impressions and constructions through hearing the language in many settings.
4. The literal-minded deaf child may find himself in a state of confusion because of the nature of language usage, such as: "The naughty boy exploded when reprimanded by his mother." The deaf child may visualize the boy exploding into space.

The Acquisition of Speechreading Ability. The first step in the development of verbal language ability is the experiencing of language as used by others and the gradual attachment of meanings to the sounds or in the case of the deaf child to lip movements of others. The dependence of language growth upon receptive opportunity and ability demands that the deaf child have many opportunities in the reception of language through speechreading, which is largely a visual process. Concerning the difficulties and problems encountered in the visual process, Costello (1958) states:

Unfortunately the very nature of vision places certain limitations upon the availability of spoken language and consequently upon the rapidity of growth and the quality of the language achieved. In fact, in the absence of hearing the reception of spoken language is greatly curtailed. The hearing sense has a wonderful spherical quality which permits the perception of sound from all directions. Speech occurring in the nearby environment is accessible at all times regardless of one's occupation with visual or manual tasks. Speechreading, however, is dependent upon vision, a sensory area essential to other activities, in particular manual activities. Reception of speech can take place only when speaker and receiver are so physically oriented that the eyes may focus upon the speaker's face. . . . Visual language experience is also limited by the absence of the alerting quality of the acoustical signal. Numerous verbal contacts are never made because the visual bond is too difficult to obtain or maintain. [P. 258.]

Speechreading introduces the child to a language system and to a world of symbols. These symbols stand for ideas and refer to events of the past, present, and future. With language growth the deaf child learns qualitative and quantitative relationships as well as abstractions. The acquisition of concepts is an important part of the language development of the deaf child. These are more difficult to

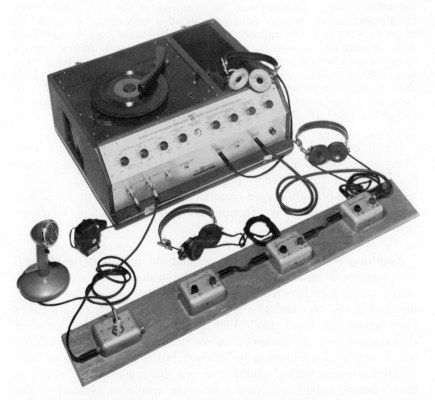

Fig. 9–2. The Warren Gated Compression Amplifier with three microphone channels. (Courtesy Jay L. Warren, Inc.)

acquire. Perceptual problems associated with speechreading present difficult learning problems to the deaf child. The rapidity of lip movements, the invisibility of certain movements, the discriminatory difficulty of movements, and the role of poor lighting conditions or distance present problems to the deaf child who must depend largely upon vision. In view of these limitations the deaf child must have ample opportunities to perceive speech in others. However, the perception of speech may come from two fundamental sources: the speech produced by others and that which he himself uses. Concerning the place of the child's own speech in language growth, Costello (1958) states:

> However, sensory stimuli important to language growth do not all come from the external environment, or should not. Speech training and talking experience can be viewed as part of language reception. The child becomes aware of his own voice, its feel and possibly its sound. With the introduction of amplification, the reception of the child's own voice takes precedence in interest value over all other environmental sounds. It is an arresting receptive experience. As word patterns become associated with meaning and representative of concepts, their use in speech forms a receptive as well as expressive experience. Self-reception of imitated word and sentence patterns associated with related situations or objects aids in the interiorization of symbol, the identification of word pattern with concept. It is this interiorization which is fundamental to the growth of verbal language. [P. 259.]

It may be noted that brain injury or damage is a descriptive term. Many of the causes of brain damage are also listed as causes of deafness. Thus, it seems likely that many deaf children may also be referred to as brain-damaged children. This may account for failure sometimes experienced in attempts to teach speechreading to a particular deaf child.

Acquiring Motor Skills. It was pointed out in Chapter 8 that except for general static ability and speed, the deaf child is not significantly handicapped in motor abilities. Results from various tests of motor skills and mechanical ability show that a wide range of abilities exist among the deaf (Doll, 1946). These studies show that deaf children are most handicapped in comparison with hearing children wherever verbal intelligence is involved, but there seems to be little difference in mechanical ability between the groups. This phase of their education should, therefore, be given special emphasis in order that they may be able to compete on more nearly equal terms at school and in later life. Certainly the deaf or hard-of-hearing child, even more than the normally hearing child, needs educational and vocational counseling not only on matters relating to the preparation for life's work but also on matters connected with his family, friends, and society at large.

Concept Formation and Problem-solving Ability of Deaf Children. The notion has frequently been expressed that deaf children are incapable of normal concept formation. Evidence gathered by Rosenstein (1960) furnished information about the ability of deaf children to form concepts. Rosenstein accepts the general formulation that children progress from perception to abstraction, and then to generalization. Data were gathered on hearing and deaf children. A factorial analysis of the data revealed differences in the two groups, supporting the notion that deaf children are inferior in the attainment of concept. Rosenstein's study on the fundamental skills of deaf children is complemented by that of Myklebust and Brutten (1953) dealing with visual perception. They found an inferiority of the deaf children on two of three standard tests used, the Marble Board test and the Pattern Reproduction test. No differences were obtained on a test of perseveration.

Stafford (1962) found that in most tests of problem-solving used in his study that hearing children surpassed deaf children. It seems likely that the symbol system of the deaf is not as subtle and efficient for solving the most abstract problems, whereas with certain types of problems the hard of hearing may be more efficient, since they have developed more completely the skill with which they use the symbol system they possess.

Instructional Procedures. Hearing is to speech what vision is to reading. A child born deaf does not learn to speak without instruction. Great strides have been made during the past half-century in teaching deaf children to speak. However, if there is no residual hearing, his reception of speech will be limited to lipreading or speechreading. Barring unusual circumstances, the postlanguage deaf child who loses his hearing at age six or later and receives prompt language instruction will not be at a significant disadvantage in educational achievement. Also, his natural speech will be well preserved. Thus, prompt and effective language instruction for elementary school children who become deaf or seriously hard of hearing is important for the child's educational development and the preservation of his natural speech.

The natural method is frequently used in teaching language to deaf children. One of the advocates of this method is Groht (1958), who espouses the use of language in natural situations through lip-reading and writing, with language principles presented later. This method is in harmony with the principles of language learning of hearing children.

Costello (1958) emphasizes the importance of feeling pleasure and satisfaction as a result of language learning. These feelings grow out of the satisfaction of the need for approval from others, of self-esteem, and of self-fulfillment. The "talk, talk, talk" procedure is advocated, not so much because of the frequency of exposure but rather the exposures associated with feelings of pleasure and satisfaction. She states: "Speechreading instruction which is repetitious, dull, monotonous, devoid of joy, without either intrinsic or extrinsic value, is a certain way to failure. Speechreading must have emotional as well as practical value" (p. 272). The fundamental principles applicable to language instruction in general will apply to the instruction of deaf and hard-of-hearing children.

1. Language should be made to serve a purpose for the child.
2. The teaching of language should be related to significant and meaningful experiences.
3. All sensory channels available should be used; the deaf child will make greater use of vision.
4. Children need varied contacts with the same words so as to understand them in different contexts.
5. Deaf children should be talked to from an early stage at home and elsewhere.
6. Deaf and hard-of-hearing children need specialized instruction to help them in their language acquisition.
7. Depending upon the readiness and ability of the child, the deaf and hard-of-hearing should be integrated into regular classes.

Enlisting Help and Cooperation from Parents. Opinions among educators are not in agreement about the advisability of help from parents both in the case of normal-hearing children and deaf children. Van Wyk (1959) has offered some useful reasons why the help of parents should be used in the education of their deaf children. Certainly most parents are keenly interested in and concerned about the speech development of their hard-of-hearing or deaf children. It would seem that, when properly motivated and guided, parents should be most helpful in the educative process. The following suggestions have been set forth as useful to parents in helping their deaf child with speech:

1. See to it that your child lives in a speaking atmosphere. Talk to him constantly. Don't use gestures to him. If the child uses one, supply the necessary word and make no further notice of it.

2. Expect your child to speak and accept the responsibility for providing him with the necessary vocabulary until he has mastered it and can give it back spontaneously in the correct situation. Start with simple words such as "Hi," "Hello," and "Bye-bye."

3. Constantly increase his vocabulary. Don't avoid new words for fear of confusing him. Use two or three words that mean the same thing so that his language will be more natural and beautiful. . . .

4. Insist that your child speak for himself in talking to relatives and friends, and later on to casual acquaintances and strangers. Don't step in and interpret. This will not help your child to develop self-confidence.

5. Send your child on the same errands as you give to your hearing children so he can learn to cope with these phases of everyday communication. At first you will need to help him with what he will say when he gets in the store. . . .

6. Never accept sloppy or careless speech. Parents have their children more hours each day than does the school. If you can train your child to speak carefully at all times, you will accelerate his school progress.

7. As you help your child to speak you will soon find it necessary to help his language. When words are in incorrect sequence, just rephrase them and let the child repeat them correctly. . . . If a child needs a certain sentence construction, he is ready to learn it and it should be given to him.

Asking questions involves many new language concepts. Children ask so many questions that parents have almost unlimited opportunities for helping. . . .

8. Discourage the use of pencil and paper when your child goes to the store. If he is to develop confidence in his speech, he will have to use it with strangers. . . . [Van Wyk, 1959, pp. 208, 227.]

OCCUPATIONAL ADJUSTMENT OF THE DEAF AND HARD OF HEARING

There are those persons who believe that a child who is deaf or hard of hearing is destined to be a burden to society, or if employed at all, he will only be able to do services that require manual work or some task very low on the scale of occupations. This conception is false. It is true that hearing defects, like any other physical handicap, may be a hindrance, but on the other hand, many persons so handicapped have achieved satisfaction and even distinction in their chosen vocations.

Vocational Guidance. The following case illustrates the need for vocational guidance and a constructive approach to the problem of the hard-of-hearing child.

Katherine's scholarship began to fall off along about the seventh grade. Altho she had shown an initial enthusiasm for girl-scout work, she began to rebel at attending meetings. She told her mother that she "did not quite know what was going on" at the meetings. Her mother was quite disturbed and influenced her father to "lay down the law" to Katherine.

However, in a routine hearing-screening program, it was discovered that Katherine had a handicapping loss of hearing and was missing oral work in the schoolroom and the instructions at the scout meetings. Katherine was equipped with a hearing aid and given instruction in lip reading. Her scholarship improved, and she participated in the activities in which she had previously had an interest.

When Katherine reached her senior year in highschool, she was determined to become a nurse. In a judicious and tactful manner, she was informed that her hearing handicap would disqualify her for optimum performance of her duties. She was guided into work as a dietitian, and, upon completing her course, found employment in a hospital. [Silverman, 1950, p. 137.]

Connor and Rosenstein (1963) noted that reading, writing, and speech skills were the keystones of successful careers for 177 females who left the Lexington School for the Deaf during the years 1935–1957. In a retrospective assessment of the school program, the interviewed women pointed out that school subjects dealing with the communicative skills were the most helpful to them. The operation of power machines and arithmetical skills were also rated as helpful to them in their later years.

Those concerned with vocational guidance of the deaf should realize that in the area of aptitude, as is true with intelligence, there appears to be a delay in maturation as compared to hearing individuals. Growth seems to continue until eighteen to twenty-one years of age before the highest level is reached. This is especially true for conceptualization and verbalization. This is important in making a diagnostic evaluation of the deaf adolescent's aptitude. It would seem that vocational guidance and training of the deaf should begin somewhat later and continue to a later date than is the case for hearing adolescents.

Vocational Training. The vocational training of the acoustically handicapped in high school need not be different from that designed for hearing students. Vocational training in the shop may include cabinetmaking, blueprint reading and drafting, physics and electricity, automobile mechanics, machine shop, welding, sheet metal work, printing, and pattern-making. Office or clerical courses may include bookkeeping, filing, typing, and the use of calculating machines.

Homemaking courses may include child care, nutrition, cooking, sewing, and household management.

Individual differences in talents and intelligence exist among those suffering from hearing defects just as they do among those who have normal hearing. Not all such persons are adapted for office work or some activity of a research nature, but there is a wide range of occupations that require different skills and different levels of mental ability and that make special demands of other sensory mechanisms. A study by Lunde and Bogman (1959), in cooperation with the National Association for the Deaf, showed that the deaf are employed in a wide range of occupational activities. A comparison of the occupational distribution of the deaf with that of the total population at the time the study was made is presented in Table 9–2. It may

TABLE 9–2

Occupational Distribution of the Employed Deaf and the Total Employed in the United States in 1957

	Employed Deaf	U.S. Population 1957
Professional, technical, and similar workers	6.6%	10.6%
Managers, officials, and proprietors	3.2	15.5
Clerical, sales, and similar workers	7.2	20.7
Craftsmen, foremen, and similar workers	35.9	13.4
Operatives and similar workers	35.2	20.1
Others (service workers, laborers, etc.)	11.9	19.7

SOURCE: After Lunde and Bogman (1959).

be noted from the occupational distribution that while the deaf are found in all the major occupational groups, there were fewer deaf in the professional, managerial, and clerical positions because of the necessity to communicate in these occupational groups. There were a greater number working as craftsmen, operatives, and in related jobs. The survey indicated further that 85 per cent of the deaf workers are successful in their occupations. This indicates that hearing loss is not an insurmountable obstacle for the realization of vocational success. If the deaf person is adequately motivated and well guided in his development, he will likely develop his talents so as to insure greater happiness and success. A boy of the authors' acquaintance, who almost completely lost his hearing during early childhood, was sent to a school for the deaf. He finished the high school course, took up cabinetmaking, and is now the foreman of a small group in a furniture plant. Other cases of similar achievement may be noted. A study of the special abilities of these individuals, with the aim to develop them further, will contribute to the happiness and welfare of the persons concerned and of those with whom they live.

The aims of education for children who are hard of hearing or deaf are similar in general to those for hearing children. However, the goal should not be that of developing individuals who imitate hearing children, but rather of well-integrated personalities who are happy in the family, community, and vocational relations. Some deaf children will learn to speak with considerable accuracy and facility; others will not. In cases where the speechreading and oral communication are not learned, other modes of language expression should be used. The child who is hard of hearing has the same needs as the child who hears normally. He has the right to grow up in an environment where he can develop his abilities without frustrations but with a feeling of belonging and security which comes from successful participation in various individual and group enterprises.

SUMMARY

The prevention of hearing defects should begin early in life. When a child suffers from an illness involving the nose, throat, or ears, special attention should be given to the conservation of hearing. If adequate treatment is given early for cases of sore throat or earache, the progress of serious infections that might destroy tissue and lead to hearing loss is stopped. As a result of medical advances, there has been a tremendous decrease in mastoid operations.

Research has contributed extensively to our knowledge of the nature and educational needs of persons who are hard of hearing. Some of the findings may be summarized as follows:

1. Wide individual differences in mechanical abilities and motor proficiency exist among the hard of hearing.
2. Many hard-of-hearing children suffer from speech difficulties.
3. Educational and vocational guidance of the hard of hearing and deaf are very important for their successful adjustment.

Certain principles and goals set forth relative to the instructional program for deaf and hard-of-hearing children may be summarized as follows:

1. The teacher should be cognizant of the abilities and needs of the individual children.

2. Efforts should be made to establish good interpersonal relations in the classroom. This means good relations with classmates and good relations with the teacher and others concerned with the program.
3. Work for the best communication possible in every situation, realizing at all times that the fundamental principles of learning apply here as elsewhere.
4. Provide continuous opportunity for the children to learn to recognize different sounds and words through lipreading.
5. Help the child understand the meaning of words and sentences, as well as to recognize them in print or on the lips.
6. Help him grow in vocabulary and thus build a better foundation for further educational growth.
7. Evaluate periodically his growth in speechreading, auditory discrimination, auditory comprehension, vocabulary, reading comprehension, articulation, and general educational growth in skills other than language.
8. Provide for special help when and where it is needed on an individual basis.

CHAPTER REFERENCES

BRILL, R. G. (1957). Education of the deaf and hard of hearing. *Except. Child.*, 23:194–98.

CONNOR, L. E., and ROSENSTEIN, J. (1963). Vocational status and adjustment of deaf women. *Volta Rev.*, 65:585–91.

COSTELLO, MARY R. (1958). Language development through speechreading. *Volta Rev.*, 60:257–59, 272.

DOLL, E. A. (1946). *Oseretsky tests of motor proficiency.* Minneapolis: Educational Test Bureau. Pp. 1–47.

DUNSDON, MARJORIE I. (1952). *Educability of cerebral palsied children.* London: Newnes Educational Publishing.

FINNETT, C. (1957). Some transatlantic differences in teaching deaf children. *Volta Rev.*, 59:204–6.

GROHT, MILDRED (1958). *Natural language for deaf children.* Washington, D.C.: The Volta Bureau.

HARDY, W. G. (1960). The assessment of hearing in children and an interpretation of the findings. In SIR A. EWING (ed.), *The modern educational treatment of deafness.* Washington, D.C.: The Volta Bureau.

HOFSOMMER, A. J. (1936). Lip reading and the intelligence quotient of the hard-of-hearing child. *J. Amer. med. Assn.*, 107:648–50.

KIRK, S. A. (1962). *Educating exceptional children.* Boston: Houghton Mifflin.

KODMAN, F., WATERS, J. E., and WHIPPLE, C. I. (1962). Psychometric appraisal of deaf children using the Columbia Mental Maturity Scale. *J. Speech & Hearing Disord.*, 27:275–79.

LUNDE, A. S., and BOGMAN, S. K. (1959). *Occupational conditions among the deaf.* Washington, D.C.: Gallaudet Coll.

MADDEN, R. (1931). *The school status of the hard of hearing child.* New York: Columbia Univer. Press.

MEYERSON, L. (1963). A psychology of impaired hearing. In W. M. CRUICKSHANK (ed.), *Psychology of exceptional children and youth.* (2d ed.) Englewood Cliffs, N.J.: Prentice-Hall.

MILLER, JUNE (1957). Classroom methods and materials for hard of hearing children. *Volta Rev.*, 59:343–45.

MONSES, EDNA K. (1959). Aphasia and deafness in children. *Except. Child.*, 25:395–99, 409.

MOTTO, J., and WAWRZASZEK, F. J. (1963). Integration of the hearing handicapped: evaluation of the current status. *Volta Rev.*, 65:124–29, 160.

MYKLEBUST, H. R., and BRUTTEN, M. (1953). A study of the visual perception of deaf children. *Acta Otol. Laryngol. Suppl.*, No. 105.

NATIONAL RESEARCH COUNCIL (1944). *The value of individual hearing aids for hard of hearing children.* Washington, D.C.: The Council.

PAULS, MIRIAM D. (1960). In H. DAVIS and S. R. SILVERMAN (eds.), *Speechreading, hearing and deafness.* New York: Holt, Rinehart & Winston. Pp. 353–67.

POULOS, T. H. (1961). Short-term rehabilitation program for hard of hearing children. *Hearing News*, 29:4–7.

ROACH, R. E. (1954). Considerations in education of children with various degrees of hearing loss. *Except. Child.*, 20:330–35, 358.

ROSENSTEIN, J. (1960). Cognitive abilities of deaf children. *J. Speech & Hearing Res.*, 3:108–9.

SILVERMAN, S. R. (1950). The hard-of-hearing child. *Nat. Educ. Assn. J.*, 39:137.

STAFFORD, K. (1962). Problem-solving ability of deaf and hearing children. *J. Speech & Hearing Res.*, 5:169–72.

STRENG, ALICE (1958). Public school programs for children with impaired hearing in small school systems. *Except. Child.*, 25:71–76.

STRIZVER, G. L. (1958). Frequency discrimination of deaf children and its relationship to their achievement in auditory training. *Volta Rev.*, 60:304–6.

VAN WYK, MARY K. (1959). Some help with speech. *Volta Rev.*, 59:207–8, 227.

WATSON, T. J. (1961). The use of residual hearing in the education of deaf children. *Volta Rev.*, 63:328–34.

WHILDIN, OLIVE A. (no date). *Hearing aid service for children.* Reprint No. 572. Washington, D.C.: The Volta Bureau.

WOODEN, H. Z. (1962). Dramatized language for the deaf. *Except. Child.*, 29:155–63.

WOODEN, H. Z. (1964). Language instruction for deaf children: an introduction to selected papers. *Except. Child.*, 30:333–35.

SELECTED READINGS

BENDER, RUTH E. (1961). *The conquest of deafness.* Cleveland: Press of Western Reserve Univer.

DAVIS, H., and SILVERMAN, R. S. (eds.) (1960). *Hearing and deafness.* (Rev. ed.) New York: Holt, Rinehart & Winston.

HART, BEATRICE O. (1963). *Teaching reading to deaf children.* Washington, D.C.: The Volta Bureau.

KIRK, S. A. (1962). *Educating exceptional children.* Boston: Houghton Mifflin. Chap. 7.

LEVINE, EDNA (1957). *Youth in a soundless world.* New York: New York Univer. Press.

MYERSON, L. (1963). A psychology of impaired hearing. In W. M. CRUICKSHANK (ed.), *Psychology of exceptional children and youth.* (2d ed.) Englewood Cliffs, N.J.: Prentice-Hall.

MYKLEBUST, H. R. (1960). *Psychology of deafness.* New York: Grune & Stratton.

O'NEIL, J. G., and OYER, H. J. (1961). *Visual communication for the hard of hearing.* Englewood Cliffs, N.J.: Prentice-Hall.

STRENG, ALICE, FITCH, J., HEDGECOCK, L. D., PHILLIPS, J. W., and CARRELL, J. A. (1958). *Hearing therapy for children.* (2d ed.) New York: Grune & Stratton.

IV

PHYSICAL
DISABILITY

Part III dealt with children with speech or hearing difficulties. Since speech and hearing are closely related and many speech problems are not organic, these were presented together in Part III rather than under "Physical Disability." Part IV will consider the special characteristics and problems of children with visual defects, and with crippling conditions. There has been considerable research in recent years on problems connected with disabilities of children. The application of scientific methods to the study of the nature and needs of these children is basic to a program of their education and training. These children have special educational needs that are better met when teachers and parents understand the significance of these needs in relation to the optimum development of the child.

In Chapter 10 different degrees of visual acuity are defined and the various visual difficulties found among children are described. Special attention is given to testing children in order to determine the nature and extent of certain visual difficulties. The role of the teacher in the screening and testing process is described. The special problems encountered by the child with defective vision and the blind child are also described. Special educational provisions for children with defective vision or who are blind are discussed in Chapter 11. In Chapter 12 the nature, characteristics, and adjustment problems of crippled children are presented. Consideration is given to problems of therapy, treatment, and guidance.

10

CHILDREN WITH VISUAL DEFECTS

Vision has been referred to as the meeting place of the sciences of physics, anatomy, physiology, and psychology. Problems of vision also occupy the attention of persons in other fields. The mathematician finds ample scope for his deductions and rigorous analytical skill. The philosopher argues whether perception of space is a property of mind or is empirically derived from the way we see, with some assistance from touch. "The artist plans his color scheme to impress the eye while the sculptor and architect associate grade and dignity of line with surface and volume for the same organ of vision. The inventor devises new sources of light which the illumination engineer effectively employs to meet the exacting requirements of sight" (Allen, 1937, p. 61). Educators, realizing the extent to which we depend upon the eyes for knowledge, perfect new visual aids for instructional use. The child responds to the various visual elements in the school situation. Through responding to these, he enlarges his knowledge and so develops a greater range and breadth of ideas.

The eye is a highly specialized sense organ that is easily stimulated by light rays and that reacts differently to various wave lengths. The eye is fairly well developed at birth. Experiments with the 1916 edition of the *Stanford Revision of the Binet Tests* have shown that the average child of five is able to distinguish the colors red, yellow, blue, and green. The ability to distinguish additional hues grows by experience and learning up through the early adolescent period. A more or less spontaneous interest in colors manifests itself during or following puberty. This fact tends to make adolescence important in conditioning an individual toward specific colors and in directing his habits of appreciation.

Structure of the Eye. The structure of the eye is similar in many respects to a camera. The eyeball is almost round in shape except at the cornea, where a slight bulge occurs. Light enters the eye through the pupil. The eyelids, when closed, serve as shutters to keep out light. The size of the pupil varies as the intensity of illumination changes. In a dark room the pupil dilates so as to permit more light rays to enter, while in bright sunlight it contracts. The light next passes through the crystalline lens which is located just behind the pupil. The lens is plastic and adjustable. When the ciliary muscles, which are attached to the lens by means of radial fibers, are relaxed, the anterior side of the lens is almost flat, while the posterior side is curved. When one focuses the eyes on nearby objects, the muscles contract, reduce the tension on the pliable lens, and thereby increase the curvature of the lens. Finally, the light passes through the vitreous humor, a transparent fluid within the fibrous walls of the eyeball, and strikes the retina.

Man is the only animal having eyes that are capable of doing such close work as reading. There is only one tiny spot on the retina, called the *macula,* which can see things sharply. When one looks at an object that must be seen distinctly, he focuses its light rays on the macula. This can be demonstrated by focusing your vision on a word in the center of this line. For the normal eye the word is clear and sharp. The words on either side fade out to an indistinguishable gray blur. In the normal adult eye the front curve, the curve of the lens, and the size of the eyeball are correctly developed for focusing on the retina the image of an object 20 feet or more away. In focusing the eye on objects that are less than 20 feet distant, and in using the eyes for close work such as reading, writing, or sewing, the ciliary muscles contract and increase the front curve of the lens. With respect to the growing child, Furniss (1940) has stated:

The child gradually appreciates varying degrees of brightness, learns to focus on near or distant objects by the efforts of "accommodation," acquires stereoscopic vision, and judges distance and color. The development of these processes is slow and conforms, with due allowances for differences in individual children, to a more or less definite pattern. The growth of the eyeball is most rapid in the first two years of life, and by the age of seven it has attained almost its maximum size. [P. 264.]

Prevalence of Visual Defects. In any group of average children the percentage of those with normal vision tends to increase as the children become older, in spite of greater use of their eyes. This is because the anatomical development of the eye is not completed until nearly the age of twenty. The problem of lack of maturation of the visual mechanism is one that should receive the careful attention of elementary school teachers. Children whose eyes have not matured to the point of accommodating readily for near objects should not be subjected to the educational discipline involved in reading.

In a study reported by Gutman (1956) 4,875 students were given the *Massachusetts Vision Test*. This test embraces a battery of three components described on page 278. The per cent of students failing the test at the different grade levels is shown in Fig. 10–1. There was an increase in failures from 18 per cent in Grade 2 to 37 per cent in high school. Hyperopia was the most frequently reported condition, comprising 47 per cent of all diagnoses. There was a close relation between the results obtained from this test and those obtained from the Snellen test. Dalton (1943) tested almost 6,000 children in California and found that 22 per cent of elementary school children and 31 per cent of high school students had visual defects. It should be emphasized, however, that any data of prevalence of visual defects will be affected by the tests and standards used and the population sample.

An exact estimate of the prevalence of blindness is not available (Hurlin, 1962). Incidence figures released by the National Society for the Prevention of Blindness show that there is approximately 1 seriously visually handicapped child for every 500 pupils (Myers, 1961). The estimated total blindness in 1960 in the United States was 385,000 or 2.14 per 1,000 of the population (Gibbons and McCaslin, 1962). Approximately 1,500,000 are reported as blind in one eye, while a much large number have some visual impairment. Gibbons and McCaslin state: "Approximately one school-age child in four needs some eye care, and it is estimated that there are 150,000 partially seeing children (including the legally blind) of preschool and school age" (p. 116).

Types of Eye Defects. The visual defects of 7,310 children enrolled in over 600 classes for partially sighted children were studied by Kerby (1952). She found that less than 30 per cent of the children

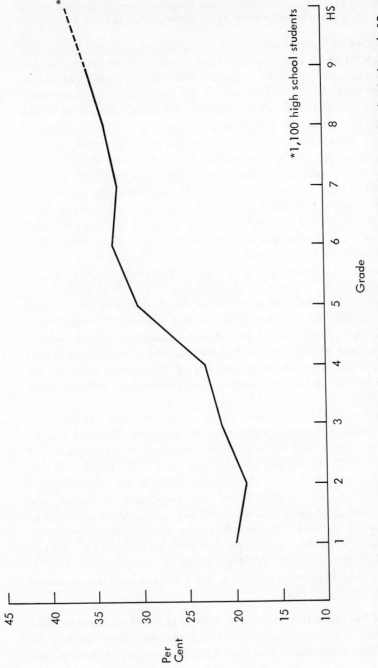

Fig. 10–1. Basic failures on *Massachusetts Vision Test* by grade in school: 4,875 students, Grades 1 through 12. (Gutman, 1956.)

fitted the visual acuity limits frequently used in defining partial sight—visual acuity between 20/70 and 20/200 after correction. Kerby reports the following types and percentages of defective vision:

Refractive errors (myopia, hyperopia, etc.)—49 per cent
Developmental anomalies of structure (cataracts, albinis, etc.)—22 per cent
Defects of muscle function (strabismus, nystagmus, etc.)—17 per cent
Disease or defects of the eye (due to infection, injuries, etc.)—11 per cent
Others, causes undetermined—1 per cent

It may be observed from the Kerby data that refractive errors constitute almost one-half of all visual defects of partially seeing children. The description and most common symptoms of refractive defects, as outlined some years ago by Berkowitz (1919), are as follows:

In cases of hypermetropia (longsight), the condition in which the eyeballs are too short from before backwards, the child can often see distant objects well but has difficulty in reading, sewing, etc. after using the eyes continually for some time. The type becomes blurred, and the letters run together; the eyeballs ache, and headache is felt, usually over the eyebrows.

These symptoms constitute eyestrain, and are chiefly due to overaction of the ciliary muscle, a small muscle situated inside the eyeball; by its action the shape and position of the lens are altered so as to allow objects at different distances to be focused on the retina at the back of the eye. This power of altering the focus of the eye is called "accommodation." . . .

In cases of myopia (shortsight), the condition in which the eyeballs are too long from before backwards, the children cannot see the blackboard when seated at the back of the class, or tell time by the clock when placed at the other side of the room; they hold books near their eyes and stoop over their work; after working by artificial light, the eyes become tired.

In cases of astigmatism the eyeball is curved unequally in different directions. Both hypermetropic and myopic astigmatism occur.

With hypermetropic astigmatism, the commoner form, eyestrain is more often associated than with any other abnormality of the shape of the eye.

Children with myopic astigmatism chiefly complain of inability to see distant objects.

Astigmatism. The discovery of the nature of astigmatism was an important medical achievement of the nineteenth century. It has been demonstrated that this condition is the result of an error in refraction due to irregular curvature of the cornea or lens of the eye.

A normally functioning eye is shown in Fig. 10–2, and an astigmatic eye in Fig. 10–3. Astigmatism is responsible for more than half the

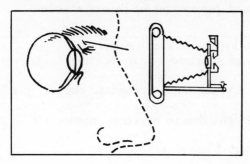

Fig. 10–2. The normal eye: parallel rays of light focus on the retina. (Adapted from Bausch and Lomb Optical Company.)

Fig. 10–3. Astigmatism: error of refraction of light rays due to irregularity in curvature. (Adapted from Bausch and Lomb Optical Company.)

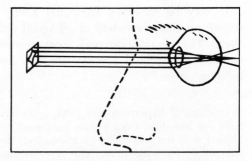

cases of seriously impaired vision and for much eyestrain. Few eyes are completely free from this defect. Since astigmatism is likely to be associated with other refractive errors, especially hyperopia, the child not only has reduced acuity resulting from blurred vision, but also suffers from eyestrain. In such cases a difficult task is imposed upon the ciliary muscle in its effort to adjust the eye to get a clearer visual image. Such efforts may result in peculiar mannerisms, nervousness, or faulty posture. Whether the child with a moderate degree of astigmatism should be advised to secure glasses depends in large measure upon age, study habits, and his general state of health. Some eyes have very little power of adjustment without some aid, and some nervous systems are more subject to reflex disturbances than are others.

Hyperopia and Myopia. An examination of Figs. 10–4 and 10–5 will make clear the nature of hyperopia (farsightedness) and myopia (nearsightedness). In Fig. 10–4 hyperopic condition is shown. The eyeball is too short from front to back, and light rays that enter the eye seem to focus the image behind the retina. Hyperopic eyes cannot see objects near at hand without placing undue strain on the

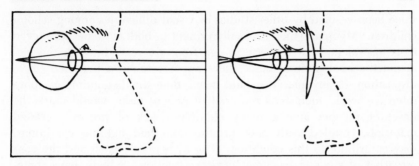

Fig. 10–4. Hyperopic or farsighted eye: rays of light focus behind the retina. Shown corrected at right. (Adapted from Bausch and Lomb Optical Company.)

muscles of accommodation. This often results in eyestrain. To test for this condition, a double-convex lens (+1.00 diopter) is used.[1] This lens brings the image to a focus more quickly. Hence, if the +1.00 diopter lens improves the vision, there is evidence of hyperopia.

Figure 10–5 shows an example of a myopic eye. Since the eyeball

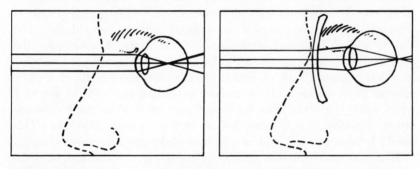

Fig. 10–5. Myopic or shortsighted eye: rays of light focus in front of the retina. Shown corrected at right. (Adapted from Bausch and Lomb Optical Company.)

is too long, the inverted image comes to a focus in front of the retina. To test for this condition, a double-concave lens (−1.00 diopter) is used. This lens causes the light to spread out and then focus closer to the retina. If the vision is improved by the −1.00 diopter lens, there is evidence of myopia.

About four decades ago Mills (1929) pointed out that vision problems usually begin in the third grade. His general conclusions have

---

[1] A diopter "is a unit of refractive power equal to that of a glass whose principal focal distance is one meter." The radius of curvature of its surface is one meter long.

since been verified by other studies of visual difficulties among school-children. Myopia, which is usually present in both eyes, becomes even more prevalent with increase in age from six years through the elementary school period. Since there appears to be a hereditary predisposition to myopia, it would seem that the beginning of more intensive work, such as is required by school tasks, would mark the onset of myopia among many children. Lack of properly graded materials, coupled with poor printing and bad lighting conditions, may contribute to this condition. The hygiene of vision and the conservation of sight is receiving greater attention. Schools have sometimes put too much stress on schoolwork that involves reading to the exclusion of many worthwhile lessons that can be learned by doing and from other methods.

Lack of Fusion. There are a number of miscellaneous types of visual problems, the majority of which may be classified under one heading. Lack of coordination of sight of the two eyes so that depth perception or some other attribute of bifocal vision is affected is termed "lack of fusion." Various types of faulty fusion are known as "strabismus"—sometimes called "heterophoria." One common type is cross-eyes, in which the eyes converge or turn in toward the nose. This is called "internal strabismus." With external strabismus the eyes so diverge that they seem to be looking in opposition directions. In a less common type of heterophoria one eyeball is tilted slightly upward or downward. Thus, in such cases one eye sees the top of a word while the other sees the lower part of it. The most common visual difficulty that is classified as lack of fusion is squint. This occurs in about 1 per cent of children under twelve years of age.

There are two common causes for squinting. In the one case the muscles are so distorted that eye movement is affected. A second cause has to do with the unequal strength of the eye muscles. One eye may be considerably weaker than the other, and this leaves the task of seeing to the stronger eye. Treatment of such defects should be left to ophthalmologists.

Symptoms of Visual Disability. If eye defects of children are listed in order of frequency of occurrence, hyperopia (farsightedness) will head the list, while astigmatism will likely be next. Myopia (nearsightedness) appears next, followed by some few cases of strabismus and by infrequent cases of inflammatory eye diseases. In order that teachers and parents may be better able to detect visual difficulties, a list of behavior characteristics is set out below (Winebrenner, 1952).

1. Blinks continually when reading or when focusing the eyes for some time on small objects.
2. Shows extreme nervousness. Displays frequent fits of temper.
3. Materials often appear blurred, and attempts may be made to brush the impediments away.
4. Holds the book in abnormal position when reading, for example, far away or very close.
5. Tilts head to one side when reading. Often looks out of side of eyes and then tries to look straight ahead.
6. Restless and irritable after using the eyes for reading or when at movies, or in other situations that require excessive use of them.
7. Inattentive during wall chart or map work. Does not like to try to follow other children in their oral reading.
8. Rubs eyes excessively; frowns and screws up the face considerably when looking at distant objects.
9. Has red-rimmed, encrusted, or swollen eyelids; recurring sties, inflamed or watery eyes.
10. Reads only a short time before stopping. Prefers play and other activities that do not tax the eyes.
11. Shuts one eye when reading. Confuses the letters very readily, and guesses, as it were, at a number of words.

Ocular Dominance. The *Miles A-B-C Test* has been found serviceable as a means of determining eye preference. It is easily administered. The subject is directed to view certain objects through a funnel made by folding a piece of papers so that the large end is pressed together in an oblong shape. This is held over the eyes. The subject is then directed to look at the observer, who is able to determine, from the focus of the eyes, which is the preferred one. The dominant eye is the one that is directed toward the observer or object, while the non-preferred eye shows greater fluctuation and does not remain focused so completely. This test presents the subject's response naturally, since he is unaware of which eye he is using. In a rather extensive study of ocular dominance among adults, the following results were obtained:

As a general rule, successive series of tests made on an individual all show the same eye as dominant. In adults, right-eye and left-eye dominance occur in the proportion of about 64 per cent and 34 per cent, respectively. About 2 per cent show no well-marked dominance habit.

Groups of right-handed individuals show ⅓ or slightly less of their number to be cases of left-eye dominance. Left-handed people are more evenly divided between right- and left-eye dominance.

Adults and children show closely agreeing results. Chinese men give results practically identical with those of American men. No significant difference appears for the women as compared with the men.

Special habits from training, as with the microscope, do not determine eye dominance. [Miles, 1930, p. 428.]

In severe cases of strabismus the dominant eye is almost as apparent as is the dominant hand in right- or left-handness. By looking at the person's eyes as he focuses them on an object, one can readily find out which eye determines his line of useful sight. A person comes to use this eye habitually, while the view of the deviating eye is completely neglected, just as the person with normal binocular vision disregards afterimages and double images.

Crossed Laterality. Most children are right-handed and right-legged, some are left-handed and left-legged, and some are truly ambilateral. In a similar manner one eye is preferred, usually on the same side as the dominant hand of the individual. In like manner, one side of the brain is dominant, the side opposite to the preferred hand. According to Blau (1946) the language process, including speech, reading, and writing, is primarily centered in one side of the brain. This is ordinarily the same half of the brain that controls the dominant eye. When the dominant eye of the child is on the opposite side from that of the preferred hand, the child is said to have crossed or mixed laterality.

Crossed laterality is not uncommon among children. The children who have it frequently do not respond well to ordinary educational methods and may need special consideration and treatment. Results from psychometric tests administered to children with crossed laterality disclose disturbances in their visual-motor integration and spatial orientation. Such children may also show evidence of a disturbed emotional state and educational difficulties in general. These youngsters need careful psychological treatment and supervision to establish one-sided control (Hume, 1951, p. 201). The importance of discovering crossed laterality lies in the fact that the teacher can then know the children who may be headed for special reading difficulties and can make special provisions for meeting their reading needs.

STUDY OF VISUAL DIFFICULTIES

The identification of school children in need of special help because of limited vision constitutes the first step in a correctional and educational program for the visually handicapped. Early recognition of potential eye difficulties furnishes the best means for preventing or ameliorating serious eye disorders and thus reducing the educational and social problems resulting from such conditions. A complete study of visual difficulties in a school population would require the services of a team of specialists from different areas. This would also demand a complete and regular eye examination of all the pupils.

Detection of Visual Difficulties. School procedures that make use of tests for the study of visual difficulties have been based upon the assumption that vision is free from impediments when, in the perception of distant objects, the acuity equals or approximates the value generally accepted as normal. Acceptance of the idea that 20/20 is perfect vision leads to the neglect of other serious problems of vision, since 20/20 is a measure of sharpness or visual acuity.[2] The assumption that the rating of visual acuity is a measure of the ease with which the eyes perform their function is to accept a standard that places major emphasis on retinal activity and almost completely ignores the muscular functions which are now known to be the basic element in the many discomforts that frequently affect the eyes. Accommodations of the eyes and the convergence of their visual axes are functions essential to vision. These require, in most phases of their activity, definite contraction of muscle groups. The mechanical act of reading is made possible through the coordination of these muscularly controlled functions, and the comfort that attends the reading process will depend upon the degree of perfection with which the muscles act.

Here is a case that illustrates a definite deficiency in visual control. A child twelve years old, with normal intelligence, was in the seventh grade. Her arithmetic computation measured slightly above the average. In oral reading she was at the fifth-grade level, but her ability in silent reading tests was below the fourth-grade level. It was noted that the child's chief difficulty was in her extremely slow rate of response. For this reason it was hard for her to accomplish the required work. Repetition of words made up most of her errors in oral reading. On an earlier examination of the child's vision no visual

---

[2] In the interpretation of 20/20 vision the first figure refers to the distance in feet at which the testing is done—20 feet. The second figure refers to the distance at which most people can distinguish the particular group of letters on a chart, such as the Snellen chart. A person with 20/20 vision can distinguish at a distance of 20 feet the letters that most people can make out at that distance. A person with 20/40 vision cannot make out the letters at a distance of 20 feet, but can distinguish larger letters at this distance, letters that most people can distinguish at a distance of 40 feet.

difficulties were observed when using the Snellen chart. When either eye was covered, it was found that she could respond correctly. However, she failed on tests that involved the use and coordination of both eyes. The difficulty was lack of motor control of eye movement. The child's slow rate of reading was the result of her inability to make rapid, coordinated eye movements.

Testing Visual Difficulties. The National Society for the Prevention of Blindness recommends as the basic minimum screening procedure for schoolchildren an annual test for distance visual acuity using the *Snellen Chart* along with teacher observations for symptoms that may be related to eye problems. Such screening should be supplemented by other tests when it seems necessary. For example, if a child persistently exhibits symptoms of eye difficulties such as those presented on page 275, he should have a competent eye examination making use of additional tests that are available.

The *Keystone Telebinocular* has been used for measuring different aspects of visual difficulties. It has an advantage over many other instruments in that tests of fusion, muscular imbalance, and coordination are included in the testing. The *Massachusetts Vision Test* checks usable distance vision on a Snellen-type chart for hyperopia and tests for vertical and horizontal balance of the extraocular muscles at distance and for horizontal imbalance at near vision. The *Telebinocular,* the *Sight-Screener,* and the *Ortho-Rater* are binocular, stereoscopic testing instruments that screen for distance and near visual acuity, fusion, depth perception, and distance and near vertical and horizontal muscle imbalance (Foote and Crane, 1954). The *Snellen Chart* is still widely used, although it is not too adequate since it will detect myopia but not hyperopia, presbyopia, or visual difficulties resulting from muscle imbalance. It still gives as accurate a measure when used by teachers as do the more expensive mechanical devices. It is also available now with glasses with + lenses to measure for farsightedness (hyperopia).

The validity and dependability of these procedures have been carefully studied by a number of investigators. Crane *et al.* (1952) report the results obtained from several methods of screening for visual defects in Grades 1 and 6. Complete ophthalmological examinations were made on 609 sixth-grade pupils and 606 first-grade pupils. The results of four different screening procedures were evaluated by comparing them with the results of ophthalmological examinations. The results revealed a low degree of correspondence between referrals by any of the screening procedures and examination results of the

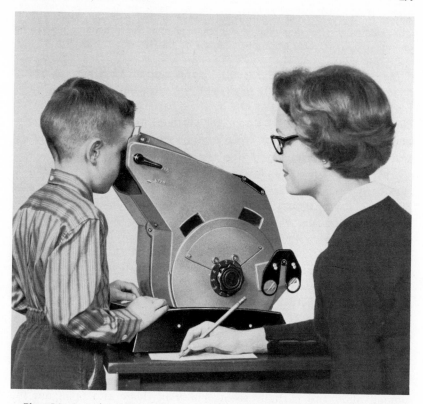

Fig. 10–6. The School Vision Tester is useful in identifying at an early age children with visual difficulties. (Courtesy Titmus Optical Company, Inc.)

ophthalmologists. In general, the greater the number of correct referrals by a particular procedure, the greater the number of incorrect referrals. Also, the greater the number of measurements involved in a procedure, the higher is the proportion of both correct and incorrect referrals. The *Ortho-Rater, Sight-Screener,* and *Telebinocular* tests correctly referred 23 to 25 per cent of the sixth graders, or about three-fourths of the 31 per cent referred by the ophthalmologist. This is a high proportion of referrals when compared with the results from the other procedures; however, these tests referred incorrectly an even larger number of students, about 30 per cent of all sixth-grade pupils. Crane and her colleagues concluded from this study that:

The efficiency of a screening procedure depends in part on the visual functions tested and the accuracy of the methods of measurement possible under ideal conditions and in part on the degree to which the tests are

suited to the nonvisual capabilities and motivations of the subject. . . .
The efficiency also depends on whether or not the procedure is simple
enough not to require elaborate training of the tester. [P. 1439.]

Motor Performance of Visually Handicapped Children. A study
conducted by Buell (1950) dealt with the gross motor performance of
blind and partially sighted children. A battery of tests, including a
50-yard dash, basketball throw for distance, standing broad jump,
and the *Iowa Brace Test*, was administered to 865 children in 12
residential schools and 8 Braille classes.

The results revealed that both groups of children fell far below
normal-seeing children on all levels of the *Iowa Brace Test*. Partially
sighted children scored better than blind children in both elementary
groups studied and at the junior high level for girls. For the boys
there was little difference at the junior or senior high school level.
The weakness of the children in motor performance seems to be general rather than specific. This was further shown in scores obtained
from track and field events. The visually handicapped children scored
lowest in the basketball throw for distance and performed significantly
better in running than in throwing. However, the visually handicapped high school boys excelled normal-seeing boys in the standing broad jump. This difference may be attributed to the intensive
training given to these boys in this particular event. These results
support findings from studies relative to certain motor deficiencies
among blind and partially seeing children. They also point out the
results that may be obtained from special training.

There is evidence, however, that the mobility of the blind may be
affected by other handicaps, especially deficient hearing ability. The
results of a study by Riley *et al.* (1964) indicate that there is a significant relationship between auditory thresholds of blind subjects
and mobility performances; the highest correlations were noted with
the higher pure-tone frequencies.

PREVENTION AND CARE OF VISUAL DIFFICULTIES

It was pointed out earlier that a complete program of eye care
requires teamwork and regular eye examinations for everyone. A
good program will certainly require comprehensive screening for early
discovery, referral for more complete examination for those who seem
to have symptoms indicating the likelihood of special eye problems,
and follow-up to carry out recommendations of the complete eye
examination. However, research reveals that an adequate screening

and identification of those in need of special help is only the first step in a program of eye care. A complete program will require careful planning by everyone concerned with the educational, medical, and other needs of a given population.

Early Attention to Eye Care. Our basic educational program is designed so as to acquire ideas and information largely through vision. It is estimated that 85 per cent or more of our learning comes by way of the eyes (Martmer, 1959, p. 333). It is therefore very important that good eye care should begin at birth and that the eyes be as near perfect as possible when the child enters school. It is also very important that eye care be continued and that children not damage their eyes as a result of educational conditions and the educative process.

The baby has not learned to fuse the image entering the two eyes during the first three months. This results in double image. There is no fixed vision pattern; therefore, the eyes may seem to wander a great deal. Concerning care at this age, Ashley (1961) states:

. . . any constant deviation in muscle balance by age six months should be referred to an ophthalmologist for careful watching. An unrecognized or neglected strabismus may lead to irreversible loss of vision in the crossed eye. During the first three years a squint is most commonly due to anatomical disturbance in the nerve supply. If the squint does not appear until three to five years, it is generally due to a refractive error. As stated, the child with a squint should always be carefully examined as soon as it is noticeable, for there may be other conditions such as congenital cataract, chorioretinitis, or retinoblastoma which may destroy the vision in one eye and cause a squint. [Pp. 26–27.]

The Problem of Eyestrain. The process that enables the eye to focus rays of light from near objects as well as from those at a distance is known as "accommodation." In reading, this process is operative and requires the continued use of certain pairs of muscles throughout the reading period. Such muscular activity inevitably leads to fatigue. Since rest is the antidote to fatigue, the eyes should be given periodic rest periods during the time when they are being used for close work. No one would think of continuing a task such as chopping wood or pulling weeds for several hours without resting his muscles, and the same principle applies in the case of reading a novel or sketching a scene. Eyestrain may be harmful to children in two ways: (1) by its effect on the entire physical system and (2) by its effect on the eyes themselves. Some common effects on the system are headaches, nervousness, irritability, drowsiness, digestive disturbances, dizziness, and car sickness. Some of the common effects on the eyes are blurring, tiring, redness, frequent blinking, dread of light, watering, sties, cross-eyes, development of astigmatism, and nearsightedness.

In the case of blurred vision some interesting answers have been obtained to the question "How does the print look to you?" Some of the more representative answers may serve as guides to the detection of eyestrain:

> "The letters all run together."
> "One letter is on top of the others."
> "I first see a letter and then it looks like another letter."
> "I see more than one line all at the same time."
> "The words are all jumbled up."
> "Part of the letters are upside down."
> "There is a skim over the letters."
> "The words and letters seem to move around."
> "After I read a line or two, I can't find my place."
> "The letters look crooked."

Early Reading and Eyestrain. The very young child is normally hyperopic, but when this condition is present in an older child, it may suggest mental, emotional, or physical immaturity. Such immaturity can contribute as much to difficulties in school as the visual disorder. Tests for measuring each child's background of interest and information and his language and mental development should be given when he enters school, in order to determine his "readiness to learn." Upon entering school, and at regular intervals afterward, each child should have his eyes examined. Witty has pointed out that more than 40 out of each 100 children in Grades 4 to 6 have serious eye defects, and that the percentage is greater in the higher grades. Learning to read when too immature may thus produce eyestrain. Very few eye defects are found among children at the time they enter school.

Early reading activities should be done by daylight or in good artificial light. After the age of seven, reading for most children may be permitted by artificial light. Experiences of pupils studying in inadequately lighted schoolrooms indicate that muscular fatigue and nervous symptoms are manifested to a greater extent than when better conditions exist. Luckiesh (1944) pointed out the effects of seeing on the total individual as follows:

Behind the eyes, operating them and performing the tasks of seeing, is the human being, or more specifically, the human seeing-machine. Except for certain aspects of health and disorders caused or aggravated by eyestrain, the human being as a seeing-machine has been too generally ignored. [P. 11.]

School Lighting Standards. Considerable research has been relative to desirable illumination in schoolroom construction. This has resulted in a changed viewpoint about the range of light intensity. Warnecke states: "Intensity of light is no longer the criterion of good lighting or seeing. Rather, proper distribution of daylight throughout the entire room and reduction of contrasts in light intensity and glare are the present-day criteria" (p. 3). There is evidence from many sources that adequate levels of illumination, with properly balanced brightness, is beneficial to the student in that it makes seeing easier and quicker. Good lighting also aids pupils with impaired vision by reducing visual fatigue; it helps in creating a more favorable climate for learning.

The levels of illumination recommended for different tasks and activities at school are presented in Table 10–1 (Illuminating Engineer-

TABLE 10–1

Levels of illumination recommended for schools (*Adapted*)

Location	Footcandles on Tasks
Classroom on desks and chalkboards	70
Study halls	70–150
Lecture rooms	70
Art rooms	70–50
Office, libraries	70
Shops and laboratories	100
Classrooms for partially seeing pupils and those requiring lipreading—on desks and chalkboards	150
Drafting room	100
Typing	70
Sewing rooms	150
Reception rooms, gymnasium	20
Swimming rooms	10
Auditorium (not for sewing)	15
Cafeterias, locker rooms	30
Washrooms	30
Corridors, containing lockers, stairways	20
Open corridors and storerooms	20

Source: Illuminating Engineering Society Handbook (1958).

ing Society, 1958). The greatest demand noted is in study halls, art rooms, and sewing rooms. There is also a need for greater illumination in the classroom for partially seeing pupils and those requiring lipreading. There is a tendency for people in the age groups from ten to twenty years to prefer more light than might be expected of young eyes. This is probably due to the lower sensitivity to glare among this group than among the twenty- to thirty-year-old group. After the age of thirty-five there is a general tendency to prefer more light for reading.

Eye Infections. Eye infections such as conjunctivitis are frequently encountered and may be very troublesome. Conjunctivitis is an inflammation of the mucous membrane of the eye resulting from bacterial infection. The symptoms include burning and watering of the eyes and an accumulation of pus under the eyelids. One of the most often observed types of conjunctivitis is that referred to as pinkeye. This condition is quite contagious and is usually spread by germs from a towel. To guard against such an occurrence children should not use the same towel.

Growing children need a well-balanced diet. An inadequate supply of protein may lead to eye infections. It has been suggested that too many sweets and an insufficiency of proteins tend to lower a child's immunity to eye infections, such as virus infections of the cornea. Such conditions always require specific care and treatment by a physician.

Sometimes disturbances of the eyes are symptomatic of a generally unhealthy condition or of disease in other parts of the body. Some diseases that may be reflected in the eyes include arthritis, diabetes, allergies, anemia, glandular disturbances, and high blood pressure. In these instances the disease condition must be treated before one can expect any permanent improvement in the eyes.

Visual Defects and Emotional Maladjustment. The first needs of the visually handicapped child should be met by his family. He needs the love and security of his parents as much as his brothers and sisters do. The importance of a favorable emotional climate for the personal, social, and educational development of the individual has been established through a number of studies. Eye specialists point out that even cross-eyes may result from serious emotional upsets or frustrations. Some children cross their eyes when scolded by their parents or when some other member of the family appears to get all of the attention. It has been suggested that nearsightedness may result in part from the child's wish to exclude from his vision the large, threatening world that he encounters. Persistent winking of the eyes or the "screwing up" of the eyes may be traced to the individual child's shrinking from danger. In such cases of visual defects the trouble may be cleared up once the underlying causes are removed. Intelligent and sympathetic parents and teachers, through understanding the child's problems, can contribute a great deal to the alleviation of such conditions.

Eye Surgery. In recent years surgery has been extensively used in the treatment of cross-eyes or strabismus. Crossed eyes can be straightened by surgery to the eye muscles or through glasses especially prepared to correct the condition. Cross-eyes can be corrected by surgery more easily where the treatment is started when the patient is very young. Furthermore, the sooner the treatment is begun, the better the chances are of producing normal vision.

The correction of cross-eyes may have great psychological value to the individual by relieving him of self-consciousness. Every child should have a thorough eye examination before he enters school. This examination should furnish a basis for special treatment that might be needed as well as for the educational guidance of the child.

Operations to prevent permanent blindness include the removal of cataracts from the eyes. Cataract is a condition in which the lens of the eye has become opaque and light cannot pass through. This condition usually occurs among older people, but it is occasionally found in children. The removal of the cataract is an operation in which the opacity that prevents the passing of light is removed. In selected cases blindness due to a damaged cornea may be corrected by the surgical transplantation of a healthy cornea to replace the damaged or diseased one.

Conservation of Vision. Although much is known about the nature, needs, and care of the eyes, the general public often relies on "common sense" and outmoded practices where vision is concerned. Too many are willing to trust the care of their eyes to a druggist, to a general medical practitioner, or to something from the counter of the drugstore. The notion still prevails that keen eyes mean good eyes and that once vision is slightly affected there is need for trying some glasses. There is a rapidly growing recognition that more attention given to the improvement of the eyes through eye exercise, diet, and other means will be valuable in improving vision without resorting to glasses. The National Society for the Prevention of Blindness works closely with official and private agencies in developing and promoting programs for the prevention of blindness and the preservation of eye health. It is just as important to have one's eyes examined regularly as it is to have a regular check of heart or kidneys.

The classroom teacher can assist children in the prevention of visual difficulties by instructing them (1) to read only when there is good light, (2) to sit in a position so that there will be no glare on the reading surface, (3) to hold reading materials in the correct position, (4) not to read while lying down, (5) not to read while riding in a bus, train, or automobile, (6) to rest the eyes periodically when engaged in reading or other close work, (7) to avoid reading during a period of acute illness, and (8) to employ good sanitary practices in the care of the eyes.

Fatigue and weakness of the eyes from eyestrain must be taken into account in any program of prevention and correction. Sometimes the lens of the eye may not function in the best manner even when glasses are used. There may be a weakened condition of ciliary muscles and also a lack of toughness of the sclerotic coat which provides protection to the eye.

Many of the pupils enrolled in classes for partially sighted children are myopic, for not all cases of myopia can be corrected sufficiently to enable the child to take part in all the learning activities of the regular class. However, special classes as such are largely disappearing. Each case should be considered individually, and treatment should be based upon results obtained from eye examinations, observations of the condition of the eyes and the behavior of the child when using his eyes, and the judgment of the ophthalmologist. The skilled services and scientific knowledge of the ophthalmologist are basic to any program for preventing serious visual difficulties and blindness. Everyone concerned with the development and training of children should understand, however, the problems related to the conservation of vision and should be aware of means for safeguarding eyesight. The tragedy of blindness—partial or complete—is no longer solely a personal problem involving only the patient and his physician. Parents, educators, public health officials, nurses, social workers, industrialists, and illuminating engineers have important responsibilities in the conservation of vision and the care of the eyes.

CHILDREN WHO ARE BLIND OR PARTIALLY SEEING

It was pointed out earlier that there is approximately 1 seriously visually handicapped child for every 500 pupils. These are the children classified as blind and partially seeing.

Fonda (1961) has offered the following definition of blindness:

(1) Vision of 20/200 or less in the better eye, or in both eyes, with best corrective glasses.

(2) Vision better than 20/200 in the better eye with best corrective glasses and with a visual field constricted to 20 degrees or less in the widest diameter, using a 3mm, or an equivalent isopter. [P. 169.]

Total blindness has been defined as inability to distinguish light from darkness, or complete lack of light perception. The Federal Bureau of Public Assistance (1936) provided a definition of economic blindness as a condition for eligibility for assistance in the general state aid-to-the-blind programs. The professional definition (Hurlin, 1962) notes:

. . . central visual acuity of 20/200 or less in the better eye with correcting glasses is considered as economic blindness. . . . An individual with central visual acuity of more than 20/200 in the better eye with proper correction is usually not considered blind unless there is a field defect in which the peripheral field has contracted to such an extent that the widest diameter of visual field subtends an angular distance no greater than 20 degrees. [P. 8.]

Causes of Blindness. The major causes of blindness have been listed in broad categories: infectious diseases, injuries, poisonings, tumors, general diseases, prenatal influences, and etiology not reported. In a study reported by Hatfield (1963) eye examination reports were collected for 7,757 pupils, or 58 per cent of the nearly 13,500 legally blind school children in the 1958–1959 school year. The estimated prevalence rates for selected school years are given in Table 10–2. A breakdown of the data by sex showed that 55 per cent of the pupils were boys and 45 per cent girls, a ratio of 122 to 100. Boys outnumbered girls in all age groups studied although the differential was smallest for 5 to 9 year olds. For practically all causes the rate of blindness for boys is greater than for girls. The one notable exception was retrolental fibroplasia, in which the rate of blindness for girls was 16 per cent higher than for boys. It is interesting to note that important changes occurred during the 25 year period studied in the cause of blindness among school-age children.

The specific cause of blindness may have important educational and psychological implications for parents, teachers, and the children concerned. The attitudes of parents may be influenced by whether the blindness is thought to be the results of hereditary or environmental conditions. Studies indicate that most blindness is of prenatal origin, although it is not always clear as to what specific factors operate to produce the condition. Some of the important factors related to eti-

TABLE 10–2

Estimated Rates of Blindness in School Age Children by
Etiology, Selected School Years

	Rate per 100,000 Pupils Enrolled			
Etiology	1933–34	1943–44	1954–55	1958–59
Infectious diseases	6.1	5.0	1.5	1.3
Toxoplasmosis	–	–	0.1	0.3
Rubella	–	–	0.1	0.2
Ophthalmia neonatorum	2.3	2.3	0.3	0.1
Syphilis	1.1	1.1	0.3	0.1
Tuberculosis	0.1	✿	0.1	0.1
Measles	0.2	0.2	✿	✿
Other	2.4	1.4	0.6	0.5
Injuries	1.6	1.5	1.0	0.8
Poisonings	✿	✿	3.8	11.3
Excessive oxygen (RLF)	–	–	3.8	11.3
Other	✿	✿	✿	✿
Tumors	0.5	0.8	1.0	1.2
General diseases	0.3	0.3	0.1	0.6
Prenatal influence	10.8	12.1	11.2	16.3
Not reported	1.9	2.2	1.3	2.6
Total, all causes	21.2	21.9	19.9	34.1
Number in study	2,702	3,749	4,426	7,757

✿ Less than one-tenth of 1 per cent.
SOURCE: Hatfield (1963).

ology and incidence of blindness over the years, suggested in the
study by Kerby (1958), are as follows:

1. Blindness rate due to infectious diseases has been progressively
   decreasing. The estimated rate for 1954–1955 is 75 per cent
   less than that for 1933–1934. Those resulting from ophthalmia
   neonatorum decreased during this period from 6.1 per 100,000
   to 1.5, while the decrease for those resulting from syphilis was
   from 2.3 to .3 per 100,000.
2. There was a notable increase in blindness resulting from excessive oxygen, producing retrolental fibroplasia—a maldevelopment
   of the retina. (Because of the high prevalence of retrolental
   fibroplasia among children born around 1950, it was responsible
   for approximately 50 per cent of the blindness in preschool
   children in Kerby's study. Medical advancements in the years
   that followed have reduced this to a rather low point.)
3. Heredity and prenatal influences unspecified remain the most
   consistent and the major cause of blindness among children.
4. There has been a steady decline in the percentage of blindness
   resulting from injuries since the high of 1.7 per 100,000 children
   of school age in 1941–1942.

Learning Problems of Blind Children. It has been estimated that the normal child learns almost 90 per cent through sight. A blind child must do all of his learning by other means. There are many examples of different kinds of learning among blind children. In various preschool programs, such as the Los Angeles Nursery School for Visually Handicapped Children, blind children are being taught to do things that in the past would ordinarily have been regarded as impossible.

It has been observed that blind babies, when allowed to creep freely, take bumps better than children with normal sight. The blind children at the Los Angeles Nursery School learn to bathe, dress and undress themselves, and to play together like any other group of children. Each has his own crib, clothes locker, drawer, and cupboard for shoes and toys. By the age of five the children have learned to button their own clothes, to lace and tie their shoes, to brush their teeth, and to manage bathroom duties. The classroom and playground equipment is selected with the needs and abilities of blind children in mind, although they make use of climbing bars, slides, and swings.

Blind children may become adept in the use of other senses in learning. Through training and guidance they may be able to pursue and enjoy many of the activities normally pursued and enjoyed by seeing children.

Speech Problems of Blind Children. Information available on speech problems of blind children is not in complete agreement. One report estimated the incidence of serious speech defects as high as 48 per cent (Brieland, 1951). A survey by Rowe (1958) of children in the Northern California area indicated that 6.7 per cent of the children would benefit from speech therapy. Miner (1963) conducted a study of speech deviations among 293 elementary school children from the Michigan School for the Blind and the Illinois Braille and Sight Saving School. Both schools had kindergartens through the sixth grade represented, along with several "special" classrooms for the mentally retarded and emotionally disturbed.

Miner found 99 children with speech deviations. This included over one-third of the children studied. Articulation problems led the list of defects, followed by voice problems as the next highest number. Only 1 child of the 293 studied was troubled with stuttering. This boy was a partially sighted student with a history of extensive neurological damage at birth. In some respects he did not fit into the patterns of speech behavior generally regarded as stuttering. Rowe pointed out earlier in her study that "No child was considered by the therapist to be a stutterer." Although one should not generalize too freely from the results of these studies, there is good evidence that the incidence of speech deviations in visually handicapped children is higher than most estimates from the general school population.

Intelligence and Achievement. The 1930 *Hayes-Binet Scale* was developed specifically for testing the intelligence of blind children. Reports from the use of this scale in 17 residential schools with 2,372 blind pupils yielded mean IQ's from 92 to 108.1, with standard deviations from 15.24 to 22.62, indicating a wide range of IQ's (Hayes, 1941). A larger percentage of blind children was found in both the above-average and below-average groups than in the general population. A more recent study by Bateman (1962) of blind children in school and in special programs gave a mean IQ of 97.5 for 53 girls and a mean IQ of 101.7 for 47 boys. These studies are based upon blind children in school rather than the total population. These data are further supported by data from a study reported by Karnes and Wollersheim (1963), and indicate that the mental development of partially sighted children in school does not deviate from that of seeing children.

Lowenfeld (1945) in reporting on the age-grade status of 481 blind pupils in the third, fourth, fifth, and sixth grades noted the following amounts of average overageness: third and fourth grades, 2.5 years; sixth grade, 2.9 years; and seventh grade, 2.8 years. Retarded academic achievement among blind children was noted in a more recent study by Ashcroft (1959), although this was less than that found among the deaf. The overageness for grade seems, according to Ashcroft (Dunn, 1963), to result largely from the following causes:

(1) late entry to school, (2) years of failure in unspecialized programs before placement in appropriate programs, (3) loss of time in school due to surgery or treatment for eye conditions or illness, (4) lack of opportunity for schooling, and (5) the slower rate of acquiring information from reading in braille, large type, or through auditory means. [P. 432.]

Adjustment Problems. A 1933 study by Cutsforth (1951) revealed considerable insight into the problems and psychological effects of blindness, and many research studies have tended to confirm his findings and assumptions. His case studies show some of the major problems that still confront blind children. Some problems relate to language activities and limited experiences resulting from lack of vision.

According to Cutsforth (1951), the phantasies observed in studies of the blind may be classified with three categories:

(1) Phantasies in which the individual eradicates the source of social annoyance; (2) phantasies in which the individual attains marked superiority or security; (3) phantasies in which the individual withdraws from the active situation in a surrender to a simple, regressive preoccupation, largely emotional in nature. [P. 75.]

The daydreaming frequently encountered among those with serious visual handicaps is no doubt closely related to their inability to participate freely in many social activities. This, however, does sometimes contribute to the development of imaginative abilities which appear frequently among some of the more intelligent individuals with serious visual handicaps. The immaturity and insecurity of the blind child can best be explained by the limitations imposed by blindness. Major limitations are upon the range and variety of experiences, mobility, and control of the environment and one's relation to it (Karnes and Wollersheim, 1963).

Some of the personality problems most often found among the visually handicapped and blind are: phantasies and daydreaming; blindisms; emotional instability; speech problems; unfavorable attitude toward self and others; and limited interests and lack of initiative. Concerning personality disturbances of the blind, Barker et al. (1953) came to the following conclusion as a result of their survey of the somatopsychological significance of impaired vision:

Probably the most impressive fact yet discovered about the psychology of the blind is the relatively small amount of personality disturbance that accompanies it. How persons can accommodate to so radical a shift in psychological living conditions without greater changes in behavior would seem to have important implications for students of personality as well as for those concerned with the adjustment of the blind. [P. 290.]

The Visually Handicapped Adolescent. The effects of being visually handicapped are frequently intensified with the onset of adolescence. The developing social-sex drive, the needs for independence, and the growth from the dependency of childhood toward the realization of adulthood present difficult adjustment problems for the visually handicapped teenager. The child grows into adolescence frequently unprepared for meeting the new demands that are geared toward helping him function independently. Frequently there has been a close identification with the mother, with the result of a low self concept and little identification with the father. The result is likely to be more difficult for the adolescent boy. The case of Arnold illustrates the problems of the emotionally disturbed visually handicapped adolescent (Wagner, 1961).

Arnold, age eighteen, had been known to our agency for approximately ten years. Diagnosis: Retrolental Fibroplasia. Initially his mother requested simple services; i.e., talking book machines, recreation, etc. Both parents were well educated, successful, and set high standards for their son. The mother had previously sought help at a time when there were no direct services for blind children in the area, and hence had to work out her conflicts and problems the best she could. At the time of contact, she was seeking direct material advice as to what to do, while running away from the kind of involvement that would help her understand the why's of her own behavior and Arnold's. She was full of self-blame, and seemed to be using this as a defense against further self-involvement. The parents' attitude was one of forcing him to develop up to their expectations and not according to his readiness.

After Arnold graduated from high school, where he attended special classes, he came to the rehabilitation center for evaluation and training, so that he might prepare for the goal that his parents had set for him—college.

Arnold was a likeable person, but otherwise ill prepared for coping with life. He had little ability to comprehend even the most simple concepts of his environment. Although his intelligence was bright-normal he had not been allowed or given the opportunity to learn what goes on around him daily, i.e., he had little concept of what a city block was, what a head of lettuce looks like, etc. Nor did he have too much curiosity about himself or his environment. He did not even know the color of his hair or eyes. Arnold expressed hostility toward his parents and seemed to blame much of his shortcomings on them. Although there was some reality in this, he also used it to avoid taking any responsibility on himself.

Arnold had great difficulty in spacial conceptualization, and poor coordination. Progress was limited in travel but although he might some times get lost coming from the railroad station to the rehabilitation center, he could use the public systems to get there. This was a new experience for him. [Pp. 300–301.]

The Blind Adolescent's Concern for the Future. The blind adolescent has throughout the earlier years met many frustrating conditions resulting from his blindness. Based upon studies of adolescents and the blind and many observations of the blind, Lowenfeld (1959) has made a good presentation of the blind adolescent's concern for the future.

In a world in which the older blind adolescent has already experienced some of the negative attitudes toward blindness and a good many of the actual difficulties caused by it, it is only natural that he will harbor increased feelings of anxiety about his future. He knows that he needed special help in learning to read and write, in reading, in some of his school assignments, in getting about, and in various other areas. . . . A certain degree of anxiety about the future is characteristic of all adolescents, but the adolescent who is blind in most cases feels it more intensely. His anxieties center around his economic future, his material future, and his future family.

Not too many decades ago, there was a profound difference between the vocational opportunities which were open to seeing and to blind adolescents. It is one of the most encouraging changes that the blind adolescent today can look with justified optimism into the future, insofar as his employment opportunities and his economic security are concerned. The Aid to the Blind Program guarantees a subsistence minimum for all blind persons, and beyond that there are almost unlimited employment possibilities for blind men and women, provided they have skills and personality characteristics to offer which make their employment desirable. The services of vocational rehabilitation agencies provide individual help if assistance in rehabilitation or placement is necessary. The blind adolescent has before him the numerous examples of successful blind people in his community, as well as throughout the nation, and all these factors contribute to brighten his economic outlook. . . .

So far as the older blind adolescent's marital future is concerned, it depends largely on other personality factors than blindness and its effects. However, his experiences, during adolescence, with members of the opposite sex often give him reasons for anxiety. His contacts with girls may cause him doubts about finding the right one and since these contacts are more limited, he may not yet have met any girl who really appealed to him. This situation is still more pronounced with blind girls whose initiative in meeting boys is further curtailed. [Pp. 314–15.]

These conditions of anxiety on the part of the blind adolescent have important bearings on his personality. In addition, the influences of his parents affect his concern about the future, as well as his ability to accept himself as a blind person.

SUMMARY

The National Society for the Prevention of Blindness has estimated that there is approximately 1 seriously visually handicapped child for every 500 pupils. Hyperopia is the most frequently reported visual difficulty among children failing a battery of visual tests. This along with other refractive errors accounts for about half of the eye defects among children enrolled in classes for partially sighted children. The teacher, by observing a list of symptoms, should be able to detect those pupils needing a special visual examination. However, an annual test for distance visual acuity along with teachers' observations is recommended by the National Society for the Prevention of Blindness.

Good eye care should begin at birth and continue throughout life, with special care that children do not damage their eyes as a result of school conditions and the educative process. Eye infections are frequently encountered and may be seriously harmful to the child's development if not cared for. The visually handicapped preschool child needs the love and security of his parents. He needs special consideration when he reaches school, but should not be overprotected. The conservation of vision is continuously receiving more attention. This begins in the home, although the school has a very important responsibility to help the child in the prevention of further visual difficulties.

The major causes of blindness have been listed in broad categories: infectious diseases, general diseases, accidents and injuries, traumas and poisonings, prenatal influences, and heredity. Prenatal influences (genetic origin and causes not specified) account for approximately 50 per cent of the cases. Blindness rate due to infectious diseases has been progressively decreasing. Likewise, there has been a steady decline in the percentage of blindness resulting from injuries.

Most studies indicate that the incidence of speech deviations in visually handicapped children is higher than in other children. The development of the partially sighted child in school does not deviate from that of seeing children except that as a group they are retarded in their academic achievement. This may be accounted for by (1) their late entrance into school, (2) greater loss of time in school, (3) lack of specialized programs to take care of their needs, and (4) the slower rate of acquiring information from reading braille or large type or through auditory means. The partially sighted child is frequently socially and emotionally immature, when compared with other children. However, there is a relatively small amount of personality disturbances that accompanies visual difficulties, although the lack of identification with the father on the part of many visually handicapped boys sometimes presents a problem.

CHAPTER REFERENCES

ALLEN, F. (1937). Color, from substance to sensation. *Sci. mon.*, 44:57–61.

ASHCROFT, S. C. (1959). The blind and partially seeing. *Rev. educ. Res.*, 29:519–28.

ASHLEY, C. (1961). Eye problems in early childhood. *Sight Sav. Rev.*, 31:25–28.

BARKER, R. G., WRIGHT, B. A., MYERSON, L., and GONICK, M. R. (1953). *Adjustment to physical handicap and illness: a survey of the social psychology of physique and disability.* (Rev. ed.) New York: Social Science Research Council. Pp. 269–309.

BATEMAN, BARBARA D. (1962). Reading and psycholinguistic processes of partially sighted children. Unpublished doctor's dissertation, Univer. of Illinois.

BERKOWITZ, J. H. (1919). *The eyesight of school children. U.S. Bureau of Education Bulletin, No. 65.*

BLAU, A. (1946). *The master hand: a study of the origin and meaning of right and left sideness and its relation to personality and language.* Research Monograph, No. 5. New York: American Orthopsychiatric Association.

BRIELAND, D. (1951). Speech education for the visually handicapped child. *Int. J. Educ. Blind,* 1:9–12.

BUELL, C. (1950). Motor performance of visually-handicapped children. *Except. Child.,* 17:69–72.

CRANE, MARIAN M., SCOBEE, R., FOOTE, F., and GREEN, E. (1952). Study of procedures for screening elementary school children for visual defects. *Amer. J. Pub. Hlth.,* 42:1430–439.

CUTSFORTH, T. D. (1951). *The blind in school and society.* (Rev. ed.) New York: American Foundation for the Blind.

DALTON, M. M. (1943). A visual survey of 5,000 school children. *J. educ. Res.,* 37:81–94.

DUNN, L. M. (1963). *Exceptional children in school.* New York: Holt, Rinehart & Winston.

FEDERAL BUREAU OF PUBLIC ASSISTANCE (1936). *Instruction regarding procedure in determining blindness.* Washington, D.C.: Federal Bureau of Public Assistance, Social Security Board.

FONDA, G. (1961). Definition and classification of blindness with respect to ability to use residual vision. *New Outlook for the Blind,* 55:169–72.

FOOTE, F. M., and CRANE, MARIAN M. (1954). An evaluation of vision screening. *Except. Child.,* 20:153–61, 180.

FURNISS, A. (1940). The school ophthalmic service. *Sight Sav. Rev.,* 10:263–72.

GIBBONS, HELEN, and McCASLIN, M. F. (1962). Prevention of blindness —the contributions of medical, social and statistical research. *Educ. Blind,* 11:116–20.

GUTMAN, ELEANOR (1956). School vision screening. *Sight Sav. Rev.,* 26:212–19.

HATFIELD, ELIZABETH M. (1963). Causes of blindness in school children. *Sight Sav. Rev.,* 33:218–33.

HAYES, S. P. (1941). *Contributions to a psychology of blindness.* New York: American Foundation for the Blind.

HUME, A. C. (1951). Helping the left-handed child. *Except. Child.*, 17:201–3, 214.

HURLIN, R. G. (1962). Estimated prevalence of blindness in the United States and in individual states. *Sight Sav. Rev.*, 32:4–12.

Illuminating Engineering Society handbook (1957). New York: The Society.

KARNES, MERLE B., and WOLLERSHEIM, JANET P. (1963). An intensive differential diagnosis of partially seeing children to determine the implications of education. *Except. Child.*, 30:17–25.

KERBY, C. EDITH (1952). A report on visual handicaps of partially seeing children. *Except. Child.*, 18:137–42.

KERBY, C. EDITH (1958). Causes of blindness in children of school age. *Sight Sav. Rev.*, 28:10–21.

LOWENFELD, B. (1945). *Braille and talking book reading: a comparative study.* New York: American Foundation for the Blind.

LOWENFELD, B. (1959). The blind adolescent. *Except. Child.*, 25:310–15.

LUCKIESH, M. (1944). *Light, vision and seeing.* New York: Van Nostrand.

MARTMER, E. E. (1959). *The child with a handicap.* Springfield, Ill.: Charles C Thomas.

MILES, W. R. (1930). Ocular dominance in human adults. *J. gen. Psychol.*, 3:412–30.

MINER, L. E. (1963). A study of the incidence of speech deviations among visually handicapped children. *New Outlook Blind*, 57:10–14.

MYERS, R. S. (1961). Program needs of visually handicapped children in Oregon. *Sight Sav. Rev.*, 31:35–40.

RILEY, L. H., LUTERMAN, D. M., and COHEN, M. F. (1964). Relationship between hearing ability and mobility in a blind adult population. *New Outlook Blind*, 58:139–41.

ROWE, EMMA D. (1958). *Speech problems of blind children: a survey of North California area.* New York: American Foundation for the Blind.

WAGNER, GEORGIANA (1961). The caseworker faces the adolescent. *New Outlook Blind*, 55:299–302.

WARNECKE, J. C. *Cragmont Test—a study in schoolroom construction.* Berkeley, Calif.: The Professional Press.

WINEBRENNER, D. K. (1952). Finding the visually inadequate child. *Vis. Dig.*, 16:21–34.

SELECTED READINGS

CUTSFORTH, T. D. (1951). *The blind in school and society.* (Rev. ed.) New York: American Foundation for the Blind.

KIRK, S. A. (1962). *Educating exceptional children.* Boston: Houghton Mifflin.

LOWENFELD, B. (1963). Psychological problems of children with impaired vision. In W. M. CRUICKSHANK (ed.), *Psychology of exceptional children and youth.* (2d ed.) Englewood Cliffs, N.J.: Prentice-Hall. Chap. 5.

LUCKIESH, M. (1944). *Light, vision and seeing.* New York: Van Nostrand.

McNALTY, SIR A. S. (1958). *The preservation of eyesight.* Bristol, England: John Wright.

MARTMER, E. E. (1959). *The child with a handicap.* Springfield, Ill.: Charles C Thomas.

SCHOLZ, R. O. (1960). *Sight: a handbook for laymen.* New York: Doubleday.

11

THE VISUALLY HANDICAPPED

The goals of an educational program for visually handicapped children are similar to those for seeing children. The visually handicapped child needs first of all acceptance by his parents, classmates, and teachers. Such acceptance is fundamental in providing an environment in which the visually handicapped child will be able to develop his potentials and make satisfactory adjustments to the forces and conditions in his environment. The American Foundation for the Blind recognizes three types of educational provisions for partially seeing and blind children. These are:

1. Education in a public or private residential school for the blind
2. Education with sighted children in public or private schools with a resource of special class teachers available during the entire school day
3. Education with sighted children in public or private schools with itinerant special teachers available at regular periods or when needed

Need for Identifying Partially Seeing Children. These are the children whose capacities to achieve in school commensurate with their ability are limited by their visual problem. A commonly used criterion for identifying these children for educational purposes is based upon visual acuity involving correct vision of 20/70 or less in the better eye. It is estimated by the Advisory Committee on Education of Partially Seeing Children of the National Society for the Prevention of Blindness that "one child in 500 of school-age enrollment is in this category" (1961, p. 170).

The majority of these children are receiving instruction in regular classrooms in their home community, often without the special services that might enable them to receive an education commensurate with their ability. The first step in any remedial program is identification. A total school-wide screening program involving testing for distant vision and careful observations by teachers with adequate follow-up of those referred for eye examination is essential if these children are to be given an educational opportunity equivalent to that of their normal-seeing classmates.

Intelligence Test Results. Considerable attention has been given to the standardization of tests for the blind. Hayes (1941) reported the results of the use of the *Hayes-Binet Intelligence Tests* in 17 residential schools for the blind. The report covers results obtained from testing 2,372 children. Of the total, 9.2 per cent had IQ's of 70 and less, while 10.3 per cent had IQ's of 120 or more. The mean IQ for the total group studied was 98.8. Results from more recent adaptations of the Binet scale and the Wechsler scale show that the percentage of children falling within the 50 per cent for seeing children (an average group) is less than the 50 per cent. There was a slightly higher percentage in the superior groups and a substantially higher percentage in the subnormal or inferior group.

The question of whether the congenitally blind differ in intelligence from those who became blind after birth was carefully examined in the studies by Hayes. He found no correlation between the age at which the child became blind and intelligence. He concludes: "The *mental constitution* of those born blind may well be essentially different from that of the other group, but the *functioning* of their minds as measured by our tests shows no such difference" (1950, p. 144).

Considerable attention is being given to the use of performance tests to supplement the Binet and Wechsler scales. The results of intelligence testing have given both parents and teachers an assurance that mental retardation is not necessarily associated with visual limitations or blindness and that most children with visual limitations have mental ability somewhat commensurate with that of their seeing classmates.

Achievement Test Results. The hypothesis that greater strain on the nervous system is required to adjust hyperopic eyes to the conditions that must be satisfied in reading seems to be confirmed by the findings of various studies. Farris (1936), for example, carried on a study among more than 1,600 seventh-grade pupils in the Oakland, California, public schools to determine the influence, if any, of visual defects on achievement in reading. He found that 44 per cent of the pupils had visual defects of varying degree, and that both hyperopia and strabismus were associated with less than normal progress in reading, while myopia and myopic astigmatism were associated with more than normal progress in reading. Of distinct significance was the fact that pupils whose visual perception was monocular made better progress in reading than those with poor coordination of the two eyes. The results of the study did not bear out the assumption that children with defects in visual acuity, regardless of type, are always handicapped in learning to read.

A more recent study reported by Eames (1959) centered on the influence of visual difficulties on reading achievement. A population of 3,500 schoolchildren, half of them reading failures and half unselected was studied. A significantly greater incidence of hypermetropia and exophoria at the reading distance was noted in the reading failure group, while myopia was noted with equal frequency in both groups. In an earlier study Eames (1955) noted that refractive errors had little statistical relationship to reading achievement among pupils doing satisfactory schoolwork, but apparently contributed to reading retardation among those classified as failures.

Adaptations of timing and administration of achievement tests for blind children have reduced the differences in scores between those obtained by the visually handicapped and seeing children. Ashcroft (1959) noted that blind children, while showing some educational retardation, were less retarded than deaf children. However, blind children are frequently found to be overage for their grade placements. The factors related to the causes of overageness among blind children were enumerated on page 290. Lack of sensory experiences involving vision is most serious to the child when, because of lack of specialized services, he is not taught to make the maximum use of other sensory avenues. Also, restrictions placed on motility will limit the child's range of experiences. The adverse effects of these factors will be determined in part by the extent to which specialized educational services are available.

Psychological Evaluation of Blind Children. A psychological evaluation must be more than an assessment of a child's intellectual ability if it is to be of value in planning an educational program suitable to his needs and abilities. The IQ has proved to be of limited value in planning an educational program for the blind child. After all, the IQ furnishes a basis for widespread and frequently erroneous generalizations.

The psychologist who attempts a psychological appraisal of the blind child must have considerable background information. A full history of the child's physical, mental, educational, emotional, and social development is an important part of a complete evaluation. The psychologist should have access to the ocular report; he needs to know the nature and extent of the visual handicap. Knowledge of the prognosis of the child's handicap is important to any educational program. A number of investigators have adapted existing psychometric tests and scales for use with partially seeing and blind children. The following psychometric devices have been used with blind children.

Interim Hayes-Binet Intelligence Test for the Blind
Wechsler Intelligence Scale for Children, Verbal Scale
Merrill-Palmer Scale of Mental Tests
Maxfield-Bucchold Scale of Social Competence, for use with blind preschool children
Situation Projective Test A
Situation Projective Test B
Guess-Why Game
The parent interview
Rating devices by the teacher

A psychological evaluation is an attempt to gather information that subsequently might serve the persons especially concerned with the child's development in all aspects. It is based upon the premise that the more information one has about the characteristics, needs, and problems of the child, the better he will be able to plan an effective program for guiding and stimulating the child in his growth and development. Thus, a final task of the school psychologist is to interpret and integrate the information collected into a report helpful to those concerned with the education, guidance, and therapy of the child.

TYPES OF EDUCATIONAL PROVISIONS

Public school services to the visually handicapped have continued to increase throughout the United States. The findings of a questionnaire addressed to 106 urban school health officers and superintendents furnish a good picture of modern educational services for blind children (Wallace, 1959). The communities from which replies were obtained had a combined population of 41,686,921 persons and a school enrollment of 6,840,105 children in the age range five to seventeen years. The principal findings are presented in Table 11–1. The most frequent type of educational plan noted was the special class. Other types of educational plans include in descending order placement in a regular class, placement in a special day school, and placement in a residential school.

TABLE 11–1

Age of Admission to School and More Frequent Type of Educational Plan

	Number of Systems
1. Age of admission	
Under age five	
Blind	17
Partially seeing	11
Delay beyond age five	
Blind	31
Partially seeing	53
2. Most frequent type of educational plan—special class	
Blind	34
Partially seeing	42

Source: After Wallace (1959).

In the large majority of cases the educational program for partially seeing and blind was supported by a combination of local and state tax funds. Most of the school systems had established criteria for the educational placement of partially seeing and blind children. In making a review of applications in a system, from 1 to 12 professional personnel may be involved.

The philosophy of education for visually handicapped children in the public schools of New York City has been stated by Fields (1961) as follows: ". . . given proper resources, children who are visually handicapped are capable of functioning effectively with their sighted classmates" (p. 337). Basic to the implementation of such a philosophy is a careful consideration of the emotional, social, and psychological needs of the child as well as his intellectual abilities. An atmosphere of good living furnishes the soil for successful work with visually handicapped children. Four kinds of supportive services have been developed for these children. These are: "(1) resource class-

The development of useful skills helps the blind child satisfy his needs for achievement and belongingness.

rooms in elementary, junior high and senior high schools, (2) itinerant teaching services, (3) classes for the emotionally disturbed, blind child, and (4) classes for the mentally retarded, blind child" (p. 337).

The Residential School. The residential school is a boarding school for blind children. Here they live, go to school, and ultimately prepare for a vocation. The first residential school for the blind in the United States was organized in 1829, and was named "The New England Asylum for the Blind." When boarding schools were established in this country, they were considered the most desirable educational facility available. They seemed to furnish the better of two possible alternatives—either to send the child to the boarding school or to train him and care for him as best as could be done at home. In spite of the disadvantages that may appear in residential schools, they offer children opportunities for socialization, certain educational techniques, and experiences with trained teachers. Thus, for the child from a home or community where educational opportunities for partially seeing and blind children are not available, the residential school would seem to offer opportunities and advantages that outweigh the disadvantages that seem to exist.

Today every state has some type of legislation enabling the development of residential or local educational programs or both for the partially seeing and blind children (Jones, 1962). The goals of the residential school have been set forth by Best (1963) as follows:

1. Maximum development of the total child.
2. A superior academic achievement.
3. A vocational education which meets the needs of the individual.
4. College preparation for students who will profit from it.
5. Post-high school counseling for students.
6. Preservation of home and community ties.
7. Total independence.
8. Helping the individual to help himself. [P. 130.]

The Regular Classroom. Under this plan the visually handicapped child is enrolled in the regular classroom and has the services not only of his regular teacher but also a qualified teacher of visually handicapped children. In addition, he may have the facilities of a resource room. The partially seeing and blind child should be encouraged to participate in most of the regular classroom activities, although some substitution may be necessary for such activities as sewing, industrial arts, drawing and painting, blueprint reading, mechanical drawing, and other activities demanding close eyework and discrimination of fine details.

The regular classroom furnishes a significant and continuing opportunity for the visually impaired child to develop an identification with his sighted peers. When this occurs, dramatic and significant differences may be observed in the manner in which he reflects his growing confidence (Bourgeault, 1961). His self concept becomes more positive in nature with a minimum of distortion and dependency. Bourgeault states: "The positive elements of the segregated, cooperative, resource, and itinerant services must be molded into a total comprehensive program which is sufficiently flexible to meet the needs of every visually impaired child regardless of where he falls on the continuum of disability" (pp. 250–251).

A braille instruction program should be offered for those children who are unable to use printed materials as a tool for learning. The teacher of braille must first of all help the blind child to develop ability to get about the school and particularly within the classroom without too much dependence upon others. The establishment of a familiarity with things in his immediate environment is an important aspect of readiness for classroom instruction in reading and writing. The braille teacher is responsible for instructing the child in the technique of braille reading and writing and in the use of special instructional equipment. The teacher may also instruct the child in touch-type on a standard typewriter when he has reached a readiness for such instruction. In New York City the keynote and ultimate objective of all teaching within the special class is to prepare the child to participate effectively in regular classroom activities (Fields, 1961, p. 338).

The Advisory Committee on Education of Partially Seeing Children (1961) suggested the following considerations in a seating arrangement for partially seeing children in a regular classroom:

1. Preferential seating should be emphasized according to the eye condition.
2. Arrange desks and location of teacher so that pupils do not face the light. Avoid possibility of pupil's sitting in his own shadow.
3. Provide adjustable desk tops or desk easels to insure better light reflectance on work, and ability to bring material close enough to eyes while maintaining good posture.
4. Permit child to sit as near chalkboards and demonstrations as necessary to obtain the best view. [P. 172.]

The Itinerant Teacher Program. In this plan the task of the regular teacher is to cooperate with an itinerant teacher who furnishes advice, special instruction, and special materials. The itinerant teacher may be employed by a large school unit, cooperatively by several smaller units, or by a state agency. The work of the itinerant teacher will include teaching braille reading and braille writing to the extent that this is needed. Tape recordings have been found useful in the education of the blind. The Special Service Division of the Oregon State Department of Education makes available to blind students in the tenth, eleventh, and twelfth grades, who have proved to be proficient braille readers, tape recordings of state-adopted textbooks, articles of special educational value, selected stories, and other useful educational materials (Stakovich, 1963). The student is issued a tape playback machine or a portable tape recorder to aid him in listening to the recordings. With a tape recorder the student is able to record class lectures and to make verbal notes and personal comments for reference and further study.

There are many advantages in the use of tape recordings and tape recorders. Many taped textbooks, articles, lectures, and other materials are already available for blind students. The blind student will, with the use of recordings, be able to use supplementary materials assigned and will be able, with the use of the recorder, to go over lectures on different topics and problems. The blind student will be able to make the maximum use of this modern educational facility, either during a regularly scheduled period or when he is working alone.

INSTRUCTION AND GUIDANCE

The Bureau of Public Assistance, Social Security Board, offered in 1936 a definition of economic blindness based upon central visual acuity of 20/200 or less in the better eye with correcting glasses. A differentiation of the visually handicapped or partially seeing and the blind as presented by Myers (1961) for instructional purposes is useful to the educator. He states: "The terms visually handicapped or partially seeing apply to any child whose visual acuity is 20/70 or less in the better eye after all medical or surgical treatment has been given and compensating lenses have been provided when necessary" (p. 35). These children must, however, be able to use their residual vision as their main avenue of learning. Such a child would be classified as blind if he is largely dependent upon the braille system, audio aids, and special equipment for learning. Because of physical, psychological, and social or environmental forces, it should be noted that one child with 20/200 vision may need to be classified as partially seeing while another child with the same vision will function as a blind child.

The instructional program should be concerned with the whole child—his mental, emotional, physical, and social self. The concept he has of himself as well as the concept of others of him are important. A study by Bertin (1959) dealt with the attitudes of students in Grades 4 through 12 toward blindness. Of the 271 children studied, 71 per cent felt that the person without sight was worse off than persons lacking other senses. Only 3 per cent of the children would choose the loss of sight to that of other senses.

The Visually Handicapped Infant and His Parents. The education of the blind infant, like that of other children, begins at birth. Early education is largely in the hands of the parents. Thus, it is most important for parents to have a favorable attitude toward the infant so that he will develop in a good emotional climate. The parents should be informed of the child's condition as early as possible, and with complete candor (Cerulli and Shugerman, 1961). Parents of visually handicapped children encounter tremendous difficulties when they discover that their child is blind. Frequently they refuse to accept the condition. Many parents develop feelings of guilt, torment, and blame. They meet with serious frustrations when they are told that little can be done to restore the child's vision.

In counseling parents, it is especially important that they are told of the child's true condition, possibilities for the future, and his immediate needs. The needs of the blind child are similar to those of the seeing. He especially needs the affection and security of his family since he is seriously limited in his explorations of the physical and social environments. He needs opportunities to develop his potentialities to the full. In this connection, it should be pointed out to the parents that the blind child may, through proper care and training, become a useful citizen. Overprotectiveness, rejection, pity, and sentimentality during infancy do untold harm to the growing child.

The Blind Child in Kindergarten. The blind child should have as many preschool experiences as possible as preparation for kindergarten experiences. These experiences enable the child to adapt himself more readily to a school situation with sighted children. His ability to do and understand things that sighted children do is a constant source of satisfaction to him. This insures a greater confidence on his part and reassurance to the teacher and other children of the class that he will be able to function effectively as a member of the group. The blind child will in most cases have developed good auditory and tactual perception. Thus, in some activities he may actually be at an advantage, especially in games where auditory or tactual perceptions are important (Orphan, 1962).

For many teachers placing a blind child in a kindergarten might impose a staggering problem. Such a problem is not insurmountable if the teacher follows certain principles in dealing with the total situation. In addition to love, understanding, and patience, the following guiding principles should be followed:

1. The teacher should take a rational and realistic attitude toward problems encountered, not a sentimental or emotional one.
2. The teacher should avoid excessive verbalizations in dealing with specific problems involving the blind child.
3. The blind child's work should be rated on its quality, not upon the fact that the child is blind.
4. The blind child should be accepted as a classmate, not a peculiar addition to the class to be given special consideration.
5. The blind child will need special help in some situations and with some problems. This should be given in as unobtrusive a manner as possible.
6. Overprotection as well as undue permissiveness for the blind child should be avoided.
7. The standard of behavior for the blind child should in general be the same as that for the seeing child.
8. The needs and educational goals for the blind child are not different from those for the seeing children.

Reading Readiness of the Blind Child. Readiness is an important aspect of all learning. Readiness to read begins early in life, being dependent upon experiences as well as maturation and ability. Reading readiness of the blind as well as other children depends on mental, physical, emotional, and educational readiness. Mental readiness refers to general mental maturity. Standardized tests may not give the whole, or even a very accurate, picture of a blind child's readiness for reading. The blind child's physical readiness must of necessity depend upon the use of his senses other than vision. Hearing becomes an extremely important avenue of learning for the blind child. The typical six-year-old blind child has developed unusual ability to discriminate aurally and make choices on the basis of what he hears. Thus, he should not find it difficult to recognize words that rhyme, to know which words begin with similar letters, and to learn other auditory skills that are useful to the beginning reader. Emotional readiness will depend largely upon the attitudes the parents have displayed toward the blind child. If he has been overprotected at home, he is likely to expect the same treatment at school. Cutsforth (1951) reports that overprotection is the greatest single source of maladjustment among blind children.

Participation in a good nursery school and kindergarten program should be helpful in preparing the blind child for school readiness. Nolan and Morris (1960) used a 30-item test requiring the subjects to name small common objects for testing the level of concept development of preschool and primary grade children. The mean correct responses and standard deviations are shown in Table 11–2. A small but regular increase in mean scores appears with grade progression, with considerable variability at each level.

TABLE 11–2

Performance of Each Grade on the Object Recognition Test

Grade	N	Mean Correct Response	S. D.
Junior nursery	9	16.33	6.96
Senior nursery	21	19.95	4.28
Kindergarten	25	23.32	2.82
First grade	23	24.91	3.94
Total	78	22.08	5.06

SOURCE: Nolan and Morris (1960).

There are many factors that contribute to reading readiness. This must be kept in mind by parents and teachers. The strength of the blind child will be his ability at auditory discrimination, memory, attention span, and verbal skills. His weakness is his inability to visualize things in his environment including printed materials. He will be helped most by a teacher who recognizes his limitations and strengths, accepts him as he is, recognizes his successes, and encourages him in his efforts to solve problems within his grasp (Karnes and Wollersheim, 1963).

Haupt (1964) has pointed out that clay modeling is a useful medium to help the child acquire perceptions through tactual sensory avenues that when integrated with other experiences are helpful to the educational growth of the child. She states:

Through working with clay the child can be made aware of what his hands and fingers tell him; he can learn how to apprehend an object and he can learn to use his fingers in new and different ways. Each step in learning to work with clay can be so devised that it involves certain basic uses for hands and fingers—alone and in concert. It gives specific training in the use of both hands at one time in different but coordinated movements. It promotes awareness of shape. The fingers learn to discover spatial relationships as well as to develop their kinesthetic sense. [P. 173.]

Visual Handicaps in Reading. Since the original stimulus in reading is the printed word, any interference with the perception of that word becomes a barrier to learning to read. Consequently, much research has been conducted bearing on the relation between vision and reading. Materials from studies conducted by Eames and others were presented earlier in this chapter.

Experiences in teaching children with impaired vision indicate that perhaps most of those whose corrected acuity is found to approximate 20/200 are able to become reasonably effective readers. Thus, serious questions have been raised about the 20/200 cutoff point for legal blindness which has frequently been used. Concerning this, Jones (1962) points out:

The analysis conducted in the Office of Education, included 4,400 children who were reported to have approximately 20/200 visual acuity. Almost 82 per cent of these were registered as reading print, about 12 per cent braille, and 6 per cent both print and braille.

Included in this same analysis were data on 600 students reported to the American Printing House for the Blind as having approximately 15/200 visual acuity. Among this group it was found that about 67 per cent were listed as readers of print, 27 per cent braille, and 6 per cent both. Study of data on 1,250 students whose visual acuity approximated 10/200 showed that 59 per cent were registered as readers of print, 32 per cent braille, and 9 per cent both. [P. 119.]

Vocational Counseling. Studies of the employment of partially sighted individuals show that they are able to enter into a wide range of activities. Also, employers are in general willing to hire such persons, especially on jobs where there are no pronounced accident hazards. A survey of the employment status of former students of the California School for the Blind by Buell (1956) revealed that about three-fourths were gainfully employed, including housewives. The occupations of the former pupils are shown in Table 11–3. Less than half of the former pupils entered white collar jobs. Of those entering college about two-thirds graduated. About half of these graduates entered the professions. These include teachers, social workers, rehabilitation workers, lawyers, chiropractors, and music teachers with a private clientele.

Occupational surveys show that office work is quite popular with blind girls. The boys seem to prefer manual work as mechanics in service stations and shops and as construction workers. Some work at such jobs as packers in factories or in assembling activities. Girls sometimes serve as medical assistants, office nurse, laboratory technicians, waitresses, and other white collar jobs where vision is not an absolute necessity. Thus, it is obvious that vocational counseling is very important for the partially seeing and blind adolescent. The school in cooperation with different community resources and the state rehabilitation services should develop a vocational training and counseling program that will lead to the vocational placement of a very large percentage of partially seeing and blind adolescents and youth.

TABLE 11–3

Occupations of Former Pupils of the California School for the Blind

Occupations	Number of Male Blind Workers	Occupations	Number of Female Blind Workers
Unemployed	35	Unemployed	36
Industrial center	26	Housewife	69
Professions	23	Industrial center	15
Assembly work	15	Professions	13
Vending stand	15	Vending stand	7
Selling	11	Assembly work	5
Musician	9	Selling	2
Kitchen help	7	Dark room	2
Dark room	5	Self employed	2
Janitor	5	Beggar	2
Office clerk	4	Traveling companion	1
Piano tuner	4	Domestic	1
Self employed	2	Braille transcriber	1
Farming	2	Switch board operator	1
Gardener	2	Bird raiser	1
Truck driver *	2	Waitress	1
Messenger	1	Clerk	1
Upholsterer	1	Dance instructor	1
Quarry worker	1	Candy factory worker	1
Braille transcriber	1		
Merchant marine *	1	Student	7
Catering business	1		
Radio repair	1		
Laundry worker	1		
Tax consultant	1		
Minister	1		
Truck helper	1		
Student	11		
Total	189	Total	169

* Former students whose sight improved.
NOTE: Dark room refers to development of X-ray film.
SOURCE: Buell (1956).

SUMMARY

The goals of an educational program for visually handicapped pupils are the same as those for seeing children. There is a need, however, for specialized services if the visually handicapped child is to develop his complete potentialities.

The first essential in any program is that of identifying these handicapped pupils and ascertaining the nature and extent of the difficulty. Intelligence tests, adapted for children with visual difficulties are useful in determining the mental development of these children. Achievement tests have also been used for determining their educational development. The use of different psychometric devices has furnished valuable information about the educational, emotional, mental, and social growth of the visually handicapped.

Public services to the visually handicapped have continued to increase and these services have become more effective as a result of studies conducted dealing with educational procedures with visually handicapped children. The residential school came into being during the early part of the nineteenth century and furnished these handicapped children opportunities they were not receiving in their home care. However, today many of these children are enrolled in regular classes with seeing children. They are encouraged to participate in most of the regular classroom activities. However, they are given specialized instruction in accordance with their special needs.

CHAPTER REFERENCES

ADVISORY COMMITTEE ON EDUCATION OF PARTIALLY SEEING CHILDREN OF THE NATIONAL SOCIETY FOR PREVENTION OF BLINDNESS (1961). Helping the partially seeing child in the regular classroom. *Sight Sav. Rev.*, 31:170–76.

ASHCROFT, S. C. (1959). The blind and partially seeing. *Rev. educ. Res.*, 29:519–28.

BERTIN, M. (1959). A comparison of attitudes toward blindness. *Int. J. Educ. Blind*, 9:1–4.

BEST, J. P. (1963). The need for the residential school. *New Outlook Blind*, 57:127–30.

BOURGEAULT, S. E. (1961). The new outlook in special education. *New Outlook Blind*, 55:246–51.

BUELL, JOSEPHINE (1956). Employment status of former pupils of the California School for the Blind. *Except. Child.*, 23:102–3.

CERULLI, F., and SHUGERMAN, ESTELLE E. (1961). Emotional disturbance —infancy: counseling the family. *New Outlook Blind*, 55:294–97.

CUTSFORTH, T. D. (1951). *The blind in school and society.* (Rev. ed.) New York: American Foundation for the Blind.

EAMES, T. H. (1955). The influence of hypermetropia and myopia on reading achievement. *Amer. J. Ophthalmol.,* 39:375–77.

EAMES, T. H. (1959). Visual handicaps in reading. *J. Educ.,* 141:1–34.

FARRIS, L. P. (1936). Visual defects as factors influencing achievement in reading. *J. exp. Educ.,* 5:58–60.

FIELDS, HELEN W. (1961). New York City educates visually handicapped children. *New Outlook Blind,* 55:337–40.

HAUPT, CHARLOTTE (1964). Improving blind children's perceptions. *New Outlook Blind,* 58:172–73.

HAYES, S. P. (1941). *Contributions to a psychology of blindness.* New York: American Foundation for the Blind.

HAYES, S. P. (1950). Measuring the intelligence of the blind. In P. A. ZAHL (ed.), *Blindness.* Princeton, N.J.: Princeton Univer. Press.

JONES, J. W. (1962). Problems involved in defining and classifying blindness. *New Outlook Blind,* 56:115–21.

KARNES, MERLE B., and WOLLERSHEIM, JANET P. (1963). An intensive differential diagnosis of partially seeing children to determine the implications for education. *Except. Child.,* 30:17–26.

MYERS, R. S. (1961). Program needs of visually handicapped children in Oregon. *Sight Sav. Rev.,* 31:35–40.

NOLAN, C. Y., and MORRIS, JUNE E. (1960). Variability among young blind children in object recognition. *Int. J. Educ. Blind,* 10:23–25.

ORPHAN, D. (1962). Educating children who are blind. *Today's Hlth,* 40:32–37.

STAKOVICH, P. (1963). The "Oregon plan" for 1963 inaugurates a tape-recording project. *New Outlook Blind,* 57:157–59.

WALLACE, HELEN M. (1959). School services for partially seeing and blind children in urban areas. *Sight Sav. Rev.,* 29:160–65.

SELECTED READINGS

ASHCROFT, S. C. (1963). Blind and partially seeing children. In L. M. DUNN (ed.), *Exceptional children in the schools.* New York: Holt, Rinehart & Winston. Chap. 8.

BARKER, R. G., WRIGHT, B. A., MEYERSON, L., and GONICK, M. R. (1953). *Adjustment to physical handicap and illness: a survey of the social psychology of physique and disability.* (Rev. ed.) New York: Social Science Research Council. Pp. 269–309.

CUTSFORTH, T. D. (1951). *The blind in school and society.* (Rev. ed.) New York: American Foundation for the Blind.

KIRK, S. A. (1962). *Educating exceptional children.* Boston: Houghton Mifflin. Chap. 9.

LOWENFELD, B. (1956). *Our blind children.* Springfield, Ill.: Charles C Thomas.

PELONE, A. J. (1957). In M. H. FOURACRE (ed.), *Helping the visually handicapped child in a regular class.* Teachers College Series in Special Education. New York: Teachers Coll., Columbia Univer., Bureau of Publications.

Resources for the visually handicapped are very numerous. The reader is especially referred to lists available from the American Foundation for the Blind and the National Society for Prevention of Blindness.

12

CRIPPLED CHILDREN

DEFINITION AND CLASSIFICATION

In this chapter consideration will be given primarily to children with those deformities, disabilities, and restrictions that result from orthopedic impairment. Children with orthopedic or crippling disabilities are those who have all kinds and degrees of difficulty in physical movement (ambulation, hand use, speech) either temporary or permanent, due to accidents, conditions, and disease processes such as anterior poliomyelitis, muscular dystrophy, rheumatoid arthritis, fractures and amputations, or certain congenital anomalies including club feet or spina bifida. Sometimes this category is referred to as the "physically handicapped" but is meant to exclude those with defects in the physical senses of vision or hearing. Children with cerebral palsy are usually included for educational placement among those with orthopedic disabilities, but they will be considered in a subsequent chapter.

Any statistical estimate of the number of crippled children is influenced considerably by the definition used. For vital statistic records every congenital deformity must be reported. Special surveys conducted by school systems or other agencies furnish additional aids in identifying the crippled child. One of the causes of discrepancies in various data regarding the number of physically disabled persons is differences in the sources of information.

The following definition was used by Barker *et al.* (1952) in studying the frequency of physical disabilities among individuals under twenty-one years of age: "A physically disabled person is one who is *generally perceived* in his cultural group to have a physique that prevents him from participating in *important* activities on a basis of *equality* with normal individuals of his own age" (p. 217).

Three sources were used for obtaining information regarding such physically disabled children in Jefferson County, Kansas: laymen, teachers, and physicians. A total of 226 disabled children were reported, with 255 different disabilities. The disabilities were reported by laymen in 109 instances, by teachers in 173 instances, and by physicians in 40 instances. The teachers' list would have included slightly more than three-fourths of the children found but would have failed to list 53 of the 226 reported. The adequacy of sources of information regarding particular disabilities is presented in Table 12–1.

TABLE 12–1

Adequacy of Sources of Information Regarding Particular Disabilities

Disability	Number	Per Cent of Cases Mentioned by:		
		Laymen	Teachers	Physicians
Speech	61	52	85	8
Visual	42	31	83	17
Orthopedic	26	58	62	22
Central nervous system	26	54	58	22
Heart	24	58	71	29
Auditory	23	61	70	17
Physique	18	39	78	0
Diabetes	5	40	60	20
Other	30	60	20	6

Source: After Barker *et al.* (1952).

Prevalence of Crippling Disabilities. The White House Conference Report summarized the results of some fairly extensive surveys on the prevalence of crippling disabilities. The ratios mentioned in the survey vary from a minimum of .91 per 1,000 of the general population in cities in New York State to a maximum of 9.79 per 1,000 in cities of the neighboring state of New Jersey. There were 755,786 crippled children reported on state registers in December, 1952 (Freedman, 1955). These numbers seem staggering when it is considered that a great many of those children, who are not helped by various agencies,

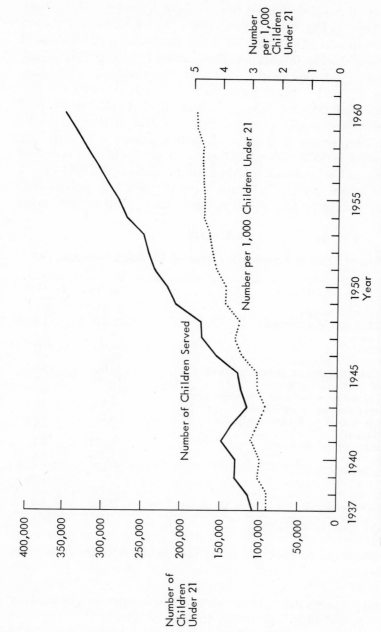

Fig. 12–1. The trend in the number of children served in the crippled children's programs and in the number per 1,000 children under twenty-one, 1937–1960. (Saffian, 1962.)

are a loss to society. There has been a continuous increase in the percentage of crippled children served in crippled children's programs. This is shown in Fig. 12–1 (Saffian, 1962). In 1960 a total of 354,883 children were served. Table 12–2 shows the disability distribution of these cases. Congenital malformations, which include a wide variety of crippling conditions, head the list, with bones and organs of movement second, and cerebral palsy third. It has been estimated that four-fifths of all crippled children become crippled under six years of age, and it is generally estimated that over half of these could be cured or improve greatly if given adequate treatment at an early age. Poliomyelitis in 1950 affected 14.5 per cent of all children in official programs and represented the third largest group. By 1960 only 7 per cent of the program children were diagnosed as poliomyelitis cases, and this group had moved to fourth place. Poliomyelitis occurs

TABLE 12–2

Diagnosis of Children Served in the Crippled Children's Programs, 1960

Primary Diagnosis	Number	Per Cent
Congenital malformations	99,586	28.1
Bones and organs of movement	61,829	17.4
Cerebral palsy	29,377	8.3
Poliomyelitis	24,889	7.0
Ear and mastoid processes	22,974	6.5
Eye, except congenital or diabetic cataract	20,925	5.9
Accidents, poisonings, violence	15,995	4.5
Diseases of the nervous system and sense organs	11,969	3.4
Rheumatic fever and heart disease	11,720	3.3
Diseases of buccal cavity and esophagus	3,511	1.0
Injuries at birth	2,577	0.7
Tuberculosis, except respiratory	1,560	0.4
Rickets	1,446	0.4
Diabetes mellitus	156	less than 0.05
Miscellaneous	24,287	6.8
Provisional or deferred diagnoses or no abnormalities	22,082	6.2

SOURCE: After Saffian (1962).

more frequently in boys and girls, and usually appears during the early years.

Causes. Congenital defects or deformities may be classified as primary or secondary. According to Shands (1957):

Primary abnormalities, which are the more common, arise from genetic causes and defects in the fertilized ovum and intrinsic irregularities in its development during the first few weeks of embryonic life. The most common nongenetic causes are dietary and endocrine disturbances, vitamin deficiencies, anoxia, undue radiation, and virus infections of the embryo. Secondary congenital defects develop in a previously normal fetus as the results of extraembryonic influences exerted during intrauterine life, usually during the last two trimesters of pregnancy. [P. 22.]

Paralysis and palsies of various parts of the body may result from birth injuries, hemorrhages, tumors and abscesses in the brain, or may follow certain diseases such as diphtheria, typhoid fever, meningitis, encephalitis, and measles. Nerve and muscle paralysis may follow fractures, dislocations, or diseases affecting tendons, joints, or bones.

Deformities of the skeletal frame are still caused by rickets, syphilis, tuberculosis of the bones, injuries at birth and later, bones that have been improperly set, and inflammation of bones and joints, as in arthritis and rheumatism. All children with any kind of physical deformity should be examined by an orthopedic specialist and the cause and diagnosis ascertained in order that adequate care and treatment may follow. While cleft lip and/or palate produce speech problems primarily, they are generally counted as crippling and are reported more frequently than any of the other congenital non-orthopedic crippling conditions found in children. About one-fifth of the congenital malformations reported in Table 12–2 fall in this category. All states furnish services to children thus affected.

Crippling Accidents. Poliomyelitis, leukemia and cancer, heart disease, pneumonia, tuberculosis, diabetes, and kidney disease are all killers of children; yet, *accidents* annually kill about as many children as do all of these diseases combined. Between 11,000 and 15,000 children are killed by "accident" in this country every year, and upwards of 50,000 other children are permanently crippled and disabled. Over half of these accidents occur to children under the age of five.

The National Safety Council (1963) indicates that for children aged one to fourteen years, accidents claim more lives than the five leading diseases combined. The number of deaths and death rates from various causes for such children in 1961 may be seen in Table 12–3. The Council reports further that among infants less than one year old, such causes as immaturity, postnatal asphyxia, and congenital malformations have the largest death totals.

Accident prevention is just as important today as the vaccines and other means for preventing crippling diseases. Such prevention begins at birth or even before. Appropriate treatment during infancy, selection of safe play materials and furniture for the home, and safety

TABLE 12–3

Causes of Death, Children Aged One to Fourteen, 1961

Causes	Number of Deaths			Death Rates *		
	Total	Male	Female	Total	Male	Female
All causes	32,877	19,065	13,812	62.1	70.9	53.1
Accidents	11,758	7,675	4,083	22.2	28.5	15.7
Motor vehicle	4,386	2,814	1,572	8.3	10.5	6.0
Cancer	4,322	2,428	1,894	8.2	9.0	7.3
Congenital malformations	3,225	1,662	1,563	6.1	6.2	6.0
Pneumonia	2,785	1,495	1,290	5.3	5.6	5.0
Gastritis, enteritis	640	357	283	1.2	1.3	1.1
Meningitis	585	337	248	1.1	1.3	1.0
Heart disease	558	284	274	1.1	1.1	1.1

* Deaths per 100,000 population.
SOURCE: National Safety Council (1963).

in the use of the automobile are essential for reducing crippling and death of children caused by accidents.

Jenkins (1960) examined the records of 728 handicapped students in Grades 9 through 12 on home instruction in the New York City school system on June 15, 1959, to see what group characteristics might be evident. While a medical diagnosis is generally prerequisite to placement on home instruction, many disabilities other than orthopedic conditions may be present, as seen in Table 12–4. In a pilot study of home instruction in Minnesota, Force (1960) found 78 spe-

TABLE 12–4

Groups of Major Disabilities of High School Homebound Students in New York City, by Number and Per Cent

Major Disability	Number			Per Cent		
	Male	Female	Total	Male	Female	Total
Emotional	110	70	180	28	21	25
Orthopedic	88	72	160	23	21	22
Neuromuscular and neurological	75	63	138	19	18	19
Heart	27	41	68	7	12	9
Upper respiratory	31	35	66	8	11	9
Gastrointestinal	12	12	24	3	4	3
Blood and blood-forming diseases	15	8	23	4	2	3
Other and unclassified	29	40	69	8	11	10
Total	387	341	728	100	100	100

SOURCE: Jenkins (1960).

cific medical diagnoses listed with fractures, rheumatic fever, scoliosis, and emotional disturbance occurring rather frequently.

The medical diagnosis is coming to be seen as of limited value in planning an appropriate educational program for children who are crippled. More attention is being given to the difficulties in functioning that a child may have without regard to the particular medical label he may "wear." Current thinking is concerned with what the child can do rather than with what he cannot do. Thus, there has been a decrease in open-air classes, cardiac classes, and other special classes for children with particular medical diagnoses. With improved school health programs and psychological and guidance services, more children are integrated into regular classrooms. One-story school buildings and other architectural considerations have made for greater possibilities of physical integration of crippled children among normal peers. Formerly the child with a heart condition was labelled "fragile" and placed in a special class; but now this child is usually placed in a regular class, after a period of home instruction, with special recommendations relative to his limitations and needs. In evaluating this trend, Fenton and Connor (1959) state:

As new special classes are being organized and the admission policies of existing ones re-evaluated, there is a growing tendency away from the organization of special classes on a medical diagnostic label only. For a period of time many of the new units that developed were organized for children with cerebral palsy only. Now the direction is toward the inclusion of all types of severely crippled children in the special education program regardless of the type of orthopedic condition. Rightfully so, the total needs of the children being served form the basis for inclusion in the program, not the diagnostic classification alone. [P. 261.]

CHARACTERISTICS

There is no close relationship between physical deformity, emotional characteristics, and specific intellectual abilities. This is a large, extremely heterogeneous category of exceptional children in which the children are "alike" in not being normal, average, or perfect physically. Beyond this fact they are rarely alike at all. Thus, it is both difficult and often dangerous to attempt generalizations about this group of children. However, some rather general characteristics may be noted upon examination of research findings and from clinical observation of crippled children.

Deprivation of early experiences important to later learning is frequently seen. Educational retardation is common, whether due to experiential deprivation, time taken for needed therapies and rest, intellectual retardation, or slowness and difficulty of physical movement. Limited social and vocational skills are also common, but the question must be raised as to whether such limitations are imposed by disability or are the result of poorly conceived and implemented education and rehabilitation programs. There is general agreement that special adjustment problems exist, but there is little agreement about the magnitude or dimensions of such problems in the face of conflicting research evidence. The social impact of crippling is quite variable. Children with visible defects may be seen as more handicapped than they are, or need be, while children with socially invisible defects, but real limitations, may be seen as less restricted than they really are, or should be. Either viewpoint obviously complicates the task of adjustment or of aspiring realistically when a child is disabled.

Intellectual Ability. Mackie (1945) studied 16,696 children, of whom 14,714 were reported with physical disabilities. Data on these children were gathered by means of a questionnaire. Chronological ages ranged from three years to over twenty-one, and the school-grade distribution extended from preschool through the twelfth year. Table 12–5 presents a summary of the age-grade placement for all types of schools and classes; 10,693 crippled children, 64 per cent of the total in the study, are represented. This table shows a high percentage

TABLE 12–5

Summary of Age-Grade Distribution of Crippled Children
for Nine Types of Schools and Classes

	Number	Per Cent
Preschool	475	4.4
Underage	406	3.8
At age	4,926	46.1
Overage	3,958	37.0
Ungraded	592	5.6
Low IQ	35	.3
Other	301	2.8
Total	10,693	100.0

SOURCE: After Mackie (1945).

of the crippled children on the overage side of the norm. Only 3.8 per cent of the children are underage; 46.1 per cent are at the correct age (the norm being based on a two-year or 24-month span for an expected grade level); while 42.6 per cent are in the overage and ungraded categories.

An early study of the mental ability of crippled children was made by Fernald and Arlitt (1925). The average IQ for 194 cases was found to be 82.35, with 86.53 for those crippled through nutritional disorders and 69.11 for those crippled through cerebral palsy. Mental examinations of 89 non-crippled brothers and sisters in 49 families indicated an average intelligence quotient of 89.2, as compared with 83.8 for these crippled children. Mackie's (1945) study provided intelligence test scores on 4,476 children. The IQ's of these ranged from 40 to 160, with a median IQ of 91. Another study of the intelligence of crippled children in Seattle, Washington, was reported by Lee (1931). The average IQ found for this group was 86.8. For those suffering from poliomyelitis and other infections the average was 92, and it was 61 for those crippled through congenital deformity.

These studies support other surveys that have been made of the mental characteristics of those crippled as a result of diseases as compared with those congenitally crippled. The congenitally crippled child is often below average in intelligence, but this does not mean that the condition itself caused the inferiority. It is more likely that crippling conditions at birth are associated more often with biological or social inadequacy. Furthermore, such factors as loss of time from school because of the physical handicap, limited opportunities for exploring the environment, and perhaps a lower level of drive in relation to intellectual pursuits may have influenced test results. Also, in many of these samples the number of children with cerebral palsy, in whom mental retardation is more than a remote possibility, would skew the distribution of intelligence test scores and give a spuriously low mean IQ for the total group.

Emotional and Social Adjustment. Children between the ages of eight and ten were used by Wenar (1956) in a study of the effects of a motor handicap on personality. The findings based on data from the *World Test* indicate that a motor handicap, per se, does not increase the incidence of emotional disturbance, as there is the same proportion of adjusted and maladjusted children in the handicapped and non-handicapped groups. There is evidence, however, that the motor handicap does entail personality changes. A weakening of the ability to erect defenses that would result in a more stable kind of self-control was observed along with a greater vulnerability to feelings of threat, either from his own destructive impulses or from a world that he perceives as dangerous. This study, supported by others, suggests that emotional instability rather than rigidity is a primary effect of the motor handicap on personality.

Findings from the Cruickshank study (1952) of 264 physically handicapped children in junior and senior high school indicated that, with regard to family adjustment, the handicapped group was more closely identified with the mother than was the case for a normal group. In relation to adjustment to society the handicapped group felt greater dissatisfaction with adults and adult society than the non-crippled group. Thus, the handicapped group showed a definite tendency to withdraw from social contacts and relations. The handicapped group was less able to evaluate interpersonal relations than the normal group. They also displayed a greater amount of self-interest. They indicated a great need for acceptance and were more willing than the normal group to be satisfied with minimal acceptance.

Donofrio (1951) investigated the effects of type, severity, and duration of crippling on intelligence, school achievement, and emotional adjustment for 270 physically handicapped children, aged five through sixteen, who attended a special school. There were 32 different medical diagnoses for the sample with poliomyelitis the most common diagnosis. Among his findings were:

1. Measured intellectual ability was within the normal range.
2. On the average these children were achieving up to their estimated capacity.
3. Emotional adjustment appeared to fall within the normal range.

Adjustment, evaluated by the *Brown Personality Inventory* and by teacher rating, was found to improve with age and was better among the less severely involved.

In an effort to determine the relationship between the time of a child's life when crippling occurs and certain personality characteristics, Kimmel (1958) studied 30 children of both sexes, between ten and sixteen years of age, who were being treated for orthopedic disability as outpatients at a New York hospital. Fifteen children were designated as a *congenital group* (onset of disability during or prior to birth) and equated for age, sex, intelligence, and severity of disability with 15 children who were designated as an *acquired group* (onset of disability after five years of age).

All subjects were administered the Rorschach Test and the Figure Drawing Test. Case-study data from social casework reports were utilized after completion of the test battery.

The acquired group showed significantly greater body confidence and body esteem than the congenital group. The congenital group used projection as a defense mechanism significantly more than the acquired group; the congenital group also showed significantly greater instances of loss of control, inability to meet situations adequately, feelings of insufficiency, and total anxiety indicators than did the acquired group. No significant differences were found between groups in reported instances of adjustment difficulties in areas of family, school, social relations, and attitude toward disability and rehabilitation. Duration and severity of disability were not found related to lack of body confidence or anxiety in either group. For children with acquired disabilities no relationship was found between age of onset of disability and lack of body confidence or anxiety. Children with cerebral palsy (in the congenital group) showed significantly greater use of flight from the self as defense against anxiety and significantly more adjustment problems related to attitude toward disability and rehabilitation than did non-cerebral-palsied children with other congenital disorders.

Kimmel (1958) concluded that the nature of the personality problems created by orthopedic disability are closely related to age of onset, and that children with acquired defects (onset after five years of age) have greater confidence in and esteem for their bodies and can cope more adequately with anxiety than can children with congenital orthopedic defects. His conclusion seems to point to the importance of the normality of early development in helping children to cope with disability. The child with a congenital defect has no personal standard of normality to which he can refer in his attempts to adjust satisfactorily.

In a study of 18 crippled children, matched with siblings and other children, Gates (1946) compared social and emotional adjustment and suggested that "cultural backgrounds and personal-social relationships, particularly in the home, may affect personal-social adjustment more than crippling" (p. 240).

The relationship of physical disability to fear and guilt feelings was studied by Cruickshank (1951), who used a *Projective Sentence Completion Test*. The results showed that "children with various types of orthopedic, cardiac, and neurological handicaps see themselves as having more fears and feelings of guilt than do children of normal physical characteristics" (p. 298).

Force (1954) studied the social relationships operating in a situation where physically handicapped and normal children were deliberately educated together in the same classroom. Subjects, drawn from three Michigan schools, included pupils from the first through the sixth grade. There were 63 physically handicapped children and 361 normal children in these classes, with all of the children possessing at least normal intelligence. The disabilities represented in the sample included cardiac (16), poliomyelitis (14), cerebral palsy (6), congenital anomalies (7), miscellaneous orthopedic (5), partially sighted (5), blind (2), oral deaf (6), brain injury—no motor damage (1), and epileptic (1).

The results, presented in Table 12–6, reveal that in terms of playmates, friends, and workmates the physically handicapped children as a group were chosen a significantly lower number of times than normal children. The orthopedically handicapped children as a group and those with vision defects received significantly lower numbers of choices on all three criteria, and the children with hearing defects and the miscellaneous group were significantly underchosen as playmates. These results indicate that those concerned with the training of these boys and girls are faced with the task of guiding all students in understanding and accepting those with handicapping conditions as members of the total group.

The importance of the home and parental attitudes for the personality adjustment of the crippled child is also more significant than for the normal child. Overprotection, which may be manifested through overindulgence, was found to be present in the majority of cases studied by Kammerer (1940). As is the case for other children subjected to overprotection, the child becomes very dependent upon the parent for everything and comes to expect special attention and consideration. The results of overprotection, combined with inadequacy and inferior economic circumstances, are illustrated in a case presented by Kammerer:

This is a fourteen-year-old boy of average performance level who has a moderately severe curvature. Since the child's father died he and his mother have lived with the paternal grandfather. They are in very poor circumstances and there is much quarreling in the home over money matters. The grandfather, according to the child's aunt and uncle, is very old and irritable and has been alcoholic. The mother is believed to be somewhat retarded mentally and has been careless about raising the child. He has always been spoiled because he was small and undernourished, but since developing scoliosis, spoiling has been much worse. He has been allowed to eat anything he wants and to have anything the parents could afford to buy him. The child's own attitude is that he has not been indulged because his mother has not been able to afford everything he wished. According to the child's teacher, neighbors of the family have helped him considerably and have treated him as one of their own children.

The child seemed to be lacking in self-confidence and his attitude was one of discouragement. He is very anxious to get well again so that he

TABLE 12-6

Mean Number of Choices of Normal and Physically Handicapped Subjects as Friends, Playmates, and Workmates

Type of Disability	No.	Friends Mean		C. R.	Playmates Mean		C. R.	Workmates Mean		C. R.
Normal	361	3.094	.134	–	3.180	.144	–	3.138	.149	–
All handicapped	63	2.238	.247	3.04	1.745	.209	5.65	1.889	.263	2.70
Orthopedic	48	2.375	.30	2.28	1.917	.229	4.68	1.937	.318	3.42
Cardiac	16	2.688	.412	.93	1.815	.425	3.04	2.312	.422	1.84
Poliomyelitis	14	2.000	.563	1.90	2.000	.429	2.61	1.786	.744	1.78
Cerebral palsy	6	.667	.45	5.17	.167	.048	19.80	.667	.451	5.45
Congenital anomaly	7	4.143	.899	1.16	3.286	.895	.91	2.714	.928	.94
Other orthopedic	5	2.000	.634	1.57	2.200	.525	1.80	1.600	.345	4.09
Vision defects	7	1.286	.598	2.95	1.429	.446	3.73	1.286	.774	2.35
Hearing defects	6	2.333	.561	1.21	.833	.366	5.98	1.833	.685	1.86
Miscellaneous	2	2.000	.707	1.52	1.500	.250	5.84	3.000	.000	.93

Source: Force (1954).

can play games with his friends at school. He likes all sports, and basketball in particular. He seems to have become more stubborn and moody
since the development of scoliosis, but does not seem to show worse than
average adjustment. [P. 82.]

Larson (1958) made a study of the availability of general experiences, viewed by experts as significant in the development of the
young child, to physically handicapped children. One hundred and
thirty-five physically handicapped boys and girls of ages three through
six years were matched with 135 physically normal children of the
same age, sex, social status, and community background. Seventy-
four of the crippled children had cerebral palsy. Larson interviewed
the parents of all 270 subjects using a 95-item interview guide derived
from an earlier study of preschool experiences. Significant differences
were found between the two groups in the major areas of socialization,
recognition, outside experience, knowledge and experience, and on
52 of 61 individual items. Although there are some real limitations
imposed by disability, Larson concluded that the majority of experiences could have been provided in more abundance if parents
of handicapped children had simply known of their importance to
development.

Jordan (1963) has considered the effect that disability in a child
can have on the life adjustment of families with handicapped children. He looked at the developmental cycle and discussed problems
delineated by research at particular points in life. His final comment
is noteworthy:

> In conclusion it may be observed that we are slowly turning our atten-
> tion to nonmedical aspects of physical disability. As we apply our en-
> ergies to the family aspects of physical disability in children we contribute
> in a fuller way to the understanding of human behavior. We begin to
> see that the behavior of handicapped persons is explained partially by dis-
> ease processes and partially by social factors. When all aspects of dis-
> ability are considered, we may well conclude that the challenges to our
> professional ingenuity posed by psychological and social factors are at
> least as important as those produced by medical considerations. [P. 336.]

Attitude Toward Self. The attitude of the crippled child toward
himself depends in a large measure upon the attitudes assumed toward him by his associates. In a study reported by Cruickshank
(1951) a projective sentence-completion test was administered to
264 physically handicapped children. The test consisted of 45 sentences designed to evaluate the self concepts of children in several

life adjustment areas. The physically handicapped children were characterized by 24 different medical diagnoses, although the largest number were handicapped by cardiac conditions, poliomyelitis, and cerebral palsy. Each of the subjects in the handicapped group was matched for age and sex with a non-handicapped child in a control group.

Table 12–7 gives figures on the responses to the sentence beginnings: "I feel most concerned about . . ."; "I am worried about . . ."

TABLE 12–7

Analysis of Responses of Handicapped and Non-handicapped Adolescents to Sentences Eliciting Guilt Feelings

| | Uncompleted Sentence | | | |
| | "I feel most concerned about . . ." | | "I am worried about . . ." | |
Response	Handi-capped (Per Cent)	Non-handi-capped (Per Cent)	Handi-capped (Per Cent)	Non-handi-capped (Per Cent)
Family	24.4	26.5	14.8	13.9
Omission	4.8	2.3	5.5	4.0
Neutral	3.7	6.7	5.1	4.0
Handicapped people	1.7	0.6	–	–
My handicap	5.5	0.0	8.7	0.0
People	12.6	8.7	3.5	5.1
Education	20.1	22.8	24.9	39.1
My health	2.4	1.0	0.0	1.4
My future	5.5	7.0	7.4	7.3
My appearance	2.4	3.0	1.3	1.4
Recreation	4.8	6.0	2.2	0.7
Vocation	2.0	2.0	0.0	2.9
Animals	2.0	1.0	1.3	0.7
My home	1.3	0.0	0.0	0.7
Myself	3.1	3.7	0.6	0.3
The world	0.0	1.3	0.6	2.5
Music	0.0	2.3	–	–
My behavior	2.0	1.6	–	–
Being a success	0.0	1.0	0.6	1.4
Money	0.0	0.6	0.6	1.8
Disease	–	–	0.6	0.0
Hospitals	–	–	1.3	0.0
Nothing	–	–	4.8	2.9
Many things	–	–	0.0	1.9
My personality	–	–	0.0	1.1

SOURCE: After Cruickshank (1951).

The responses indicate that the handicapped group expressed more concern over "my handicap," "people," "health," "my home," and "handicapped people." They worried more about their handicap, disease, hospitals, and recreation. These results illustrate the fact that children with various types of orthopedic, cardiac, and neurological handicaps see themselves with different fears, problems, and feelings of guilt than do children with normal physical characteristics.

Force (1954) concluded from his study of the social status and self-perceived status of physically handicapped children that: "Orthopedically handicapped children differ significantly from normal children in the relationship between their actual status and their guessed status as friends, but they and other physically handicapped children see as clearly as normal children the numbers liable to choose them as playmates" (p. 208). Force also summarized the findings of a large number of studies dealing with factors affecting an individual's status within a group, factors affecting friendship choices, factors affecting the status of subgroups, and self-perceptions of status within social groups. These studies generally revealed that the social structure of a group evolves developmentally through the elementary school years. The studies disclosed also that school achievement, intelligence, socioeconomic background, emotional climate of the home, special skills and abilities, personality traits, physical structure, sex, nationality, race, and religion may influence the social status of an individual. These varied factors may operate differently at different age levels but could certainly complicate the social adjustment process for children who are crippled.

Krider (1959) studied the self concepts of crippled children and non-crippled children to see if there were either quantitative or qualitative differences. Eighteen crippled children, 9 boys and 9 girls, randomly selected from Grades 7, 8, and 9 at a special orthopedic school, were matched individually with 18 non-crippled children randomly selected from a regular junior high school. Data were obtained by the Q Sort Technique, the *Mooney Problems Checklist*, a study of cumulative records and interviews with both parents.

The major hypotheses that there would be demonstrable differences in the self concepts of these crippled and non-crippled adolescents were not sustained by the data. There was evidence that the more severely disabled children tended to give more negative concepts of the self, that the crippled children seemed to attach more significance to culturally and socially valued self-characteristics than did the non-crippled, and that the crippled children seemed less able to admit damaging self-descriptions than did the non-crippled.

EDUCATION AND TREATMENT

Need for Treatment. In primitive times, especially among the Greeks, the ideal of physical perfection and military dominance went hand in hand. Such a premium was placed upon physical perfection that those who were congenitally malformed were exposed to the elements and allowed to perish. The growth of Christianity gradually

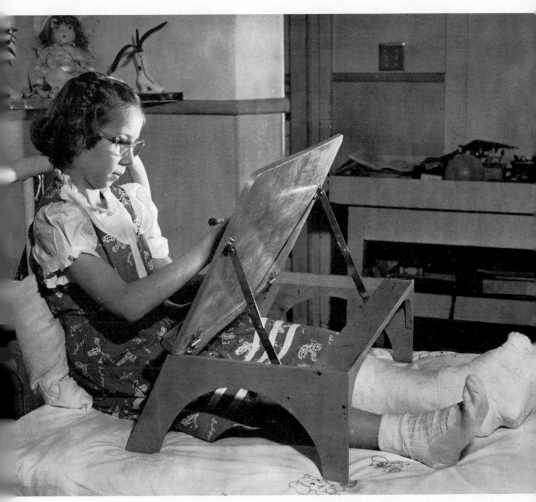

Shrine Hospital, Atlanta, Georgia

A crippling condition may be a serious handicap to a child's learning unless steps are taken to provide special instruction.

brought a more humanitarian attitude toward those who were crippled, and they came to be looked upon with pity and compassion. They were accepted as worthy of alms and were permitted to go forth and live off the generosity of others. This attitude prevails somewhat today so that the public still looks with pity upon those who are crippled, malformed, or who suffer from some other physical deformity or disability.

The first national and international lay organization for crippled children was organized in 1919. This was later broadened to include handicapped adults and is now called the National Society for Crippled Children and Adults, Inc. In 1935 the first crippled children's program of the federal government was established by the Children's Bureau of the United States Department of Labor. The entrance of the federal government into the field of medical care of crippled children led to great improvements in the program and to the establishment of state children's programs by all states. Each state program has a system of out-patient clinics for case finding, diagnosis, and follow-up examinations. Many of the clinics are operated in conjunction with the hospitals. During 1950 there were 247,000 crippled children who received service in the state programs. There are no statistics available relative to the total number that are helped through private sources rather than state or federal agencies, but there has been a steady increase in the percentage of crippled children receiving such services.

Diagnoses that have been made of crippled children in the last 40 years reveal important changes. There have been pronounced decreases in the numbers of children with tuberculous-joint conditions, pyogenic osteomyelitis, and poliomyelitis, but the number of congenital malformations in the crippled children's clinics is increasing.

One of the earliest and most comprehensive studies of methods for caring for and educating crippled children was made by Reeves (1914). In her report she emphasized the importance of early treatment and especially the early recognition of those suffering from crippling conditions. Although this is an early study of the care and education needed for crippled children, the general philosophy of the treatment needed for exceptional children is the same as that held by most students of exceptional children today.

Some of the changes in therapy stem from developments in child psychology. It was emphasized earlier that the needs of the exceptional child are in general similar to those of the normal child. Society should learn to accept a child's deviation from average in a realistic manner—as part of his total personality, but not as his most important characteristic. Furthermore, the crippled child himself should be helped to accept his disability in the same manner.

Increased knowledge of conditions leading to crippling has brought about important changes in methods of dealing with crippled children. Increased funds to the states through federal legislation assist more disabled boys and girls to take their places in the social and economic structure of our society.

Results of Therapy.   An analysis of the results of therapy shows that the best brains and best abilities do not always spring from the most healthy circumstances but that individuals suffering from physical, mental, or nervous disorders may also make their contribution. Franklin D. Roosevelt might well be held up as a splendid example of how this truth applies in the case of a physical disorder. Stricken with poliomyelitis in 1921, he fought his way to the White House as President of the United States a decade later in a show of personal power, iron will, and determination that astounded the nation.

The results of the work that is being done by various specialists and health agencies in the prevention of crippling diseases and the treatment and therapy of crippled children are remarkable. The Polio Vaccine Assistance Act of 1955 provided $30 million for grants to assist states in vaccinating expectant mothers and children under twenty years of age. Enough Salk vaccine was available so that all children through age nine could be included by 1956.

Public health clinics are being made available more and more for formerly neglected children. The results of orthopedic surgery show that many deformities can be corrected or considerably modified. Among the items that should be considered in any treatment are the following: First, the case must be discovered and brought to the attention of the agencies responsible for care and treatment. Second, this should be done at an early date so that the program of therapy can be planned during the growing period. Third, there is a fundamental need for cooperation of home and school with the different agencies concerned with the correction and treatment of various types of defects. Such cooperation will enable the program to be more extensive in its scope and more effective in its results.

Educational Needs.   The aim of the special education program for crippled children is to fit them to take adequate places in the social and economic world and to train them to apply their abilities and knowledge with the greatest efficiency of which they are capable. Natural but rather serious restrictions may come from the limitations on normal social and cooperative relations imposed by physical conditions. Inability to assume a full part as members of the social group may be due to feelings of isolation which in turn may stem from consciousness of the handicap.

Insofar as possible the crippled child should be placed in an environment filled with satisfying, wholesome group fellowship and be given an opportunity to participate in group experiences. He should not be permitted, by means of segregation or by shielding, to delay adjustment to the normal life of the community, to develop a "cripple psychology" and a feeling of being vastly different from others. He should be given the opportunity, and encouraged, to develop initiative and independence. Musical experience is one means that has been found useful in dissolving frequent emotional and social blockings resulting from the crippled conditions. Special feats, drawing activities, certain specialized forms of professional and technical services, stenographic and bookkeeping activities, as well as a range of occupations extending almost throughout the entire scope of vocations, may, with some modifications, be followed by the crippled.

The crippled child should be taught the rules of society and helped to realize that standards are not going to be entirely altered to fit his special condition. He should develop a spirit of cooperation in order that he may ultimately assume responsibility and function as others in the community do. He should not be treated dramatically but, rather, as normally as possible. His work in school should not be organized for unusual display, although this does not mean that he should receive no encouragement. He should be motivated, but when this motivation overemphasizes the crippled condition, there is the danger of personality distortion.

Acceptance. Important to the best development of crippled children is that they be accepted as members of the group. Parents should be helped in efforts to face the condition realistically and to accept the child with his disabilities. Parents should come to recognize the child's limitations and his assets and accept him as any other member of the family. The child should be expected to share in the responsibilities, obligations, and benefits of family life just as do the other members.

How a child feels about his handicap is a more important factor in his social and personal adjustment than is the handicap itself. If he feels inferior or if he feels that he should be given unusual privileges, he may resort to various undesirable adjustment mechanisms that tend to breed social and personal adjustment problems. With no other group is the general goal of knowing the self, accepting the self, and being the self more important than with the crippled. The cooperation of the teacher and parent in the guidance of the crippled child is important.

Soldwedel and Terrill (1957) studied the attitudes of handicapped and non-handicapped children and their parents toward the physically handicapped child in an integrated classroom situation. The total sample consisted of 32 children and their parents. There were 10 physically handicapped children and 22 non-handicapped children in a combined seventh- and eighth-grade class in a special laboratory school on a college campus. Children ranged from twelve to fourteen years and had been together the entire year. Sociometric instruments were administered to the children and to their mothers. The handicapped children in this sample saw themselves as more integrated psychologically than did their mothers, and the fact of disability appeared to make little real difference to the parents of the normal children. This study, although limited in scope, raises interesting questions about adolescence and disability, teacher influence on integration, and parent education.

Special Education. In a descriptive study of the public school program for orthopedically handicapped children in New York City, McCormick (1941) found many limitations that still exist in varying degrees among programs around the country; many special facilities and desirable program modifications were missing; many children were judged able to function in regular grades; many could have been in special classes but remained on home instruction; few received vocational counseling or were enrolled in available vocational courses taught in the system's schools.

A further study (Wrightstone *et al.*, 1954) of the educational program for fifth- and eighth-grade crippled children in New York City revealed that level of intelligence was less important in determining school achievement than were neurological involvement, motivation, and previous atypical school experience.

It has been widely suggested that one-story school buildings and improved school planning make it possible for more crippled children to attend regular classes. The Neil School for Physically Handicapped Children (Mullen, 1957) in Chicago provides many opportunities for special and integrated services for crippled children.

Special education for crippled children is more a matter of bringing appropriate education to the child where he may be found—at home, in the hospital, in a special class or school—than it is a matter of a special teaching methodology for children in an extremely heterogeneous group. However, Usdane (1960) feels that the special teacher has a great responsibility in guiding crippled children and that vocational training cannot be delayed. He asserts:

> . . . the handicapped child must be prepared to deal adequately in interpersonal relationships with other workers, the boss, the personnel interviewer, and the consumers; he must be adequately trained in abilities and skills to sustain interest in his work. Both these needs must start to be met in elementary school and must be reinforced and broadened at the secondary level. [P. 252.]

Condon (1962) has described the methods by which various colleges and universities have established programs to facilitate integration of crippled students into college. A great deal is being done across the country to remove or reduce architectural barriers in schools, colleges, and other public buildings of all kinds.

SUMMARY

Children who are crippled make up one of the most heterogeneous groups of exceptional children. They may have a wide range of medical diagnoses and may have greatly varying special educational needs. Thus, there is little agreement on definition or numbers. More important than a particular medical diagnosis are the restrictions or limitations produced by a certain disease process or condition. Congenital malformations, defects of bones and organs of movement, and poliomyelitis have been leading causes of crippling although the prevalence of polio is decreasing dramatically with use of the Salk and Sabine vaccines. Accidents permanently cripple up to 50,000 children each year and produce more deaths in children than the five leading diseases combined.

The development of home instruction and hospital instruction and construction of one-story school buildings have combined to provide appropriate educational opportunities for increasing numbers of crippled children. As a group they are likely to be educationally retarded and to have distortions in growth and experiences which complicate educational planning. There may be problems in emotional and social adjustment, but these are hardly general to all crippled children and depend upon a great many variables that are, as yet, not very clearly understood. Good family attitudes and adjustment are as important to the well-being of the crippled child as to other exceptional children.

Medical treatment and the various therapies can do much to reduce or prevent physical disability and dependence. Early detection and treatment are important. Special education for crippled children is seen more frequently as special placement and a special program rather than as a special or unique teaching methodology. The development of satisfactory interpersonal and vocational skills is important, and they are emphasized from the outset of schooling.

The crippled child does not need to be a serious liability to society or maladjusted in his personal and social relations. He should be treated realistically by both parent and teacher, with a general recognition of his handicaps and need. He should be expected to enter into the regular activities of the community and school insofar as his handicaps do not interfere seriously with such participation.

CHAPTER REFERENCES

BARKER, LOUISE S., et al. (1952). The frequency of physical disability in children: a comparison of three sources of information. Child Developm., 23:215–26.

CHILDREN'S BUREAU, U.S. DEPARTMENT OF HEALTH, EDUCATION, AND WELFARE (1955). Diagnosis of children served in crippled children's programs, 1952. Statistical Series, No. 25. Washington, D.C.: U.S. Government Printing Office.

CONDON, MARGARET E. (1962). The facilitation of the education of the physically disabled college student. Rehabilit. Lit., 23:266–74, 281.

CRUICKSHANK, W. M. (1951). The relation of physical disability to fear and guilt feelings. Child Developm., 22:291–98.

CRUICKSHANK, W. M. (1952). A study of the relation of physical disability to social adjustments. Amer. J. occup. Ther., 6:100–109.

DONOFRIO, A. F. (1951). A study of crippled children in an orthopedic hospital school. Except. Child., 18:33–38.

FENTON, J., and CONNOR, FRANCES P. (1959). The changing picture in the education of children with crippling conditions and special health problems. Except. Child., 26:261–62, 277.

FERNALD, MABEL R., and ARLITT, ADA H. (1925). A psychological study of crippled children of various types—a preliminary report. Sch. & Soc., 21:449–52.

FORCE, D. G. (1954). A comparison of physically handicapped children and normal children in the same elementary school classes with reference to social status and self-perceived status. Unpublished doctor's thesis, Univer. of Michigan.

FORCE, D. G. (1960). Pilot study of home instruction in Minnesota, 1959–60. Unpublished manuscript.

FREEDMAN, LILLIAN (1955). Chief, Health Statistics Section, Department of Health, Education, and Welfare. Personal communication, April 29.

GATES, MARY F. (1946). A comparative study of some problems of social and emotional adjustment of crippled and non-crippled girls and boys. *J. genet. Psychol.*, 68:219–44.

JENKINS, SHIRLEY (1960). Some characteristics of homebound adolescents in New York City. *Except. Child.*, 27:175–82.

JORDAN, T. E. (1963). Physical disability in children and family adjustment. *Rehabilit. Lit.*, 24:330–36.

KAMMERER, R. C. (1940). An exploratory study of crippled children. *Psychol. Rec.*, 4:82.

KIMMEL, J. (1958). A comparison of children with congenital and acquired orthopedic handicaps on certain personality characteristics: an evaluation of self-concept, anxiety, defense mechanisms, and adjustment in children with orthopedic handicaps. Unpublished doctor's dissertation, New York Univer.

KRIDER, MARY (1959). A comparative study of the self concepts of crippled and noncrippled children. Unpublished doctor's dissertation, Wayne State Univer.

LARSON, L. (1958). Preschool experiences of physically handicapped children. *Except. Child.*, 24:310–12.

LEE, MARY V. (1931). The children's orthopedic hospital: a survey of the intelligence of crippled children. *J. educ. Res.*, 23:164–66.

McCORMICK, H. W. (director) (1941). *Orthopedically handicapped children.* New York City: Board of Education.

MACKIE, ROMAINE P. (1945). *Crippled children in American education, 1939–1942. Contribution to Education, No. 913.* New York: Teachers Coll., Columbia Univer., Bureau of Publications.

MULLEN, FRANCES A. (1957). Chicago opens a new school for the physically handicapped. *Except. Child.*, 23:296–99, 332.

NATIONAL SAFETY COUNCIL (1963). *Accident facts.* Chicago: The Council.

REEVES, EDITH (1914). *Care and education of crippled children in the United States.* New York: Russell Sage Foundation.

SAFFIAN, SADIE (1962). *Program trends in crippling conditions, 1950–1960.* Child Health Studies Branch, Division of Research, U.S. Department of Health, Education, and Welfare. Washington, D.C.: U.S. Government Printing Office.

SHANDS, A. R. (1957). *Handbook of orthopaedic surgery.* (5th ed.) St. Louis, Mo.: C. V. Mosby.

SOLDWEDEL, BETTE, and TERRILL, ISOBEL (1957). Sociometric aspects of physically handicapped and nonhandicapped children in the same elementary school. *Except. Child.*, 23:371–72.

USDANE, W. M. (1960). Vocational guidance for crippled children: a positive force in future job training and placement. *Rehabilit. Lit.*, 21:252–54.

WENAR, C. (1956). The effects of a motor handicap on personality: III. The effects on certain fantasies and adjustment techniques. *Child Developm.*, 27:9–15.

WRIGHTSTONE, J. W., *et al.* (1954). Studies of children with physical handicaps: II. The child with orthopedic limitations. *Bureau of Educational Research, Publication No. 33.* New York City: Board of Education.

SELECTED READINGS

CRUICKSHANK, W. M. (1963). *Psychology of exceptional children and youth.* (2d ed.) Englewood Cliffs, N.J.: Prentice-Hall. Chap. 6.

HARWAY, VIVIAN T. (1962). Self-evaluation and goal-setting behavior in orthopedically handicapped children. In TRAPP and HIMELSTEIN (eds.), *The exceptional child.* New York: Appleton-Century-Crofts. Pp. 568–82.

CHILDREN'S BUREAU, U.S. DEPARTMENT OF HEALTH, EDUCATION, AND WELFARE (1962). *Program trends in crippling conditions, 1950–1960.* Statistical Series, No. 67. Washington, D.C.: U.S. Government Printing Office.

SHANDS, A. R. (1955). The care and treatment of crippled children in the United States. In FRAMPTON and GALL (eds.), *Special education for the exceptional.* Vol. 2. Boston: Porter E. Sargent.

WARE, LOUISE E. (1955). Parents of the orthopedically handicapped child. In FRAMPTON and GALL (eds.), *Special education for the exceptional.* Vol. 2. Boston: Porter E. Sargent.

WILSON, MARGUERITE (1963). Crippled and neurologically impaired children. In L. M. DUNN (ed.), *Exceptional children in the schools.* New York: Holt, Rinehart & Winston. Chap. 9.

For additional material the reader is referred to the National Society for Crippled Children and Adults, Inc., Chicago, and the National Foundation, Inc., New York, formerly called the National Foundation for Infantile Paralysis.

V

NEUROLOGICAL AND OTHER PHYSIOLOGICAL IMPAIRMENT

The grouping of neurological impairments and special health problems together is one of convenience for study rather than one based upon common factors or problems. Chapter 13 deals with brain-damaged children. These children have been affected in various ways by an early injury to the brain or by a disturbance in the development of the brain. Among the symptoms to be treated in this chapter will be those subsumed under the label "Strauss syndrome." In Chapter 14 cerebral-palsied children are studied. "Cerebral palsy" is a general term used in describing one group of children with neurological disorders resulting from an injury to the brain. The chief characteristic found in these children is some kind of difficulty in physical movement. The various kinds of neuromuscular disabilities and related disabilities found among those with cerebral palsy are presented. Chapter 15 deals with special health problems including rheumatic fever and other heart conditions, diabetes, allergies and asthma, and epilepsy.

13

BRAIN-DAMAGED CHILDREN

Great confusion frequently exists in the use of the term "brain damaged," and it is always necessary to ascertain a particular writer's or speaker's meaning in his use of the term. A crucial question may be this: Does the term refer to etiology or to implicit symptoms?

Brain damage may be considered as either *cause* or *effect*. It may cause certain symptoms or sequelae, but it is in turn caused by antecedents that are often not very clearly understood. Brain damage may occur before, during, or after birth at any time as the result of a variety of causes, chief among which are hemorrhage or anoxia, which in turn have antecedents in a variety of circumstances. The "endogenous-exogenous" argument may be used in an attempt to determine etiology in particular cases of mental retardation. Children may be cerebral palsied or epileptic as a result of some physical insult to the brain.

Possible manifestations of brain injury may be categorized in the following manner:

BRAIN DAMAGE OR INJURY (Physiological Fact)

	Result	*Label*
Differential symptoms	Intellectual development	Exogenous mental retardation
	Movement difficulties	Cerebral palsies
	Consciousness	Epilepsies
	Language development	Aphasias
	Behavior control Concept development Perception	Strauss syndrome—"brain injured"

343

The term "brain damaged" or "brain injured" is often used to imply some or all of the symptoms now assumed under the label "Strauss syndrome." The fact is that these various broad symptoms may occur together in any number or combination. A child may be brain damaged in fact, but have none of the symptoms of the Strauss syndrome. Further, there may be no demonstrable evidence of a brain lesion and yet a child may perseverate or have perceptual difficulties of the type first delineated by Strauss. In debating the question of whether a child is brain injured or not, educators, medical doctors, and psychologists often fail to take constructive action about symptoms that are now fairly well understood.

In commenting about the heterogeneity possible among children with brain injuries, Fouracre (1958) says: "Brain-injured children are as individually different as any group of children; and, consequently, some brain-injured children will present all symptoms in varying degrees, some will present combinations of these symptoms, and still others only a single symptom" (p. 211).

The Concept of the Brain-Injured Child. The term "brain injured" was introduced in this country by Strauss (1939) prior to World War II. The concept was further developed by Strauss and Lehtinen (1947) who pointed out that the brain-injured child, in contrast to the familial or hereditary mental retardate, is a result of brain injury and that these children tend to be hyperactive, poorly coordinated in their motor performances, faulty in their perceptions, unpredictable in their behavior, and frequently mentally retarded.

This concept has been rather widely accepted by students working with handicapped children for several reasons, according to Wortis (1956):

First, it relates the disturbance and disability of a certain group of defective or problem children to a known or supposed actual deficiency of the brain; second, it more or less correctly describes a recognizable clinical grouping of children who have had demonstrable brain injury and who display a similar combination of symptoms; and third, and perhaps most important of all, it prescribes a carefully contrived and apparently useful plan of management or education for dealing with these children. [P. 204.]

However, Wortis points out that the concept of the brain-injured child should be enlarged "to include a much greater variety of patterns and possibilities and to make allowance for quite varied handicapping conditions that may impede the educational process" (p. 206). This would include injuries resulting from anoxic and other nutritional lacks, injury from hemorrhage, injury to subcortical centers, and small cortical injuries or scars. Thus, we now note a variety of brain-injured children whose difficulties and problems are quite varied and whose conditions call for greatly refined methods of analysis.

However, as Birch (1964) more recently has noted:

> . . . the *fact* of brain damage in children and the *concept* "the brain damaged child" are quite different matters. . . . As a *fact*, brain damage refers to any anatomic or physiologic alteration of a pathologic kind present in the nerve tissues of the brain. . . . The *concept* "the brain damaged child" . . . is, rather, a term that has been used to designate a certain pattern or set of patterns of behavior disturbance. [P. 35.]

Causes. The etiology of brain injury is diffuse, although there are certain operative causes that are generally accepted among medical specialists. Brain injury may occur prenatally, paranatally, or postnatally, involving any of the following conditions or circumstances set forth by Fouracre (1958):

> 1. Pre-natal: The pre-natal injury may be due to unknown genetic or developmental factors, to various noxious agents carried by the mother during her pregnancy; it may result from rubella, the Rh factor, or toxemia. It is a recognized fact that the early intra-uterine life is a particularly vulnerable period for the embryo.
> 2. Para-natal: Injuries at the time of birth are of all types and may result from precipitous delivery or prolonged labor; sedatives or anesthesias during delivery; anoxemia, hyperoxemia, or intracranial hemorrhages related to traumatic birth. Prematurity in itself may be serious. . . .
> 3. Post-natal: The brain damage following birth may be due to a multiplicity of causes such as injuries and accidents, the Rh factor, and to various inflammatory producing viruses, pyogenic organisms or toxins, such as arsenic and lead poisoning. [P. 210.]

The nervous system is a highly organized pattern of structures and is vulnerable to damage from many environmental forces. There are many types of damage that may be manifested and a variety of causes for such damage. Damage to the developing organism during fetal life may result in such abnormalities as microcephalus or hydrocephalus. The child's brain is easily damaged as a result of trauma or infection before or during birth. A detailed study of the causes and nature of the various types of injury operating at birth is beyond the scope of this volume. Any mechanical difficulty that results in cerebral hemorrhage, and difficulty in breathing that may lead to anoxia, are likely to produce damage to the brain cells.

Congenital Malformations.   Cerebral abnormalities may result from congenital malformations that imply some interference or alteration of the growth process from conception, usually during the early fetal period. It has been observed that some maternal infections may be transmitted to the fetus and adversely affect its development. Various observations, supplemented by experiments with animals, have shown that factors such as vitamin deficiencies may adversely influence the development of the fetus.

Infections during pregnancy that may contribute to brain damage and mental retardation are rubella, toxoplasmosis, and certain toxic brain lesions of the fetus due to Rh-factor incompatability or abdominal X rays of the mother. A report on 11 children born of women who, during pregnancy, lived within a radius of 1,200 meters of "ground zero" in Hiroshima revealed that 7 were microcephalic and mentally retarded, whereas none of the children examined whose mothers had been living outside this area during pregnancy suffered from such conditions (Plummer, 1952).

Sex Differences in the Prevalence of Malformations.   It was pointed out in Chapter 3 that there are more males than females in institutions for the mentally retarded. Findings from relatively recent surveys seem to support the view that mental retardation resulting from brain injury is more prevalent among males than among females. The larger average birth weight of male babies may partially account for this difference.

A study by Murphy (1940) furnished evidence that congenital malformations were more prevalent among male infants than among female infants, with a ratio of 115.4 males to 100 females, while the general sex ratio for births was 103.2 to 100. For hydrocephalics, without spina bifida, the sex ratio was 170.2 males to 100 females.

The results of Murphy's study were supported by findings from a New York State survey reported by Malzberg (1953). The results, presented in Table 13-1, show a preponderance of malformations among the males in all of the categories. The greater incidence among the males is for mongolism and cranial anomalies, while malformations resulting from infectious diseases show the least sex difference.

ENCEPHALITIS

Definition.   Encephalitis is a neurological disease that may strike people of all ages. It is a form of brain inflammation that is believed to be caused by a virus that is present in the secretions in the nose

TABLE 13–1

Sex Ratios of Malformations, Based Upon First Admissions
in New York State

	Males	Females
Total population	95.4	100
Mongolism	151.0	100
Birth traumas	128.1	100
Cranial anomalies	164.3	100
Infectious diseases	116.3	100

SOURCE: After Malzberg (1953).

and mouth, although there are several varieties of this condition. It often follows an acute fever brought on by influenza, whooping cough, measles, or mumps. (Neal, 1942.) Its onset may be gradual or sudden. Intellectual deterioration and other difficulties may or may not result from this disease.

An analysis of 77 cases of measles encephalomyelitis, by Fox *et al.* (1953), observed over a period of 25 years, furnishes further information about the nature and symptoms of encephalitis. The mortality rate was 28.6 per cent. The ages of these patients ranged from five months to thirty-two years, with 62.3 per cent from four through seven years of age. A diminished or absent cough reflex was one of the earliest sign noted in 74 per cent of the patients.

Symptoms. Some of the more unique symptoms of encephalitis are blurred vision; inequality of size of the pupils of the eyes; localized paralysis, usually of muscles of the face; and rigidity of the neck muscles. Some behavior characteristics noted by Jenkins and Ackerson (1934) include listlessness, restlessness, crying spells, emotional instability, and a defiant attitude. The child who was formerly active and cooperative may become inert or assume a defiant attitude.

Postencephalitic Behavior. Ewalt and Farnsworth (1963) indicate that only some patients will show residuals, or "chronic encephalitis." They point out: "The chronic states are manifested principally as disturbance in impulse control, overactive or overaggressive behavior, and in some cases Parkinson symptoms with or without the behavior disturbance due to mental symptoms" (p. 159).

Listlessness, emotional instability, disorderly behavior, and irritability characterize the behavior of the postencephalitic child. Studies of the intelligence of postencephalitic children yield mean IQ's of

75 to 90. A marked tendency for intelligence to deteriorate was noted in a study by Brown *et al.* (1940). A decrease of 1.4 points per year in the average IQ from one examination to another was reported for a group of 108 postencephalitic patients.

There are difficulties encountered in patterned perceptual-motor functions, such as those involved in spatial orientation, and in visual and auditory memory. Like the so-called brain-damaged child, the postencephalitic child often encounters difficulties in integrating perceptions into meaningful patterns. He may be deficient in copying designs from memory and in reproducing figures from memory. In comparison with his mental age he is retarded sometimes two or more years in the *Goodenough Draw-A-Man Test.*

Kastein (1952) presents a case history of a postencephalitic boy that furnishes good insight into the development, characteristics, and difficulties (especially speech and language) of such children:

The history given by the mother revealed normal first pregnancy, high forceps delivery. Uneventful neonatal period up to six months when the child developed laryngitis and an ear condition which the family physician treated by what was described as "minor surgery," which was performed in the home. Subsequently, according to the mother, the boy ran temperatures ranging from 102 to 106 degrees for a period of six months. This condition was later diagnosed as virus pneumonia and encephalitis.

The child sat up at eleven and a half months; walked at nineteen months; said "mama" and "dada" at eighteen months. He was toilet trained; could feed himself and chew solid food. He could not sip or blow.

Observation during the first interview revealed a boy who looked small for his age. His gait was awkward and he stumbled frequently. His motor coordination was poor, he could not dress or undress himself, nor could he hold a pencil. He was ambilateral. Functions of the articulators were limited; attempts at protrusion of the tongue resulted in curling, there was no lateral protrusion, no elevation. Lips were slightly retracted, but could not be protruded.

Although sight and hearing were good, Kenneth showed almost complete lack of visual and auditory perception; there was no evidence of symbol behavior; he could not recognize or match simple colored pictures, or point to pictures named. He did not respond to spoken language beyond the simplest commands, such as "come here," "sit down." Attention span was exceedingly short; he could not be made to continue any activity for more than a few minutes at a time. [P. 570.]

Special Characteristics. The onset of encephalitis may be sudden or it may first appear as a form of drowsiness, from which the name sleeping sickness was derived. The disease usually runs its course in a period of less than two weeks. It has been estimated that one-fourth of the patients die from the disease, while approximately the same number have complete recovery. It is the other 50 per cent, those who retain certain unusual emotional and personality characteristics, with whom educators, social workers, and others are especially concerned. Many of the conduct disorders are impulsive in nature, but it is very difficult to produce behavior changes, since the disorders are due to organic lesions in the brain. Emotional instability, restlessness, egocentrism, impudence, and abusiveness characterize the individual during the chronic stage of encephalitis.

CHARACTERISTICS AND PROBLEMS OF THE BRAIN-DAMAGED CHILD

Beck (1961) surveyed the literature to determine the amount of agreement among writers concerning *symptoms* of brain injury and their detection. He noted some 43 symptoms which could be grouped under 15 more general headings:

perseveration	disparity in development
distractibility	hyperactivity
disorganization or	emotional instability
lack of integration	insecurity
perceptual difficulties	irritability
conceptual difficulties	convulsions
language disorders	mental deficiency
motor incoordination	poor retention

The following deviations in the psychological make-up of some brain-damaged children were first differentiated by Strauss and Lehtinen (1947) and are of major interest in this chapter.

(a) disturbances in perception,
(b) disturbances in concept formation (thinking and reasoning),
(c) disturbances in language,
(d) disturbances in emotional behavior. [P. 4.]

Whether or not intellectual impairment follows brain damage will depend largely upon the particular area or areas involved. If the lesion is in the cortex, which in the case of man is larger and more differentiated than in lower forms of life, intellectual impairment is a definite possibility, although not inevitable. Intellectual impairment is far less likely when the lesion is restricted to the subcortical areas.

The behavior of the infant is difficult to interpret. This fact accounts in part for different interpretations and conclusions about the effects of brain damage in infant children. Knoblach and Pasamanick (1959) stressed the belief that undetected cerebral injury is relatively frequent and may account for a range of conditions, from severely disabling neurological damage to minor behavioral deviations. Clinical observations show that brain-damaged children of average or superior intelligence frequently show a striking deficit in performance or visual-motor and visual-perceptual tasks (Taylor, 1959). Thus, tasks of these types are frequently used as an aid in evaluating the possibility of brain injury.

Tactual-kinesthetic Localization.   Error of tactual localization has been widely used as a standard neurological test to indicate brain lesions. This test is based upon the hypothesis that brain damage would be indicated by a larger than normal error of tactual localization on those areas of the skin likely to be affected by the damaged cortical area. A study by Satter and Cassel (1955) dealt with tactual-kinesthetic localization in three groups of mentally retarded children, grouped according to etiology (organics, familials, and psychogenics). These three groups were matched on the basis of chronological age and IQ and compared with a group of normal children in ability to make tactual-kinesthetic localization on six skin areas. The mean error scores earned by the four groups of children are presented in Fig. 13–1. In general the results confirmed the hypothesis of differences in tactual-kinesthetic localizations between mentally retarded and normal children. The brain-damaged children made larger errors in their localizations than did the children retarded as a result of either familial or psychogenic factors. Further, "correlations between right and left members support the hypothesis that when brain damage does occur, it is likely to be confined to a particular cerebral region" (Satter and Cassel, 1955, p. 657).

Orientation.   The brain-injured child's space and time orientation is often poor because of the disturbances in perception of spatial relations. Laterality is often not well established. Also, the child's notion of laterality is confused even in cases where dominance appears definite.

Halpin (1955) presented evidence that "brain-injured" retarded children, considered as a group, make more errors on tasks that require visual-motor integration than do matched familial retardates.

Studies show that children whose mental retardation is related to early acquired damage to the brain are impaired in sensory-motor functions and in perceptual integrations. Such children also display

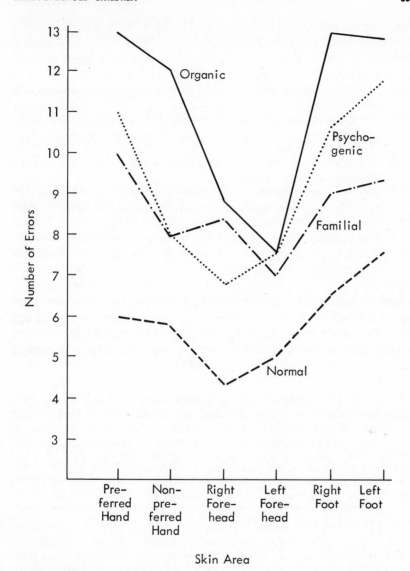

Fig. 13–1. The mean error scores earned by normal and mentally retarded children in test of tactual-kinesthetic localization. (Satter and Cassell, 1955.)

disturbances in conceptual thinking, which distinguish them on the Binet tests from non-brain-damaged children. In a study by Werner (1945) a number of significant differences were observed in the perceptual and conceptual behavior of brain-damaged and non-brain-damaged children on the Rorschach test. Among these are the following:

1. A predominance of piecelike detailed responses among the brain damaged.
2. Reversals in the normal relationship between figure and background appeared as a tendency of the brain-damaged children to react to the white spaces.
3. A tendency on the part of brain-damaged children toward fantastic interpretations.
4. The greater meticulosity of the brain-damaged children was evidenced by their attitude toward the test and their apologetic nature in certain interpretations given.
5. The smaller total number of responses of the brain-damaged children provided some evidence for the greater rigidity in their responses.

Speech Difficulties. Speech difficulty among the brain damaged may be manifested in an inability to speak clearly and enunciate distinctly. They may also have difficulty mastering a phonetic approach to a new word. This is observed in their inability to remember phonetic sounds. Dinsmore (1954) states:

Errors of visual perception of the brain-injured are noted (1) by their confusing similar letters when the letters are encountered as separate units or as integrals of words, i. e.: h, d; m, w; b, p; p, q; h, n; o, e, c; m, n; a, s; i, j; etc., (2) they mistake words in which the general form is similar and in which the same letter or letters appear, for example, "then" is read as "the," "you" as "yes," or "should" as "shouted," (3) they read the word incorrectly even in context on the basis of some prominent detail, as when "again" is read as "began," (4) they also have difficulty in organizing letters accurately in their spatial sequence, for instance, "stop" will be confused with "spot" and "tap" as "pat." [P. 432.]

Perception. Unusual visual perceptions on the part of brain-damaged children have been observed by a number of students of this problem. Strauss and Lehtinen (1947) indicated that minute cerebral lesions, even in the absence of gross neural pathology, operate to produce critical changes in perceptual behavior.

Two groups of subjects, one exogenous and one endogenous, were used by McMurray (1954) in a study of the visual perception of mentally retarded children. The subjects in each group were paired on the basis of sex, chronological age, and intelligence. The exogenous group, compared with endogenous mental retardates, exhibited unusual perception, as revealed by their tendency to perceive fewer reversals in moving figures projected on a screen. Closely related to these results are those reported by Halpin (1955). She noted that brain-damaged children, as a group, made more errors on tasks requiring visual-motor integration than did matched familial retarded children.

Perseveration is frequently present in the brain-damaged child. He may repeat over and over what he has just done. In writing he will repeat a letter or word when he is unable to proceed with a sentence. He appears to be attracted to the details of an object, rather than to the general pattern. This may be noted further in his observation of a tree, where he may be attracted to the bark or leaf on the tree, rather than the tree as an object. In his reading activities he becomes lost in a few words, rather than in attempting to grasp the meaning of a sentence.

The individual's inability to differentiate the elements making up a configuration or pattern was observed by Werner and Bowers (1941) in their study of the auditory perception of children. They tested the ability to reproduce simple patterns of melody. The brain-injured children exhibited an erratic type of behavior, with a greater deficiency than normal children in the ability to grasp the essential melodic whole.

A comparison of results obtained on a block design test, when accuracy and speed of performance were analyzed separately, suggested that brain-damaged subjects show differential impairment in accuracy of performance but do not show differential impairment in speed of performance (Heilbrun, 1959).

Behavior Disturbances. Case studies of individuals with brain lesions show that not all areas of the cerebral cortex are equally important for normal intellectual activity. For example, lesions of the occipital lobe may cause serious visual difficulties without impairment of learning capacity. Such a disability may, however, provoke serious behavior disturbances, as noted by Cobb (1944):

Lesions of the brain may affect personality in a direct and primary way, or secondarily by complex psychological reactions such as fear and discouragement. A person may have a hemianopsia from a lesion of the occipital areas and never notice the visual defect. After a neurological examination has brought this blind area to his attention, he may become preoccupied with his defect and become anxious, afraid to cross the street and restricted in social relations. In this case the lesion itself did not cause a psychological effect, because it was a lesion of the lowest cortical level of integration. Fear, aroused by discovering the trouble, did cause psychological reactions of the highest levels. A more obvious example is the varied responses of old people to hemiplegic "strokes" from thrombotic lesions of the motor cortex. This common neurological disorder is borne by some with courage and equanimity. Others are thrown into a deep depression. The variability of reaction is rarely a question of the type or location of the lesion, but an expression of the whole life experience of the person who gets the stroke. [P. 553.]

Bond and Appel (1931) noted that feelings of inferiority and insecurity appeared in the histories of 48 postencephalitic children admitted to classes of the Pennsylvania Hospital. The following describes the sense of insecurity experienced by James, which is somewhat typical:

James, small, delicate, sensitive, was described as always insecure, unsatisfied, and afraid. He was afraid that his father might be burned, that his mother might be dead, that his sister might fall and crack her head open. He feared magic; he had dreams of death, coffins, and seizure. He thought his mother loved his sister better. [P. 22.]

The growth and development of the brain-damaged child brings to a focus problems involving parental relations. The adolescent is faced with the reality and meaning of his disability. Adamson *et al.* (1961) state: "This awareness of reality is heightened by an intensification of parental concern and a resurgence of unrealistic parental expectations, strongly influenced for years by patterns of denial or partial acceptance of their brain-damaged son or daughter as a handicapped person" (p. 157). At this time both child and parent need extra support and guidance.

TREATMENT AND EDUCATION

The first step in any treatment and educational program for brain-damaged children is to analyze carefully the nature and extent of the functional disability that results from the damage. After this is done, one should consider the psychological and educational implications of these disabilities. There is also the possibility that psychological factors arising from the social-emotional climate of the home, and deprivations of psychological needs due to hospitalization or institutional isolation, may be as damaging to the personality development and intellectual growth as the organic pathology itself. Again, the whole child must be studied and treated.

The treatment of children suffering from neurological lesions is still in its infancy. Cerebral surgery has raised the hopes of some parents of afflicted children, although most of the results have been disappointing. Positive results have been obtained in some cases where mental retardation was clearly predicted (McLaurin and Matson, 1952).

In discussing the results of his study of matched groups of 24 brain-injured mentally retarded children and 24 familial mentally retarded children who were compared on measures of perception, learning aptitude, intellectual scatter, language development, quantitative ability, and personality characteristics, Gallagher (1957) makes this statement about diagnosis: "It would seem reasonable to expect the educator to make his own educational diagnosis of each child's perceptual development, personality skills or language development and make his plans accordingly whether or not a diagnosis of brain injury has been medically determined" (p. 69).

Scherer (1961) studied a sample of 46 brain-injured children in an attempt to identify relevant variables that would aid in long-range prediction of academic achievement. At an average age of five years, four months these children were given a battery of psychological tests, and ratings were obtained on several variables thought relevant. Patients were retested later (average interval was five years, two months) with added measures of academic achievement. The *Stanford-Binet* was the only variable that could predict academic achievement. As Scherer points out: "None of the other factors which had been thought to be related to academic achievement, i.e. social adjustment, test adjustment, organic traits, emotional adjustment, and physical status were of any value" (p. 106).

Bateman and Kirk (1963) reviewed several studies done through the Institute for Research on Exceptional Children at the University of Illinois. In discussing Gallagher's study (1957) they emphasize one of his points in saying:

Gallagher points out that while the two groups do differ significantly from each other in some characteristics, there were many characteristics, perhaps more important for educational planning in which the groups did not differ. The educational importance of the personality differences, especially the tendency of some brain-injured children to be disinhibited and distractible, and the desirability of a behavioral (rather than neurological) approach to those perceptual difficulties shown by some brain-injured children are discussed. [P. 21.]

Gallagher's main contention was that the area of disturbance should determine the kind of modification of educational procedures that is desirable.

In considering symptoms suggestive of brain injury and the teacher's task, Beck (1961) suggested: "If he displayed learning difficulties suggestive of brain injury, he would be taught by techniques designed to overcome these difficulties. If a child displayed difficulty in perception or concept formation, the teaching techniques would be the same whether he turned out to be brain injured or not" (p. 61).

Frey (1961) found that the brain injured who had been in special classes for brain-injured children read significantly better than the non-brain-injured children in ordinary special classes or regular grades.

Kaliski (1959) listed a number of teaching techniques that she found useful with brain-injured children. Among these were (1) use of flashlights, color, rhythm, rhythmic speech, or special auditory stimuli to focus a child's attention while teaching him, (2) modifying language in verbal instructions, (3) use of diversified concrete interpretation for number work, (4) use of phonic and kinesthetic approach in reading, (5) use of "stories" (concrete experience for reading), (6) spelling—have the child say the word as he writes it, (7) stressing directions in cooking and systematic procedures in general, and (8) physical education—focus on body image. She summarized her approach by saying (1) take nothing for granted, (2) structure the daily living (simplified and not overstimulating), and (3) use a variety of approaches to suit educational needs.

The educational program for the brain-damaged child must have as its central concern his functional disabilities. Strauss (1952) points out that education should focus upon the individual child from three viewpoints:

(1) normal growth patterns of basic mental processes, i.e., perception, reasoning, language, and emotional behavior.

(2) organic defects of basic mental processes.

(3) disparity of growth, i.e., normal development in some function, defective development in others, resulting in specific individual disturbed patterns of part or all basic mental processes. [Pp. 716–17.]

Word study has been found to be important to the brain-damaged child's readiness for, and progress in, reading. The teacher should call his attention to components of the word, both visually and phonetically. A number of techniques have been found useful in securing and retaining the interests of brain-damaged children. They may cut out familiar pictures from magazines and paste them on heavy paper. Then the pictures of objects beginning with similar sounds may be grouped together, or pictures that illustrate words beginning with two-letter sounds, such as *chair, chimney,* etc., or pictures that illustrate some specific sound may be selected.

Earlier it was pointed out that there was an intensification of parental concern and renewed unrealistic parental expectations as the individual reaches adolescence. At this time the child may have reached puberty though delayed in mental and social maturation. "It is at such a time that a residential school setting, by virtue of its control and stability can offer a healthy opportunity for both parents and teen-agers to experience a constructive working-through of the psychological conflicts and reality problems at hand" (Adamson *et al.,* p. 157).

SUMMARY

There are certain types of brain-damaged children that can be classified into special categories according to the factors responsible for the condition or according to developmental characteristics. There are sufficient data available to furnish a rather full and accurate description of the different types of brain-damaged children. This chapter has been especially concerned with such types as congenital malformations, postencephalitic behavior, and other symptoms of brain damage.

The educational and emotional problems of the brain-damaged child can usually be traced to organic restlessness and instability. Since the brain lesions are frequently not helped by medical treatment, the teacher's efforts should be extended to (1) helping the child manipulate and control his environment and (2) training the child to exercise increased voluntary control over the *self.*

CHAPTER REFERENCES

ADAMSON, W. C., HERSH, A., and CREASY, W. T. (1961). Some psychological aspects of the management of the brain-damaged adolescent in a residential setting. *J. Child Psychiat.,* 2:156–64.

BATEMAN, BARBARA D., and KIRK, S. A. (1963). Ten years of research at the Institute for Research on Exceptional Children, University of Illinois, 1952–1962. Unpublished manuscript.

BECK, H. S. (1961). Detecting psychological symptoms of brain injury. *Except. Child.,* 28:57–62.

BIRCH, H. G. (1964). Brain injured children, a definition of the problem. *Rehabilit. Lit.,* 25:34–39.

BOND, E. D., and APPEL, K. E. (1931). *The treatment of behavior disorders following encephalitis.* New York: The Commonwealth Fund.

BROWN, A. W., JENKINS, R. L., and CISLER, L. E. (1940). Influence of lethargic encephalitis on intelligence of children as determined by objective tests. *Amer. J. Dis. Child.*, 59:238–54.

COBB, S. (1944). Personality as affected by lesions of the brain. In J. McV. HUNT (ed.), *Personality and behavior disorders.* New York: Ronald.

DINSMORE, MAYME (1954). Teaching reading to the brain-injured child. *Amer. J. ment. Def.*, 58:432.

EWALT, J. R., and FARNSWORTH, D. L. (1963). *Textbk. Psychiat.*, New York: McGraw-Hill.

FOURACRE, M. H. (1958). Learning characteristics of brain-injured children. *Except. Child.*, 24:210–12, 223.

FOX, M. J., KUZMA, J. F., and STUHLER, J. D. (1953). Measles encephalomyelitis. *Amer. J. Dis. Child.*, 85:444–50.

FREY, R. M. (1961). Reading behavior of public school brain injured and non-brain-injured children of average and retarded mental development. Unpublished doctor's dissertation, Univer. of Illinois.

GALLAGHER, J. J. (1957). *A comparison of brain-injured and non-brain-injured mentally retarded children on several psychological variables.* Monograph of the Society for Research in Child Development. Vol. 22, No. 2.

HALPIN, VIRGINIA G. (1955). Rotation errors made by brain-injured and familial children on two visual-motor tests. *Amer. J. ment. Def.*, 59:485–89.

HEILBRUN, A. B. (1959). An immediate memory modification of the block design test: relative performances of brain-damaged and control subjects. *J. consult. Psychol.*, 23:390–94.

JENKINS, R. L., and ACKERSON, L. (1934). The behavior of encephalitic children. *Amer. J. Orthopsychiat.*, 4:499–503.

KALISKI, LOTTE (1959). The brain injured child—learning by living in a structured setting. *Amer. J. ment. Def.*, 63:688–95.

KASTEIN, S. (1952). Speech and language habilitation in a postencephalitic child. *Amer. J. ment. Def.*, 56:570–77.

KNOBLACH, H., and PASAMANICK, B. (1959). Syndrome of minimal cerebral damage in infancy. *J. Amer. med. Assn.*, 170:1384–387.

McLAURIN, R. L., and MATSON, D. D. (1952). Importance of early surgical treatment of cranio-synostosis. *Pediatrics*, 10:637–52.

McMURRAY, J. G. (1954). Visual perception in exogenous and endogenous mentally retarded children. *Amer. J. ment. Def.*, 58:659–63.

MALZBERG, B. (1953). Sex differences in the prevalence of mental deficiency. *Amer. J. ment. Def.*, 58:301–5.

MURPHY, D. P. (1940). *Congenital malformations.* Philadelphia: Univer. of Pennsylvania Press.

NEAL, J. B. (1942). *Encephalitis, a clinical study.* New York: Grune & Stratton.

PLUMMER, G. (1952). Anomalies occurring in children exposed in utero to atomic bomb in Hiroshima. *Pediatrics*, 10:687.

SATTER, G., and CASSEL, R. H. (1955). Tactual-kinesthetic localization in the mentally retarded. *Amer. J. ment. Def.*, 59:652–57.

SCHERER, I. W. (1961). The prediction of academic achievement in brain injured children. *Except. Child.*, 28:103–6.

STRAUSS, A. A. (1939). Typology in mental deficiency. *Amer. J. ment. Def.*, 44:85–90.

STRAUSS, A. A. (1952). The education of the brain-injured child. *Amer. J. ment. Def.*, 56:712–18.

STRAUSS, A. A., and LEHTINEN, LAURA E. (1947). *Psychopathology and education of the brain-injured child.* New York: Grune & Stratton.

TAYLOR, EDITH M. (1959). *Psychological appraisal of children with cerebral defects.* Cambridge: Harvard Univer. Press.

WERNER, H. (1945). Perceptual behavior of brain-injured defective children: an experimental study by means of the Rorschach technique. *Genet. Psychol. Monogr.*, 31:51–110.

WERNER, H., and BOWERS, M. (1941). Auditory-motor organization in two clinical types of mentally deficient children. *J. genet. Psychol.*, 59:85–89.

WORTIS, J. (1956). A note on the concept of the "brain-injured child." *Amer. J. ment. Def.*, 61:204–6.

SELECTED READINGS

BENDER, LAURETTA (1955). *The psychopathology of children with organic brain disorders.* Springfield, Ill.: Charles C. Thomas.

BIRCH, H. G. (ed.) (1964). *Brain damage in children, the biological and social aspects.* New York: Williams & Wilkins.

CRUSE, D. B. (1962). The effects of distraction upon the performance of brain-injured and familial retarded children. In E. P. TRAPP and P. HIMELSTEIN (eds.), *Readings on the exceptional child.* New York: Appleton-Century-Crofts.

HOOD, O. E. (1957). *Your child or mine; the brain-injured child and his hope.* New York: Harper & Row.

LEWIS, R. S., STRAUSS, A. A., and LEHTINEN, LAURA E. (1960). *The other child: the brain-injured child.* (2d ed.) New York: Grune & Stratton.

STRAUSS, A. A., and WERNER, H. (1962). Disorders of conceptual thinking in the brain-injured child. In E. P. TRAPP and P. HIMELSTEIN (eds.), *Readings on the exceptional child.* New York: Appleton-Century-Crofts.

14

THE CHILD WITH
CEREBRAL PALSY

In recent years the child with cerebral palsy has been studied intensively. As a result of these studies, much information is available about the etiology of cerebral palsy and the potentialities for habilitation and education of the cerebral-palsied child.

Cerebral palsy is a general term used to include a group of neurological disorders caused by injury to the brain and characterized by lack of muscular control. (The motor field of the brain is shown in Fig. 14–1). These muscular manifestations vary considerably in their nature and intensity from person to person. Perlstein (1955) pointed out that: "Of all the cerebral palsied, 25 per cent are so mildly handicapped that they need no special treatment" (p. 115). He also states: "Twenty-five per cent are so severely involved that they may be confined to wheelchair or bed, and cannot be rehabilitated. The remaining 50 per cent have moderate involvement and can be rehabilitated only by special help" (p. 115).

TERMINOLOGY AND CLASSIFICATION

Definition. The term "cerebral palsy" is generic; it covers a group of related conditions, rather than an isolated entity. This is indicated

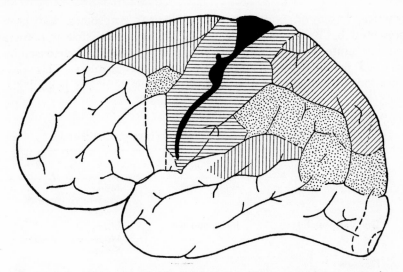

Fig. 14-1. The motor field of the brain. The pyramidal area is shown in black. The extrapyramidal areas are inside at the base of the brain—beneath the cortex. (Adapted by permission from Grinker, *Neurology* (3d ed.), Charles C Thomas, Springfield, Ill., 1943.)

in the definition by Wishik (1954): "Cerebral palsy is a group of conditions resulting from brain disturbance and having in common a disorder of muscular control" (p. 158). Thus, the term "cerebral palsy" does not delineate a specific condition any more clearly than does the term "headache," which may be symptomatic of a number of conditions or factors that are operating.

Although cerebral palsy is a condition resulting from damage to the brain, the characteristics of cerebral-palsied children are different in most instances from the traits of brain-injured cases described in Chapter 13, in that physical disabilities are factors of major importance. The intellectual, emotional, and social problems present in the training of other groups may also be present in the training of the cerebral palsied. However, physical limitations overshadow all other problems and should be given prime consideration in any training program.

Classification. Classification of the cerebral palsies is made easy by the different manifestations of disability. Attempts to apply any classification, however, are made difficult because various types of disability may be observed in the same individual. A classification that has been found useful for research purposes and for clinical practice, based on well-defined neurological syndromes, has been presented by Balf and Ingram (1955). They claim that it permits more accurate descriptions of cases than other classifications based on assumed pathology, etiology, or single clinical features. This classification, presented in Table 14–1, lists six major types: hemiplegia,

TABLE 14–1

Classification of Cases of Cerebral Palsy in Childhood

Neurological Diagnosis	Distribution	Severity
Hemiplegia	Right or left	Mild
		Moderately severe
		Severe
Double hemiplegia	Right and left	Mild
		Moderately severe
		Severe
Diplegia		
Hypotonic	Paraplegic	Mild
Dystonic	Triplegic	Moderately severe
Rigid or spastic	Tetraplegic	Severe
Ataxic diplegia		
Hypotonic	Paraplegic	Mild
Spastic	Triplegic	Moderately severe
With contracture	Tetraplegic	Severe
Ataxia		
Cerebellar	Predominantly	Mild
	unilateral	Moderately severe
Vestibular	Bilateral	Severe
Dyskinesia		
Dystonic	Monoplegic	Mild
Choreoid	Hemiplegic	Moderately severe
Athetoid	Triplegic	Severe
Tension	Tetraplegic	
Tremor		

SOURCE: After Balf and Ingram (1955).

double hemiplegia, diplegia, ataxic diplegia, ataxia, and dyskinesia.

A neurological diagnosis of the condition or injury is essential and should be made with as much accuracy as possible. Aside from the neurological analysis, there is the orthopedic aspect of cerebral palsy, in which the patient is viewed from a motor standpoint. A classification based largely upon motor functions and disturbances has been described by Phelps (1949). The six terms that he uses in his classification can be explained as follows:

1. *Flaccid paralysis.* Flaccid paralysis is perhaps the best-known disturbance of muscle function. Joint motion in the direction

of contraction does not exist. The muscle is flabby and lifeless. All attempts at direct stimulation fail.

2. *Spastic paralysis.* True spasticity in a muscle is a type of hyperactivity to contraction from any stimulus. When the muscle is stimulated by its own voluntary nerve stimulation, a greater degree of contraction results than in a normal muscle.

3. *Athetosis.* This is an involuntary movement or series of movements. It appears as a twisting wormlike series of muscular contractions, progressing down a limb in waves, a second wave following in the proximal joints as the first reaches the distal joints.

4. *Ataxia.* The types of incoordination in spasticity and athetosis are definitely secondary, while that of ataxia is primary. Ataxia or primary incoordination is an inability to control the magnitude or direction of a voluntary motion once it has been initiated.

5. *Tremors.* Tremors are of various types, but are usually classified as coarse or fine and rapid or slow. The tremors usually seen are those produced by violently resisted exertion. They may be organic or functional in origin. They may be found in individuals who are in all other ways normal. They may be intentional and voluntary or non-intentional and involuntary in nature.

6. *Rigidity.* Rigidity, as applied to muscles, is a sustained, nonvoluntary condition of contractibility and loss of elasticity. Rigidity, being postural, suggests an exaggeration of postural or plastic tone. The chief forms of rigidity described are decerebrate rigidity and rigor mortis.

Electromyography has been found useful in arriving at a physiological classification. According to Putnam (1949), the following physiological states, alone or in combination, can be recognized:

1. *Spasticity or hyperreflexia.* This is found in injuries or disturbances of the corticospinal tracts. The clinical picture is usually that of a variable amount of motor deficit, with some awkwardness in management, and sometimes spasm of the antigravity muscles, which may lead to contractions in severe cases. . . .

2. *Athetosis and dystonia.* These are similar physiologically, but athetosis is manifested in the extremities chiefly by abnormal movements, dystonia chiefly in the axial muscles by abnormal tension and postures. . . . The patient may have some degree of voluntary control, which is, however, usually overcome by the torrent of purposeless involuntary impulses.

3. *Alternating tremor and Parkinsonian rigidity.* These two entities are rarely seen in children. . . .

4. *Ataxia due to cerebellar deficit.* This is fundamentally a lack of con-

trol and coordination, rather than of involuntary movement, as in athetosis. . . .

· 5. *Transverse lesion of the spinal cord.* . . . Extreme hyperflexia and spread of impulses through the isolated segment is observed. [P. 173.]

Using a five-type classification, Bice (1950) has presented the number and per cent of 1,158 children falling into the different types. The data, presented in Table 14–2, show that the category of spasticity

TABLE 14–2

Classification of 1,158 Children According to Type of Cerebral Palsy

Type	Boys	Girls	Total	Per Cent *
Athetosis	176	126	302	26.1
Spasticity	334	204	538	46.5
Rigidity	61	50	111	9.6
Ataxia	94	46	140	12.1
Tremor	15	12	27	2.3
Mixed	19	21	40	3.5
Total	699	459	1158	100.1

SOURCE: After Bice (1950).
* Calculated to the nearest tenth of a per cent. Consequently, the total is 100.1 per cent.

contains the largest number, 46.5 per cent of the entire group being identified as this type. Phelps and Turner (1948) report, however, that about 45 per cent of children suffering from cerebral palsy might be classified as athetoids. Efforts to coordinate their motor activities in some cases cause these youngsters to set up tensions in some muscle groups, and these tensions may be mistaken for spasticity. This may account for differences sometimes given for the percentages found in this group and the spastic group. Spasticity and athetosis are seen in the great majority of cases of cerebral palsy. This fact may be seen graphically in Fig. 14–2.

Incidence of Cerebral Palsy. Although a number of surveys have furnished a general guide, existing data do not furnish an accurate basis for estimating the prevalence of cerebral palsy. An incidence of between 2 and 2.5 cases of cerebral palsy per 1,000 children in Edinburgh, Scotland, was reported by Ingram (1955). It is estimated that more than 250,000 children in the United States are afflicted with cerebral palsy. But Richards (1956) has stated: "The total number of cerebral palsied is estimated at half a million, with 10,000 cerebral-

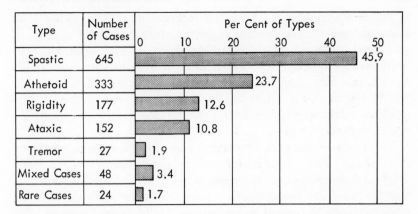

Type	Number of Cases	Per Cent of Types
Spastic	645	45.9
Athetoid	333	23.7
Rigidity	177	12.6
Ataxic	152	10.8
Tremor	27	1.9
Mixed Cases	48	3.4
Rare Cases	24	1.7

Fig. 14–2. Types of cerebral palsy—an analysis of 1,406 cases, 1936–1951. (Hopkins *et al.*, 1954.)

palsied children being born annually" (p. 67). An earlier survey (Perlstein, 1949) of Schenectady County, New York, revealed a prevalence of 590 per 100,000, with the highest percentage in the lower age groups (see Table 14–3). The lower rate in the upper age groups results mainly from the inability to locate the cerebral palsied in

TABLE 14–3

Numbers of Cerebral-palsied Persons in Each Age Group Estimated for Schenectady County and New York State, 1949

Age Group	Percentage of Cases, Schenectady County	Estimated Number of Cases, New York State
Under 5	16	3,250
5–9 years	28	6,160
10–14 years	17	3,740
15–19 years	8	1,760
20–24 years	13	2,860
25–34 years	9	1,980
35 and over	9	1,980
Total	100	22,000

SOURCE: Perlstein (1949).

these groups rather than a greater mortality rate of cerebral-palsied children and youth.

Causes of Cerebral Palsy. There are certain factors that predispose infants to cerebral palsy. It is more common among premature than among full-term infants. According to Perlstein (1949), *anoxia* is an important cause. The brain is highly sensitive to lack of oxygen. If prolonged, anoxia causes irreparable damage. The newborn baby must breathe quickly. The infant brain is able to withstand anoxia for a longer time than the adult brain, but anoxia both in the adult and in the newborn affects the higher cortical centers first. In the newborn infant who suffers anoxia the midbrain and basal nuclei are more commonly involved.

Next to anoxia the most important cause of brain damage is *cerebral hemorrhage.* These hemorrhages are primarily submeningeal. Intracerebral hemorrhages, in the sense of explosive isolated episodes inside the brain, are less common. Most cerebral hemorrhages occur in close proximity to cortical motor areas or to the internal capsule. The pyramidal tract area is, therefore, more likely to be involved, and the resulting condition is usually spasticity.

Rh-factor incompatibility between the blood of the mother and infant may result in agglutination of blood cells and either death or physical disability. Infants suffering from such a disorder may be afflicted with involuntary movements, paralysis, and mental defects. Factors that may precipitate damage to the brain may also be divided according to the period of the individual's life:

1. Those which occur during the prenatal period.
2. Those which occur at the time of birth.
3. Those which occur some time in the individual's life after birth. [Usher, 1946, p. 196.]

In a study by Deaver and Greenpan (1952) an analysis was made of the predisposing and prenatal factors as physiological agents in 94 cases of cerebral palsy selected at random from a preschool cerebral palsy clinic. The results revealed that in most cases two or more etiological factors were involved. Some of the most frequent probably predisposing factors included prematurity of birth, excessive birth weight, prenatal anoxia, Rh-factor incompatibility, and toxemia. Contrary to commonly held opinions, maternal age, sex of the baby, and being the firstborn were not found to be significant factors. However, Nesbitt (1959) indicates that the perinatal period, from the twentieth week of gestation through the twenty-eighth day of life (after birth), presents a "greater hazard . . . than any other period . . . to old age" (p. 123).

A statistical survey of the etiology of cerebral palsy among a group of institutionalized cases is reported by Gauger (1950). These data are in harmony with those presented previously. The etiological factors presented in Table 14–4 indicate the wide range of agents or conditions that are associated with cerebral palsy during the prenatal, natal, and early childhood period. Prematurity, anoxia, injuries at birth, and infections of various types stand out as prominent causes of cerebral palsy among children.

TABLE 14–4

Major Factors in the Etiology of 141 Institutionalized Cerebral Palsy
Patients at the Pacific Colony, Spadio, California *

Etiology	Major Factor	All Reports
Traumatic		
Prematurity	19	24
Anoxia	9	9
Unspecified birth injury	8	8
Prolonged labor	7	12
Difficult labor	7	15
Precipitate labor	6	8
Postnatal trauma	6	8
Instrumental delivery	4	10
Postmaturity	2	3
Induced labor	2	5
"Big baby"	–	1
Total	70	103
Infections		
Encephalitis		
Type unspecified	4	5
Pertussis	4	4
Measles	1	1
Polio	5	11
Influenza	1	1
Meningitis	3	3
Maternal infection	4	7
Unspecified infection	3	4
Lues (syphilis)	4	5
Vaccination	1	1
Chorea	–	1
Total	30	43
Developmental	7	
Unknown (probably developmental)	34	
Total	141	

* This table shows both the number of times a certain factor was reported and the number of times it was considered primary.
SOURCE: Gauger (1950).

ASSOCIATED CONDITIONS AND DEFECTS

Since any area of the brain may be damaged, many associated conditions and defects may be found among those who have cerebral palsy. There is no relationship between geographical factors and the prevalence of cerebral palsy (Duryea, 1941). No differences have been found in the incidence in rural and urban areas. There are a number of physical and mental defects that may be found among cerebral-palsied children. The same brain damage that produces a motor handicap may produce mental retardation. Speech is a motor act and there may be involvement of the voice mechanism as well as of hands and arms, or legs and trunk. The cerebral-palsied child may also be subject to epileptiform seizures. The presence of these multiple handicaps often complicates greatly the task of diagnosis and treatment.

Intelligence Evaluation. The usual test for measuring intelligence consists largely of verbal materials or items requiring motor manipulation. However, the speech of the cerebral-palsied child is often indistinct, while motor abilities are impaired so as to handicap him in tests involving motor manipulation. Furthermore, some of these children suffer from defective vision or hearing. In testing the cerebral-palsied child, the examiner therefore has the problem of trying to determine from the child's responses whether he failed certain test items because of lack of intellectual development or because of physical disabilities.

A number of investigators have seriously questioned the use of existing intelligence tests for evaluating the mental ability of these subjects. Phelps (1948) suggested that the *Stanford Revision of the Binet Tests* might be used satisfactorily, provided that the examiner is aware of the disabilities that may affect the individual's responses to the test items. A study reported by Jewell and Wursten (1952) bears on this problem. One hundred of a group of 325 children examined by an individual intelligence test were retested within a median time of nine months. The intelligence quotients of 27 of these children showed increases of five or more points. The changes in IQ were more frequent and greater for those with initial IQ's above 50 than for those with initial IQ's below 50.

Intelligence Test Scores of Children with Cerebral Palsy. In a study by Fouracre *et al.* (1950) the mental abilities of 129 orthopedically handicapped children were measured by the *Stanford Revision of the*

Binet Tests, Form L. The data presented in Table 14–5 show that those crippled by cerebral palsy ranked lowest in mean IQ compared to all other groups of children examined. These results have been largely substantiated by other studies.

TABLE 14–5

Distribution of Intelligence Quotients of 129 Orthopedically Handicapped Children

Group	Number of Children	Intelligence Mean	Quotient Range
Cerebral palsy	65	79.3	18–146
Polio sequelae	19	102.6	55–137
Congenital anomalies of skeletal-muscular system	15	93.4	49–130
Arthritis, tuberculosis of bone, etc.	30	90.3	48–124
All groups	129	86.7	18–146

SOURCE: After Fouracre *et al.* (1950).

A survey of studies by Heilman (1952) indicated that the average intelligence of cerebral-palsied children is lower than for normal children. In five studies of a total of 1,002 children, approximately 45 per cent were classified by investigators as mentally retarded, while roughly 30 per cent were classed as slow learning. The distribution of intelligence quotients of 1,741 children included in four studies (Fouracre and Thiel, 1953) is presented in Table 14–6. According to

TABLE 14–6

Distribution of Intelligence Quotients Among Children with Cerebral Palsy

Study	Number of Children	Percentage with IQ			
		0–69	70–89	90–109	110 and above
Bice *et al.*	992	49.0	22.5	21.9	6.6
Miller and Rosenfeld	330	50.0	22.5	23.0	4.5
Asher and Schonell	354*	45.2	26.8	20.1	4.0
Fouracre *et al.*	65	41.5	23.1	24.6	10.8

* Test results in 14 cases (3.9 per cent) were not recorded because the children were not yet assessable.

SOURCE: After Fouracre and Thiel (1953).

these data, over 70 per cent of cerebral-palsied children have intelligence quotients below the normal range of 90–109.

In an earlier study (Ross and Davidson, 1947) psychometric data were computed on 587 cerebral-palsied children ranging in age from infancy to twenty-one years. Their IQ's, based on scores from the *Stanford-Binet Test*, were distributed as follows:

IQ	Per Cent
Below 35	9
35 to 75	42
75 to 105	41
Above 105	8

Miller and Rosenfeld (1952) studied 330 cerebral-palsied children, ranging from infancy to twelve years old. Form L of the *Stanford Revision of the Binet Tests* was administered to the younger ones. However, subjective examinations were necessary for 67 cases whose physical impairments were so severe that they were unable to respond to any other testing procedure. The results were classified according to the usual types. A wide range of IQ's appeared among the subjects of each type studied (see Table 14-7).

TABLE 14–7

Percentage of Children of Different Palsy Types
Falling Within Certain IQ Ranges

Types	Percentage with IQ			
	Below 70	70–89	90–109	110 and above
Spastic	51	19	25	5
Athetoid	52	30	16	2
Ataxia	33	30	26	11
Mixed	55	18	27	0
All types	50	22.5	23	4.5

SOURCE: After Miller and Rosenfeld (1952).

Hohman and Freedheim (1958) obtained IQ's on 1,003 cases of cerebral-palsied children referred to a medical clinic. The distribution of IQ scores of these children are shown in Table 14–8, indicating that the majority of these children had IQ's below 70. These data are somewhat similar to data obtained by Schonell (1956) from a sample of 354 children in England. Schonell found that 75.9 per cent of the cerebral-palsied children had IQ's below 90 compared to 27 per cent in a normal population.

Considerable research has been done in adapting testing procedures and interpreting test results in ways designed to make allowances for

TABLE 14–8

Distribution of 1,003 Estimated IQ's of Cerebral-palsied
Group of Children

IQ Level	Per Cent of Cerebral Palsy Group
110 and above	3.1
90 to 109	13.0
70 to 89	25.1
69 and below	58.8

Source: After Hohman and Freedheim (1958).

the problems presented by cerebral palsy. Based upon results obtained from these procedures, investigators have consistently found the incidence of mental retardation high, with approximately 50 per cent having IQ's below 70 with at least 25 per cent showing extreme retardation, that is, IQ's below 50 (Cruickshank and Raus, 1955).

Concept Formation and Integrative Ability of Children with Cerebral Palsy. In an early investigation two groups of 26 children were studied by Cotton (1941); one was a group of cerebral-palsied children, the other a group of physically normal children. The groups were matched in sex, chronological age, and mental age (estimated for cerebral-palsied children). The results indicated that the cerebral-palsied children differed from the normal group in three respects. They displayed (1) a wider range of individual differences of the type of response within a test situation, (2) a greater tendency toward concrete types of responses, and (3) a greater tendency toward stereotyped types of responses.

More recent experiments have served to corroborate the findings of Cotton. Dolphin and Cruickshank (1952) used two groups of 30 children as subjects, one a cerebral palsy group and the other a group of physically normal children. The test involved determining the relationships in life situations. The task of the children was to select from miscellaneous objects the particular ones that go with different life situations represented in pictures. The cerebral palsy group selected a significantly greater number of objects. Some qualitative differences were also noted between the two groups, in that the cerebral palsy group:

1. Made more selections based on secondary qualities of the objects
2. Chose a large number of uncommon objects
3. Dramatized the pictures in their selection of objects

4. Extended the pictures into time and space
5. Frequently rejected an object after having initially selected it
6. In some cases were unable to organize the picture into a meaningful whole

Results from a study by Wenar (1954) reveal that a significant decrease in integrative ability in children accompanies increase in the severity of a motor handicap. Integrative ability is here considered in terms of richness and organization of ideas. Thus, Wenar concludes that "the handicapped child cannot bring the variety, flexibility, and coherence of ideation to life situations that the non-handicapped child brings, and that he cannot handle the complexities of life as effectively. Instead he prefers to take on fewer and simpler activities and to have a more limited area in which to function" (p. 292). However, no evidence appeared that the motor handicap produces a particular kind of deviant thinking in the child.

Some Secondary Defects. According to Guibar (1955), ocular defects exist in over 50 per cent of cerebral palsy patients. A study by Miller (1953) dealt with all such secondary defects potentially affecting the educability of children crippled by cerebral palsy. A sample of 165 cases, taken at random from a file of cerebral-palsied children, was used in her study. The over-all distribution of the 165 cases among seven types of cerebral palsy was: athetoid—23 per cent; tension athetoid—18 per cent; spastic—36 per cent; rigidity—15 per cent; ataxic—1 per cent; tremor—1 per cent; and mixed types—6 per cent. Nearly one-fourth of the sample were reported emotionally maladjusted. Some kind of visual defect was found in 41 per cent of the cases, with strabismus (24 per cent) and nystagmus (13 per cent) occurring the most frequently. Approximately one-third (27 per cent) of the cases had no speech; 62 per cent had speech sufficient for communication at their mental age level. The incidence of these and other secondary defects found by Miller is summarized here:

Visual defects	41 per cent
Auditory defects	7 per cent
No speech	27 per cent
History of convulsive disorders	30 per cent
Emotionally maladjusted	23 per cent
Non-self-feeders	38 per cent

Dunsdon's (1952) careful study of the educability of 916 cerebral palsy cases in England and Wales revealed that nearly 60 per cent (about 500 cases) had a measured IQ of less than 70. Of these low-IQ cases speech retardation was found in 40 per cent, and no speech in 16 per cent. Obviously, cerebral-palsied children are handicapped by tests requiring such skills as motor coordination, speech, and auditory, visual, or perceptual acuity. In the study of 208 cases by Ingram (1955), referred to earlier, 49 per cent were found to have significant speech defects, and 8 per cent revealed symptoms of aphasia.

Irwin (1955a) designed a study to test the hypothesis that phonetic differences exist among three groups of cerebral-palsied children from one to twelve years of age. The groups included 128 spastics, 86 athetoids, and 52 tension athetoids. The findings of the study revealed no strong statistical evidence of differences in the mastery of speech sound elements among the three groups.

An evaluation by Irwin (1955b) of the vowel and consonant profiles of 225 cerebral-palsied children indicated the following: (1) a deficiency of the back vowels and the front consonants in the phonetic equipment of the cerebral palsied; (2) a ten-year period to eliminate glottal sounds from their phonetic equipment in comparison with about two years for normal subjects; (3) a similar retardation of the cerebral palsied in a mastery of the back vowels.

According to Mecham et al. (1960), the incidence of hearing losses among cerebral-palsied children varies widely according to the different investigators. These differences may be the result of variation in reference points for hearing loss, the sample studied, or methods of testing. In spite of differences found, the studies tend to agree that the hearing problems among the cerebral palsied is sufficiently serious to warrant special consideration in any educational or therapeutic program. Hopkins et al. (1954) reported 5 per cent, while Rutherford (1945) had earlier reported a figure of 41 per cent in his sample. In her study of 1,293 cerebral-palsied children Shere (1960) found hearing defects in 7.2 per cent of those with spasticity, 18.4 per cent of those with ataxia, and 22.6 per cent of those with athetosis.

Emotional Complications and Problems. Physicians, social workers, and others who have studied and treated children having cerebral palsy have almost constantly observed disturbing emotional reactions in the patient and family. The cerebral-palsied child may be kept from school, or if he is sent to school, he may be avoided by his teachers and not accepted by his classmates. A study by Force (1954) of the social acceptance of physically handicapped children revealed that the cerebral-palsied subjects were chosen less often as friends, playmates, and workmates than were any other handicapped children.

Bice's (1954) careful classification of 250 quotations from parents regarding attitudes toward their children with cerebral palsy showed that 74 per cent of the quotations were negative in nature. Comments ranged from mild rejection to a frank expression of death wishes. An earlier study reported by Little (1949) revealed that of the families of 22 cerebral-palsied children studied, only one family showed no marked evidence of emotional disturbance resulting from having a child with cerebral palsy. This finding is not surprising in light of the frequently obvious nature of the disability, which sets the child apart from other children. Although the observations of the 22 children whose families were studied were not complete at the time the study was reported, the evidence indicated clearly that the attitudes of the home and other agencies have a profound effect on the severity of the disturbance and the extent to which it yields to treatment.

In Miller's (1953) study it was noted that the cerebral-palsied child's emotional maladjustments ran the gamut of such behavior symptoms as enuresis, hyperactivity, aggressiveness, withdrawal, stuttering, no speech, infantilism, temper tantrums, destructiveness, and excessive crying. On the *California Test of Personality* her subjects scored higher on social adjustment than on self-adjustment. Their egocentric natures were reflected in low scores on the subtests of "feeling of belonging," "self-reliance," and "sense of personal worth." On various projective tests they revealed basic insecurities that were intensified during adolescence.

From a later study of parent-child relationships, when the child was cerebral palsied, Miller (1958) concluded:

1. Problems in the parent-child relationship appear to be an important factor in the maladjustment of the mildly handicapped cerebral palsied child.
2. The handicap itself does not appear to remain the child's basic problem, though it may have triggered the beginning of the problem.
3. The child with a mild handicap appears to have more severe adjustment problems arising from disturbed parent-child relationships than does the child with a severe handicap.
4. The typical "brain-injury" response appears to have a strong emotional component and may be subject to modification. [P. 305.]

Perlstein (1955) had earlier commented:

Emotional disturbances frequently play a more important role in handicapping the cerebral palsied individual than do his physical defects. As a result of their physical incapacity, these children do not have opportunities for ordinary social experience, and thus for normal social maturation.

In the families of cerebral palsied children, parental attitudes are naturally colored by having such a handicapped child. [P. 119.]

A group of 40 cerebral-palsied children were found by Portenier (1942) to be characterized by emotional immaturity, lack of persistence, and inadequate socialization. In the Tracht (1946) study the *Guilford Inventory of Factors* was administered to 90 cerebral-palsied adults. These subjects showed significantly greater social and thinking introversion, more depression, and more emotional instability than a non-cerebral-palsied control group.

Of special interest is the fact that one etiological factor, virus infection, may have a direct relationship on the emotional maladjustments of cerebral-palsied children. In the Miller (1953) study etiology was attributed to encephalitis in 12 cases and to meningitis in 3 cases. These cases represent 9 per cent of the total sample. Six of these cases were diagnosed as emotionally maladjusted. The syndrome of behavior factors seen were well known to teachers who had post-encephalitic or postmeningitic children in their classes. Benda (1952) points out:

It is not uncommon that neurologic symptoms are inconspicuous while mental symptoms, in the form of behavior disorders and mental retardation, are in the foreground. . . .

.   .   .   .

The older the child is at onset of the virus, the more marked are abnormal behavior patterns, while neurologic evidence of brain damage may be vague and nonconclusive. [Pp. 292–93.]

THERAPY AND EDUCATION

Major emphasis in the investigations and treatment of children with cerebral palsy has been on the neuromuscular syndrome, although it is generally recognized that mental retardation or perceptual disturbances may result from the same trauma that produce the neuromuscular syndrome. Thus, the syndromes of "brain injury" and cerebral palsy both arise from damage to the brain. The differences in the manifestations result from non-selective damage that may occur to the brain. Strauss (1952) presented the following summary of the relationship of the areas of disturbance in regard to cerebral palsy:

(1) cerebral palsied child without mental or psychological complications—a medical problem.

(2) cerebral palsied child with organic mental involvement, ranging from behavior and learning difficulties to mental retardation—a medical, educational, psychological problem.

(3) cerebral palsied child with secondary psychological reactions caused by maladjustment resulting from the handicap—a medical and psychological problem.

(4) cerebral palsied child with organic mental involvement and with secondary psychological reactions—a medical, educational and psychological problem. [P. 714.]

Importance of Therapy. A general timetable of care and training for the cerebral palsied should begin with the onset of the condition. The importance of early recognition and evaluation is important in such a timetable. Special health supervision, parental counseling, and therapy based upon individual needs are essential in a therapeutic program. A detailed muscle test should be given to the cerebral-palsied child and treatment outlined that is based upon his condition, needs, and readiness. Special exercises in physical therapy should be designed primarily to develop normal joint motion, rhythm, and speed. Occupational therapy should consist of learning the basic skills used in feeding and dressing one's self. It may also consist of certain activities, such as weaving and carpentry, that enable the cerebral-palsied child to acquire certain muscular skills.

Education and Training. The school records of 500 cerebral-palsied children included in a statewide survey by the New Jersey State Crippled Children's Commission (McIntire, 1947) showed that approximately 78 per cent were retarded one or more grades for their age. This may be accounted for by a number of factors, any of which may be present in a given case, such as lack of school opportunity, late school-entrance age, mental retardation, speech defects, and sensory defects. The extent to which some of these factors were present in the New Jersey group of school-age children is shown in Table 14-9.

The behavior of some cerebral-palsied children is characterized by distractibility and hyperactivity. These children find it difficult to withstand the impact of varied or intense stimuli. The typical classroom, characterized by a wide range of colors, displays, and bulletin boards filled with pictures, disregards the basic perceptive nature of these cerebral-palsied children. Stimulation of a psychological nature should be controlled to the point where extraneous stimuli will not interfere with the learning process. The types of classrooms and buildings provided for the education of the cerebral-palsied child will

TABLE 14–9

Factors Contributing to School Retardation of Cerebral-palsied Children

Contributing Factor	Per Cent
Mental retardation	
Feebleminded intelligence	27.6
Borderline intelligence	5.6
Dull-normal intelligence	11.0
Lack of educational opportunity	23.0
Late school-entrance age	38.0
Visual defects	42.0
Hearing defects	11.0
Speech defects	55.0

SOURCE: After McIntire (1947).

play an important role in his educational growth and adjustments. The physical environment in which he goes to school may be the determining factor in his educational and physical development.

Educational leaders in the field of cerebral palsy advocate the establishment of special classes as a part of the regular program. Such practice permits a certain amount of interplay between the handicapped and normal children. It also permits the cerebral-palsied child who is physically able to participate in many school activities with normal children. Such placement should be made on the basis of a careful study of each case, since some cerebral-palsied children may be overstimulated or otherwise harmed by activities with normal children. However, they do need to become a part of a social group and to participate in as many activities designed for normal children as their conditions will permit. Extensive use of paints, pencils, crayons, modelling clay, and similar materials is important during the early years.

Concerning the educational program for the cerebral-palsied child, Fouracre and Thiel (1953) have stated:

The school curriculum for the child with cerebral palsy, particularly if he is limited in mental ability in some or all areas, should provide continuous realistic guidance which will enable him in spite of his neuromuscular disability to make a wholesome adjustment as a contributing member of society. . . . The curriculum should include a systematic sequence of meaningful, satisfying experiences aimed at developing sound attitudes and basic physical, social, and mental skills that can be directly related to the functional demands and resources of the environment in which he presently finds himself, as well as in the situation which he will meet when he has completed his school years. [P. 408.]

Educators working with cerebral-palsied children have increasingly come to recognize the importance of normal maturation and the points at which the cerebral-palsied child has not grown normally or had the kinds of experiences by which other children are helped to become ready for school experiences. Thelander (1956) has noted the following aims for a nursery school program:

1. To give these children as many experiences of normal children as possible, that is, to see, touch, feel, explore, hear, and smell the world around them;
2. To be with other children, see and share with them; and
3. To be accepted by adults as individuals, not as objects of pity or aversion. [P. 50.]

The classroom teacher of cerebral-palsied children, in his efforts to achieve learning, is frequently blocked by the pupils' emotional problems. The cerebral-palsied child is often a fearful child; he is especially afraid of failure. He needs most of all to succeed at some tasks he deems worthwhile.

It has been noted among cerebral-palsied children in intensive habilitation training that the measured IQ shows a substantial increase, sometimes as much as 20 to 30 points over a two-year period. Berko (1955) pointed out that this increase is more commonly found in children with a "rugged psychometric profile," that is, scattered levels of ability in different functions.

Machek and Collins (1960) reported a study of 102 clients screened for a work-study program in a rehabilitation center. They found no correlation between IQ level and performance and found that the appearance of normality and neatness, both of which have some importance for vocational placement, to be poor in a majority of the clients accepted for the program. However, their most striking finding is:

. . . the most important prognostic factors are not I.Q. and job sample performance. The psychosocial considerations such as emotional stability, and motivation are of greater importance. A patient's low level of maturity, an inability to accept himself and an unrealistic attitude toward employment lowers his chances for vocational rehabilitation. [P. 436.]

They further concluded that a majority would appear able to be productive only in a sheltered, sympathetic environment. The tensions of competitive employment were felt likely to increase musculoskeletal and emotional defects.

In a consideration of the psychoeducational problems of cerebral palsy, Reed (1959) comments on the deprivation of experiences common to cerebral-palsied children and its effect on later learning:

The studies of children who have been deprived sensorially in their early years have shown that beyond a certain point of maximal learning, it would appear that certain kinds of losses cannot be made up. . . . Normal learning is a complex process involving genetic components of maturation, perceptual organization and affective integration. Cerebral palsy may affect adversely all of these areas. [P. 6.]

Reed (1959) lists the following kinds of difficulties that may be found among cerebral-palsied children:

(a) Impaired exploratory capacity
(b) Impaired capacity for differentiating objects in dynamic processes
(c) Impairment of affective controls
(d) Greater energy required to learn
(e) Resulting overprotection and/or rejection
(f) Lowered frustration tolerance
(g) Reduced motivation and effort—reduction of effectiveness of rewards
(h) Reduced early learning and increased gaps between the knowledge of cerebral palsy patients and peers and decreased later adaptability.

Perlstein (1955), in considering the rehabilitation of persons with cerebral palsy, outlined the following goals that he felt desirable to achieve:

1. He should be capable of some form of locomotion either independently or with crutches or other apparatus.
2. He should be capable of self-care and self-help in eating, dressing, toileting, and similar activities.
3. He should have an effective method of communication, either by speech, writing, or by other means.
4. His appearance should be as normal as possible.
5. He should be able to earn money or its equivalent in competitive industry, in a sheltered workshop, or by self-employment.
6. He should be able to employ his own spare time in satisfying avocations and in social contacts. [Pp. 117–18.]

Importance of Parental Attitudes. It is essential not only that the cerebral-palsied child receive educational help but also that his parents cooperate with various agencies in helping their child. The records of cerebral-palsied children show a preponderance of parental rejection, overprotection, and indulgence, with immaturity and insecurity frequently resulting. This is a critical problem involving the attitudes, goals, and aspirations of the parents. First, parents must be helped to accept the child with his limitations. Second, they must realistically bring their goals, immediate and long term, to the level actually attainable by the cerebral-palsied child. Third, they should recognize the unique rate of development of the child, which in many cases will be slower than that of the average child.

Group meetings of cerebral-palsied children and their parents brought forth three significant problems of the cerebral-palsied child (Doob *et al.*, 1955). These were (1) the dependence of the cerebral-palsied child upon his parents, (2) the need for social contacts, and (3) the problem of obtaining sufficient educational and vocational training for him to become to some degree independent and self-supporting.

SUMMARY

Cerebral palsy is a term that includes a group of conditions having in common disorders of muscular control. Manifestations vary considerably in nature and severity, and several classifications have been established. In most cases cerebral palsy exists from birth or begins during early infancy. Surveys show its estimated occurrence is from 3.5 to 7 children in each 1,000 of school age.

Speech defects, hearing disorders, and visual difficulties appear frequently among cerebral-palsied children. Also, personal and social maladjustment are often present in a large percentage of cases. The disturbing emotional reactions frequently found among parents of cerebral-palsied children complicate the problems of these children. Although the National Society for Crippled Children and Adults and the United Cerebral Palsy Association have strived for many years to provide better educational and rehabilitation facilities for crippled and cerebral-palsied children, some states have not as yet made provisions specifically designed for their education and rehabilitation. There are indications that parents and educators are becoming better informed about the characteristics, needs, and problems of cerebral-palsied children. Increased attention is being given to special defects frequently associated with cerebral palsy.

Many cerebral-palsied children are mentally retarded, and a greater number are educationally retarded. The excessive degree of educational retardation seems to result from (1) lack of school opportunity,

(2) late entrance to school, (3) mental retardation, (4) speech defects, and (5) sensory defects. The establishment of special classes as a part of the regular program permits a greater amount of interplay between the handicapped and normal children than do completely separate schools and classes. Educational and vocational guidance are essential for the optimum development of these boys and girls.

CHAPTER REFERENCES

BALF, C. L., and INGRAM, T. T. S. (1955). Problems in the classification of cerebral palsy in childhood. *Brit. med. J.*, No. 4392, pp. 163–66.

BENDA, C. E. (1952). *Developmental disorders of mentation and cerebral palsies.* New York: Grune & Stratton.

BERKO, M. J. (1955). Psychometric scatter: its application in the clinical prediction of future mental development in cases of childhood brain injury. *Cerebral Palsy Rev.*, 16:16–18.

BICE, H. V. (1950). *Psychological services for crippled children.* Trenton, N.J.: New Jersey State Department of Health.

BICE, H. V. (1954). Some factors that contribute to the concept of self in the child with cerebral palsy. *Ment. Hyg.*, 36:120–31.

COTTON, CAROL B. (1941). A study of the reactions of spastic children to certain test situations. *J. genet. Psychol.*, 58:27–44.

CRUICKSHANK, W. M., and RAUS, G. M. (1955). *Cerebral palsy, its individual and community problems.* Syracuse, N.Y.: Syracuse Univer. Press.

DEAVER, G. G., and GREENPAN, L. (1952). Clinical approach to the etiology of cerebral palsy. *Arch. phys. Med.*, 34:478–85.

DOLPHIN, JANE E., and CRUICKSHANK, W. M. (1952). Psychology of concept formation in children with cerebral palsy. *Amer. J. ment. Def.*, 56:386–92.

DOOB, DOROTHY, BOLES, G., and ROBRICK, GLADIS (1955). Simultaneous group meetings of cerebral palsied children and their parents. *Educ. Res. Bull.*, 34:141–52.

DUNSDON, MARJORIE I. (1952). *The educability of cerebral palsied children.* London: Newnes Educational Publishing.

DURYEA, L. C. (1941). The cerebral palsy problem. *New York State J. Med.* P. 1819.

FORCE, D. G. (1954). A comparison of physically handicapped children and normal children in the same elementary school classes with reference to social status and self-perceived status. Unpublished doctor's thesis, Univer. of Michigan.

FOURACRE, M. H., JANN, GLADYS R., and MARTORANA, ANNA (1950). Educational abilities and needs of orthopedically handicapped children. *Element. Sch. J.*, 50:331–38.

FOURACRE, M. H., and THIEL, ELLEN A. (1953). Education of children with mental retardation accompanying cerebral palsy. *Amer. J. ment. Def.*, 57:401–14.

GAUGER, ADELINE B. (1950). Statistical survey of a group of institutionalized cerebral palsy patients. *Amer. J. ment. Def.*, 55:90–98.

GUIBAR, G. P. (1955). Cerebral palsy: a practical routine for discerning oculomotor defects in cerebral palsied children. *J. Pediatr.*, 47:333–39.

HEILMAN, A. (1952). Intelligence in cerebral palsy: a new interpretation of research studies. *Crippled Child*, 30:11–13.

HOHMAN, L. B., and FREEDHEIM, D. K. (1958). Further studies on intelligence levels in cerebral palsy children. *Amer. J. phys. Med.*, 37:90–97.

HOPKINS, T. W., BICE, H. V., and COLTON, KATHRYN C. (1954). *Evaluation and education of the cerebral palsied child.* Washington, D.C.: International Council for Exceptional Children.

INGRAM, T. T. S. (1955). A study of cerebral palsy in the childhood population of Edinburgh. *Arch. Dis. Childh.*, 30:85–98.

IRWIN, O. C. (1955a). Phonetic equipment of spastic and athetoid children. *J. Speech & Hearing Disord.*, 20:54–57.

IRWIN, O. C. (1955b). Phonetic speech development in cerebral palsied children. *Amer. J. phys. Med.*, 34:325–34.

JEWELL, B. T., and WURSTEN, H. (1952). Observations on the psychological testing of cerebral palsied children. *Amer. J. ment. Def.*, 56:630–37.

LITTLE, S. (1949). A note on an investigation of the emotional complications of cerebral palsy. *Nerv. Child*, 8:181–82.

MACHEK, O., and COLLINS, H. A. (1960). Preliminary report of evaluating and classifying the vocational potential of the cerebral palsied. *Arch. phys. Med. Rehabilit.*, 41:434–37.

McINTIRE, J. T. (1947). On the education of the cerebral palsied. *J. educ. Res.*, 40:561–68.

MECHAM, M. J., BERKO, M. J., and BERKO, FRANCES G. (1960). *Speech therapy in cerebral palsy.* Springfield, Ill., Charles C Thomas.

MILLER, ELSA A. (1958). Cerebral palsied children and their parents. *Except. Child.*, 24:298–302, 305.

MILLER, ELSA A., and ROSENFELD, G. B. (1952). The psychologic evaluation of children with cerebral palsy and its limitations in treatment. *J. Pediatr.*, 41:613–21.

MILLER, MELBA (1953). An investigation of secondary defects potentially affecting the educability of children crippled by cerebral palsy. Unpublished doctor's dissertation, Univer. of Southern California.

NESBITT, R. E. L. (1959). Perinatal casualties. *Children*, 6:123–28.

PERLSTEIN, M. A. (1949). Medical aspects of cerebral palsy. *Nerv. Child*, 8:128–51.

PERLSTEIN, M. A. (1955). Cerebral palsy: medical and educational implications. *Amer. J. ment. Def.*, 60:115–21.

PHELPS, W. M. (1948). Characteristic pathological variations in cerebral palsy. *Nerv. Child*, 7:10–13.

PHELPS, W. M. (1949). Description and differentiation of types of cerebral palsy. *Nerv. Child*, 8:107–27.

PHELPS, W. M., and TURNER, T. A. (1948). A doctor looks at cerebral palsy. *Hygeia*, P. 188.

PORTENIER, L. G. (1942). Psychological factors in testing and training the cerebral palsied. *Physiother. Rev.*, 22:301–3.

PUTNAM, T. J. (1949). The neurology and neurosurgery of cerebral palsies and related disorders. *Nerv. Child*, 8:170–76.

REED, M. R. (1959). Psycho-educational problems of cerebral palsy. *Cerebral Palsy Rev.*, 20:3, 6.

RICHARDS, E. (1956). A study of a selected group of cerebral palsied persons to determine minimal occupational profiles and abilities associated with vocational success. *Dissert. Abstr.*, 16:67–68.

ROSS, A. T., and DAVIDSON, VIDA T. (1947). Psychologic handicaps of cerebral palsied children. *Publ. Welf. Ind.*, 57:15–16.

RUTHERFORD, B. R. (1945). Extraneous movements in cerebral palsy. *Physiother. Rev.*, 25:63–67.

SCHONELL, F. ELEANOR (1956). *Educating spastic children.* Edinburgh: Oliver & Boyd.

SHERE, MARIE O. (1960). The cerebral palsied child with a hearing loss. *Volta Rev.*, 62:438–41.

STRAUSS, A. A. (1952). The education of the brain-injured child. *Amer. J. ment. Def.*, 56:712–18.

THELANDER, H. E. (1956). Pediatric management of brain-damaged children. *Cerebral Palsy Rev.*, 17:32, 50.

TRACHT, V. S. (1946). A comparative study of personality factors among cerebral palsied and non-handicapped persons. Unpublished master's thesis, Univer. Chicago.

USHER, E. (1946). An integrated approach to cerebral palsy. *Del. State med. J.*, 18:196–99.

WENAR, C. (1954). The effects of a motor handicap on personality: II. The effects on integrative ability. *Child Developm.*, 25:287–94.

WISHIK, S. M. (1954). An outline of administrative guides for the community cerebral palsy program. *Amer. J. Pub. Health*, 54:158–65.

SELECTED READINGS

ALLEN, R. M., and JEFFERSON, T. W. (1962). *Psychological evaluation of the cerebral palsied person.* Springfield, Ill.: Charles C Thomas.

BOLES, G. (1959). Personality factors in mothers of cerebral palsied children. *Genet. Psychol. Monogr.*, 59:159–218.

CARDWELL, VIOLA E. (1956). *Cerebral palsy, advances in understanding and care.* New York: Association for the Aid of Crippled Children.

CROTHERS, B., and PAINE, R. S. (1959). *The natural history of cerebral palsy.* Cambridge: Harvard Univer. Press.

CRUICKSHANK, W. M., BICE, H. V., and WALLEN, N. E. (1957). *Perception and cerebral palsy.* Syracuse: Syracuse Univer. Press.

CRUICKSHANK, W. M., and RAUS, G. M. (1955). *Cerebral palsy: its individual and community problems.* Syracuse: Syracuse Univer. Press.

DEAN, VERA (1957). *Three steps forward.* London: Faber & Faber.

LEARNING, P. A. (1959). *The challenge of cerebral palsy.* Christchurch, N.Z.: Whitcombe & Tombs.

MECHAM, M. J., BERKO, M. J., and BERKO, FRANCES G. (1960). *Speech therapy in cerebral palsy.* Springfield, Ill.: Charles C Thomas.

PHELP, W. M., HOPKINS, T. W., and COUSINS, R. (1958). *The cerebral palsied child: a guide for parents.* New York: Simon & Schuster.

RUSS, J. D., and SOBOLOFF, H. R. (1958). *A primer of cerebral palsy.* Springfield, Ill.: Charles C Thomas.

USDANE, W. (1959). Employability of the multiple-handicapped. *Rehabilit. Lit.,* 20:3–9.

15

SPECIAL HEALTH PROBLEMS

Besides vision and hearing difficulties, crippling, and cardiac conditions, there are a number of special health problems among children. Common among the conditions are allergies, diabetes, malnutrition, and tuberculosis. Most children with these conditions will be enrolled in regular classes, and many of them will make satisfactory progress. Some of them are reminiscent of Dickens' description in *Nicholas Nickleby* of children in early nineteenth-century London:

Pale and haggard faces, lank and bony figures, children with the countenances of old men, deformities with iron upon their limbs, boys of stunted growth, and others whose long, meager legs would hardly bear their stooping bodies, all crowded on the view together. There were the bleareyed, the harelip, the crooked foot, and every ugliness of distortion that told of unnatural aversions conceived by parents for their offspring, or of young lives which, from the earliest dawn of infancy, had been one horrible endurance of cruelty and neglect—with every kindly sympathy and affection blasted in its birth, with every revengeful passion that can foster in swollen hearts eating its way to their core in silence, what an incipient hell was breeding there!

The major causes of death among children have changed considerably during the past several decades. For children aged one to fourteen years accidents claimed more lives than the five leading diseases combined during the year 1962 (National Safety Council, 1963). By 1962 heart disease had dropped to fifth place as a cause of death in this age group while cancer moved into the first position. (See Table 15–1.)

TABLE 15–1

Leading Causes of Death Among Children Aged One to Fourteen Years, 1962

| | Death Rate per 100,000 | | |
	Males	Females	Total
All causes	68.3	52.4	60.5
Accidents	27.7	15.2	21.9
Motor-vehicle	10.6	6.4	8.5
Cancer	8.4	7.2	7.8
Congenital malformations	5.7	5.7	5.7
Pneumonia	5.7	5.2	5.4
Gastritis, enteritis	1.2	1.1	1.2
Heart disease	1.0	1.1	1.0
Meningitis	1.1	0.9	1.0

SOURCE: National Safety Council (1963).

Health and Growth. In 1935 (Hoefer and Hardy, 1935) the health records of 40 children with high increments of mental growth, as found by measurement of consecutive yearly mental ages, showed them to be in better physical condition throughout this growth period than were 41 children with low increments of gain in mental age. An association of vigorous health with an accelerated mental growth rate was strongly suggested, for not only did the average health scores point to a real difference between the groups, but 75 per cent of the mentally accelerated cases were described by the physician as in good or excellent health at each yearly inspection. (See Fig. 15–1.)

When the health groups were equated on the basis of age, IQ, and socioeconomic level, the healthy children ranked above both the physically handicapped and the average children with respect to school progress as judged by educational tests and by teachers' marks. The differences were not large, but they were consistent. When IQ and health varied, even though the groups were alike in the other factors and had had the same degree of continuity of school experience, as judged by regularity of attendance and by number of transfers, the children differed markedly in the gains on school tests given during the health program. The very healthy children were consistently more

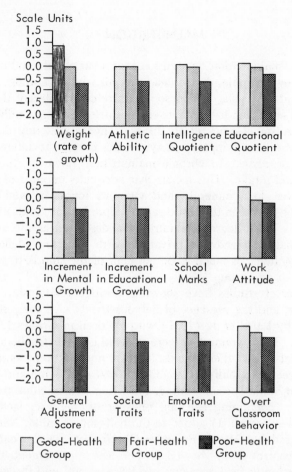

Fig. 15–1. Physical, mental, and social development of groups (equated for chronological age and socioeconomic status) of children in good health, fair health, and poor health. The scale units are expressed in terms of standard deviations above and below the mean. (Hoefer and Hardy, 1935.)

successful than the children in poor health. Similar tendencies were observed from a comparison of the results of those at the extremes of the test scores. In measures of muscular strength and robustness, in physical endurance, in relative freedom from physical defects, in nutrition, and, in general, all-round physical condition, pupils who made the largest gains in educational achievements ranked above both the average pupils and the pupils showing little school improvement.

MALNUTRITION

The term "malnutrition" is used to cover a variety of conditions such as anemia, hypotrophia, dystrophia, atrophia, decomposition, pellagra, dystonia, and athrepsia. All these names refer to different degrees or aspects of a condition in which essential nutrients are not fully utilized by the organism (Gomez et al., 1954). They are merely descriptive indicators of certain symptoms or syndromes present at different stages of specific processes. In chronic malnutrition, however, there is insufficient food intake. This means that adequate amounts of proteins, carbohydrates, fats, minerals, and vitamins found in well-balanced diets are not available for tissue repair, reproduction, and other work of the cells. Third-degree malnutrition is described as the final stage of nutritional deficiency or privation, with a serious deficiency in weight—sometimes as much as 50 per cent of the standard weight for the particular age group.

A number of studies have shown a positive relationship between malnutrition and the presence of nervous habits. An early study was conducted by Laird et al. (1931) with children in Grades 1, 3, and 5 as subjects. These youngsters were selected by their teachers as being the most nervous in their classes. One group was kept as a control, a second received a half-pint of milk at 9:30 A.M. daily, and the third group was given a special feeding, consisting of a calcium metabolism concentrate (containing calcium, phosphorus, maltose, lactose, vitamin D, and some cocoa) added to the half-pint of milk. Nervousness was measured by Olson's Behavior Check List. At the end of two weeks the control group showed 2.3 per cent improvement; the group that received milk feedings improved 8.2 per cent; and the group that was fed milk plus the concentrate improved 15.6 per cent. Marked improvement was shown by 85 per cent of the children in the third group; in fifteen traits the improvement was 25 per cent or more.

There is evidence that the growth lag of children with chronic malnutrition may be reduced significantly by daily milk supplements to an inadequate diet. In one study (Dreizen et al., 1950) 40 children with retarded skeletal growth associated with chronic malnutrition were given a dietary supplement of reconstituted milk solids equivalent in protein value to one quart of cow's milk. The supplements were given six days per week over a period of 20 months. Despite the fact that the diets of these children remained deficient in calories and several other nutrients, the children gained an average of 1.23

centimeters in height and 1.35 kilograms in weight over and beyond the gains of a nutritionally comparable group not given the added milk supplement. Withdrawal of the supplements was followed in almost all cases by a regression in the growth pattern. In a more recent report by Spies *et al.* (1953) it was pointed out that: "The retarding effect of prolonged nutritive failure on skeletal maturation is to a great extent reversible provided the nutrient value of the dietary supplement is sufficient to overcome the accumulated deficiencies" (p. 12). However, according to Platt *et al.* (1963), caloric restrictions or deficiencies of single nutrients brought on by infectious episodes or other stress that may impair appetite at a time when the needs of the body are high are reflected in bones as striations or arrested growth lines.

Since Williams coined the term "kwashiorkor" in 1933 for the nutritional syndrome of weanling children in the Gold Coast of Africa, the phenomenon, with variations, of protein malnutrition in such children has been recognized around the world. It is receiving broad attention through research and direct aid from organizations such as the World Health Organization, the Food and Agriculture Organization of the United Nations and UNICEF. Scrimshaw (1963) has pointed out that infant mortality in underprivileged areas of the world is 3 to 6 times higher than in the United States and Western Europe but may go 30 to 60 times higher in certain localities. Infant deaths are due to a wide variety of causes, and not all are prevented by good nutrition or improved hygiene and medical care. However, malnutrition is directly or indirectly involved in all of the excess mortality. Protein malnutrition is the most universal kind of nutritional deficiency.

The time lapse between initial exposure to nutritional inadequacy and the onset of nutritional disease may be short or long, depending upon the initial level of nutritional reserves and the degree of nutritional inadequacy (Jolliffe, 1962).

Brock and Hansen (1962) state that where kwashiorkor exists "There is widespread ignorance of the importance of cow's milk or other protein foods for children who have been weaned from the breast. This is as important a cause of protein malnutrition as poor socioeconomic conditions" (Brock and Hansen, 1962, p. 102).

Nutritional Anemia in Children. Infants are usually supplied with an adequate supply of iron during the first six months of life. There is, however, a greatly increased demand for iron following this period. This is a result of the expanding blood volume and the total hemoglobin associated with rapid growth. Nutritional anemia appears when there is an insufficient amount of iron in the diet. Clinical symptoms secondary to anemia may not be manifested during the early stage. Thus, parents are usually unaware that the child is suffering from a dietary deficit. Pallor and susceptibility to fatigue are symptoms that may be observed. If the anemic condition is not corrected, irritability, anorexia, and failure to grow ultimately appear. A case reported by Pollock and Richmond (1953) illustrates the nature of nutritional anemia during early childhood.

W. M. W., a 2-year-old Negro male, was admitted to the hospital because of vomiting, failure to gain weight, anemia, and frequent colds. On admission, physical examination revealed no pathological condition, but his red blood count was 2.59 and hemoglobin 4.1 Gm.

The patient was an only child and was unplanned for. The mother vomited throughout her pregnancy. The patient was bottle fed from birth until 15 months of age. Although solid foods were introduced at 7 months, they were poorly taken and the diet consisted mainly of milk and cereal. Mother's attitude about the child's feeding habits was grossly pessimistic. . . . The family lived with the father's sister, who was also married and had two of her own children. The housing was most inadequate and there was overcrowding. Since the patient has been a year old, the mother has been forced to work to assist in the economic situation. [P. 478.]

In the study by Pollock and Richmond (1953) it was noted that a constellation of circumstances, varying from patient to patient, may be observed in nutritional anemia. They conclude from their observations:

In general, our study indicated that social, economic, and emotional factors served to disturb the feeding pattern, with resultant development of feeding problems. Thus, a disturbance in the parent-child relationship reflected as feeding problems was responsible for the development of anemia in this group. Some of the specific problems observed were inability to breastfeed; regressive anorexia associated with toilet training or with anemia; perpetuation of anorexia, which may occur with teething or acute infections; and perpetuation of physiological anorexia, which may occur in the second year of life. Immaturity of parents, marital incompatibilities, sexual problems, as well as the social and economic factors associated with poor housing and financial privation, all were factors causing a poor parent-child relationship. The most consistent single finding perhaps was the failure of any single mother in this series to breastfeed her infant. [P. 483.]

Food Habits of Children. Nutritional needs differ at various age levels and will vary considerably from child to child of the same age level. The mean daily intakes of food energy and ten nutrients were estimated from seven-day dietary records for 1,188 Iowa schoolchildren at successive age groups from six through eighteen (Eppright and Roderuck, 1955). Except for calcium, the boys at successive age levels had progressively larger daily intakes of food energy and nutrients. The mean daily intake of the girls tended to be greatest from age six to twelve. The mean daily nutritive value of the diets of both the boys and the girls approximated or exceeded the recommended dietary allowances of the National Research Council. After age twelve the girls tended to have diets below the recommended allowances in most nutrients. However, a fairly large proportion of the children—both boys and girls—had diets that were not well fortified by certain nutrients. Table 15–2 shows the per cent of children whose daily intakes of specified nutrients were less than 67 per cent of the allowances. These data show that the percentage with a low mean daily intake of calcium was high. Many of the children used little of the vitamin-C and carotene-rich fruit and vegetables.

The agricultural experiment stations of Maine (Clayton, 1952)

TABLE 15–2

Per Cent of Children with Food Energy Value and Nutrients in Average Daily Diets at Levels Less than 67 Per Cent of the National Research Council Recommended Allowances

		6–8 Years	9–11 Years	12–14 Years	15 Years and Above
Food energy	Boys	0.0	2.4	5.1	4.9
value	Girls	2.1	4.4	4.2	4.3
Protein	Boys	0.0	2.4	1.7	1.9
	Girls	2.1	3.3	7.9	9.6
Calcium	Boys	10.9	14.7	29.7	20.7
	Girls	19.8	25.2	29.7	45.6
Iron	Boys	2.0	3.7	6.2	2.9
	Girls	4.9	6.0	16.3	31.5
Vitamin A	Boys	2.0	6.8	6.8	4.9
value	Girls	3.5	6.0	9.7	19.3
Thiamine	Boys	0.0	4.3	5.1	6.9
	Girls	1.4	6.0	8.4	12.2
Riboflavin	Boys	0.0	4.9	5.1	3.9
	Girls	2.8	6.0	10.9	13.1
Niacin	Boys	0.0	1.2	2.8	4.9
	Girls	1.4	2.2	3.6	7.0
Ascorbic acid	Boys	11.6	11.0	22.8	18.8
	Girls	12.1	10.4	20.0	22.8

SOURCE: After Eppright and Roderuck (1955).

undertook a project to obtain information relative to the diets of 780 junior high school pupils. The information was compiled from four-day and seven-day diet records; blood tests for hemoglobin, vitamin A, carotene, and vitamin C; and physical examinations for nutritional defects. Physical examinations showed that several types of defects, probably relating to nutritional conditions, frequently appeared. These included "overweight, underweight, signs of previous rickets, fol-liculosis (rough, dry, 'goose-pimply' skin), marginal blepharitis (in-flammation of the eyelids), thickening of the conjunctiva of the eyes, atrophic cheilosis (reddened peeling lips), angular stomatitis (red-ness, cracks, and sores at the angles of the lips), changes in the papillae of the tongue, gingivitis (inflamed gums), and dental caries" (p. 967). The results of the blood tests for carotene, vitamin A, and vitamin C supported the conclusion that these defects were related to poor nutrition. In comparison with the National Research Coun-cil's recommended daily dietary allowances, the diets of the junior high school girls were low in calories, protein, calcium, iron, and vita-min C. The boys' diets were low in calories, calcium, and vitamin C. Deficiencies in vitamin C, iron, and calcium are definitely related to the low consumption of citrus fruits and juices, green leafy vegetables, raw vegetables, and milk products.

Nutrition Education. Nutrition education is essential to any school health program. Instruction on what, when, and how to eat, along with the why, should be included. It is not sufficient to present in-formation about health; children must also become conscious of the importance of practicing good health habits. Health awareness, as an attitude, should be a major goal of health instruction. Such awareness becomes more meaningful and significant when it is related to home, school, and community problems. The school lunchroom should pro-vide opportunities for students to put into practice good health habits taught in the classroom and elsewhere. Children should experience tasting of unfamiliar food under pleasant circumstances and should have opportunities to select good lunches under guidance.

DIABETES

Nature and Symptoms. Diabetes is not exactly an endocrine dis-order, but rather a disorder of the body metabolism—marked by an interference of the body's ability to use food substances, particularly sugar. Thus, there is an abnormal concentration of sugar in the blood and in the urine. A secondary and sometimes serious result is that fats, which depend upon the presence of sugars for their effective conversion into usable forms, are not adequately utilized. Diabetes is particularly severe during childhood, since the demands of the growing body are great and most activity is at a high rate. Before the discovery of the use of insulin in treating this condition, the average child with diabetes lived two years after the onset of the disease.

As a rule diabetic children appear healthy and well at first. An important symptom is persisting fatigue, which is due to the unavailability of sugars and the secondary inability to use fats. Also, hunger becomes important as a symptom, since foods are not properly converted into usable nutritive substances.

According to Grishaw (1962), other symptoms usually found include excessive thirst, excessive urination, loss of weight, slow healing of cuts and bruises, changes in vision, intense itching, pain in fingers and toes, and drowsiness.

Prevalence. Estimates of the prevalence of diabetes in the United States as of 1959 were 2.9 million, of which only slightly more than one-half were known cases (Forsham, 1959). This is an incidence of approximately 16.9 per 1,000 population. The incidence is less than .5 per cent for children under twelve years of age. According to Danowski (1957) about 150,000 children under the age of fifteen were afflicted with diabetes in 1957. The seriousness of the disease results from the complications and short life expectancy unless treated, rather than its great prevalence among children.

Importance of Psychological Factors. A number of investigators have emphasized the importance of psychological factors. Experimental evidence reported by Hinkle et al. (1951) supports the hypothesis that psychological and cultural factors affect the onset and course of this disease. These investigators described diabetes as a disorder of adaptation. Children who have diabetes react to various life situations as though they were deprived of food. Their adaptive reactions are those that are appropriate to conditions of starvation. The onset of diabetes occurs after a period of stress, such as that caused by the death of a loved one, or the loss of a job or some relationship that was highly valued.

The importance of emotional factors in diabetes has been observed by a number of investigators. It is not clear, however, why some cases develop diabetes and others do not. It appears likely that emotional stress acts as a precipitating factor, setting off a condition to which the individual is already susceptible. Rosen and Lidz (1949) studied 12 patients selected at random from a group of over 50 diabetics who had been readmitted to the medical wards with disturbances in the acid-base balance of the body two or more times after their initial regulation. All 12 patients indicated serious emotional disturbances. However, few suffered from psychiatric syndromes that could be readily classified. The following case was somewhat typical of the group:

A 19-year-old youth who had been diabetic for four years had been very poorly adjusted long before the onset of his diabetes, playing truant, fighting with teachers, demanding attention from his mother in very infantile ways. The onset of his diabetes, at about the time a younger sibling was born, increased his negativistic attitude. He became increasingly seclusive, blaming his diabetes because everyone treated him as being different. His third admission occurred after he had stopped taking insulin because he no longer cared to live. The fourth admission came after he had lost his job because he could not stand being bossed, when he took a suicidal dose of sedatives in addition to stopping diet and insulin. [P. 212.]

Parental reactions to the diabetic child are likely to be either of two: oversolicitous coddling or resentment and rejection (Podolsky, 1955). The manner in which the child is treated by his parents, siblings, and others will determine to a marked degree how he will react to his ailment. Thus, diabetic children show great variations in their behavior and personality characteristics. They are often frightened children because their mode of life is different from that of others. They find themselves restricted and regimented with relation to diet. Since there is apparently no end to this restriction, they may acquire the notion that they are suffering from an incurable condition. It is at this point that sympathetic and realistic guidance on the part of parents and others is most important.

ALLERGIES AND ASTHMA

Allergic and asthmatic conditions have received increased attention from specialists in different fields of science within recent years. There is increasing evidence of an intimate relation between a child's emotional life and the occurrence of these conditions. This is implied in a statement by Harold S. Tuft, Medical Director of the Jewish National Home for Asthmatic Children in Denver, Colorado. "Asthma is caused by an allergy, and no one ever really gets cured of an allergy. But we do say that we can *control* asthma. We can remove the emotional overload which is preventing these children from recovering" (*Newsweek*, November 28, 1955).

Allergies of Childhood. While there is no general agreement on the incidence of allergic disorders, there is an indication of its prevalence that under a liberal definition would include half the population. A study by Rapaport *et al.* (1960) of 2,169 children under fifteen years of age revealed that 20 per cent had major allergic conditions. The nature and severity of cases vary from the person who sneezes when confronted with moldy bread to the one who gasps with asthma or groans with the severe pains of migraine headaches. A basement musty from dampness and dust, feathers of the bed pillow, dandruff, or milk and eggs for breakfast may be sufficient stimuli to produce the sneezing state. Much attention has been given in recent years to the causes of this condition, and a number of rather effective forms of relief have been developed.

It is likely that allergies can develop in a baby even before birth because of the diet of the expectant mother. Two other very vulnerable periods in a child's life are infancy and during any convalescence. If, during infancy, the child is given an excess of allergenic foods (foods capable of creating antibodies if they invade the bloodstream), there is danger that an allergy for such foods may develop. If the baby is given new foods during a period of gastrointestinal disturbances such as diarrhea or dysentery, there is grave danger of the development of an allergy for such foods. Also, if the growing child is given special foods in excess during a convalescence following an operation or disease, an allergy to such foods may result. One precaution to be observed, then, is not to give the child special foods to an excess, and to be especially careful about introducing new foods during a critical period in his life. A further precaution is to provide the child with allergenically denatured foods during such periods. If the foods are well heated or steamed sufficiently so that the proteins have been temporarily denatured by a coagulation process that makes them more readily digestible, there will be little danger of allergic conditions developing.

During critical periods in the lives of growing children allergies may develop to substances other than food. Cotton and feather pillows, rag rugs that are great catchers of dust, or overstuffed furniture that provides a haven for dust particles provide good stimuli to the development of allergic conditions. A principle important in connection with the development of an allergy is that an individual cannot acquire a food, dust, or pollen allergy without first being exposed to that particular food, dust, or pollen in some form. Thus, a preventive program should begin with the child's early contacts with conditions that may be stimuli. A child who is aware of precautions necessary for the prevention of an allergic condition is not as likely to develop an allergic state as the child who grows up without this awareness (Roberts, 1947).

Allergies and Emotions. There is considerable evidence that not all allergies result from pollens and foods, but that many have a psychological basis. In a study reported by Miller and Baruch (1957) 97 per cent of the mothers of 201 allergic children interviewed expressed a rejecting attitude toward these children, whereas only 37 per cent of the mothers of a control group of 110 non-allergic children expressed such an attitude.

However, not all rejected children find the allergic state the best procedure for solving conflict. It has been observed in large psychiatric hospitals that the incidence of allergic manifestations is significantly less among psychotic patients than among the population at large. A number of investigators have found that schizophrenic and manic-depressive patients are rarely sensitive to the usual allergens used in making skin tests. In the McAllister-Hecker study (1949) comparisons were made between a control group of 757 individuals and a test group of 1,875 neuropsychiatric patients for symptoms and signs of allergy. The survey revealed an incidence of major allergic symptoms by history of 21 per cent and by physical signs of 13 per cent among the control subjects. Among the test group from the same geographic location the incidence of symptoms by history was 5.7 per cent and by physical signs 2.9 per cent. The incidence of physical signs among the patients was further broken down with these results: schizophrenic patients, 2.9 per cent; manic-depressive psychotics, 1.4 per cent; organic psychoses, 3.0 per cent; and epileptics, 13 per cent. Only among the epileptics was the incidence of physical signs equal to that among the controls.

Asthma Among Children. At least half of the country's asthma victims are children. Of this group about 10 per cent have chronic, intractable asthma, which may be fatal. Chronic, intractable asthma is characterized by coughing, wheezing, and gasping for breath. Drugs, helpful to 90 per cent of asthma sufferers, do not relieve asthmatic conditions that are chronic.

Neuhaus (1954) noted that asthmatic children of eight through fourteen years were more maladjusted than normals in that they displayed greater anxiety, insecurity, and dependency. No significant differences were found between an asthmatic group and a cardiac group of children. Data from this study indicated personality traits common to both illnesses, and perhaps common in general to protracted chronic illnesses.

According to M. Murray Meshkin, chief medical consultant of the Jewish National Home for Asthmatic Children, asthmatic children need a change from their home environment, no matter how sympathetic and conscientious their parents or relatives may be (*Newsweek,* November 28, 1955). Most asthmatic children are in serious conflict with one or both parents. They feel the lack of parental affection and the security that goes with such affection. Thus, they become over-dependent and demanding and display periodic outbursts of anger and rebellion. Studies of the children at the Jewish National Home indicate that about 10 per cent of them do not want to get well, the doctors finding it difficult to wean them away from dependency on their illness for attention and consideration. The cure found most effective for these children is termed "parentectomy"—the separation of children from their parents, homes, and other members of their families.

TUBERCULOSIS

The National Tuberculosis Association was founded in 1904. At that time tuberculosis was the number one killer in this country. Since then the death rate has been reduced over 90 per cent. However, it is still one of the most prevalent debilitating diseases of infancy and early adulthood. It is caused by the *bacillus mycobacterium tuberculosis,* which can infect almost any tissue of the body, although it most often affects the lungs.

Tuberculosis in Childhood. There are two types of tuberculosis, the primary infection and the reinfection. The primary infection takes place most often during childhood and was formerly referred to as "childhood tuberculosis." Such an infection may occur at any stage in life, the term "primary" indicating the stage or process that follows the first implantation of the bacilli in body tissue. It has been estimated that as many as two-thirds of the population of the United States develop primary infection at some time in their lives, but less than 1 in 100 develop any further tuberculosis disease. The primary infection during childhood is a benign one that is seldom accompanied by any pronounced illness (Solomon, 1952).

Because of the preventive measures in schools and elsewhere, a remarkable change has occurred during recent decades in the age distribution of those suffering from tuberculosis. The incidence of primary tuberculosis has become considerably higher in the group beyond forty years of age, and the disease is now beginning to be referred to as a disease of older people (Dubos, 1953).

The extent of tubercular infection varies in accordance with economic circumstances. It is a disease of misery and is most often found among those living in poor, squalid, and disadvantageous conditions. The death rate from tuberculosis gives a rather accurate index of the economic level of people. When high wages prevail, tuberculosis is not a serious problem, for high wages mean better food, housing, and medical care. These conditions are not closely associated with tuberculosis.

When the disease is contracted during childhood, there are four possibilities: (1) spontaneous recovery may occur without manifest symptoms; (2) the disease may become definitely organized and lead quickly to death; (3) after becoming manifest, the disease may disappear, following some evident illness; or (4) there may be a relapse after an apparent recovery. Which of these conditions will follow is determined both by the native vitality of the individual and by the general conditions of his environment and mode of life.

The site of infection in children of school age is less often in the lungs than in the lymphatic glands or in the bones. Swollen glands of the neck, often considered of little importance, are frequently a symptom of tuberculosis. With tuberculosis of the bone, as with the pulmonary form of the disease, the greatest stress should be placed upon early diagnosis. The most effective prophylaxis would be the protection of children, especially during the first three or four years of life, from severe infection. When treatment is begun early enough, recovery is almost certain, and in a majority of cases without resulting deformity. But it appears that in most cases (probably 95 per cent) of spinal tuberculosis, deformity is already present before the diagnosis has been made. The child with frequent or occasional pains, slight rigidity, or tenderness in the joints should be an object of concern, since these symptoms are significant.

Means of Preventing Tuberculosis. Any successful campaign against tuberculosis must focus its attention mainly upon infants and children. Since there is good evidence that the pulmonary tuberculosis of adults is only the tertiary form of a primary infection that occurred in infancy, and since the gland and bone infections of schoolchildren are the secondary form, the logical and most effective method would be to prevent the infection of infants by removing them from all contact with persons who are tuberculous. Sanitary laws relating to housing and community conditions may accomplish something by lessening the chances of infection. What a child needs most to keep him well is room to live, sunlight, air, and the opportunity to play. An early life of poverty and conditions that condemn children to a life of squalor and insufficient nutrition are factors that contribute greatly to susceptibility and that do not yield readily to the efforts of those seeking to prevent tuberculosis.

The importance of parents and teachers having some knowledge of tuberculosis is well recognized, and the X-raying of teachers themselves has become an accepted part of the school personnel program. The prevention of tuberculosis at all school-age levels depends largely upon good personal hygiene that goes beyond acceptable standards of cleanliness, and on periodic X-raying of all the children, good nutrition, and good home and school adjustments.

Problems in the Diagnosis and Care of the Tubercular. Tuberculin testing is useful as a diagnostic procedure and as an indication of the prevalence of infection in a community. The Mantoux test and the Patch test have been widely used to determine whether or not the child has taken into his body at any time in his life some tubercle bacilli. A positive tuberculin test indicates the need for an X-ray examination of the lungs and further clinical study. Further diagnostic procedures should then depend upon results obtained from such X rays. Increased emphasis is being placed on early detection through stepped-up X-raying of all schoolchildren.

Prolonged bed rest has been the basic treatment for tuberculosis for over a half-century. However, the treatment of tuberculosis has undergone a radical change since the advent of antimicrobial therapy. Overprotection and overindulgence of the tubercular child are hazards to be avoided in the treatment. Bakwin (1950) has pointed out that hospitalized children with active tuberculosis show specific psychological reactions to their condition. They resist bed rest and the limitations placed upon their physical activity. Diffuse motor activity, emotional outbursts, and refusal or inability to cooperate are frequently encountered. The psychological needs of the child should be given special consideration. Opportunities for creative activity, social participation, and positive identification with the parents or other adults about him are essential in the care and treatment program.

HEART CONDITIONS

It was noted earlier in this chapter that heart conditions ranked sixth as the leading cause of death among children aged one to fourteen in 1962. Brownell (1952) has listed three main groups of children in school who may be referred to as cardiac:

1. Children with a heart murmur or some other abnormal physical finding but for whom at the time a definite diagnosis of heart disease cannot be made
2. Children with congenital defects of the heart
3. All children who have had rheumatic fever, whether or not they are afflicted with heart trouble

Classification. There are two types of cardiac conditions—congenital and rheumatic. The child with a congenital cardiac condition is affected from birth. Those with rheumatic hearts acquire the condition from rheumatic fever, which affects both the heart and joints, and usually strikes between the ages of five and sixteen. Concerning differential diagnosis, Wedum and Rhodes (1955) state: "It is probably safe to say that every child, at some time in his life, has a functional or normal systolic murmur. The incidence of organic heart disease, both congenital and acquired, seldom runs over 1 per cent in school children. When a systolic murmur is heard in a child the overwhelming probability is that it is not organic" (p. 981).

Congenital Heart Conditions. Parsons (1954) claims that congenital heart conditions are usually due to arrested fetal development during the period of organogenesis in the first three months of pregnancy. Malformations of the heart vary from those that do not interfere in any manner with the child's activities to those so serious that the infant is unable to survive. The majority of children who reach school age with congenital heart conditions are handicapped little, if at all. Recent advancements in surgery have made possible a normal or near-normal life for many who formerly were severely affected. Considerable education and psychological adjustments are often necessary for those so treated. It may be necessary to teach them to live with a normal heart, engaging in activities in which they were formerly not allowed to participate.

During recent decades more progress has been made in understanding congenital heart defects than any other type of heart condition. There is ample evidence that links congenital heart defects to German measles in the mother during the first two or three months of pregnancy. Improved maternal and infancy care has lowered significantly the mortality rate among children with congenital heart malformations.

Prevalence of Heart Disease Among Children. Accurate information about the prevalence of heart disease among children is difficult to obtain. Estimates vary from 1 per cent to 6 per cent or more (White, 1951). In a study conducted in Connecticut (Quinn et al., 1950) the prevalence of rheumatic fever in three factory towns was compared with the incidence in a nearby control town that was largely residential, with good living conditions. The rheumatic fever rate among seventh- and eighth-grade schoolchildren in the three factory towns was 6 per cent while that of the control town was 2.5 per cent. In the control town there was significantly more crowding in the homes of those who had rheumatic heart disease than in the other homes. In general the factor of crowding in the home appeared to be more prominently associated with the prevalence of rheumatic heart disease than did the factor of substandard housing.

The incidence of heart disease in school-age children in the city of Philadelphia (see Table 15–3, Cahan, 1953), based upon a census taken in 1953, is much lower than that discovered in the Connecticut study. In general the rate of heart disease has been found high in New England and the Rocky Mountain states, especially for rheumatic-cardiac cases. Differences in diagnostic procedures might also account for some of the differences in the findings. In the Philadelphia study the majority of cases were diagnosed upon the basis of the clinical opinion of a cardiologist. The largest percentage of cases were found in the junior high schools, and the lowest percentage in the elementary grades. This situation seems to result largely from the greater number with acquired heart disease in junior high schools.

The studies reported by Jackson et al. (1947) indicated that the recurrence rate of rheumatic fever was decreased in children whose environment had been improved. Of the various environmental factors studied, the most significant association was found between the dietary ratings and the recurrence rate of the disease. If the heart

TABLE 15–3

Organic Heart Cases, Philadelphia Public Schools, February, 1953

	Elementary Schools and Special Classes (age 5–11)	Junior High Schools (age 12–14)	Senior High and Vocational Technical Schools (age 15–17)	Total
Enrollment *	129,886	38,193	39,383	207,462
Number of school units	189	24	20 †	233
Total heart cases				
Number of cases	700	317	277	1,294
Per cent of enrollment	.53	.82	.7	.62
Congenital heart anomaly				
Number of cases	247	77	69	393
Per cent of enrollment	.2	.2	.2	.2
Per cent of total heart cases	35.29	24.29	24.91	30.37
Acquired heart disease				
Number of cases	453	240	208	901
Per cent of enrollment	.34	.62	.52	.43
Per cent of total heart cases	64.71	75.71	75.09	69.63

*Does not include kindergarten children.
† Two units are combined: junior-senior high schools.
SOURCE: After Cahan (1953).

escapes damage during the first attack, it is more likely to be damaged if there are repeated attacks. Experiments with modern drugs have offered great promise in preventing recurrence and possible serious damage to the heart.

The National Safety Council (1963) reported that the mortality rate for children aged one to fourteen from organic heart disease was 1 per 100,000. This was a substantial decline from that of a decade or more ago. The mortality rates from rheumatic fever and chronic rheumatic heart disease has shown a steady decline. The National Office of Vital Statistics (1952) reported data for different age groups. These data, presented in Table 15–4, indicate that, while the mortality rate from rheumatic fever tended to be highest in the age group under forty-five, the mortality rate from rheumatic heart disease shows a continuous increase with age.

Rheumatic Heart Disease. Rheumatic fever may attack several parts of the body simultaneously. The characteristics commonly ob-

TABLE 15–4

Mortality from Rheumatic Fever and Rheumatic Heart Disease,
United States, 1950

Age Group (Years)	Mortality Rates per 100,000 Population	
	Rheumatic Fever	Rheumatic Heart Disease
Under 1	0.6	–
1–14	1.5	0.7
15–24	1.3	3.2
25–34	1.7	5.2
35–44	2.5	12.4
45–54	0.9	24.2
55–64	0.4	32.8
65–74	0.9	42.3
75–84	1.9	70.4
85 and over	2.1	168.5
Total	1.4	13.2

Source: National Office of Vital Statistics (1952).

served, from which the disease got its name, are acute inflammation of the joints and a high fever. Other characteristics which frequently accompany the disease are chorea, skin rash, frequent bleeding of the nose, and abdominal pains that may be confused with appendicitis. The seriousness of the disease stems from the damage and scarring that often occur in the heart during recovery.

Due to the inadequacy of diagnostic criteria used in some cardiac clinics, rheumatic heart disease may be either overdiagnosed or underdiagnosed. The classic description of rheumatic fever in terms of explosive attacks, fever, and elevated sedimentation rate does not appear in a large percentage of cases. The results of 10- and 20-year studies of patients followed from childhood reveal that many had had carditis, despite the absence of the symptoms usually associated with such a condition (Bland and Jones, 1951). Davis and Greene (1954) point out that the diagnosis of rheumatic heart disease and rheumatic fever in the absence of a classical history has become a clinical problem of major importance. They propose three categories of diagnostic criteria: (1) positive evidence, (2) presumptive signs, and (3) helpful diagnostic criteria.

As a lead they suggest that the occurrence of rheumatic heart disease in other members of the immediate family has positive value. They state further:

General inspection of the child usually yields our most telling diagnostic information. In our opinion, marked pallor may be the first noticed physical finding. This clue is often the first and most important one pointing to the presence of acute heart disease. Should the child have other general signs of heart disease, such as shortness of breath, cyanosis, or venous engorgement, the patient no longer presents a problem in the diagnosis of heart disease, but rather a problem in classification as to the type of heart disease and the disposition of the case. [P. 433.]

Streptococcal infections are usually regarded as the forerunners of attacks of rheumatic fever. Although such infections, which are extremely common, are not usually followed by rheumatic fever, over half the cases of rheumatic fever are preceded by sore throat and tonsillitis. In others there may be a history of acute infection of the upper or lower respiratory passages. Furthermore, those suffering from rheumatic fever seem quite prone to develop chronic or recurrent forms of sore throats and tonsillitis. Susceptibility to conditions that may lead to rheumatic fever is more common in some families than in others. The nature of this susceptibility is not clear, but there is some evidence that suggests that it is hereditary. Other evidence suggests that it is the same type of susceptibility common to tuberculosis and other diseases.

Sometimes the condition of the heart is the only diagnostic indication of rheumatic fever. Increased pulse rate, unexplained fever, and systolic murmurs may provide important clues. The child may either be obviously sick or may show no outward appearance of being sick.

When the heart is permanently injured, the scarring is usually the result of inflammation of the valves between the chambers on the left side of the heart. Cardiac complications develop in approximately two-thirds of the children with rheumatic fever. An attack does not convey immunity but actually appears to make the individual more prone to recurrent attacks.

The most obvious and important change in behavior is nervous instability, accompanied by movements that may best be described as fidgety. The child becomes seemingly alert, overresponsive, excitable, emotional, and is easily depressed. Other conditions frequently encountered include insomnia, sleepwalking, night terrors, enuresis, tics, etc. Bland and Jones (1952) report that chorea occurs in 51 per cent of all rheumatic fever patients during some phase of their illness.

Campbell and Reynolds (1949) have pointed out that, when children with heart disease are given adequate instruction at home, they are not likely to become educationally retarded. Also, the close contacts with adults that their disability makes necessary furnishes needed social stimulation. Thus, in terms of actual educational accomplishment most of these children were achieving satisfactorily. White (1951) has pointed out that, once the disease becomes inactive, the child can safely attend school and should not be placed in a special group or class. The modern educational trend is toward integration, with special considerations where the need exists, rather than separation.

Some Problems. Physical illness in a child may have serious implications because of the attitudes he develops toward his condition and himself (Langford, 1948). With rheumatic fever this situation is frequently complicated by its long-term character. Convalescence is not a matter of days but of weeks and months, and is sometimes extended by a recurrence into an even longer period of confinement and convalescence. The child does not understand why this happens to him. Sometimes he develops feelings of guilt that actually aggravate the problem of personality orientation to the condition.

A child with heart trouble is greatly handicapped in his social relations. Rheumatic fever in particular affects most often individuals who are in their latent period of emotional maturation. Josselyn (1949) points out:

The long period of isolation from a social group and normal social activities lessens the opportunity for friendships to partially replace the parents. Furthermore, and more significant, aggressive behavior, expressed in the healthy patterns of the normal child through aggressive, active games, is again dangerous. Such expression of aggression carries with it the possible punishment of death! The danger in aggressive behavior thus becomes a real one, and the sublimation usually found by children is forbidden. [P. 99.]

However, in a study by Force (1954) of the social acceptance of physically handicapped children among normal peers (see also pp. 326–27), cardiac children were pretty well accepted as friends but not as playmates.

At home the cardiac child is likely to be pampered because he must not be permitted to do much work around the house, fight his own battles lustily, or receive severe punishment. As a consequence he may become overbearing, egotistical, selfish, or lazy. Neuhaus (1954) noted that cardiac children, aged eight through fourteen, exceeded normal children of the same age in degree of neuroticism and dependency. These findings are readily understood when the long period of convalescence and nature of the physical treatment required for the cardiac child is realized.

After the period of bed rest is over, the child is still not allowed to resume normal activities. His activities may be seriously limited at first, particularly if there appears to be a rather serious impairment of the heart. Since it is difficult to determine the exact rate and amount of recovery, the doctor cannot assure the child that he may return to normal activity if he follows a prescribed routine. The child can only be assured of probable gradual entrance into more normal life activities.

The seriousness of rheumatic fever in the fact that the heart or the protective membrane that encloses the heart is permanently damaged in some way. For certain types of damage, surgery has been utilized with reasonable success.

There may be a murmur or an irregularity in rhythm of the heartbeat. Heart murmurs are particularly common among school-age children, and often these murmurs are caused by some peculiar course of the vessels in the neck, producing what is referred to as a "venous hum." Some such murmurs are transmitted into the chest, where they are then erroneously diagnosed as organic heart disease. Only after a careful study is made can an accurate judgment be made about the seriousness of a murmur. Irregularities in the heartbeat are found frequently among children and adults. Although a great many of these irregularities are due to heart disease, erratic beats sometimes occur in people who have normal hearts. Such people are usually rather nervous. It is not uncommon for variable pulse rates to appear in children at an early age. In order to determine whether or not irregular heartbeats are serious, a complete diagnosis including a cardiac study is necessary.

Children with congenital heart disease are more likely to suffer from too much restriction of their activity than from too much freedom. However, this will depend in a large measure upon the individual child. A follow-up study of 699 survivors of 1,000 rheumatic fever patients who 20 years earlier had acute attacks showed that 3 out of 4 had little or no limitations on their activities (Keith *et al.*, 1958).

EPILEPSY

As with other exceptional children, it should be emphasized that the child with epilepsy is first of all a child. He differs from other children only in that he may have an occasional seizure or take medicine to control seizures. This viewpoint should be the beginning point for understanding and successfully dealing with epileptic children. It should be further emphasized that modern neurologists consider "epilepsy" merely a synonym for "seizures" rather than a term representing a specific disease entity (Rupp, 1958).

Definition. "Epilepsy" is from a Greek word, *epilambanein,* meaning to seize or attack. An unfortunate aspect of the word is the unfavorable connotations usually associated with it. During the Dark Ages seizures were regarded as visitations supernatural in origin. Because of the generally unfavorable connotation associated with the word "epilepsy," Lennox (1941) has argued against the use of the term and has suggested the term "cerebral dysrhythmia" (brain rhythm disorder). This term is based upon research and observations of the brains of those with epilepsy and means a periodic disturbance of the brain rhythm. Livingston (1954) has given a broader definition of the term. He states: "Epilepsy may be defined in a broad sense as a term used to designate a variable symptom complex characterized by a *tendency toward recurrent paroxysmal signs or symptoms of disturbances of cerebral activity*" (p. 20).

The term "epilepsy" is so general as to be virtually meaningless. It tells nothing of the site of disturbances in electrochemical activity in the brain cells nor does it give any clues to the severity or extent of the manifestations that result from such disturbances, although the electroencephalograph continues to be the most widely used laboratory procedure for diagnosing epilepsy.

Classifications and Symptoms. The epileptiform seizure itself is made up of several different symptoms that may be present in varying degrees in different persons. The seizures may vary almost infinitely in character and number. Lennox (1941) points out, however, that the main elements of seizures are: first and foremost, the impairment or loss of consciousness; second, involuntary muscle movements; third, abnormal sensations; and fourth, psychic or mental disturbance. The various combinations of these symptoms differentiate the clinical types of seizure.

Since epilepsy is a condition that may have many different origins, it presents great difficulties in diagnosis. According to Lennox (1945), the real problem in diagnosis lies in the detection and separation of the genetic from the acquired causes. Most students of this problem agree that overt seizures of some form, recognized as epileptic seizures, are still the most reliable guide in a clinical diagnosis of epilepsy. The physician usually supplements these observations with the electroencephalogram, commonly referred to as the brain-wave record (see Fig. 15–2). These brain-wave records of a subject may

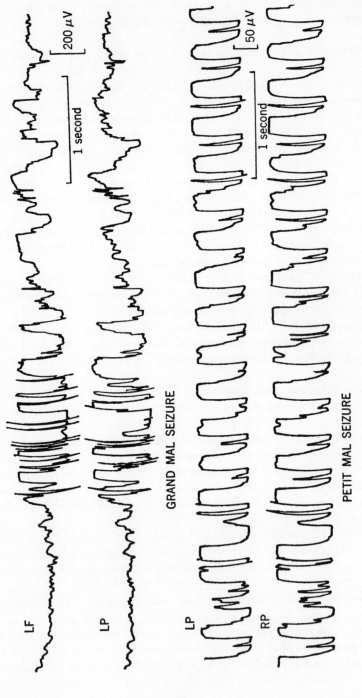

GRAND MAL SEIZURE

PETIT MAL SEIZURE

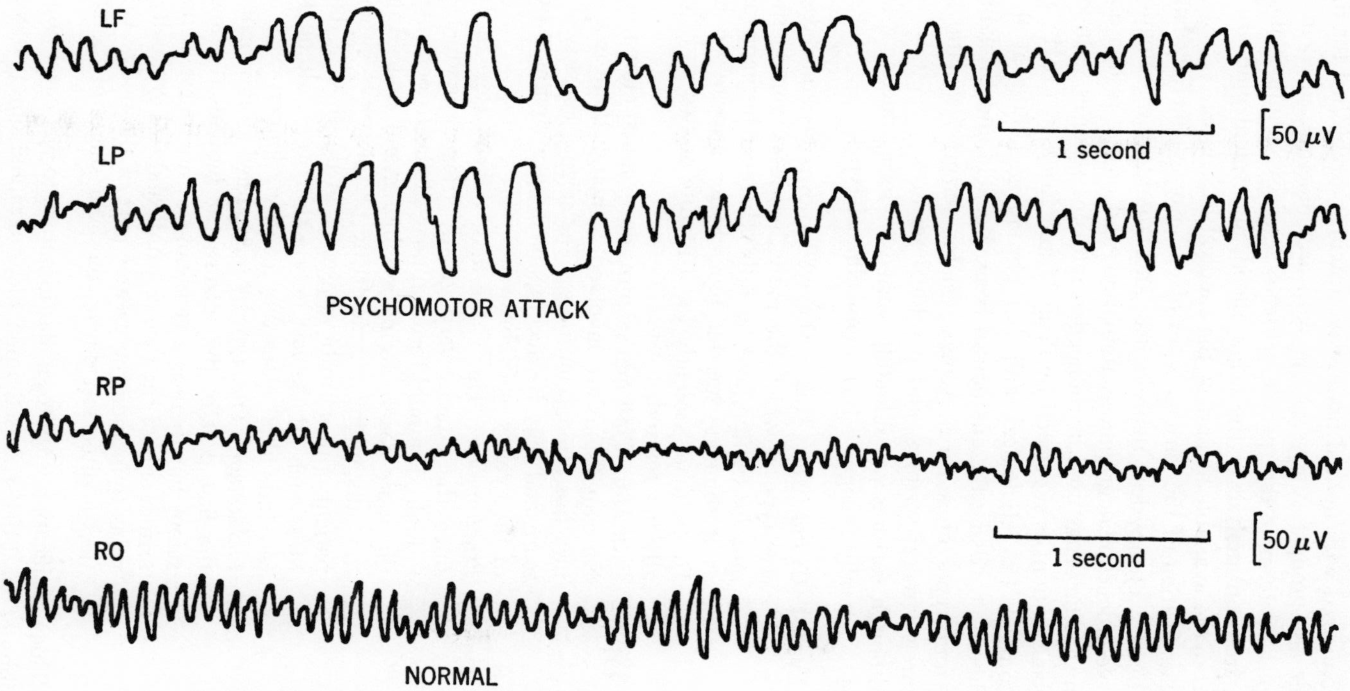

LF

LP

PSYCHOMOTOR ATTACK

50 μV

1 second

RP

RO

NORMAL

50 μV

1 second

Fig. 15-2. Characteristic electroencephalograph tracings. (Thorpe and Katz, 1948.)

be compared with normal brain-wave tracings established for the different age groups. X rays of the skull are sometimes used in an attempt to determine the specific cause of seizures. Routine laboratory data from an analysis of the urine, blood, and spinal fluid are sometimes made available as part of the medical diagnosis.

Classification of the various types of epilepsy is generally based on the history, on physical, neurological, and laboratory examinations, on the electroencephalographic examination, and on the results obtained from specific drugs used in connection with the seizures. Three bases of classification, as suggested by Penfield and Erickson (1941) are (1) anatomical, (2) etiological, and (3) chronological age at the time of the onset. Using the anatomical basis, Penfield and Erickson identify four types of seizures: somatic motor seizures, somatic sensory seizures, visceral seizures, and psychical seizures.

Although seizures are infinitely varied in form, doctors (Yahraes, 1954) generally recognize four main clinical types:

Type 1. *Grand Mal.* This is the well-known generalized convulsive type in which the individual loses consciousness, his muscles tighten, and he falls wherever he happens to be as if someone has hit him. Saliva appears on his lips. He twitches violently for a minute or two and then usually lies relaxed.

Type 2. *Petit Mal.* Petit mal seizures occur much more frequently. No convulsions are involved, although there is a momentary loss of consciousness. The seizure consists of a brief stare and may be accompanied by a rhythmic twitching of the eyelids or eyebrows.

Type 3. *Psychomotor.* This is the most difficult type to diagnose, since the attacks vary greatly from individual to individual. The mild forms appear similar to petit mal, while the more severe forms are like grand mal. Amnesia is the outstanding characteristic of this type, although the patient appears to be conscious at the time of the attack. Most such attacks last only a short time, although with a few individual cases they continue longer.

Type 4. *Jacksonian.* This type is a modified grand mal. During the first part of the seizure the individual remains conscious but there is a twitching or numbness of one leg or arm or side of the face or trunk, and this gradually spreads so as to include the greater part of the body. Consciousness is often lost during the later stages of the attack.

This classification is quite similar in nature to one early proposed by Gibbs *et al.* (1938), based upon electrographic observations during clinical seizures of various kinds. The four types they observed were:

(1) grand mal, (2) petit mal, (3) petit mal variant, and (4) psycho-motor. Although many patients suffer from a mixture of seizures, the great majority of cases may be classified into one of the four groups. The results of a study by Kaye (1951) of the electroencephalogram records of 17 cases with petit mal are given in Table 15–5. The lack of uniformity of the EEG results reveals that the clinical diagnosis of petit mal epilepsy is an individual problem not easily resolved through a single test or observation.

TABLE 15–5

Distribution of Children According to Type of
Electroencephalogram Record

Electroencephalogram Record	Number of Children
Consistent with petit mal	10
Normal	2
Not specific but abnormal	4
Not a clearly abnormal record	1
Total	17

Source: After Kaye (1951).

Prevalence. Epilepsy usually has its beginning during childhood or adolescence. From a study of 8,823 children from 2,653 families in Boston, Thom (1942) found that 6.7 per cent had had one or more seizures. This is somewhat higher than the findings reported about draftees for both World War I and World War II, in which about 5 per 1,000 were rejected for military service because of epilepsy (War Department, 1944). The various surveys show that epilepsy is about equally prevalent among males and females, with a slight excess among the males.

Although exact figures are not available, there has been a rather definite consensus that approximately 80 per cent of the cases have seizures before the age of twenty. Lennox (1951) reported that epilepsy started in the first decade of life in 47 per cent of 4,000 epileptic cases. This fact tends to add significance to the possible role of the schools in dealing with epilepsy.

Etiology. The most frequent type of convulsive seizure encountered during the first month of life is that which occurs in connection with a cerebral birth injury. In the case of seizures having their onset between the ages of two and ten, the cause is usually attributed to injury at birth, cerebral thrombosis during a febrile illness, or postnatal injury. Peterman (1946) reported that in 122 of 176 cases in which the initial seizure occurred between birth and one month of age the cause was a cerebral birth injury. The study by Livingston (1954), referred to earlier, indicates that the causes of epilepsy are complex.

Lennox (1955) found evidences of an inherited predisposition to idiopathic seizures based on a study of 20,000 near relatives of approximately 4,000 epileptic patients. In this group of near relatives the incidence of persons with a history of one or more seizures was 3.2 per cent, and of these approximately one-half had chronic epilepsy, more than three times the percentage of chronic epilepsy among the general population. This evidence is further supported by Lennox's data on 173 pairs of twins who had seizures. Among the 77 identical twins there was agreement in 70 per cent of the cases, while among the 96 fraternal twins there was agreement in only 12.5 per cent of the cases. These findings support the view that heredity may play an important role in epilepsy.

Hereditary predisposition is also assumed to be a factor in other medical conditions, such as diabetes, cancer, tuberculosis, high blood pressure, obesity, etc. With regard to epilepsy this theory means that under certain conditions an individual hereditarily predisposed may develop epileptic seizures while a non-predisposed individual under similar conditions would have no such seizures. Precipitating causes are thought to affect those with a predisposition to epilepsy in such a way as to actually produce a seizure. Yahraes (1954) enumerates the causes as follows:

1. *Brain injury.* Brain injury "may occur before a person is born, or during birth. It may be the result of an infection that has settled in the brain after diseases like sleeping sickness, measles, meningitis, or whooping cough. It may come from a severe head injury or from a tumor in the brain" (p. 6).
2. *Bodily disorders.* "A disorder in some other part of the body may react unfavorably upon the brain and lead to seizures. A kidney disease may have such an effect, or a gland disturbance" (p. 6).
3. *Emotional upsets.* These upsets are "common in adolescence and occasionally seizures are attributed to them" (p. 6). Emotional disturbances may also be a factor in seizures that develop later in life.

Controlled experiments with the electroencephalograph suggest that seizures may be induced by means of appropriate emotional stress applied to known epileptic individuals. Due to the diversity of personality patterns found among those who are epileptic, one cannot set forth a particular classification of psychological factors that would precipitate a seizure. However, evidence based on clinical and therapeutic studies indicates that childhood fears, frustrations, rejections, and sexual stimulation without adequate discharge are precipitating factors.

Epilepsy resulting from permanent cerebral changes or damage due to known causes is referred to by Livingston (1954) as secondary, organic, or symptomatic epilepsy. When the specific cause cannot be determined, the condition is classified as cryptogenic epilepsy, also known as idiopathic, primary, essential, genuine, or true epilepsy. Of 4,158 epileptic children studied by Livingston 2,224, or 53 per cent, were classified as having cryptogenic epilepsy. Livingston suggests, however, that all types of epilepsy are due to some anatomical or physiological cerebral defect. In this connection he states:

> It should be emphasized that *a diagnosis of crytogenic epilepsy is an admission of our failure to uncover the nature of the underlying cerebral lesion.* It is probable that many patients so diagnosed have sustained cerebral damage or have malformations of such a minimal nature as to escape detection. It is also possible that with increasing skill and knowledge and with newer techniques some of these cases will be removed from this group and classified according to cause. [P. 23.]

Livingston's analysis of the case histories of the 4,158 epileptic children revealed that 1,934 of them presented signs or symptoms indicative of cerebral damage prior to the appearance of epilepsy. There was evidence of brain damage specific enough to be considered significant in 1,518 cases. A classification of the types of brain damage found or suspected in these cases is presented in Table 15–6. Cerebral birth injuries and congenital developmental diseases of the brain account for approximately 83 per cent of these 1,518 cases. These data support the generally accepted hypothesis that cerebral birth injuries are a frequent cause of epilepsy.

Intelligence. In one study, of 103 epileptic children in a children's hospital, a mean Stanford-Binet IQ of 88 was reported (Sullivan and Gahagan, 1955). This was significantly below that of other hospital children tested.

The distribution of IQ's of 248 children with convulsive disorders, studied by Mullen (1953) in Chicago, is shown in Table 15–7. There is a wide range of IQ's in the group, with 56.7 per cent falling in the 50–79 range. The mean IQ of the group was 71.8. These data support the hypothesis that seizures occur relatively frequently among those of lower intellectual ability. This does not indicate a causal

TABLE 15–6

Classification of Types of Brain Damage Found or Suspected in 1,518 Patients with Secondary Epilepsy

Type of Brain Damage	Number of Patients
Cerebral birth injuries	650
Congenital developmental diseases of the brain, including tuberous sclerosis, Sturge-Weber syndrome, and miscellaneous types	602
Vascular occlusions	103
Familial cerebral degenerative diseases	19
Meningitides, encephalitides, encephalopathies	44
Posttraumatic	71
Lead poisoning	14
Brain abscess	3
Brain tumor	3
Parasitic diseases	6
Syphilis	3
Total	1,518

SOURCE: Livingston (1954).

TABLE 15–7

Distribution of Intelligence Quotients of 248 Children with Convulsive Disorders *

IQ	Number of Cases	Per Cent † of Those with Known IQ
120–129	1	
110–119	1	
100–109	14	
90–99	24	
Total 90–129	40	17.9
80–89	31	13.8
70–79	47	
60–69	51	
50–59	29	
Total 50–79	127	56.7
40–49	13	
30–39	12	
20–29	1	
Total 20–49	26	11.7
Total known IQ	224	
IQ not reported	24	
Total studied	248	

* In 90 per cent of the cases the results are based on individual examinations, chiefly the Stanford Revision of the Binet Test.

† To nearest tenth of a per cent.

SOURCE: After Mullen (1953).

relationship necessarily. Brain damage which produces one can also (and frequently does) cause the other. Convulsive disorders are relatively common in a mentally retarded population. However, Sarason (1953) points out, "In the large majority of these cases the convulsive disorder is not considered the cause of the mental deficiency and does not have a deteriorating effect on intellectual functioning" (p. 195).

One difficulty in evaluating the results of many studies is that institutionalized cases have been used. This makes it difficult to make generalizations about non-institutionalized epileptics since it is often impossible to separate the effects of convulsions from those of prolonged institutionalization. Also, the epilepsy may not be the primary reason for institutionalization. Sarason (1953) points out: "Studies of the effects of institutionalization indicate that even in the absence of epilepsy a decrease in the intelligence quotient is by no means surprising" (p. 197).

Broida's (1955) review of the results of studies of the intelligence of non-institutionalized cases indicates that for these individuals, intelligence does not differ significantly from that of the general population. Furthermore, efforts to establish characteristic subtest patterns for epileptics indicate that there is no typical epileptic pattern.

Personality Characteristics. While there is general agreement among students of epilepsy that emotional and social problems of one type or another often accompany epileptic conditions, the concept of the epileptic personality is an erroneous stereotype that has its roots in prescientific thinking. The results of the study by Kogan et al. (1947) with the Rorschach Test were contrary to the notion that there is an "epileptic personality." Studies of epileptic children in Detroit's Special School Program by Tenny (1955) substantiated the results of the study by Kogan et al. He concluded:

In response to the limitations associated with their handicap, the children appeared to follow no single pattern, which might be characterized as a typical personality pattern. Rather they reacted in various ways, some tending to withdraw, others to behave aggressively, the majority following a middle course. The pattern seemed to be dictated less by the common handicap of epilepsy than by their own personality variations. [P. 165.]

Problems. Children who are handicapped may be handicapped socially because of anxiety in others. Teachers, pupils, and others look upon the epileptic with awe and fear at the time of seizure. Seizures may be quite disturbing to the onlooker, especially if he is not accustomed to seeing them. Teachers are likely to fear the possible occurrence of seizures in individuals who are labeled epileptic.

The special concern over epilepsy is not only the immediate reaction to a seizure or possible seizure, but is also a reflection of the attitude society has too often manifested toward epilepsy. In most cases the epileptic child needs regular schooling, and studies show that many of them have been given an adequate education for living in regular classes (Hyslop, 1941). They need to be exposed to life experiences similar to those provided for the average child.

It appears that epilepsy may have some detrimental effect upon school progress. This is clearly indicated by Tenny (1955) in a summary of data on epileptic children in Detroit's special school program:

1. Of 734 pupils for whom data were clear, 67 per cent were retarded one grade or more at admittance to the special school.

2. Over 62 per cent of 195 children entering kindergarten or first grade were retarded in grade placement, indicating that epilepsy had delayed their admittance to school.

3. Although intellectual retardation was a contributing factor in grade placement, pupils of normal intelligence and above were likewise retarded in grade placement.

4. In addition to initial retardation in grade placement, almost 60 per cent of the pupils failed one-half or more grades during their stay at the special school.

5. Achievement test scores revealed a retardation somewhat greater than that indicated by actual grade placement and progress.

6. A comparison of achievement test ages and mental ages of 540 pupils revealed that 50 per cent of these pupils had academic achievement below the expected average for their mental ages, while only 32 per cent achieved above the expected average for their mental ages.

7. On final achievement tests of 417 pupils, 60 per cent achieved below the expected average for their mental ages and only 22.5 per cent above the expected average for their mental ages. [Pp. 165–66.]

In their vocational adjustments epileptics are frequently handicapped by the attitudes of society toward their education and employment. However, an abundance of evidence from the experiences of vocational training programs and the employment of these individuals indicates that a large percentage can be successfully trained and placed on different kinds of jobs. Schechter (1955) gives the following results on 1,450 cases accepted for service by the Illinois Division of Vocational Rehabilitation: 756 gainfully employed; 321 still pending; 296 closed, for various reasons, as ineligible; 41 committed to state institutions; and 36 dead.

In a study reported by Lennox and Mohr (1950–1951) 22 unselected male clinic epileptic patients, ages twenty to fifty-two, were studied with reference to social, work, school, and marital adjustment. The results showed that work adjustment was better for patients whose medical handicap was marked, while social and school adjustment were better when the medical handicap was slight. Work adjustment was more apt to be good when the patient told friends and the employer about his condition. A positive relationship was noted between good work adjustment and the ability and willingness of the individual to accept his condition. The results of this study point to the importance of a favorable and realistic personal attitude toward his own condition in the patient's social and vocational adjustment.

Control of Seizures. In many patients there is some kind of warning before a seizure begins. Parents, teachers, and others may suspect an approaching attack because of unusual pallor, or enlarged pupils of the eyes, or increased irritability. The patient should be taught to recognize sensations indicative of an impending seizure. In many cases the control of seizures is made more difficult by not knowing the exact cause of them. A seizure should be regarded as symptomatic. When the first seizure at school occurs, school officials should determine whether or not the child is receiving medical attention and what recommendations or treatments have been made.

When the school has received information about the child's condition and recommendations for his care and treatment, it should then cooperate with other agencies concerned with the medical treatment of the child. A periodic physical checkup is needed so that the child will not be handicapped by any needless restrictions placed upon him. The school can also make an important contribution to the care and treatment of the individual by adequately providing for certain psychological needs. This means that the school should direct him into school activities or pursuits from which he will secure a real sense of achievement and feeling of personal worth needed for wholesome personal-social development. However, he should not be pushed beyond his abilities.

Situations in school that produce an intense amount of anxiety or that produce undue emotional stress should be avoided. It has been observed that many children with a history of convulsive disorders at home are free of these in a school situation where their needs are met and undue pressures avoided. A favorable social and psychological environment will do much to relieve the problems of many epileptics. Medical research has advanced, and promises continued advancement, to such a degree that the handicaps associated with epilepsy may be reduced to a minimum for all but a small number of persons with epilepsy.

SUMMARY

There are many adverse conditions that may affect a large proportion of boys and girls and lower their vitality.

Malnutrition looms large in a survey of the health problems of children. The term "malnutrition" covers a wide range of conditions. The growth lag of children suffering from malnutrition may be considerably reduced by supplementary diets. The emotional concomitants associated with malnutrition should be taken into consideration in any sound program dealing with this problem.

The diabetic child has been the subject of considerable study. These children usually appear to be healthy until the onset of the condition. Hunger is an important symptom since foods eaten are not properly converted into usable nutritive substances. The incidence of diabetes among children is not high, being less than .5 per cent in children under twelve years of age. The importance of psychological factors has been emphasized by a number of investigators.

Cancer is a disease more frequently encountered among adults than among children. Perhaps 50 per cent of cancer among children appears as leukemia, a condition that has sometimes been mistaken for anemia. Leukemia among children develops more rapidly than among adults and is more likely to prove fatal.

Allergies and asthmatic conditions have received increased attention within recent years. There is considerable evidence that such conditions are closely associated with emotional factors in a child's life. The most vulnerable periods for the onset of allergies are infancy and during convalescence. Asthma appears as frequently among children as among adults. Asthmatic children are more maladjusted than normal children, with most of them in serious conflict with one or both parents.

Although tuberculosis during childhood has been very much reduced, it is still a significant debilitating disease of infancy and early adulthood. Unlike cancer, it develops slowly and in its early stages is seldom accompanied by any readily apparent symptoms. Early diagnosis is most important. Due to diagnostic and preventive measures in our schools, a remarkable change has occurred in the age distribution of those suffering from tuberculosis. The disease is becoming more and more a disease of older people.

The emphasis on periodic health examinations for all children is reducing many health hazards that are frequently present in childhood.

Two types of cardiac conditions appear frequently among children and adolescents: congenital and rheumatic. Malformations of the heart at birth vary from those that do not interfere in any manner with the child's activities to those so serious that the infant is unable to survive. The majority of children with congenital heart conditions are not seriously handicapped in their educational and social development. Improved health care of infants and expectant mothers has significantly lowered the mortality rate among children due to congenital malformations of the heart, while advancements in surgery have made a normal or near-normal life possible for many who would otherwise be seriously handicapped.

Rheumatic fever may attack several parts of the body simultaneously. Its seriousness, however, results from the damage that often appears in the heart. Prevalence of the disease varies with climatic and living conditions, with the largest percentage of cases found among junior high school pupils. Susceptibility to rheumatic fever is more common in some families than in others, although the exact nature of this susceptibility is not clear. The diagnosis of rheumatic fever in the absence of a classical history is a clinical problem of major importance. The condition of the heart is sometimes the only diagnostic indication. Cardiac complications develop in about two-thirds of the cases. Some personality changes frequently associated with the presence of rheumatic fever are nervous instability, over-responsiveness, periods of depression, sleepwalking, night terrors, enuresis, and tics.

The long period of convalescence required for the patient tends to complicate problems associated with rheumatic fever.

Epilepsy has been broadly defined as a tendency toward recurrent symptoms of disturbances of cerebral activity. It is a condition of many different origins. The epileptic seizure consists of different manifestations that may be present in varying degrees in different persons. The first and foremost element in the seizure is the loss of consciousness. Several bases for the classification of types of epilepsy have been used. Lennox estimates that 90 per cent of all seizures may be classified into one of four groups, although many individuals suffer from a mixture of seizures. Epilepsy usually has its beginning during childhood or adolescence. The causes of epilepsy are complex but there is considerable evidence for believing that a predisposition to the occurrence of the condition can be inherited. Anxiety, aggressiveness, deficient intellectual control, and mental retardation also are characteristics frequently encountered. Persons with epilepsy are frequently handicapped in their social adjustments. Their educational and vocational adjustments may be made more difficult by the attitudes of society toward them. A positive relationship has been noted between good work adjustment and the willingness on the part of the individual to accept his condition. For these reasons the epileptic child presents a challenge to those concerned with his education and guidance.

CHAPTER REFERENCES

BAKWIN, H. (1950). The child with tuberculosis. *J. Pediatr.*, 37:936–37.

BLAND, E. F., and JONES, T. D. (1951). Rheumatic fever and rheumatic heart disease: a 20 year report on 1,000 patients followed since childhood. *Circulation*, p. 836.

BLAND, E. F., and JONES, T. D. (1952). The natural history of rheumatic fever: A 20 year perspective. *Ann. intern. Med.*, 37:1006–26.

BROCK, J. F., and HANSEN, J. D. L. (1962). Protein deficiency. In NORMAN JOLLIFFE (ed.), *Clinical nutrition*. (2d ed.) New York: Harper & Row. Pp. 88–121.

BROIDA, D. C. (1955). Psychological aspects of epilepsy in children and youth. In W. M. CRUICKSHANK (ed.), *Psychology of exceptional children and youth*. Englewood Cliffs, N.J.: Prentice-Hall.

BROWNELL, KATHERINE D. (1952). The child with rheumatic fever or heart disease. *Except. Child.*, 19:65–67, 70–73, 83.

CAHAN, J. M. (1953). School cardiac census—1953. *J. Sch. Hlth*, 23:276–80.

CAMPBELL, M., and REYNOLDS, G. (1949). The physical and mental development of children with congenital heart disease. *Arch. Dis. Child.*, 24:294–302.

CLAYTON, MARY M. (1952). Food habits of Maine school children. *Amer. J. Publ. Hlth*, 42:967–68.

DANOWSKI, T. D. (1957). *Diabetes mellitus*. Baltimore: Williams & Wilkins.

DAVIS, L. L., and GREENE, MARJORIE H. (1954). Rheumatic fever and rheumatic heart disease in children as seen in clinic practice. *Amer. J. Dis. Child.*, 88:427–38.

DREIZEN, S., et al. (1950). The effects of milk supplements on the growth of children with nutritive failures: II. Height and weight changes. *Growth*, 14:211.

DUBOS, R. J. (1953). Biologic and epidemiologic aspects of tuberculosis. *Amer. Rev. Tubercul.*, 68:1–8.

EPPRIGHT, E. S., and RODERUCK, CHARLOTTE (1955). Diet and nutritional status of Iowa school children. *Amer. J. Publ. Hlth*, 45:464–71.

FORCE, D. G. (1954). A comparison of physically handicapped children and normal children in the same elementary school classes with reference to social status and self-perceived status. Unpublished doctor's dissertation, Univer. Michigan.

FORSHAM, P. H. (ed.) (1959). Current trends in research and clinical management of diabetes. *Ann. New York Acad. Sci.*, 82:231.

GIBBS, F. A., GIBBS, E. I., and LENNOX, W. G. (1938). Cerebral dysrhythmias of epilepsy: measures of their control. *Arch. Neurol. Psychiat.*, 39:298–314.

Gomez, F., Galvan, R. R., Cravioto, J., and Frenk, S. (1954). Studies on the undernourished child. *Amer. J. Dis. Child.*, 87:684–93.

Grishaw, W. H. (1962). The diabetic child. *NEA J.*, 51:16.

Hinkle, L. E., Evans, F. M., and Wolf, J. (1951). Studies in diabetes mellitus. *Psychosom. Med.*, 13:160–83.

Hoefer, Carolyn, and Hardy, Martha C. (1935). Some influences of a health education program during the elementary school years. *Elem. Sch. J.*, 35:368–439.

Hyslop, G. H., and Committee (1941). *Epileptic children*. New York City: Board of Education.

Jackson, R. L., Kelly, Helen G., Rohret, Cecilia H., and Duane, Julia M. (1947). Rheumatic fever recurrences in children without sulfonamide prophylaxis: evaluation of environmental factors. *J. Pediat.*, 31:390–402.

Jolliffe, N. (1962). The pathogenesis of deficiency disease. In Norman Jolliffe (ed.), *Clinical nutrition*. (2d ed.) New York: Harper & Row. Pp. 1–27.

Josselyn, Irene M. (1949). Emotional implications of rheumatic heart disease in children. *Amer. J. Orthopsychiat.*, 19:87–100.

Kaye, I. (1951). What are the evidences of social and psychological maladjustment revealed in a study of seventeen children who have idiopathic petit mal epilepsy? *J. Child Psychiat.*, 2:115–60.

Keith, J. D., Rowe, R. D., and Vlad, P. (1958). *Heart disease in infancy and childhood*. New York: Macmillan.

Kogan, Kate L., *et al.* (1947). The personality reaction patterns of children with epilepsy, with special reference to the Rorschach method. *Epilepsy, Assn. res. nerv. ment. Dis. Proc.*, 26:616–30.

Laird, D. A., Levitan, M., and Wilson, V. A. (1931). Nervousness in school children as related to hunger and diet. *Med. J. Rec.*, 134:494–99.

Langford, W. S. (1948). Physical illness and convalescence: their meaning to the child. *J. Pediatr.*, 33:242–50.

Lennox, Margaret A., and Mohr, Jennie (1950–1951). Social and work adjustment in patients with epilepsy. *J. Psychiat.*, 107:257–63.

Lennox, W. G. (1941). *Science and seizures: new light on epilepsy and migraine*. New York: Harper & Row.

Lennox, W. G. (1945). Epilepsy. *Clinics*, 4:504–30.

Lennox, W. G. (1951). The heredity of epilepsy as told to relatives and twins. *J. Amer. med. Assn.*, 146:529–36.

Lennox, W. G. (1955). The social and emotional problems of the epileptic child and his family. In Frampton and Gall (eds.), *Special education for the exceptional*. Vol. 3. Boston: Porter E. Sargent.

Livingston, S. (1954). *The diagnosis and treatment of convulsive disorders in children*. Springfield, Ill., Charles C Thomas.

McAllister, R. M., and Hecker, A. O. (1949). The incidence of allergy in psychotic conditions. *Amer. J. Psychiat.*, 105:843–50.

MILLER, H., and BARUCH, D. W. (1957). The emotional problems of childhood and their relation to asthma. *AMA J. Dis. Child.*, 93:242–45.

MULLEN, FRANCES A. (1953). Convulsive disorders among educable mentally handicapped pupils. Paper read at Amer. Educ. Res. Assn., Atlantic City, N.J., February 16.

NATIONAL OFFICE OF VITAL STATISTICS (1952). Estimated number of deaths and death rates, for specified causes, 1950. *Curr. Mortal. Anal.*, May 9, pp. 12–15.

NATIONAL SAFETY COUNCIL (1963). *Accident facts.* (Source of data: National Vital Statistics Division.)

NEUHAUS, E. C. (1954). A personality study of asthmatic and cardiac children. Unpublished doctor's thesis, New York Univer. *Newsweek*, November 28, 1955. For the forgotten. P. 70.

PARSONS, C. G. (1954). The general practitioner and her child with heart disease. *Brit. med. J.*, 2:208–12.

PENFIELD, W., and ERICKSON, T. C. (1941). *Epilepsy and cerebral localization.* Springfield, Ill.: Charles C Thomas.

PETERMAN, M. G. (1946). Convulsions in childhood, twenty year study of 2,500 cases. *Amer. J. Dis. Child.*, 72:399–410.

PLATT, H. S., STEWART, R. J. C., and PLATT, B. S. (1963). Bones of malnourished children. *Proc. Nutr. Soc.*, 22:29.

PODOLSKY, E. (1955). Physical ailments and the frightened child. *Ment. Hyg.*, 39:489–97.

POLLOCK, G. G., and RICHMOND, J. B. (1953). Nutritional anemia in children. *Psychosomat. Med.*, 15:478, 483.

QUINN, R. W., LIAO, S. J., and QUINN, JULIA P. (1950). An environmental and sociological study of rheumatic heart disease. *Amer. J. Publ. Hlth*, 40:1285–95.

RAPAPORT, H. G., APPEL, S. J., and SZANTON, V. L. (1960). Incidence of allergy in a pediatric population. *Ann. Allergy*, 18:45–49.

ROBERTS, W. C. (1947). Protecting your child from allergy. *Hygeia*, August, pp. 602, 607.

ROSEN, H., and LIDZ, T. (1949). Emotional factors in the precipitation of recurrent diabetic acidosis. *Psychosom. Med.*, 11:211–15.

RUPP, C. (1958). The management of epilepsy. *J. Amer. med. Assn.*, 166:1967–70.

SARASON, S. B. (1953). *Psychological problems in mental deficiency.* (2d ed.) New York: Harper & Row.

SCHECHTER, D. S. (1955). Helping epileptics in jobs. In FRAMPTON and GALL (eds.), *Special education for the exceptional. Vol. 3.* Boston: Porter E. Sargent.

SCRIMSHAW, N. S. (1963). Malnutrition and the health of children. *J. Amer. Diet Assn*, 42:203–8.

SOLOMON, S. (1952). *Tuberculosis.* New York: Coward-McCann.

SPIES, T. D., DREIZEN, S., SNODGRASSE, R., PARKER, G., and CURRIE, CATHERINE (1953). Skeletal maturational progress of children with chronic nutritive failure. *Amer. J. Dis. Child.*, 85:1–12.

SULLIVAN, E. B., and GAHAGAN, L. (1955). On intelligence of epileptic children. *Genet. Psychol. Monogr.*, 17:309–76.

TENNY, J. W. (1955). Epileptic children in Detroit's special school program. *Except. Child.*, 21:162–67.

THOM, D. A. (1942). Convulsions of early life and their relation to the chronic convulsive disorders and mental defects. *Amer. J. Psychiat.*, 98:574–80.

THORPE, L. P., and KATZ, B. (1948). *The psychology of abnormal behavior.* New York: Ronald.

WAR DEPARTMENT (1944). *Physical examinations of selective service registrants during wartime.* Medical Statistics Bulletin No. 3. Washington, D.C.: U.S. Government Printing Office.

WEDUM, BERNICE G., and RHODES, P. H. (1955). Differential diagnosis of rheumatic fever in office practice. *J. Amer. med. Assn.*, 157:981–86.

WHITE, P. D. (1951). *Heart disease.* New York: Macmillan.

YAHRAES, H. (1954). *Epilepsy—the ghost is out of the closet.* Public Affairs Pamphlet No. 98.

SELECTED READINGS

BAKER, H. J. (1959). *Introduction to exceptional children.* (3d ed.) New York: Macmillan. Chap. 8.

BRIDGE, E. M. (1949). *Epilepsy and convulsive disorders in children.* New York: McGraw-Hill.

ELLENBERG, M. (1962). *Clinical diabetes mellitus.* New York: McGraw-Hill.

KRAM, C. (1963). Epilepsy in children and youth. In W. M. CRUICKSHANK (ed.), *Psychology of exceptional children and youth.* (2d ed.) Englewood Cliffs, N.J.: Prentice-Hall.

LIVINGSTON, S. (1963). *Living with epileptic seizures.* Springfield, Ill.: Charles C Thomas.

MARTMER, E. E. (ed.) (1959). *The child with a handicap.* Springfield, Ill.: Charles C Thomas. Chaps. 10, 11, 20.

NEWMAN, J. (1963). Psychological problems of children and youth with chronic medical disorders. In W. M. CRUICKSHANK (ed.), *Psychology of exceptional children and youth.* (2d ed.) Englewood Cliffs, N.J.: Prentice-Hall.

PARK, GLADYS M. (1955). Psychological Aspects of Tuberculosis. In FRAMPTON and GALL (eds.), *Special education for the exceptional.* Vol. 2. Boston: Porter E. Sargent.

PATTISON, H. A. (1957). *The handicapped and their rehabilitation.* Springfield, Ill.: Charles C Thomas. Chaps. 7, 15.

WRIGHT, G. N., GIBBS, F. A., and LINDE, SHIRLEY M. (eds.) (1962). *Total rehabilitation of epileptics—gateway to employment.* Washington, D.C.: Office of Vocational Rehabilitation.

YASUMURA, M., and BALL, JANET S. (1955). Occupational Therapy for Rheumatic and Cardiac Children. In FRAMPTON and GALL (eds.), *Special education for the exceptional.* Vol. 2. Boston: Porter E. Sargent.

VI

EMOTIONAL AND
SOCIAL ADJUSTMENT

The manner in which children behave must be interpreted in terms of the interaction of the individual and his environment. Diversified personalities emerge as a result of inherent constitutional differences and the various environmental conditions that have affected the individuals at different stages in their development.

Chapter 16 deals with children with emotional and adjustive difficulties. Behavior is described as a function of biological, psychological, and social needs. Both adjustive and maladjustive behavior are attempts to satisfy needs. Chapter 17 deals with children who display more serious personality disturbances. Special attention is given to the large group of these children referred to as schizophrenics. In Chapter 18 children displaying antisocial and delinquent behavior are studied. The major factors or conditions associated with juvenile delinquency are presented and analyzed.

The educational provisions for emotionally disturbed and/or socially maladjusted children are presented in Chapter 19. During the past decade considerable research has been conducted relating to the education of emotionally disturbed children. The philosophy and nature of work now being done with emotionally and socially disturbed children are presented in this chapter.

16

EMOTIONAL AND SOCIAL MALADJUSTMENT

The roots of personality disorders among adults can usually be traced to childhood experiences. Many types of mental and emotional disturbances first appear, or certain symptoms are displayed, during the early years of life (Schonell, 1952). If emotionally disturbed children can be identified during the beginning stages of their disturbances and measures can be taken to help them, much can be done to prevent personality maladjustments at a later period.

This chapter is concerned with those children who fall between the well-adjusted child and the child with serious personality disturbances, while the chapters that follow deal with antisocial and delinquent behavior, and personality disturbances during childhood and adolescence. Misbehavior may be regarded as psychologically normal even though it constitutes a problem for the teacher. Wattenberg (1960) points out that behavior bespeaks emotional disturbance when it consistently shows the following characteristics:

1. *The behavior has a peculiar compulsive or driven quality.* The pupil in question really knows better but "cannot help himself." Something made him do it and he cannot tell you what. Such behavior calls for professional diagnosis.
2. *The behavior has a quality of soliciting punishment.* Helen, in sev-

427

enth grade, consistently goes out of her way to provoke the wrath of her teachers and does not stop until the teacher swoops down on her, shouting, "You have been asking for this!" The teacher's outburst is a fairly accurate diagnosis. . . .

3. *The misbehavior is accompanied by inappropriately intense emotion.* When Carl gets into a fight, he completely loses control of himself and becomes almost murderous. Although fighting among boys is not unusual, widely destructive rage is another matter. . . .

4. *The misbehavior itself is inappropriate to the age level or situation.* Jennie, although 12, has temper tantrums in which she acts like a six-year-old. Larry, although living in a rather reserved middle-class suburb, uses four-letter obscenities in class. Either form of conduct is so far out of line it indicates some serious personality disorder.

5. *There is a consistent pattern of offenses followed by intense remorse, which is quickly forgotten because there are new offenses and further remorse.* For a conscience to be able to punish after a misdeed but be incapable of giving effective advance warnings is hardly normal. Again, professional diagnosis is needed.

6. *After relatively serious events, some youngsters appear preoccupied with their parents' probable reaction.* It is quite possible that the child's conflict is motivated by hostility to a parent. Such behavior can be the result of a neurotic pattern. . . . [Pp. 17–19.]

Empirical research studies show that certain recurrent, observable symptoms of problem behavior appear among children and these tend to cluster into two major symptom-clusters—acting-out or conduct problems and withdrawn or personality problems (Quay, 1963, p. 18). Serano *et al.* (1962) list the categories of adjustment during adolescence. They state: "These categories are: the infantile maladjustment reaction in adolescence; the childish maladjustment reaction in adolescence; the juvenile maladjustment reaction in adolescence; and the preadolescent maladjustment reaction in adolescence" (p. 897). These types are supported by data gathered on the developmental histories, clinical observations, and psychological testing of 63 disturbed adolescents. These categories of adolescent disturbances are closely related to the materials presented in subsequent chapters dealing with disturbed children and adolescents. Preadolescents who are maladjusted frequently exaggerate their bonds with their peers and fall easy prey to the activities and notions of older peers. They are frequently maladjusted at home and at school.

INCIDENCE OF MALADJUSTMENT

The extent of maladjustment found among a group of children and adolescents will be determined first of all by any definition of maladjusted behavior. If, for example, conformity is the key to good adjustments, children who are taught to conform will show the least amount of maladjustment. Materials presented later in this chapter show that many factors affect the child's adjustment. Thus, one would expect the frequency of maladjustment to vary with such factors as the emotional climate of the home, membership in a minority group, social class of the child, level of intelligence, school achievement, physical disabilities, and other forces either within or without a particular individual.

Emotionally Disturbed Children in the Classroom. It is recognized that any school population varies as much in emotional behavior as it does in intellectual ability. It appears that developments in school mental hygiene have not kept pace with developments in intelligence testing and classifications. In the first place, many teachers fail to recognize emotional problems in children with whom they work; second, they often fail to attach due significance to the problems that do present themselves.

A distinction should be made between problem behavior that interferes with normal classroom activities and problem behavior that leads to serious personal and social maladjustments. Such a distinction was made in the study by Sparks (1952) in which a comparison was made between traits rated by one group of teachers as most detrimental to the future of the child and those rated as most troublesome in the classroom. The teachers were to rate the 55 problems from the Wickman list of traits. The ten traits rated by the teachers as most serious to the child and the ten rated as most troublesome in the classroom are presented in Table 16–1. It seems clear from the results of this

TABLE 16–1

The Ten Traits Rated by Teachers as Most Serious to the Child and the Ten Rated Most Troublesome in the Classroom

Rank	Serious to Child	Troublesome to Teachers
1	Stealing	Interrupting
2	Untruthfulness	Carelessness in work
3	Unreliableness	Inattention
4	Cruelty and bullying	Restlessness
5	Cheating	Silliness, smartness, etc.
6	Heterosexuality	Whispering and note-taking
7	Impertinence	Tattling
8	Impudence	Thoughtlessness
9	Selfishness	Disorderliness
10	Laziness	Inquisitiveness

SOURCE: After Sparks (1952).

study that teachers consider those traits that are contrary to our social and moral code as the most detrimental to the future adjustments of the child.

Bower (1960) noted that at least three children in each class of 200 classrooms studied could be regarded as having educational problems of sufficient severity to warrant the label "emotionally handicapped children" (p. 62). He also noted that 87 per cent of the clinically known emotionally handicapped children were rated by their classroom teachers as among the most poorly adjusted children in the class. As perceived by teachers, 4.4 per cent of all the children in the 200 classes studied were overly aggressive or defiant most of the time, while 6.1 per cent were overly withdrawn or timid most of the time.

Identifying Emotionally Handicapped Children. Many problems are encountered trying to determine which children in a school population are markedly handicapped by emotional problems at present or will be later in life. Bower (1959) has described the emotionally handicapped child in the following manner:

The emotionally handicapped child is therefore circumscribed as one having a higher degree of vulnerability to behavior problems and one who, as an adult, will exhibit this vulnerability in general health problems, or interpersonal relationships, inability to function sexually, or economically, inability to profit from experience, or lead a happy life. In its more pervasive form this vulnerability may lead to psychosis, neuroses, suicide, repetitive automobile accidents, alcoholism, narcotics addiction, or criminal behavior. One can, therefore, describe the emotionally handicapped child as a child who is unable or will be unable to take the slings and arrows of life without caving in, becoming immobilized, or exploding. [P. 8.]

The study reported by Bower (1960) included results from fourth-, fifth-, and sixth-grade classes, each of which contained at least one child who could be clinically designated as "emotionally handicapped." The results on the inventory, "Thinking About Yourself," showed that emotionally handicapped boys exhibited greater self-dissatisfaction than other boys about their personal lives and a significantly greater discrepancy between the self and wanted self. In most cases their dissatisfaction related directly to difficulties in school. "However, the items which showed the greatest discrepancy between self and wanted self for the emotionally handicapped boys were the same items of greatest discrepancy for other boys" (pp. 46–47). This is an illustration of the similarity of human nature, referred to in Chapter 1. A comparison of emotionally handicapped girls with their male counterparts showed that the girls related their difficulties and dissatisfactions more to personal and family matters than did the boys. The girls also showed a more passive relationship between self and wanted self than did their male counterparts. Concerning these differences, Bower writes:

The differences in the responses between the emotionally handicapped boys and girls were consistent with the culturally assigned roles of each. The boys reacted to their difficulties in a direct, forceful and non-introspective manner. The girls were perhaps more insightful and thoughtful but less inclined to voice or act upon their difficulties. Undoubtedly these differences in personality play a large part in making emotionally handicapped boys more numerous and more difficult problems in an institution such as a school. [P. 47.]

Another method used by Bower for identifying emotionally handicapped children was "A Class Play." In this technique each pupil, assuming the role of a director of a play, is asked to nominate pupils from the class to play different parts in a class play. This naming was found to be a highly valid method for screening emotionally handicapped children. Bower suggests that, if only one method were available for class analysis, this would undoubtedly be the best single procedure. This method makes use of peer evaluations, which have been found to be most useful and highly predictive. Concerning peer evaluations, Bower states:

Almost all studies of peer perception point to a strong relationship between emotional adjustment and peer judgments. Most, if not all, confirm the reciprocity of school adjustment and school success. The child who is most accepted by his peers gets the best grades, has the higher IQ, comes from a higher socioeconomic level, and has fewer emotional problems. Conversely the child who is least accepted by his peers gets the poorest grades, has the lowest IQ, comes from a lower socioeconomic class, and has more emotional problems. [P. 55.]

A classification of behavioral items and traits made by the California Association of School Psychologists and Psychometrists, Research Committee (1954) shows something of the nature of deviant behavior observed at school. This study, like other studies of this type, shows that boys with behavior problems outnumber girls approximately three to one. It seems likely that much of the difference in behavior problems between boys and girls stems from the greater conformity on the part of girls, which is part of our cultural expectations. Certainly the student that does not conform to a rather marked degree to the program, regulations, and general social and cultural pattern of the school tends to run into difficulty. This was suggested in an earlier chapter in connection with difficulties frequently encountered by many talented and creative children and adolescents. The types of behavior reported by the California psychologists and psychometrists are shown in Table 16–2, which indicate that personality problems,

TABLE 16–2

Type and Per Cent of Social and Emotional Problems Among Disturbed Children

Type	Per Cent
Personality problems, such as withdrawal	17
Learning and academic difficulties	16
Emotional problems, temper outbursts	13
Social relationships, dangerous acts	14
Behavior problems, stealing, lying	11
Nervous habits, enuresis, thumb-sucking	10
Somatic symptoms, fatigue	5

SOURCE: California Association of School Psychologists and Psychometrists, Research Committee (1954).

emotional problems, and problems involving social relations are most frequently encountered by school psychologists.

Referral Problems. The behavior problems encountered in child guidance clinics furnish a guide to the incidence of behavior disorders and to the varieties of child behavior patterns regarded as *undesirable* in our culture. However, since it has been shown that children are often referred for more than one reason, most studies include from one to three or more reasons in their tabulations of reasons for referral.

Gilbert (1957) reported the results of a survey of referrals to child guidance clinics in four major metropolitan areas. Two types of general clinics were included: (1) community orthopsychiatry clinic, and (2) the school psychoeducational clinic or guidance bureau. The two community orthopsychiatric clinics were the Child Guidance Center of Metropolitan Detroit (500 cases) and the Child Guidance Clinic of Philadelphia (500 cases). The two psychoeducational guidance services were the Bureau of Child Guidance of the New York City Board of Education (680 cases) and the Bureau of Pupil Guidance of the Chicago Board of Education (820 cases).

The composite distribution of the four metropolitan clinic caseloads on a common base of ten referral problem categories, broken down by age and sex, is shown in Table 16–3. While there are 2,500 subjects,

TABLE 16–3

Composite Distribution of "Referral Problems" in Four Metropolitan Child Guidance Centers
(Number = 2,500 Children; Average 1.9 Complaints per Child)

Referral Problems	Under 6		6 to 10		10 to 14		14 to 18		All Ages			Total as Per Cent of Number	Per Cent of All Cases in Two Community Clinics	Per Cent of All Cases in Two School Clinics
	Male	Female	Male	Female	Male	Female	Male	Female	Male	Female	Total			
Academic difficulties	3	0	358	126	322	117	146	54	829	297	1,126	45	27	56
Mental retardation	16	9	166	94	180	123	50	35	412	261	673	27	6	40
Aggressive and anti-social behavior	45	12	242	65	192	39	115	45	594	161	755	30	45	20
Passive, withdrawn, asocial behavior	38	15	174	74	110	50	60	25	382	164	546	22	32	14
Emotional instability and anxiety symptoms	45	16	205	86	108	46	49	25	407	173	580	23	34	16
Hyperactivity and motor symptoms	24	12	139	59	69	24	20	5	252	100	352	14	22	8
Sexual behavior problems	6	1	12	10	13	6	6	6	37	23	60	2%	4	1
Toilet training	27	7	50	25	36	14	0	2	113	48	161	6%	12	1
Speech defects	25	9	62	19	26	9	10	1	123	38	161	6%	6	7
Miscellaneous	14	17	90	38	71	51	34	29	209	135	344	14	20	9

SOURCE: Gilbert (1957).

433

the total number of referral problems approaches 5,000 with academic difficulties leading the referrals in school clinics and aggressive and antisocial behavior being most frequent in the community clinics. Boys were referred for guidance more frequently than girls in all age groups and for all problem categories—the over-all ratio being about 2.5 to 1. For aggressive and antisocial behavior the ratio is almost 4 to 1, which is about the same as that for juvenile delinquents brought before the courts. A further analysis of the data by grades showed that problems involving insecurity were relatively more frequent in the early school years, reflecting problems related to adjustment to school.

SYMPTOMS OF MALADJUSTMENT

Symptoms of personal and social maladjustment are not the same for all children. There are, however, some symptoms that appear frequently among the different groups of maladjusted children. Also, some symptoms are more readily observed than are others. Jane, for example, may be quiet in school, but given to fantasy. On the other hand, her cousin, Sally, may be aggressive and given to lying, showing-off, and quarreling. The inexperienced or uninformed teacher is likely to brand Sally as a seriously maladjusted person while the withdrawn pupil (Jane) is overlooked or regarded as a model pupil.

Recent studies show that it is the frequency of appearance of certain symptoms that is especially important in evaluating personality maladjustments. Most children appear to show some of these symptoms at irregular intervals, but certain children display them in most situations and quite regularly. The persistence of such symptoms is an important clue to their seriousness.

Some cases of maladjustment arise as a result of needs that the teacher and school can easily satisfy while others may require the services of a psychiatric social worker, a clinical psychologist, or a psychiatrist. There are many signs indicative of emotional and social maladjustment. These symptoms have been classified by different investigators in various ways. They are so interrelated that no clear-cut classification can be presented. The writers have attempted a threefold classification involving (1) physical signs, (2) behavior deviations, and (3) emotional manifestations.

Physical Signs

Facial twitching	Rocking feet
Nervous spasms	Drumming with fingers

Stuttering   Twisting hair
Biting nails   Restlessness
Scratching self   Fidgeting
Vomiting   Rapid, nervous speech
Enuresis   Crying easily
Digestive disturbances

Behavior Deviations

Aggressiveness   Retiring
Negativism   Easily embarrassed
Night terrors   Sleep disturbances
Bullying   Walking in sleep
Lying   Masturbation
Voluntary mutism   Stubbornness
Poor schoolwork   Regression
Overly sensitive

Emotional Manifestations

Given to worry   Disposition to hate
Feelings of inferiority   Resentful
Abnormal fears   Temper tantrums
Pouting   Extreme timidity

Aggression as Symptomatic. According to the Yale frustration-aggression hypothesis, one form of response to frustration frequently found among children is belligerency. In the case of the small child this behavior often appears in the form of temper tantrums. It may be noticed when a toy is taken from the two-year-old. The child is likely to resort to crying, kicking, biting, or some other form of aggressive behavior, especially if he has not been trained to respond otherwise. It also has been observed that frequent anger responses during childhood are closely associated with illness, sleep disturbances, constipation, and certain psychosomatic responses, notably gastrointestinal reactions.

The child who fails is frustrated in his desire to achieve. The force of the "norm" is one of the most important sources of feelings of insecurity resulting from failure. This feeling, which may be accompanied by violent outbursts, is frequently encountered by those dealing wih mentally retarded or brain-damaged children. It was early observed by Goldstein (1939) in her work with brain-injured soldiers.

The child or adolescent who is frustrated may resort to a form of projection in which he blames other persons or things for his troubles. Or he may use aggressive displacement by breaking street lights or damaging property at school when frustrated by the reactions of his teacher to his failure or misbehavior. Attempts to handle conflicts and frustrations through regression, displacement, and related devices are rarely entirely satisfactory since such methods do not actually solve the causal problem. The case of Philip illustrates how the operation of fear of people, no doubt growing out of harsh treatment in early childhood, led to aggressive behavior in group situations.

Philip was referred to the social worker by the classroom teacher when he was in the second grade because of his overly aggressive behavior. He would frequently become so angry that he had to be removed bodily from the classroom to prevent him from physically harming other children. The social worker conferred with the mother and the child. It became evident that the boy had strongly exaggerated fears. He felt that people were "mean." This was a threat to him, and he was sure that adults wanted to hurt him. When these feelings were explained to the teacher, she immediately made every effort to assure him of her friendly attitude and found opportunities to praise him for any constructive classroom activities. He was admitted to an after school club. His first few weeks in the club were marked by frequent fights with the other children. The group teacher discovered he had ability in dramatics, and was skillful in handling puppets. This won him recognition from the other children in the club. His presentation of a puppet play developed after school helped to establish him both in the club and in the classroom. As his need for aggressive behavior diminished it was evident that he had a better than average mental ability. With the friendly attitude of the teachers and the administrative staff he was gradually able to mobilize his aggression into greatly improved accomplishment in academic skills. . . . [Franklin, 1954, pp. 372–73.]

The extent of aggressive behavior observed among elementary schoolchildren has increased during the past two or more decades (Redwine and Wainwright, 1955). This is quite likely a result of the increased permissiveness in the American home and the emphasis on competition in so many aspects of children's lives. Children can be aided in the acquisition of friendliness and cooperative behavior if parents and teachers will guide them in the development of their abilities and in the pursuance of useful activities that will help them feel worthwhile and secure social approval.

Restlessness and Irritability as Symptomatic. Closely related to aggression is the child characterized by excessive restlessness and irritability. It already has been suggested that such behavior is symptomatic of emotional disturbance. Failure in reading or other important learning activities often leads to such behavior. When childred become fatigued and disturbed because of difficulties in their environment that lead to frustrations and tensions, restlessness and irritability are likely to result. On the other hand, the child who is unable to concentrate in school and is generally inefficient in the performance of his school activities, particularly reading, may be suffering from emotional disturbances.

From a study of emotional symptoms in schoolchildren Cummings (1944) found that restlessness, anxiety, and lack of concentration were closely associated with a high incidence of emotional symptoms. Specific fears were found in over one-fifth of the children, with 8 per cent showing fear of animals.

Restlessness is not as poorly received by other children as it is received by teachers. This trait may be symptomatic of emotional disturbance. In a study of peer status of sixth- and seventh-grade children Laughlin (1954) obtained a correlation of —.484 between restlessness and social acceptance among sixth-grade pupils and a correlation of —.535 at the seventh-grade level. A high positive correlation was obtained between restlessness and both talkativeness and attention-seeking. The negative correlations obtained between restlessness and friendliness, enthusiasm, cheerfulness, physical attractiveness, and likability indicate that restlessness is more likely to be associated with undesirable traits than with desirable traits. This finding also implies that emotional maladjustment tends to interfere with the total adjustment of the child.

Evasion and Withdrawal as Symptomatic. Aggression and withdrawal are reaction patterns simultaneously present in every child. It is only when they appear in an exaggerated form that they are indicative of a relatively serious disturbance. Furthermore, these exaggerated behavior patterns develop out of similar circumstances. The constitutional nature and early experiences of a child will largely determine the preponderance of aggressive or withdrawal behavior patterns exercised in different environmental settings.

Evasion or withdrawal may be observed in the growing child's world of fantasy or daydreams. The teacher calls on Linda, but Linda is staring into space, seeing nothing in particular but thinking of things she would like to have or activities she would like to pursue. Linda does not understand what the teacher said, except that she faintly recalls that her name was called and she realizes that at the present time her classmates are staring at her. Linda is living in a world of fantasy. Such a world may be more satisfying to Linda than the real world.

Parents, teachers, and other adults working with children should be alert to early symptoms since the younger the child the more easily he can be helped to tear down any wall he may have built up between himself and others.

Defective Speech as Symptomatic. One of the frequently observed symptoms of emotional disturbance appears in relation to speech. This may appear in rapid irregular forms of speech. In a most serious form this behavior appears as stuttering. The relationship may be noted in connection with the observations by Baker and Holzworth (1961), presented in Table 17–1. Relative to speech difficulties Josselyn (1948) found "a definite correlation between the development of talking and the adequacy of early care; not only did the well-mothered babies vocalize sooner but their speech maintained a smoother and easier progress" (p. 20).

In a study reported by Moncur (1955) a group of stutterers consisting of 42 boys and 6 girls, ranging in age from 62 to 98 months (median 79.6 months), was compared for maladjustments with an equivalent group of non-stutterers. The findings indicated that young stutterers on the whole display a number of symptoms of maladjustment other than stuttering itself. The stutterers averaged more than twice as many symptoms of maladjustment as did the non-stutterers. According to the parents, "young stutterers characteristically appear to be very nervous, are enuretic, have nightmares and night terrors, display aggressive behavior, are 'fussy' eaters, and need to be disciplined often" (p. 96).

Adjustment problems appear to plague youngsters in other phases of their language development. Spache (1957) made a study of 125 elementary school reading disability cases, using the *Rosenzweig Test* to assess adjustment. The cases studied were children retarded from one to two years in grade placement. He found that these youngsters could be classified into five groups: (1) the aggressive or hostile children in conflict with authority, (2) the adjustive children who sought only to be inoffensive, (3) the defensive children who were sensitive and resentful, (4) the solution-seekers or peacemakers, and (5) the autistic who were characterized by blocking or withdrawal.

Reading Difficulties. Directors of reading clinics have constantly observed a close relationship between reading difficulties and emotional disturbances in many children having reading problems. Tjossem *et al.* (1962) state:

In children of apparent normal intelligence and without evidence of frank central nervous system disorder, the diagnosis of reading failure is not a simple matter. Such possible factors as lateral dominance, mild central nervous system dysfunction, maturation slowness, specific disability in visual-motor functions, genetic predisposition, methods of reading instruction, school changes and emotional disturbances are often suggested as the basis for reading failure in children. [P. 1104.]

An intensive study of 24 children with reading difficulty was conducted by Tjossem *et al.* The mean age of the children was eight years, ten months. Reading tests showed an average reading retardation of 1.4 grades below grade placement. Occurrence of the developmental and behavioral variables isolated for analysis are presented in Table 16–4. Motor awkwardness and speech problems were fre-

TABLE 16–4

Frequency of Developmental Problems and Behavioral Signs
in 24 Retarded Readers

	Frequency
Motor awkwardness	10
Speech problems	14
Developmental delay	5
Behavior signs	
Hyperactivity	8
Accidents	9
Enuresis	16
Nervous habits	14
Allergic reactions	9
Headache or stomachache	13

SOURCE: Tjossem *et al.* (1962).

quently found. The materials of this table support the observations of a number of students of reading problems. Stress reactions in otherwise healthy children of early school age may either be a result or cause of reading difficulties. The investigators conclude:

The majority of the children with reading difficulty were found to have a family history characterized by reading problems and/or laterality other than right in two or more generations. Atypical pregnancy, birth, or neonatal development was characteristic of other children with reading difficulty and subtle nervous system dysfunction seems likely to be a factor in the reading performance of these children. [P. 1112.]

Emotional Immaturity. The emotionally immature child is handicapped in his social and educational development since he is unable to participate in the varied school and out-of-school activities. Nancy, a first-grader, pouts or cries when she is not allowed to do something she very much desires to do. Jeff, a fourth-grader, invites teasing from the other members of his class because he does not take part in their games during the recess period. These and similar cases are frequently observed among emotionally immature children in the elementary school.

Emotional maturity is directly related to the task of social adjustment, which has been studied by a number of students of child development. Using the *Rorschach Ink Blot Test,* Robbertse (1955) obtained significant differences in the personality structure of socially adjusted and socially maladjusted pupils ten to thirteen years of age. The socially well-adjusted pupils surpassed the socially maladjusted in such characteristics as willingness, desire, and ability to establish harmonious relations with their environment. The maladjusted gave more responses indicative of emotional immaturity, such as irritability, impulsiveness, depressive moods, and inability to adjust normally to outer reality. Emotional immaturity seems to arise primarily from home conditions in which the child has been overprotected. This may be initiated in a period of illness. Emphasis on the child's participation with peers in a variety of experiences will be helpful in developing more mature ways of meeting emotional and social situations.

FACTORS AND CONDITIONS INFLUENCING MALADJUSTMENT

The determinants of emotionally disturbed and socially maladjusted behavior may be found in three categories: biological, psychological, and social. However, overlap and integration are observed continuously. The importance of separating these categories stems from the fact that rational treatment demands an understanding of the pathological behavior pattern. For example, the effective treatment of disturbed behavior arising from chronic nutritional deficiency would be quite different from the treatment used for a child suffering from emotional deprivation during the period of infancy and early childhood. Eisenberg (1953) has pointed out: "The child is first of all, a biological entity; the integrity of his central nervous system is the precondition for psychological and social function. That integrity depends in turn upon all of the organ systems of the body that support and nourish nervous tissue" (p. 31).

Explanations of a child's emotional and social maladjustments are frequently inadequate, since they do not take into account the varied forces affecting the child. Most cases of maladjustments cannot be traced to a single cause although a particular factor may be of paramount importance. Where many difficulties combine to cause a disturbance and no single factor stands out as of special importance, the case may become a baffling one. The most difficult cases require the services of specialists. The role of the school in the identification, guidance, and referral of the difficult cases is extremely important.

Individuality of the Child. Attempts to place all the blame for childhood disturbances on the home, especially the mother, fail to take into consideration the individuality of the child's reaction pattern, which begins to appear very early in life. It also seems likely that parental behavior that is undesirable for a particular child might be constructive and desirable for another. Parents are constantly bewildered over differences existing among their children. Concerning differences, Chess *et al.* (1959) have pointed out that "if the child's patterns of behavior and emotional responses are determined not only by parental attitudes and other environmental factors, but also by his own specific reaction pattern, then caution must be imposed on the common tendency to assume that disturbances in a child are necessarily the exclusive results of unhealthy parental functioning" (p. 801).

The individuality of children is further observed in their perception of their parents. Serot and Teevan (1961) noted that the child's perception of his relationship with his family was extremely important to him and is directly related to his adjustment as measured by the *California Test of Personality, Elementary Series AA.* The well-adjusted child perceives his parent-child relationship as relatively happy and close to the ideal. This study indicated further that the parent's perception of the relationship is unrelated to the child's social adjustment, the correlation being .04 between the mother's scores on the *Swanson Child-Parent Relationship Scale* and the children's scores on the *California Test of Personality,* while the correlation with the father's scores was .16. These results are quite significant, indicating a close relationship between the child's perception of his home relations and his adjustment.

The Role of the Home. The importance of the home in the personal and social development of the individual child appears during the first year of life.

A parent-child relationship affecting the child's emotional security is the most frequent source of children's problems. Evidence of the effects of favorable or unfavorable parent-child relationships are abundant. Anxiety states and conditions associated with such states are found most frequently among children from homes in which there is considerable tension or outright rejection. The anxieties of children who withdraw as a result of lack of affection or rejection are difficult to treat. Bobby's recognition of his father's disappointment because he could not measure up to his father's standards indicates the seriousness of a feeling of rejection.

> Bobby was ten when his father brought him to the psychologist. By then, he was a completely defeated child. He did not think he could do anything successfully; he did not even want to try any more. He was poor in work, afraid of contacts, and almost tired of life. "I wish I was never born," were his words. When he played a game in which he could make a wish, he would say, "I wish I was different, but it's no use."
>
> Very early Bobby failed to satisfy his father's wish for an athletic son. His father, a strong and athletic man, did not get enthusiastic response to his roughhouse plays, and thus when Bobby was two or three, the disappointment began.
>
> This was not the type of son he had hoped for, the father admitted to the psychologist. "Why couldn't we have a strong athletic boy instead of this 'softy'?" [Buhler, 1952, p. 128.]

By means of interviews Abbe (1957) compared the attitudes toward child behavior of mothers of disturbed children. She found the mothers to be restrictive, lax, and overindulgent more than mothers of children making normal adjustments. Since attitudes do not remain stable, studies dealing with the role of maternal attitudes must give special attention to the attitudes existing during various periods of the child's life.

An investigation by Peterson *et al.* (1959) dealt with the attitudes of parents in relation to the adjustment of their children. They compared 31 families with children six to twelve years of age selected from the clientele of a guidance clinic with 29 families in which the children were judged by teachers as displaying acceptable adjustment. They found that both mothers and fathers of problem children seemed to be less well adjusted and sociable, more autocratic, and experienced more contention regarding discipline than did non-clinic parents. One of the more significant findings was that the attitudes of fathers were as significant as were the attitudes of mothers to the occurrence and form of the maladjustments among children. This study supports others that emphasize the importance of the father as well as the mother in shaping the child's emotional adjustment.

The Census Bureau reports that one out of five Americans shifts his home each year. Such mobility frequently presents problems to children who are required to adjust to new school conditions, new friends in the neighborhood, and new activities on the playground. Data presented by Gordon and Gordon (1958) show that children are adversely affected, as indicated by the higher incidence of emotional disorders and delinquency rates.

Social-Class Influences. The social class of a child's family frequently determines not only the neighborhood in which he lives and the group with whom he associates and plays, but also the goals, aspirations, and social skills of the individual child. There is evidence from many sources that children from low socioeconomic neighborhoods are likely to have feelings of insecurity and to display hostility to a greater extent than children from more privileged neighborhoods (Goldstein, 1955). A recognition of the operation of these forces should help teachers and others better to guide children from underprivileged home and neighborhood conditions.

Closely related to this matter are the problems encountered by children from minority groups. The prejudice of one group toward another, variations in the patterns of living, values of the different cultural groups, and straining by the less privileged to be accepted by the more privileged present difficult adjustment problems to children in the elementary school. Recent research in the general area of child development has produced considerable evidence to show that class and cultural tensions are sources of many adjustment problems among children. Children of foreign-born parents are often caught in the conflict of trying to gain acceptance of their classmates without losing the support and affection of their parents.

Children from some minority groups frequently find themselves friendless and unwanted by their classmates. *Prejudice* is a social reality full of social and psychological consequences. The child who is not accepted by other children because of accident of birth involving race, religion, nationality, or social class faces a difficult problem in developing a healthy concept of the self. He sees himself and his parents devalued because of certain conditions over which he has no control. The effects of contradictions imposed by cultural forces may be observed in a case presented by Eisenberg (1953):

John, a Negro boy of 10, had been doing poorly in school, and he frequently attacked his younger brother, Albert, and stole from his family.

He had made up his own song, whose chorus ran, "I don't like people and they don't like me." His light-skinned father could "pass" as white, but not when dark-pigmented John was with him. For this reason, among others, he much preferred the lighter Albert. Nothing that John did pleased him. Every day when John went to school he was forcibly reminded of his status since the school was segregated and on his way there he had to bypass a white neighborhood that was unsafe to traverse. When he went shopping with his mother, they couldn't buy in certain stores and there was no place to lunch in town. Treated as inferior by the dominant culture and rejected by his own father for the very same reason, he was bitter and aggressive. The clinic was able to provide at least one place where he was accepted as a person and praised for his accomplishments. The clinic visit was the one event in the week for which John showed any enthusiasm. John's adjustment at school improved and he became a leader in his scout troop, though his hostility toward the favored Albert showed little change. Social factors could not be altered but personal support was given to the child, at the same time that an effort was made to help his mother understand his needs. [P. 33.]

Peer Conformity and Emotional Adjustments. Conformity to group mores and norms has often been associated with good emotional adjustment. In a study by Langner (1954) designed to test this hypothesis various clinical and social-psychological tests were administered to a sample of 600 schoolchildren from the fourth to the twelfth grade, one-third of whom were Indian, one-third white Protestant, and one-third "Spanish" or Mexican.

The results revealed that, while conformity to peer group behavioral norms was correlated with emotional adjustment, deviation did not necessarily indicate maladjustment. Several factors or conditions made it possible for the individual to deviate from the peer group norms and not suffer an emotionally bad consequence for such a deviation. Deviation from peer group norms produced emotional maladjustments mainly when such deviations separated the individual from the group, producing an "isolate." This action automatically cut off an important source for the satisfaction of certain needs of the individual. Those children who had friends but thought they had none were seriously disturbed. The feeling of isolation was a greater determinant of maladjustment than actual isolation, indicating further the importance of the individual's concept of *the self*.

A study reported by Davis and Parenti (1958) had as one of its purposes to investigate relations between social choice and measures of personality in groups of normal children and emotionally disturbed children. The children in each group studied were asked to name their three best friends on four occasions with a one-week period between each interview. In addition, the children were rated for eight personality traits. Correlations obtained between popularity and the eight personality traits and between mutuality of friendship choice and the eight personality traits for the two groups of children are presented in Table 16–5. The Bradley group consisted of emotionally

TABLE 16–5

Correlations Between Sociometric Measures and Personality Ratings of Emotionally Disturbed Children and a Group of Normal Children

Personality Attributes	Bradley (48 Children)		Camp (80 Children)	
	Popularity	Mutuality	Popularity	Mutuality
General emotional adjustment	−.44	−.24*	−.31	−.42
Eccentricity	−.43	−.27*	−.19*	−.35
Pessimism	−.42	−.28*	−.24*	−.30
Distrust	−.36	−.24*	−.28	−.34
Anxiety	−.45	−.26*	−.36	−.39
Resentment	−.44	−.34	−.28	−.71
Socientricity	.47	.30*	.25*	.43
Optimism	.43	.25*	.35	.43
Trust	.38	.27*	.34	.42

Source: Davis and Parenti (1958).
* Significant at the .05 level.
† Significant at the .01 level.

disturbed children, while the Camp group was made up of normal children. The findings revealed that popular children tend to be well adjusted emotionally and to possess socially desirable personality traits. In the group of emotionally disturbed children it was noted that the disliked subjects tended to be more emotionally disturbed than the ignored ones. A significantly higher percentage of mutual choices was found in the normal group. Furthermore, the mutuality of friendship scores was significantly correlated with good emotional adjustment and the possession of desirable personality traits.

Self-Acceptance and Adjustment. A number of investigations have shown that there is a relationship between self-acceptance and social adjustment. Taylor and Combs (1952) found that children who were better adjusted tended to see themselves in a more matter-of-fact manner than did those who were less well adjusted. According to the results of a study by Cohen (1954), both very high and very low goal-setting reflect self-rejection. This is in harmony with the results of an earlier study by Sears (1941) in which it was noted that both groups of children were insecure and uncertain of their own abilities.

The setting of a very high goal was for some the goal itself; for others the setting of a very low goal was a means of protection.

Bruce (1958) used a scale to measure the self-acceptance of sixth-graders. He defined self-acceptance as the congruence or lack of discrepancy between self concept and ideal self. He found that children with the smallest discrepancy between self concept and ideal self tended to be less anxious and insecure. The results of this study have important implications for parents and teachers. For example, if Janet's ideal self is that of a girl who has many friends, even though her schoolwork is of an inferior quality, Janet will not feel insecure if her schoolwork does not measure up to her teacher's expectations. She will, however, show more anxiety about her friends. If she does not feel that she has many friends, there will be a high degree of discrepancy between her self concept and her ideal self. Such a condition does not make for wholesome personality integration.

Educational Retardation and Maladjustment. There is considerable evidence that overage children are not accepted by their younger classmates. Studies bearing on this were presented in an earlier chapter. In a study by Bedoian (1954), sixth-grade pupils were divided into three age levels: the underage, the at-age, and the overage. Results from sociometric testing showed that the scores of the overage children were significantly lower than those received by the at-age and underage children. The results of this study have been verified by other studies. The educationally retarded child is likely to be maladjusted in school if he is unable to achieve status and satisfy his need for achievement through some endeavors in school or in out-of-school activities.

Consideration of the relationship between emotional maladjustment and academic failure has often led to much confusion. Children who appear dull in school because of their educational retardation may actually be suffering from serious frustration and emotional maladjustment. The emotional problems thus keep them from showing their potential mental and educational abilities. Such children, too, may be classified in a field-cultural group of actually retarded. Intelligence test scores alone do not differentiate such children from those who are mentally retarded as a result of hereditary factors or birth injury.

Intelligence and Maladjustment. There is considerable evidence that maladjustment looms large among mentally retarded children.

An early study by Lurie (1935) dealt with the types of problems encountered by 1,000 mentally retarded boys and girls referred to a child guidance clinic. Incorrigibility and delinquency characterized the mentally retarded children. With these children it was also noted that school failure problems began around the fourth-grade level. This period seemed to coincide with the beginning of aggressiveness and antisocial behavior.

Problems of adjustment are often acute among the mentally retarded who are capable of making some academic progress in school. Such children may appear normal, especially when they have had favorable home and community advantages. Their learning problem may go largely undetected until they reach the fourth or fifth year in school. A study by Hinkelman (1951) was designed to determine the areas in the field of adjustment that seems to be most seriously affected by retarded intelligence. The groups of seventh-grade boys and girls were given the *California Test of Personality* and the *Kuhlman-Anderson Intelligence Test*. The mean differences of the pupils in the upper and lower intelligence groups revealed some interesting and significant differences in adjustment. The greatest difference noted among the self-adjustment items was for freedom from withdrawing tendencies. The differences between the two groups were not as great in the social adjustment items as in the self-adjustment items. The greatest differences were on the items of family relations, school relations, and social standards. The smallest differences were on the items of community relations and social skills. These results indicate that low intellectual ability among seventh-grade pupils is more likely to lead to maladjustment at home and at school than in the community at large. This maladjustment no doubt results from the premium that the home in general and the school in particular place upon verbal intelligence and academic achievement.

Emotional Adjustment of the Physically Handicapped Child. The concept of self involves the individual's awareness of himself in relation to his environment (Cruickshank, 1947). The normal child is propelled into his environment by means of what he sees through visual cues, of what he hears through auditory cues, and through other sensory contacts with things about him. Any condition that is a potential source for disturbing the normal growth process is likely to affect the individual's understanding of himself in relation to his environment. If any of the sensory avenues or mechanisms involved in learning are impaired, a limitation or distortion is likely to be placed upon the learnings and adjustments related to the impairment or deficiency.

In a study by Cruickshank (1951) involving 264 physically handicapped pupils in junior and senior high school, three crippling conditions accounted for most of the cases—heart pathology, poliomyelitis, and cerebral palsy—with the remainder including 21 other diagnoses. These handicapped pupils were matched with normal pupils for age and sex. A projective sentence-completion test, consisting of 45 sentences, was used to examine the self concepts in five areas: (1) family, (2) society, including peer group, (3) other persons with physical disabilities, (4) goals and wishes, including attitudes toward thwarting situations, and (5) fear and guilt situations.

The data from this study indicated that the physically handicapped pupils related better to the mother than to the father, while the opposite was true for the control group. Also, the handicapped group felt greater dissatisfaction with adults and society than did the control group. There was a definite tendency shown for the handicapped group to withdraw from social contacts and relations. The handicapped group was not as well able to evaluate interpersonal relations as was the normal group. Their personal adjustment was characterized by concern for self, while that of the normal group was allocentric in nature. However, the handicapped desired to be treated like others rather than singled out as individuals with handicaps.

Pringle (1964) presents the following conclusions from a review of the literature on the behavior and personality development of the physically handicapped:

> While most comparative studies show the handicapped child to be less mature and more disturbed than those without any disabilities, the consensus of opinion and weight of evidence—at present at any rate—seem fairly heavily balanced against the view that the handicapped are inevitably maladjusted. That behavior and personality are bound to be affected where the disabled physique has seriously limiting, depriving effects, whether physically, socially or both, is unlikely to be disputed. . . . Furthermore, available data have failed to show any evidence of a definite association between a particular disability and a particular behavior characteristic. [Pp. 213–14.]

SUMMARY

The importance of early identification and treatment of maladjusted children has been emphasized. There are various symptoms that may be recognized by teachers and others in identifying maladjusted children. Some of the most important are aggressiveness, withdrawal, irresponsibility, temper tantrums, and rebelliousness. The most frequent causes for referral of children to guidance clinics were seen to be academic difficulties, aggression, and antisocial behavior. Studies show that teachers tend to consider those traits that are contrary to our social and moral code as the most serious, while mental hygienists and clinicians regard withdrawal, daydreaming, and related traits as most serious.

The child's personality presents a complex pattern changing with maturation and experience. The complexity of this pattern and the interplay of the various elements make it very difficult to classify maladjustments into certain categories. The task of determining a specific cause or causes for such behavior patterns is a difficult one. One cannot set forth a simple formula to explain childhood adjustments. However, teachers can be made aware of symptoms of maladjustment, of factors and conditions that may lead to maladjustment, and of ways to help the child overcome the less serious forms of maladjustment.

Case studies show that many factors contribute to the development of maladjusted behavior patterns. Considerable research has shown the importance of the home, socioeconomic conditions, peers, and the school in the emotional and social adjustments of children and adolescents.

CHAPTER REFERENCES

ABBE, ALICE C. (1957). Maternal attitudes toward behavior and their relationship to the diagnostic category of the child. *J. genet. Psychol.,* 92:167–73.

BAKER, J. W., and HOLZWORTH, ANNETTE (1961). Social histories of successful and unsuccessful children. *Child Developm.,* 32:135–49.

BEDOIAN, U. H. (1954). Social acceptability and social rejection of the underage, at-age, and overage pupils in the sixth grade. *J. educ. Res.,* 47:513–20.

BOWER, E. M. (1959). The emotionally handicapped child and the school. *Except. Child.,* 26:6–11.

BOWER, E. M. (1960). *Early identification of emotionally handicapped children in school.* Springfield, Ill.: Charles C Thomas.

BRUCE, P. (1958). Relationship of self-acceptance to other variables with sixth-grade children oriented in self-understanding. *J. educ. Psychol.,* 49:229–38.

BUHLER, CHARLOTTE (1952). *Childhood problems and the teacher.* New York: Holt, Rinehart & Winston.

CALIFORNIA ASSOCIATION OF SCHOOL PSYCHOLOGISTS AND PSYCHOMETRISTS, RESEARCH COMMITTEE (1954). Emotionally disturbed children in California. *Calif. J. educ. Res.*, 5:116–20.

CHESS, STELLA, THOMAS, A., and BIRCH, H. (1959). Characteristics of the individual child's behavioral responses to the environment. *Amer. J. Orthopsychiat.*, 29:791–802.

COHEN, L. B. (1954). Level of aspiration behavior and feelings of adequacy and self-acceptance. *J. abnorm. soc. Psychol.*, 49:84–86.

CRUICKSHANK, W. M. (1947). The mental hygiene approach to the handicapped child. *Amer. J. occup. Ther.*, 1:215–21.

CRUICKSHANK, W. M. (1951). The effect of physical disability on personal aspiration. *Quart. J. Child Behav.*, 3:323–33.

CUMMINGS, J. D. (1944). The influence of emotional symptoms in school children. *Brit. J. educ. Psychol.*, 14:151–61.

DAVIS, A., and PARENTI, ANITA (1958). Personality, social choice, and adults' perception of these factors in groups of disturbed and normal children. *Sociometry*, 21:212–24.

EISENBERG, L. (1953). Treatment of the emotionally disturbed preadolescent child. *The Pre-adolescent exceptional child.* Proceedings of the 25th Conference of the Child Research Clinic of the Woods Schools, held in Philadelphia, May 23.

FRANKLIN, ADELE (1954). Teachers—not therapists. *Nerv. Child*, 10:368–77.

GILBERT, G. M. (1957). A survey of referral "problems" in metropolitan child guidance centers. *J. clin. Psychol.*, 13:37–42.

GOLDSTEIN, A. (1955). Aggression and hostility in the elementary school in low economic areas. *Understanding the Child*, 24:20–21.

GOLDSTEIN, RUTH (1939). *The organism.* New York: American Book Co.

GORDON, R. E., and GORDON, KATHERINE K. (1958). Emotional disorders of children in a rapidly growing suburb. *Int. J. soc. Psychiat.*, 4:85–97.

HINKELMAN, E. A. (1951). Intellectual level and personality adjustment. *Elem. Sch. J.*, 52:31–35.

JOSSELYN, IRENE M. (1948). *Psychosomatic development of children.* New York: Family Service Association of America.

LANGNER, T. S. (1954). Normative behavior and emotional adjustment. Unpublished doctor's thesis, Columbia Univer.

LAUGHLIN, FRANCES (1954). *The peer status of sixth and seventh grade children.* New York: Teachers Coll., Columbia Univer., Bureau of Publications.

LURIE, L. A. (1935). Conduct disorders of intellectually subnormal children. *Amer. J. Psychiat.*, 91:1026–38.

MONCUR, J. P. (1955). Symptoms of maladjustment differentiating young stutterers from non-stutterers. *Child Developm.*, 26:91–96.

PETERSON, D. R., BECKER, W. C., HELLMER, L. A.; SHOEMAKER, D. J., and QUAY, H. C. (1959). Parental attitudes and child adjustment. *Child Developm.*, 30:119–30.

PRINGLE, M. L. K. (1964). The emotional and social adjustment of physically handicapped children. *Educ. Res.*, 6:207–15.

QUAY, H. C. (ed.) (1963). *Research in psychopathology*. Princeton, N.J.: Van Nostrand.

REDWINE, ELEANOR, and WAINWRIGHT, LETITA (1955). The development of a power context. *J. Indiv. Psychol.*, 11:172–77.

ROBBERTSE, P. M. (1955). Personality structure of socially adjusted and socially maladjusted children according to the Rorschach test. *Psychol. Monogr.*, Vol. 69, No. 19.

SCHONELL, F. J. (1952). The development of educational research in Great Britain. Part IV. Maladjusted pupils. *Brit. J. educ. Psychol.*, 22:30–31.

SEARS, PAULINE S. (1941). Level of aspiration in relation to some variables of personality; clinical studies. *J. soc. Psychol.*, 14:311–36.

SERANO, A. C., McDANALD, E. C., GOOLISHIAN, H. A., MacGREGOR, R., and RITCHIE, AGNES M. (1962). Adolescent maladjustment and family dynamics. *Amer. J. Psychiat.*, 118:897–901.

SEROT, NAOMI M., and TEEVAN, R. C. (1961). Perception of the parent-child relationship and its relation to child adjustment. *Child Developm.*, 32:373–78.

SPACHE, G. (1957). Personality patterns of retarded readers. *J. educ. Res.*, 50:461–69.

SPARKS, J. N. (1952). Teachers' attitudes toward the behavior problems of children. *J. educ. Psychol.*, 43:284–91.

TAYLOR, C., and COMBS, A. W. (1952). Self-acceptance and adjustment. *J. consult. Psychol.*, 16:89–91.

TJOSSEM, T. D., HANSEN, T. J., and RIPLEY, H. S. (1962). An investigation of reading difficulty in young children. *Amer. J. Psychiat.*, 118:1104–13.

WATTENBERG, W. W. (1960). What is "normal" misbehavior? *NEA J.*, 49:17–19.

SELECTED READINGS

BOWER, E. M. (1962). Comparison of the characteristics of identified emotionally disturbed children with other children in classes. In E. P. TRAPP and P. HIMELSTEIN (eds.), *Readings on the exceptional child*. New York: Appleton-Century-Crofts. Pp. 610–28.

COLEMAN, J. C. (1960). *Personality dynamics and effective behavior*. Chicago: Scott, Foresman.

KING, G. (1960). *The mentally ill child in America*. New York: National Organization for Mentally Ill Children.

KIRK, S. A. (1962). *Educating exceptional children.* Boston: Houghton Mifflin. Chap. 13.

LINDGREN, H. C. (1959). *Psychology of personal and social adjustment.* New York: American Book Co.

PATE, J. E. (1963). Emotionally disturbed and socially maladjusted children. In L. M. DUNN (ed.), *Exceptional children in the schools.* New York: Holt, Rinehart & Winston. Pp. 239–84.

SARASON, S. B., DAVIDSON, K. S., LIGHTHALL, F. F., WAITE, R. R., and RUEBUSH, B. K. (1960). *Anxiety in elementary school children.* New York. Wiley.

YATES, A. J. (1962). *Frustration and conflict.* London: Methuen.

See also references for Chapters 17, 18, and 19.

17

PERSONALITY DISTURBANCES

Personality disturbances frequently appear early in the life of the individual child. Unless these disturbances are outstanding, they may go undetected by the parents and others closely identified with the child. The school more than any other community institution affords an early opportunity for the detection of personality disturbances.

The increasing number of emotionally disturbed children needing treatment, better means of identifying emotionally disturbed children, and improved facilities for dealing with these children have brought forth the demand for extending clinical services into the schools. In addition, these factors have led to a recognition of the need for special classes for these children. The goals of the program as set forth by Rubin and Simson (1960) are "to identify disturbances early in the child's school adjustment and provide prophylactic care through special education methods integrated with clinical understanding" (p. 153).

ANXIETIES AND FEARS DURING CHILDHOOD

Anxiety and childhood appear to go together. It is commonly observed that children display greater anxiety and fear than adults. Despert (1946) observed manifestations of anxiety in a group of 78 preschool children. Although not one of the 78 children was found to be totally free of anxiety manifestations, marked differences were noted in intensity and frequency. Instances of undifferentiated excitement were observed in emotionally immature and intensely anxious children.

By the time a child reaches nursery school age, anxieties and fear appear in organized and differentiated reactions and are regarded as part of general nursery school behavior. A lack of anxiety and fear reactions at this stage may be regarded as symptomatic of an organic or mental maladjustment.

Definitions. There is considerable confusion about the meanings of terms such as "fright," "anxiety," and "fear." At times these terms are used interchangeably. Although a clear line of distinction cannot be drawn, definitions are helpful in delimiting these forms of behavior.

Fright may be regarded as denoting a shock reaction, a startle pattern of behavior appearing very suddenly in response to an intense or surprise stimulation.

Anxiety, on the other hand, refers to a feeling of impending danger. According to Kramer (1946), the anxiety reflex is present within all living beings. It is one of the reflexes that help to preserve life. The term "anxiety" includes not only the anxiety reflex but also the various degrees of learning that have become interrelated with it. Concerning the nature and origin of anxiety, Blau and Hulse (1956) state:

> The significant point regarding the etiology of anxiety neurosis is that it is a reaction to a real provocation, and in the case of childhood anxiety neurosis, this is the lack of parental care. A child needs the direction, support and loving care of a parent as much as he needs other essentials for life, growth and development. . . . Lacking as yet an adequate ego organization of his own, he depends upon the outside one which promotes his own ego by identification, education and support. Without these supporting influences, he is truly deprived and threatened. The resulting anxiety and behavior are a direct reaction to real noxious neglect and any treatment is wanting if it is short of recognizing this provocative factor. [P. 111.]

Anxiety alone is not abnormal but should be regarded as symptomatic of emotional disturbances when it is excessive or inappropriate. It is natural for one to become anxious when faced with a difficulty, conflict, or some frustrating situation. Since frustration is a normal part of life, anxiety is expressed by human beings from the earliest stages of childhood. However, the infant or child is limited in his capacity to meet threats to his ego and security. The etiology of childhood anxiety lies in home conditions characterized by rejection or actual hostile attitudes toward the expression of the ego.

Fear has been described as a protective reaction of the organism. Bergman (1946) describes its development and operation as follows:

When the ego perceives some danger in the environment, it directs attention to the place from which the danger is expected and either initiates action appropriate for fight or flight, or inhibits action altogether.

As soon as the child's personality reaches a stage or organization in which he understands the connection between an impulse in himself and stimulation from the outside world, the fear reaction is extended to some of his own impulses also. He touches the stove and gets burned. He bites his mother and is punished. If the child is right in his expectations of danger, then such fears, both of impulses from the inside and of dangers from outside must be considered as normal emotional reaction. . . . [P. 37.]

There is no sharp line of demarcation between anxiety and fear. The term "anxiety" is usually employed in a more general manner, while the term "fear" is used in relation to particular objects, persons, or situations. Anxiety is regarded as the spilling over of impulses from the central nervous system into the autonomic nervous system. Such a condition produces a specific feeling tone—a sort of uncomfortable feeling—along with peripheral motor disturbances such as rapid heartbeat, increased blood pressure, rapid breathing, and hyperadrenia.

As a result of maturation and learning the child acquires a better understanding of his environment and comes to relate certain environmental forces and conditions to the sources of his anxieties and fears. As he continues to grow, he comes to realize that his anxieties and concerns are not always based upon real dangers. The sources of his present anxieties are better understood and his reactions are more in harmony with reality. There are, however, cases where this is not true and these children face difficulties in adjusting to anxiety-provoking situations.

The Fears of Children. A degree of maturity and learning sufficient for the child to anticipate an unpleasant event is necessary for the development of anxiety. However, fear, with its intellectual counterpart, requires a still greater degree of maturity. It is not easy to evaluate and describe the fears of small children. They have often been confused with fright or the startle pattern. The untrained observer is quite likely to describe the fears of children in terms of adult behavior patterns.

The school-age child exhibits a wide range of fears. As the child increases in age, important changes occur in the types of situations that provoke fear. In one study 27 per cent of children reported a fear of animals at ages five and six, but only 11 per cent reported such a fear at ages eleven and twelve (Jersild, 1943). There is, however, a pronounced increase in fear of the dark and being left alone during this period of development.

The children with whom we are primarily concerned in this chapter are the withdrawn, fearful ones. Their difficulties stem from numerous sources, but in the classroom they are often termed "misfits." Some of their difficulties may be observed in their display of nervous habits. They usually are emotionally fearful children who find it difficult to make friends and fit into a normal classroom situation. These children are often overlooked since they conform to most of the prescribed behavior patterns of the typical classroom.

Feelings of Inadequacy.   Many children develop feelings of inferiority and inadequacy. Such feelings have an adverse effect on their personal and social adjustment. Feelings of inferiority are likely to occur among younger children in connection with motor skills and other activities in which they do not possess the skills or abilities of older, more capable children. Normally the child outgrows early feelings of inadequacy as he becomes more proficient and becomes more able to make evaluations and comparisons on the basis of age differences.

EMOTIONAL DISTURBANCES

Emotionally disturbed children have been defined by Kirk (1962) as "those who have inner tensions and show anxiety, neuroticism, or psychotic behavior" (p. 331). These children are further described by Haring and Phillips (1962) as follows:

Emotionally disturbed children are children who have more or less serious problems with other people—peers and authority figures such as parents and teachers—or who are unhappy and unable to apply themselves in a manner commensurate with their abilities and interests. In general, one might say that an emotionally disturbed child is one who has a sizable "failure pattern" in living instead of a "success pattern." [P. 1.]

A child may be unable to function in a purposeful or goal-directed manner. His perspective of the realities about him varies markedly from those of his peers. Thus, his adaptations to varying situations are likely to be unrealistic, ineffective, or inappropriate.

The social histories of 71 children in a state mental hospital were compared with those of a matched control group of 71 children composed of 35 boys and 36 girls (Baker and Holzworth, 1961). The incidence of early psychosocial problems is presented in Table 17–1.

TABLE 17–1

Incidence of Early Psychosomatic Problems

Type of Problem	Per Cent	
	Patients	Controls
Enuresis*	44	14
Severe temper tantrums	35	13
Fears or phobias	25	–
Speech difficulties	23	4
Rocking or head banging	16	1
Encopresis	8	–

* Beyond three years.
SOURCE: Baker and Holzworth (1961).

Enuresis led the list of psychosomatic problems in both groups. With one exception the control group's enuresis had ceased by school age. Temper tantrums, fears, speech difficulties, and rocking or head banging characterized a relatively large percentage of the hospitalized children during their early lives.

A composite picture of the patient group shows some striking contrasts with the control group. More of the patients' mothers told of having difficulty during their pregnancies. The patient group experienced serious school achievement and adjustment problems during their early years at school. "A large majority of the patients had poor relations with their peers and did not belong to any social group outside their family and classroom" (p. 147).

PSYCHONEUROSES AND PSYCHOSES

Patterns of behavior for groups and individuals within a society should be interpreted within their cultural context. The adjustment process involves a dynamic relation between the individual and his environment. The neurotic individual is generally regarded as one who is unable to make satisfactory adjustments to the many situations and conditions of everyday living.

Freud refers to the *superego*, which is the individual representation of the total behavior pattern and experiences of the individual. A person's ideals, values, and aspirations are included in the superego.

The psychoneurotic is in a state of conflict between his individual needs and the ideals and values of his superego. These conflicts appear at all stages of maturation and learning. Concerning childhood conflicts, Benda (1954) states:

In children, psychoneurotic conflicts manifest themselves on two levels: first, in socalled "psychosomatic" manifestations and, second, in behavior disorders with a great variety of expressions. The psychosomatic manifestations are often associated with either disorders of breathing, e.g., in the form of asthma, or disorders in function of the intestinal tract in the form of persistent constipation or diarrhea. Later in life, the same type of disorder may lead to severe spasms and the development of ulcers. On a higher psychological level, psychoneurotic conflicts are often expressed in children in the refusal to learn to talk and to use language as a common means of communication. During school age, reading and spelling difficulties are often of an emotional nature. In more severe cases, the emotional disorder manifests itself in a regression to stages of earlier development and the patterns of a younger child are adopted. . . .

From a general psychological point of view it has to be realized that emotional disorders change the set of motivations of a child, and, therefore, his contact with the outer world may be changed in its essential pattern. Children of school age revolt by refusing to learn what they are supposed to learn, by lack of attention or short attention span, by inability to memorize, and by excessive dealing with dreams, especially in the form of ambitious dreams. Such emotional behavior may lead to complete failure in school, and many children with emotional difficulties are considered stupid, of inadequate intelligence, or even feebleminded. . . . It has also been demonstrated in discussing the marginal group that hardly any child coming from the marginal strata is spared from severe emotional conflicts which further interfere with the development of an intelligence which may be somewhat inadequate anyway. . . . [Pp. 1153–54.]

Functional Disorders. Ideas and feelings that are unpleasant in nature may be repressed to such a degree that the individual is no longer conscious of them. Once ideas and feelings are repressed, they are no longer under conscious control. Repressed ideas and emotions may find release or expression in some physical or physiological form such as pains, tics, allergies, headaches, sensory and motor disturbances, and gastrointestinal disorders. These functional disturbances may take on the guise of almost any physical disease and are sometimes confused with them. In many cases these disturbances are evidenced by motor or sensory conditions of an abnormal nature (Preston, 1940). The case of Jerry, seen by the senior author, is illustrative:

When he was four years of age, Jerry began having vomiting spells every morning immediately after his breakfast period. A careful physical examination revealed no organic trouble. Jerry was large for his age, was above average in intelligence, and came from a home that might be termed in the upper middle social and economic level of society.

A more careful study of the problems of Jerry revealed that the home was characterized by severe domestic discord between the father and mother. Jerry was very fond of both his father and mother, but had looked upon his father as a playboy. Due to the domestic turmoil, the father ate his breakfast earlier and left for his office. Jerry and his mother ate together at a later hour. The mother was a nervous type and this was accentuated by the family troubles. She was also determined that Jerry should eat a well-balanced breakfast every morning. This constant observation and insistence on the part of the mother, coupled with the adjustment which he was being forced to make of eating without his father, seems to have been the major factors responsible for the vomiting.

Comparison of Psychoneuroses and Psychoses. The functional disorders have been divided into two main groups—the neuroses or psychoneuroses and the psychoses. Boundaries between these are not always clear. However, the psychoneuroses consist of the milder disorders which are manifested in certain, fairly well-defined ways. These are less pronounced and less serious in nature than the psychoses. The psychoses affect the total personality, sometimes to the extent of complete disorganization or the development of a dual personality. A girl may think, for example, that she is a movie star or Cinderella. In such a case the individual finds an adjustment through an escape into fantasy to such a degree that she is unable to distinguish between the real and the imaginary. Lehner and Kube (1955) have furnished a descriptive differentiation in terms of psychiatric criteria:

1. No organic basis can be detected in neurosis. This does not necessarily mean that the neurotic person is free from organic disease, but any such disease from which he may be suffering is irrelevant as far as his neurosis is concerned.

2. Unlike the psychotic, there is no consistent and lasting deterioration of the neurotic's intellectual functions.

3. The neurotic's experiences and mood changes are less sudden than those of the psychotic and more related to specific changes in the environment.

4. The neurotic suffers no persistent distortion of external reality, such as hallucinations and delusions. Although the neurotic may withdraw from social relations to some extent, he does not lose contact with reality as does the psychotic. [P. 141.]

Every neurosis can be classified according to the social situation in which it occurs. The neurosis, as distinct from the psychosis, is influenced by the individual's social life. This may be observed in the case of a child whose behavior at home, at school, and on the playground is at variance with that of the other children. Schneersohn (1955) presents an interesting case of home neurosis which illustrates this variability.

M., 9 years old, a fifth-grade pupil in a private elementary school, had an I.Q. of 117. The father had called for his daughter at her school and on the way home had asked her to stop for a moment into the flat of an acquaintance of his. Immediately on entering my flat, the child realized that she was taken to a physician. She began to scream so hysterically that the neighbors, in alarm, rushed in. Tumult reigned. The child had to be taken away. The scene had later on a special significance.

The parents later described the child's behavior at home in the following terms. M. was an unruly, wild, and aggressive child. She hit other children and even her mother; and yet in almost sadistic way she loved her mother. She liked her mother to kiss her, but if her mother was disinclined, she would strike her, scream, and curse. Her mother used the rod on the child with such force that weals were raised on her back. Despite the fact that she chastised her daughter so severely the mother often kissed the child and spoiled her.

Already in her first year M. was a difficult infant. She cried at night and was soothed by being taken to her mother's bed. (Thus already at that early stage her parents gave in to her.) In her seventh year she commenced to attend school. She progressed successfully each year to the next higher grade. At home she became more aggressive from day to day.

The school report was in surprising contrast to the evidence of the child's behavior at home. The teachers and the headmistress were all agreed that M. was obedient and well-behaved: "She never quarrels with her schoolmates and is courteous in her relations with them. . . . In class she is quiet and well mannered." [P. 50.]

This is an extreme case of home neurosis, not only because the extremely aggressive behavior appeared only at home, but because this behavior was induced by home conditions. The child was above average in intelligence and displayed interest and energy in connection with school tasks. Her neurotic disposition, observable during infancy, was aggravated by the vacillating behavior of her mother. There developed a sort of hate-love relationship between the child and the mother.

Anxiety Neurosis in Childhood. Anxiety per se during childhood is not abnormal. It is only when anxiety becomes excessive or inappropriately directed that it should be regarded as damaging to personality integration. The child is limited in his ability to withstand frustration and threats to his security. Ego involvement is important at this point, and the continuous experience of defeat or rejection inhibits self-expression and produces varied symptoms of behavior disorders such as temper tantrums, destructiveness, acts of mischief or violence, and running away.

The etiology of childhood anxiety, first described by Freud in 1894, frequently is related to a rejecting, hostile attitude in the family environment. A rejecting attitude on the part of one or both parents may be unconscious in nature and thus may take the form of over-protection as a compensatory reaction. An anxiety neurosis frequently appears among children from homes where the level of what is expected of the child is beyond the child's ability. These children most frequently come from middle-class homes where the families have higher aspirational levels for their children than do parents from lower socioeconomic groups (Stendler, 1951). The case of Jane which came to the attention of one of the authors illustrates excessive anxiety resulting from parental pressure.

Jane was the third member of a middle-class family of four children. She had two older brothers and a younger sister. The older boys had made an above-average record in school and measured up fairly well to the father's and mother's scholastic aspirations for their children. The parent's expectations for Jane seemed to involve a form of dramatics to an even greater degree than superior grades. The mother displayed considerable interest and some ability in dramatics when in high school and college, and was quite ambitious for Jane to be active in dramatics even when she was enrolled in the first and second grades. When Jane was in the second grade she was not chosen for a major role in a pageant related to the development of the American flag. This upset the mother very much. On other occasions the mother continued to try to place Jane in the limelight, and in this she had the hearty support of the father who saw in Jane the possibilities of everything he could hope for in a daughter as well as something he appreciated in Jane's mother prior to their marriage. Jane found the competition at school rather keen and she simply could not fulfill all the expectations of her parents. This brought forth a loss of interest on the part of Jane in her schoolwork and a withdrawal from social contacts with other pupils.

Psychoneuroses During Childhood. Certain reaction patterns are common to different groups of individuals who suffer from various adjustment problems. Investigators have distinguished three rather clear-cut psychoneurotic disorders. These are:

1. *Neurasthenia.* A condition characterized by chronic fatigue, irritability, and aches and pains.
2. *Psychasthenia.* A condition characterized mainly by abnormal

fears, obsessions, and compulsions. The fears are known as phobias.

3. *Hysteria.* A condition characterized by a wide variety of physical conditions such as palpitation of the heart, convulsive seizures, and paralytic states similar to those produced by definite organic diseases.

Neurasthenia. The neurasthenic child shows great susceptibility to mental and physical fatigue. He complains of being tired, of having a headache or an upset stomach. He does not eat well. He complains of dizziness or of pains in the chest and stomach. Physical examinations reveal no organic trouble. It should be pointed out, however, that these pains and other discomforts are very real to the child. The following case illustrates a fairly typical neurasthenic condition:

Sam had been complaining of pains in his stomach and of dizziness for some time before he was brought to the attention of the school physician. After a careful examination the latter stated that he couldn't observe anything wrong with Sam except that he was spoiled and was just using this as an excuse to get out of some tasks at school.

The diagnosis, although in part correct, did not reveal the whole story. The boy was eleven years of age and the youngest member of a family of three children. His brother was eighteen years of age, had made a very good record in school, and was at this time a freshman in college. His sister was almost sixteen years of age, and received more than her share of the attention of the family, especially from the father. Sam was perhaps an unwanted child, although he was accepted as a member of the family. He started to school at the age of six, and had a difficult time adjusting during the first year of his career. At home he was usually left out of planning on the part of the family and was often left with an aunt when the family made special trips out of town.

He got along fairly well in school, although he was given to daydreaming a great deal. It seems that his aches and spells of dizziness appeared when he reached the fifth grade and his brother left for college. The parents pointed out to him his average ability in school and the success that his older brother was having. The boy, apparently unable to face these facts and conditions, found refuge in physical difficulties.

Although there are different viewpoints about the exact cause of neurasthenia, many authorities have pointed to the presence of mental and emotional conflicts as the outstanding feature. This seems to be the case with Sam. It was pointed out previously that children are born with certain urges or drives. Furthermore, it is now recognized that there are psychological needs that must be met in a fairly satisfactory manner if the child is to develop into a normal well-adjusted personality. Sometimes conditions arise that conflict with these drives and needs. Unpleasantness, emotional tension, and dissatisfaction result from such a thwarting of drives. Pains and other physical disorders provide a means for meeting such a conflicting situation and for avoiding the unpleasantness and tension associated with it. Thus Sam adjusted to the situation by avoiding his schoolwork through physical illness.

Psychasthenia. Psychasthenia is a condition of chronic uneasiness, with feelings of insecurity and inferiority. It is not often encountered in school, but tendencies in this direction are frequently present among children. The term is applied to several disorders that are no doubt related in origin and development. These are (1) phobias, (2) obsessions, and (3) compulsions.

A *phobia* is an unusual or morbid fear of some object or situation. In such a case an individual shows an intense fear of something, even though he realizes that there is no real reason for it. A child who is afraid of darkness (nyctophobia) will show extreme fear and suffer much discomfort when placed in a dark room. He is, however, unable to give a rational reason why he is so afraid. Some of the most common phobias found among children are:

    Acrophobia—fear of high places
    Algophobia—fear of pain
    Aquaphobia—fear of water
    Claustrophobia—fear of closed places
    Nyctophobia—fear of night or darkness
    Pyrophobia—fear of fire
    Zoophobia—fear of animals

An *obsession* is present when an individual is confronted with continuously recurring ideas that interfere with orderly thinking. These tend to persist even though their illogical or absurd nature is recognized by the subject. This condition may sometimes be closely related to a phobia. If the idea of fire keeps recurring, it may come to evoke a morbid fear or dread of fire in the individual.

A *compulsion* originates in the same general way as an obsession. It is a seemingly irresistible act that the individual is compelled to perform in order to affect a reduction in tension created by some frustrating or conflicting situation. The distinction between obsession and compulsion is not always clear, as in the case of *arithomania*, in which an individual may have an almost irresistible urge to count every telephone pole or other object he passes. *Kleptomania*, which is a strong impulse to steal, with little regard for value, is one of the most common forms of compulsion. *Mythomania,* an abnormal tendency to lie or exaggerate, is also a common compulsion.

Some compulsions result from early childhood experiences where the child is taught to perform some act, such as touching a trinklet or other object. This may be highly emotionalized in the life of the child during the period of repeating the act. Children's games, unusual social customs and fads, or special rituals may contribute to the development of such compulsions. Most compulsions, however, develop from a psychological need, as is shown by the following case of a child with kleptomanic tendencies.

Mary came from a home of average circumstances. She was the youngest of a family of four children—a brother of nineteen, a sister of sixteen, one of fourteen, and herself. She was nearing her twelfth birthday and was in the fifth grade at school. She didn't seem to get along as well with her schoolwork as had the other children of the family, and she was constantly reminded of this by a persistent and somewhat domineering mother. Mary showed much interest in her personal appearance, and went to great pains to adorn herself with jewelry, lipstick, and other cosmetics which would affect her general appearance. Although she had an allowance which was ample for her general needs, she would take jewelry from the desks, dressing rooms, or any other places at school where she was able to find it. She kept this hidden fairly securely in her locker at school. She didn't make use of most of it, and had acquired quite a collection, when the case came to the attention of the principal near the end of the school year. It seems that the compulsion to take jewelry was an outgrowth of a need for recognition.

School phobia is generally thought of as similar in nature to other phobias of childhood in that the child's anxiety involves the general school situation or some specific aspect of the school such as the teacher, reciting in class, classmates, tests, report cards, some school subject, or the recess period. When the child actually resists going to school because of some fear connected with the school situation, he is displaying a school phobia. According to Eisenberg (1958), the reports of 4,000 admissions to one particular clinic over a period of eight years show the number of cases diagnosed as having school phobia rose from 3 per 1,000 to 17 per 1,000 cases. These figures perhaps reflect an increased recognition of this condition as a result of better diagnostic procedures rather than an actual increase. The modal age for school phobia is usually six years, when children are beginning to realize the demands of the school. Most studies indicate that the majority of children with school phobia are actually above average in intelligence with a low incidence of academic achievement problems.

When the findings of the various studies are considered in relation to the basic factors that contribute to school phobia, one may observe a family pattern operating. The interpersonal relationship in the family involving the child and his mother stands out clearly. The school-phobic children more frequently appear in families where the father is a white-collar worker and where mothers are likely to be quite anxious about their children. Where sex differences are found, girls are almost always more frequently seen to be more anxious. Sibling position appears to play a role in some studies with the youngest or only child more frequently having a phobia about school. The family constellation often includes a mother whose own unsolved dependency needs have been irritated by the early efforts of the child toward autonomy. Concerning this, Sarason *et al.* (1960) point out the following:

The mother of the school phobic child keeps her child in a state of neurotic dependence in an unconscious attempt to satisfy her own needs and diminish the pain of re-experiencing archaic conflicts which are manifest in deep feelings of inadequacy and anxiety about her ability to cope with her child's conflicting need to obtain gratification of his dependency requirements while at the same time acquiring some degree of autonomy and independence. . . . This attitude of discouraging the development of autonomous and self-reliant behavior keeps the child in a state of immature dependency and fear of aggression, since it effectively deprives him of the opportunity of learning to deal masterfully with his own inner feelings (including those of hostility) as well as with external events and relationships. [P. 53.]

Hysteria. The term "hysteria" refers to a condition in which the individual exhibits, without any identifiable organic basis, characteristic behavior symptoms that are similar to those found among diseased, crippled, and sensory-impaired individuals. It has no connection with the term "hysterics" which is loosely used to indicate excited behavior. Symptoms of hysteria are many and varied; they can assume almost any form that the individual is capable of manifesting. Some of the more common symptoms are sensory disturbances, excessive sensitiveness, motor disturbances, tremors, twitching, disturbances of speech, disturbances of sleep, crying out, seizures with falls, and loss of consciousness. Few clear-cut cases are to be found in our schools, but the peculiar mental traits that lead toward hysteria are frequently met. "Neuromuscular manifestations of hysteria and other abnormal psychosomatic conditions often simulate primary orthopaedic affection. Nearly all orthopaedic conditions may be aggravated by psychologic disorders" (Shands, 1957, p. 23).

Psychoses. The ways of dealing with fears and anxieties will vary enormously, ranging from those that have social value to those that disorganize the personality. Concerning this, Noyes and Kolb (1963) state:

> The degree of anxiety from which one suffers, its manner of expression, and the types of defenses which one utilizes against it largely constitute the difference between mental health and mental sickness. . . . The methods of dealing with anxiety may so disturb personality functioning that social adjustment is destroyed. The more the individual is threatened and the less his tolerance for conflict, the more he is driven to defend himself. Among the less malignant devices for minimizing anxieties are the phobic, conversion, and compulsive reactions—neuroses which do not seriously disorganize the personality. Devices which may serve a similar purpose but disorganize the personality and produce a serious break with reality are called psychotic. [P. 109.]

The Diagnosis of Childhood Psychosis. Based upon the published reports of diagnoses, there has been an increased frequency of childhood psychosis during the past two decades. Any increase in numbers may stem from more accurate diagnostic procedures, from a greater awareness of its existence, or increased attention to this condition during childhood and thus a tendency to diagnose varying conditions as childhood psychosis. The nomenclature presents some problems in identifying mental illness during childhood. Concerning this, Strob (1960) states:

> The name-giving itself is always a matter of some controversy. Are we going to call it childhood psychosis, or schizophrenia, or autism, or atypical development, or shall we call it dementia? . . . My own feeling is that, at least for the purpose of further discussion, we should consider the existence of a mental illness in childhood and call it, for the time being, childhood psychosis. [P. 238.]

The search for a single factor as the causative agent has been most fruitful in the scientific study of many diseases. This procedure has been less successful in the study of childhood mental illness. In psychological illness multifactoral causations often operate. Further, there is often a close and tangled interrelation of these factors. This can be observed in case studies presented later in this chapter. The search for a single, indispensable incident or factor as the cause is not only unlikely to be helpful in diagnosing childhood psychosis but most likely to be a hindrance.

As pointed out earlier, the "fact-finding" stage is an essential part of any successful diagnosis. There are many clinical descriptions that help to set boundaries of childhood psychosis. Putnam (1955) states: ". . . there is general agreement that in spite of the considerable divergence in the clinical picture depending on age of onset, severity of the illness and the types of defiance used, there is a core problem which manifests itself as a lack of clarity in the child's perception of himself as a person separate from his environment" (p. 521).

Diagnostic criteria differ from school to school or from clinic to clinic. These differences frequently result from the basic frame of reference or the point of departure in studying each case. Also, attempts to oversimplify the causes of childhood psychosis by looking for a single cause have produced various theories and differential interpretations of diagnoses. Any framework for understanding childhood psychosis must be rooted in knowledge of child psychology, particularly those phases that deal with the dynamics of behavior. Studies of the onset of childhood psychosis in a particular child should follow the longitudinal approach described in Chapter 1. Careful observations must be conducted over a period of time. History-taking is valuable; however, records obtained from the recollections of mothers may be more harmful than good since the facts are frequently colored and distorted by the mother's emotional involvement with her child. Nonetheless, observations without some framework are useless. Clinical observations must be an integral part of the diagnostic procedure conducted within the framework of present knowledge of the dynamics of child behavior (Strob, 1960, p. 242).

Difficulties in Diagnosis. The difficulties in diagnosing psychoses in children have long been recognized by investigators who generally agree that the problems encountered in differentiating emotional illness resulting from outright rejection, hostility, or deprivation and those resulting from a psychological defect that is not easily observable may be very confusing. Another difficulty lies in the unreliability of histories given by parents who are unable to deal with their children and their own problems in a more or less detached and objective manner (Szurek, 1956). The inability to secure an accurate history of a child's mental and emotional characteristics and development makes it extremely difficult to determine the nature and amount of changes that have taken place in a given period of time.

A further tendency to view the child in terms of theoretical behavior standards and to look upon deviant behavior as normal and childlike has appeared in psychological and psychiatric thinking as well as the thinking of the public in general. Concerning the diagnosis of psychotic illness during childhood, Bellak (1958) states:

The difficulty in diagnosing psychotic illness in children has long been pointed out by many authors who basically agree that the combination of the psychologic need to deny severe emotional illness in children and the individuality, fluidity, and disorganized quality of any symptom complex, resulting from its occurrence prior to the completion of emotional organization, have been the major deterrents in this regard. Perhaps the greatest difficulty stems from the unreliability of histories given by parents who cannot see their children, past or present, in an objective or detached manner. . . .
Another diagnostic difficulty has been suggested by the peculiar developmental position of schizophrenia in adolescence. Here the question is raised as to whether the illness existed within the personality since early childhood or infancy, or whether it is new in onset and the product of a new developmental stage. [P. 590.]

Several investigators have avoided the difficulties involved in the diagnosis of childhood illness by using the term "atypical development," (Kaplan and Kaplan, 1956; Putnam, 1955).

Etiology.　From a study of the etiology of mental illness Cobliner (1963) concluded that a disruption in the family of orientation is the principal source of mental disorders. He states:

Any disruption in that family is likely to result in emotional deprivation of the child so that he does not receive the optimal care he might get otherwise. However, the events and conditions which bring about this deprivation vary with the family's social position. Our figures indicate that in the lower class physical separation from the parents is decisively more harmful for the child than it is for children in the middle and upper classes. Conversely, in the upper and middle classes disturbing relations within the family which find their repercussion in corresponding attitudes toward the child seem relatively more damaging to the child than is the case in the lower class. [P. 209.]

A review by Atkins et al. (1962) of 42 emergency cases of emotionally disturbed children brought before the Eastern Diagnostic and Evaluation Center of the Pennsylvania Department of Public Welfare revealed the presence of "an enduring and pervasive disturbance in the child which has been the focus of past ineffective planning on the part of the family and services. There is a common history of expedient solution to past crises, which have broken down and increased the child's disturbance as panic spreads through the surrounding matrix of personal and professional supports" (p. 218). The typical picture in the family of these children was one of extreme family instability throughout most of the child's history. "In the majority of cases there had been an indication of a disturbed maternal-child interaction in infancy" (p. 219).

CHILDHOOD SCHIZOPHRENIA

Understanding of childhood schizophrenia has passed through several important phases in recent decades. Whereas its existence was formerly denied, it is "now regarded as being of such a global, all-encompassing nature, that for purpose of differential diagnosis its possibility must be considered in every serious emotional and mental disturbance of childhood" (Bellak, 1958, p. 693). It has been estimated that over 50 per cent of those hospitalized in mental institutions are schizophrenic. There is a tendency on the part of some clinicians to classify almost all unusual conditions during childhood and adolescence as schizophrenic. This, of course, should be avoided. There is, however, considerable evidence that many so-called psychopathic adolescent personalities are actually schizophrenics.

Definition and Developmental Pattern. The schizophrenic sequence usually begins as a withdrawal process. Concerning its nature, Jenkins (1952) notes: ". . . Schizoid withdrawal is a relative withdrawal of attention and interest from the outer environment, particularly from empathic contact with the human environment. Autistic fantasy tends to replace external reality as a focus of attention, and the capacity for reality testing is reduced" (pp. 738–39).

Early infantile autism has frequently been considered as the earliest form of psychotic disturbance. It is generally regarded as a specific type within the larger area of childhood schizophrenia, although Kanner (1958) did not provide such a classification, preferring the term "early infantile autism."

The basic nature of childhood schizophrenia according to Eisenberg and Kanner (1956) is dependent upon the child's own psychological structure, resulting from inherent factors combined with the dynamics of parent-child relationships. It is a psychobiological disorder, resulting from the combined operation of innate and experiential factors. The clinical terms that are used to describe childhood schizophrenia or atypical ego development are full of paradoxes. This is well pointed out by Szurek (1956) as follows:

The child whose disorder is extreme can be recognized by his marked or extreme unresponsiveness, even negativism, to the approach of others— adults or coevals. Yet, at certain times, with certain people—particularly adults—in reaction to certain attitudes he responds with intense vigor, with great and often violent speed, all of which is so disproportionate to the immediate precipitating event that the latter is difficult to notice or to reconstruct later. He is quite indifferent, often especially to his mother. Yet, on closer observation, he is, as we may say, particularly "dependent" upon her. . . .

He gives the impression of stupidity at one moment, and of Machiavellian precision in his cunning at another. He is phobic about some things and situations and foolhardy in his apparent fearless and heedless activity about others. He appears altogether absorbed in his own inner processes, yet gives evidence of being acutely sensitive to all that goes on around him. He seems at times almost self-destructively content to do nothing for himself, yet suddenly on a few occasions he shows unusual skill and expertness in some activity of his own choice, at his own pace and timing. [P. 524.]

After 20 years on the Psychiatric Division of Bellevue Hospital, in which she studied and treated schizophrenic children two to twelve years of age, Bender (1956) arrived at the following definition of childhood schizophrenia:

Childhood schizophrenia involves a maturational lag at the embryonic level characterized by a primitive plasticity in all areas from which subsequent behavior develops. It is genetically determined and activated by a physiological crisis such as birth. Anxiety is both the organismic and physiological response calling forth defense mechanisms. Three types of clinical pictures are presented depending in part upon the defense mechanisms: (1) the pseudo-defective or autistic, retarded, inhibited child; (2) the pseudoneurotic with any number of neurotic mechanisms and evident anxiety; (3) the pseudo-psychopathic with paranoid ideation, and a tendency to act out in anti-social behavior. [P. 499.]

Incidence. Several writers have noted the wide variability among reports from different hospitals on the incidence of schizophrenia and the discrepancies in diagnoses. Studies by Arnhoff (1954), Ash (1949), and Mehlman (1952) show a lack of agreement in psychiatric diagnoses of schizophrenia. When the psychiatrists were asked to diagnose 52 patients, Ash noted complete agreement in 48 per cent and complete disagreement in 31 per cent. When we consider the multiple frames of reference from which diagnosis can be made, this is to be expected. Thus, it is likely that different observers focused their attention on different aspects of the patient's behavior.

According to estimates presented by Bellak (1958), it would appear that the true incidence of schizophrenia in a Western European society can hardly be less than 50 per 100,000 and should not exceed 250 per 100,000. However, the given incidence in any society will depend upon a number of factors, some of which are: (1) the definition used, (2) the extent of treatment and care, (3) the age of population, and (4) the nature of the society—urban versus rural. First admissions to mental hospitals under the older diagnostic entity of dementia praecox have been used as one basis for determining the prevalence of schizophrenia. This does not furnish a basis for judging the entire population. Such a study would most likely reveal a much greater incidence of schizophrenia. This general assumption is certainly consistent with the operation of our medical system. Bellak has suggested that a conservative estimate of cases in a community generally exceeds hospital admissions by at least 15 per cent (p. 71).

Problems of Diagnosis. Although childhood schizophrenia is a diagnostic entity that has become rather firmly established in the literature dealing with childhood psychosis, there are a number of investigators of childhood personality disorders who question the use of the term. Asman (1960) suggests the use of the term "ego pathology" to replace "childhood schizophrenia" since it appears to be more consistent with present knowledge of severe personality disturbances in childhood. Certainly much confusion has arisen about the precise clinical referents of those classified as childhood schizophrenics. Because the diagnoses of childhood schizophrenia are based upon different theories, behavioral observations are interpreted in different terms, and etiological viewpoints vary. Thus, the genetic-organic or psychogenic origin is controversial. This may be noticed in the different descriptions and expectations of childhood schizophrenia.

The greatest difficulty in the diagnosis of schizophrenia appears during its early stages. It is for this reason that diagnosis during childhood and adolescence is frequently inaccurate. Bellak (1958) states: "When symptoms are fully fledged, the disturbances in relationship to others, speech patterns, thinking, effect, and motility should cause no major difficulty" (p. 112). Studies conducted by Goldfarb (1961a) and other investigators clearly indicate that schizophrenic conditions are not of a single pattern. A group of 20 seriously disturbed, schizophrenic children was compared with a control group of normal children in public school, matched in age and sex. An extensive battery of tests and appraisals furnished physical, behavioral, and familial data on both groups of children. From these comparisons Goldfarb presented the following summary and conclusions:

Schizophrenic and normal children were not different in simple physical characteristics such as height and weight, or in auditory, visual, and tactile acuity. However, the two groups were clearly different in more complex behavioral functions. The schizophrenic children were uniformly inferior to normal children in perceptual processes involving figure-ground discrimination and configurational closure. They were far below the normal children in conceptual functions requiring abstractions and categorization and deviated markedly in speech and communicative ability. Finally, the schizophrenic children were extremely deficient in psycho-motor capacities. [P. 188.]

On the basis of manifest behavior and certain secondary symptoms Fenichel *et al.* (1960) presented a description of five categories of children at the League School who had been diagnosed "childhood schizophrenia" by an outside psychiatrist or agency. These are described as follows:

1. *The autistic child.* The primary source of stimulation for these children is from their own body. "They have little or no speech, rarely display any affective awareness of people, and maintain a level of activity which has the barest relation to objects or events in the real world" (pp. 131–32). Two subgroups may be observed:
   a) Those who have been retarded in maturation from birth
   b) The child who has a history of regression
2. *The organic type of schizophrenic child.* These children manifest certain symptoms associated with organic conditions although they present no clear-cut history of cerebral damage or dysfunction.
3. *A neurotic variety of schizophrenia.* Some of these have at one time been autistic. The clinical picture is marked by anxieties and anxiety defenses such as phobias, obsessive-compulsive symptoms, and bodily preoccupations.
4. *An asocial aggressive type.* "These are generally somewhat older children who are poorly related, aggressive, difficult to manage, often somewhat paranoic" (p. 133).
5. *The schizophrenic child in transition.* "These are children who have a meager relatedness but are distinguished from the remaining children by their maintenance of continual contact with their environment, however meager this contact may be" (p. 133). They have not yet developed any structural defenses.

Etiology. It was pointed out earlier that the etiology of childhood psychosis is not easy to ascertain. However, evidence supports the viewpoint that behavioral deficiencies such as appear among childhood schizophrenics can be produced by a neurological defect in the child or by abnormal conditions in his early environment (Goldfarb, 1961a). Goldfarb states: "This concept of two general classes of causes of behavioral defects of the schizophrenic child (a neurophysiological inadequacy in the child, or a primary disturbance in the psychosocial atmosphere in the family life) seems to fit the clinical impression of a grossly bimodal clustering of schizophrenic children" (p. 190). These clusters have been designated as *organic* and *nonorganic*. In the study by Goldfarb standardized forms of clinical neurological tests of perceptual, postural, and motor response showed a greater trend to organicity or impaired neurophysiological organization in the schizophrenic group of children than in the normal group. However, the neurological tests confirmed the success of the investigators in distinguishing between organic and non-organic schizophrenic children and showed in greater detail the nature of the differences.

The Autistic Child. The syndrome labelled "early infantile autism" was originally described by Kanner (1943) as an *"inability to relate themselves* in the ordinary way to people and to situations from the beginning of life" (p. 242). At a later time he modified his original definition to include children who developed normally for the first eighteen to twenty months of life, only to undergo at this time a behavior pattern of withdrawal, manifested by the loss of language function, failure to develop socially, and a loss of interest in normal activities. In 1958 he gave as the most important criteria of infantile autism the following:

1. "An extreme self-isolation, or an inability to relate themselves in the ordinary way to people or situtaions from early in life."
2. "An obsessive insistence on the maintenance of sameness."

Cunningham and Dixon (1961) studied the language development of an autistic child who had progressed normally up to the age of two years, after which there was an arrest in his development and, in the case of speech, with no apparent physical cause. The following symptoms, characteristic of infantile autism, as described by Kanner, were observed:

(1) An inability to relate in the ordinary way to people. He took no notice of adults when they came into the room. He would avoid looking at an adult who approached him.

(2) He showed a desire for the preservation of sameness. For example, he persisted in repetitive activities, such as rocking, or manipulating shiny objects, and resented any interference with these activities. He also showed great reluctance to leave the house to play in the garden.

(3) He showed a preoccupation with certain sensory characteristics of objects without regard to their accepted functions. For example, he would become preoccupied with the reflection of light on a shiny object. He would wave a toy car in front of his eyes, being interested in the interruption of the light. He did not run the toy car along the floor as a normal child would do.

(4) He showed an ability for skilled manipulation of objects which was considerably in advance of his level of development in other respects. When given the performance tests of the Merrill-Palmer Scale, he scored at a level of 4 years 9 months. But at this time his language was at about a 2-year level, and his emotional and social behavior resembled that of a 2-year old. [P. 195.]

It has been pointed out that these children usually have good cognitive personalities (Kanner, 1943). This may be observed in the extraordinary use of language, although frequently perverted, and unusual memory manifestations. This syndrome differentiates these children from childhood schizophrenia by the detachment from people being present no later than the first year of life and by the evidence of good intellectual potentialities. Eisenberg and Kanner (1956) state further: "Physical examination failed to reveal any consistent organic abnormality that could be related to the clinical picture. Family background was striking in the universal presence of high intelligence, marked obsessiveness, and coldness" (p. 557).

Clinical History of Infantile Autism. It was suggested earlier that children described as manifesting infantile autism come out of an intelligent, obsessive, and emotional frigid background. It might be stated that emotional care, recognized as very important to the infant's well-being, is absent from the lives of these children. This is clearly brought forth in the case of Brian presented by Eisenberg and Kanner (1956):

The mechanization of care and the almost absence of emotional warmth in child rearing may be exemplified by the case of Brian, who was one of twins born despite contraceptive efforts, much to the distress of his parents whose plans centered about graduate study and had no room for children.

Pregnancy was quite upsetting to the mother and caused the father, who was already immersed in study, to withdraw still further from the family. The mother, a psychology graduate student, decided that the children were to be raised "scientifically"—that is, not to be picked up for crying, except on schedule. Furthermore, an effort was made to "keep them from infections" by minimizing human contact. What little care was dispensed was centered on Brian's twin who was physically weaker and, according to the mother, more responsive. At five months of age, the twin was found dead after an evening in which both twins had been crying loudly but had not been visited, in accordance with the rigid principle. Following this tragedy, the mother withdrew from the remaining child even more completely, spent her days locked in the study reading, and limited her concern almost exclusively to maintaining bacteriological sterility, so that Brian was isolated from children and almost all adults until he was well over two. During the period he was content to be alone and to occupy himself, just how the parents rarely bothered to inquire. It was only when he reached the age of four without the development of speech and began to display temper tantrums when his routine was interrupted that they began to recognize the fact that he was ill. So distant were the members of this family each from the others that the parents failed to be concerned about, if they did not actually prefer, Brian's indifference to them. [Pp. 561–62.]

There is little likelihood that any single etiologic agent is solely responsible for this pathology although parental indifference seems to stand out. Their parents had other interests and activities with which they were much preoccupied. However, these children appeared in some ways to be different from a very early stage. "Present knowledge leads to the inference that innate as well as experiential factors conjoin to produce the clinical picture" (Eisenberg and Kanner, 1956, p. 564).

Speech Patterns. Clinicians working with schizophrenia are impressed with the strange nature of the voice patterns and the frequency of different kinds of speech disorders. Although deviation in language content is the difficulty most frequently reported, disturbances in the production of speech and voice are significant, especially to the clinical observer. Goldfarb *et al.* (1956) reported results of clinical judgments of deviations from normal speech, based on observations and recordings. These judgments were based on a year's experience with the speech behavior of most of the children.

The reported speech deviations from expected normal of 6 children with reactive behavior disorders and 12 childhood schizophrenics are presented in Table 17–2. The children with reactive behavior

disorders were used as a contrasting group to the group of schizophrenic children. The schizophrenic children show a greater number and wider range of speech deviations from normal in every

TABLE 17–2

Speech Deviations from Expected Normal in Specified Areas of
6 Children with Reactive Behavior Disorders and 12 Children with
Childhood Schizophrenia

Deviation in	Reactive Behavior Disorder	Childhood Schizophrenia
Phonation		
Quality	6	12
Volume	0	9
Pitch	1	9
Duration	1	9
Rhythm	0	8
Intonation	1	8
Articulation	1	9
Facial and body reinforcement	0	12

Source: After Goldfarb *et al.* (1956).

category except voice quality. All children in both groups were
judged as deviants from the normal in voice quality, which included
nasality, denasality, breathiness, hoarseness, throatiness, and glot-
tization. A kind of voice quality charaterized as dull or wooden
(flatness) was noted among the schizophrenics but in only one child
with reactive behavior disorder. The schizophrenic child has an
excessively high pitch level although pitch changes unrelated to
meaning are more often observed. Complete omission of normally
required sounds or substitution of sounds is common among schizophrenics. The speech of the schizophrenic child lacks the type of
rhythm observed among normal children. They frequently place
stress on syllables and words of little importance to the meaning of
the phrase. Facial and bodily gestures unrelated to the spoken words
are much in evidence while a stolid facial expression may be observed. Goldfarb *et al.* (1956) state: "Over-all, the complex deviations noted in the case of the schizophrenic children add up to a
global impression of flatness. Flatness appears to be compounded of
insufficiency of volume, pitch, rhythm, stress and intonation" (p. 550).

Thought Disturbances. The thinking of schizophrenic children is
frequently characterized by thought disturbances. These are varied

in their manifestations. However, studies of thought in schizophrenic children must take into consideration that the language and thought of children are characterized by their egocentric nature, immaturity, and tendency to fantasy. Thus, allowances should be made for a child's age and limited experience (Despert, 1940).

A study by Cobrinik and Popper (1961) had as its purpose to investigate by means of the Rorschach technique the nature of thought disturbance in schizophrenic children of different ages. The subjects consisted of 48 boys between the ages through seven years, one month and thirteen years, eleven months in residential treatment. These children demonstrated deviation in many areas of mental functioning. Case histories of the boys revealed a very high incidence of thought symptoms with many subjects having a history of delayed motor and language development. The responses to the Rorschach Test were scored for perceptual and thought disturbances. Analysis of the data showed that 25 of the 48 boys demonstrated some form of thought disturbance. A decline was noted in the manifestation of thought disturbance in early adolescence, that is, after eleven years of age. These results support those of earlier studies by Bender (1947) bearing on the decline of thought disturbances as schizophrenic children approach adolescence.

Social Background of the Schizoid Child. The inability of the schizoid child to form a satisfactory emotional attachment to others has been noted by clinicians. Despert (1947) observed that these children constantly refer to themselves in the third person and look upon their own behavior with a kind of detached attitude.

Significant social background factors may be noted among schizophrenic children. In one study involving 392 such children it was noted that a total of 180, or 46 per cent, came from homes in which there was severe rejection or overprotection on the part of one or both parents (Wahl, 1954). One of the most significant background factors appears to be the perfectionistic mother.

Family variables were studied by Lucas (1964) in 100 schizophrenic subjects and in 100 control subjects selected with special care. "Three environmental variables, other than age and marital status, were found to be related to the incidence of schizophrenia—the psychological climate of the family of orientation, the absence of the father during the first six years and the degree of kinship of the persons who reared the S_s during the first 20 years of their lives" (p. 533). These findings give support to the emphasis by Goldfarb (1961b) to the importance of the physical intactness of the family in the development of an integrated personality. The rated psychological climate of the family emerged as the most significant variable studied. This variable yielded a correlation of .77. This would seem to emphasize the quality of the relationships in the family structure. This variable was based upon ratings including seven descriptive anchoring points. The correlations between the psychological climate of the family and other independent variables, shown in Table 17–3, were significant and high.

TABLE 17–3

Correlations of Ratings of the Psychological Climate of the Family
with Other Independent Variables

Independent Variable	Correlation
Absence of mother (0 to 6 years)	.63
Absence of father (0 to 6 years)	.32
Absence of mother (0 to 20 years)	.44
Absence of father (0 to 20 years)	.41
Distance of kinship of those who reared S_s (0 to 6 years)	.37
Distance of kinship of those who reared S_s (0 to 20 years)	.46
Mental illness of mother	.33
Mental illness of father	.30
Mental illness of sibling	.29

SOURCE: After Lucas (1964).

A group of hospitalized mental patients all of whom had been studied by the staff and diagnosed as schizophrenic was selected by Bower et al. (1960) for study. The high school record of this group was compared with that of a control group. In addition, data were gathered from members of the high school staffs about the characteristics of the boys making up the two groups. Using pictures from high school yearbooks as means of identifying the boys, interviews were held with members of the school staff relative to the subjects of the study. These interviews indicated that high school students who later became schizophrenic were significantly different from a control group, although only a small number of the preschizophrenic group were perceived by school personnel as emotionally sick.

The results presented in Table 17–4 show significant differences between the two groups with respect to grades, school attendance, participation in extracurricular activities, subjects failed, and course of study followed. Interviews with the school staff showed further that the schizophrenic boys tended to have less interest in girls, group activities, and athletics. They were inclined to be more submissive, anxious, dependent, and careless than the control group of boys. Although they were not usually perceived as being emotionally disturbed, they were less liked by their peers and teachers and displayed less leadership skill than the control group. In general their mental health and school adjustment were rated lower than those of the control group.

TABLE 17–4

Significant Comparison of Preschizophrenic and Control Boys on Selected Items in Their School Records

Item	Major Difference
1. Graduation	Fewer graduated
2. Course of study followed (college preparatory or general)	Enrolled in general course of study
3. Best subjects	Did best in foreign languages; did poorest in physical education and mathematics
4. Subjects failed	English, social studies, and mathematics
5. Over-all grade pattern	Declining
6. Grade average	One grade below
7. Attendance	Poorer
8. Extracurricular activities	Less interest in sports and dramatics
9. IQ score	Preschizophrenics—mean, 99:3; control —mean, 106.3

SOURCE: After Bower *et al.* (1960).

Treatment of Schizophrenia. It seems clear that childhood schizophrenia is an instance of disordered behavior function involving especially the ego processes of self-awareness and self-identity. However, the specific characteristics and forms of defensive behavior established in any given child can only be understood in connection with the child's unique characteristics and the interpersonal dynamics of his family background. Goldfarb (1961a) states:

. . . to understand the symptoms of a schizophrenic child, one must study the child himself in terms of physiology, ego organization, and intrapsychic dynamics. It is also necessary to study the family as a psychosocial unit and the individual members of the family, including the schizophrenic child, in terms of family role behavior and intrapsychic organization. Finally, it is most important to understand the uniquely individualized interplay between intrinsic processes within the schizophrenic child and extrinsic processes within his family. [P. 730.]

Through psychiatric help much can be accomplished, especially if the schizoid child is recognized during early years and the co-operation of the parents can be secured. A study by Donnelly (1960) showed that fathers of psychotic children were passive in nature and able to see the child as an individual more than the mother. Mothers were inclined to overbaby such children and displayed overanxious proclivities as well as a high degree of emotionality. The greater objectivity of the fathers' attitudes, as shown in their behavior toward such children, stood out as the most important result of this study. This would indicate that the clinician, social worker, and teacher should attempt to get the fathers of such children to take a more active part in child-rearing and therapy for such children.

Mild cases can be treated at home and placed in special classes at school while the more severe cases will require hospitalization. Many of these can be helped through psychotherapy and an educational program developed for them. Concerning the outlook for improvement, Eisenberg and Kanner (1956) state:

If one factor is significantly useful, it is a sympathetic and tolerant reception by the school. Those of our children who have improved have been extended extraordinary consideration by their teachers. They constitute a most trying group of pupils. School acceptance of behavior that elsewhere provokes rejection is undoubtedly a therapeutic experience. [P. 560.]

In recent years tranquilizers have become a popular therapeutic agent with children. However, drug therapy as a treatment procedure is not a new technique. Reluctance to use electric shock and the need for quieting many children led to the investigation of chemical compounds. Benzedrine and Dexidrene have been used since 1937 (Bradley, 1957) for quieting children with serious personality disorders. Chlorpromazine was used by Miksztai (1956) and Ayd (1957) in the treatment of schizophrenic children. Basing themselves on the results of their studies, both investigators endorsed chlorpromazine as a valuable support in the treatment of such children. Lehman *et al.* (1957) used reserpine in the treatment of nine autistic children. They reported that all children showed some improvement as indicated by less hyperactivity, improved perspective of their surroundings, and easier control. Other drugs that have been used with some apparent success are diphenylmethane, meprobamate, ataractic, and prochlorperazine. The widespread research now in progress, along with the success thus far obtained, offers much promise. However, the results must be carefully studied in terms of controls used, possible side effects, and reasons for failure with some children. These agents seem to offer greatest promise not as cures but as means of improving the child's behavior so that he can participate more effectively in different kinds of therapeutic programs.

SUMMARY

Anxiety and fear appear to go with childhood, although marked differences may be noted in the intensity and frequency of their occurrence among children. Excessive timidity among children is indicative of emotional maladjustment. The child who feels inadequate will be handicapped in social development. Excessive anxiety and feelings of inadequacy lead to withdrawal as a means of averting the realities of life. Children often develop nervous habits which trouble parents a great deal. These take the form of nail-biting, enuresis, stuttering, psychogenic vomiting, sleep disturbances, and temper tantrums.

The more serious type of personality disturbances are classed as psychoneuroses and psychoses. No clear line of demarcation can be drawn between these types, although the psychoses are the most serious. Three rather clear-cut psychoneurotic disorders are described in this chapter: neurasthenia, psychasthenia, and hysteria.

One of the most serious of the functional disorders is schizophrenia. This usually begins as a withdrawal process. The schizoid child is characterized by such traits as boastfulness, hyperactivity, selfishness, nervousness, apathy, inability to get along with other children, shyness, lack of interest in others, and guilt feelings. Early infantile autism has frequently been considered as the youngest form of psychotic disturbances in children. It is frequently classified as one form of schizophrenia.

Although considerable research involving childhood psychosis has been conducted during the past decade or more, the outlook for most children suffering from serious personality disturbances is not promising. Therapy is most effective if it can be started during the early years before the disturbance has become so deep seated. Such therapy will in most cases involve the treatment of the child in his total environment setting, which will include further special attention to interpersonal relations within the family.

CHAPTER REFERENCES

ARNHOFF, F. N. (1954). Some factors influencing the unreliability of clinical judgments. *J. clin. Psychol.*, 10:272–75.

ASH, P. (1949). The reliability of psychiatric diagnosis. *J. abnorm. soc. Psychol.*, 44:272–76.

ASMAN, A. H. (1960). Childhood psychosis and "childhood schizophrenia." *Amer. J. Orthopsychiat.*, 20:391–96.

ATKINS, T. E., ROSE, J. A., and SMITH, O. R. (1962). Emergency care of disturbed children. *Children*, 9:217–21.

AYD, F. J., JR. (1957). Emotional problems in children. The use of drugs in therapeutic management. *Calif. Med. J.*, 87:75.

BAKER, J. W., and HOLZWORTH, ANNETTE (1961). Social histories of successful and unsuccessful children. *Child Developm.*, 32:135–49.

BELLAK, L. (1958). *Schizophrenia: a review of the syndrome.* New York: Logos Press.

BENDA, C. E. (1954). Psychopathology of childhood. In L. CARMICHAEL (ed.), *Manual of child psychology.* (2d ed.) New York: Wiley. Pp. 1153–54.

BENDER, LAURETTA (1947). Psychopathic behavior in children. In R. M. LINDER and R. V. SELIGER (eds.), *Handbook of correctional psychology.* New York: Philosophical Library.

BENDER, LAURETTA (1956). Childhood schizophrenia: clinical study of one hundred schizophrenic children. *Amer. J. Orthopsychiat.*, 26:499–506.

BERGMAN, P. (1946). Neurotic anxieties in children and their prevention. *Nerv. Child*, 5:37–55.

BLAU, A., and HULSE, W. C. (1956). Anxiety (actual) neuroses as a cause of behavior disorders in children. *Amer. J. Orthopsychiat.*, 26:108–18.

BOWER, E. M., SHELLHAMER, T. A., and DAILY, J. M. (1960). School characteristics of male adolescents who later became schizophrenic. *Amer. J. Orthopsychiat.*, 30:712–29.

BRADLEY, C. (1957). Behavior of children receiving Benzedrine. *Amer. J. Psychiat.*, 94:577.

COBLINER, W. (1963). Social factors in mental disorders: a contribution to the etiology of mental illness. *Genet. Psychol. Monogr.*, 67:151–215.

COBRINIK, L., and POPPER, LILY (1961). Developmental aspects of thought disturbance in schizophrenic children: a Rorschach study. *Amer. J. Orthopsychiat.*, 31:170–80.

CUNNINGHAM, M. A., and DIXON, CYNTHIA (1961). A study of the language of an autistic child. *J. Child Psychol. Psychiat.*, 2:193–202.

DESPERT, LOUISE J. (1940). A comparative study of thinking in schizophrenic children and children of preschool age. *Amer. J. Psychiat.,* 99:189–213.

DESPERT, LOUISE J. (1946). Anxiety, phobias, and fears in young children. *Nerv. Child,* 5:8–24.

DESPERT, LOUISE J. (1947). The early recognition of childhood schizophrenia. *Med. Clin. N. Amer.,* May, pp. 680–87.

DONNELLY, ELLEN (1960). The quantitative analysis of parent behavior toward psychotic children and their siblings. *Genet. Psychol. Monogr.,* 62:331–76.

EISENBERG, L. (1958). School phobia: a study in the communication of anxiety. *Amer. J. Psychiat.,* 114:712–18.

EISENBERG, L., and KANNER, L. (1956). Childhood schizophrenia symposium, 1955. 6. Early infantile autism, 1943–55. *Amer. J. Orthopsychiat.,* 26:556–66.

FENICHEL, C., FREEDMAN, A. M., and KLAPPER, ZELDA (1960). A day school for schizophrenic children. *Amer. J. Orthopsychiat.,* 30:130–43.

GOLDFARB, W. (1961a). *Childhood schizophrenia.* Cambridge, Mass.: Harvard Univer. Press.

GOLDFARB, W. (1961b). The mutual impact of mother and child in schizophrenia. *Amer. J. Orthopsychiat.,* 31:738–47.

GOLDFARB, W., BRAUNSTEIN, PATRICIA, and LORGO, I. (1956). Childhood schizophrenia symposium, 1955. 5. A study of speech patterns in a group of schizophrenic children. *Amer. J. Orthopsychiat.,* 26:544–55.

HARING, N. G., and PHILLIPS, E. L. (1962). *Educating emotionally disturbed children.* New York: McGraw-Hill.

JENKINS, R. L. (1952). The schizophrenic sequence; withdrawal, disorganization, psychotic reorganization. *Amer. J. Orthopsychiat.,* 22:738–48.

JERSILD, A. T. (1943). Studies of children's fears. In BARKER, KOUNIN, and WRIGHT (eds.), *Child behavior and development.* New York: McGraw-Hill.

KANNER, L. (1943). Autistic disturbances of affective contact. *Nerv. Child,* 2:217–50.

KANNER, L. (1958). The specificity of early infantile autism. *Revue de Psychiatrie Infantile,* 25:108–13.

KAPLAN, H., and KAPLAN, HELEN S. (1956). Emotional problems and vocational adjustments. *Psychiat. Quart. Suppl.,* 30:34–60.

KIRK, S. A. (1962). *Educating exceptional children.* Boston: Houghton Mifflin.

KRAMER, HILDE C. (1946). Orthogenesis of anxiety. *Nerv. Child,* 7:25–36.

LEHMAN, E., HABER, J., and LESSER, S. R. (1957). The use of reserpine in autistic children. *J. nerv. ment. Disord.,* 125:351–56.

LEHNER, G. F., and KUBE, ELLA (1955). *The dynamics of personal adjustment.* Englewood Cliffs, N.J.: Prentice-Hall.

LUCAS, L. (1964). Family influences and schizophrenic reaction. *Amer. J. Orthopsychiat.*, 34:527–35.

MEHLMAN, B. (1952). The reliability of psychiatric diagnosis. *J. abnorm. soc. Psychol.*, 47:577–78.

MIKSZTAI, M. W. (1956). Chlorpromazine (thorazine) and reserpine in residential treatment of neuropsychiatric disorders in children. *J. nerv. ment. Disord.*, 123:477–79.

NOYES, A. P., and KOLB, L. C. (1963). *Modern clinical psychiatry.* (6th ed.) Philadelphia: W. B. Saunders.

PRESTON, M. I. (1940). Physical complaints without organic basis. *J. Pediatr.*, 17:279–304.

PUTNAM, M. (1955). Some observations on psychosis in early childhood. In G. CAPLAN (ed.), *Emotional problems of early childhood.* London: Tavistock.

RUBIN, E. Z., and SIMSON, C. B. (1960). A special class program for the emotionally disturbed child in school: a proposal. *Amer. J. Orthopsychiat.*, 30:144–53.

SARASON, S. B., DAVIDSON, K. S., LIGHTHALL, F. L., WHITE, R. R., and RUEBUSH, K. K. (1960). *Anxiety in elementary school children.* New York: Wiley.

SCHNEERSOHN, F. (1955). Play and neuroses of children. *Amer. J. Psychiat.*, 112:47–52.

SHANDS, A. R. (1957). *Handbook of orthopaedic surgery.* (5th ed.) St. Louis, Mo.: C. V. Mosby.

STENDLER, CELIA B. (1951). Social class differences in parental attitudes toward school at grade 1 level. *Child Developm.*, 22:37–46.

STROB, G. (1960). On the diagnosis of childhood psychosis. *J. Child Psychol. Psychiat.*, 1:238–43.

SZUREK, S. A. (1956). Childhood schizophrenia: psychotic episodes and psychic maldevelopment. *Amer. J. Orthopsychiat.*, 26:519–43.

WAHL, C. W. (1954). Some antecedent factors in the family histories of 392 schizophrenics. *Amer. J. Psychiat.*, 110:668–76.

SELECTED READINGS

BENDA, C. E. (1954). Psychopathology of childhood. In L. CARMICHAEL (ed.), *Manual of child psychology.* (2d ed.) New York: Wiley. Chap. 18.

BERKOWITZ, PEARL W., and ROTHMAN, ESTHER P. (1960). *The disturbed child.* New York: New York Univer. Press.

EISENBERG, L. (1962). School phobia: a study in the communication of anxiety. In E. P. TRAPP and P. HIMELSTEIN (eds.), *Readings on the exceptional child.* New York: Appleton-Century-Crofts. Pp. 629–38.

HARING, N. G. (1963). The emotionally disturbed child. In S. A. KIRK and BLUMA B. WEINER (eds.), *Behavior research on exceptional chil-*

dren. Washington, D.C.: Council of Exceptional Children, National Education Association.

HOCH, P. H., and ZUBIN, J. (1955). *Psychopathology of childhood.* New York: Grune & Stratton.

MYERS, J. K., and ROBERTSON, B. H. (1959). *Family and class dynamics in mental illness.* New York: Wiley.

WERKMAN, S. L. (1962). Present trends in schizophrenia research: implications for childhood schizophrenia. In E. P. TRAPP and P. HIMELSTEIN (eds.), *Readings on the exceptional child.* New York: Appleton-Century-Crofts. Pp. 585–91.

See also Selected Readings for Chapter 16.

18

ANTISOCIAL AND
DELINQUENT BEHAVIOR

An important developmental task is to achieve socially responsible behavior and to contribute to the life activities and the welfare of the society in which one lives. This requires both interdependence and personal independence, both conformity and individuality, both social development and the development of individual abilities. Within recent years much publicity has been given to the irresponsible behavior of teen-agers and teen-age gangs although not all antisocial behavior and delinquency is to be found among this age group. Also, the great majority of teen-agers (95 per cent or more) are not juvenile delinquents in any sense. However, the problem of juvenile delinquency has become sufficiently serious to receive the attention of our various social agencies. These boys and girls are basically normal individuals but have become rebellious, irregular in attendance at school, irresponsible, careless of ownership rights, and filled with the urge to injure others.

DEFINITIONS

Antisocial Behavior. Antisocial behavior is especially characterized by aggressiveness, self-indulgence, and rebelliousness. It is observed in the ten-year-old girl who is described by her mother as quarrelsome, argumentative, defiant, and untrustworthy. It also appears in the case of the eleven-year-old boy who plays hookey from school and who is described as disturbing, ill-tempered, disobedient, and disrespectful to his teachers.

Antisocial behavior is frequently associated with nonconformity. Sex differences in conformity have been noted with girls showing a greater tendency to conform than boys. This compliance accounts in part for the greater amount of child and adolescent delinquency among boys than among girls. Meyer and Thompson (1956), in an investigation of sixth-graders, found that boys tended to receive more disapproval from their teachers than did girls. They interpreted their findings as suggesting that teachers attempt to socialize pupils by using counteraggressive behavior in response to aggressive behavior characterized by nonconformity.

The Delinquent. From a social point of view delinquency means any form of behavior detrimental to the well-being of society. Such a definition, however, does not provide for any practical limits. Juvenile delinquency is a legal term. In most states a juvenile delinquent is an individual under eighteen years of age who is adjudged guilty of violating the law. However, if delinquency is defined in terms of acts detrimental to the well-being of society or breaking the law, almost all children and adolescents are delinquent at some time or other. Cohen (1957) has emphasized the need for studying delinquency as collective behavior. In American culture many child and adolescent activities usually regarded as part of the child's way of life may be regarded as delinquent acts when regarded in terms of the definitions usually presented for delinquency. For example, parades without permits, Halloween activities, bonfires, and celebrations related to activities at school or elsewhere may be a violation of the law or detrimental to the well-being of some group or individual.

In 1961, for the first time since 1948, juvenile delinquency cases referred to juvenile courts decreased from the previous year (U.S. Department of Health, Education, and Welfare, 1962). Delinquency cases continue to be primarily a boys' problem; boys are referred to the court more than four times as often as girls. The percentage changes between 1960 and 1961 were approximately the same for boys' and girls' cases. The largest decrease in 1961 occurred in the unofficial cases handled by rural courts. The trends in juvenile court delinquency cases and child population ten to seventeen years of age are shown in Fig. 18–1.

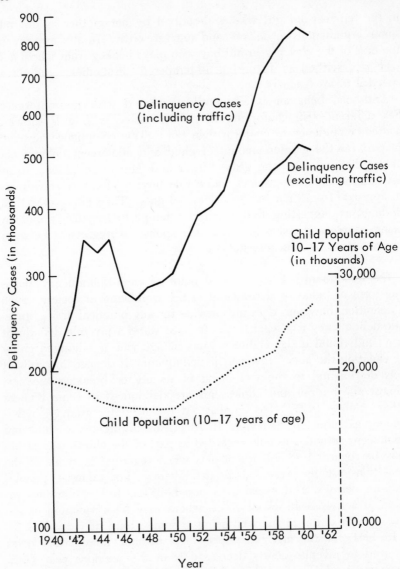

Fig. 18–1. Trends in juvenile court delinquency cases and child population ten to seventeen years of age, 1940–1961 (semilogarithmic scale). (U.S. Department of Health, Education, and Welfare, 1962.)

Most studies of delinquency deal with the extreme delinquent, those continuously in trouble with the law. The study by Miller *et al.* (1961) dealt with a group that falls near the center of a range of behavior from highly delinquent to negligibly delinquent, and is therefore fairly representative. A group referred to as the "Junior Outlaws" consisted of boys thirteen to fifteen years of age. It was noted that the most frequent delinquent acts were directed against other groups of adolescents. Other aggressive acts were directed, in descending order of frequency, against neighborhood adults in frequent contact with the Junior Outlaws, other adults in regular contact with the Junior Outlaws, and family members. The investigators concluded from a study of 1,490 aggressive acts that the mechanisms utilized by the Junior Outlaws could scarcely be characterized as abnormal.

On the contrary, they appear as an organized, efficient, and dynamically balanced system, performing stabilizing and integrative functions for both the group and its members. From this perspective, this type of adolescent group appears not as a defective or pathological organism, but as a highly effective device for accommodating a universal human problem in a manner particularly well geared to the condition of its cultural milieu. [P. 298.]

Delinquent vs. Neurotic Children. At times some students have confused delinquent and neurotic children. A study conducted by Bennett (1960) was designed to test certain psychoanalytic theories about the development of neurotic and delinquent children ranging in age from five to seventeen years with a median age of ten years. Fifty pairs of cases were chosen, one child of each pair selected as delinquent and the other selected as neurotic. The pairs were matched on the basis of sex, age, and IQ. Thirty pairs were boys; 20 pairs were girls.

The picture of the delinquent group was that of unsocialized aggressive children. They differed from the neurotic group in that their behavior was characterized by stealing, lying, truancy from school, aggressiveness in the form of torturing others, destruction of property, running away, defiance of authority, and extreme disobedience. The neurotic group's behavior was characterized by such elements as obsessions, fearfulness, anxiety, inhibited behavior, inferiority feelings, and reaction formations such as overcleanliness and excessive modesty.

The backgrounds of both groups showed a dearth of stabilizing influences, with the discipline in the homes of delinquents being much more inconsistent than was the case for the neurotic.

PSYCHOLOGICAL TYPES OF DELINQUENCY

Attempts have been made to ascribe special characteristics to delinquents. Donet (1951) concluded from a study of the psychiatric aspects that delinquency is a biosocial phenomenon the common psychological denominator of which is a feeling of insecurity. Case studies of delinquents reveal that these boys and girls have the same basic needs and, in general, face the same problems as non-delinquents (Resnick, 1956). Any attempt to draw a clear-cut psychological line between delinquents and non-delinquents will be fraught with difficulties.

Attempts have been made by a number of investigators to classify delinquents into types or special groups. However, it is generally recognized that much overlapping exists in any classification. In many cases such classification does furnish a basis for better studying delinquents and their problems. Hewitt and Jenkins (1941) classified delinquents as (1) socialized, (2) unsocialized, and (3) maladjusted or withdrawing. Beck (1956) has briefly described four types of delinquents that might be encountered in the school setting: (1) the social delinquent, (2) the asocial delinquent, (3) the neurotic delinquent, and (4) the organic or "accidental" delinquent. These classifications are similar to that of Reiss (1952), who, from data obtained in the records of 1,110 white male juvenile delinquent probationers of the Cook County Juvenile Court, was able to isolate three psychological types of delinquents: (1) the relatively integrated delinquent, (2) the delinquent with markedly weak ego control, and (3) the delinquent with relatively defective superego control. The classification given by Reiss will be used as a basis for discussing characteristics of delinquents.

The *relatively integrated* delinquent is rather well adjusted emotionally and will in all probability become an emotionally mature adult. These children are socialized delinquents and show no symptoms of maladjustments other than the delinquent act. They are classified by some psychiatrists as "normal" although individuals of this group are repeatedly engaged in delinquent acts. The range of behavior is wide, ranging from stealing an automobile for joy riding to selling protection to younger children or committing holdups with loaded pistols. The case of Walter is illustrative of one who is a "normal" or integrated delinquent:

Walter, the second of two brothers and a younger sister, was 13 years of age. He, along with three pals, played hookey from school frequently. On several occasions the boys stole fruit from a neighborhood fruit stand. Walter often came home late at night. His mother worked as a cashier at a laundry to support the family as her husband had died when Walter was eight.

Results on psychological tests given at different periods showed an IQ range from 78 to 90. Walter's lowest score was on test items involving language activities, including reading. His highest score was on the non-language type of tests. His school record was poor, and he showed a pronounced deficiency in reading ability. His older brother was in the tenth grade and doing satisfactorily in his school work. Walter also assumed some responsibility for his own needs as well as those of the family. He worked at a neighborhood grocery store on Saturdays.

At the center of Walter's life activities and interests was the gang of boys with whom he associated. He resented very much the times when he had to stay at home with his younger sister. The mother had little time to spend at home. Her work and church activities took up a major portion of her time. Walter had no educational goals and regarded school as a place where he had to go as a matter of course. He maintained a friendly relationship with his brother who gave him some spending money each Saturday after being paid for work at the store. Walter was friendly with his teacher and counselor, especially when they did not pressure him about his school work.

The delinquent with *markedly weak ego control* is generally regarded as either an insecure person with low self-esteem or as a highly aggressive and hostile person. Such delinquents make up the "maladjusted or withdrawing" group in the threefold classification of Hewitt and Jenkins (1941). They tend to withdraw from social participation and are often "lone wolf offenders." A case described by Topping (1941, pp. 490–92) illustrates this type of delinquent:

Harold, white, 14½. One of probably identical twins, of a family of seven children. When he was four, his mother died and his father deserted. The twins, two brothers, and a sister were placed in an orphanage where they remained four years, until the sister died. The other twin became delinquent. Harold stated his own delinquent conduct was due to his desire to be with his brother. His studied efforts to emulate the gangster smack of adolescent theatricals. He has a warped and scarred personality and is capable of deadly attack. Bitter hostility and a philosophy of futility became an integral part of his personality. Outstanding in his reaction were disappointment and bitterness arising from the loss of his parents; dread of being thought a sissy by his twin; loss of emotional security through separation from his siblings; determination to rejoin his twin by becoming delinquent.

Delinquents referred to as having *relatively defective superego control* have not developed society-conforming behavior. They are characterized by emotional immaturity. Hewitt and Jenkins (1941) refer to them as "unsocialized delinquents." However, they may be socialized with respect to their own peer group. An important task faced by adolescents as they grow toward maturity is that of reconciling individual desires and characteristics with the demands of society.

We honor the hero who is daring, we magnify power and speed, and we glorify the machine for what it can do. However, teenagers are cautioned to drive the automobile at a restricted speed and not to race or take chances by passing other cars on curves or on the brow of a hill. The difficulty that the emotionally immature adolescent has in reconciling these demands and conditions may be observed in the reckless driving of many youth.

The Psychopath. Presently available diagnostic methods and clinical observations indicate that some individuals with behavior problems cannot be classed as neurotic. Neither are they mentally defective. Rarely do they appear at a clinic before the case has become an aggravated one. These individuals make a failure of living, especially in social relations. They display a lack of self-control, poor judgment, and little, if any, self-understanding. They lie freely; and when challenged about their behavior, they blame all of the trouble upon others or upon society in general. They have been described by Cleckley (1950) as inconsistently unreliable, inconsiderate of others, and shameless. When frustrated, they are sometimes aggressive to the point of doing injury to others. Such persons are labeled as *psychopathic.*

Johnson (1955) has said: "The psychopathic personality or 'psychopath' of later years is the grown-up delinquent child with defects in conscience, who is in court for theft, burglary, forgery, or worse" (p. 474). There is good evidence from the social histories of adult psychopaths that even as children they were regarded in their home communities as "problem children." However, one should not conclude that all problem children are potential psychopaths. Bender (1947), for example, has estimated that from 5 to 10 per cent of the problem children whom she studied would be classified as psychopaths. This is about the same percentage of the prison population that criminologists estimate as psychopaths.

Juvenile Sex Offenders. The results of a survey of all sex offenders appearing before the psychiatric clinic of the Toronto Juvenile and Family Court between the years 1939 and 1948 were reported by Atcheson and Williams (1954). During this ten-year period, 3,112 juvenile delinquents were referred to the clinic, 2,516 males and 596 females. The percentage of the boys involved in sexual misbehavior was 5.8 and of the girls, 34.5. The charges were classified into three categories: 7.2 per cent of the female sex offenders and 68.9 per cent of the male sex offenders were placed in the category of *specific* charges. On the other hand, 79 per cent of the females and 18.9 per cent of the males were classified in the category of *non-specific* charges. Thirteen per cent of the females and 12 per cent of the males were classified in the category of *unrelated* charges involving theft, truancy, or malicious mischief, in which sexual misconduct was also present. These data also indicate that of the specific charges, those involving sexual deviations were usually found among the males, while of the non-specific charges, those implying promiscuity were usually found among the females.

There were six times as many males with psychiatric disorders among the sex offenders as among the males of a control group. No significant differences were observed between the female groups in this regard. "Normal" female delinquents are promiscuous in an attempt to gain status, affection, and security. For the male, promiscuous acts appear to be based in a large measure on a developing sex curiosity. Atcheson and Williams (1954) conclude: "The eventual understanding of the etiology and psychopathology of abnormal sexual behavior in the adult must come from an intensive and systematic study of the emotional disorders of the sex delinquent child" (p. 370).

Results from an analysis of the histories of 83 neurotic, delinquent girls of ages fourteen to eighteen, most of whom were arraigned for stealing, were reported by O'Kelly (1955). Significant differences were noted between the sexual and non-sexual delinquents:

> . . . the sexual delinquents tend to have conjugally unstable mothers and a distorted relation to the father, but their early history in relation to the mother tends to be relatively tranquil. These findings do not preclude a connection between maternal loss or gross rejection and sexual delinquency; but they suggest that any such connection is much less close than is the case in thieves. [P. 66.]

CHARACTERISTICS OF JUVENILE DELINQUENTS

It was suggested earlier that a distinction should be made between groups of socialized children and adolescents with "time on their hands" and those in conflict with society described by Blake (1958) as follows: "Groups of frustrated, confused youths direct their hostility toward institutions they see as symbols of society" (p. 8). A need of the first group is that of acceptance into the activities of the adult society, while the needs of the latter involve counseling and therapy of the individual. The discussion that follows gives a description of characteristics frequently found among juvenile delinquents, but it should not be inferred from this discussion that there is a specific delinquent type.

Self Concept and Juvenile Delinquency. Reckless *et al.* (1957) have pointed to a good or poor concept of self and others, as manifested by twelve-year-olds, as a basis for predicting juvenile delinquency. It is suggested that a child or adolescent with a good self concept has a sort of built-in insulator against juvenile delinquency while the individual with a poor self concept frequently succumbs to delinquency. He finds security and acceptance in the juvenile gang, which in our cities has frequently become the most effective and rewarding group of a particular neighborhood. With this group he is able to protect his ego and prove his worth from episode to episode, in accordance with the code of the gang.

A study reported by Lively *et al.* (1962) dealt with the stability of the direction of socialization in adolescents twelve to fifteen years of age. A total of 1,171 students from the sixth, seventh, eighth, and ninth grades supplied usable information and completed a socialization scale consisting of 46 items from the *California Personality Inventory*. The results, presented in Table 18–1, show the mean scores by grades, sex, and area of residence (good or bad). Scores in the middle 30's and beyond were considered as representing a veering toward socialization while scores in the low 30's and 20's are less favorable in direction. The results indicate a trend toward stability of scores from twelve to fifteen years of age. There is also a constancy in the differences between boys and girls and between good and poor neighborhoods.

These findings give considerable assurance to those working with teen-agers. In view of the fact that the direction of socialization and a favorable self concept have been found to have insulation value against a propulsion toward delinquency, stability in the direction of self concept and socialization becomes very important in the prediction and control of delinquency. Concerning the task of the behavioral scientist, Lively *et al.* (1962) state:

He can attempt to fortify the favorable components, so as to strengthen the insulation against delinquency, although this is probably not necessary. He can also attempt to change the unfavorable direction of socialization and self concept in those children who are veering toward delinquency, an effort which would amount to mobilizing the child to internalize values, norms, goals, expectations, responsibilities, limits, status, belongingness, identification, alternative approaches—concepts which in turn would steer him away from delinquency, provided there is no basic damage and no

TABLE 18-1

Variations in Mean Socialization Scores by Grade, Sex, and Area of Residence

	Grade 6			Grade 7			Grade 8			Grade 9		
	Number	Mean	Standard Deviation	Number	Mean	Standard Deviation	Number	Mean	Standard Deviation	Number	Mean	Standard Deviation
Sex												
Male	92	35.5	6.4	156	36.2	6.6	153	34.4	7.3	154	33.8	7.8
Female	100	38.7	6.3	168	39.4	6.1	172	38.9	6.9	176	38.8	7.2
Area												
Good	95	38.4	6.3	175	38.8	6.1	177	37.8	7.2	176	37.4	7.3
Bad	97	35.9	6.8	149	36.8	6.7	148	35.6	7.3	154	35.5	7.5

SOURCE: After Lively et al. (1962).

basic antisocial character formation. . . . The task ahead is to design a program which will enable the 12-year-old child who is spotted as showing an unfavorable direction of self to strengthen this self and to develop defense against pressures, pulls, and pushes. [P. 167.]

Defensive Behavior and Delinquency. Defensive behavior frequently takes the form of aggressive behavior in an attempt to cover up an inadequacy. This means that many delinquencies originate in mechanisms such as attention-getting and compensation. Aggressive behavior of a serious nature in delinquents shows many pattern factors such as:

1. The individual has no basis for maintaining self-esteem, such as love or proper attention.
2. He is overly motivated to secure recognition and admiration, either from his peer group or from older delinquents.
3. He is driven by anxieties originating in physical, social, and intellectual inferiorities, and can gain satisfactions from the feeling that his aggressive behavior gives.
4. Quite often he has developed a deep hostility toward his parents, and employs his delinquent behavior as a means of hurting and punishing them.
5. Flagrant sexual delinquency among girls is thought to be a response to an unsatisfied need to have someone love them and pay attention to them.

An adjective checklist of 75 words was used by Shippee-Blum (1959) to compare the ego strength of rebellious and cooperative adolescents. Each subject was asked to mark as true (1) the adjectives that described him as he really was, (2) all adjectives that described his father as he (the adolescent) saw him, and (3) those that described his mother correctly. On the adjective checklist the rebels "revealed unrealistic self-regard, which differed from the realistic self-appraisal of the cooperatives. Rebels were found to regard themselves more highly than they regarded their parents; cooperators admired their parents more than themselves" (p. 50).

Personality Characteristics. Healy and Bronner (1936) compared 105 pairs of delinquents and their non-delinquent brothers or sisters on certain personality characteristics. The delinquent in their study was distinguished from his non-delinquent brother by his marked feelings of inferiority, ascendant behavior, restlessness and hyperactivity, and greater number of nervous habits. His dislike for school and his teachers was plainly related. He displayed the picture of an insecure individual attempting to satisfy certain unfulfilled needs through aggressive acts, belligerency, showing off, excessive movie attendance, and other activities.

Through the factor analysis of two sets of questionnaire items previously found to differentiate between delinquents and non-delinquents, Peterson et al. (1959) attempted to determine personality and background factors related to delinquency. The combined questionnaire was administered to 116 delinquents and 113 non-delinquents, matched with respect to age and place of residence. Three personality dimensions and two background factors emerged from this study. The first personality dimension was characterized by a number of psychopathic qualities and was named accordingly. Tough, amoral, rebellious qualities are obviously implied by the factors presented in Table 18-2, which shows the factors with the highest loadings.

TABLE 18-2

Dimension 1: Psychopathy

Factor	Loading
1. The only way to settle anything is to lick the guy.	64
2. Winning a fight is more fun than anything.	62
3. The people that run things are usually against me.	62
4. Cops usually treat you dirty.	61
5. If you don't have enough to live on it's OK to steal.	60
6. A lot of times it's fun to be in jail.	54
7. The only way to make big money is to steal it.	53
8. A person is better off if he doesn't trust anyone.	52
9. If the cops don't like you, they will get you for anything.	51
10. Life usually hands me a pretty raw deal.	48

SOURCE: After Peterson et al. (1959).

In the second personality dimension impulsive antisocial behavior appeared along with expressions of regret, depression, and other negative affects. This dimension, interpreted as a neurotic dimension, bears a close resemblance to the type of delinquent sometimes labeled the "disturbed delinquent." Items in this dimension having the highest loadings are shown in Table 18-3. The third personality dimension is characterized by a sense of incompetence and failure, and is labeled "Inadequacy." The meaning of this dimension is perhaps less clear than that of the others although many delinquents are characterized by a history of failure, which leads to a feeling of inadequacy. The items in this dimension having the highest loadings are shown in Table 18–4.

TABLE 18–3

Dimension 2: Neuroticism

Factor	Loading
1. I often feel that I am not getting anywhere in life.	68
2. Sometimes I used to feel that I would like to leave home.	56
3. I seem to do things that I regret more often than other people do.	56
4. I have often gone against my parents' wishes.	55
5. My parents often disapproved of my friends.	54
6. I sometimes wanted to run away from home.	52
7. I often feel as though I have done something wrong or wicked.	52
8. I don't think I'm quite as happy as others seem to be.	51
9. People often talk about me behind my back.	48
10. With things going as they are, it's pretty hard to keep up hope of amounting to something.	47
11. I would rather go without something than ask for a favor.	44

Source: After Peterson et al. (1959).

TABLE 18–4

Dimension 3: Inadequacy

Factor	Loading
1. I have never been in trouble with the law.	−43*
2. I am behind at least a year in school.	41
3. I'd quit school now if they would let me.	39
4. When I was going to school I played hooky quite often.	38
5. When something goes wrong I usually blame myself rather than the other fellow.	35
6. I hardly ever get excited or thrilled.	34
7. I enjoy work as much as play.	31
8. My folks move (or used to move) from place to place a lot.	30

Source: After Peterson et al. (1959).
* The negative sign indicates that a false response is associated with the positive pole of the factor.

Intellectual Status of Juvenile Delinquents. The notion is still quite prevalent that most juvenile delinquents are of low intelligence. Such a notion stems largely from the negative relationship usually found between school achievement and delinquency. It is also likely that certain interpretations given to intelligence test scores of delinquents have given support to this notion. Glueck and Glueck (1950) reported differences in the components of the intelligence of delinquents and non-delinquents as revealed in the verbal and performance aspects of the *Wechsler-Bellevue Scale*. The delinquents were inferior to the non-delinquents in verbal intelligence while the two groups resembled each other closely in performance intelligence. A distribution of verbal and performance IQ's of the 500 delinquents is shown in Fig. 18–2. The delinquents are more successful in those

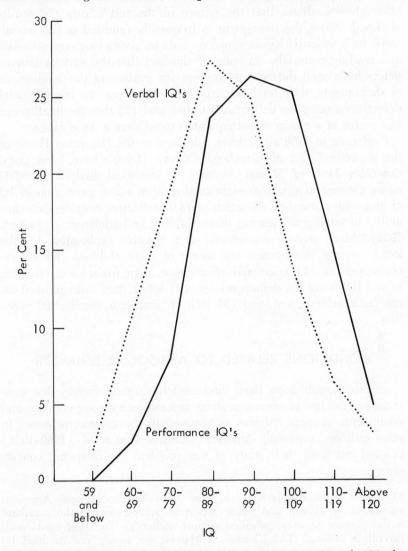

Fig. 18–2. Distribution of verbal and performance IQ's of 500 delinquent boys. (Glueck and Glueck, 1950.)

tasks in which the approach to meaning is direct rather than through symbols. They are generally inferior in vocabulary and information. These findings indicate a source of learning difficulty for them in much of the traditional school program, and no doubt account in a large measure for their retardation in school.

The study by Glueck and Glueck, substantiated by results from other studies, shows that the nature of the test affects the results obtained. Since the delinquent is frequently retarded in his school-work, he is seriously handicapped on tests involving language activities and reading materials. In spite of the fact that the various investigators have used different techniques for evaluating the intelligence of delinquents, they tend to agree (1) that there are many mental defectives among the delinquents tested, and (2) that the intelligence test scores of a group of delinquents extend over a wide range.

Beginning in 1956 all children admitted to the Detention Home of the Juvenile Court of Cuyahoga County (Ohio) have been given the *Ohio Tests of Mental Abilities*. A statistical analysis of 8,003 cases, ranging in age from eight to seventeen years, gave a mean IQ of 91.4 with a standard deviation of 14.0, indicating considerable variability in intelligence among these children and adolescents (Siebert, 1962). Many reasons are offered as a possible explanation for the lower average intelligence test scores of these children and adolescents such as (1) emotional effects that stem from events relating to and following the delinquent act, (2) lower than average need for scholastic achievement, and (3) lack of interest in intellectual activities.

CONDITIONS RELATED TO ANTISOCIAL BEHAVIOR

Anthropologists have been interested in cultural factors that contribute to the low incidence of stress and violence among children and adolescents in some cultures as opposed to the greater incidence in other cultures, especially American culture. Hsu *et al.* (1960–1961) pointed out from their study of this problem the following conclusion:

The most striking difference, in fact, between the Chinese American adolescent in Hawaii and white American adolescents on the mainland is the absence of overt rebellion against authority. The "big fight" with parents is lacking. The Chinese in Hawaii are simply not troubled by adolescent difficulties. Both police files and interviews with parents and social workers suggest that the "problem adolescent," when found, is an exception. [P. 43.]

Parental Attitudes.   There are some who would blame the working mother for most cases of juvenile delinquency. There is, however, no recent evidence to substantiate such a claim. The *quality*
of the parent-child relationship is more important in this connection
than the *quantity*. Children need guidance and supervision in their
development. However, too much supervision at all stages in the
child's development will not permit the child to grow in independence
—the ability to accept responsibility and to practice initiative. At the
ages of ten or eleven most children are satisfied to spend much of
their leisure time with their parents at home. With the onset of
puberty, the wider range of interests, and broadened social activities,
adolescents begin to seek companionship and activities outside the
home. Parents sometimes deplore this condition and fail to realize
the adolescent's need for emancipation from the emotional ties of the
home.

Testing the hypothesis that parental attitudes are closely related to
juvenile delinquency, the Glueck and Glueck (1950) investigated the
kinds of parental discipline employed in the homes of delinquents
and non-delinquents. It was observed that parents of delinquents re-
sorted to punishment and to a lesser extent to reasoning than did the
parents of non-delinquents. It was further noted that mothers of
delinquents were inclined to be lax and erratic in their discipline
while fathers were erratic, lax, and overstrict. Both the mothers and
fathers of non-delinquents displayed firm but kindly measures of discipline (p. 131).

Sometimes the delinquent behavior of the child or adolescent is
reinforced by parents who consciously or unconsciously sanction the
delinquent activity. The case of Jack reported by Baittle (1961)
illustrates this:

An example is Jack, who was a popular member of the group. He was
constantly involved in serious fighting with other boys and was expelled
from school many times. His father frequently boasted of getting into
trouble when he was Jack's age, and refused to recognize the seriousness
of his son's fighting. He felt Jack would straighten out as he himself had.
Moreover, the father felt that Jack could not possibly compete with his
own delinquencies in adolescence, and therefore blinded himself to what
the boy was doing. The mother, although verbalizing wishes to impose
controls on Jack, could not because of her unconscious fear of hurting
him. Unconsciously, she wished the boy to get into trouble and be punished, and he acted this out. [P. 708.]

Glueck and Glueck (1950) have provided a measuring device designed to indicate the possibility of future delinquency in a particular

child. Their instrument is made up of factors having to do with parent-child relationships. The five factors making up the subcategories of the prediction table are shown in Table 18–5.

TABLE 18–5

The Glueck Social Prediction Table

Social Factor	Failure Score
1. Discipline of boy by father	
Overstrict	72.5
Lax	59.8
Firm but kindly	9.3
2. Supervision of boy by mother	
Unsuitable	83.2
Fair	57.5
Suitable	9.9
3. Affection of father for boy	
Indifferent or hostile	75.9
Warm (including overprotective)	33.8
4. Affection of mother for boy	
Indifferent or hostile	86.2
Warm (including overprotective)	43.1
5. Cohesiveness of family	
Unintegrated	96.9
Some elements of cohesion	61.3
Cohesive	20.6

SOURCE: After Glueck and Glueck (1950).

Character and Personality of Parents. A factor closely related to parental attitudes is the character of parents. During early childhood the individual identifies closely with his parents. He not only accepts their behavior as a desired standard of behavior but tends to imitate them. Thus, parents are usually the first and most important teachers whom the child encounters. In a study by Lumpkin (1931) of delinquent girls it was noted that their parental background was very unsatisfactory. Social-defective tendencies such as crime, alcoholism, and sexual irregularities appeared 443 times in 189 families studied.

In the study by Glueck and Glueck (1950) comparisons were made between the parents of delinquents and non-delinquents with respect to physical, mental, and emotional handicaps. Table 18–6 shows that the parents of delinquents are much more burdened with serious physical ailments, mental retardation, emotional disturbances, drunkenness, and criminality than are the parents of non-delinquents. Over 60 per cent of the fathers of delinquents drank to the point of intoxication, as compared with 39 per cent of the fathers of non-delinquents. Seri-

TABLE 18–6

History of Serious Physical Ailments, Mental Retardation, Emotional
Disturbances, Drunkenness, and Criminality of Parents
of Delinquents and Non-Delinquents

Condition	Delinquents		Non-Delinquents		Difference (Per Cent)
	Number	Per Cent	Number	Per Cent	
Mother					
Serious physical ailments	243	48.6	165	33.0	15.6
Mental retardation	164	32.8	45	9.0	23.8
Emotional disturbances	201	40.2	88	17.6	22.6
Drunkenness	115	23.0	35	7.0	16.0
Criminality	224	44.8	75	15.0	29.8
Father					
Serious physical ailments	198	39.6	143	28.6	11.0
Mental retardation	92	18.4	28	5.6	12.8
Emotional disturbances	220	44.0	90	18.0	26.0
Drunkenness	314	62.8	195	39.0	23.8
Criminality	331	66.2	160	32.0	34.2

SOURCE: After Glueck and Glueck (1950).

ous physical ailments, mental retardation, and emotional disturbances
were significantly more in evidence among parents of delinquents than
among parents of non-delinquents.

Family Breakdown and Delinquency. For many years the broken
home has been listed as one of the main causes of juvenile delinquency. To substantiate this claim, many studies of the broken home
has been listed as one of the main causes of juvenile delinquency. To
substantiate this claim, many studies of home backgrounds have been
conducted. Almost without exception these studies show broken
homes in the background of a large percentage of cases. However,
the broken home is, in most cases, the climax of a long series of events
and simply indicates underlying adjustments that affect all members
of the family. There is evidence that it is not the broken home as
much as the factors often associated with this condition, especially
among the lower economic groups. In an early study bearing on this
problem Campbell (1932) showed that it was the tension, neglect,
and poverty accompanying broken home conditions that caused an
increased percentage of delinquency in these groups. Using records
of 604 juvenile delinquents of both sexes, Hirsch (1937) interpreted
the results as showing broken homes a consequence of constitutional

abnormalities and temperamental instabilities of parents rather than a direct contributing factor to delinquency. Many siblings from broken homes are untouched by this factor.

Congested Neighborhoods. The detrimental effects of bad home conditions are usually supplemented by undesirable neighborhood influences. In the first place, congested home conditions are most frequently found in congested neighborhood conditions. Such is the case with the slum areas in some of our cities. It has been noted in various studies that juvenile crime rates are relatively higher in such areas. In Maller's study (1936) of juvenile delinquency in New York City, it was observed that delinquency was generally concentrated in certain underprivileged areas. Such areas are characterized by (1) low rents, (2) low educational levels of the parents, (3) excessive retardation of pupils in school, (4) poor recreational facilities, (5) overcrowded home conditions, (6) high adult crime rate, and (7) lack of organized activities for children and adolescents. These results are similar in nature to results obtained from subsequent studies in other cities.

Delinquents are more frequently found within the lower-class group although petty crimes involving mischief and the destruction of property are frequently found among middle-class children and adolescents with "time on their hands." The individual brought before the courts is often a person rejected or neglected by both his parents and the community. The lower-class delinquent usually does not have the orientation toward developing a regard and respect for attitudes of foresight, self-control, responsible independence, and the developing of initiative for achievement that is found in the middle-class gang; nor does he have the opportunity or the training in the fundamentals of good manners, good taste, and consideration of others found among children and adolescents with more favorable home conditions.

Delinquent Gangs. The gang often furnishes the teen-ager with a pattern of life that satisfies certain basic needs. The child or adolescent who feels unwanted at home or who is unable to identify himself with organized activities at school or elsewhere drifts naturally into a gang. In fact, if a boy lives in a certain neighborhood where gang activities flourish, he is well-nigh forced to join a gang for self-protection. Although gangs are made up largely of boys, it has been pointed out that in New York City three out of four teen-age gang wars are caused by girls (Sundell, 1961). Although these girls are not members of the all-male gangs, they associate with them and are frequently a source of conflict between opposing gangs, leading opposing gang members to commit crimes ranging from misdemeanors to murder. These gang girls are usually sexually promiscuous, truant from school, and violent in their behavior. Many of them are petty thieves, alcoholics, drug addicts, and prostitutes. Some of these transmit venereal disease or give birth to illegitimate children or smuggle deadly weapons and dope to gang members. A broken home, a poor parent-child relationship, a slum neighborhood, lack of recreational facilities —all these factors contribute to the making of a gang girl. Without a favorable adult identification and with a failure to satisfy her psychological needs otherwise, she shifts her allegiance and activities from socially acceptable groups and institutions to those of the gang.

A study of the records of 5,878 boys between the ages of ten and sixteen years contacted on complaint of Detroit police revealed that gang members are more likely to come from "easygoing" homes and low neighborhoods than are non-gang members (Wattenberg and Balistriori, 1950). The gang members were more likely to come from substandard homes and racially mixed neighborhoods, which at the time of the study tended to be less well to do. The non-gang group had a higher proportion of youngsters living in good neighborhoods. Gang activities thrive in neighborhoods where no community provisions have been made for meeting the needs of children and adolescents for achievement, belongingness, and ego enhancement.

The general characteristics and spirit of the neighborhood and community are important factors in the cause and prevention of juvenile delinquency. There is evidence from many sources that organized educational, recreational, and work programs help in the prevention of juvenile delinquency. The need for such programs is borne out in the results of a study by Glueck and Glueck (1950) comparing the play places of delinquents and non-delinquents. The results, presented in Table 18–7, show that 95.2 per cent of the delinquents, as compared with 58.4 per cent of the non-delinquents, hung around street corners while 86.8 per cent of the delinquents, as compared with 14.2 per cent of the non-delinquents, sought their recreation in neighborhoods at a considerable distance. A larger percentage of delinquents than non-delinquents played in vacant lots, on the waterfront, and in railroad yards. On the other hand, a much lower percentage of delinquents spend part of their leisure time at home and on the playgrounds (p. 162).

TABLE 18–7

Comparison of Play Places of Delinquents and Non-Delinquents

Description	Delinquents		Non-Delinquents		Difference (Per Cent)
	Number	Per Cent	Number	Per Cent	
Street corners	476	95.2	292	58.4	36.8
Distant neighborhoods	434	86.8	71	14.2	72.6
Vacant lots	232	46.4	135	27.0	19.4
Waterfronts	152	30.4	79	15.8	14.6
Railroad yards	102	20.4	5	1.0	19.4
Poolrooms, cheap dance halls, etc.	76	15.2	4	0.8	14.4
Home	208	41.6	466	93.2	−51.6
Playgrounds	147	29.4	305	61.0	−31.6

Source: After Glueck and Glueck (1950).

The School. Although the schools are playing an increasingly important role in the training of boys and girls for responsibilities as future citizens, there are certain conditions and practices sometimes maintained that contribute to juvenile delinquency. Some of the major problems listed by teen-agers relate to the school. This stems largely from the fact that school attendance is required of all the boys and girls. Teachers and administrators often attempt to make all of these boys and girls fit a similar mold. The pupil who doesn't get along well in reading or is otherwise not academically inclined frequently finds himself at odds with his teachers and other school personnel. This may lead to truancy which is very often the first step toward juvenile delinquency. Teachers and administrators should concern themselves with the causes of truancy since truancy is closely related to stealing and sex offenses. A study by Williams (1947) showed the importance of truancy in relation to juvenile delinquency. His study was based on the results from 98 cases referred to a clinic during the school year 1944–1945. Truancy, stealing, incorrigibility, and sex misdemeanors were the chief causes for referral of half the cases. There were few cases, however, where one factor alone was noted. Truancy was the chief complaint in 21 cases. Further study of the 98 cases showed that certain conditions seemed to favor truancy. Listed in descending order of frequency, these were: (1) poor parental control, (2) no goal, (3) gangs, (4) pushed against a low IQ, (5) low economic status, with a desire to keep up with peers in style and dress, (6) inability to keep up with the educational program of the class after a severe illness, (7) punishing parents, and (8) dislike of teachers.

Effects of Failure. The problem of individual differences in innate ability, background of experiences, interests, and goals loom large in connection with many problems discussed in earlier chapters. Any interpretation of individual behavior and development must take into consideration these differences. The importance of this is brought forth in a study by Wattenberg (1954) of factors associated with re- peating delinquent acts among preadolescent delinquents. The rec- ords of 90 "repeaters" were compared with those of 235 boys with only one police contact. Repeating delinquencies was found to be closely associated with poor schoolwork, low intellectual ability, membership in unruly gangs, and reputation for trouble. The seriousness of con- tinued school failure is supported by data reported by Zabolski (1949) in which a comparison is made between 50 delinquent boys with a mean age of 15.5 years and a control group of 50 non-delinquent boys. The delinquent boys were characterized by a psychological deficit. Their behavior was attributed to a series of inadequacies or failures. The delinquent boy in this case was attempting to satisfy basic needs not being satisfied at school or elsewhere. Delinquency was for him a positive form of socially unaccepted behavior made in an attempt to satisfy his needs, especially the need to protect and enhance the ego.

PREVENTION AND TREATMENT

An effective prevention program must have for its inception the determination of the causes of delinquency. Methods of prevention will then be based upon these causes. Much could also be done in the prevention and rehabilitation of the young delinquent if he could be located before his delinquent behavior pattern has been completely formed. Concerning the rehabilitation of the delinquent, the effort to make him a useful member of society, Jenkins and Blodgett (1960) state:

The problem of the delinquent presents a challenge to which we have as yet no wholly satisfactory answer. Aside from questions of prevention, we are faced with a problem of reintegrating a young offender with a so- ciety which he may have rejected and which is certainly inclined to reject him. The society will not basically change, and such a reintegration can come about only as the result of a change within the delinquent profound enough to influence the whole course of his behavior. Such a change is not likely to occur as long as his delinquent techniques remain effective. To the delinquent his way of life may be natural and justifiable enough. In general, he must meet an experience sufficiently moving to force him to reorient himself. . . . We must frustrate his delinquent technique without eliciting a frustration stereotype. This creates problems of judgment and control and timing—particularly since we are rarely able to deal with delinquents in isolation. We do find our results in harmony with the idea that one is more likely to be successful through dealing with a delinquent in terms of his interest in himself than through effort expended more directly in teaching moral values. [P. 753.]

Prognosis of Delinquency. Kvaraceus (1961) concludes from his study of the use of predictive instruments for predicting delinquency that: "The behavior ratings of experienced teachers showed more promise than the revised form of the *Kvaraceus Delinquency Proneness Scale*" (p. 434). This finding indicates that future behavior can best be predicted from the behavior activities as observed by teachers and other adults able to make objective observations. It has been often observed that parents are usually unable to make objective observations as noted recently by one of the writers. A college instructor who had just received her doctorate degree related how her son had recently had an automobile accident, doing almost $400 worth of damage to the family car and demolishing an old car parked near the highway. This was his fifth wreck within a period of 12 months and he was at the time of this last wreck on probation. Yet, the mother stated: "My son is a very careful driver. I'm sure he never exceeds the speed limit. He just has hard luck. I always feel safe riding in the car when he is driving."

It was pointed out earlier in this chapter that the delinquent has a low self concept. He also mistrusts others and is unable to accept responsibility. This was noted in a relatively recent study by Jenkins and Blodgett (1960). Using the results of studies conducted with delinquent boys at two schools, they conclude:

At both, increased acceptance of others is an important favorable prognostic sign, and increased rejection or mistrust is an unfavorable sign. Increased assumption of personal responsibility is a favorable prognostic sign and reduced sense of personal responsibility is an unfavorable prognostic sign. Dedifferentiation of responses or developing confusion is an unfavorable prognostic sign. [P. 756.]

The Home. Since the home seems to be the focal point in the development of antisocial forms of behavior, an effective prevention and treatment program should consider the home. Just as the present trend in psychiatric treatment of a member of a family includes other members of the family, so should a remedial program for a delinquent child include other members of his family, especially the father and mother. This is clearly implied in the results of a study reported by Wilson (1962).

The patterns of living of 52 problem families were selected by Wilson for study on the basis of performance-inadequacy. The most disabling feature of the problem family noted in this study is its social isolation. Delinquency is part of the behavior pattern of the child in which there seems to be a complete lack of awareness of the moral significance of his actions. This is noted particularly among families exhibiting child neglect, with the main factors dominating the children's lives being poverty and weak relations with their parents and other adults. If parents can be brought to see the ill effects of neglect, many would be motivated to respond differently toward their children.

This does not mean that parents should practice overprotection or indulgence. The role of consistent discipline in child development is important. However, the nature of the discipline and the spirit in which it is administered will largely determine its effectiveness.

The Neighborhood. A large proportion of delinquency has its origins in the streetcorner subculture of lower-class society. Kvaraceus (1959) points out that we should take a close look at the forces in this milieu that tend to generate norm-violating behavior for a large segment of the delinquent population. The lower-class culture, referred to throughout this chapter, indicates a particular way of life and is followed by a large percentage of our population, especially in large urban areas. Their values, characteristics, concerns, and pattern of behavior are the product of a well-formed culture system. Juvenile delinquents frequently emerge from such a cultural pattern. They are children and adolescents with problems. Almost all of the difficulties each encounters can be traced directly to his attempts to adhere to forms of behavior and to achieve standards and values as they are defined in his or her gang. Kvaraceus (pp. 15–16) describes three general processes by means of which this culture milieu contributes to the youngster's involvement in delinquent behavior. These are:

1. The youngster can engage "in certain cultural practices which comprise essential elements of the total life pattern of lower-class culture" and "automatically" violate "certain legal norms."
2. ". . . in some instances where alternative avenues to valued objectives are available to the youngster, the law-violating route frequently entails a relatively smaller investment of energy and effort than the law-abiding route."

3. ". . . the *demanded* response to certain situations recurrently engendered within lower-class culture may call for the commission of illegal acts."

Adjustment to streetcorner living is not easy. Members of lower-class streetcorner groups frequently possess stamina, physical fitness, and the capacity to interact and to subordinate their own selfish desires to the over-all needs of the group to a greater degree than youngsters from more privileged neighborhoods. These qualities, when directed toward constructive and socially acceptable goals, are important ingredients for success in school, in community activities, and on the job as a useful citizen. In the case of the middle-class boy similar skills and drives are often directed toward the Eagle Scout Badge or 4-H Club awards. It is these motives and qualities of the lower-class boys and girls that need to be channeled into law-abiding activities and that can eventually develop a good, productive citizen who will assume a responsible role in the adult world of tomorrow.

The School and Juvenile Delinquency. According to Kvaraceus (1958), many youngsters who are given the delinquency label are not true delinquents. He describes the school delinquents as being educationally bankrupt: their report cards show marginal or failure marks; they tend to be average or below average for their grade; their attitudes toward school are heavily charged with hate and hostility; they change school frequently; truancy is frequent or habituated; leaving school as soon as the law will allow is the rule; they seem to enjoy little feeling of belonging to the classroom; "book learning" as such is likely to be frowned upon; they very rarely participate in volunteer extracurricular activities; they tend to play the bully role on the playground; and they frequently take their frustrations out on school property.

Seven factors are listed by Kvaraceus (1958) that would act and react in positive and negative fashion to spark antisocial aggression and delinquency. These are as follows:

1. *Good schools must maintain and enforce ordered patterns of living in the daily experiences which they provide all children.* Most delinquents come from homes and neighborhoods which are singularly devoid of any patterns of systematic living.

2. *The good school demands self-denial, self-control, self-restraint, and a focus on distant goals.* The delinquent personality structure reveals an infantile self-indulging, here-and-now makeup operating on a strong pleasure principle, allergic to the hard work and continuous-effort principles implicit in the learning process.

3. *The good school presents the face of a benign authority figure.* The delinquent's concept of authority is generally on the negative side in view of the emotional damage and deprivation which he has often suffered at the hands of the inconsistent, disloyal, betraying, and rejecting authority figures which often frequent his preschool life.

4. *The good school tries to retain all youngsters in their school program even after they reach the age of school-leaving.* The delinquent child intends to drop out of school and does so at the earliest opportunity, thus conveying his true feelings and estimate of the school's worth.

5. *The good school remains always the bastion of the virtues of fair play, honesty, cleanliness, and good and clean speech.* The delinquent's value system rates these virtues as weaknesses and finds greater prestige in swearing, stealing, and sex play—all anathema to the school.

6. *The school places a high priority and prestige on abilities to verbalize and abstract which find best expression through the academic phase of the curriculum.* The delinquent more often than not is lacking in the quality of abilities and interests he can bring to bear on the academic program.

7. *The good school must remain a center for learning and teaching and avoid becoming a community convenience for the emotionally disturbed and socially maladjusted.* Many true delinquents, when appraised emotionally, are found to be sick and are more in the need of therapy than instruction. In a sense, many true delinquents are sitting in the wrong institution. [Pp. 14–15.]

The Classroom Teacher. The delinquent must have some one reliable and important adult with whom he can identify himself. This may be a Scout leader, a religious leader, a club leader, the coach at school, or some other adult in a position of leadership. In some cases this might be a classroom teacher although the usual role of the classroom teacher would be supportive. Darling (1963) has offered a good description of attitudes necessary on the part of the classroom teacher if he is to carry out this supportive role.

(1) *Draw a circle and take him (or her) in.* This is sometimes difficult. It requires personal maturity on the part of the teacher; however, the teacher cannot bring about desirable change in another person, no matter how eloquent the teacher may be, if he cannot communicate with that person. There is no communication with a child who has been isolated emotionally.

.   .   .   .

Psychologically, the adolescent youngster is almost entirely shaped by his heredity and environment. He has done little independent thinking or living as yet. Like the old revivalist who saw the drunkard in the gutter, it could well be said of the delinquent, "There but for the grace of God, am I." None of us chooses our parents or our childhood environment.

Most teachers are from stable families. Most aggressive or delinquent youngsters are from unstable families. Teachers must continually remind themselves that not all people live in stable, middle-class homes. School people dare not judge others on the basis of their own limited experiences.

Our Judeo-Christian tradition teaches that we are all made of the same stuff and that each person is of priceless value. No matter how a person appears, he is of inestimable value in the scheme of things and entitled to the same consideration as are we ourselves. There is every practical, psychological, and philosophical reason to "draw a circle and take him in"; yet as immature human beings we sometimes fail. Emotional acceptance is the first step in helping a person who has problems. Without this step no results can ensue.

(2) *Expect the best.* Expectations as well as emotional acceptances or nonacceptances are apparent. Like the proverbial slip, expectations show when least anticipated. Children read us like books and our every personality flaw basks in an exposed light. This is teaching!

Someone has said that only an optimist should teach. Expectations, whether negative or positive, are catching. These expectations should be working for the teacher and his youngsters. The teacher's sights must be focused on the potentiality of each individual. Paul in his beautiful essay on love writes that love "hopeth all things." The good teacher "hopeth all things."

.   .   .   .

(3) *Build up his self-concept.* Adolescents with problems almost uniformly have low estimates of themselves. They are at odds with their environment and basically blame themselves, protecting their inner selves with layers of rationalizations. These layers themselves are disagreeable things and are repugnant to others and cause those in authority and others to increase the feeling of failure by expressions of criticism. Thus an ever deepening cycle of self-depreciation, hostility, and withdrawal or aggression is set up.

How is such a cycle to be broken? Some techniques which have been successfully used in interrupting the cycle are:

(*a*) Seizing upon every favorable characteristic or action, recognizing this, and reinforcing it with praise or acceptance.

(*b*) Setting up opportunities for small successes and indicating approval of these successes.

(*c*) Paying no attention to failures in matters that are not overpoweringly important.

(*d*) When discipline or criticism is necessary, couching it in terms of criticism of the act—never of the person. . . . The labeling of a person as "stupid," "unthinking," "selfish," or "lazy," at once isolates that person emotionally and starts again the cycle of self-depreciation and hostility. What school person has not been extremely remorseful at times after having done this very thing as a result of being sorely tried.

(4) *Establish reasonable but clearly defined limits.* "My folks don't care when I get in. They don't care enough about me even to tell me what to do," a so-called delinquent once complained. All are entitled to the security of limits. Most delinquents have not had this security at home either because the parents have not cared or because the parents lacked the will and consistency to hold limits.

Teachers can help bring some order to the delinquent by holding to reasonable limits. School people need from time to time to re-examine their established limits, asking themselves "Have we set limits on the really important things or on picayune matters?"

Indeed, youngsters with problems will step over the limits at times, but the resultant discipline should be directed at the act, not the person. A limit is a restriction. It is likewise an indication that someone cares. If the child feels emotional acceptance, the chance of his working successfully within reasonable limits is greatly enhanced.

(5) *Be a people watcher.* There is so much to learn about how people grow, what makes them tick, how personality develops, and how it may be warped, that this can be a lifelong hobby—in fact, should be a lifelong hobby for the teacher.

To avoid having the same experiences over and over, teachers need to have contact with minds that are especially penetrating. All school people need to learn from those who they feel are especially successful in working with youngsters; and they need personally to observe the human animal under a variety of conditions. To do this, it is necessary to get out of the classroom and see youngsters live at home and at play and under all conditions. . . .

(6) *Remember that Rome was not built in a day.* The student who has serious problems has probably taken much time in acquiring them. . . . School personnel must push for progress but should also take the long view when efforts are not immediately or initially met with large success. Progress in personality development is usually marked by a series of small and faltering progressions. . . . [Pp. 484–86.]

The best effects can be expected when there is a team approach to the study of the delinquent. This is brought forth in the observations of Daniels (1960). When the psychiatrists work closely with the teachers, counselors, and others concerned with the education of junior high school boys and girls, positive results in the prevention and treatment of preadolescent delinquency can be expected.

SUMMARY

The delinquent child or adolescent does not represent a unique type although his behavior is characterized by aggressiveness, self-indulgence, and rebelliousness. Delinquent behavior may be regarded as sypmtomatic of a great variety of conditions. Three psychological types of delinquents were described in this chapter: (1) the relatively integrated delinquent, (2) the delinquent with markedly weak ego control, and (3) the delinquent with relatively defective superego control.

The personality structure of the delinquent is often an adjustive reaction resulting from failure to satisfy his needs through socially acceptable channels. A consideration of the types of delinquents presented in this chapter in the light of forces closely associated with delinquency might lead to a better clarification of how certain syndromes or patterns of factors may operate to produce a certain delinquent. Maladjustments alone do not cause delinquency; psychoneurotic tendencies alone do not cause delinquency; inferior intelligence alone does not cause delinquency. Delinquent children differ from non-delinquents in a number of significant ways. One of the outstanding differences is in the history of failure for a large percentage of delinquents. They are often educationally retarded in school, or are not accepted by their classmates, or are underprivileged in the community.

The needs of the delinquent are not different from the needs of non-delinquents. Delinquent behavior is fostered by an atmosphere of insecurity and rejection. It might be stated as a fundamental principle that every child has the potential of becoming a delinquent. The group of children classed as delinquent comes from all races, creeds, and social classes. The school is the one social institution that has contact with all of these children. It is in a strategic position to meet this problem, and teachers show much ability in the prognosis of delinquency.

The delinquent has a low self concept. The classroom teacher and other leaders of youth must be concerned with the background, problems, and needs of teen-agers. They must be cognizant of conditions that lead to delinquency and to methods useful in the prevention of delinquent behavior acts. In many cases, however, their role must be a supportive role. The best results can be expected when there is a team approach by all the agencies concerned with the education and guidance of teen-agers.

CHAPTER REFERENCES

ATCHESON, J. D., and WILLIAMS, D. C. (1954). A study of juvenile sex offenders. *Amer. J. Psychiat.*, 111:366–70.

BAITTLE, B. (1961). Psychiatric aspects of the development of a street corner group: an exploratory study. *Amer. J. Orthopsychiat.*, 31:703–12.

BENDER, LAURETTA (1947). Psychopathic behavior in children. In R. M. LINDER and R. V. SELIGER (eds.), *Handbook of correctional psychology.* New York: Philosophical Library.

BENNETT, IVY (1960). *Delinquents and neurotic children: a comparative study with one hundred case histories.* New York: Basic Books.

BLAKE, MARY (1958). *Youth groups in conflict.* U.S. Department of Health, Education, and Welfare, Social Security Administration, Children's Bureau. Washington, D.C.: U.S. Government Printing Office.

CAMPBELL, M. W. (1932). The effect of the broken home upon the child in school. *J. educ. Sociol.,* 5:274–81.

CLECKLEY, H. (1950). *The mask of sanity.* St. Louis, Mo.: C. V. Mosby.

COHEN, A. K. (1957). Sociological research in juvenile delinquency. *Amer. J. Orthopsychiat.,* 27:781–88.

DANIELS, E. M. (1960). Psychiatrists in the school. *J. nat. Educ. Assn.,* March, 49:11–12.

DARLING, G. H. (1963). The delinquent in the school. *Clearing House,* 37:483–86.

DONET, L. (1951). *Psychiatric aspects of juvenile delinquency.* World Health Series, Monograph Series No. 2. Geneva: World Health Organization.

GLUECK, S., and GLUECK, ELEANOR (1950). *Unraveling juvenile delinquency.* Cambridge, Mass.: Harvard Univer. Press.

HEALY, W., and BRONNER, A. P. (1936). *New light on delinquency and its treatment.* New Haven, Conn.: Yale Univer. Press. Pp. 73–78.

HEWITT, E., and JENKINS, R. L. (1941). Case studies of aggressive delinquents. *Amer. J. Orthopsychiat.,* 11:485–92.

HIRSCH, N. D. M. (1937). *Dynamic causes of juvenile crime.* Cambridge, Mass.: Sci-Art.

HSU, F. L. K., WATROUS, BLANCHE G., and LORD, EDITH M. (1960–1961). Culture pattern and adolescent behavior. *Int. J. soc. Psychiat.,* 7:3–53.

JENKINS, R. L., and BLODGETT, EVA (1960). Prediction of success or failure of delinquent boys from sentence completion. *Amer. J. Orthopsychiat.,* 30:741–56.

JOHNSON, ADELAIDE M. (1955). Individual antisocial behavior. *Amer. J. Dis. Child.,* 89:472–75.

KVARACEUS, W. C. (1958). *Juvenile delinquency.* Washington, D.C.: Department of Classroom Teachers, National Education Association.

KVARACEUS, W. C. (1959). Culture and the delinquent. *NEA J.,* 48:14–16.

KVARACEUS, W. C. (1961). Forecasting delinquency, a three-year experiment. *Except. Child.,* 27:429–35.

LIVELY, E. L., DINITZ, S., and RECKLESS, W. C. (1962). Self concept as a predictor of juvenile delinquency. *Amer. J. Orthopsychiat.,* 32:159–68.

LUMPKIN, K. D. (1931). Factors in the commitment of correctional school girls in Wisconsin. *Amer. J. Sociol.,* 37:222–30.

MALLER, J. B. (1936). Juvenile delinquency in New York City. *J. Psychol.,* 39:314–28.

MEYER, W. J., and THOMPSON, G. G. (1956). Sex differences in the distribution of teacher approval and disapproval among sixth grade children. *J. educ. Psychol.*, 47:385–96.

MILLER, W. B., GEERTZ, H., and CUTTER, H. S. (1961). Aggression in a boys' street corner group. *Psychiatry*, 24:283–98.

O'KELLY, ELIZABETH (1955). Some observations on relationships between delinquent girls and their parents. *Brit. J. med. Psychol.*, 28:59–66.

PETERSON, D. R., QUAY, H. C., and CAMERON, G. R. (1959). Personality and background factors in juvenile delinquency as inferred from questionnaire responses. *J. consult. Psychol.*, 23:395–99.

RECKLESS, W. C., DINITZ, S., and KAY, BARBARA (1957). The self component in potential delinquency and potential non-delinquency. *Amer. sociol. Rev.*, 22:566–70.

REISS, A. J. (1952). Social correlates of psychological types of delinquency. *Amer. J. Sociol.*, 17:710–18.

RESNICK, J. (1956). Why antisocial children? *Educ. Form*, 21:101–4.

SHIPPEE-BLUM, EVA M. (1959). The young rebel self-regard and ego-ideal. *J. consult. Psychol.*, 23:44–50.

SIEBERT, L. A. (1962). Otis IQ scores of delinquents. *J. clin. Psychol.*, 18:517.

SUNDELL, A. (1961). Report of the gang girl. *Amer. Girl, special ed.*, May, p. 44.

TOPPING, RUTH (1941). Case studies of aggressive delinquents. *Amer. J. Orthopsychiat.*, 11:485–92.

U.S. DEPARTMENT OF HEALTH, EDUCATION, AND WELFARE (1962). *Juvenile court statistics—1961.* Children's Bureau Statistical Series, No. 69. Washington, D.C.: U.S. Government Printing Office.

WATTENBERG, W. W. (1954). Factors associated with repeating among preadolescent delinquents. *J. genet. Psychol.*, 84:189–95.

WATTENBERG, W. W., and BALISTRIORI, J. J. (1950). Gang membership and juvenile misconduct. *Amer. sociol. Rev.*, 15:744–52.

WILLIAMS, E. Y. (1947). Truancy in children referred to a clinic. *Ment. Hyg., N.Y.*, 31:464–69.

WILSON, HARRIET (1962). *Delinquency and child neglect.* London: George Allen & Unwin.

ZABOLSKI, F. C. (1949). Studies in delinquency: personality structure of delinquent boys. *J. genet. Psychol.*, 74:109–17.

SELECTED READINGS

COHEN, A. K. (1955). *Delinquent boys: the culture of the gang.* Glencoe, Ill.: Free Press.

GARRISON, K. C. (1965). *Psychology of adolescence.* (6th ed.) Englewood Cliffs, N.J.: Prentice-Hall. Chap. 18.

GLUECK, S., and GLUECK, ELEANOR (1962). *Family environment and delinquency.* Boston: Houghton Mifflin.

KVARACEUS, W. C. (1954). *The community and the delinquent.* Yonkers, N.Y.: World Book Co.

KVARACEUS, W. C. (1962). Delinquent international-ambivalent obsession. *NEA J.,* 51:22–24.

MAYS, J. B. (1955). *Growing up in the city.* Liverpool, England: Univer. Press of Liverpool.

MICHAELS, J. F. (1955). *Disorders of character.* Springfield, Ill.: Charles C Thomas.

ROUCEK, J. S. (ed.) (1958). *Juvenile delinquency.* New York: Doubleday.

WILSON, HARRIET (1962). *Delinquency and child neglect.* London: George Allen & Unwin.

19

EDUCATING DISTURBED AND/OR MALADJUSTED CHILDREN

The often quoted statement that "all men are created equal" is a political axiom expressing our belief in social justice; it is not an expression of a scientific truth. The fact is that all human beings are both like and unlike each other. This may seem to be a paradox. It was, however, pointed out in Chapter 1 that the human race is structured in accordance with a pattern involving many similarities. It was also pointed out that vast differences may be observed within any group, even a group that is characterized as emotionally disturbed.

The classic method of teaching that has been handed down historically is group instruction, based upon assumed similarities of the individuals making up the particular class or group. Increased knowledge of individual differences has brought forth a realization that learning is a highly individual matter and that individualized service must be provided if the maximum results are to be obtained. Thus, it is becoming more and more clear that group instruction and individual help and guidance are indispensable and complementary methods in the educational process.

Educational Goals of Emotionally Disturbed Children. Not only do emotionally disturbed children differ, but there are also differences and similarities in the educational goals set up for them. Theoretically the end goals for emotionally disturbed children are the same as those for normal children. There are, however, certain immediate practical goals that the teacher of emotionally disturbed children must bear in mind. These are basically somewhat prerequisite to the long-range goals to be achieved. These goals have been described by Lavietes (1962) as follows:

1. Making the child feel adequate, hopeful, and unafraid in the group teaching experience through
   a) undoing distortions in interpersonal relationships by means of the teacher's behavior toward the child;
   b) reducing anxiety in the child through the reduction of inappropriate expectations from him;
   c) presenting benign social reality to a child who has experienced distortions in reality perceptions in the past or who has withdrawn from adapting to reality;
   d) overcoming resistance to learning through stress on nonpainful, nondangerous, pleasurable, ego-building aspects of learning.
2. Substitution of mutual aid (cooperation, sharing, awareness of others' needs) for competition and suspicion of others. [P. 856.]

These additional and more immediate goals set forth as prerequisite to goals for normal children have certain technical implications. These are set forth in Table 19–1. It should be pointed out that there is not necessarily a higher value on the items in Column B than on those in Column A. Rather, the emphasis in Column B grows from the goals for the teaching of disturbed children. It is perhaps the planned aspect of Column B with emphasis upon smaller classes and individual instruction that should be stressed.

BASIC PRINCIPLES

There are certain basic principles that all people concerned with education and treatment of emotionally disturbed children should understand. Parents and teachers in particular should be aware of these principles in their dealings with emotionally disturbed children. Some of these principles are set forth in the following discussions (Newman, 1961).

The Emotionally Disturbed Child Can Learn. The emotionally disturbed child has already learned many unfortunate and unhappy

TABLE 19–1

Technical Implications of Educational Goals for Normal and
Emotionally Disturbed Children

Column A	Column B
Technical Implications of Goals for Normal Children	Technical Implications of Goals for Disturbed Children
1. Larger classes	1. Smaller classes
2. Group process always dominant over individual process	2. Individual process dominant over group most of the time
3. Emphasis on content, curriculum, materials	3. Emphasis on child's feeling about self, group, teacher, and learning process
4. Expectation of verbal and motor control	4. Tolerance of verbal and motor discharge
5. Personality of teacher less significant to process	5. Personality of teacher strong influence in achievement of goals
6. Teaching techniques designed for average child	6. Teaching techniques devised on individual basis using knowledge of child
7. Expectations usually held higher than performance and geared to group	7. Expectations usually held to level of performance and variable with each child
8. Use of pressure, reproach, guilt, and competition in stimulating conformity. Goal of learning justifies means to it	8. Avoidance of such methods. Means of learning are a large part of the goal
9. Distance and formality of relationship between teacher and child	9. Closeness and informality of relationship; more physical closeness unless contraindicated
10. Displays of achievement by chronological age standards	10. Recognition of achievements suitable to capacities
11. Teacher's relationship to parent haphazard, mostly decided by individual teacher	11. Teacher's relationship to parent calculated for benefit of child, decided clinically
12. Thinking dominated by survival of the fittest with exclusion of the deviant	12. Survival of all is dominant. Tolerance of the deviant
13. Standard equipment, room design, furniture with displays, etc. designed for average children and augmented by individual teacher	13. Planned room size, furniture, displays, etc., with effect on child as basis for arrangements
14. Teacher has clerical responsibility during class	14. Teacher must be free of clerical responsibility when with children

SOURCE: Lavietes (1962).

things that interfere with what society would have him more preferably do.

What we would like him to learn cannot be learned without the presence of a complex of factors; factors involving such things as the mental health of his parents, or at least one parent, of his and his parents' physiological health, their economic and physical situations, their conflicts and concerns, their needs and deprivations, their manner of handling life and the manner in which life has handled them, their constitutional make-up, and their economic and cultural opportunities. In any event, these children have not had the climate to teach them what we would like them to learn. . . . In accordance with the human organism's adaptive ability, these children have learned what life has taught them about people, objects, danger, helplessness, terror, and survival. [Newman, 1961, p. 201.]

Extinction of Old Patterns. The extinction of old patterns of behavior, even in the simpler instances of lower animals, is never as simple as that of establishing behavior patterns in the growing child who has not developed unfortunate or undesirable patterns of behavior.

For indeed the behavior patterns that these children [*emotionally disturbed children*] have developed for themselves, be it intense withdrawal into a world of their own making or hostile attack, or diffuse, ill-coordinated stabs at the environment, have been the only way they have had to deal with the problems that beset them. To relinquish these tools for survival, regardless of how uneconomical, how unhappy, how inappropriate and self-defeating they may be, simply because we ask them to do so, is an absurd simplification of human processes. [Newman, 1961, p. 201.]

The extinction of old patterns of behavior requires first of all motivation on the part of the learner. The question may well be raised: Will the new patterns of behavior better serve his needs than the old patterns? The relinquishing of old patterns of behavior in favor of new ones may seem quite ridiculous and unrewarding to the emotionally disturbed child.

Demonstration of New Patterns. In the re-education process Hobbs (1963) emphasizes that we assume that the individual has acquired bad habits. He states further: "We assume that he has learned to construe the world in such a way that his world must reject him, and that he has acquired specific ways of coping that are immediately rewarding but ultimately defeating. The task of reeducation is to help the child learn new and more effective ways of construing himself and his world and to learn habits that lead to more effective functioning" (p. 5).

Newman (1961) has emphasized the need to demonstrate to the emotionally disturbed child over and over again that his old learnings are not valid in the situation at school, that old behavior patterns only lead to trouble for him. Adults in the child's world need to demonstrate that the school-world is not hostile to him, even though much of the world outside the school may appear to be hostile and untrustworthy. He needs to be taught through experiences at the school that he is capable of achieving, and that he is accepted by his teachers and other adults at school. The emotionally disturbed child needs to be guided in facing reality and to see from demonstrated experiences that he can develop skills that are useful to him in meeting life problems and at the same time maintain respect and love of peers and adults.

Reinforcement of New Learning. Until the emotionally disturbed child is able to see that old behavior patterns are unrealistic and frequently useless to him in his efforts to meet daily problems, the problem of extinguishing old behavior patterns will not be met; neither will new learnings be securely established. Reinforcement of new learnings takes place best when the child finds that the new learnings are in the end rewarding, that they elicit the support and love of his parents, teachers, and other adult figures. This may call for a system of guides for behavior with immediate reward and punishment administered again and again. Concerning these guides or rules, Quay (1963) states: "These positive and negative reinforcers may have to be rather rudimentary in the beginning (e.g., physical restraint and isolation) but at the same time a determined effort should be made to pair them with the more verbal social reinforcers to which the child must eventually learn to respond" (p. 30).

School Is a Place Where Gratification Exists. The activities of the school must convey to the child the recognition that gratifications exist here. Concerning the timing of such gratifications, Newman (1961) states:

At first the gratifications must come immediately in the wake of the task. Later the interval between the problem and its fulfillment can be lengthened out. At first the task must bring with it success, no matter how easy the job. Later the success can be postponed. Some errors can be encompassed on the way to success, some snags met and handled. Part of the reward of tolerating frustration need not be verbalized; it just happens that the subject matter becomes more interesting and involving as more frustrations can be tolerated. [P. 202.]

The timing of activities must depend largely upon the insight of the teacher or other adults concerned. If the interval is too long the child may become contemptuous of his teacher as well as of himself.

School Is a Place with a Predictable Environment. This calls for the existence of structure. The child must learn that the school exists for a purpose, that certain things are done at school, that the teacher has certain responsibilities, and that certain things are expected of him (the child). The school is a place where the child can live and maintain his ego and integrity; it is also a place where certain things are done at a given time and in accordance with certain structured patterns.

School Is a Place Where Help Is Available. The school should be a place where the child's personal interests can be explored and his potential developed. The environment should be such that his personal needs are satisfied, and guidance is available from understanding teachers. Such help and guidance from teachers and others should be constructive and designed according to structured patterns set forth by the objectives and procedures of the school. However, if the child comes to regard the school as a place where his efforts are rewarding and where he can be guided and helped in doing certain tasks and in learning new tasks, he will no longer regard the school as a place "where he is sent."

Timing in Reference to Props. The young disturbed child may feel insecure without some of his toys or other familiar objects during the first days at school. The disturbed child in a new school will feel most insecure in the presence of things, conditions, and people that are entirely unfamiliar to him. The need for props in the form of familiar objects, friends, or books should be recognized by the teacher. After a time, when the reality has come through that the school is not necessarily a terrifying place but instead a place where he can learn new tasks and where he can get help in learning, these props will no longer be needed.

Timing in Reference to Self Concept. The child brings his past to school with him. This includes his self concept. For a while the teacher may deem it necessary for him to continue this self concept. But, to continue this too long is to convey the notion that this is an acceptable self concept or that the school is not concerned about the kind of self concept he has. The child's self concept may be that of a "bully" or a vile person. The teacher is faced with the problem of how far to allow him to maintain such a self concept. Group reaction to overt aggressiveness may help the child in breaking down an undesirable self concept. The child's self concept tends to change in harmony with his learning that certain reactions lead to disapproval of his peers and teachers. The importance of *protecting the ego* while developing a changed self concept should be recognized by the teacher. When the child learns that he cannot change the school, but must accept certain regulations and conditions, important changes are likely to occur in his self concept.

Expect Backsliding. Finally, the message that the school is different from what the child expected begins to break through. He is somewhat upset by this new perception; it calls for a reorientation of much of his thinking and behavior. Until his old habit patterns are replaced by changed habit patterns, he will continue to try certain "old tricks" at times. His behavior may appear to be in the "old patterns," but actually the tone of it has changed. Teachers and others are usually able to recognize that changes have taken place and that this reversion at times during the early stages of his relearnings is frequently to be expected.

Enter: Reality About the Self. Children are in school to explore themselves and to develop their potentials. The school helps the child more accurately to define himself and to understand his capabilities and limitations. He learns that he cannot always win, that he is inferior in certain abilities while good or perhaps superior in others. His grandiose ideas about the self is challenged in the schoolroom and on the playground. The child needs to be guided in the development of a realistic concept of the self and at the same time in the protection of his ego. The task of the teacher is to guide the child in the development and realization of worthwhile and realistic goals. This means that the child must be brought to understand better himself in relation to the tasks at school and elsewhere.

Enter: Reality About the Teacher. Much of the success of the educational program for emotionally disturbed children depends upon the ability and skill of the teacher to establish with the pupil a mutually perceived climate of understanding and trust. Most emotionally disturbed children display lack of self-control and inability to get along with age mates. The teacher must frequently provide a group situation structured for learning desired ways of behaving. Hollister and Goldston (1962) state:

She needs to use her understanding of individual and group functioning to lessen and prevent maladaptive behavior that interferes with relationships, group productivity, and individual learning. The procedures include structuring expected behaviors, use of peer controls, group-wide guidance methods, control of group misbehavior, and methods for coping with poor individual behavior. [P. 354.]

The teacher of the emotionally disturbed child directs his efforts toward helping the child overcome undesirable attitudes and habits and build up favorable self concepts. The child's image of the teacher is modified as a result of satisfying relations experienced in the classroom. His image of the teacher has an important bearing on his behavior at school and carries over into his relationship with others at school and elsewhere.

THE DISTURBED CHILD IN THE CLASSROOM

The presence of an emotionally disturbed child in the classroom raises the tension level of a group. Thus, the members of the group tend to avoid the emotionally disturbed child, isolating him from the group. Such isolation makes for social distance, and may be observed in the interaction between the disturbed child and his social environment. Such interchanges are characterized by formality, hostility, extreme politeness, failure to maintain contact, or rudeness. The group may sometimes pity the emotionally disturbed child and display a protective attitude. Such behavior is an acknowledgment of the group's feelings toward the child and contributes to his isolation from the group.

The Teacher. Tallman and Levine (1960) list three questions the teacher should attempt to answer in evaluating the existence and extent of a child's emotional disturbance. "Is the child's behavior appropriate in terms of his goals and aspirations? Does the child have the ability to live with some tolerance and respect for himself? Finally, does the child deal with his environment in an effective manner?" (P. 125.)

The disturbed child, because of his life experiences, is not able to function in an integrated manner. His behavior is described by Tallman and Levine (1960) as follows:

(a) Rigid, stereotyped, vacillating or inconsistent attitudes and actions which lack purposefulness and goal direction; indications of anxiety manifested by tension, withdrawal, nervousness, and irascibility which interfere with the child's experiencing personal satisfaction; (c) indications that the child sees his situation somewhat differently than others around him, so that he is not able to recognize what is expected of him in his immediate environment. [P. 126.]

The emotionally disturbed child presents a challenge to the teacher. Concerning this, Tallman and Levine state:

The need of the disturbed child for close personal attention and for an intensive relationship may come into conflict with the necessity for getting across a prescribed body of knowledge to the entire class. If the teacher over-emphasizes his one-to-one relationship with the disturbed child, it may be detrimental to his relationship with the group. The classroom structure, in general, is established for the purpose of group learning and the children may be confused and distracted by an intensive relationship between the teacher and one child. [P. 115.]

Classroom Organization.   One of the most important and practical matters faced by the school administrator in dealing with any group of exceptional children is whether or not the cost of special classes and programs can be justified. Usually special classes add to the cost of the total school program. The question then involves whether or not children in special classes show more improvement or greater educational growth than children in regular classes.

Three educational methods of handling classes for emotionally disturbed children were subjected to experimentation by Haring and Phillips (1962). The children in the study were moderately to severely emotionally disturbed. Their emotional characteristics were reflected in a wide range of behavior symptoms. Three groups of children were used in the study. Group I is described as a structured special class. Children were assigned work on the basis of intellectual and achievement tests and on the basis of information in each child's personal file. They were held to the completion of assigned work before play or recreation opportunities were available. The children of Group II were in regular classrooms in six elementary schools. The teachers used methods of teaching emotionally disturbed children generally employed in a regular classroom setting. The following considerations were uppermost in the practices of teachers in Group II:

1. All assigned work was well within the child's ability.
2. Wherever possible, the school work was modified to suit the child's interest.
3. The child was given experience in which he could find success.
4. The child was given opportunities to find accomplishments and recognition.

5. Extra privileges and responsibilities were provided in order to give the child attention.

6. Punitive responses to the child's aggressive, rebellious behavior were avoided by the teachers. [Pp. 72–73.]

The children of Group III were assigned to a special class. The group is referred to as the permissive group. The following teaching methods, classroom environment, and program comprised the educational setting for this group:

1. The curriculum was modified to suit the interests of the children.

2. The teacher reflected friendliness and warmth with the children.

3. An atmosphere of relative permissiveness was established, so that the children felt free to express their feelings and anxiety.

4. The teacher recognized the children's feelings and reflected these feelings back to them.

5. When limits were set, the teacher still made sure that the children's feelings were accepted and reflected back.

6. The teacher believed in the importance of meeting the real emotional needs of the child, not only the material, academic needs. [P. 73.]

Before and after tests were administered to the three groups in the first year of the program. The modifications of behavior and academic achievements of the three groups were then compared. The gain in achievement of the special-class groups surpassed that of the regular-class group. The pre- and posttesting results on behavior ratings are presented in Fig. 19–1. In general it appears that both in academic achievement and behavior adjustment the child who was placed in the structured special class made the greatest gain. It may be argued that these are overt changes and that the emotionally disturbed child still may have within him the disturbed feelings, fears, and anxieties, which must be resolved before there can be fundamental changes in his behavioral adjustments. It is not possible to evaluate these inner emotional states from the data here presented. However, the results of this study do show that special classes for emotionally disturbed children, staffed with competent teachers who have an understanding of the problems of such children, can be educationally productive. Haring and Phillips conclude: "A structured classroom is one in which clear direction, firm expectations, and consistent follow-through are paramount; this is presumably a healthy state of affairs for normal children, as well as necessary for optimal growth of emotionally disturbed children" (p. 80).

Anxiety and Learning. An investigation by Palermo *et al.* (1956) was concerned with attempting to determine the relationship of anxi-

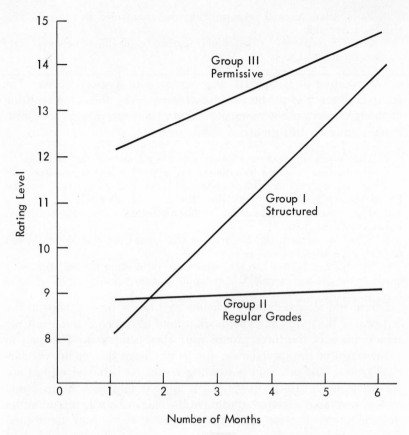

Fig. 19–1. Pre- and posttesting results on behavior ratings by Groups I, II, and III. (Haring and Phillips, *Educating emotionally disturbed children,* McGraw-Hill Book Company, 1962, by permission.)

ety in children to performance in complex learning situations where one or more competing incorrect responses is dominant. The learning task of the subjects involved turning off different colored lights by buttons arranged on a panel and connected to the lights. The subjects were instructed that they were to learn which button turned off each light and that if an error was made, correction would be allowed.

The subjects consisted of 36 fourth-grade pupils selected on the basis of extreme scores on the children's form of the *Taylor Scale of Manifest Anxiety.* Anxiety scores for the non-anxious group ranged from 3 to 11 and for the anxious group from 23 to 33. Figure 19–2

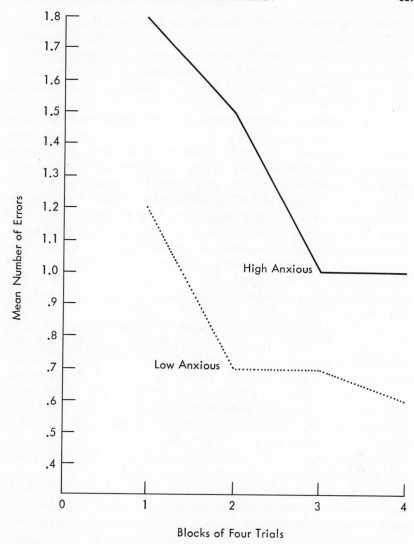

Fig. 19–2. Error curves for the anxious and non-anxious subjects plotted in blocks of four trials. (Palermo *et al.,* 1956.)

presents the learning curves of the anxious and non-anxious groups. On each block of trials the non-anxious subjects made fewer errors than the anxious subjects. Thus, it appears that in difficult learning situations where the dominant response is not correct, the anxious subjects show inferior performance in comparison to the performance of the non-anxious subjects. These results have important educational implications. In discrimination-learning problems where the dominant response is not correct, the discriminations are more readily learned by the less anxious subjects. The high degree of anxiety in this case acts as a deterrent to learning.

Another experiment involving classroom situations compared threat of failure and security with regard to promotion as a motivating procedure (Otto, 1935). The gains made on the *Stanford Achievement Test* of a group of second- and fifth-grade children periodically threatened with failure of promotion were compared with the gains made by a group of second- and fifth-graders reassured that they need not have any fear of not being promoted. In both grades the non-threatened group made greater gains than the threatened group although the differences were not statistically significant. The ill effects of insecurity have been emphasized by psychiatrists as well as by clinical psychologists. Thus, it appears that using threat of failure of promotion to children in the elementary school has little positive value to offer the teacher.

General emotional stability is one of the personal factors essential for optimum learning. There is evidence from many sources that children who are emotionally immature are not ready for the learning tasks found at school. Likewise, sixth- and seventh-grade pupils who are emotionally immature frequently lose interest in their school activities and fail to develop realistic and worthwhile goals related to learning activities. Combs (1958) suggested that most failures in reading and spelling are a result of unfortunate attitudes toward the subject. The children see themselves as inadequate; hence, he points out, this leads to increased inadequacy at school.

Learning through the problem-solving process appears as a threat to the speculative and indecisive nature of the emotionally disturbed child. Towle (1954) states:

Learning becomes a precarious quest fraught with hostility, guilt, and anxiety. With so much at stake in his goal-striving he is often unable to contain the anxiety and tension, so that defenses are erected which interrupt learning. These children experience much failure in social situations, and sometimes they fail in school, and notably they are prone to do so at the stage of adolescent revolt against parents. Often, however, they become constricted, task-centered achievers who shut out experiences which would contribute to their emotional development, and their relationships notably become constricted and distorted. [P. 14.]

THERAPY FOR CHILDREN WITH
PERSONALITY DISTURBANCES

When a child has developed serious personality disturbances characterized by anxiety neuroses, childhood psychosis, or character disturbances such as are seen in the psychopath, it is obvious that preventive measures have been unsuccessful. The child now has an illness or disorder that should be treated. The first step in such a treatment is to determine the etiology of the behavior—both organic and functional—in order that an accurate diagnosis may be made. When possible, the diagnosis should include information about genetics, conditions before birth, treatment during infancy and early childhood, and experiences during the developmental period. Such a diagnosis requires time and painstaking inquiry.

Therapy Involving the Environment. The therapy for emotional disorders may well be divided into three categories for special consideration: (1) that directed toward changing the individual, (2) that directed toward altering the general environment, and (3) that involving interpersonal relations with parents or other adult-authority figures who bear directly upon one's personal development.

Therapy involving the environment must take into consideration the child's physical world. Materials were presented in previous chapters showing something of the nature of results of an underprivileged environment. If the child is undernourished, poorly clothed, and ill-housed, his health and physical, intellectual, emotional, and social development will be adversely affected (Della-Dora, 1962). If he lives in a slum area with overcrowded home conditions and has no place for play and recreation, he will not develop desirable emotional and social characteristics. Good character development is not nourished by forces found in a delinquency area. Although nutrition, housing, slum clearance, crime prevention, and other wholesome environmental conditions are problems of a sociological and economic nature, they have a direct bearing on the emotional development of children. Thus, they are indirectly problems of the therapist in his work. It becomes the duty of the therapist both as a professional worker and as a citizen to attempt to improve the child's environment so as to furnish a basis for good emotional development. A child suffering from malnutrition must first be better fed before we can hope for an improvement in emotional disturbances such as restlessness or nightmares.

Therapy Involving Parents or Parent-Figures.   Any therapy involving the parents will depend upon what can be done within the bounds of the legal-cultural environment. It is not an easy matter to take the child from a parent, except in extreme cases of cruelty or neglect. Even in such cases much damage has already been done to the child. A second consideration in therapy directed toward parents is the psychodynamics of the parents' behavior. If the parent, because of his ignorance of child training, is following a course that leads to emotional disturbances, guidance in the form of information may be very helpful. The senior author observed this several years ago in the case of a father who set forth very high standards for his first child, a daughter. The daughter enrolled in school a few months before she was six years of age. In the first and second grades she had much difficulty keeping up with other members of the class. She had an average IQ. The father expected her to excel, and when she failed to do this in the second grade, she developed nervous mannerisms such as blinking the eyes and restlessness along with sleep disturbances. The school psychologist discussed the matter with the parents. The girl was then allowed to go at her own pace, repeating the second grade with another teacher the following year. Ultimately she finished high school with a good record.

A parent's behavior toward a child may be a result of prejudice. He may be prejudiced against permissive training and demand complete obedience from the child, not allowing the child to ever question his authority or word. Such an attitude cannot usually be treated by direct instructional methods, although the parent may be influenced by someone in whom he has absolute confidence. The therapist usually finds it difficult to deal with the parent whose attitude and behavior toward the child is based upon prejudice.

The parent may demand certain activities of the individual child in an effort to satisfy his own unmet needs. The mother may find that her social life is very limited, so she finds gratification through directing her daughter into a whirlpool of social activities. The father fails to satisfy his need for self-esteem through his life activities but perhaps this can be vicariously satisfied through some glamorous performance of his son as a football hero or earlier in life as a little champion at something.

The parent may actually be suffering from a serious emotional conflict. In such a case the parent is himself or herself in need of therapy. Concerning these, Pearson (1949) states:

Parents who suffer from frank neuroses—conversion and anxiety hysteria and compulsion neurosis—may also manifest adverse behavior toward the child as a symptom of their neurosis, but they are too ill to be helped regarding their behavior toward the child by instructional therapy. . . . There are also parents whose behavior toward the child is the result not of neurotic character but of ambulant psychosis. Although they seem to get along, they are actually psychotic people. For such cases, even psychoanalysis is frequently of little help. [P. 310.]

Therapy Directed Toward the Individual Child. Too often therapy is directed toward changing the child without any consideration of his environment. The therapist observes that changes in the child's immediate environment are unlikely and focuses all of his attention upon the child. In the treatment of the child it is important to ascertain the actual strength of his ego. Does he have a favorable concept of himself? In cases where he has a weak ego or unfavorable concepts of the self, efforts should be directed toward the development of more favorable concepts of the self. The child who is guided in the development of worthwhile aspirations and then helped in his efforts to reach his aspirations will likely develop more favorable concepts of the self through his successes.

The child's ego and self-esteem must be protected. In some cases it is essential for the therapist to guide the child in the development of a stronger ego and more favorable self-esteem. In this he will need the cooperation of teachers, parents, and others. The child's ego is strengthened by successes, by favorable relations with others, and by identification with ego ideals.

Group Therapy. An important trend in psychotherapy is the use of therapy, either exclusively or in cooperation with individual therapy. The results of an early experiment (Hewitt and Gildea, 1945) in group psychotherapy, using a small group of girls in a day camp of 100 children, indicates some of the values to be derived from group therapy. It was observed that the children "gradually became freed emotionally to a point where they could openly express their feelings and face some of their personal conflicts and the dangerous consequences, since they felt reassured by the consistent accepting attitude of the therapist" (p. 118). The results of this and subsequent studies of group therapy with children show first the importance of the learning process in the development of a close interpersonal relationship among the children making up the group. Second, the experimenter observed that the personality of the therapist was extremely important to the success of any program of group therapy. This indicates that the role of the therapist, technique, and patients cannot be separated in evaluating the results of the program.

No one method or no one theory can be set forth as the one that should be followed in group theory. The group serves as the learning situation through which the learning process operates. It is important in this connection that the children involved be carefully selected on the basis of their problems of adjustment in the larger group, and on their past history of adjustment in group situations. The activities must be so organized that the children are not made to feel that they are different from other children. Discussion groups, play activities, work projects, and reading and study programs have been found useful. These should be adapted to the problems and nature of the children. The therapist must assure the children through his relations with them of his sincere interest in them and of his acceptance of them, even though they may not be wholly accepted by many members of the larger group.

Residential Treatment.   The past decade has witnessed the development of residential treatment centers for the emotionally disturbed child. This is largely an outgrowth of the recognition by child guidance clinics and others concerned with the treatment of emotionally disturbed children that their efforts are frequently made difficult by the tension and conflicts in the home situation of the patient. The residential center is better able to treat the whole child and is based upon a philosophy of multidisciplinary treatment. It is especially designed to furnish long-term treatment of children whose emotional disorders disturb all phases of their social and academic adjustments. The goal of such treatment is to return the child to relatively normal family living. This is frequently complicated by stress and conflicts in the home. To return a child to a home atmosphere that fails to provide for his basic needs will not solve his problems. Too often he is returned to a home situation that inevitably only leads to a return of his emotional disturbances.

There are, however, limitations to residential treatment, as suggested by Rubin and Simson (1960) who state:

Living in an institutional environment can be detrimental to the growth and development of the personality if continued too long. There is a tendency to develop undue dependence on external controls and supports, and this is especially true of the closed ward hospital environment. A return to a more normal pattern of family life is often required if personality growth is to continue. This may be true even before the child is ready to tolerate a full day at public school or unsupervised peer group exercises. [P. 147.]

The educator's role in the residential treatment of children has been well stated by Rabinow (1955): "The educationist's role may be defined as helping the child to self-realization through the exercise of available potential within culturally approvable modes, while the therapist has as his role the child's self-realization through the liberation of the unavailable potential which is coerced by the emotional problem" (p. 685).

The Role of Drugs. The controversy concerning the use of drugs in treating emotionally disturbed children has caught the attention and raised the emotions of psychologists, social workers, teachers, and parents. The attitudes and expectations of physicians vary from the one extreme in which psychotherapy is regarded as the only treatment that will serve a real purpose, and in which it is held that drugs function only as placebos or tranquilizers, to the other extreme in which drugs are thought to attend disturbed functions at the physiological level—the place at which the difficulty is believed to lie.

Eisenberg (1964) attempted to determine the effects of drugs on the behavior of emotionally disturbed children encountered in a clinic. The children were rated at the end of a seven-week treatment period on the basis of mothers' reports, teachers' reports, and clinical observations. No differences were noted for the three treatment conditions —placebo, meprobamate, and prochlorperazine. Differences were found in outcome for the major diagnostic categories. The outcome distributions are shown in Table 19–2. Children with psychotic dis-

TABLE 19–2

Outcome in Relation to Diagnosis

	Improvement Rating			
Diagnosis	Marked	Mild	None	Total
Neurotic	15	6	0	21
Hyperkinetic	14	9	10	33
Defective	0	9	4	13
Antisocial	1	2	7	10
Total	30	26	21	77

SOURCE: After Eisenberg (1964).

orders do not respond as dramatically to drug treatment as adult patients, although tranquilizers can be useful, when used with cautions, in checking destructive and impulsive behavior. Neurotic disorders seem rarely to respond in a decisive fashion to available medications. Psychological management is regarded as the preferred modality of treatment. Eisenberg concludes: "Drugs can be useful agents in managing pediatric psychiatric disorders when chosen appropriately and applied with discrimination" (p. 172).

SUMMARY

The importance of prevention and early identification of behavior disorders has been emphasized. The most important single factor in helping children with behavior problems is to begin early before the problem has become acute. A great deal that can be done for a child in the early stages of difficulty is impossible by the time a maladjusted behavior pattern has become well established. Thus, the immediate goals for the education of emotionally disturbed children require first of all small classes. Furthermore, the individual process must be followed to a marked extent since each child's difficulties are unique. Certain basic principles that must be recognized by the teacher and others dealing with the emotionally disturbed have been set forth. These are:

1. The emotionally disturbed child can learn.
2. Consideration must be given to the extinction of old patterns of behavior.
3. The new learnings will need reinforcement.
4. The school is a place where gratification exists.
5. The school is a place with a predictable environment.
6. The school is a place where help is available.
7. The need of props for the child may be important.
8. The teacher must give due regard to the child's self concept.
9. Backsliding frequently takes place.
10. The child should be encouraged to face reality.
11. The child's image of the teacher is important.

The nature of the classroom organization is important with the structured classroom providing a better climate for the child's development. Using threat or failure has little positive value to offer and may be detrimental to the individual's emotional adjustment and learning.

The development of serious personality disturbances is obvious evidence that preventive measures have been unsuccessful. Thus, the child now has an illness or personality disturbance that should be given special consideration. Therapy may well be directed toward changes in the individual, changes in the general environment, and changes involving interpersonal relations. Frequently therapy, if it is to be successful, must include parents, especially in parent-child relations. Therapy directed toward helping the child develop a favorable and realistic concept of the self will be helpful to the child with a weak ego or with an unrealistic concept of the self. Residential treatment is more amenable to treatment based upon a multidisciplinary philosophy of therapy and is most needed by children from homes involving tension and conflicts.

CHAPTER REFERENCES

Combs, A. W. (1958). New horizons in field research: the self concept. *Educ. Leadership*, 15:315–17.

Della-Dora, D. (1962). The culturally disadvantaged, educational implications of certain social-cultural phenomena. *Except. Child.*, 28:467–72.

Eisenberg, L. (1964). Role of drugs in treating disturbed children. *Children*, 11:167–73.

Haring, N. G., and Phillips, E. L. (1962). *Educating emotionally disturbed children*. New York: McGraw-Hill.

Hewitt, Helen, and Gildea, Margaret (1945). An experiment in group psychotherapy. *Amer. J. Psychother.*, 15:112–27.

Hobbs, N. (1963). The process of re-education. A paper delivered at the first annual workshop for the Staff of Project Re-ED, in Gatlinburg, Tennessee, September 1.

Hollister, W. G., and Goldston, S. E. (1962). Psychoeducational processes in classes for emotionally handicapped children. *Except. Child.*, 28:351–56.

Lavietes, Ruth (1962). The teacher's role in the education of the emotionally disturbed child. *Amer. J. Orthopsychiat.*, 32:854–62.

Newman, Ruth (1961). Conveying essential messages to the emotionally disturbed child at school. *Except. Child.*, 28:199–204.

Otto, H. J. (1935). An attempt to evaluate the threat of failure as a factor in achievement. *Elem. Sch. J.*, 35:588–96.

Palermo, D. S., Castaneda, A., and McCandless, B. R. (1956). The relationship of anxiety in children to performance in a complex learning task. *Child Developm.*, 27:333–37.

Pearson, G. H. J. (1949). *Emotional disorders of children*. New York: W. W. Norton.

QUAY, H. C. (1963). Some basic considerations in the education of emotionally disturbed children. *Except. Child.*, 30:27–30.

RABINOW, B. (1955). The role of residential treatment for children symposium, 1954. 5. The role of the school in residential treatment. *Amer. J. Orthopsychiat.*, 25:685–91.

RUBIN, E. Z., and SIMSON, C. B. (1960). A special class program for the emotionally disturbed child in school: a proposal. *Amer. J. Orthopsychiat.*, 30:144–53.

TALLMAN, I., and LEVINE, S. (1960). The emotionally disturbed child in the classroom situation. *Except. Child.*, 27:114–26.

TOWLE, C. (1954). *The learner in education for the profession.* Chicago: Univer. Chicago Press.

SELECTED READINGS

ASSOCIATION FOR SUPERVISION AND CURRICULUM DEVELOPMENT (1950). *Fostering mental health in our schools.* 1950 Yearbook. Washington, D.C.: National Education Association.

BAKWIN, H., and BAKWIN, RUTH M. (1953). *Clinical measurement of behavior disorders in children.* Philadelphia: W. B. Saunders.

CAPLAN, G. (ed.), (1955). *Emotional problems of early childhood.* New York: Basic Books.

ELKINS, DEBORAH (1955). How the classroom teacher can help the emotionally disturbed child. In FRAMPTON and GALL (eds.), *Special education for the exceptional.* Vol. 3. Boston: Porter E. Sargent.

JOSEPH, H., and ZERN, G. (1954). *The emotional problems of children: a guide for parents.* New York: Crown.

REDL, F., and JACOBSON, S. (1958). The emotionally disturbed child. *NEA J.*, 47:609–11.

SCHNEIDERS, A. A. (1955). *Personal adjustment and mental health.* New York: Holt, Rinehart & Winston.

See also Selected Readings for Chapters 17 and 18.

SELECTED ANNOTATED BIBLIOGRAPHY

CRUICKSHANK, W. M. (ed.) (1963). *Psychology of exceptional children and youth.* (2d ed.) Englewood Cliffs, N.J.: Prentice-Hall. Eleven authorities from different areas of exceptionality combined their experiences and training in the production of this volume. The text is designed as a survey of the field for teachers and prospective teachers.

DUNN, L. M. (ed.) (1963). *Exceptional children in the schools.* New York: Holt, Rinehart & Winston. Seven scholars representing different areas of special education contributed to this book. It is divided into ten chapters dealing with mentally retarded, gifted, emotionally disturbed and socially maladjusted, speech-impaired, deaf and hard-of-hearing, blind and partially seeing, crippled and neurologically impaired children.

Education of exceptional children. *Rev. educ. Res.,* Vol. 33 (1963), No. 1. Summaries of research studies on organization, administration, and supervision of special education for all types of exceptional children.

JORDAN, T. E. (1962). *The exceptional child.* Columbus, Ohio: C. E. Merrill. This book is divided into three parts. In the first part the general dimensions of the problem presented by the exceptional child are set forth. The second part deals with handicapped children, and two chapters on the gifted are presented in the third part.

KIRK, S. A. (1962). *Educating exceptional children.* Boston: Houghton Mifflin. The problems of exceptional children are approached through the concept of discrepancies in growth, thus furnishing a better understanding of exceptional children and their educational needs.

KIRK, S. A., and WEINER, BLUMA N. (eds.) (1963). *Behavioral research on exceptional children.* Washington, D.C.: The Council for Exceptional Children, National Education Association. This volume contains 12 chapters, each authored by a research specialist in a particular aspect of special education. The main body of each chapter consists of reviews of specific research studied in the form of extended abstracts of selected studies.

LOUTTIT, C. M. (1957). *Clinical psychology of exceptional children.* (3d ed.) New York: Harper & Row. This volume is a product of 7 authorities with Louttit furnishing 5 of the 13 chapters. It reflects the point of view and specialization of the different scholars. An abundance of materials is included which makes this a useful source for superior and advanced students interested in the clinical approach to studying exceptional children.

MAGARY, J. F., and EICHORN, J. R. (1960). *The exceptional child: a book of readings.* New York: Holt, Rinehart & Winston. Materials in the various areas of special education are brought together in this book consisting of 71 readings, each by a recognized authority. Special emphasis is given to the child rather than his particular handicap.

MAGNIFICO, L. X. (1958). *Education for the exceptional child.* New York: McKay. The problems and methods of special education are discussed. The book is designed as a text for the teacher in training and as a guide for the teacher in service.

TRAPP, E. P., and HIMELSTEIN, P. (eds.) (1962). *Readings on the exceptional child.* New York: Appleton-Century-Crofts. An introduction, giving the incidence figures of exceptional children in the United States, is followed by 47 readings. These readings cover the areas of mental deficiency, the gifted, the aurally and visually handicapped, the speech handicapped, the aphasics, the physically handicapped, the brain damaged, and the emotionally disturbed.

GLOSSARY

The definitions here presented are intentionally brief and non-technical. They are intended for the beginning student as an aid in studying this text.

Aberration.   A deviation, usually regarded as abnormal.

Ability.   Actual power, whether inherited or acquired, to perform an act.

Academic aptitude.   Combination of abilities needed for schoolwork.

Acuity.   Acuteness or clearness; amount of sensory perception, especially of vision.

Adjustment mechanism (*see* **Defense mechanism**)

Agraphia.   Inability to write words, although motor functioning is normal—a type of aphasia.

Alexia.   A language disorder in which the individual, although having normal vision, is incapable of interpreting written words.

Ambivalence.   A combination of opposing feelings simultaneously toward a person or situation.

Amentia.   Mental deficiency.

Amnesia.   Loss of memory due to a brain injury, shock, or similar cause.

Anomaly.   A deviation from the general or normal pattern.

Anoxemia.   Deficient aeration of the blood; deficiency in the oxygen supply of the blood.

Anoxia.   Oxygen deficiency resulting from a diminished supply of oxygen to the brain tissues.

Anxiety neurosis.   A condition characterized by apprehension and fear, and accompanied by other symptoms such as irritability, excitability, and depressed states.

Aphasia.   A loss or impairment of the ability to communicate or understand written or spoken language due to injury to the language centers of the brain.

Aphonia.   Inability to utter vocal sounds, due to some structural or functional defect in the vocal cords.

Apraxia.   A brain disorder characterized by loss of ability to manipulate and use common objects and to execute planned movements.

Articulatory defects. Indistinct or confusing speech resulting from failure or inability to produce the commonly accepted speech sounds.

Astigmatism. Defective curvature of the refractive surfaces of the eye as a result of which a ray of light is not sharply focused on the retina but is spread over a more or less diffused area.

Ataxia. Injury to the cerebellum resulting in a muscular incoordination characterized by a lack of balance.

Bilateral. Having two sides; pertaining to both sides.

Birth trauma. An injury to the infant received during or due to the process of being born.

Capacity. A potential ability, or one largely inherited but not fully developed.

Cardiograph. Instrument for recording action of the heart.

Cerebral meningitis (*see* **Meningitis**)

Chorea. Spasmodic twitching of a muscle, indicative of disorder of motor-control areas of the nervous system.

Compensation. A defense mechanism by which an individual covers up or counterbalances a real or imagined inferiority in an effort to reduce tension.

Conflict. A condition that arises when an individual is faced with motives that are incompatible.

Congenital. Existing at birth, as for example a brain injury; not necessarily hereditary.

Conjunctivitis. Inflammation of the mucous membrane that lines the inner surface of the eyelid and is reflected over the forepart of the eyeball.

Correlated. Closely connected; systematically or reciprocally related.

Cretinism. A type of mental deficiency resulting from a deficiency in thyroid secretion.

Convulsion. Violent involuntary contractions of an extensive set of muscles.

Defense mechanism. A technique by means of which anxiety and tension may be reduced.

Delinquency. Violation of the code of the large social group.

Dementia praecox (*see* **Schizophrenia**)

Diplegia. Paralysis affecting like parts on both sides of the body; bilateral paralysis—legs more often affected than arms.

Drooling. Dripping or flowing of saliva from the mouth.

Dysarthria. A condition in which the individual is deficient in normal use of the speech organs, such as the lips, jaws, tongue, and vocal cords.

Dysfunction. Absence of complete normal function—differs from paralysis, in which there is loss of function.

Dyslalia. Difficulty of speech due to abnormality in the tongue or other organs of speech.

Ego. The self; in psychoanalytic usage, the conscious part of the mind which acts as the mediator between the id and the obstacles to its satisfaction.

Egocentric. Centering around the self.

Electrocardiogram. A graphic picture of electrical charges caused by contraction of the heart muscles.

Emmetropia. Refractive condition of the eye in which vision is normal or perfect.

Encephalitis. Inflammation of the brain; brain fever.

Endocrine glands. Organs that produce secretions called hormones which pass into the blood or lymph stream.

Endogenous. From within—often used to describe condition arising from factors within, such as an hereditary condition.

Exogenous. From without—often used to describe a condition arising from factors without, such as a non-hereditary condition.

Extroversion. Literally, a turning outward (*see also* **Introversion**).

Facing reality. Accepting the conditions and objects in the world as they actually exist.

Field-cultural. The impact of cultural forces in relation to the environmental setting in which they operate.

Frustration. The perception of an interference with the satisfaction of a need or drive.

Group therapy. Group psychotherapy; the treatment of several individuals as a group.

Grand mal. An epileptiform seizure in which there are severe convulsions and a loss of consciousness.

Hemiplegia. Paralysis of the arm and leg on one side of the body.

Heterosexual. Referring to the opposite sex in matters relating to love and sexual attraction.

Homosexual. Referring to the same sex; preference for members of the same sex as potential sex objects.

Hydrocephalus. A condition usually characterized by an abnormally large head due to excessive fluid in the cranium.

Hypertonia. Excessive muscle tone.

Hysteria. A psychoneurosis characterized by emotional disturbances, and often partial loss of memory, paralysis, etc.

Id. In psychoanalytic usage, the unconscious, dynamic part of the self; reservoir of the primitive drives which constantly demand satisfaction.

Idiopathic. Of unknown cause.

Idiosyncrasy. Characteristic or trait peculiar to an individual.

Identification. The defense mechanism by which an individual identifies himself with persons, groups, institutions, or objects as a means of satisfying certain needs or relieving frustrations.

Incidence. Range of occurrence or influence of a condition or disease.

Individuality. That which differentiates one person from another.

Infantile. Reverting to infant characteristics or traits.

Inferiority feeling. An attitude characterized by lack of confidence, with feelings of unworthiness and inadequacy.

Introversion. Literally, a turning inward (*see also* **Extroversion**).

Jacksonian epilepsy. A form of epilepsy in which the seizure is limited to one leg or to one part of the body, usually without the loss of consciousness.

Lesion. Change in tissue resulting from injury or disease.

Leukemia. A fatal disease of the blood-forming organs, characterized by a marked increase in the number of white blood cells in the blood and the presence of immature cells.

Level of aspiration. Goal or standard of achievement one sets for himself.

Libido. A psychoanalytic concept referring to psychic vital drive of the individual.

Macrocephaly. Abnormal condition involving an enlargement of the head.

Malformation. Any congenital irregularity or irregular development in the formation or correlation of parts in an organism.

Malnutrition. Imperfect assimilation and nutrition.

Mannerism. Habitual, automatic oddity of behavior.

Maturation. Growth and development resulting from inner forces.

Meningitis. Inflammation of the meninges. Cerebral meningitis may be due to trauma, tuberculosis, or to extension of inflammation from neighboring structures. Spinal meningitis is an inflammation of the membranes of the brain and spinal cord.

Mental age. Level of intelligence in terms of the age when the average child reaches that level of intellectual development.

Mental deficiency. Often used as a synonym for feeblemindedness.

Microcephalus. Unnatural smallness of the head due to imperfect development.

Muscle spasm. An involuntary, convulsive muscular contraction.

Muscular dystrophy. Metabolic disorder where there is degeneration and wasting of muscle tissue.

Myopia. Nearsightedness.

Myxedema. A disorder characterized by lethargy and dullness resulting from a lack of thyroid secretion.

Negativism. A form of behavior characterized by rebelliousness, stubbornness, or refusal to follow suggestions or to face reality.

Neurasthenia. A psychoneurosis characterized by aches, pains, fatigue, irritability, and bodily discomfort.

Neurosis (*see* **Psychoneurosis**)

Nystagmus. An involuntary, rapid, jerking movement of the eyeball, —may be either lateral, vertical, rotary, or mixed.

Obesity. The accumulation of fat that is detrimental to health.

Occupational therapy. Any activity, mental or physical, medically prescribed and professionally guided, to aid a patient in recovery from disease or injury.

Organismic age. Age of an individual based upon the average of a number of different ages, such as skeletal age, mental age, educational age, social age.

Orthopedic. Pertaining to the correction of physical (skeletal) deformities.

Orthopsychiatry. The field of psychiatry especially concerned with mental disorders during childhood and adolescence.

Ossification. Formation of bone; state or process of being converted into bone.

Paraplegia. Paralysis of the lower part of the body, including both legs.

Pathology. Condition produced by disease or injury.

Personality profile. A graphic representation of the personality characteristics or traits of an individual.

Petit mal. A mild epileptiform seizure characterized by dizziness or other sensations—a momentary lapse of consciousness.

Physical therapy. Treatment of disability, injury, and disease by such measures as massage, exercise, application of heat, light, water, and electricity.

Physique. Bodily structure and organization.

Poliomyelitis. Inflammation of the gray matter of the spinal cord.

Potential. Existing in possibility, not in actuality; the highest level at which a person could perform.

Precocious. Early or rapid development.

Profile chart. Graph or curve formed by uniting the points representing one's scores on each of several kinds of tests or performances.

Projection. Ascribing to others the ideas, feelings, or attitudes that the individual himself has but does not desire to recognize or face.

Projective technique. A testing method in which the subject is required to ascribe his own thoughts and feelings to a stimulus of relatively high ambiguity—designed to determine personal characteristics.

Psychasthenia. A psychoneurosis characterized by abnormal fears, obsessions, and compulsions.

Psychogenic. Originating in one's mental and emotional life.

Psychoneurosis. A mental or emotional disturbance that affects only part of the personality and that is not of sufficient severity to make a person dangerous to society. In this text, used interchangeably with **neurosis.**

Psychopath. A person suffering a mental or nervous disorder characterized by a lack of moral sensibility and emotional control.

Psychosis. A personality disorder of sufficient severity to alienate the person from reality and endanger the safety of others.

Psychosomatic. Pertaining to impaired bodily function of psychological origin.

Psychotherapy. Treatment of mental and emotional disorders by psychological methods.

Quadriplegia. Paralysis or involvement of all four extremities.

Rationalization. The justification of one's behavior through plausible and acceptable but actually irrelevant and unimportant motives.

Repression. The closing off from conscious awareness of painful memories or thoughts distasteful to the self.

Retrolental fibroplasia. A dense, fibrous growth behind the lens of the eye which prevents normal vision—usually producing blindness.

Schizophrenia. Synonym for dementia praecox, literally meaning a splitting off from reality.

Spasm. Involuntary contraction of a muscle or group of muscles.

Spastic hemiplegia. A condition in which one hemisphere or side of the body is affected with spasticity.

Spastic paraplegia. A condition in which both legs are affected with spasticity.

Spasticity. Involuntary contraction of affected muscles when they are suddenly stretched—called stretch reflex—resulting in tenseness and inaccurate, difficult voluntary movement.

Spinal meningitis (*see* **Meningitis**)

Strabismus. Squint or "cross-eyes"; failure of the two eyes to direct their gaze at the same object because of muscle imbalance.

Sublimation. Redirection of energy into acceptable or realistic channels.

Superego. Used synonymously with conscience; in psychoanalytic usage, that part of the self that produces strife and difficulty when the ego follows primitive urges from the id.

Syndrome. An aggregate of symptoms that characterize a certain disease or disorder.

Therapy. Any method used to treat a disease or condition.

Tic. A spasmodic moving or twitching of a group of muscles that, on the surface, bears no relation to the individual's problems.

Tonus. Partial contraction of a muscle, leading to muscle firmness or rigidity.

Trauma. Any injury to the body caused by violence; a physical wound or an emotional shock leaving a deep psychological impression.

Traumatic experience. A sudden difficult situation that arouses a feeling of helplessness.

Tremor. A condition of trembling of any part of the body, such as the hands, head, or fingers.

Triplegia. Paralysis of three limbs.

Unconscious. A psychoanalytic concept referring to that portion of the mind that influences the individual's thinking and actions, and of which the individual is not consciously aware.

Withdrawal. Avoidance of facing an annoying unpleasant situation.

SELECTED DIRECTORY OF 16MM FILMS °

Accent on Use, sound, 19 min. (31). Produced for the National Foundation, Inc., this film shows the part played by physical therapy in restor-
ing infantile paralysis patients to health.

Angry Boy, sound, 33 min. (13). Tommy Randall, caught stealing at
school, is treated at a guidance clinic, rather than as a juvenile criminal.
Through a team approach involving the services of a psychiatrist,
Tommy's troubles are determined.

Arts and Crafts for the Slow Learner, color, 27 min. (33). Craft activities
suitable for six-year-old educable retarded children are presented along
with uses that can be made of free and inexpensive materials.

The Bobath Approach in Cerebral Palsy Habilitation, color, 30 min. (26).
Furnishes a description of the neuromuscular basis for speech problems
of the cerebral-palsied child along with methods useful for helping him
in vocalization.

Boy in Storm, black and white, 25 min. (22). The medical aspects of
epilepsy are shown. The social consequences and problems associated
with epilepsy are also presented.

Camp Cheerful, black and white, 15 min. (24). Shows the method used at
a residential camp for dealing with crippled children and the results obtained in terms of their social and psychological development.

The Cerebral Palsied Child, black and white, 29 min. (20). Three major
types of cerebral palsy are described. Special problems and needs of
the cerebral-palsied child are presented.

° Parenthetical numbers identify the film source. See the Directory of Film
Sources, pp. 553–54.

Cerebral Palsy: Methods of Ambulation, color, 20 min. (24). Shows the methods used in teaching motor skills to preschool cerebral-palsied children including crawling, standing, and walking.

Challenge of the Gifted, color, 11 min. (15). Surveys the program in a Unified School District (Vallejo, California) in reaching gifted children of the fourth, fifth, and sixth grades.

Children in Search of a Self, black and white, 30 min. (16). The autistic child is the central theme. Characteristics and methods of therapy are presented.

Children Limited, color, 30 min. (39). The emphasis is on residential treatment of the mentally retarded.

Class for Tommy, black and white, 21 min. (30). Shows a special class for Tommy, a six-year-old educable mentally retarded child.

Debbie, black and white, 27½ min. (11). Debbie, an emotionally disturbed teen-ager, is helped through the efforts and services of a child welfare agency.

A Desk for Billie, black and white, 57 min. (19). The true story of an intelligent child of migrant parents and the problems she faced in her attempts to secure an education.

Diagnosis of Childhood Schizophrenia, black and white, 40 min. (28). The importance of mental health and mental health symptoms in the identification of schizophrenia during childhood are brought forth.

Discovering Individual Differences, black and white, 23 min. (31). Demonstrates how one teacher was able to know and understand each pupil. Presents techniques of observation, records, behavioral journal, shared information, interviews with parents, and staff conferences.

Educable Mentally Handicapped, black and white, 29 min. (20). The characteristics and programs for handicapped children, especially the mentally retarded, are shown.

Education of Exceptional Children, black and white, 30 min. (38). Teaching methods used with various types of handicapped children are illustrated.

A Fair Chance for Tommy, black and white, 11 min. (25). Tommy, one of an estimated 78,000 partially seeing children in our schools today, is enrolled in a regular public day school. Ways in which the itinerant special teacher helps Tommy and other partially seeing children are shown.

Families First, sound, 22 min. (30). The abuses of tensions, frustrations, and antisocial behavior are demonstrated. Two contrasting family situations are illustrated.

The Feebleminded, sound, 44 min. (37). The various types of mental defectives found in an institution are shown, and also physiological and psychological differences between the clinical types described.

Give Them a Chance, black and white, 12 min. (30). Typical activities in a class of educable mentally retarded where the chronological ages range from seven to thirteen are shown.

Good Speech for Gary, color, 30 min. (31). Gary, a second-grader, is helped through a well-organized speech correctional program in which there is cooperation between his classroom teacher and a speech correctionist.

Growing Up with Deafness, color, 37 min. (6). A ten-year documentary presentation of the progress of a group of deaf students first studied when three to twelve years of age.

Hard Brought Up, black and white, 40 min. (13). Different aspects of juvenile delinquency are presented, such as environmental forces leading to delinquency, services of child welfare agencies, and methods of dealing with delinquents.

Individual Differences and Psychological Tests, black and white, 30 min. (21). The measurement of human abilities and individual differences is explained.

The Intelligence Testing of Tom, black and white, 52 min. (9). The correct method of administering the *Wechsler Intelligence Scale for Children* is illustrated. The reactions of a gifted child who originally scored a 196 IQ on the Binet-Stanford is shown.

Introduction to Aphasia, sound, 25 min. (34). An animated presentation of the anatomical basis of language, types of aphasia, and the relation of various lesions in the type of aphasia.

Johnny's New World, color, 16 min. (25). Describes how teachers detect and deal with children's eye problems.

The Least of These, color, 20 min. (31). Shows the operation of a residential facility program for severely mentally retarded children.

A Light to My Path, color, 15 min. (14). Describes a community program of services for trainable mentally retarded children from nursery school through workshops in the different grades.

No Less Precious, black and white, 14 min. (2). A descriptive account of programs for the mentally retarded throughout the United States.

Overdependency, sound, 32 min. (35). A case history of Jimmy, an attractive young man whose life is crippled by behavior patterns resulting from a too-dependent childhood, is presented.

Pay Attention, sound, 30 min. (31). Shows some of the educational and personality problems faced by children of all age levels who are hard of hearing.

The Perkin's Story, color, 40 min. (5). Describes the activities of the Perkin's School for the Blind.

Problem Children, sound, 20 min. (32). This is the story of two school boys, one a shy, withdrawn type, the other an aggressive, antisocial type. Shows how the school may help such boys.

The Right to Hear, color, 28 min. (31). Problems of the deaf and severely hard of hearing are shown in cases illustrating mild, moderate, and total deafness.

Sensory Processes and Perception, black and white, 30 min. (21). The role of the sensory processes in gathering and processing information is presented.

Shyness, black and white, 29 min. (23). Shyness in children is studied.

The causes of shyness and methods useful in dealing with it are brought forth.

Somatic Endocrine Types of Neuropsychiatric Disorders, silent, 19 min. (13). Different types of endocrinological malformations are shown, such as albinism, hydrocephalus, microcephalus, cretinism, and mongolism.

Speech Disorders: Physical Handicaps, black and white, 29 min. (20). Describes the different kinds of speech disorders, their etiology, diagnosis, and therapy.

Speech Disorders: Stuttering, black and white, 29 min. (20). Several children who were aided in overcoming stuttering are interviewed. Therapy used is brought forth in these interviews.

Stuttering, black and white, 27 min. (15) (State University of Iowa). This is a presentation of a comprehensive report from the Speech Clinic on progress in determining the causes and methods for the treatment of stuttering.

A Survey of Children's Speech Disorders, color, 29 min. (31). Methods of identifying speech disorders and their prevalence are shown.

Symptoms in Schizophrenia, silent, 18 min. (30). A variety of symptoms of schizophrenia is shown, including stereotypes, posturing, and simple hebephrenic reactions.

The Temple City Story, color, 22 min. (33). Presents an integrated educational program for blind children. The role of the resource teacher for the blind working with the regular teacher is shown.

Testing Intelligence with the Stanford-Binet, 18 min. (30). The method of administering and scoring the *Revised Stanford-Binet Scale* is shown. The student is given a glimpse of the uses of intelligence test results in teaching and guidance.

That Boy Joe, sound, 17 min. (2). This is the story of Joe Hastings, a delinquent boy, who is tried and convicted for burglary.

Thursday's Children, black and white, 22 min. (7). The teaching of language, speechreading, and speech for children four to seven years of age at Margate School for the Deaf (England) is presented.

A Time for Talent, color, 29 min. (8). Three outstanding school programs for the gifted students are presented.

Too Young to Say, color, 13½ min. (10). Illustrates the procedures used in testing the hearing of preschool children.

Toward Tomorrow, black and white, 42 min. (1). A descriptive series of nine totally blind preschool and school-age children taken in their homes or in the schools where they are enrolled.

Trainable Mentally Handicapped, black and white, 29 min. (20). Classroom scenes are used to show the training methods used with mentally retarded children.

Tuesday's Child, color, black and white, 14 min. (18). A short but clear explanation of characteristics and problems of the mentally retarded.

The Valiant Heart, black and white, 27 min. (17). The case history of a valiant eight-year-old child with rheumatic fever is depicted.

Persons interested in films and other audio-visual materials dealing primarily with programs for the mentally retarded are referred to *Audio-Visual Material on Mental Retardation,* National Association for Retarded Children, New York.

An annotated list of 67 films on hearing and deafness appeared in *The Volta Review,* 64 (1962): 77–83, 104.

Films on other handicaps, particularly directed to professional personnel, are described in *Films on the Handicapped,* Council for Exceptional Children, Washington, D.C.

DIRECTORY OF FILM SOURCES

1. American Foundation for the Blind, New York, New York.
2. Associated Films, Chicago, Illinois.
3. Bailey Films, Inc., Hollywood, California.
4. Bureau of Community Services, New Jersey Department of Institutions, Trenton, New Jersey.
5. Campbell Films, Saxton River, Vermont.
6. Campus Films, Inc., New York, New York.
7. Contemporary Films, Inc., New York, New York.
8. Division of Press and Radio Relations, National Education Association, Washington, D.C.
9. Educational Film Library, Syracuse University, Syracuse, New York.
10. Harsche-Rotman and Druck, Inc., Chicago, Illinois.
11. Health and Welfare Materials Center, New York, New York.
12. Indiana University, Indianapolis, Indiana.
13. International Film Bureau, Chicago, Illinois.
14. Junior League, Tampa, Florida.
15. McGraw-Hill Book Co., Text-Film Department, New York, New York.
16. Memorial Guidance Clinic, Richmond, Virginia.
17. Motion Picture Library, American Medical Association, Chicago, Illinois.
18. National Association for Retarded Children, New York, New York.
19. National Education Association, Washington, D.C.
20. National Educational Television Film Service, Indiana University, Bloomington, Indiana.
21. National Educational Television and Radio Center, New York, New York.
22. National Epilepsy League, Chicago, Illinois.
23. The National Film Board of Canada, New York, New York.
24. National Society for Crippled Children, Chicago, Illinois.
25. National Society for the Prevention of Blindness, New York, New York.
26. Newington Hospital for Crippled Children, Newington, Connecticut.
27. New York State Department of Commerce, Film Library, Albany, New York.
28. New York University Film Library, New York, New York.
29. Ohio Division of Mental Health, Columbus, Ohio.
30. Pennsylvania State University, Audio-Visual Aids Library, University Park, Pennsylvania.
31. State University of Iowa, Bureau of Audio-Visual Instruction, Iowa City, Iowa.

32. SWS Films, Hollywood, California.
33. Temple City Public Schools, Audio-Visual Department, Temple City, California.
34. United World Films, Government Film Department, New York, New York.
35. University of California at Berkeley, California.
36. University of Illinois, Visual-Aids Service, Champaign, Illinois.
37. University of Minnesota, Audio-Visual Instruction, Minneapolis, Minnesota.
38. Visual Aids Service, University of Illinois Extension, Urbana, Illinois.
39. Washington Association for Retarded Children, Seattle, Washington.

AUTHOR INDEX

555

SUBJECT INDEX